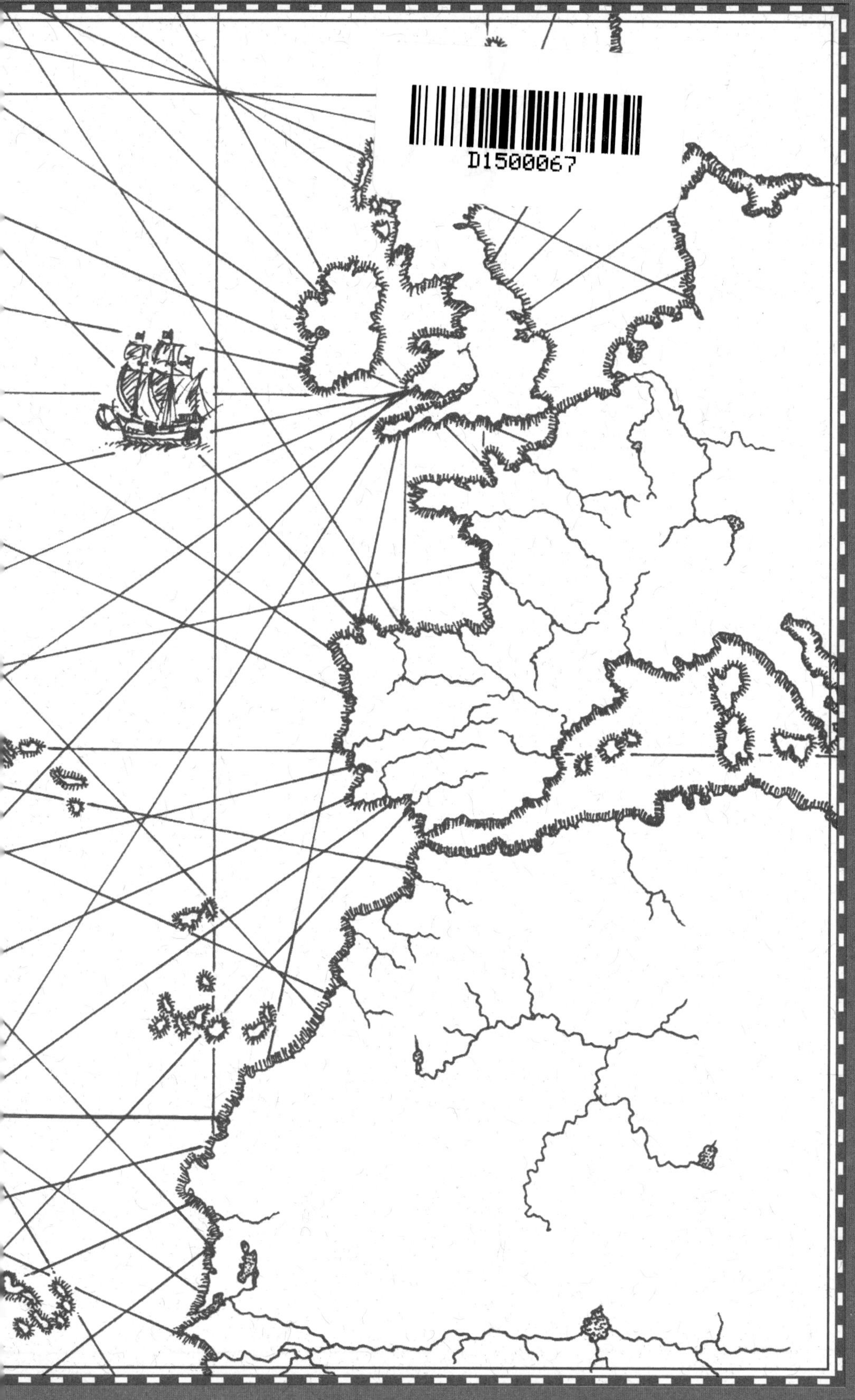

# THE HATCH AND BROOD OF TIME

Portrait of Eliza (Ayres) Phelps (1808–1880)

Painted after her marriage to George Alexander Phelps in New York City, 8 September 1825. Oil on wood, possibly Waldo & Jewett, New York, ca. 1826, in the possession of Ann-Elisa Wetherald Black.

*Photo by Fogg Art Museum, Harvard University*

# *The Hatch and Brood of Time*

## *Five Phelps Families in the Atlantic World 1720–1880*

by
Peter Haring Judd

*with a foreword by*
David Hackett Fischer

NEWBURY STREET PRESS
Boston, Massachusetts
1999

*Published and distributed by*

NEWBURY STREET PRESS
101 Newbury Street
Boston, Massachusetts 02116-3007

special publications imprint of the
New England Historic Genealogical Society



Judd, Peter H.
The hatch and brood of time : five Phelps families in the Atlantic world, 1720–1880 / by Peter Haring Judd.
p. cm.
Includes bibliographical references and indexes.
ISBN 0-88082-092-6 (alk. paper)
1. Phelps family. 2. Wheelock family. 3. Herring family. 4. Dennison family. 5. Nova Scotia Biography. 6. New England Biography. I. Title.
CT274.P52J83 1999
929'.2'0973—dc21 99-38131
CIP

To

Julia Phelps (Haring) White

1851–1928

*who planted the seeds*

There is a history in all men's lives
Figuring the natures of the times deceased,
The which observed, a man may prophesy,
With a near aim, of the main chance of things
As yet not come to life, who in their seeds
And weak beginnings lie intreasurèd.
Such things become the hatch and brood of time . . .

*Henry IV 2*, 3:1

# CONTENTS


List of Figures viii
List of Tables x
"The History in All Men's Lives"
Foreword by David Hackett Fischer xi
Preface xxv
Acknowledgments xxxi
Key to Citations xxxiii
Abbreviations xxxvi

PART ONE: A FAMILY NARRATIVE 1

I *Land and Society* 3
II *Colonial Lives* 19
III *A Rebel Pastor in Nova Scotia* 71
IV *Making the Wilderness Bud and Blossom* 119
V *Opportunity in the New Republic* 187
VI *Leaning on the Lever of Archimedes* 237
*Epilogue* 293

PART TWO: GENEALOGICAL & BIOGRAPHICAL NOTES 297

Prefatory Remarks 299
*Phelps I* 301
*Wheelock* 334
*Haring* 352
*Phelps II* 389
*Denison* 398

Select Bibliography 413
Index 435

# FIGURES


Portrait of Eliza (Ayres) Phelps (1808–1880) frontispiece

1. James Demarest Haring (1819–1868) xxvi
2. Caroline Eliza (Phelps) Haring (1828–1868) xxvii
3. Connecticut River Valley Settlement, Later 1600s 6
4. Connecticut Towns and Cities Associated with the Phelpses 18
5. T. Johnson's View of Yale College, 1745 21
6. Land Ownership in Hebron, Connecticut, 1744 28
7. The Davenport Lineage 31
8. The Rev. Eleazar Wheelock (1711–1779) 33
9. Theodora Phelps's Letter to her Father, Eleazar Wheelock, March 1769 43
10. A Nineteenth-Century Representation of the Rev. Wheelock and Dartmouth Students at the Founding of the College 55
11. "A New and Accurate Map of the Province of Nova Scotia in North America from the Latest Observations," 1781 73
12. Nova Scotia, near Port William 76
13. Title Page of Benajah Phelps's Sermon on the Death of Jane Chipman, 1775 96
14. Imaginative Portrait of the Rev. Henry Alline (1748–1784) on Itinerancy 102
15. The Champlain Corridor and Quebec 118
16. Davenport Phelps's Letter to the Rev. Samuel Peters, 22 April 1786 138
17. Niagara Falls 145
18. Navy Hall, Niagara 150
19. Fort Niagara and Newark 151
20. A Portion of Glanford Township 154
21. Joseph Brant 158
22. The Connecticut River Valley, New York State, and Upper Canada 166
23. Memorial Panel at Trinity Church, Geneva, New York 170
24. Memorial Tablet for Davenport Phelps at Trinity Church, Geneva, New York 174
25. "Rough sketch of ye relative situation of our churches" 175
26. View of Geneva, New York, 1807 180

27. The First Trinity Church Building, Geneva, New York 181
28. Eleazar Wheelock Phelps's Letter to His Wife, 25 September 1818 186
29. Major Turnpikes Linking Stafford to Points in Massachusetts and Connecticut 210
30. At the Corner of Greenwich Street 224
31. "Plan of the City of New York" 226
32. Phebe (Phelps) Phelps (1770–1861) 235
33. The Phelps House in Fairfield, Connecticut, 1872 239
34. The Phelps Family House in Fairfield, Connecticut, 1836–1870 257
35. James Demarest Haring (1819–1868) 266
36. John Samuel Haring (1810–1860) 267
37. Liverpool Commercial District: Walmsley's Map of Liverpool and Its Suburbs, 1884 278
38. Julia Phelps Haring (1851–1928) 283
39. Julia Phelps Haring 285
40. George Alexander Phelps House, ca. 1871, Fairfield, Connecticut 287
41. Eliza (Ayres) Phelps (1808–1880) 289
42. George Alexander Phelps (1803–1880) 289

# TABLES

1. Household Furnishings in Alexander Phelps's Estate Appraisal 61
2. Real Property and Livestock in Alexander Phelps's Estate 62
3. Personal Items in Alexander Phelps's Estate 63
4. Partial List of Creditors to the Estate of Alexander Phelps 68
5. Episcopal Parishes Organized by Davenport Phelps in New York State 182
6. Securities in the George Alexander Phelps Estate, Valued at $110,000 in 1880 291

# THE HISTORY IN ALL MEN'S LIVES

*A foreword by David Hackett Fischer*

For readers with an interest in history and genealogy, here is a book that brings the two disciplines together with high success. Its approach is fresh and creative. Its narrative is graceful and fluent. And the best of it is to be found in the substance of the work. Peter Haring Judd has joined history and genealogy in a way that gets results. He uses genealogical materials to enlarge our understanding of American history. At the same time, he works with historical sources in a way that expands the process of research and writing in genealogy. Altogether, Peter Judd has made a highly original contribution to both disciplines. More important, he has developed a method by which other contributions might be made.

The book draws its subjects from the history of the Phelps family in New England. Its protagonists were descendants of William and Ann Phelps and five children who left their home at Crewkerne, Somerset, and joined the Puritan Migration. They sailed to America in 1630 aboard the ship *Mary and John*, that great ark of West Country Puritanism.

In the New World, they were among the founders of the settlement at Dorchester in the Massachusetts Bay Colony. They were people of substance, and William Phelps was a leader from the start. He was Dorchester's representative in the General Court as early as 1632, and its selectman in 1634 and 1635. Their East Anglian neighbors in Boston welcomed them but looked upon them as a group apart. John Winthrop called them "the western men." There were tensions over land, politics, religion, and probably other differences of ancient origin. The western men grew increasingly restless in Massachusetts. In 1636 William Phelps and many others left the Bay Colony and moved to Connecticut.

William and Ann Phelps settled in the seed town of Windsor, on the Connecticut River. There they faithfully obeyed the biblical injunction to increase and multiply. To the five children who sailed with them, at least three more were added in America. Seven of that number (five of them sons) married and produced children of their own. The result was a teeming progeny of Phelpses, who intermarried with many other families in Connecticut, and very often with one another, through as many as sixteen generations from the Great Migration to our own time.

Peter Judd has not attempted a rounded genealogy of the Phelps family—a labor that would require many volumes, and a long life. He has given us something different here, and more interesting. From the great ganglia of the Phelps genealogy, he has extracted five Phelps families, all in his own line. Their lives span the broad middle period of American history from 1724 to 1880.

The book is a sequence of five stories—each centered on a man, a family, and a period of American history. Every story discovers in its historical sources something that adds interest and meaning to its genealogy. It also finds in its genealogical materials something that makes a serious contribution to historical knowledge.

The first story is about Alexander Phelps (1724–1773) and the history of colonial Connecticut. A large historical literature has interpreted that world as static, stable, and highly stratified—a "land of steady habits" closely ruled by a "standing order" of ministers and magistrates, in sharp contrast to American society in the nineteenth and twentieth centuries.

The saga of Alexander Phelps and his family gives us a different perspective on the history of colonial Connecticut. It is the story of an open and fluid society; of constant striving and continuing movement; of hard choices and unexpected consequences; of large risks, small gains, and dramatic reversals of fortune. It is also a story about family relationships as human resources of high importance in a dangerous and unpredictable world.

Alexander Phelps was of the fourth generation from William and Ann. He was born and raised in the town of Hebron, Connecticut, a new hill town between the Connecticut and Thames Rivers. It was not a tidy, close-built New England community of modern memory, but a raw and open settlement of separate farmsteads, jagged stumps, and girdled trees, where Puritan families struggled desperately to serve God and improve their lives.

Alexander's father, Nathaniel Phelps, was a founder of the town and also its first clerk, innkeeper, militia captain, and one of its largest landowners. He divided his property among his children on the biblical rule of double partible inheritance. The eldest son was given 40 acres and the homestead. Alexander, the youngest, got 20 acres, a cow scale, and a college education. He went to Yale and was destined for the ministry. On graduation he refused the offer of a pulpit and chose to be a country lawyer and landowner. Back he went to Hebron. He became active in the affairs of his town and represented it in many sessions of the Connecticut General Assembly. Eventually he became an officer in the militia and was titled "Colonel Alexander Phelps, Esq."

Alexander Phelps became a member in good standing of Connecticut's standing order, but his life was a continuing struggle for wealth, reputation, security, and stability. He borrowed heavily to buy land, speculated dangerously in Susquehannah lands, and invested in foreign trade throughout the Atlantic world. He was full of restless energy, often on the road, sometimes at sea; but his goals eluded him, and his fortunes rose and fell through periods of prosperity and depression, war and peace, health and sickness.

In 1749 he married his cousin Anne Phelps Jones. A year later he suffered a shattering blow. His wife and two newborn infants died suddenly in a single terrible month. In 1752 he married Theodora Wheelock, daughter of Eleazar Wheelock, a leading Congregational minister and "religious politician" of high eminence and the founder of Dartmouth College.

Alexander's affairs prospered in the 1750s. Then came the world depression of the 1760s. It hit New England very hard. Alexander was overextended, and lost heavily. It also was a difficult time for him in other ways. He was deeply caught up in religious questions, as his Puritan forbears had been. As the Awakening continued to reverberate in Hebron, a New Light town, Alexander went the other way and chose to join the Anglican Church, a difficult and painful decision. In politics he strongly supported the Whig cause in the Stamp Act crisis, but tried to maintain warm relations with imperial leaders in New England—not an easy task.

All the while, his business affairs went from bad to worse during the 1760s. Family connections kept him afloat, and helped shelter assets from insistent creditors, and also opened new opportunities. His wife's kin were doing well in New Hampshire, a colony that was growing very rapidly. In 1771, Alexander decided to move his family 250 miles north to the town of Lyme, New Hampshire, to be closer to his powerful father-in-law Eleazar Wheelock, and to find land and fortune on New England's northern frontier.

In New Hampshire his prospects began to improve. He acquired land and established a homestead. He helped his father-in-law with the founding of Dartmouth College, and his estate began to flourish. Then suddenly Alexander was caught in a controversy between two rival towns who both wanted the college, and he was accused of bribery. The accusation appears to have been false, but it wounded his reputation in an honor-bound society.

With some difficulty, Alexander got clear of the controversy, and began to find his feet again. He borrowed, invested, and prospered as never before. Then suddenly, at the peak of his success, he died in 1773, at the early age of 49. He left his affairs in extreme disorder, with no will and many creditors. His widow, Theodora, picked up the pieces and held the household together, with much help from her family. She married again, and the Phelps family went on to other struggles.

Altogether, the life and early death of Alexander Phelps is a short story, but it is significant for historians in several ways at once. It reveals a society where in Peter Judd's words "there came to be increasing ability to make choices of religion, profession, and dwelling place." The life of Alexander Phelps and his family was a complex web of choices. The decisions were not easy, and their consequences were often very difficult to bear.

We also find evidence in his troubled life that colonial New England was not a set of closed corporate communities, but an extraordinarily open, free, and dynamic society. The more open it became, the more difficult and complex were the choices that people such as Alexander Phelps had to make. Its freedom and openness were not the consequences of the American Revolution, but its cause, and the medium in which it moved.

The second story is about the choices of the Reverend Benajah Phelps (1737–1817) in the era of the American Revolution. Here again, we find a new perspective on a major period of American history. Benajah was the fifth child of Alexander's older half-brother Nathaniel Phelps, who had inherited 40 acres and the homestead in Hebron, where Benajah was born.

Like so many younger sons of Connecticut's landed families, Benajah went to Yale (A.B. 1761) and became a Congregational minister. Times were hard, and good pulpits were not easy to find in Connecticut. In 1766 Benajah made a bold decision. He chose to move 600 miles northeast to Nova Scotia, where an opportunity presented itself.

After the French and Indian War, a large body of Connecticut families moved to Nova Scotia in search of land that had been taken from the French Acadian settlers. These Connecticut settlers founded a New England-style town at Cornwallis, and asked Eleazar Wheelock to recommend a Congregational minister. Wheelock thought first of his family, and put forward the name of Benajah Phelps, half-step-nephew-in-law of his daughter Theodora Wheelock, and kinsman of Alexander Phelps.

The Connecticut people of Cornwallis were too poor to support Benajah, but he was given a generous grant of 666 acres by the royal governor of Nova Scotia. He also won the hand of Phebe Denison, of a prominent and affluent family. His prospects were bright, and he accumulated assets that were worth $1,500 and more, in addition to his large landholdings.

But then the troubles began. Times were hard and harvests short in Nova Scotia during the 1760s. Benajah's congregation scraped together enough money to build a meetinghouse, but they argued bitterly about its location, and the result was a permanent breach between the minister and some of his flock. Benajah's salary was not paid. A charismatic New Light itinerant minister from Rhode Island came to town and began to make converts. Benajah could not compete with him. Sickness struck his household, and he came down with smallpox. He recovered, but sometime before 1778 he either resigned or was dismissed from his pulpit, and decided to move to his wife's town of Horton, Nova Scotia.

Then came the American Revolution. Benajah chose to support the Whig cause, a brave decision in a royal province under imperial control. When a Yankee privateer raided Nova Scotia and plundered the homes of Loyalists, British authorities suspected Benajah of involvement. He fled hastily to escape imprisonment, leaving his wife and children behind.

Benajah tried desperately to return for them, but he was captured at sea by a British warship and set adrift in an open boat in the Gulf of Maine. He was lucky to reach the coast alive. Benajah tried again overland and failed once more—the Royal Navy controlled the coast of the Maine and Nova Scotia. Benajah consumed all of his liquid assets in these attempts to rescue his family, and his lands were seized by British authorities.

When the money was gone, he returned to Connecticut and got a calling as pastor in what is now Manchester. In 1782 he at last scraped together enough money to bring his family away from Nova Scotia. The family was reunited in Connecticut, and more children began to arrive. Their fortunes brightened. In 1784 the Connecticut legislature compensated Benajah generously for the loss of his property in Nova Scotia.

But Benajah began to have trouble with his congregation, and he was dismissed yet again in 1794. He left the ministry and lived in retirement in his former parish, short of money, selling and mortgaging land. His wife, Phebe, died in 1816, and Benajah passed away in 1817 in his eightieth year.

It is a long, sad story, full of irony and pathos. For an historian it suggests a new way of thinking about the era of the American Revolution. Benajah Phelps was a strong supporter of that "glorious cause," which ended in victory for the independent colonies. But for him and his family, it brought much pain and suffering.

Benajah was not a passive victim of circumstance. His life was a sequence of individual choices, actively made in conjunction with public events. Some of these events opened choices for him that had not existed before (the French and Indian War and the conquest of Nova Scotia). Other events changed the results of his choices in unexpected ways (the American War of Independence) Along the way there were many dramatic reversals of fortune.

Through it all, the brightest star in Benajah's life was his family. It sustained through the dark years. After his death it is his family for which he is remembered.

The third story is of Davenport Phelps (1755–1813), son of Alexander Phelps, protagonist of the first story. Born in Hebron, he briefly attended Yale. When his family moved to New Hampshire, he was one of the first students to enroll at Dartmouth College. He was still there when his father died suddenly. His mother, with help from her family, found the means to support him to graduation in 1775.

After commencement Davenport joined the Continental army. He served in the invasion of Canada and fought at the Battle of Bennington. On the field at Bennington his New Hampshire regiment stormed the redoubt that was held by Queens Loyal Rangers, who included many Connecticut Tories, some of whom had lived in Hebron. In the struggle for the redoubt, Davenport Phelps found himself fighting some of the friends of his youth in a great struggle that was at first called not the American Revolution but the American Civil War.

After the war this footloose veteran settled in Orford, New Hampshire, and tried to organize the upper Connecticut Valley as a separate state. He had strong support from many others, but the statehood movement failed. In 1785 he married Catharine Tiffany, daughter of a physician in Hanover, New Hampshire. The new family began to grow in the usual Phelpsian way. To support them, Davenport decided to move down the Connecticut River to Hartford. There he started a "mercantile business" with his mother's half brothers, James and Eleazar Wheelock, Jr. That venture failed in the deep depression of 1785–86.

In 1786 Davenport returned to New Hampshire and became a lawyer in Piermont. He was an active participant in his new home. He joined the militia and rose rapidly to the rank of colonel in 1788. He also became a Freemason and helped to form a Grand Lodge at Hanover for the state of New Hampshire. It was a great event in Freemasonry. Paul Revere rode north from Boston to Hanover specially for the occasion.

Like Revere and many other veterans of the Revolution, Davenport Phelps was deeply worried about the prospects for the new American republic that he had helped to found. In 1786 this Whig veteran of the War for Independence started a correspondence with a Tory friend of his Hebron youth, the Reverend Samuel Peters, who had moved to London. Davenport wrote at length on the "depressing conditions" and "disorder of society." He was dismayed by the "great commotions" of Daniel Shays, and deeply troubled by the prospects for America, as were so many Americans at that time.

As his doubts grew, Davenport Phelps made a momentous choice. He decided to emigrate to Canada, where opportunities seemed brighter. He moved to Newark, then the capital of Upper Canada, took an oath of allegiance to the Crown, became the king's attorney, and received a grant of 84,000 acres. It appeared that he had made a wise decision.

But he continued to be deeply troubled, and seems to have gone through a spiritual crisis of the sort that came so often to the descendants of the Puritans in difficult times. Many others of New England stock had similar experiences at the same time. The result was the religious revival miscalled the Second Great Awakening (it was the First Great Revival), which began in the 1780s.

Davenport Phelps, like others of his family, chose to go a different way. He resolved his spiritual crisis by joining the Anglican Church. Further, he decided to become an Anglican missionary to the Indians. He had formed a friendship with Joseph Brant, the great Iroquois leader, who was also an active Freemason. Brant supported Davenport in his determination. But the British authorities doubted his loyalty and refused his request for ordination.

Davenport was a man of strong will, after the model of his Puritan ancestors, and not easily deterred from his own errand. He returned to the United States and was ordained to the deaconate at Trinity Church in New York City and to the priesthood at St. Peter's, Albany. Afterwards, he went north again, settled his family in the frontier village of Geneva, and began to work as a missionary and Episcopal circuit rider, ministering to white settlers among the Finger Lakes. He founded twelve churches and labored in his faith until his death in 1813.

The career of Davenport Phelps offers us another way of thinking about the era that scholars call the "Critical Period"—the difficult years between the end of the American Revolution and the beginning of the new national government. The history of that era has been written backward from the framing and ratification of the Constitution. Some of Davenport's friends and comrades in the war chose to build a new republican system on a scale that no republic had ever reached before. Davenport himself chose to go a different way. He sought a brighter future for America in reunion with Britain, peace with the Indians, and an ecumenical revival of Christian faith. It was noble idea, but the road to America's future led in a different direction.

The career of Davenport Phelps reminds us that the Critical Period was a crisis in the classical sense. It was a moment when the destiny of a great nation lay in the balance, and there were many open choices to be made. It is easy to believe that there were no other roads to the future but the one that was actually taken. The life of Davenport Phelps leads us to think again. There were many possibilities in that pivotal moment. It was not clear which one would succeed.

The fourth story braids together two lines in the Phelps family. It is about Eleazar Wheelock Phelps (1766–1818) and his wife Phebe (Phelps) Phelps (1770–1861). It too suggests new ways of thinking about the period in which it unfolds, called the era of the early republic by historians.

Eleazar was born at Hebron, Connecticut, in 1766. He was the seventh child of Alexander Phelps. His future wife, Phebe, was born in Cornwallis, Nova Scotia, in 1770, the second daughter of Benajah Phelps. Both were children of misfortune. Eleazar was seven when his father died and thirteen when he lost his grandfather and namesake, the family patriarch—another heavy blow. Phebe Phelps suffered many misfortunes as the daughter of Benajah. She was eight years old when her father fled their home, twelve when her family was reunited in Connecticut, and not much older when her father lost his pulpit there.

In 1785 Eleazar went to Dartmouth, where his uncle was the new president, but he did not take a degree. He withdrew from college and moved to Connecticut, perhaps to help his brother Davenport Phelps in the ill-fated mercantile venture at Hartford. Somewhere near Hartford he met his relative Phebe Phelps, who lived nearby. They would have discussed the complexities of their family relationship. She might have explained that she was the daughter of the half step-nephew of his father. She could also have said that she was the daughter of his father's half-blood first cousin. Or maybe she told Davenport that she was his half first cousin, once removed. All of these statements were correct. In any case, they were sufficiently removed from one another to be safely beyond the strictest rule of consanguinity, but close enough to have much in common. They were married in 1793.

The young couple decided to settle in Stafford (now Stafford Springs), in northern Connecticut, directly on the Massachusetts line. A reason for their choice was the presence in Stafford of their fifth cousin, John Phelps, who owned a successful iron foundry, the largest industry in town. He was also a prosperous and powerful landowner and judge.

Eleazar became clerk of the probate court in which cousin John Phelps presided. The relationship was so close that Eleazar later became executor of John Phelps's very large estate. With his cousin's help, he hung out his shingle as a lawyer and was appointed justice of the peace. He also became an active member of the Federalist party, which was highly organized in Connecticut and fiercely challenged by Jeffersonian Republicans. In Stafford some of them tried to have him removed as justice of the peace, but he held on to his office and in 1811 became judge of probate as well.

He also chose to become active in the Worcester & Stafford Turnpike Corporation and accepted responsibility for the building of the road through his own town. Turnpike companies were a source of little profit and much pain and litigation. It was a decision he came to regret. Eleazar and his colleagues hired members of the Lyon family to do the actual construction, and they failed to perform to satisfaction. Eleazar won a judgment against them, which would have required a payment of $5,000.

A bizarre incident followed. The Lyons and their lawyer responded with an orgy of violence against Eleazar. They invaded his home, smashed doors, scattered belongings, and threatened his family. When this act produced no result they broke in again, plundered the house while the family was in it, and stripped the house so completely that it became uninhabitable.

The first attack had appeared to be a drunken binge. The second was more calculated. The attackers brought a wagon to carry away Eleazar's property. It was (and is) a shocking event. Under English and American law, a man's home was strongly protected against this sort of violation. The criminal sanctions in New England were very severe. But so complete was the breakdown of order in Stafford that there appears to have been no criminal prosecution. Eleazar sought damages in a civil suit, and his lawyer won another judgment against members of the Lyon family and their friends. But now the Turnpike Corporation went to court against Eleazar, and won a civil action in the amount of $40,000 for failure to have the road constructed. It was a very large sum, far in excess of his real estate, or even the value of the road. Eleazar Phelps resigned his judgeship, closed his legal business, and left town with his wife and six small children. His real estate was seized by the sheriff.

But he appears to have carried with him a considerable fortune. Perhaps in fear of litigation, he moved with his wife and six children to Europe. They left the country before the War of 1812 and remained abroad until 1815, traveling widely.

After the war they decided to move back to America and made their home in New York City. Eleazar set himself up in foreign trade. By 1817, when New York City was beginning its great period of commercial expansion, he appeared to be doing well. In 1818 he decided to sail to Cuba on business. Then suddenly came yet another reversal of fortune. His vessel was attacked by pirates who plundered it so completely that they even took the clothes off Eleazar's back. But they let him live, and he made his way to Havana. A letter to his family assured them that all was well. Then suddenly he was stricken by a tropical fever. A few weeks later Eleazar was dead.

His widow, Phebe Phelps, somehow was able to pick up the pieces, and supported her children in New York until they began to prosper in trade and were able to support her. She lived until 1861, and died in a comfortable country home in Connecticut, surrounded by her family.

The strange story of Eleazar and Phebe Phelps offers a new perspective on America in the era of the early republic. The state of Connecticut in that period appears in the historical literature as a place of order and internal peace. The career of Eleazar Phelps tells a different tale. It offers evidence of a turbulent society, full of internal stresses, conflict, and violence. In the case of the Phelps family, the system of law and order in Connecticut broke down entirely. One of the richest and most powerful families in Stafford was driven out of town by two vicious mob assaults. The violence was done with apparent impunity.

At the same time, Eleazar appears to have succeeded in extracting from Stafford a fortune large enough to take his entire family to Europe for an extended period, and then to set himself up as a merchant in New York. Perhaps he gained his wealth by methods that did not endear him to his neighbors. In any case, this remarkable incident tells us that Connecticut was very far from the "land of steady habits" that appears in the scholarly literature. It tells us that historians of the early republic have work to do.

The fifth and last tale is about George Alexander Phelps (1803–80) and America in the era that historians call the "middle period" of the nineteenth century.

George Alexander was the son of Eleazar and Phebe Phelps, and a direct descendant of all the protagonists in these stories. In 1818 he was fifteen years old when his father died miserably of fever at Havana.

Unlike his father and grandfathers, George Alexander never graduated from college. He went into business in New York. By 1825, at the age of 22, he had sufficient capital to be set up as a "fruiter." He did well and advanced quickly from "fruiter" to "importer" to "commission merchant." He became a partner in a firm that specialized in the highly lucrative business of importing oranges, lemons, dates, raisins, and figs from the Mediterranean to Manhattan.

George Alexander worked on Front Street, near other fruit merchants on the East River. He appears to have associated with a coterie of Connecticut Yankees who controlled much of the business in that neighborhood, and also with artisans and merchants from other regions. The range of his friends was different from all of his forbears and significant of a change in the texture of American society. In 1825 he met and married Eliza Ayres, the daughter of a silver plater with Virginia roots. He was the first of the protagonists to marry outside the narrow boundaries of New England culture.

The marriage appears to have been happy and fruitful, and the business continued to flourish. George Alexander appears to have been careful and very prudent. He survived the major panics of 1837 and 1857 and got through many other vicissitudes in the turbulent business history of New York City. Credit reports in the files of R. G. Dun and Company show steady growth in his wealth and reputation. By 1854 his firm was described as a "first rate house" with a capital of $300,000.

The family also grew rapidly. By 1849 there were twelve children. George Alexander moved from a modest home in lower Manhattan to a fashionable brownstone house on 14th Street. His children and grandchildren intermarried with wealthy merchants in New York and Connecticut. He also acquired a country house and estate of 20 acres in Fairfield, Connecticut, where his mother lived until her death.

Four of George Alexander's sons entered the family firm, and greatly expanded its operations. They opened offices in Palermo (1859) and Liverpool (by 1873) and began trading in cotton and other goods. By 1866 Dun's credit reporters estimated the firm's worth at between $500,000 and $1 million. George Alexander retired from his business, which began to be called Phelps Sons. He moved to Fairfield, bought an even bigger house, and died there in 1880, leaving a large estate entirely to his family.

Peter Judd observes that "the pursuit of wealth and the maintenance of family life" were the two great themes of George Alexander's life. His sphere of activity as a successful import merchant was larger in geographic terms than any Phelps who came before him, but it was tightly centered in other ways. We find no evidence of interests outside his highly specialized business and his family, no indication of engagement in politics, religion, culture, or other sorts of economic activity, and no sign of involvement in large events. George Alexander was a businessman, absorbed in the pursuit of wealth and the support of his family. In many ways the life of this "modern" master of business enterprise was more constrained than that of his early New England ancestors.

There is a curious paradox here. The structure of American society was growing more complex in the nineteenth century, but the condition of individual lives was becoming more narrow and more specialized than early American lives had been. Here again we find a very interesting and suggestive way of rethinking our views on another period of American history in the nineteenth century.

These five stories become even more interesting when they are read together. One finds strong continuities from one Phelps generation to the next. Always there was the same restless striving that brought William and Ann Phelps to America in 1630. Every generation took an entrepreneurial approach to life and assumed risk for the sake of profit. They worked very hard, but Max Weber, in his *Protestant Ethic and the Spirit of Capitalism*, clearly misunderstood them.* They were not driven by an ethic of work, but by an ethic of striving. Through many generations that attitude changed its object but not its nature.

There were also continuities in the world where they lived. In every generation that American world was open, fluid, dynamic, turbulent, disorderly, and very dangerous. In all but the last generation there was extreme instability in their lives. Peter Judd observes, "research expands and enlivens family memory," adding, "it also tears at the heart."

Every generation of Phelpses lived in a time of great events and sweeping change. They were caught up in large historical processes, but they were not merely the objects of history. All of them were autonomous actors whose lives might be understood as a series of choices. The future was open for them. Their decisions always made a difference, but the results were not as anyone could have desired or foreseen.

Always there is a very strong sense of family, and a broad web of kin-connections, which are vitally important to the welfare of each individual member. Vital figures in the maintenance of this system of support were the women who often took over entirely the management of the family's affairs in the face of misfortune. That happened in three of the five Phelps families who appear in this book. In every generation, the scope of a woman's responsibility was not confined to separate spheres, as the literature suggests. In all these many Phelpses, male and female, there was an extraordinary strength and resilience, which appeared most of all in moments of defeat.

---

* Max Weber, *The Protestant Ethic and the Spirit of Capitalism*, trans. Talcott Parsons, 2d ed. (London: Allen and Unwin, 1976).

All this emerges from Peter Haring Judd's remarkably successful way of bringing history and genealogy together. It comes from his extraordinary research in primary materials, and his close reading of the secondary literature, and most of all from his warmth and sensitivity to the people who appear in every part of the book. In all of these ways Peter Judd's book is a model for research and writing in history and genealogy. His own striving for excellence in the work, and his success in achieving it, is true to the spirit of his remarkable family.

DAVID HACKETT FISCHER *received his Ph.D. at Johns Hopkins University in 1962. Since then he has taught at Brandeis University, where he has served as Chair of the Crown Program in American History intermittently since 1973. He has also taught at Harvard University, the University of Washington, Seattle, Oxford University, and at various institutions in New Zealand. Professor Fischer has received numerous awards for teaching and scholarship, and his contributions to the field have been recognized with the St. Nicholas Society's Irving Medal (1996) and the Ingersoll Foundation's Ingersoll Prize (1997). His many publications include the award-winning* Albion's Seed: Four British Folkways in America *(1989),* Paul Revere's Ride *(1994), and* The Great Wave: Price Movements in Modern History *(1996), all published by Oxford University Press. He currently resides in Wayland, Massachusetts, with his wife Judith. He has been a member of the New England Historic Genealogical Society since 1995.*

# PREFACE

Above the prickly horsehair sofa in the front hall of my grandmother's house there were three portraits in oval frames. Two were husband and wife, I was told. The husband was an ethereal-looking young man with dark hair. He wore a high white collar and a black jacket with a matching bow tie below his chin, accented by the white shirtfront. He looked directly at me. The same hand painted his wife, whose gaze tilted slightly, as though in deference to her husband. She struck me as composed and reserved. A white lace collar brought out the paleness of her face. They both had dark brown eyes, like my mother, like me.

The third portrait showed a woman with red hair, unlike anyone I knew in our family. A prominent nose gave her face an angular, noble cast. She seemed to come from a different world. Before I knew the word "elegance" she embodied it for me. These images were imprinted on my imagination as indelibly then as the Remington mounted Indian warrior on the mantle nearby, whose lance was perpetually aimed at an imagined buffalo. Grandmother surely told me many times who these august persons were, but to me they were simply ancestors who had lived in a remote and unreachable time. I shared with many children the sense that my family faded into impenetrable obscurity when no one remained who had known them.

I knew my grandmother's parents from framed photographs on her bureau, and because she told me stories about them they lived for me in a past I could understand. I liked the elderly lady seated on a bench in a garden who held out her hand to a magnificent collie named Pierrot, and I believed I would recognize her if she walked into the room. I remember feeling sad on my eighth birthday when my mother told me that her grandmother would have been 88; I knew that people did live that long and that I could have known her. Great-grandfather was present in several photos. The ends of his moustache were trimmed so that they turned up slightly, and his hat was slightly tipped. In informal poses he looked as though he was about to say something wry. He was portly, and in a formal picture he looked like a senator, impossibly remote. There was one photo that I particularly liked. It was a souvenir of a visit to an Atlantic City photographer with a set of mirrors and showed half-a-dozen great-grandfathers seated around a table, each with a twinkle in his eye. I knew he was a man who would *stride* into a room. The faces in the portraits in the oval frames were not as remote as I thought. The man and wife were the parents of the elderly woman with the collie, and the elegant lady was her grandmother.

1. James Demarest Haring (1819–1868)
The images of Haring and his wife, painted photographs on glass, were probably made in New York City at the time of their marriage, 1 September 1846.

I grew up in the 1930s in Waterbury, Connecticut. All my relatives seemed to live in houses within a few minutes' walk. My mother early taught me the gradations of cousins, aunts, uncles, "greats," and "removeds." I had a lively sense of how we were all related and enjoyed reciting the distinctions.

I thought then that it was the natural course of things for all relatives to live nearby. I had no idea that they lived near each other because our common great-grandfathers had come to Waterbury and its factories less than a hundred years before. Those men were energetic lads from villages in eastern Connecticut, attracted to a place where others were putting their mechanical and organizational skills to new uses. Their factories in the rapidly growing city transformed copper, brass, and steel wire into oil and gas lamp fixtures, fasteners, eyelets, plumbing, stays for clothing, and hardware for the nation's houses. In my childhood, their sons and grandsons carried on in those factories.

2. Caroline Eliza (Phelps) Haring (1828–1868)

As I write, it is over 150 years since those pioneers came to the city of factories. Not one of this family remains in Waterbury or its environs, and no descendant has been involved in manufacturing for a third of a century. What was the vivid present in my childhood seems nearly as remote to me as the world in which the people in the oval portraits lived.

The great-grandmother on the garden bench by Pierrot was born Julia Phelps Haring in 1851 on Monroe Street, where Manhattan bulges to the east. The house was within walking distance of her father's office on Peck Slip, near the piers where he and his brother were flour brokers. He was James Demarest Haring, the fine-looking young man with the steady gaze. His wife was born Caroline Eliza Phelps, the lady in the white lace collar. William Phelps, her immigrant ancestor, born in the West Country of England, came in the Great Migration to Massachusetts Bay and thence to Windsor on the Connecticut River. In the six fecund generations that followed him, Phelps sons and daughters could be found throughout Connecticut, up and down "Great River," and in New York State and City. It was in the city that Caroline Eliza's father was a prosperous importer in the Mediterranean fruit trade. Her husband's Harings emigrated from

Holland, the first arriving in New Amsterdam in the 1630s. James was mostly Dutch, but he had Huguenot blood as well. Doubtless more important to him was the tradition of leadership. His grandfather was active in the rebel cause in New York and served three terms as a member of the Continental Congress. His father was an officer in the northern army during the frustrating campaigns around Lake Ontario in the War of 1812.

In 1874, six years after her parents died, their only child, Julia Phelps Haring, married George Luther White, of Waterbury. He was the son of one of those inventors and entrepreneurs who had come to the city in the 1840s. The Whites lived in that city all their lives, and their three children were born and died there.

Julia prepared a notebook for her granddaughter's sixth birthday in 1913, in which she set down the family lines that came down to the child. Filling its pages in her scrawling hand were the names of the Dutch Harings, the Puritan English Phelps, Davenport, and Wheelock families from which she descended, and her husband's White, Ranney, Eels forebears from the lower Connecticut River valley. There is not a blot in it, and letters in her collections showed me that she had consulted the authorities of the day for the older generations.

Julia's concern for preserving her family's history had its roots, I believe, in her effort to keep hold of the past that had been taken from her when both her parents died when she was 17. With her father gone there were no more visits to Kip, Roosevelt, Haring, and Jones cousins in New York. When his older sister died four years later, Julia's touch with the Haring past vanished as "old New York" had disappeared in the transforming midcentury city. The Phelps relatives remained close, but she doubtless looked back on her life with her mother and dashing father (as the ethereal young man became) as a time all the more golden through its disappearance. The lists in the notebook probably helped her recapture the happy moments of her youth.

The notebook came to me 60 years later and was the talisman that led me to this study. Like many other researchers into family history, I became curious about the persons and stories behind the names, titles, and dates. What did an "Esq." do in colonial Connecticut? How was it that the eastern Connecticut town of Hebron produced such determined and enterprising men? What was Alexander Phelps's relationship with his well-known father-in-law, Eleazar Wheelock? What was Alexander doing in New Hampshire when he died? One of his sons in this family with a Puritan-Congregational past was noted as an Episcopalian missionary in New

York State. What was his life like? Another son, named for his grandfather, was a judge in Federalist Connecticut but died in Havana, Cuba. This last amazing fact was entered in the notebook without comment. Could I ever uncover his story? And why, as the notebook also reports, had he left Connecticut to travel in Europe during the War of 1812? How came it to pass that his wife—also named Phelps—had been born in Cornwallis, Nova Scotia, a place not on modern maps?

The queries multiplied early in my research, whetting the appetite. As I moved from secondary works and printed sources to archives and manuscript collections, the discoveries increased. I soon came to focus on the experience of the Phelps family line from the 1720s to the 1880s and on five heads of family who were related by blood and marriage: father, two sons, half-brother and father-in-law, and grandson. Their experience covered the last years of colonial America and the early national period through the centennial. It included radically different enterprises that went to the heart of the interests of their day, from the evangelical revival known as the Great Awakening to the opening up of New York City to the world as a center of trade, finance, and immigration.

I wanted to understand how families in three successive generations responded to the social and economic challenges of their times. The physical and social conditions of the life of the colonial official, Alexander Phelps, who died before the Revolution, are nearly as different from those of his grandson, the New York merchant, George Alexander, who died over 100 years later, as they are to mine.

Among the women in these families, two were widowed early and raised children to adulthood. All of the mothers here bore children over periods from 16 to as many as 22 years; they cared for small children for half a lifetime. They experienced the loss of infants and small children—never more than in the nineteenth century—and the satisfaction that most survived them. Three of these women endured the absence of their husbands for long periods of time and had to take on "outside" tasks—caring for farm animals and the minding the crops—as well as run the household. They all lived to old age themselves and could look back on vanished worlds.

The geography of this narrative is expansive. It involves Connecticut towns, Portsmouth, New Hampshire, the upper Connecticut River valley, Nova Scotia, western New York and Upper Canada, New York City, Bermuda, and the Caribbean and the transatlantic world of Europe, Liverpool, and the high seas. Within this geography, five men and their families collectively lived through a transformation of the world that affected every aspect of social and economic relations and the man-made environment. I have sought to place the lives of individuals in this larger historical context.

# ACKNOWLEDGMENTS

A New Yorker researching colonial and early national Connecticut and New York has access to an abundance of riches within the city. The Irma and Paul Milstein Division of United States History, Local History and Genealogy at the New York Public Library, with its helpful staff and pleasant working space, has been the locus of much of my research. The library of The New York Genealogical and Biographical Society provides an accessible and comprehensive collection and a congenial staff. The New-York Historical Society's library is an essential resource for the city in this period.

The Dartmouth College Library graciously supplied copies from the college archive of the correspondence of Alexander and Benajah Phelps, Eleazar Wheelock, Eleazar Wheelock Phelps, and Josiah Bartlett. Excerpts are quoted in the following pages by permission. I am grateful to Anne Ostendarp and Barbara L. Krieger for their expert comments and assistance.

Staff members of the Public Archives of Nova Scotia, the Connecticut Historical Society, the Worcester Historical Museum, the American Antiquarian Society, the Archives of the Episcopal Diocese of New York (Wayne Kempton, Archivist), the Grafton County (N.H.) Probate Court, the Ontario County (N.Y.) Probate Court and the Lycoming County Historical Society are among those who responded generously to my inquiries.

Several researchers worked on my behalf in near and distant libraries and archives. Judith Plummer, now of Westbrook, Maine, combed the Connecticut State Archives and the local records with an experienced eye. Dr. Allen B. Robertson of Halifax performed similar services at the Nova Scotian archives. William Stansfield of Fairfield, Connecticut, provided information on the Phelps family in that town in the nineteenth century. T. J. Hughes of Kew, Surrey, assisted with research into the naval records at the Public Record Office in London. Susan Burton of Toronto supplied information from the Ontario Archives. Thomas S. Johnson checked the "Shipping News" columns of 1818 New York City newspapers for me.

I am indebted to a number of readers for their comments on drafts of chapters: Christopher Collier, the Connecticut State Historian; Professor Alan Taylor, History Department, University of California, Davis; Margaret Conrad, Director of the Planter Study Center, Acadia University, Wolfville, N.S.; Barry Moody, former Director of the Planter Study Center; John V. Duncanson, historian of Falmouth, N.S.; Sharon DeBartolo Carmack, C.G., historian and genealogist; Harry Macy, Jr., F.A.S.G., Editor of *The New York Genealogical and Biographical Record;* and my friends David P. Chandler, Warren Michel Swenson, Betty Fussell, Phyllis La Farge Johnson, and the late Douglas D. McKee. Dr. Howard J. Schneider restored my eyes to health so I could undertake this research. I am grateful to all for help and encouragement and add the usual disclaimer, that they bear no responsibility for the result.

I thank Henry B. Hoff, C.G., F.A.S.G., for helping me find a home for my manuscript and for reviewing the genealogical materials on the Haring family. Scott C. Steward, Editor of the New England Historic Genealogical Society's *NEXUS*, and D. Brenton Simons, Editorial Director of the Newbury Street Press, were of critical assistance in the preparation of the publication. Thomas Kozachek, Editor of the Newbury Street Press, helped enormously in completing this project, sharpening sentences and ensuring consistency of style. This book is immeasurably better as a result of our collaborative process, which was always a pleasure.

Permissions for quotations from manuscripts in their collections were given by the Dartmouth College Archives; Baker Library, Historical Collections, Harvard University Business School, for the R. G. Dun & Co. Collection: Credit Reports; the National Archives of the Episcopal Church, for the use of the Samuel Peters Collection; and The New York Public Library for the use of maps from their collection.

At the Planters Study Conference, Acadia University, September 1998, I presented a paper on Benajah Phelps, which included some of the material in chapter 3. The fall 1997 issue of *Seaport*, the magazine of the South Street Seaport, New York, includes the letters quoted in chapter 5 from and about E. W. Phelps and the account of his voyage and death in Havana.

# KEY TO CITATIONS

| | |
|---|---|
| AGC | *Archives of the General Convention, The Correspondence of John Henry Hobart*, vols. 2–6, ed. Arthur Lowndes (New York: privately printed, 1912). |
| Arch. Ont. | Archives of Ontario, Toronto, Ontario, Canada. |
| Budke | The George H. Budke Collection, Manuscripts and Archives Division, New York Public Library, New York City. |
| CSL | Connecticut State Library, Hartford, Connecticut. |
| Conn. Arch. | Connecticut Archives at the Connecticut State Library. |
| *DAB* | Allen Johnson and Dumas Malone, eds., *Dictionary of American Biography* (New York: Charles Scribner's Sons, 1928–). |
| DCA | Dartmouth College Archives, Dartmouth College Library, Special Collections, Hanover, New Hampshire. |
| *DCB* | *Dictionary of Canadian Biography* (Toronto: Toronto Univ. Press, 1966–) |
| *DNB* | Leslie Stephen and Sidney Lee, *Dictionary of National Biography* (London: Oxford Univ. Press, 1885–). |
| FHL | Microfilm, Family History Library, The Church of Latter Day Saints, Salt Lake City, Utah. |
| Force 4 | Peter Force, *American Archives Fourth Series, Containing A Documentary History of the English Colonies in North America from the King's Message to parliament of March 7, 1774 to The Declaration of Independence by the United States* (Washington, D.C.: St. Clair Clarke and Peter Force, 1843). |
| JHW MSS | Notebook, letters, and other material of Julia Phelps (Haring) White (1851–1928) in possession of Peter Haring Judd. |
| NEHGS | New England Historic Genealogical Society, Boston, Massachusetts. |
| *NGSQ* | *National Genealogical Society Quarterly* (Washington, D.C.: National Genealogical Society, 1912–). |

| | |
|---|---|
| NSARM | Nova Scotia Archives and Records Management [*olim* Public Archives of Nova Scotia], Halifax, Nova Scotia, Canada. |
| NYGBS | New York Genealogical and Biographical Society, New York, New York. |
| NYHS | New-York Historical Society, New York, New York. |
| NYPL | New York Public Library, New York, New York. |
| NYPL Mss. Div. | New York Public Library, Manuscript and Archives Division. |
| *NYT* | *New York Times.* |
| *PRCC* | *The Public Records of the Colony of Connecticut*, ed. J. Hammond Trumbull and Charles J. Hoadly, 15 vols. (Hartford, Conn.: [State of Connecticut], 1850–90). |
| *PRSC* | *The Public Records of the State of Connecticut*, ed. Charles J. Hoadly, Leonard W. Labaree, Catherine Fennelly, Albert R. Van Dusen, Christopher Collier, Bonnie Bromberger, Dorothy Ann Lipson and Douglas M. Arnold, 15 vols. (Hartford, Conn.: [State of Connecticut], 1894–1991). |
| *OED* | *The Oxford English Dictionary: A New English Dictionary on Historical Principles* (Oxford: Clarendon Press, 1888–). |
| *Peters Coll.* | Samuel Peters Collection, National Archives of the Episcopal Church, Austin, Texas. The guide to this archive is Kenneth Walter Cameron, *The Papers of Loyalist Samuel Peters: A Survey of the Contents of his Notebooks—Correspondence during his Flight to England, Exile, and the Last Years of His life* (Hartford, Conn.: Transcendental Books, 1972). |
| Phelps 1899 | Oliver Seymour Phelps and Andrew T. Servin, comps., *The Phelps Family of America and their English Ancestors with Copies of Wills, Deeds, Letters and Other Interesting Papers, Coats of Arms and Valuable Records*, 2 vols. (Pittsfield, Mass.: Eagle Publishing, 1899). |
| PRO | Public Record Office, Kew, Richmond, Surrey, United Kingdom. |

| | |
|---|---|
| *Record* | *New York Genealogical and Biographical Record*. (New York: NYGBS, 1870–). |
| *Register* | *New England Historical and Genealogical Register* (Boston: NEHGS, 1847–). |
| R. G. Dun | R. G. Dun & Co. Collection: Credit Reports, New York City, Historical Collections, Baker Library, Harvard Business School, Cambridge, Mass. |
| *TAG* | *The American Genealogist* (Warwick, R.I., 1922–). |
| VRs | Vital Records, Barbour Collection, Connecticut State Library (unless otherwise noted). |

# ABBREVIATIONS

| | |
|---|---|
| aft. | after |
| b. | born |
| bef. | before |
| bet. | between |
| bp. | baptized |
| ca. | circa |
| Co. | county |
| d. | died |
| dau. | daughter |
| m. | married |
| obit. | obituary |
| poss. | possibly |
| prob. | probably |
| resp. | respectively |
| y. | young |

# PART ONE

# *A FAMILY NARRATIVE*

# I

## LAND AND SOCIETY

*Land! Land! Has been the idol of many in New England.*

— Increase Mather, "An Earnest Exhortation to the Inhabitants of New England"

*Moreover I will appoint a place for my people Israel, and I will plant them, that they may dwell in a place of their own, and move no more.*

— II Samuel 7:10

In the seventeenth century New England was in the grip of a "little ice age"; its average temperatures were about equivalent to those of southern Labrador in the twentieth century. Far from being an impediment, the challenge to overcome the weather provided "an immensely stimulating environment for an active population."[1] The families were large since most children survived, and there was a steady growth in population throughout the century and into the next. In Connecticut this was almost entirely the result of flourishing families, as there was little immigration after the first European settlements.[2]

By the 1690s the pressure on the land in the settled towns was evident. Young men in the towns along the coast and the Connecticut River began to seek land further away, where it would be cheaper and more plentiful. The preachers railed against this appetite for more, but they "failed to sustain the ideal of the small-scale, nucleated town that inspired the earliest settlers. Men wanted elbow room, not clustered houses and outlying common or private fields."[3] In only a few years the Puritan emigrants were on the move again; they had "planted" as the prophet Samuel enjoined, but

---

[1] "Average rates of mortality in Massachusetts fell far below those of most places in the western world." David Hackett Fischer, *Albion's Seed: Four British Folkways in America* (New York: Oxford Univ. Press, 1989), 52, 54. Fischer's information on the temperature is based on Hubert H. Lamb, *The Changing Climate: Selected Papers* (London: Methuen, 1960), 16.

[2] Robert J. Taylor, *Colonial Connecticut: A History* (Millwood, N.Y.: KTO Press, 1979), 62–73.

[3] John R. Stilgoe, *Common Landscape of America, 1580 to 1845* (New Haven: Yale University Press, 1982), 45.

many wanted another and larger place of their own, and the injunction to "move no more" was lost in the richness of the land they had found.

One reason was success. The first generations of settlers had learned to raise crops and animals in quantities beyond their needs, and they developed a market for them: "Everywhere good land was at a premium, and industrious men, with a little luck, grew rich by working larger and larger holdings and speculating in land. Elbow room was not the product of sinful lust but of calculated investment."[4] Their drive to expand their living space was, of course, necessitated by their growth as a population—more land was needed to sustain ever greater numbers. Most children survived to adulthood and needed their own houses and land when they married.

## Hebron

At the beginning of the eighteenth century there still were lands within the colony not allocated to any town, abandoned by native Americans, whose population had been decimated by epidemics early in the preceding century. The legislature would approve a "plantation" and grant lands to those who agreed to build on and settle them. Our interest lies in a forested tract six miles square on the uplands east of the Connecticut River, which the legislature approved as a "plantation." Among those who arrived about 1704 to clear the land for the first houses were two young Phelps men from Windsor, grandsons of one of its founders. There were nine families in residence when Hebron was incorporated in 1707. It was named for the place of such consequence for the Children of Israel, honored as the birthplace of Sarah, Abraham's wife, and the site of a famous conquest by Joshua.[5] The first town meeting in Hebron took place in 1708, and the General Assembly recognized the settlement as a town in 1709.

---

[4] Ibid., 48.

[5] In the Old Testament, Hebron was the burial place of Sarah, wife of Abraham. Joshua reclaimed it for the Children of Israel after their return from Egyptian exile. Hebron is also said to have been a place where tribes came together; one view is that the Connecticut Hebron was so named because the settlers came from at least two communities, Saybrook and Windsor. Florence S. Marcy Crofut, *Guide to the History and the Historic Sites of Connecticut* (New Haven: Yale Univ. Press, 1937), 801: "'Society, a league, friendship' are probable meanings . . . the name possibly referred to the settlers' union into a community." Arthur H. Hughes and Morse S. Allen, *Connecticut Place Names* (Hartford: Connecticut Historical Society, 1976), 248; [Samuel Andrews Peters,] *General History of Connecticut*, by a Gentleman of the Province (London, 1781; New Haven, 1829), 138.

Present-day Hebron is somewhat smaller in area than that incorporated in 1709; in the next century portions were allocated to the towns of Marlborough and Columbia.[6]

The Connecticut General Assembly determined the boundaries of a town when it enacted its incorporation. From that point the freemen (male holders of property) could elect officers to manage the town's business—taxation, property and vital records, ways, fencing, stray animals. They also elected two delegates to represent them in the semi-annual assembly. This well-organized process reflected the ultimate authority of the colony's central government, which, however, granted the towns authority in most matters affecting the inhabitants. The pioneer families seeking to establish a new town had a tested institutional framework already in place in other towns and sanctioned by law and experience as effective in maintaining order and assuring property owners of voting powers and representation of their choice.[7] Service in local government was an important function; the name Phelps is found in all the important town offices for decades following the incorporation.

The physical arrangement of the towns created in the 1700s was no longer that of the "nucleated village" found in England and in the Phelps's native Windsor, where house lots were close to one another at the center and fields lay at a distance. The houses in Hebron and other later-established towns were scattered, set in their owners' fields and woodlots.

The incorporation of the towns provided for public space. The meetinghouse was the "center of all man-made improvements," placed where roads intersected. Nearby was the parson's house, situated on a lot also reserved for the burial ground. The prime location for private houses was near the meetinghouse, where residents had ready access to Sabbath meetings, the roads, and the trade that passed by. The incorporations also established a training field for the militia and common grazing land (the green), often trampled and muddied by cattle and sheep.[8]

---

[6] John Sibun, *Our Town's Heritage, 1708–1958, Hebron, Connecticut* (1975; reprint, Hebron, Conn.: Douglas Library of Hebron, 1992), 12, 36.

[7] Taylor, *Colonial Connecticut*, 65–75.

[8] Stilgoe, *Common Landscape*, 48.

3. Connecticut River Valley Settlement, Later 1600s
A portion of "An Exact Mapp of New England and New York."

*Map Division, The New York Public Library, Astor, Lenox and Tilden Foundations*

## Church and State

Congregationalism was the established religion in Connecticut, in a polity that did not separate church and state. In these early days, the ecclesiastical society had coterminous boundaries with the town, and its formation also required action by the legislature. It was supported by tithes levied on the property holders and enforceable by the courts. (In the course of the century this requirement was loosened to exempt members of other sects, but at the time of Hebron's founding such lenity was unthinkable.) The pastors were the most learned men in most communities, with moral authority and political influence.

New England Congregationalism, which developed in the seventeenth century, had no central authority: "A group of persons (visible saints) could form a church by agreement and consent, when they, living in the same society, would covenant to observe the ordinances of Christ." The covenant was a solemn obligation made in open meeting, which permitted the members to participate in the grace of God. The officers elected by such a group were elders, deacons, and the pastor, who was ordained by the congregation that called him. The pastorate was considered to be a lifetime appointment, and the pastor was the "leader of the community and wielded considerable power . . . shaping political, social, as well as religious convictions of his parishioners."[9]

The community was closely governed. The elected town officers regulated the maintenance of fences, stray animals, the construction and placement of houses, and the behavior of its citizens:

> Every householder kept his wife and children and any adults who lived under his roof, in the knowledge of God and His laws and in continuous obedience to local regulation, or else his neighbors entered his house and corrected his error . . . The household . . . depended on mutual aid to maintain order, but every household order depended on the town for its existence.[10]

Families were the nuclear social unit, "the root whence church and commonwealth cometh," as a Bay Colony preacher put it.[11] In Puritan thought, the covenant between God and the individual was enlarged to include parents, children, and kindred. New Englanders paid great attention to lineage, as we shall see with the Phelpses. Generations are linked through Christian names that connect one to the other: "New England's interest in genealogy . . . was not a pride in rank and quarterings, but a moral and religious idea that developed directly from the Puritan principles of the founders." [12]

Marriage was a civil contract. The ceremony was usually performed at home in the presence of a magistrate. The husband was in charge of the household and the affairs of the farm or the business. "Conjugal relations rested upon an assumption of inequality between the sexes," and the convention that women were helpmates was frequently expressed.[13] Almost

---

[9] Edwin S. Gaustad, *The Great Awakening in New England* (New York: Harper, 1957), 5.

[10] Ibid., 50.

[11] Jonathan Mitchell, "Sermon from Psalms," quoted in Edmund S. Morgan, *The Puritan Family* (New York: Harper and Row, 1966), 15.

[12] Gaustad, *Great Awakening*, 69–70.

[13] Fischer, *Albion's Seed*, 81, 83.

all women married in this period, and as wives and mothers they had several roles requiring hard work, skill, and perseverance. Basing her work on diaries, court cases, and inventories, Laurel Thatcher Ulrich describes these roles as *housewife* (having duties within the house, cooking and household management, and yard); *deputy husband* (shouldering male duties, such as planting or running the household, as Theodora [Wheelock] Phelps would have to do as a widow); *consort* (harmonizing spirituality and sexuality in marriage); *mother* (spending herself "to perpetuate the race" and society); *mistress* (training those who served her, such as her neighbor's daughters); *neighbor* (participating in the community of women who gathered to share news and help with childbirth); and *Christian* (with full membership in the meeting and often in the majority).[14] Much of the written record documents the activities and positions of males, but the health of the community in the deepest sense depended on the daily service in the home performed by women.

Mothers usually began the child's first lessons in reading and writing at home. The densely argued sermons at the Sabbath meetings required that listeners have not only a knowledge of the Bible but also the ability to follow the recondite arguments of a text that took an hour or more to deliver. The ability to read and understand the Bible and the laws of men was a key tenet of the Puritans, as they sought to maintain the beliefs that motivated their emigration to the New World.[15] Schools were as important as meetinghouses as marks of civilization and were equally supported by taxation.[16] Harvard, founded in 1636, and Yale, founded in 1707, were institutions that marked the colonists' commitment to higher education. Four of the Phelps men in this account attended college (two Yale, two Dartmouth), and Eleazar Wheelock, the father-in-law of one and mentor of another, founded Dartmouth, the third college of pre-Revolutionary New England.

---

[14] Laurel Thatcher Ulrich, *Good Wives: Image and Reality in the Lives of Women in Northern New England 1650–1750* (New York: Vintage Books, 1991), 8–9. For a vivid picture of birthing practices see the same author's *A Midwife's Tale: The Life of Martha Ballard, Based on Her Diary, 1785–1812* (New York: Vintage Books, 1991).

[15] Fischer, *Albion's Seed*, 129–34.

[16] One fifth to one half of the limited public funds available in newly created towns in Puritan New England went to the school. "The entire school system was dominated by the Congregational Society, within which authority was vested . . . at the head of the school system [after its founding in 1707] was Yale." Julian P. Boyd, ed., *The Susquehannah Company Papers* (1930; reprint, Ithaca, N.Y.: Cornell Univ. Press, published for Wyoming Historical and Genealogical Society, Wilkes-Barre, Pa., 1962), 1:xxii.

## Creating Place

The land in the vicinity of Hebron was well drained by two small rivers, one flowing into the Connecticut, the other into the Thames to the east. There are considerable changes in elevation and varied topography, with ridges that exceed 500 feet above sea level. It was thickly forested when the settlers arrived, with a few clearings left by the Indians. The Connecticut River was about 15 miles away, Windsor over 20 (overland or by the river). On the Thames River estuary, about 20 miles away, was Norwich, a center of trade and an important destination for produce and animals to be shipped to the West Indies.

The first families made a clearing for a house and planted the first year's crop among the tree stumps and ashes from burned brush. Their forebears had learned that the native corn ("Indian corn") grew well in rough conditions and could be planted among the stumps in the first season after clearing. It gave "a good yield without plowing, hoeing or manuring, and the ashes from the cleared land furnished a good fertilizer." The planters usually used the yellow or "flint" corn (because of the hardness of its kernels), which had immense advantages as a first crop since it had a high yield and ripened early.[17]

The earliest settlers preferred to kill trees by girdling them rather than chopping them down and hauling them. Colonial families used enormous quantities of wood for heating, an estimated 30 to 40 cords per year. The sawmill was one of the first enterprises in any town and consumed the forest trees to cut lumber for houses and barns.[18] In the first seasons after clearing fields the settlers would plant among the dead trunks, which would eventually fall. Later, when the stumps had been pulled out or rotted away, the fields could be plowed and planted with wheat and rye. The early settlers grew a variety of vegetables for the table, "leeks, melons, English gourds, radishes, cabbages, peas and asparagus," and most houses had herb gardens. The root crops—potatoes, carrots, turnips—"were not appreciated as food."[19] Farms prospered and an export trade gradually developed in the early 1700s.

---

[17] Bruce C. Daniels, *The Fragmentation of New England: Comparative Perspectives on Economic, Political and Social Divisions in the Eighteenth Century* (Westport, Conn.: Greenwood Press, 1988), 4.

[18] William Cronon, *Change in the Land: Indians, Colonists, and the Ecology of New England* (New York, 1985), 120.

[19] Ibid., 5.

"[D]omestic grazing animals—and the plow which they made possible," according to William Cronon's study of New England ecology, "were arguably the single most distinguishing characteristic of European agricultural practices." They critically influenced the development of an integrated economy: "Grazing animals were the quickest way for colonists to develop cash with a minimum of labor . . . [and were] one of the linchpins which made commercial agriculture possible in New England . . . Livestock production became tied to the markets of the ports by a web of relationships that extended beyond the fall drives."[20] By the latter part of the eighteenth century this trade made Hebron the richest township in its county.[21]

The settlers used animal power as the native Americans never had. Their oxen-driven plows could break land deeper and more extensively than the hoe and mattock. Oxen could also be used to remove boulders and the ubiquitous stumps. Unlike the aboriginal inhabitants of the land, the settlers bred domestic animals. Hogs were particularly useful in the early years, as the settlers could let them loose in the woods or in the partially cleared sections. Unlike sheep, they "could stand their own against wolves." They were used for meat and hides and often bred in such quantities that the surplus could be sold. Cattle, used for meat, dairy, and hides, required more care and were present in large numbers only after settlements became well established.

In the first generations the land yielded bountiful crops, but the settlers' agricultural practices were destructive and led to depletion of the soil. By mid-century there were warning signs. Jared Eliot, the scientifically-minded pastor at Killingworth on the Sound, raised a warning that tells us that the decline was evident by the 1740s. "When our forefathers settled here," he wrote, "they entered a Land which probably had never been Plowed since the Creation; the Land being new they depended upon the natural Fertility of the Ground, which served their purpose very well, and when they had worn out some piece they cleared another, without any concern to amend their Land, except a little helped by the Fold and the Cart-Dung . . . Old lands being thus worn out, I suppose to be one Reason why so many are inclined to Remove to new Places that they may raise Wheat; as they may have more Room, thinking that we live too thick."[22]

---

[20] Cronon, *Change in the Land*, 138–40.

[21] Crofut, *Guide to the History and the Historic Sites of Connecticut*, 809.

[22] Jared Eliot, *Essays on Field Husbandry*, 1747, quoted in *Susquehannah Company Papers*, 1:.xlvi.

The exhaustion of the soil no doubt played a considerable role in the 1760s emigration from eastern Connecticut towns to Nova Scotia, to the northern Connecticut valley in the 1760s (drawing a Phelps family and others from Hebron), and westward to New York.

A generation after the first clearings, Hebron presented an open landscape, with houses scattered amid their own fields; there was no closely built-up village center. The first meetinghouse was built in 1716 on the highest ridge, at the intersection of roads, where it was easily seen by all (the site of the present-day Congregational Church).[23] It was almost certainly the largest building in the town. In those years many churches were built with towers and spires, "dwarfing nearby houses and trees, and, suddenly, in the first years of the eighteenth century, ordering not only individual towns but the landscape emerging from the forest wilderness."[24] By 1756 there were an estimated 1,856 people in Hebron, and by the Revolution 2,337.[25] (The colony as a whole had an estimated 130,000 and 198,000 respectively in those years.)

Farmers in eastern Connecticut towns had surplus livestock and grain to sell to merchants for resale to the West Indies, where the plantations required large imports of food to maintain the slave population. Traders in the port cities sent livestock, packed meat, flour and cheese, and lumber to the islands in exchange for imported molasses, sugar, and rum. Most trade was conducted with bills of exchange and accounts of barter; specie was always scarce.[26]

As the price of foodstuffs rose during the century, farmers expanded their plantings and their production of livestock for the island trade. Hebron animals and surplus grains went to markets via the Connecticut River and the eastern ports of Norwich and New London. There were ups and downs: the trade with the islands was often interrupted by wars; many transactions primarily benefited merchants in the neighboring states, and

---

[23] Sibun, *Our Town's Heritage*, 20.

[24] Stilgoe, *Common Landscape*, 57.

[25] Evarts B. Greene and Virginia D. Harrington, *American Population Before the Federal Census of 1790* (New York, 1932); Gaspare John Saladino, "The Economic Revolution in Late Eighteenth Century Connecticut" (Ph.D. diss., Univ. of Wisconsin, 1964), appendix 2. Estimates from muster rolls and other sources indicate there were about 38,000 people in the Connecticut colony in 1730. By 1749 this had increased to 70,000 and by 1774 to 198,000. *Susquehannah Company Papers*, 1:xlix.

[26] Daniels, *Fragmentation of New England*, 11. According to Saladino, "The Economic Revolution," 2, "In the late colonial period, Connecticut vessels annually carried out 15,000 head of livestock, 20,000 barrels of beef and pork, and 15,000 pounds of cheese."

the perennial shortage of specie led to debts and lawsuits. Nonetheless, the export trade was the most dynamic element in the colonial economy until the Revolution. Hebron farmers were full participants in what was an evolving economic revolution, the move from a subsistence and barter system to a market economy.[27]

The first settlers had come to Hebron by trails and paths, but by mid-century there were well-traveled cartways connecting the town to Lebanon and Windham to the north and east, Colchester and Norwich and New London to the southeast, and the Connecticut River ports to the west. Hartford and New Haven were a day's journey by horse, Boston or New York two full days away.

Virtually all heads of household owned a house and land, and there were few mature men without a house or lot.[28]As the trading economy developed there came to be an increasing disparity of wealth. A study of assessments of households in colonial Connecticut revealed a progression. In the early 1700s the "wealthiest group owned 37 percent of the total, increasing that to 46 percent during the 1720s. There it stood . . . until the 1750s when it rose to over half, ending at 55 percent."[29] While these are colony-wide estimates and reflect the greater wealth in the larger trading towns, there was probably a similar increase in the share of total wealth by the well-to-do families in Hebron. Through their skills, strength, health, and application, some farmers, including the Phelps settlers in Hebron, were more successful than others and accumulated wealth.

The inhabitants of Hebron and other towns east of the river in colonial Connecticut had, in some respects, a different cultural and social orientation from those of the western towns. This is seen in their more fervent response to the religious revivals of the 1730s and 1740s and their more extensive emigration. The furor over the Stamp Act in 1765 was intense in the eastern towns. In the Revolution there were fewer Loyalists in the east than in the west. Most students of the subject consider the eastern Connecticut inhabitants to have been less conservative, more prey to popular movements, and under greater pressure of overpopulation. The east-west differences were always a factor in late colonial politics.[30]

---

[27] Daniels, *Fragmentation of New England,* 10. Saladino develops this theme in detail.

[28] "The proportion of men without even a house or lot a was one seventh for the first thirty years, less than one fourth thereafter. [They were] mostly young laborers, half under 30." Jackson T. Main, *Society and Economy in Colonial Connecticut* (Princeton: Princeton Univ. Press, 1985), 125.

[29] Ibid.

[30] *Susquehannah Company Papers*, 1:lii.

## Religious Revivals and Eleazar Wheelock

Religion was a major driving force behind the Puritan emigration, and it continued to be the central thread in the organization of their society in America. The families in this book lived their lives amid the aftereffects of the great religious revival called the Great Awakening. Hebron was profoundly affected by the revival's precursor, the local frontier revival of the 1730s.

By the 1720s the religious impulse had slackened as the first generations of the migration passed from the scene. The "Halfway Covenant," adopted by New England churches early in the 1700s, permitted membership in an ecclesiastical society without the full confession and covenant formerly required. To its supporters this was a moderate step that would open up membership to a wider circle, deemed important as the population increased. To traditionalists it showed a falling off from the discipline and commitment necessary to create the "New Jerusalem foretold by the prophets." Religion became more a matter of form than commitment, and there seems to have been a general decline in piety as much observance was centered on long, intellectual sermons by learned pastors.[31]

The Rev. Benjamin Trumbull, a historian of Connecticut late in the century, described the apparent decline of religion in society on the eve of the revivals of the 1730s and 40s:

> Young people became loose and vicious, family prayer and religion were greatly neglected. The young people made the evenings after the Lord's Day, and after lectures, the times for their mirth . . . taverns were haunted . . . It seems also to appear that many of the clergy, instead of clearly and powerfully preaching the doctrines of original sin, or regeneration, justification by faith alone, and the other peculiar doctrines of the gospel, content themselves with preaching a cold, unprincipled and lifeless morality.[32]

As religious feeling and commitment waned, the colonial economy expanded. Some were able to support the luxuries of dress and household furnishings then developing in England and imitated in Boston and New York. The improvements in trade were beginning to provide outlets for

---

[31] Gaustad, *Great Awakening,* 11, 14–15.

[32] Benjamin Trumbull, *A Complete History of Connecticut, Civil and Ecclesiastical, from the Emigration of its First Planters from England in the year 1650 and to the close of the Indian Wars* (New Haven: Maltby, Goldsmith, and Samuel Wadsworth [completed in 1797], 1818), 2:137.

energies that might in the previous century have gone into theological disputations. Church life became less central. "As sainthood became more synonymous with respectability," writes a historian of the revival, "Congregationalism became more like the world in which it lived, less like a pure fellowship of saints called out from society . . . New England, nodding sleepily, was soon to be awakened with a start."[33]

On 29 October 1727 there was an earthquake in New England that resulted in "a greater resort to ministers than the days before." The tremors were seen by many as God speaking to the feckless latter-day Children of Israel. The next sign that could be interpreted as the displeasure of God came in 1735 when an outbreak of "throat distemper" (diphtheria) swept New England, the worst epidemic since the emigration.

Whether directly related to these portents or not, as Jonathan Edwards famously observed of the Northampton to which he had recently come, "In 1735, the town seemed to be full of joy . . . [there were] remarkable tokens of God's presence in almost every house." The excitement spread down the Connecticut valley and into eastern Connecticut.[34]

The preachers who spurred the revival offered their listeners mighty themes. They spoke of God's majesty and His implacable anger at sinners; the terrors of the hellfire to which the unrepentant would be condemned for eternity; the potential of confession of sin and the sweetness of God's grace in Christ to welcome the confessed sinner when born again.

The revival brought emotionalism into the austere Calvinism of the established churches; members of the congregation cried out in agony, wept, spoke in tongues, sang for joy. Such manifestations were distasteful to traditionalists and many meetings split into what became termed "New Lights" and "Old Lights." The greater challenge was theological. Calvinist orthodoxy was based on the all-powerful God who had chosen His Elect and whose Will could not be influenced by human good works. The message of these revivalists (and of those in the Great Awakening that followed it) was that an individual could come into God's grace through self-examination and an autonomous act of confession. It was intention and behavior that signified, not the inscrutable will of God. Read this way, the revival opened up a challenge to clerical and, ultimately, to secular authority. Although the burst of excitement in the frontier revival lasted scarcely

---

[33] Gaustad, *Great Awakening*, 15.

[34] Ibid., 18.

more than a year, the implications were profound and were to be built upon by the more widely experienced Great Awakening.

The unanticipated results were a schism in Congregationalism, the emergence of competing sects, and the acceptance of individual autonomy as a mainspring of action. Such qualities fitted in with the developing world economy led by the British empire; this was expanding the wealth and goods available. This new abundance made existence in the world more inviting. Linked with the rationalism of the European Enlightenment and the material abundance of North America, it brought to an end the Puritan era of collective endeavor in New England and set in train the new spirit of entrepreneurial individualism. These changes influenced in varying ways the lives of the subjects of this book.

Hebron and neighboring Lebanon in the mid-1730s were, in the words of Trumbull, who had known several of the prominent preachers, "visited with an uncommon effusion of the holy spirit . . . Convictions were powerful, and terrible, at once bowing down sinners to the very dust, stripping them of every self-justifying plea."[35] There was also dissension, the eruption of what he called "violent opposers." The Hebron minister and several members of the congregation, dismayed by the emotionalism, left the Ecclesiastical Society to found St. Peter's Anglican Church, among the first in the colony.[36]

The North Society of Lebanon called Eleazar Wheelock (1711–79) to be its pastor in 1735, the year of the stirrings of the frontier revival.[37] He was 24 years old and a recent graduate of Yale (1733). He had shared the Dean Berkeley donation for outstanding students of divinity with Benjamin Pomeroy, the future pastor of the Hebron Society and future brother-in-law to Wheelock. Both had been inspired at Yale by an early pietistic

---

[35] Trumbull, *Complete History of Connecticut*, 2:137–42; James Dow McCallum, *Eleazer Wheelock, Founder of Dartmouth College* (Hanover, N.H.: Dartmouth College Publications, 1939), 4. Wheelock signed his name with "Eleazar," the spelling used here.

[36] Trumbull, *Complete History of Connecticut*, 2:534; Sibun, *Our Town's Heritage*, 21.

[37] Lebanon abutted Hebron to the east and had been founded a few years earlier, in 1797. Its North Society was within the limits of present-day Columbia. See Bruce Purinton Stark, "Lebanon, Connecticut: A Study of Society and Politics in the Eighteenth Century" (Ph.D. diss., Univ. of Connecticut, 1970).

revival. With the evangelical enthusiasm he had acquired at Yale, Wheelock led the congregation to become New Lights within a few months.[38]

Wheelock threw himself into the cause of awakening the spirit and began what he called his "itinerancies," in which he toured the towns of eastern Connecticut, Massachusetts, and Rhode Island and often preached in the open air. (Preaching outside of the meeting was a direct challenge to the authority of the local pastor and was bitterly controversial.) He corresponded with Jonathan Edwards and preached where the latter suggested the revival needed support. (Wheelock was present at Enfield, Connecticut, in the later revival of 1741 when Edwards gave the most famous of his sermons, "Sinners in the Hands of an Angry God.") Trumbull described Wheelock as "a gentleman of comely figure, of a mild and winning aspect . . . His preaching and addresses were . . . winning, beyond almost all comparisons, so that his audience would be melted even into tears, before they were aware of it."[39] At the height of the revival he gave in one year "one hundred more sermons than there are days in the year."[40] Wheelock managed to maintain his own base throughout the two revivals, challenging but not separating from the established Congregationalists. Wheelock is a major figure in the family narratives that follow.

The New Light pastor who led the Hebron congregation at the height of the revival—and for many years thereafter—was the Reverend Benjamin Pomeroy (1704–84), the classmate of Wheelock who married the latter's sister, Abigail.[41] Trumbull recalled that when Pomeroy preached he "appeared to have a deep concern for the salvation of his hearers; and often, in his address to them, and in his expostulations and pleadings with them to be reconciled to God, to forsake the foolish ways, would melt into tears and weep over them." He could also "set the terrors of the Lord in awful array before sinners, and show them, in an alarming manner, the slippery places on which they stood."[42] The man and his mission are typical of the forces that helped to shape an impressionable American culture.

---

[38] Jonathan Edwards wrote that "many places in Connecticut have partook in this same mercy." He noted "outpourings" in Coventry, Lebanon (under Eleazar Wheelock), Durham, Ripton in Stratford (under Jebidiha Mills), Mansfield (under Eleazar Williams), Tolland, Hebron, and Bolton. All but Stratford are east of the river. Gaustad, *Great Awakening*, 19.

[39] Trumbull, *Complete History of Connecticut*, 2:158.

[40] McCallum, *Eleazer Wheelock*, 14.

[41] See "Wheelock" in the Genealogical & Biographical Notes.

[42] Trumbull, *Complete History of Connecticut*, 2:157; Sibun, *Our Town's Heritage*, 21.

The history of North America's towns and cities in the late eighteenth and nineteenth centuries is the history of enterprising and industrious men and women like the Phelpses and Wheelocks. It is fitting and instructive to cast the times in the light of their personal stories, for their fortunes and misfortunes reflect those of society. To do so, however, requires not only biographical precision but also imagination. The physical texture of these lives cannot be conjured solely from what we know of the material culture of the times; letters and inventories are the interstices. Other dimensions must be taken into account with sympathetic understanding.

There was the landscape of Hebron and Lebanon—cleared fields, wood lots and woodpiles, unshaded box-like houses, dusty or muddy paths and roads. There were grazing animals, the noises of wagon wheels, axes against wood, and horses' hooves. At home there were fires, the smell of wood smoke, the sights, sounds and smells of the barnyard animals, insects, the mess of farm equipment, the noise of children. Within, at night, there were aureoles of light around the candles, deep shadows, the glow of pewter, cold away from the fire. There was no privacy. Beds were in every room, so too were the smells of unwashed bodies and clothing, of ashes and smoke. The seasonal changes influenced every aspect of life. Travel was close to the weather; the nights were dark and the woods were dangerous—it was easy to lose one's way.

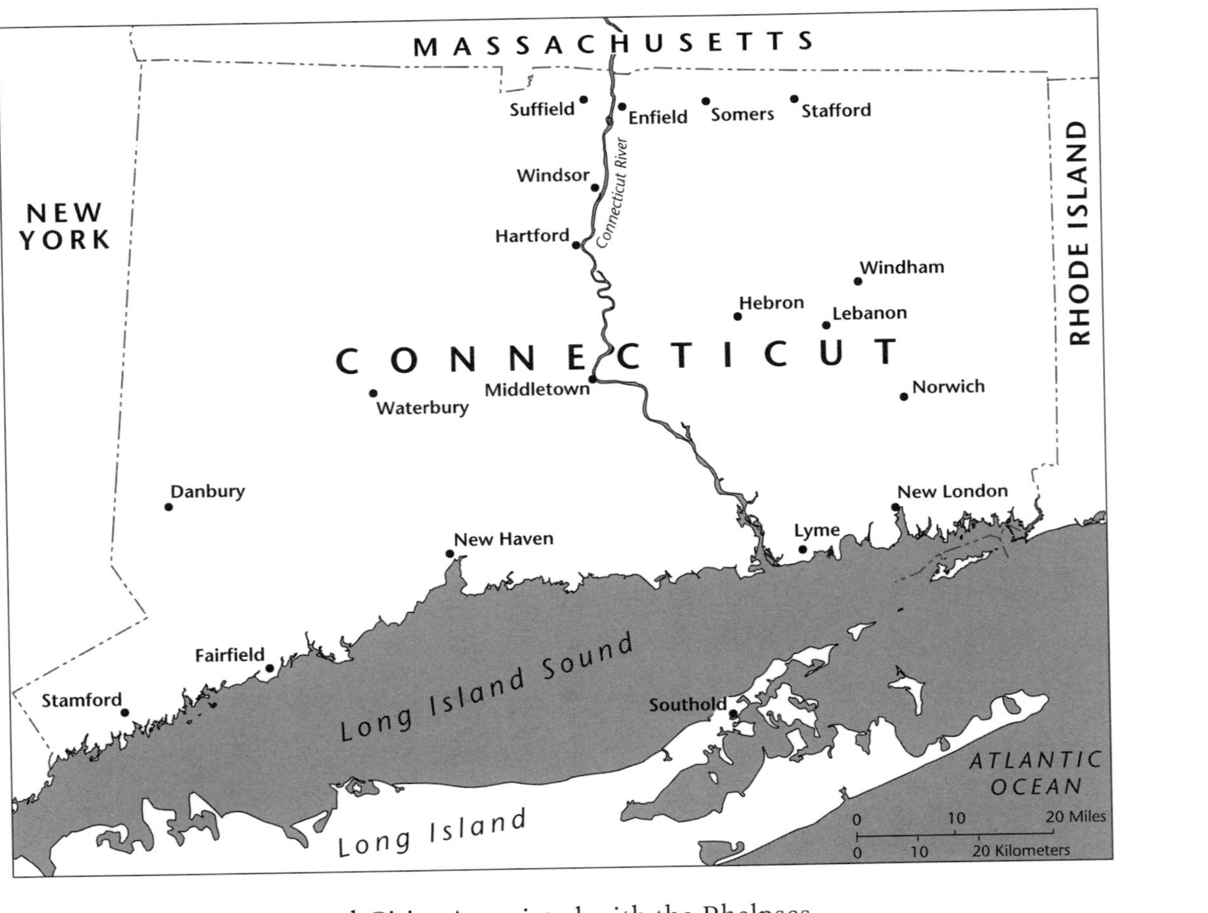


4. Connecticut Towns and Cities Associated with the Phelpses

# II

## COLONIAL LIVES

*God alloweth a man to remove, when he may employ his talents and gifts better elsewhere, especially when where he is, he is not bound by special engagement.*

—John Cotton, "God's Promise to His Plantation," preached at Southampton in 1630 to those departing with John Winthrop

### Alexander Phelps, Esq., and His Lady, Theodora

Alexander Phelps must have struck an elegant figure in Portsmouth, New Hampshire, as he negotiated the charter of Dartmouth College for his father-in-law, Eleazar Wheelock. Phelps's sense of accomplishment in securing the charter for the college turned to bitterness, however. Wheelock, who, Phelps believed, had charged him with finding a site, chose Hanover without his knowledge. Worse, in a bidding contest between the sparsely settled northern Connecticut valley towns, a Hanover man accused Phelps in a "Red Letter" of having accepted a bribe from a rival town. Alexander called this a slander from "a Clubb of mean, low-lived men . . . a Set of High handed Rioters . . ." He died two years later, the breach with his father-in-law apparently never healed.[1]

Phelps, son of a founder of Hebron, Connecticut, had intended a career in the Congregational ministry, but in a change of heart characteristic of many enterprising young men in the decades after the Great Awakening, he turned to the practice of law. He found a field for his talents in his native Hebron, where he served in important town offices, was many times the town's delegate to the General Assembly, and acquired real estate. Alexander's marriage to Theodora, the eldest daughter of the Rev. Eleazar Wheelock, brought him into contact with the energetic older man and his ambition to educate Native Americans.

Alexander Phelps began life in the matrix of the New England town of Hebron, Connecticut, whose cultural and institutional characteristics were

[1] Alexander Phelps, in Hebron, to Eleazar Wheelock, in Hanover, 23 March 1771, DCA MS 771223.2.

the products of the encounter between English Puritan immigrants and the wilderness they explored and to a large extent tamed in the previous hundred years. He was born in Hebron on 6 January 1723/4, a full 20 years after its founding. He was the sole son born to Abigail Pinney, Capt. Nathaniel Phelps's second wife. The boy was old enough during the frontier revival of the mid-1730s to witness its enthusiasm and understand its arguments. He was ten years old when the pastor of the Hebron Society and some of the congregation left the town to found one of the few Anglican churches east of the river.

The Hebron Society was firmly aligned with New Light ideals. Alexander must have become familiar with the preaching at the Sabbath meetings of the Rev. Benjamin Pomeroy, well-known New Light and a sometime itinerant, who succeeded as pastor of the Hebron Society.[2] He would also have known of the latter's brother-in-law, the young Rev. Eleazar Wheelock, in neighboring Lebanon, also a leading New Light.

The Hebron fathers established a school soon after the first meetinghouse was complete, only ten years after the first settlement. Education and religion went hand in hand. Alexander was probably taught to read and write using "the ordinary road of Horn-book, Primer, Psalter, Testament and Bible."[3] *The New England Primer* had tables showing the alphabet and rhymes to acquaint children with words. The sententious, often rhyming, texts were repeated out loud by small children. As they grew older they read the Bible in the King James Version.[4] After learning basic reading and writing skills, taught by the mother and older siblings, the child was placed under the instruction of the schoolmaster, who taught grammar, "cyphering" (sums), religious texts, and Latin and Greek.

The classics were as necessary as religious instruction in the education that led to Yale, which required its entering students to know how to read Greek and compose in Latin. Alexander was an apt pupil, for he became one of the first men in the town to go to Yale College, the apex of the edu-

---

[2] Franklin Bowditch Dexter, *Biographical Sketches of the Graduates of Yale College* (New York: Henry Holt, 1896), 1:485–88. Benjamin Pomeroy was a graduate of the class of 1733 with Eleazar Wheelock. He was ordained at Hebron on 16 Dec. 1735. In the Whitefield-inspired revival of the 1740s he became an itinerant preacher, in violation of a law passed by the General Assembly at the time. In May 1744 he was found guilty and was fined. He married Abigail, sister of Eleazar Wheelock, on 24 Oct. 1734.

[3] John Locke, 1690, quoted in Alice Morse Earle, *Child Life in Colonial Days* (1899; reprint, Stockbridge, Mass.: Berkshire House, 1995), 107.

[4] Ibid., 107–49.

5. T. Johnson's View of Yale College, 1745

*Yale Picture Collection, Manuscripts and Archives, Yale University*

cational system in the colony. He entered in the fall of 1740. A Scottish visitor described the town and its college at the time in terms favoring the older Harvard College but pointing out a parallel with Jerusalem that would have pleased the college fathers:

> Newhaven is a pretty, large, scattered town, laid out in squares, much in the same manner as Philadelphia, but the houses are sparse and thin sown. It stands on a large plain, and upon all sides (excepting the south, which faces the Sound) it is enclosed with ranges of little hills, as old Jerusalem was, according to the topographical descriptions of that city. The burying place is in the center of the town, just facing the college which is a wooden building about 200 feet long, and three stories high, in the middle front of which is a little cupola, with a clock upon it. It is not so good a building as that at Cambridge, nor are there such a number of students.[5]

[5] Alexander Hamilton, *Itinerarium* [1744] (1907; reprint, New York: Arno Press, 1971), 203.

Yale was an institution for the education of future Congregational pastors, but by Alexander's time only half of its graduates became ordained ministers. By this date Yale was educating for leadership. Whether or not graduates became ministers (which usually required three more years of study), the training in rhetoric and oratory and the practice given the students in disputation and declamation fitted graduates to become upholders of the standing order of colonial Connecticut.[6] Alexander intended to become a minister and continued his studies after his graduation, serving as a tutor. However, though a candidate for ordination at one time, he became part of that half of the Yale graduates who followed secular pursuits.

Alexander's years at Yale began during one of the most turbulent periods in its history.[7] The trigger was the Rev. George Whitefield's preaching in New Haven in late October 1740. He had landed a month before in Newport, Rhode Island, to begin a tour that set off a religious revival whose intensity and extent soon led it to be called the Great Awakening. Alexander would have been familiar with his message of repentance and rebirth, akin to those of the earlier frontier revivals.

Whitefield was a charismatic in the tradition of St. Paul. He preached out of doors to anyone who came, using a voice that was said to carry to a crowd of 5,000. Dr. Samuel Johnson said of him that "he would be followed by crowds were he to wear a nightcap in the pulpit, or were he to preach from a tree."[8] Benjamin Franklin heard him often in London and described how with his "loud and clear voice" he

---

[6] Yale was an integral part of the Congregational establishment in Connecticut colony. Its rector was an ordained minister who, like the faculty, was appointed by the General Assembly. Out of the nearly 500 graduates up to 1744, when Phelps graduated, only half became ordained ministers. He became one of a tiny minority in this period (35 of 485) who became lawyers. Yale moved to New Haven from Saybrook in 1718. Dexter, *Biographical Sketches,* 1:773. Taylor, *Colonial Connecticut,* 140.

[7] See the excellent account of Yale in these years in Carter Stone Hayner, "The Reaction of Yale to the Great Awakening, 1740–1766" (Ph.D. diss., Univ. of Texas, 1977). The furor of the religious revival confronted the Rev. Thomas Clap within a few months of his induction as rector April 1740. He was 37, a Harvard graduate, and had been pastor in Windham in eastern Connecticut. He set out to establish a stringent standard for the college but found in September of the year of his inauguration that the students and the New Haven townspeople were swept up by Whitefield's preaching which directly challenged the orthodoxy that Clap had intended to strengthen.

[8] Quoted in Frank Lambert, *"Pedlar in Divinity": George Whitefield and the Transatlantic Revivals, 1737–1770* (Princeton: Princeton Univ. Press, 1994), 67.

> Articulated his words so perfectly that he might be heard and understood at a great distance, especially as his auditors observed the most perfect silence . . . By hearing him often, I came to distinguish easily between sermons newly composed and those which he had often preached in the course of his travels. His delivery of the latter was so improved by frequent repetition, that every accent, every emphasis, every modulation of the voice, was so perfectly well tuned and well placed, that, without being interested in the subject, one could not help being pleased with the discourse.[9]

In the fall of 1740 in Boston the newspapers reported that the roads coming into the towns where he preached were jammed with wagons and people on horseback coming to hear Whitefield. He used an impromptu, emotional, inspired style in contrast to the closely formulated, cerebral arguments of the Yale- and Harvard-educated pastors. "Preaching almost universally by Note," he wrote, "is a certain Mark they have, [but] in a great Measure, [they have] lost the old Spirit of Preaching—it is a sad Symptom of Decay of vital Religion, when reading Sermons becomes fashionable where extempore Preaching did once almost universally prevail. . . . "[10] His hearers cried out in pain or ecstasy; they publicly confessed sin and repentance and avowed a "reborn" commitment to God. Anyone could come to his meetings—unlike the Sabbath meetings in the local meetinghouses, where only the covenanted could attend. In every way his was a challenge to the Puritan orthodoxy.

Whitefield pointed out "the terrible sinfulness of man and his utter dependence for salvation on the mercy of God" and exhorted his listeners to prepare for the grace of God's mercy by publicly acknowledging their sins and repenting. He believed that any person, through self-scrutiny and willpower, could be reborn in Christ and experience the hopefulness of everlasting life.[11] There was no need for the authority of the pastor.

---

[9] Franklin added that "his writing and printing from time to time, gave great advantage to his enemies. Unguarded expression, and even erroneous opinions, delivered in preaching, might have been afterwards explained or qualified, but *libera scripta manet*." Quoted in Gaustad, *Great Awakening*, 29.

[10] Whitefield's *Journal*, quoted in Gaustad, *Great Awakening*, 30.

[11] Ibid., 135, 140; Louis Leonard Tucker, *Connecticut's Seminary of Sedition: Yale College* (Chester, Conn.: American Revolution Bicentennial Commission of Connecticut, 1974).

During Whitefield's week in New Haven he "spoke very closely to the students, and showed the dreadful ill consequences of an unconverted ministry."[12] He told them that the clergy, including the Yale rector and teachers, were living in sin if they did not publicly confess their sins and profess rebirth. He minced no words: Yale-educated ministers and teachers were "the Bane of the Christian Church." This gauntlet cast down before the establishment stirred the students, and "the public became convinced that young people were being sent to defiled seats by learning."[13]

Other itinerants followed Whitefield. Gilbert Tennent from New Jersey preached 17 sermons in a week in New Haven the next spring, three of them in the College Hall. A student reported that "many cried out with distress and horror of mind, under a conviction of God's anger, and their constant exposedness to fall into endless destruction. . . ."

The wildest of these revivalists was the Rev. James Davenport, brother-in-law of Eleazar Wheelock, great-grandson of the founder of New Haven Colony, and maternal uncle of Alexander's future wife. He claimed to have the ability to determine by visual aspect whether a person was saved ("confessed") or damned ("unconfessed"), and he would point to and condemn the latter. A student wrote of these New Haven meetings that when the uproar and confusion were greatest he prayed "for the destruction of the unconverted ministers . . . who had, in his judgment, sent thousands of innocent people to hell."[14] A vivid picture of Davenport's ability to hold an audience is attested by this account of his appearance in Boston:

> He does not seem to be a Man of any Parts, Sprightliness or Wit. His Sermons are dull and heavy, abounding with little low Similitudes. He has no knack at raising the Passions, but by a violent straining of the Lungs, and the most extravagant writhings of his Body, which at the same Time that it creates Laughter and indignation in the most, occasions great meltings, screamings, crying, swooning and Fits in some others. Were you to see him in his most violent agitations, you would be apt to think, that he was a Madman just broke from his Chains. But especially had you seen him returning from the Com-

---

[12] Quoted in Dexter, *Biographical Sketches*, 1:661.

[13] Hayner, "The Reaction of Yale to the Great Awakening," 27, 33, quoting from Whitefield's *Journal*, 95–96.

[14] Stephen Hopkins, then an undergraduate, later a leading New Light pastor, quoted in Hayner, "The Great Awakening at Yale," 41. The future president of Yale, Ezra Stiles, described James Davenport as "indecent mad." Dexter, *Biographical Sketches,* 1:447–50.

> mon after his first preaching, with a large mob at his Heels, singing all the Way thro' the Streets, he with his Hand extended, his Head thrown Back, and his Eyes staring up to Heaven attended with so much Disorder, that they look'd more like a Company of Bacchanalians after a mad Frolick, than sober Christians who had been worshipping God.[15]

Rector Clap of Yale had initially welcomed Whitefield's message, but not surprisingly opposed the "doctrine of the unconverted clergy" and Davenport's emotionalism.[16] Some students were inspired by the preacher's message, however, and one of them, David Brainerd, proclaimed of the rector that he "had no more grace than this chair." Brainerd was summoned before the entire college and expelled when he refused to admit error.[17]

The fervor inspired by Whitefield abated within a year, but the established order had been severely shaken. The experience combined a challenge to authority and turned attention to an individual's ability, indeed responsibility, to find through self-examination and without the aid of authority the direction to take in life. As Richard L. Bushman, a leading modern historian of the revival, concluded, "the truly revolutionary aspect of the Awakening was the dilution of divine sanction in traditional institutions and the investing of authority in some inward experience."[18] While the long-term effects of the revival worked their way through colonial society, the furor from Whitefield's preaching was soon spent. "Christians are Dreadful Dead here . . ." John Maltby, Wheelock's stepson, wrote two years later from Yale.[19]

---

[15] *Boston Evening-Post*, 5 July 1742, quoted in Gaustad, *Great Awakening*, 39. James Davenport (1716–57) had been minister of the Society at Southold, L.I., before this itinerancy. He was notorious for his condemnation of the "unconverted clergy" and for a book-burning in New London. In 1742 he and the Rev. Benjamin Pomeroy were charged with disturbing the peace in Stratford, Conn., for their preaching. Gaustad, op. cit., 78.

[16] Taylor, *Colonial Connecticut*, 135.

[17] Brainerd later became a missionary to the Indians and died of tuberculosis as a young man. Jonathan Edwards edited his spiritual memoir. Hayner, "The Great Awakening at Yale," 79– 80.

[18] Richard L. Bushman, *From Puritan to Yankee: Character and Social Order in Connecticut, 1690–1765* (Cambridge, Mass.: Harvard Univ. Press, 1967), 220.

[19] John Maltby to Sarah Wheelock, 18 Nov. 1742, quoted in Hayner, "The Great Awakening at Yale," 100.

The world in which Alexander and his family lived their mature lives was greatly influenced by the revival. It was the first event that was reported by newspapers throughout the colonies. People were brought together in new associations and were given an awareness of collective identity. It set on course the proliferation of sects that became a significant feature of the American democracy. The individualism and the challenge to authority that the revival nurtured were the wellsprings of the protests against the Stamp Act in the 1760s, the next great event to bind the colonies.

The revival's emphasis on individual choice and self-actuated commitment had the unforeseen effect of releasing new secular energies. "Increasing numbers of young men who started out in life to become ministers began to go into capitalistic endeavor as a road to social or political prominence."[20] Alexander did just this. And, most strikingly, he exercised a choice that would have been unthinkable to earlier generations of the family. He became an Anglican.

After his graduation in 1744, Alexander taught in Eleazar Wheelock's school, which had removed to Hebron for the year. This began what would be a lifelong association. Wheelock was a supporter of Whitefield's message, but a moderate who had not endorsed the extremes of the revival. One of the pupils in the school in this year was Samson Occum, a Connecticut Mohegan Indian, who had been drawn into the revival as a youth by James Davenport. He remained with Wheelock throughout the 1740s and became an ordained minister, the most famous of the school's graduates.[21] Later his conspicuous presence encouraged donors in England to give a large sum of money, which would eventually help to found a college. Alexander was promoting, in a practical way, the message of the revival through his association with Wheelock and the school.[22]

For a time he remained on course for the ministry. In 1746 the congregation of the Union Society in northeast Connecticut invited Alexander to be a candidate to succeed the recently deceased pastor. After some months' trial, they offered a generous salary of £200 per year and an initial settlement of £400 (old tenor). Alexander chose instead to accept an

---

[20] James Truslow Adams, *Provincial Society, 1690–1773* (New York: Macmillan, 1927), 235–36, quoted in *The Susquehannah Company Papers,* 1:xv.

[21] Frederick Chase, *A History of Dartmouth College and the Town of Hanover, New Hampshire,* ed. John K. Lord (Cambridge, Mass.: John Wilson and Son, 1892), 1:9, 67.

[22] Ibid., 1:7.

appointment as a tutor at Yale, a signal mark of respect for the young man. He received his M.A. in 1747.[23] He would have been a candidate for ordination in many Connecticut meetings, but from some inner struggle or other circumstances we can only imagine, he abandoned the ministry. After teaching for a year in the town of Monson, Massachusetts, he returned to Hebron to take up the practice of law.[24]

Prospective attorneys learned law through an apprenticeship and reading, but there is no record of Alexander's associations. From a prominent family, educated and with property of his own, he was well placed for success in the profession. His ties to his native town had remained strong. When he came of age his father had given him 20 acres of land in the town, and he "tuck y[e] freeman's oath in y[e] open meeting."[25] By the late 1740s Alexander was a man of considerable property, the inheritor of his father's lands (divided with his half-brothers).[26]

There was plenty of scope for an attorney in the numerous land transactions and actions on debt amid the litigious farmers of a prosperous and growing town. A modern student of eighteenth-century Connecticut writes that the county court caseload "was so heavy that it suggested colonial men suited one another at the drop of a hat, was growing constantly; while the population of the colony increased about three and one-half times between 1700 and 1730, the debt cases in county courts increased nineteen fold. The courts were constantly full of litigation over debt dispute, many of them involving seemingly insignificant sums of money."[27] An ambitious young man in mid-eighteenth-century Connecticut could do well in a prosperous agricultural town like Hebron. The dominance of

---

[23] Charles Hammond, *The History of Union Connecticut* (New Haven: Price, Lee, and Adkins, 1895), 65; Dexter, *Biographical Sketches,* 1:765–66. Monson is east of Springfield.

[24] Dexter, *Biographical Sketches,* 1:765, states that Phelps settled in Hebron "probably as a lawyer."

[25] Hebron Land Records, 3:175, Hebron, Conn., Office of the Town Clerk; Hebron Town Meetings, vols. 1–4 [combined], 1708–1799, 145 ("Aprill y[e] 8[th], 1745"), Hebron, Conn., Office of the Town Clerk.

[26] Capt. Nathaniel Phelps died 23 Sept. 1746. Hebron VRs, 1:44; Will of Nathaniel Phelps, Colchester Probate District, CSL, box 139, packet 2417 (FHL film 1,015,791); Hebron Conn., Town Clerk's Office, Hebron [Conn.] Land Records, 3:211, 3:313, 4:10 [land transfers].

[27] Bruce C. Daniels, "The Political Structure of Local Government in Colonial Connecticut," in Bruce C. Daniels, ed., *Town and Country: Essays on the Structure of Local Government in the American Colonies,* 44–71 (Middletown, Conn.: Wesleyan Univ. Press, 1978), 50.

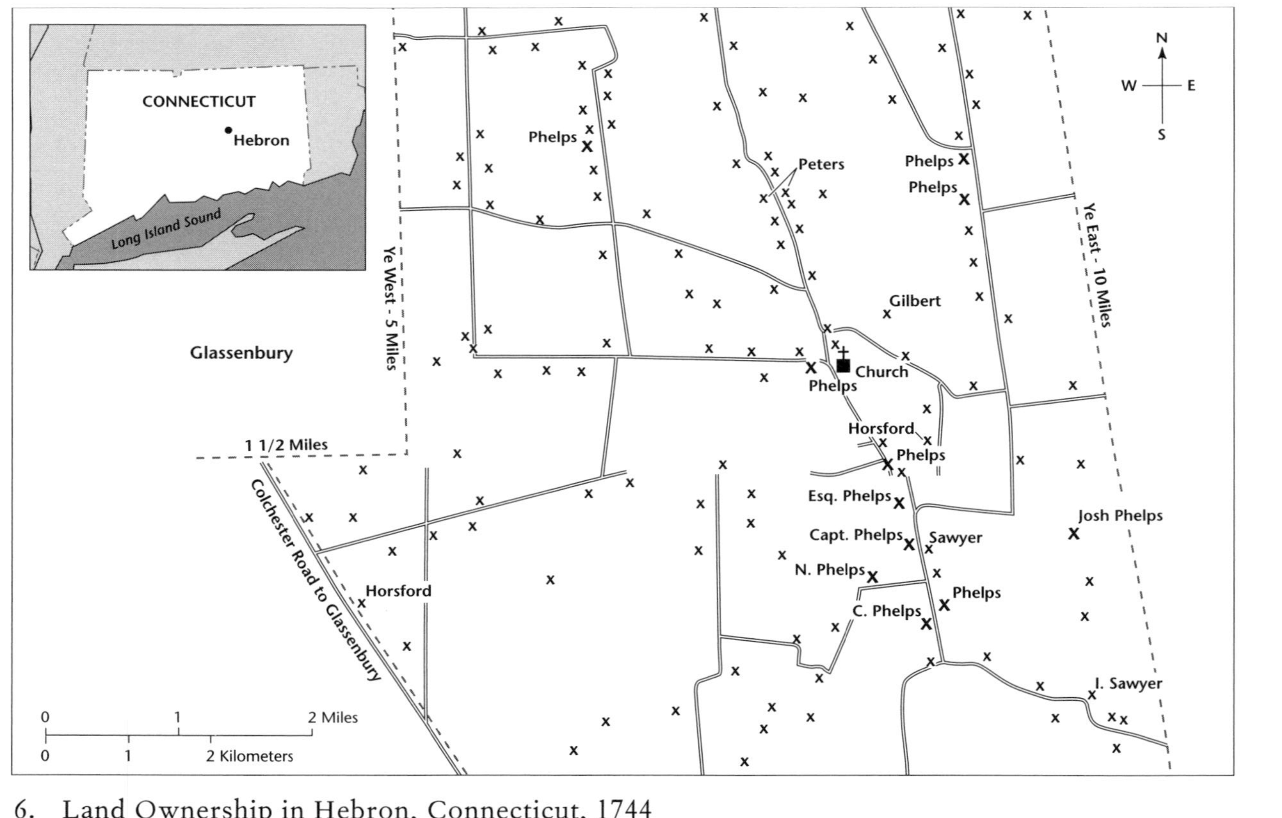


6. Land Ownership in Hebron, Connecticut, 1744

The pattern of settlement is characteristic of later New England settlements, with farms and their homesteads at some distance from one another.

*Based on Isaac Pinney's map of 1744 (Connecticut State Library)*

town culture in the colony was then at its apex, as mercantile centers and the future cities were not yet draining smaller settlements of their economic strength.

On 20 July 1749 Alexander married Anne (Phelps) Jones, a widow, in Hebron. She was his cousin, the daughter of John Phelps, a substantial landowner in the town. With the shocking brutality of nature, the marriage ended in Anne's death in childbirth along with twin infants.[28] In one fell swoop Alexander's family was gone. In what appears an act of sympathy and affection, a few months later "John Phelps & Anne Phelps his wife" granted an acre of land "for the consideration of that Good Will and regard which we have to our Son-in-Law Alex'r Phelps."[29]

The young widower set about acquiring property and building a patrimony, as his father and relatives had done. In 1752 he purchased a barn located on a one-quarter acre lot on a highway for £100 from the Rev. Benjamin Pomeroy, the pastor of the Hebron Ecclesiastical Society. Pomeroy and his son were witnesses to Phelps's purchase of an adjacent lot for £166.[30]

Land was the means for many ambitious Connecticut men in the mid-eighteenth century to acquire wealth. Pastors, farmers, and traders alike bought and sold land for profit. In the late 1750s there came to be another vehicle for investment in land, a stock company, whose subscribers expected large profits. Wheelock, Pomeroy, and Alexander Phelps were among the names listed as subscribers to stock in the Susquehannah Company in 1752.

This was an enterprise of Connecticut speculators to divide and sell land in territory claimed by Connecticut in the Susquehanna Valley, just

---

[28] Anne Phelps was born in Hebron on 25 May 1729, daughter of John Phelps and Anna Horsford (Hebron VRs). Anne married first John Jones, on 24 May 1747 (Hebron VRs, 1:43), and had two children in Hebron (Phelps 1899, 1:228); she married second Alexander Phelps, on 20 July 1749 (Hebron VRs, 1:52). She died 18 April 1750 (Hebron VRs, 1:53). Her children, probably twins, were Theodotia, born 8 April 1750, died 14 April 1750, and Anne, born 9 April 1750, died 15 April 1750 (Hebron VRs, 1:53–54). Her father, John Phelps, was born at Windsor, 21 March 1702/3 (Windsor VRs, 1:32), the son of "William Sr.," who died at Windsor 21 Nov. 1711 (Windsor VRs, 2:260). John Phelps represented Hebron in the General Assembly and served in town offices. He and his son, John Jr., had numerous dealings with Alexander Phelps in land transactions, and John Jr. was a claimant on Alexander's estate; John died in Hebron 10 Feb. 1769 (Hebron VRs, 2:338). William Sr., John Phelps's father, was probably brother to Timothy Phelps, grandfather to Alexander. John was thus Alexander's first cousin once removed.

[29] 6 Jan. 1751/2, Hebron Land Records, 4:26.

[30] Hebron Land Records, 4:56, 4:59–60, 4:71–72.

south of the New York border in territory that was disputed with Pennsylvania. Connecticut investors claimed it on the basis of a provision in the colony's seventeenth-century charter, which gave it the rights to a strip that theoretically stretched across the as yet unexplored continent to the Pacific Ocean.

The Connecticut General Assembly approved the establishment of the town of Westmoreland in the Susquehanna Valley just as it did other towns and considered it to be an integral part of Connecticut. The capital raised by the corporation was to be used to finance settlement; once a core of settlers had been established the remaining land could be sold off in smaller lots at a profit. The project and the investments were popular in eastern Connecticut (and became a major bone of contention between the eastern and western part of the state in the years before the Revolution). The company vanished without profit, however, in the Revolution, as did Connecticut's claims.[31]

It is not surprising to find the names of the two pastors and Phelps among the owners of small amounts of stock in the company in the 1750s, as it was something of a craze in the eastern part of the state. It is, of course, another example of New Lights pursuing material gain a decade after the peak of the Great Awakening.

Alexander's second marriage allied him with New Light and old Puritan families. It was a fruitful union, with healthy children, including the two sons who are the subjects of their own chapters in this narrative. Twenty months after the death of his first wife, Alexander, at the age of 28, married Theodora Wheelock in Hebron on 9 January 1751/2.[32] He thus became associated by marriage with the energetic Rev. Eleazar Wheelock, who was to provide him with a significant opportunity.

Theodora was the eldest of four children born to Sarah (Davenport) Maltby, Wheelock's first wife, a widow, who had four children in her first marriage. She died when her daughter was ten years old. Unusually for a child from a well-established family, Theodora was married at the age of

---

[31] *Susquehannah Company Papers,* 1:105, 175; Richard T. Warfle, *Connecticut's Western Colony: The Susquehannah Company* (Hartford: American Revolution Bicentennial Commission of Connecticut, 1979). The company used the older spelling of the river's name.

[32] Hebron VRs, 2:80.

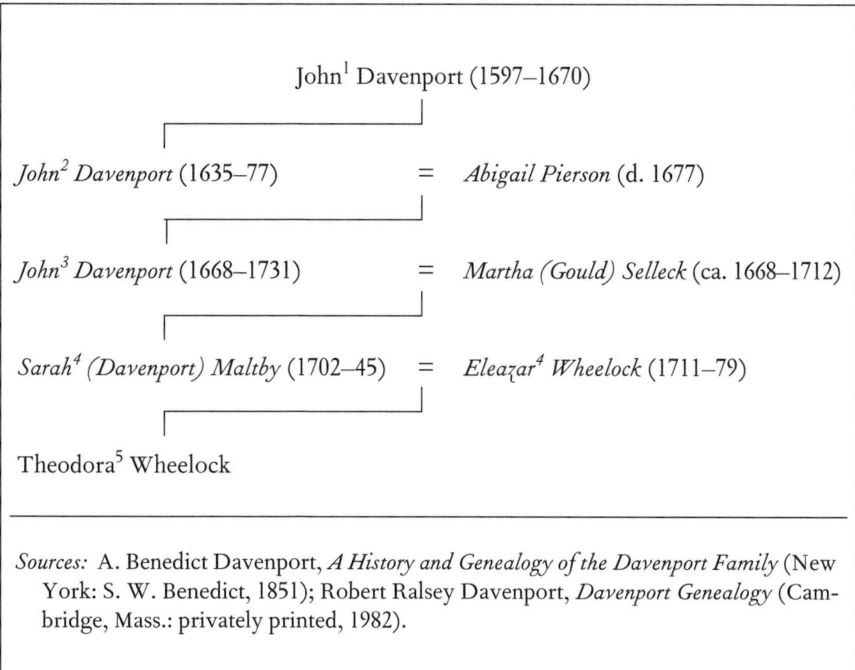


*Sources:* A. Benedict Davenport, *A History and Genealogy of the Davenport Family* (New York: S. W. Benedict, 1851); Robert Ralsey Davenport, *Davenport Genealogy* (Cambridge, Mass.: privately printed, 1982).

7. The Davenport Lineage

16, considerably earlier than the usual marriage age at that time in the early 20s.[33]

Through her mother, Theodora was descended from eminent Connecticut Congregationalists. Theodora's great-great-grandfather was John Davenport, the Puritan divine who founded New Haven Colony. Her grandfather was pastor of the Congregational Church in Stamford, a pillar of the later orthodoxy; and the notorious Rev. James Davenport was her maternal uncle.[34] Theodora's half brother (her mother's son by her

---

[33] There can be no doubt that this was Theodora's age at marriage. Her birth date was in 1736, the year following her mother's marriage to Wheelock. Lebanon VRs, 1:331.

[34] Influenced by Wheelock, James Davenport publicly recanted the views that had agitated New Haven and Yale and retired to New Jersey, where he became minister of a Presbyterian congregation in what is now Pennington, N.J. Esther (Edwards) Burr, wife of the president of the College of New Jersey (later Princeton University), recorded his visits, including one in Feb. 1757, when there was a religious revival among the college students. Burr feared that Davenport's arrival on the scene would further excite them. *The Journal of Esther Edwards Burr, 1754–1757*, ed. Carol F. Karlsen and Laurie Crumpacker (New Haven: Yale Univ. Press, 1984), 249 [23 Feb. 1757].

first husband) was the John Maltby who had reported the "deadness" in the post–Great Awakening college. He became a Presbyterian minister and was sent by the New York Presbytery to Bermuda, where Alexander would visit him many years later.

At the time of his daughter's marriage, Eleazar Wheelock had been pastor of the North Society in Lebanon for sixteen years. He had become one of the most influential of the pastors in eastern Connecticut, where the New Lights predominated. His energies after the Great Awakening were directed towards education. Like many pastors, he supported himself in part by teaching local children. In December 1743 the Mohegan youth named Samson Occum enrolled and proved himself an adept and loyal pupil. This experience gave Wheelock the idea of attracting other Native Americans. Nearly ten years later he opened a correspondence with the Rev. John Brainerd, a missionary in New Jersey, who sent two youths. (John was the brother of David, who had been dismissed from Yale during the religious revival.) By 1761 there were ten Native American students, the next year about 25.[35]

Wheelock was a gifted publicist and promoted his projects through *Narratives*, published in the colonies and in England. The school was the kernel from which Dartmouth College was to grow and with whose fortunes Alexander and Theodora would be involved.

In the 1750s the school was renamed Moor's Charity School after the donor of a house where students, ten boys and eight girls, resided in those years. There was a strict regime that required students "to be clean and decently dressed, and be ready to attend prayers before sun-rise, in the fall and winter, and at 6 o'clock in the summer." Following prayers, Scripture reading, and a short time for "diversion," lessons began at 9 A.M., and, after a midday break, ended at 5 o'clock with prayer. "Evening prayer is attended before the daylight is gone. Afterwards they apply to their studies, &c."[36] There were also practical arts: husbandry for the boys and housewifery for the girls. In what became the stuff of legend, two would-be students walked 200 miles in 1754 to be taught by Wheelock, and Iroquois children came from hundreds of miles away on foot in later years.[37]

---

[35] Eleazar Wheelock in Dexter, *Biographical Sketches*, 1:493–99. The school is described on 1:494.

[36] McCallum, *Eleazar Wheelock*, 81, quoting Wheelock in *Narratives*, 1:36.

[37] Chase, *History of Dartmouth College*, 1:9.

8. The Reverend Eleazar Wheelock (1711–1779)
Oil on canvas, 1793–1796, posthumous portrait by Joseph Steward

*Commissioned by the Trustees of Dartmouth College, Hanover, New Hampshire*

The *Narratives* kept the school in the eye of a public much taken with the prospect of converting and "civilizing" the Native Americans.[38] Lord Dartmouth headed English trustees who raised money for the furtherance of Wheelock's work. The Rev. Samson Occum's visit to England in 1765 helped them accumulate the vast sum of £12,000 (including a donation from George III), which made possible the fulfillment of Wheelock's aim to found a college.[39]

---

[38] *DAB*, s.v. "Occum, Samson"; McCallum, *Eleazar Wheelock*. In a 1765 letter Wheelock informed Phelps that, despite a rumor to that effect, the Moor's Charity School would not be moved to Hebron. Eleazar Wheelock, in Lebanon, to Alexander Phelps, in Hebron, 25 Jan. 1765, DCA MS 765125.1.

[39] McCallum, *Eleazer Wheelock*, 67. Dexter, *Biographical Sketches*, 1:495.

Joseph Brant (1742/3–1807), the Mohawk chief who led the Loyalist Indians in western New York during the Revolution, attended the school for two terms in 1761. He arrived at age 18 or 19 and between the terms returned the hundreds of miles to Iroquois lands in the west to bring back more students. He became a devout Anglican and in the 1790s was closely associated with Alexander's son, Davenport, whom he successfully encouraged to take holy orders.[40] At the time, Wheelock found Brant "of a Sprightly Genius, a manly and genteel Deportment, and of a Modest and benevolent Temper . . . I have Reason to think he began truly to love our Lord Jesus Christ Several Months ago; and his religious Affections Seem Still agreeably increasing." Brant's admiration for Wheelock's family prompted him to send two of his sons to Dartmouth in the early 1800s, when it was headed by John Wheelock.[41]

Theodora was healthy and bore eight children over a 19-year span. The first seven of these births conform to the twenty-to-thirty-month cycles of pregnancy and lactation that have been observed in the birthing patterns of New England women in these years.[42] Their birth months, March, June, August, September, October also illustrate the "deseasonalizing" of sexual behavior in New England in contrast to western Europe at the time, when most conceptions occurred in the spring and births in the winter.[43] There is a striking gap of almost six years between the seventh and last child, between Theodora's thirtieth and thirty-sixth years. These were years of financial difficulty for the family (from 1766 to 1772), but whether that prompted an effort at family limitation or there were miscarriages cannot be known. The unusual circumstances of the birth of the last child, which occurred after the family moved to New Hampshire, will be discussed below.

Theodora gave birth at home, attended by a midwife and helped by neighboring women. For the mother it was an ordeal ("travail"), but one shared by those who attended her and increasingly familiar with time. There was always the prospect of death, of the mother or of the child, as Alexander well knew, but Theodora did not lose a child at birth, and only one died when small.[44]

---

[40] See chapter 4.

[41] DCB, vol. 4, s.v. "Thayendanegea."

[42] Ulrich, *Good Wives,* 135.

[43] Fischer, *Albion's Seed,* 166.

[44] For a description of the birthing care and attendance see Ulrich, *Good Wives,* 126–28. See the Genealogical & Biographical Notes for further information on the children.

The genealogy of the family was written in the names chosen for most of the children. The firstborn was named for Sarah, the forename of Theodora's deceased mother. The first son was given the maternal family name, homage to the lineage from John Davenport. Theodora was named for her mother, and the second son was named for his father. Eleazar Wheelock was named for his maternal grandfather, and Ralph Rodolphus for his mother's brother and for his great-grandfather.[45] Only Lucey, who died as a child, and Emelia had names that have no obvious family association.[46] Although there are family associations for most of the names, the majority of them are also Biblical, in keeping with Puritan tradition. Yet family seems the most important theme in the naming of these children, with preeminence given to Theodora's heritage.

With this second marriage and the beginnings of a family, Alexander followed in his father's footsteps. He was elected by his fellow freemen to town offices and was one of the town's two delegates to the General Assembly for 11 sessions.[47] To be a delegate to the General Assembly was to participate in one of the oldest of all representative governments, one maintained in Connecticut under the 1672 charter. The governor, the members of his council, and those of the General Assembly were all elected officials. At the base of this democracy were property owners admitted to the status of "freemen" by election at semiannual town meetings. (In the mid-eighteenth century over half of adult males in the towns were freemen.) The procedure for the election of the governor, deputy governor, and assistant was more complex but still based on the votes of the freemen in all the towns.[48]

---

[45] Eleazar Wheelock Phelps's name is spelled "Eleazer" in Phelps 1899; but in his signature and in most records it is Eleazar.

[46] Of the 146 grandchildren of one colonial family, 86 percent "were named for grandparents, parents, aunts or uncles." Ulrich, *Good Wives,* 150. For the prevalence of Biblical and parental names, see Fischer, *Albion's Seed,* 97–102.

[47] Alexander Phelps served as delegate from Hebron to the General Assembly for 11 non-consecutive sessions between 1754 and 1771. The longest gap between service was between 1762 and 1771. *PRCC,* 10–14.

[48] At the September meeting "Each freeman could vote for up to twenty men as nominees . . . The constable of each town tallied the votes and forwarded them to the colony secretary, who announced at the October session of the assembly the names of the top twenty vote-getters for the entire colony. At the April freemen's meeting each freeman could vote for one of these nominees as governor, one as deputy, and twelve as assistant." Daniels, *Fragmentation of New England,* 65.

The assembly was legislature, executive branch, and final court of appeal in one. A governing council formed of delegates elected from among the assembly served the governor as an executive, and the assembly as a whole was the court of highest resort and appeal. Connecticut leaders jealously guarded the autonomy granted them by the charter of 1672 (the seizure of which by an appointed royal governor had been prevented by its being hidden in the famous hollow of an oak tree in Hartford) and were only in the legal sense "governed" by the Crown in London. There was no disruption in the continuity of government in Connecticut during the Revolution (unlike in neighboring states), and the charter's arrangements remained in effect until the new state constitution of 1818.[49]

Alexander was also elected to town offices that had more direct influence over the lives of the residents. The town was responsible for tax collection, road maintenance, and the numerous functions regarding property transactions. At the principal town meeting in December, often lasting two days, the assembled freemen elected officers, from the fence watchers and hog reeves—who administered the local ordinances against hogs roaming beyond their owners' property—to the more important selectmen and clerk.

Phelps men, including Alexander, regularly occupied these last-named, prestigious offices, which were given increasing political authority as the century progressed. Alexander was elected town clerk in 1757, the office that his uncle, Lieutenant Timothy, had been the first to hold in the town. He was re-elected each December from 1760 to 1765 and elected selectman in 1763.[50] The Governor's Council appointed Alexander justice of the peace for the first time in 1754 and reappointed him until he left the colony.[51]

Modern analyses of officeholding patterns show that in most Connecticut towns there was considerable continuity in officeholding by individuals

---

[49] With the exceptions of Massachusetts, Connecticut, and Rhode Island, the Crown appointed governors in the colonies. *PRCC,* 10:152ff.

[50] Reference to these elections and to other offices of trust for which Alexander Phelps was chosen (to lay out a highway, as agent in the case of an idiot child, to represent the town in a memorial to the General Assembly) are found in Hebron Town Meetings, vols. 1–4, 1708–1799, 184–92, 195, 226. "From every analysis of colonial New England officeholding, we know that major officeholders were usually from the upper half of the economic class structure." Daniels, *Fragmentation of New England,* 65; also see Bruce C. Daniels, "Diversity and Democracy: Officeholding Patterns among Selectmen in Eighteenth-Century Connecticut," in Bruce C. Daniels, ed., *Power and Status: Office Holding in Colonial America* (Middletown, Conn.: Wesleyan Univ. Press, 1986), 36–52.

and by members of the same family. Hebron had the highest average of terms per officeholder and was among the highest ranking for the number of terms served by members of the five leading families, of whom the Phelps were one.[52]

Hebron was an inland town, though not far from the river and Long Island Sound ports. Most of Phelps's travel was by horse on the poor roads of the day. His assembly duties involved journeys on horseback to and from Hartford and New Haven for the biannual sessions. He could probably have reached each of these in a long day's ride on a good horse and would have stayed several nights for the sessions. Except for short stretches near Hartford and New Haven, the roads were locally maintained and rough. The less affluent walked, and goods were carried in carts pulled by oxen. The surfaces were pitted and uneven at the best of times, and in rain and thaw there was mud. Hebron was not on an axis of well-traveled roads as was neighboring Lebanon, but there were routes that connected with roads to the commercial centers on the river and sound. While the roads were difficult, colonial Connecticut was a well-connected place, and all towns of any size were accessible and saw a share of the traffic as traders moved surplus crops and animals to the ports on the water. The network of roads had greatly improved by midcentury.[53] Highways to Boston, Windham County, and Albany connected to New Haven and Hartford.

There was regular postal service at the time on the New York–Boston route along the shore, New Haven–Springfield by the western bank of the Connecticut River, and New Haven–Boston through Colchester, Lebanon, and Killingly in the northeast corner of the colony. Newspapers, let-

---

[51] Justices of the peace supervised elections and, with the selectmen and constables, "named the tavern keepers, bound men to keep the peace, and apprehended suspects." They could decide criminal cases involving modest fines as established by the legislature, similarly in civil cases. "Cases of drunkenness, swearing, Sabbath-breaking, debts, unlicensed taverns, unlawful lottery tickets, were brought to their attention. Appeals could be taken to the legislature in all cases save those of swearing or Sabbath breaking." In practice each town had one or two JPs, though it was nominally a county-wide appointment. Richard J. Purcell, *Connecticut in Transition 1775–1818* (1918; reprint, Wesleyan Univ. Press, 1963), 132–33. See also Daniels, *Fragmentation of New England*, 43.

[52] Daniels, "Diversity and Democracy," 43, table 1; see also 26–27.

[53] "Middletown was linked by cartway to Saybrook; two roads connected Connecticut with the Hudson River Valley, and Norwich became the hub for a network of highways in eastern Connecticut . . . every town was connected . . . By the end of the decade, the transportation of the colony had been transformed to one that enabled large amounts of goods to be moved." Ibid., 19.

ters and travelers' reports along the post roads linked New England to New York and the other colonies. It was along them that the news of the excitement caused by Whitefield's preaching spread and, later, the news of the demonstrations against the Stamp Act and the subsequent trading restrictions.[54]

The evolved network of roads encouraged the movement and exchange of goods and people and news. Alexander was on these roads a good deal for the assembly sessions, and later to and from Portsmouth, New Hampshire, via Boston. Regular travel brought a delegate like Phelps into contact with those in the towns along the way, fellow travelers, and, of course, his fellow deputies. In a time when much news was transmitted orally, these contacts would have given him a wide view of the affairs and trade of the colony and of a larger world.

Alexander was a delegate in the years of the French and Indian War from 1756 to 1760, when the British forces were victorious.[55] Connecticut supported the war more consistently than the other colonies, and the assembly in these years raised troops for garrison and engineering tasks in the north. A recent study concludes that the council and the assembly effectively administered a war effort involving several thousand men sent north with their supplies.[56] It was a prosperous time for Connecticut merchants, who benefited from contracts to supply clothing, food, and animals to the expeditions sent to fight the French in the northern woods. Phelps regularly attended sessions of the assembly, but since debates were not recorded we have no record of his political views and he did not serve on committees most involved in the war effort.

In the buoyant wartime economy Alexander expanded his landholdings. In 1757 he purchased three parcels, "about 20 acres with a dwelling house standing thereon bounding east on highway," 14 acres with "a gristmill thereon standing with all y^e privileges thereunto belonging," and a lot consisting of "about 38 acres." For these properties he paid £200.[57] To put such a sum in perspective, a study of estate inventories of New Englanders

---

[54] Isabel S. Mitchell, *Roads and Road-Making in Colonial Connecticut* (New Haven: Yale Univ. Press, for the Tercentenary Commission of the State of Connecticut, 1934); Charles O. Paulin, *Atlas of the Historical Geography of the United States* (Washington, D.C.: Carnegie Institution of Washington, American Geographical Society, 1932), pl. 138H.

[55] The treaty of peace was not completed until 1763, when it was signed at Paris.

[56] Harold E. Selesky, *War and Society in Colonial Connecticut* (New Haven: Yale Univ. Press, 1990).

[57] Hebron Land Records, 4:233.

before the Revolution showed that a net worth of £240 placed the owner within the top one-third of the well-to-do.[58] His investments in the next decade show a confident effort to expand his holdings, probably because his optimism had been fueled by wartime prosperity, and the effects of the postwar economic depression had not yet been felt. In 1764 he paid substantial sums for two purchases, £600 for four parcels of land in Hebron with 276 acres and £185 for almost 100 acres, including land abutting that of the governor, William Pitkin.[59] However, there was much risk, as virtually all of Phelps's property was subject to a mortgage on property owned by him and Obadiah Horsford, a fellow townsman with whom he had several land transactions. A mortgage deed for £600 from Alexander's cousin and former father-in-law, John Phelps, Esq., of Hebron, was recorded in 1765, indicating that these large purchases were funded with borrowed money. John Phelps had evidently borrowed this sum from Boston merchants, as the mortgage stipulated: "Provided that if y^e^ above named Alexander Phelps & Obadiah Horsford . . . shall well & truly cause to be paid to Wm. & Dan'l Hubbard of Boston their heirs etc 3 several notes of hand by them with John Phelps executed to y^e^ said Hubbards dated 18 Sept. 1765." Interest was payable exactly three years after that date.[60]

Military success in the war was long in coming for the British and their colonials. After three years of unsuccessful campaigns in the north, forces under Lord Jeffrey Amherst took Ticonderoga and Crown Point in the Champlain Valley in 1759, and Quebec fell to Wolfe. In 1760 Amherst and his army encircled Montreal and forced its surrender. New France in North America was no more.

The northern frontier of New England and New York was now secure from French-financed Indian raids. Nova Scotia, strategically crucial to

---

[58] Alice Hanson Jones, *Wealth of a Nation to Be: The American Colonies on the Eve of the Revolution* (New York: Columbia Univ. Press, 1980), 327.

[59] Hebron Land Records, 5:124, 5:64, 5:69. The third parcel bore the restriction "Exclusive of y^e^ widows Right of Dower with y^e^ Dwelling House thereon." Phelps's purchases in 1764 included those in association with Israel Morey and Obadiah Horsford, both of whom would be involved in his affairs at the end of his life, when all three had emigrated to the upper Connecticut valley in New Hampshire. Morey would help Phelps in a dispute with his father-in-law and was the judge of probate for his estate; Horsford was a substantial creditor of the estate. The governor's son, William Pitkin, Jr., witnessed the first deed. Tillotson also owed Phelps's estate £183 in 1773—that is, the £150 Phelps had given him plus interest.

[60] Hebron Land Records, 5:498.

control of the North Atlantic, was in British hands. Both of these developments would affect the Phelps family. The secure frontier encouraged settlement in northern New Hampshire, which would lead to the fulfillment of Wheelock's vision for a college and encourage Alexander to emigrate in search of new opportunities. His half-nephew and fellow townsman, Benajah Phelps, was sent to Nova Scotia after the peace by Wheelock and other Congregationalists to be a pastor to eastern Connecticut families who had emigrated there.[61]

Connecticut's economy had prospered during the war. There was adequate currency, and the merchants enjoyed military and naval orders for food, clothing, and equipment.[62] However, peace brought an end to military orders and ushered in a severe economic depression. The cramping effects of the postwar depression reveal themselves in a curious memorial Phelps and two others submitted to the General Assembly in October 1765. With "Great Pains," the petitioners told the assembly, they had "made Discovery of a plant on a distant part of this Continent bearing such Resemblance in Fragrance and Taste to the genuine Bohea Tea." They requested a twenty-year patent for "curing & also vending such plants." The product is "highly interesting and beneficial to this Community to people of all Ranks in this Day of Distress as it will be not only much Cheaper but also more easily purchased than that which is imported."[63]

Bohea was a black tea of high quality first imported from the hills of western China to England in 1704. The plant that Alexander and his partners had found and its location were not revealed. The assembly, unconvinced, did not grant the patent. The reference to the "Day of Distress" is, however, a reminder of the postwar depression and the impending imposition of import duties by the Crown.

Borrowing for the last land purchases had indebted the Phelps family. Evidently spurred by a desire to find a venture to improve his strained finances, Phelps, whose experience had up to that time been confined to Connecticut, journeyed to Bermuda in 1767. Ships from the port of New London regularly went to and from the West Indies, and a further voyage to Bermuda would not have been unusual. "[T]is y^e^ most Barren piece of

---

[61] References are by date to *PRCC*, 11.

[62] Taylor, *Colonial Connecticut*, 106.

[63] Industry, 1st ser., vol. 2, 123, Conn. Arch., box 71, roll 92–75.

Ground of Rocks that I ever Saw;" Alexander wrote his father-in-law from that island, "and would almost be useless, were it not for y$^{e}$ Red Cedar with which it abounds." Prospects for business were not promising: "the State of this Island is Such that Trade Can not be Advantagious here . . . Money is very Scarce in this land."[64] At the time, Bermuda was in a postwar depression more severe than Connecticut's.[65]

There was a family connection on the island; Theodora's half-brother, the Rev. John Maltby, who had written of the collapse of the spirit of the revival at Yale, was minister of the Warwick Presbyterian Church. He had been there 18 years, sponsored by New York Presbyterians in the interests of maintaining a Dissenting church in the Anglican colony.[66] Phelps wrote that he expected to travel southward, "and Mr. Maltby will go with me." Whether that voyage ever took place is unknown, but Maltby was soon to leave the island.

Phelps's finances had deteriorated badly by 1768. Jonathan Mason of Boston successfully brought judgment against him and Obadiah Horsford for £290, resulting in their loss of "a certain piece of land lying a little northward of the Meeting House in said Hebron."[67] A year later in a letter acknowledging Wheelock's payment of a bill for him, Alexander

---

[64] Alexander Phelps, in Bermuda, to Eleazar Wheelock, in Lebanon, 14 Sept. 1767, DCA MS 767514.1.

[65] There were about 10,000 inhabitants on the island at this time, about evenly divided between white and black, with many out of work. Wilfred Brenton Kerr, *Bermuda and the American Revolution: 1760–1783* (Princeton: Princeton Univ. Press, 1936), 1–9; Henry C. Wilkinson, *Bermuda in the Old Empire: A History of the Island from the Dissolution of the Somers Island Company until the End of the American Revolutionary War: 1684–1784* (London: Oxford Univ. Press, 1950), 365, 367.

[66] Like Phelps, Maltby foresaw poor prospects: "This island seems to be running fast to destruction and the people, it is probable, will be very greatly depressed." One solution was emigration "as we have so many hundred living badly nay rather perishing very miserably." (He himself shortly left and settled in Georgia in 1768. Soon thereafter he contracted tuberculosis and in his final illness in 1771 was taken in by Wheelock in Hanover.) The Rev. John Maltby to a merchant of South Carolina, 25 Jan. 1765, PRO, Colonial Office, 5:540, quoted in Kerr, *Bermuda and the American Revolution*, 9; Georgia Lord (Morehouse) Maltby, *Family Record of the Maltby–Morehouse Family* (privately printed, 1895), 203.

[67] Hebron Land Records, 5:498. The deed (5:624) from Alexander Phelps to the executors of John Phelps, Esq. (d. in 1769) in 1772 in the amount of £700 in 1772, the year after Alexander Phelps removed to New Hampshire, probably is for the same property as was in the mortgage deed. Mason could be the merchant of that name who had an office in Cornhill, Boston, from the 1760s to 1780s. See *Register* 84 (1930), 152, 375. See also Ann Smith Lainhart, ed., "John Haven Dexter and the 1789 Boston City Directory," *Register* 140 (1986): 23–62.

expressed the "hope that providence will so order my Affairs that I shall be able Sooner or later to make some Satisfaction Answerable."[68]

Wheelock had helped his daughter's family in time of need. There were then six children at home, ranging in age from three to sixteen. (A seventh, Lucey, died at age five two years before.) Providing for a household of that size would have required considerable cash as well as the labor of non-family members on the farm. These years must have been exceptionally difficult for Theodora, who still had small children to care for and educate. In March 1769 she sent a note to her father by "Salley" to request that he send "Dinah" to help her. She could not make the request in person because of illness, and the legal difficulties of the Phelps household were such that there was a remote risk of Dinah (who must have been a slave in the Wheelock household) being attached by creditors, which could have caused Wheelock not to send her. She mentions the names of the two men who had dealings with her husband. The letter shows the knowledge this wife had of the family's money affairs. She addresses her father as "Revd & Hond Sir."

> After my Duty to you I would Inform that I send Salley to y$^{r}$ house to know if you will Lend Dinah, I intended to come my self but indisposition of Body is Such with me that I am not able to Leave home the affairs of our Debts are at present Such that there is no Danger of any attachment that will touch her Coll$^{n}$ Pitkins affair is settled on good Termes Horsfords Case has had a hearing but is adjourned till y$^{e}$ week after next, but by the Judgement of them who are to be Regarded it Looks prosperous on our Side & that Mr. Phelps is not much mistaken in his former [guess] if upon the whole Sir you think it unsafe to send her we must rest untill Better Security can be had from Y$^{r}$ Dutifull Daughter[69]

The extant county court records for Windham County, which included Hebron until 1785, have no court cases 1763–69 involving Pitkin, Horsford, or Phelps. Thus a more detailed look at the legal struggle Theodora refers to is not possible, but it is clear enough that Alexander's finances were seriously strained at this time.

There was a bright moment in these depressed years, however. The General Assembly bestowed on Alexander the treasured honorific of a high military title and appointed him "Lieutenant Colonel of the 12th

[68] Alexander Phelps, in Hebron, to Eleazar Wheelock, in Lebanon, 29 Jan. 1769, DCA MS 769129.

[69] Theodora Phelps, in Hebron, to Eleazar Wheelock, in Lebanon, March 1769, DCA MS 769240.1.

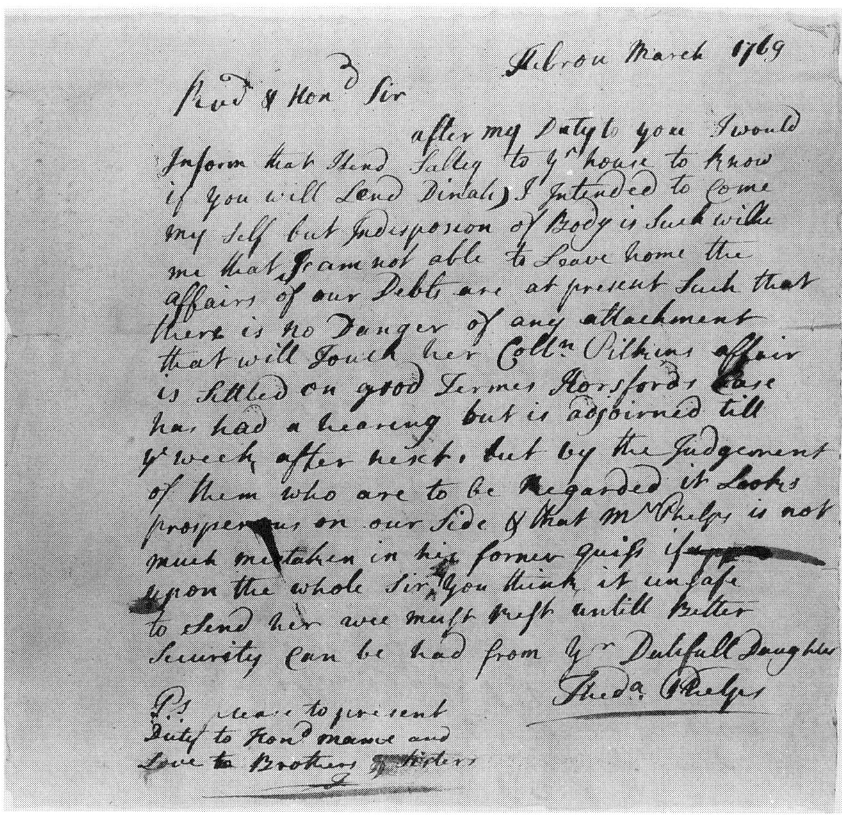

Hebron March 1769

Revd & Honrd Sir

after my Duty to you I would
Inform that I send Salley to yr house to know
if you will Send Dinah, I Intended to Come
my Self but Indispotion of Body is Such with
me that I am not able to Leave home the
affairs of our Debts are at present Such that
there is no Danger of any attachment
that will Touch her Colln Pitkins affair
is Settled on good Termes Horsfords Case
has had a hearing but is adjourned till
ye week after next, but by the Judgement
of them who are to be Regarded it Looks
prosperous on our Side & that Mr Phelps is not
much mistaken in his former guess if
upon the whole Sir you think it unsafe
to send her wee must rest untill Better
Security Can be had from Yr Dutifull Daughter

Theda Phelps

P.S. please to present
Duty to Honrd mamme and
Love to Brothers & Sisters

9. Theodora Phelps's letter to her Father, Eleazar Wheelock, March 1769

*Dartmouth College Library*

regiment in this colony" in May 1766. Henceforth he was addressed as Col. Alexander Phelps, Esq.[70]

For all his upbringing, ties through his and his wife's family to the Dissenting tradition, and filial relationship with Wheelock, the evidence indicates that Alexander was sympathetic to the Anglicans and became a communicant. Two documents point to this conclusion. In 1771 he responded to a charge that had been conveyed to his father-in-law by the Rev. Benjamin Pomeroy that he had attended an Anglican service. "[A]s to my Going to Chh.," Alexander wrote in explanation, "if that be scandal-

[70] This title occurs in records beginning in the early 1760s. That of 1766 is listed in *PRCC,* 12:459.

ous I am quite willing to bear ye Scandal I believe ye Chh of England to be ye Chh. of Christ and you have known my Sentiments for many years." He had not been attending meeting, for he added of the Hebron Congregational pastor, Pomeroy, that "I have not had one minutes Conversation with him Since Octr last, tho' I have not endeavored to avoid him . . ."[71] Short of an explicit statement of his allegiance, this is convincing evidence of his adherence to the institution that his forefathers had deplored. It also indicates that Wheelock was living in a more religiously tolerant world, as his son-in-law's views were a matter of concern, not of abhorrence. The Anglican Church in Hebron was St. Peter's, established in Hebron in 1733 at the time of the frontier revival and, at the time of this letter, under the Rev. Samuel Peters.

The second piece of evidence came years after his death, in the correspondence of his eldest son, Davenport, with the Rev. Samuel Peters, then a Loyalist exile in London. The young man introduced himself with the sentiment that "Your former friendship to my Father & affectionate attention to his family merit my sincerest gratitude." Davenport, who himself later became an Anglican priest, seemed to regard Peters as a mentor in subsequent correspondence.[72] Though this is less compelling evidence than the first, it adds to the conviction that the one-time candidate for ordination among the Congregationalists had joined the church of his pre-immigrant forebears in England. Puritan New England was changing in the aftermath of the Great Awakening.[73]

In Hebron the Anglican church was formed about 30 years after the town was founded, unusual for eastern Connecticut, where there were only six Anglican churches before the Revolution. St. Peter's was founded when the Rev. John Bliss left the Congregational meeting in 1734 with about a dozen families. Twenty-five years later, it had grown in membership to 30–40 families, about 10–15 percent of the households, the highest

---

[71] Alexander Phelps, in Hebron, to Eleazar Wheelock, in Hanover, 23 March 1771, DCA MS 771223.2. This is the same letter in which he accused Wheelock of not clearing his name in response to a charge that he had a accepted a bribe to locate Dartmouth College when acting as his father-in-law's agent. See below. It seems that Alexander Phelps and the Rev. Benjamin Pomeroy did not get on. In 1755 Jonathan Edwards's daughter, Esther (Edwards) Burr, heard the latter preach in Princeton, and it weighed upon her. "I have been at meeting all day and heard Mr Pomeroy, a gentleman very famous in New-light circles—he preached well but his delivery is so slow that a bodies thoughts have time between his words to run throu the World and my head has ached all day and I fear I have got no good." *The Journal of Esther Edwards Burr*, 126–27 [22 Jan. 1755].

[72] Davenport Phelps, in Piermont, N.H., to Samuel Peters, in London, 22 April 1786, *Peters Coll.*

percentage of Anglicans in towns east of the Connecticut River.[74] Until 1761 St. Peters did not have an ordained minister. Since the Church of England held to the principle of apostolic succession through the episcopate, and as there were no bishops then in North America, candidates for ordination had to go to England. Through illness and loss at sea no less than three candidates for rector of St. Peter's died before ordination. Samuel Peters, son of the landowner who had given the property to the church, graduated from Yale in 1757. The family wealth allowed him to travel to England, where he was ordained two years later. He returned to be installed as rector in 1761.[75] He inherited the family lands and a large farm and was one of the few slave owners in the town.

Peters became notorious for his support of the mother country when tensions with the colonies increased in the 1770s (after Alexander Phelps's move to New Hampshire). In the summer of 1774, as recounted by the nineteenth-century historian of the Anglican church in Connecticut,

> His impudent conduct and intense loyalty had involved him in serious trouble. He was charged with communicating intemperate articles to the newspa-

---

[73] Pomeroy exemplified the New Light emotionalism with which Alexander had grown up and from which he had evidently turned. He was not alone, as others in the years following the Great Awakening had responded to New Light enthusiasm by becoming Anglicans. An example comes from a congregation in Northbury (later Plymouth, Connecticut) who wrote to the Society for the Propagation of the Gospel in Foreign Parts (SPG), the Anglican missionary wing. They were repelled by the New Light revivalists with their "insufferable enthusiastic whims and extemporaneous jargon [who] brought in such a flood of confusion among us, that we became sensible of the unscriptural method we had always been accustomed to take in our worship of God, and of the weakness of the pretended constitution of the churches (so called) in this land; whereupon we fled to the Church of England for safety, and are daily more and more satisfied we are safe, provided the purity of our hearts and lives be conformable to her excellent doctrines." Petition sent to the SPG in 1844, quoted in E. Edwards Beardsley, *The History of the Episcopal Church in Connecticut from the Settlement of the Colony to the Death of Bishop Seabury* (New York: Hurd and Houghton, 1874), 1:132.

[74] Stephen Reed Grossbart, "The Revolutionary Transition: Politics, Religion and Economy in Eastern Connecticut, 1765–1800" (Ph.D. diss., Univ. of Michigan, 1989), 374. A few towns west of the river had larger shares of Anglicans; Waterbury and Stamford, for example, each exceeded 20 percent. Grossbart's analysis shows that Anglicans were not discriminated against for political office, which many of them held. He does not identify Hebron as having an Anglican delegate to the General Assembly. Ibid., 372.

[75] Beardsley, *History of the Episcopal Church in Connecticut*, 207; Sheldon S. Cohen, *Connecticut's Loyalist Gadfly: The Reverend Samuel Andrews Peters* (Hartford: The American Revolution Bicentennial Commission of Connecticut, 1976), 7–8.

> pers for publication, and making false representations to his friends in England. A mob of about three hundred persons assembled at his house in August of that year and again in the ensuing month, and made known their determination to obtain from him satisfaction and an acknowledgment of his errors. He met them, arrayed in his canonical robes for protection; but the exasperated mob had as little respect for these as for the wearer, and seizing him violently, to the damage of his garments, they carried him to the Meeting-house Green, where he was forced to read a confession which had been previously prepared for him and with this offering their lawless patriotism was satisfied and he was set at liberty . . . a few days later he set out for Boston "in good spirits" . . . a letter to his mother was intercepted that described with pleasure the potential arrival of six regiments from England [and expected that] the "hanging work will go on, and destruction will first attend the sea port towns; the lintels sprinkled, and the side-posts, will preserve the faithful."[76]

From London the sharp-penned Peters shortly published what purported to be a *History of Connecticut* in which he settled scores with the Congregationalists and made witty and often outlandish claims. His indignant account of the August 1774 incident was meant to warn of the dangers of mob rule. He returned to the American shores early in the next century and died in New York City at the age of 91. His affection for the native town from which he was routed so rudely fifty years before was such that he provided that his body be buried in the St. Peter's churchyard.[77] We will return to this lively character and his family in later chapters.

There is no evidence that Alexander's friendship with Peters or his Anglicanism put him in the camp of those supporting the mother country in the events that led up to the Revolution. His only recorded political stand on one of the issues that stirred the colonies that led to the rebellion suggests the contrary. The tensions began in 1764 when Parliament imposed a tax on the stamps affixed to legal transactions, at a time when merchants and artisans in the colonies were suffering from severe economic depression. Eastern Connecticut towns were the hotbed of anti–

---

[76] Beardsley, *History of the Episcopal Church*, 1:306.

[77] The inscription on the monument reads: "Rev. Samuel Peters, LL.D., b. Hebron Nov. 20, 1735, O. S., d. New York April 29, 1826 AE. 91, ordained in England Deacon and Priest 1759, and while residing in that country after the Revolution was elected though not consecrated Bishop of Vermont. Erected by his grandson, Samuel Jarvis Peters of New Orleans, 1841." Lucius B. Barbour, "Hebron, Connecticut," in *Genealogical Data from Connecticut Cemeteries.*

Stamp Tax activity, and when the news came of its repeal in 1766 church bells in Hebron and throughout the colony were rung in celebration.

Parliament returned to the theme of taxes on the colonies, however, and in 1767 imposed duties on imports, decrees the colonists dubbed the "Intolerable Acts." In a coordinated effort, Connecticut traders followed the lead of those in Massachusetts and New York and pledged "non-importation" agreements in which all would join in protest of what they deemed an unjust tax.[78]

To strengthen the non-importation sentiment in the port towns, which had waned after several years, the Hebron freemen, assembled in a town meeting in September 1770, resolved "that it is our mind that the new [non] importation agreement come into by the Americans be Closely adhered to & preserved Inviolate by all at s[d] meeting that it is our mind that the violation of it ought to be [treated] with all that contempt and Disregard which a Breach of Public Faith to their Country's Cause Justly Deserves."[79] The freemen chose Alexander Phelps to represent this view at a colony-wide meeting to be held in New Haven. At this early stage he is thus on record as supporting the "Country's Cause" that would lead most of his fellow townsmen into rebellion five years later.

There were still hard times, and Alexander saw a new field of opportunity. Like many in Hebron and eastern Connecticut in the late 1760s, he was attracted by the possibilities for settlement and land trading in the now-secure upper Connecticut River valley of New Hampshire. This could allow him to rebuild his finances after the reverses of the 1760s. As early as 1761 a number of Hebron men, including Alexander Phelps and several of his relatives, were among those granted a charter to the empty town of Thetford, on the east side of the upper Connecticut River, in what was then territory claimed by New Hampshire.[80] Few moved in the early years, but by the end of the decade interest in New Hampshire lands stirred. In 1771 Alexander decided to move the family north and start a new community, just as his father had done in Connecticut 70 years before.

---

[78] Albert E. Van Dusen, *Connecticut* (New York: Random House, 1961), 125, 129.

[79] The town meeting took place 10 Sept. 1770. Hebron Town Meetings, 200. Samuel Gilbert, Esq. (a sometime delegate to the General Assembly) was the other delegate chosen by the meeting.

[80] Abby Maria Hemenway, ed., *The Vermont Historical Gazetteer: A Magazine* (Burlington, Vt.: privately printed, 1871), 2:1002.

It was not only landless younger sons who were making such moves in the late 1760s and early 1770s; the "removals" included leading families. The migrations were doubtless precipitated in part by the decline in agricultural productivity in Connecticut as well as the persistence of the post-war depression. There was also the attraction of being the first purchasers, able to sell land to later arrivals in what promised to be an extensive settlement. In the case of this Phelps family, there was the added incentive to be near Eleazar Wheelock's Dartmouth College.

## Dartmouth

In the late 1760s Gov. John Wentworth of the royal colony of New Hampshire at Portsmouth began to promote the offer of interior land grants.[81] His goals were to encourage immigration to increase tax revenues and to strengthen the colony's claims against those of New York for lands on and west of the Connecticut River. He also welcomed a college in New Hampshire to attract the sons of the colony's elite away from the rebellious influences at Harvard and Boston, then under military occupation.

The grants were taken up by eastern Connecticut men, sometimes in groups, and several of the towns in the upper valley were given the names of the towns from which the original settlers came. New Hampshire came to have its own Hebron, Lebanon, and Lyme. The early town meetings of Hanover were held in Mansfield, where a number of those intending to migrate north then lived.[82] Alexander Phelps was one of 60 proprietors granted a share of the lands in the township of Bath in March 1769. This namesake of the fashionable spa in western England was a forested tract six miles square, its bounds marked on trees—a "Pine Tree" and "Beech Tree" are cited in the deed. (Bath is about 40 miles north of Hanover and borders the river.) The reverberant title of the grantor was "George the Third, by the Grace of God King of Great Britain, France, and Ireland

---

[81] Wentworth strongly supported Wheelock's proposal to establish a college in the colony. Brian C. Cuthbertson, *The Loyalist Governor: Biography of Sir John Wentworth* (Halifax, N.S.: Peteric Press, 1983), 13. John Wentworth, born in America, was appointed governor by George III in 1766 and was forced to flee by revolutionaries in 1775. He later was appointed governor of Nova Scotia and died in 1820.

[82] From 1761 to 1766 Hanover town meetings took place in Mansfield. *Records of the Town and Selectmen of Hanover N.H., 1761–1818* (Hanover, N.H, 1905), iv.

King, Defender of the Faith, &c." The grant was made "with the Advise of our Truly and well beloved John Wentworth, Esq., Governor and Commander in Chief of our said Province of New Hampshire in New England."[83]

Reflecting New England practice, the grant required that ". . . a Tract of Land as near the Center of the said Townships as the Land will admit, shall be reserved and markt out for Town Lots, one of which shall be allotted to each Grantee of the Contents of one Acre." The proprietors were also required to build one wagon road through the property.

Alexander's involvement in New Hampshire deepened in the fall of 1769, when his father-in-law employed him to negotiate a charter for what became Dartmouth College. The one-time itinerant preacher had become in his maturity a builder of educational institutions. He realized by the mid-1760s that Moor's Charity School had not been as effective in developing missionaries to the Native Americans as he had hoped, and had come to the view that a college that could educate "white scholars rather than . . . Indians for teachers and missionaries" would be more useful.[84] He set about raising funds and finding a site. A site in Connecticut was not possible, as chartering of a college there would require amendment of the 1672 charter, which the governor and assembly were unwilling to risk for fear of Crown interference. Sir William Johnson, the *de facto* Crown representative in Iroquois territory in western New York, had refused Wheelock's request to locate a college there, anticipating, perhaps, a challenge to his own authority.

The opening up of the New Hampshire lands became Wheelock's opportunity. The colony's governor and council were eager for new settlement, and the proprietors in the virtually empty northern townships sought to attract an institution that would draw settlers to buy their lots. The trustees under Lord Dartmouth, in London, held the ample purse of £12,000, the funds raised in part by the Rev. Occum. It was partly to reassure these English donors that Wheelock sought a location that would permit the college to be given a royal charter. New Hampshire was a royal colony, and the support that Wheelock had generated among influential men in England, including George III, meant that there would be no opposition from His Majesty's government. Wheelock assigned the task of negotiation with the colonial government to his son-in-law.

---

[83] Grafton County [N.H.] Register of Deeds, 3:334.

[84] McCallum, *Eleazer Wheelock*, 167.

In the autumn of 1769 Alexander committed himself to an extended stay in Portsmouth to work out the agreement with Governor Wentworth and the leaders of the assembly. His letters are preserved in the Wheelock papers, making this the most fully documented portion of his life. The episode they describe is crucial to understanding the origins of what became an enduring institution. Previous accounts, however, have understandably focused on Wheelock, the founder. In the aftermath of the success of the charter negotiations, Phelps became bitterly disappointed with Wheelock, and this account attempts to present his point of view.

Portsmouth was then an elegant and prosperous port with a society centered on the governor. Phelps would undoubtedly have appeared in the city fashionably dressed. According to the inventory of his estate at his death, a little over three years later, there were several items that would have shown up well in that society: "1 pair silver Connecticut Buckles," a gold ring, "8 rufled Shirts," a "Chints Gown, best Blue Coat & claret Jackcoat," an orange jackcoat, a blue cloak, a pair of Nankeen breeches (yellow or pale buff cotton from China).[85] Despite the strained financial circumstances he mentions to his father-in-law, this representative of the venerable Congregational New Light could look the eighteenth-century English gentleman in his meetings with the governor and council.

At the outset of the negotiations it appeared that Anglican–Congregational rivalry could prove an obstacle to the charter. Would the governor insist that the college be Anglican in a colony where the Church of England was the established religion? Would Wheelock insist that it be Congregational? This raises the possibility that Wheelock may have chosen Phelps as his mediator because of his Anglican affiliation as well as his negotiating skills.

In October 1769, Phelps reported to Wheelock in Lebanon that the governor "appears very Friendly to you personally and to y$^{e}$ School." However, he had insisted that the Anglican bishop of London serve on the London trust *ex officio*. Phelps feared this would be unacceptable to Wheelock because of the Anglican presence, and *ex officio* representation was contrary to the Connecticut tradition of elections. He tested the proposal with local churchmen, "whose Judgt I think you would value, Strict

---

[85] "An Inventory of the real and Personal Estate of Col. Alexander Phelps late of Lime Deceas'd, submitted January 15, 1774," Grafton County [N.H.] Probate Court. These are all items that mark Alexander, for all his financial difficulties, to be among the well-to-do. Jones, *Wealth of a Nation*, 330.

Dissenters . . ." As the bishop was to be "only a nominal member of y^e^ Trust in England," their view, as reported by Phelps, was that his presence would be "but a meer matter of moon shine; and not worthy of much Consideration. . . ."[86] This was persuasive, and Wheelock agreed to the arrangement, which further illustrates the lessening of sectarian rivalry at this point in the century.

Wheelock was so pleased with the governor's attitude that he considered naming the college for him. "You see I proposed the calling the House by his Name & had almost concluded to call the College itself so. But my obligations in points of gratitude to the Earl of Dartmouth are great. . . ." It was an honor Wentworth tactfully refused in deference to Lord Dartmouth.[87]

With the charter all but signed, Wheelock instructed Alexander to select the site from among townships competing with offers: "let your Eye be upon having as much near, & convenient for Speedy improvement for the present support of my Family & School as may be." It was a canny procedure to encourage competing bids. The proprietors who sought the college in their townships would have to compete with generous offers of land, labor, and building materials. Wheelock deputized Phelps to act for him: "I need only give you some general Hints and leave You to conduct the Whole Affair according as your Own Prudence." Here was the basis of the later grave misunderstanding between the two men.

Wheelock told Phelps to "See what Donation may be had by charitable [ ] Gentlemen, of Materials Which Shall be necessary for the Buildings . . . Glass, Putty, coloring, papering, Spikes, Nails, for floors, Ceiling, lathing, Shingling, clapboarding, [ ], Locks, Latches, Ackes, Hinges, [ ], Tongs, Handirons &c." As the college must be self-supporting for food from the outset, he should also "See what Provision May be Made Most conveniently for putting Seed of all kinds in to the Ground Seasonably for the Support of My Family & School."[88]

That November Alexander returned home, the charter agreed to but not signed. After a few days, however, Wheelock insisted he return to

---

[86] Alexander Phelps, in Portsmouth, to Eleazar Wheelock, in Lebanon, 18 Oct. 1769, DCA MS 769568.3. The issue vanished when the Bishop of London declined to serve.

[87] Eleazar Wheelock, in Lebanon, to Alexander Phelps, in Portsmouth, 25 Oct. 1769, DCA MS 769575.3.

[88] Eleazar Wheelock, in Lebanon, to Alexander Phelps, in Portsmouth, 20 Nov. 1769, DCA MS 769620.

Portsmouth forthwith to complete the negotiation. Phelps was reluctant, "Especially on acct. of my wife's illness . . . but as She Consents though with Great Reluctance, I Conclude to Go,—yet my affairs are Very Deficient . . ." He agreed to be on his way "by Tuesday Noon, So as not to be hindered by y^e^ Thanksgiving," and hoped "to have an able Horse, and an Easy one, [as] y^e^ Journey is long, and Tedious."[89]

The charter was completed in December, ready to be signed early in the new year. Alexander concerned himself with choosing the site and assembling materials and remained in Portsmouth. He reported that "Nails, Glass are very Scarce," a reflection on the state of colonial manufactures at the time and the effect of the non-importation agreements on materials from Britain. He would "soon" be on his way to look at prospective sites, and "money for Expense will be very Short. I hope I can Borrow of You."[90]

In January 1770, Alexander reported the receipt of bids from towns seeking to have the college within their bounds. The leading proprietor of Littleton (near the White Mountains, then only boundaries marked on a map) offered 1,000 acres and "Ten Thousand Feet of Boards to be delivered at said Place, Ten Thousand 10d Nails." For Wheelock himself he offered 400 acres and "Four Thousand feet of Boards & Four Thousand 10d Nails."[91]

As charged, Alexander negotiated a site for the college. He chose one overlooking a horseshoe bend in the Connecticut River in Haverhill, north of Hanover. By March 1770 he had purchased lumber and committed to laborers so that construction could start when the ground could be worked in keeping with Wheelock's sense of urgency. Unbeknownst to him, Wheelock had received an offer from the proprietors of Hanover, on the river to the south of Haverhill, that promised extensive lands for the college and a sizable package for the Wheelock family. To strengthen the town's case, its representative planted doubt in Wheelock's mind about Phelps's integrity. He was said to be "trying to advance his own interest" in Haverhill, and there was an insinuation that he had accepted a bribe.

---

[89] Alexander Phelps [in Hebron] to Eleazar Wheelock, in Lebanon, 19 Nov. 1769, DCA MS 769619.

[90] Alexander Phelps, in Portsmouth, to Eleazar Wheelock, in Lebanon, 19 Dec. 1769, DCA MS 769669.

[91] Leonard Whiting, in Littleton, N.H., to Alexander Phelps, in Portsmouth, 20 Jan. 1770, with a note by Benjamin Whiting of Charlestown, 5 March 1770, DCA MS 770120.

None of Wheelock's biographers or historians of Dartmouth College supports this accusation.

Wheelock traveled to Hanover in March accompanied by his brother-in-law, the Rev. Benjamin Pomeroy, one of the Connecticut trustees of the college. To the English trustees he wrote that the site was "near White River falls . . . upon a direct line from Portsmouth to Crown Point, to which we were informed a good road may be had and its distance but 60 miles; and about 140 to Montreal and but 40 miles land portage to each of these places . . . the Indian tribes far and near have been well acquainted with this place . . ."[92] He accepted the town's offer without informing Phelps.

The latter shortly learned that he had been undercut, that his commitments in Haverhill were empty, and that his word had been impugned. He concluded that the "Connecticut trustees," of whom Pomeroy was the most influential, were behind the decision and implied that he had been conspired against.[93] He was stung by the charge of bribery. From Hebron in late March he wrote bitterly to his father-in-law, "being anxious to right Especially where your Honour, my own & y[e] Publick good are Concern'd." The letter that survives is a copy he made of the original, kept for the record and sent the next year when the controversy flared up again.

He told his father-in-law that he had been "Expressly instructed by you to 'Transact the whole affair relative to y[e] College according to my own Prudence with y[e] advice of such as I should think fit to Consult, & also that when y[e] Charter should be obtaind and Recorded, then I should proceed to take the Deeds of Land given to the School and your Self, in Doing which your Express Direction was that I should keep my 'Eye upon getting as much near and convenient for Speedy—'improvement for the present Support of your Family & School as might be & that I should bring home y[e] Several offers to Know y[r] Preference 'for a Site of the School in the Several places and the Gov[r]. Reasons for Preferring y[e] Place he Should Choose to fix it in & also that I should see what provisions Could be made for putting Seed in to the Ground 'Seasonably for the Sup-

---

[92] Letter of 29 July 1770, quoted in McCallum, *Eleazer Wheelock*, 176.

[93] The accusatory letter was from James Murch, of Hanover, to Wheelock, 13 March 1770. Chase, *History of Dartmouth College*, 1:133. There were seven Connecticut trustees and five from New Hampshire. All of the Connecticut trustees were Congregationalists, and all but one graduates of Yale (the exception was Wheelock's son-in-law, the Rev. William Patten of Hartford, a Harvard graduate). Ibid., 121. See the Genealogical & Biographical Notes.

port of your Family & School and also that I should see what 'Materials for Buildings might be had on the Spot viz. Boards, &c . . ."[94]

Alexander refuted the "hint which is Spreading that in my late Tour in y$^{e}$ Affair of the College, I acted without Book . . .": to jeopardize his name in New Hampshire would be folly because "my Carrecter with the Govr. is to Dear to me to be willing to loose it, Since I have interested my Self so much in Land in his Province, & my Difficult Circumstances in this Colony which by long absence from my own affairs at home, are the more Difficult; make it the more necessary that I take good care of my name and Interest in New Hampshire." He appealed to Wheelock to clear his name and signed the letter "your very Dutifull Son." Given the tone and substance of this letter, the irony must have been evident to both men.[95] A year later Phelps was to point out that he had received no reply.

Wheelock moved to Hanover in August 1770 to supervise the clearing and planting of the land and the construction of the first buildings. Remarkably energetic at 60, he was in the process of fulfilling the project of many years' planning and the achievement for which he is known to posterity.

The first building was a log hut 18 feet square for Wheelock and his family. "In a few years more than 2,000 acres of land in the immediate vicinity of the college were fitted for cultivation and pasturage and a village grew up, which in 1775, besides the college buildings, mills, barns, a brew and a malt-house and blacksmith shop, comprised eleven comfortable private dwellings within sixty rods of the college of which at least four were of two stories."[96]

The pines on the site were "of the largest size" and under the jurisdiction of the governor according to the masting regulations of the Royal Navy. These reserved the tallest and best pines in the colony for its ships, but because of the importance of the college project, Governor Wentworth gave permission for cutting them. One is said to have measured 270 feet from butt to top.

---

[94] Copy in Phelps's hand of his letter of 22 March 1770, DCA MS 770222.1, enclosed in his letter to Wheelock of 23 March 1771, DCA MS 771223.2, to remind him of his earlier defense of his actions. On it is written: "The foregoing is a true copy of my letter to Doctr. Wheelock—which was Delivered to him before he Sett out on his first tour to Coos."

[95] Ibid.

[96] *Gazetteer of Grafton County, New Hampshire, 1709–1886,* ed. Hamilton Child (Syracuse, N.Y.: 1886), 305.

10. A Nineteenth-Century Representation of the Rev. Wheelock and Dartmouth Students at the Founding of the College

*John Warner Barber,* Historical, Poetical, and Pictorial American Scenes; Principally Moral and Religious, Being a Selection of Interesting Incidents in American History *(New Haven: J. H. Bradley, 1851), Dartmouth College Library*

Davenport Phelps, eldest son of Theodora and Alexander, was enrolled in Dartmouth as soon as instruction began and in 1775 was among the first students to graduate.[97] (In the first years of the college there were about twelve English students and six Native Americans enrolled.) Wheelock described his plan for the institution at the outset:

---

[97] *General Catalog, Dartmouth College and Related Schools* (Hanover, N.H.: Dartmouth College, 1940).

> The college will stand upon the body of lands designed for cultivation, which situation will be well accommodated to my plan of introducing labor, as the principal or only diversion and way for students health &c which means they may not only contribute much to their own support, under the conduct of a prudent and skillful overseer, but young Indians with English boys may be instructed and improved in the arts of agriculture without the least impediments to their studies.[98]

There were four in the first (1771) graduating class, including John Wheelock, the founder's son and his successor as president.[99]

A year after his aggrieved letter of March 1770, Alexander wrote again. This time he was helped by a personal intervention from a Hebron friend who had established himself successfully in the northern province. Israel Morey, once a blacksmith in Hebron, had become a considerable landowner, sawmill operator, and a judge and was influential in Orford, north of Hanover. General Morey, as he was titled after his service in the militia during the Revolution, was an original proprietor in Orford and a founder of the First Church there. He had been a strong supporter of the college along with his fellow Orford townsman, Daniel Tillotson, also from Hebron.[100] Both of these men had dealt in land with Alexander in Connecticut. (Morey would be the judge of probate that assisted Theodora with Alexander's estate and also would oversee the settlement of Wheelock's estate.)

Morey brought to Wheelock on Phelps's behalf the copy of the earlier letter and this one written 23 March 1771. The latter is tightly written on three and two thirds foolscap pages, in a hand that reveals the writer's distress. Phelps pointed out that Wheelock had not publicly denied "a

---

[98] McCallum, *Eleazer Wheelock*, 176.

[99] David McClure and Elijah Parish, *Memoirs of the Rev. Eleazar Wheelock, D. D.* (Newburyport, Mass.: Edu and Little, 1811), 63.

[100] Israel Morey (Lebanon, Conn., 1735–Orford, N.H., 1809) m. on 14 July 1757 Martha Palmer (Lebanon, Conn., 1733–Fairlee, Vt., 1810), Alice Doan Hodgson, *Thanks to the Past: The Story of Orford, N.H.* (1965; reprint, Orford, N.H.: Historical Fact Publications, 1992), 421, 424, 432 (and index entries). Their son Samuel (Hebron, Conn. 1762–Fairlee, Vt., 1843) invented an early steamboat, which he demonstrated on the Connecticut River. Ibid., and Elmer Munson Hunt, *New Hampshire Town Names* (Peterborough, N.H.: 1970), 26. Morey and Tillotson supported Wheelock's proposal to establish the college in the north; Morey wrote Wheelock on 4 Sept. 1767 "rejoicing at the news of the School being fixt within the province of New Hampshire." Chase, *History of Dartmouth College*, 1:127–28.

Report, that I had Sold y^e^ College and & that I was uneasy with you &c." which had "Spread and passes Current for Truth."[101] He had wished to let the issue drop, but "a Number of your present Townsmen had at Diverse places in this Colony, industriously spread that & Sundry other Reports, as false as that . . . I had acted in your affair without your Direction &c." Alexander termed them "a Clubb of mean, low-lived men . . . [a] Set of High-handed Rioters . . ."

He bitterly recalled the sacrifices he and Theodora had made, "my fatigues in your Business, my Suffering, in Body and Estate, the Sufferings of my family by reason of my absence, my wife left Linguering through a Long winter with Bodily indispositions . . ." Once there had been "your Kind Reception of me when I brought your Charter; your urging me to visit you the next Tuesday; Consult with you . . ." But then came "your Almost perfect Silence Launching y^e^ Affair, when I waited on you . . . [and your] Consulting those and almost only those who you Knew to be unfriendly to me . . ."

Alexander's grievances were formidable charges: "Sudden Changes of mind; your Secreting all your then future plans from me, after I had Done So much, which you often Said was well Done; your Confusing &c . . ." There was even a question of the fee, for after "your urging me, to Give you my Bill of Charge, telling me as an inducement to make my Charge low, that probably I should be much Benefited by the College; . . . when I told you I had made a mistake in Charging my honest wages; your Geting my first Bill [ ] and approved by one who neither you nor I have esteemed friendly; & who would not have Done what I Did for 20/p^r^ Diem for which you allow me 6/- . . ."

Finally he accused Wheelock of "total neglect of Corresponding with me, Since you left Connecticut, while you wrote frequently to a number who live near me . . ." He does not mince words: his father-in-law's behavior was "unbecoming y^e^ Scholar, y^e^ Freind, the Gentleman, y^e^ Christian and even the Child to hear with insensibility all that has been thrown at me and up on me . . ."

It is an unlovely story. Since history belongs to the winners, Alexander's disappointment has been long forgotten in the success of the institution founded by the indefatigable Wheelock. Ezra Stiles, when president of Yale, summed up Wheelock: "He had much of the religious politician in

---

[101] Alexander Phelps, in Hebron, to Eleazar Wheelock, in Hanover, 23 March 1771, DCA MS 771223.2.

his Make. It is said that amidst a great Zeal and show of piety he was very ambitious & haughty. And yet there was something piously sweet, amiable & engaging in his Manner. Such a mixture of apparent Piety & Eminent Holiness, together with the love of Riches, Dominion & Family Aggrandizement is seldom seen. He was certainly as singular a Character as that of Ignatius Loyola."[102] "For the sake of Wheelock's reputation," writes a twentieth-century historian of Dartmouth, "it is to be hoped that he had better evidence of wrong-doing on Phelps part . . . Unless there was more evidence against him than that which is now available, he seems to have been hardly used."[103]

While in Portsmouth, Alexander added to his ownership of New Hampshire lands. Israel Morey sold him two proprietors' rights in the town of Orford for £50. In light of the later controversy, there is no indication that "there was anything out of character in the transaction."[104] Back in Connecticut, Phelps was elected a delegate to the General Assembly for a final time by Hebron freemen and took part in the session of May 1771.[105] This was his last public office in the town and colony since he moved north later that year.

Wheelock had been in Hanover since the previous summer, and whatever Alexander's disagreements with him, with the move north, Theodora and the children would be close to their distinguished father and grandfather. Alexander was already a large landowner there and followed the lead of Israel Morey and other well-to-do Hebron residents. Davenport had just entered Yale at the age of 16, but in order to keep him with the family, his father took him out to complete his education at Dartmouth.[106]

Alexander cut his losses for the new venture. He sold the three Hebron pieces containing the gristmill and a house (possibly the family residence)

---

[102] Quoted in Leon Burr Richardson, *History of Dartmouth College* (Hanover, N.H.: Dartmouth College Publications, 1932), 189–90. Ezra Stiles (1727–95) entered Yale College in 1742, graduating in 1746, thus overlapping with Alexander Phelps's final two undergraduate years. He was pastor in Newport, R.I., and was called to Yale as president in April 1778, where he served until his death. *DAB*.

[103] Richardson, *History of Dartmouth College*, 95.

[104] Chase, *History of Dartmouth College*, 1:124. The transaction with Morey was recorded 2 Feb. 1770, Grafton County [N.H.] Register of Deeds, 1:226. Other transactions involving Phelps are found in 9:710, 1:275, 277–79, 281–83.

[105] *PRCC*, 13.

[106] John N. Norton, *Pioneer Missionaries or the Lives of Phelps and Nash* (New York: General Protestant Episcopal & School Union and Church Book Society, 1859), 18.

at half their purchase price five years before (£100 in 1772 versus £200 in 1767). He transferred four parcels valued at £700 to the executors of the John Phelps (d. 1769) estate, doubtless representing the repayment of the mortgage.[107]

Sometime after that May assembly session, the family moved north. It would have been an arduous process. Theodora had to dismantle one household, supervise the packing of the furnishings and other of their goods into wagons for the journey. There would have been several cart-loads to take the furnishings and farm equipment that were in the new house at Alexander's death less than two years later. Four of the children were of an age to be helpful. Sarah, the eldest, was 18, Davenport 16, Theodora 14, and young Alexander 12. But there were two who needed minding, Emelia, 7, and Eleazar Wheelock, 5.

Their destination was almost 250 miles north of Hebron. It had taken the first of the families to leave the town for the lands in the upper Connecticut valley eight days to reach their destination, young husband and wife on horseback, an oxen-drawn sledge behind. The last sixty miles had been nothing but a track.[108] That was six years before; in the interim the steady stream of settlers had probably widened and cleared the route, and there were more settlements en route for overnight stays. Although there were no great natural obstacles, there were stream crossings, some doubtless requiring a detour, and the cartway must have had bumps and snags.

For Theodora there was another challenge. In early summer of that year she became pregnant with her eighth and last child. She was 35, by no means at the limit of the child-bearing age, but not in the full strength of youth and with many pregnancies and household cares behind her. If the family moved in the autumn, when the roads were best, she would have been several months pregnant. It was not unusual for women to travel during pregnancy, but it would have been an ordeal.[109]

Apart from the move, it was an unusual and difficult pregnancy, judging by the condition of the baby. Ralph Rodolphus was born on the first

---

[107] Hebron Land Records, 5:552, 5:578, 5:624, 6:290.

[108] This was young John Mann and his wife, Lydia (Porter) Mann, who were sent off by their Hebron neighbors on 16 Oct. 1765 and arrived in Orford, N.H., on the 24th. Lydia was two months pregnant with the first of 15 children. Hodgson, *Thanks to the Past: The Story of Orford, N. H.*, 90–98. See the references to Benning Mann in chapter 5.

[109] Ulrich, *Good Wives*, 141–42, cites examples of women traveling up to the fifth month of pregnancy.

day of spring in 1772. A few days later a chatty note appeared in the *Massachusetts Gazette* with a somewhat arch sense of geography. It reported a startling fact about the child. "We hear from Orford, an excellent Town, 16 Miles from New-Hampshire, or Dartmouth College, that on the 21st of March, the Lady of Col. Phelps was delivered of a son, weighing Sixteen Pounds and an half."[110] Though the birth weight is twice or more what might have been expected, it is not, however, without precedent, and modern obstetricians observe such weights from time to time. The birth would have been difficult, but as Theodora had already given birth numerous times there may not have been other complications. In any event, she lived for another 39 years and the boy to his seventh decade.[111]

While pregnant and in the conditions of the northern winter, Theodora was responsible for setting up a new household, caring for and educating the smaller children. It was an achievement, not of the kind that gets mentioned in the records of offices held and transactions conducted, but of fundamental importance to the health of family life. Theodora was soon to be challenged further.

The family settled in Lyme, adjoining Hanover to the north, "Lime" in early spelling, and the namesake of the Connecticut town. Their house must have had sizable acreage with it, for Alexander paid £500 to a resident of Windham County, Connecticut for the tract where his house and barn were located.

We know from the inventories made two years after the family's move that they lived comfortably; the house and its furnishings were not those of a struggling pioneer. For all the credit that Alexander was using for his land purchases, the household economy depended in large part on their farm. The equipment and the animals probably came with the family on the trek north, so this household is also a reflection of what they had in Hebron. Like all but city-dwellers at the time, the family kept farm animals and raised subsistence crops. The stock included a "Black Cow and a speckled," a red cow with "Gallows horns," one being grazed at neighbor Green's another at Gilbert's, five hogs, and a yoke of oxen[112] In the barn were the plow, saddles, a yoke, a potash "Cittle," and "an old horse."[113]

---

[110] *Massachusetts Gazette*, 13 April 1772.

[111] Currently practicing physicians report occasional incidences of birth weights on this order of magnitude, sometimes as a result of a diabetic condition. Personal communication from Carolyn Westhoff, M.D., obstetrician, Columbia-Presbyterian Hospital, New York City, March 1998.

Table 1
Household Furnishings in Alexander Phelps's Estate Appraisal

| Item | Value in £ |
|---|---|
| Best Bed and Furniture plane Ticking | 7 |
| 2nd best Bed & Furniture strpd Tickg Cotton | 4 13*s* |
| 1 Bed Stripd woolen Ticken | 3 15*s* 7*d* |
| 1 Bed & Furniture | 7 8*s* |
| 1 Rug at 35/ & Trundle Bed | 4 1*s* |
| 1 Bed English Ticken | 6 4*s* |
| 1 do Linseywoolsey Do | 5 7*s* |
| 3 Table Cloths | 0 18*s* |
| 1 pair Sheds & 1 Desk | 1 15*s* |
| 1 Table, 1 Dozen Chairs | 1 10*s* |
| Looking Glass | 4 10*s* |
| 4 old chests at 1 staff | 0 11*s* |
| 3 prs of Handirons | 0 18*s* |
| 1 pair Handirons & 1 Warming Pan | 1 4*s* |
| old Pewter: | |
| Platters Plats and Basons | 4 12*s* |
| Earthen Do | 1 12*s* |
| 3 Brass kettles | |
| Ironware, Tea Kettle | |
| 2 Trammels,[a] Teapot | |
| 4 [?] Copper & 3 Tubs | |
| 1 Wafer Iron, Salt Bucket | |

*Source:* Phelps Testamentary Documents.

a. "A series of rings or links or other device to bear a crook at different heights over the fire." *OED.*

The "House and Well" was valued in the inventory at £80—a sum that in that new community indicated a building of more than basic quality. Inside it was well equipped with "best" and "2nd best" "beds and

[112] Ebeneezer Green, Esq., a signer of the inventory, owned abutting property and later had many transactions with Phelps's estate. Thomas Gilbert, yeoman, sometimes referred to as "Capt.," with a surname from a Hebron family, was a creditor of the estate.

[113] "An Inventory of the real and Personal Estate of Col. Alexander Phelps late of Lime Deceas'd," 15 Jan. 1774, "Phelps, Alexander," 1773 et seq., Testamentary Documents, Grafton County [N.H.] Probate Court [hereinafter cited as Phelps Testamentary Documents].

Table 2
Real Property and Livestock in Alexander Phelps's Estate

| Item | Value in £ |
|---|---|
| One Barn | 7 10*s* |
| one House and Well | 80 |
| one Home Lot | 112 10*s* |
| 4 Ten Acre Lots | 56 |
| One right of Land in the Township of Fairleigh | 14 |
| Three rights of Land in Strafford excepting the three first Division Lots | 20 |
| Ten Acres of Land in Lime adjoining to the Land of Mr. Green | 45 |
| 1 ox yoke and Staple & Ring | 15 |
| 1 Yoke of Oxen and old Horse | 15 |
| 1 Black Cow at 4.10 & 1 speckled | 4 5*s* 0*d* |
| 1 red Do Gallows horns | 9 0*s* 0*d* |
| 1 Sley and Tackling | 3 10*s* 0*d* |
| 5 Hogs | 4 10*s* 0*d* |
| 1 Cow at Greens | 5 10*s* 0*d* |
| 1 Cow at Gilberts | 3 5*s* 0*d* |
| 2 potash Cittle [kettle] | 11 10*s* |
| 1 Shovel and Tongues | |
| 1 Plow, & Staple and Ring | |
| 1 Waterpot at 4&1 Chane | 0 11*s* 0*d* |
| 4 Old Axes | |
| 1 pair small Stilyards no 350 | |
| 1 Saddle | 0 16*s* |
| 1 old Surtout & 2 Hunter's saddle | |

*Source:* Phelps Testamentary Documents.

furniture" and two other beds, presumably shared by some of the children; the small ones may have used the trundle bed. There was bed ticking, one of which was "English," another of linseywoolsey, and table-cloths. There were a dozen chairs, which could seat the grown family, a servant or two, or visitors. There were also signs of some luxury: pewter "Platters Plats and Basons" and "earthen" same. The family could afford to buy tea and had both a kettle and tea pot; there were brass kettles and copper tubs, sturdy equipment for daily living, cooking, washing, and laying up food.

Table 3
Personal Items in Alexander Phelps's Estate

| Item | Value in £ |
|---|---|
| 4 Silver Stone Rings | 0 18*s* 0*d* |
| two pair Stone buttons | 0 6*s* 0*d* |
| one Gold Ring | 0 10*s* |
| 1 pair silver Buckles | 0 9*s* |
| 7 large Silver Spoons | 1 4*s* |
| 1 Silver salt Spoon | 0 3*s* |
| 8 rufled Shirts | 4 |
| 2 white Jackcoats | 0 12*s* |
| 1 old wig | 0 9*s* |
| best Blue Coat & claret Jackcoat | |
| 1 blue Cloak | |
| 1 straight bodied white Do | 0 12*s* |
| 1 pair blue Breeches | 0 12*s* |
| 1 pair leather Do | 0 6*s* |
| 1 pair Nankeen Do | 0 6*s* |
| 1 orange Jackcoat | 0 6*s* |
| 1 Chints Gown & ~~1 old pale Blue Jack~~ | 1 4*s* |
| 1 Beaver hat & 5 pair black Gloves | 1 2*s* |
| 5 pair blue gloves | 0 5*s* |
| 4 pair worsted Stockings | 1 4*s* |
| 4 pair Cotton & Linnen Do | 1 0*s* |
| 2 pair Yard Do | 0 4*s* |
| 1 pair Shoes & [ ] pair Spurs | 0 10*s* |
| 1 Silk Jackcoat | 1 2*s* |

*Source:* Phelps Testamentary Documents.

There were many mouths to feed, clothes to wash, and much to do to keep up the farm. Theodora could have had a servant to help her, and the older girls would have done so, but there would have been little leisure time.

After the move, Alexander continued to amass property, now in smaller parcels for small sums; the sellers were probably those who had received grants earlier and were unable or unwilling to occupy the land. In June and July 1772, there were eight deeds recorded in Grafton County, seven of them transactions in which he bought or sold rights in land for £10.[114] He

[114] Grafton County [N.H.] Register of Deeds, 9:710, 1:275, 277–79, 281–83.

was moving along to recoup his fortunes, and it is clear that he saw in this new frontier the opportunity he had lost in the depressed Connecticut economy. There was considerable risk, as the purchases were supported with borrowed money, but he was descended from long-lived men and doubtless expected more years for his investments to ripen.

It was not to be. Alexander was only 49 when death put an end to his plans and called in the risk. He died on 19 April 1773, less than two years since the family had moved north. The *New Hampshire Gazette* emphasized his education and integrity: "Died at Orford, in this Province, the 19th instant, Alexander Phelps, Esq.; a gentleman of a liberal Education, and who had sustained several Offices of Trust in Connecticut, which he discharged with Fidelity."[115] Theodora's brother, Ralph, wrote their sister Ruth Patten in early May "of the broken state of our dear sister Phelps, and her family, by the death of our worthy brother, the Colonel—a heavy breach, not only to the widow and the fatherless ones, but to the public, as he was just entering into a large and useful field in a civil life—but he is gone!"[116] His may have been a sudden death as his brother-in-law Ralph's letter implies, and for the fact he had made no will.

The widow Theodora was left with challenging responsibilities. The seven children were under age at their father's death, although Sarah was nearly of age. Davenport was in his eighteenth year and a student at Dartmouth. There were still three children under 10, including the large baby who was then only a year old. Theodora was the executrix of the estate, an experience which would give her knowledge of the practical affairs of the world that her husband had probably handled before. She had to make decisions about the assets and the creditors and keep records.

The children would have been responsibility enough had there been available cash, but the estate was heavily indebted. Though ultimately the assets in land would be sufficient to pay off the creditors and leave some left, there were few liquid assets at hand for living expenses. For the next several months every outlay to maintain the household had to be recorded, a tedious chore for the widow, but giving us insights how she ran the household.

The inheritance laws as they had developed in New England provided that one third of an estate of a man who died intestate should go the widow and two thirds to the children. There were provisions for the eldest son to receive a double share of the "personalty" (personal effects, chattels) of

---

[115] New Hampshire Gazette, 30 April 1773. Orford adjoined Lyme to the north. The testamentary documents place Alexander Phelps in Lyme; Chase, *History of Dartmouth College,* 1:134.

[116] Ralph Wheelock, in Hanover, to Ruth Patten, in Hartford, 3 May 1773, in *Interesting Family Letters of the Late Mrs. Ruth Patten of Hartford, Conn.* (Hartford: D. B. Moseley, 1845), 43.

the estate.[117] (As there is no statement of the distribution in the records, it is not known whether Davenport received this double share.)

The composition of Alexander's estate was similar to others in New England. About three quarters of the estates of the well-to-do in these years were in land, the balance divided about equally between the equipment needed for farming or other occupation and the house furnishings and personal items. The total of this estate puts Alexander into the category of what a recent commentator terms "Middle or high-income lawyers, doctors, ministers."[118]

Three days after their father's death Theodora purchased "13 yds of Callico for Davenport & Theod[a]," a few days later "a Breeches Pattern" and a thimble. The mother and older daughters were busy making clothes. Their purchases included needles, thread, buttons, braids, skeins of wool, "Satten," "Taffety (For Sally & Theod[a])." The materials needed for the family's clothing between the April of Alexander's death and the following spring amounted to £40, and the list of items runs to two pages. Some were bought for the family by Ebeneezer Green, the neighbor who is cited as having bought £35 of these supplies for the family. Theodora raised immediate cash by selling him in October 1773 three acres from a 50-acre parcel across the river in the town of Thetford.[119]

In a second account there are items or services purchased for the household that run to three pages. These include "Quart of Orange, for Davenport," "Stick Sealing Wax," sugar, tea, tea kettle, horse bought of Capt. Gilbert for £20 (by far the most expensive item). The family also bought rum in barrels (several entries), paid "B. Rich for quilting," paid "Harry with oxen," charges for ferrying, "To Hanover to procure provisions," "Bill for Smith Work To Silvanus Pingry," and horse hire. They bought (some in large quantity): "Wheat of Sml. Bell, Corn of T. Bartholomew, wheat of Mr. Pattinson, 200 lbs. of Pork, Lamb, potatoes, Beef, Rye of Nelson, Sugar, Molasses, Rum, at Esq Summers." An expense on 1 February 1774 was cash "for daughter Sally's Journey to Connecticut and

---

[117] Carole Shammas, Marylyn Salmon, and Michel Danin, *Inheritance in America from Colonial Times to the Present* (New Brunswick, N.J.: Rutgers Univ. Press, 1987), 32.

[118] Jones, *Wealth of a Nation*, 330–31, table 173.

[119] "Account of Cloathing had for Col. Phelps Family after his Death under administration of Theodora Phelps," Phelps Testamentary Documents. The deed for the sale of the land to Green in Thetford (later Vermont, then in Gloucester County, New York) was dated 2 Oct. 1773. DCA MS 77352.

expenses for her sickness on the road." Another was for Davenport's tuition.[120]

There is a virtual social and economic history in these documents. It is clear enough that Theodora could tap the help of neighbors to carry the family through the difficult time. It is also clear that the family lived well, could eat well, and were well-clothed through their own efforts. We learn of the eldest child Sally's (Sarah's) trip to Connecticut, suggesting the ties with the family there; there is the clothing for young Theodora ("Theod[a]") and Davenport's essential support at Dartmouth. Curiously, there are no references to the other children.

There were seventeen large creditors to be satisfied and nearly thirty smaller ones. The estate could not pay them without liquidation of some of its assets in real estate. The largest of the debts was the cost of a bond to "Horsford" due to John Dennis at £228; this is almost certainly Obadiah Horsford, who is listed as creditor elsewhere for a small amount and who had been involved in several of Phelps's Hebron land transactions. There were also obligations to prominent people: the estate owed Governor Wentworth "half" of £118, Silas Deane £58 (as administrator to Joseph Webb), and the Rev. Samuel Peters £38. There were over a dozen other creditors for small amounts as shown in table 4.[121]

The books listed in the inventory reveal Alexander to have been, as would be expected, an educated man.[122] There were Bibles and grammars for Latin and Greek and English, although literature is represented only by Ovid. This country lawyer had law books and, not surprisingly for one so involved with land, a surveyor's guide:

Attorneys practice 2 vol
Lord Cook 1 vol
Willistons Works
1 Greek Testament
a Latin Bible
Pramon ad Sectorem

Astronomy
a Latin Book
a Latin book
Hails Pleas of Crown
Hawkins Pleas of the Crown
Jacobs Law Dictionary

[120] "Account for Provisions and other necessary Family Articles for Colo Phelps Family since his death (exclusive of Clothing) under Adm. of Theod[a] Phelps)," Grafton County [N.H.] Probate Court.

[121] In Hebron, Conn., Phelps's estate was considered "insolvent." Eleven years later a parcel that had remained in his ownership in Connecticut was sold by Joshua Phelps, "Administrator on the Estate of Col. Alex'r Phelps Late of Hebron Dec'd Represented Insolvent . . ." Hebron Land Records, 7:101.

[122] "An Inventory of the . . . Estate of Col. Alexander Phelps," Phelps Testamentary Documents.

| | |
|---|---|
| Office Execr. | 1 Latin Dictionary |
| Connecticut Lawbook | Gordons Geography |
| Justice Pracie | Martins Philosophy 3 vol |
| Green Bible | Surveyors Guide |
| Sectorum & Calender & Baxter | Ovids |
| E. Pemberton | 1 Greek Testament |
| Annotations on Physic | 1 Greek Grammar |
| Carrel on Job | Milton, Corderii & Academy |

Two years after her husband's death, Theodora wrote a letter to her father to introduce the neighbor, Capt. Ebeneezer Green, who had been helpful to her. He was to pass through Hanover en route to a meeting of the assembly. "Capt. Green has Earnestly Injoyned it, that I should write you that he will set out, to go to the Assembly, and that he should be ready to receive any of y[r] Commands by Trivet [?] Letters, and Greate promises of Friendship to do all he Can in part of y[r] affairs—this from Y[r] Ever Dutifull Daughter, Theod[a] Phelps, Lime Feby 20 1775."[123]

Theodora's note is scrawled, brisk, to the point, the note of a busy woman but also one who had a sense of what help her father might need of the assembly. Agitation against the British was mounting at the time, with the tinder to be lit in only a few weeks at Lexington. Wheelock had much on his mind, with the prospect of an interruption in the funds available to him from England.

Theodora took a big step three years after her husband's death when she petitioned the court for permission to sell the lands in Lyme and Apthorp "in order to . . . pay to the Creditors of the Estate their just demands." The judge of the probate court was her late husband's friend, Israel Morey, who approved the distribution.[124] The estate was not fully released from debt until 1778, when John Young certified that "he will meet the unsatisfied claims on the estate of Alexander Phelps." Davenport Phelps, then a Dartmouth graduate and veteran of the Battle of Bennington, was present at the signing. Although the estate was free of debt, there

[123] Theodora Phelps, in Lime (Lyme), N.H., to Eleazar Wheelock in Hanover, 20 Feb. 1775, DCA MS 775170.

[124] Statement by Theodora Phelps to Israel Morey, Esq., Judge of the Probate of Wills for Grafton County, 2 Nov. 1776. Grafton County [N.H.] Probate Court.

Table 4
Partial List of Creditors to the Estate of Alexander Phelps

| Claimants | Amount in £ |
|---|---|
| Isaac [Bringe?] Esq. by Note | 34 11*s* 11*d* |
| ditto for acct | 1 16 10*d* |
| Bond to Horsford for £1,000 to pay John Dennis Esq. | 228 12*s* 7*d* |
| Phelps & Green to Gov. Wentworth £118.13.5 half to be paid by the Estate | 61 14*s* 9*d* |
| Silas Deane Admr to Joseph Webb, a Note Primly Interest | 58 6*s* 0*d* |
| Saml Peters Note | 38 16*s* 2*d* |
| John Phelps Esq Balance | 73 0*s* 6*d* |
| Ob. Horsford acct. Ballance u Agreement | 13 3*s* 1*d* |
| Proprietors of Abthorp Taxes | 56 |
| Jonathan Child Collector of Rates | 7 0*s* 0*d* |
| Tho. Johnson | 18 5*s* 5*d* |
| Dr. Henry Willes fr Acct | 1 1*s* 0*d* |
| Israel Smith ditto | 0 13*s* |
| Capn. David Barbu[t] Note | 5 17*s* |
| Ditto in Acct | 50 13*s* 6*d* |
| John Green acct | 48 8*s* 3 |
| Aaron Stiles Acct | 5 16*s* 0*d* |
| Capt. Daniel Ingraham | 10 |
| Sub total | 707 10*s* 4*d* |
| *Other names for small amounts on notes or accounts*[a] | |
| Sub total | 854 8*s* 6*d* |
| *Additional claimants for small amounts*[b] | |
| Due on note £150 given by Col. Phelps to Danl. Tillotson dated June 8, 1763, assigned by [ ] Tillotson to the [p] Wm. Pitkin, Esq, Principal & Interest | 183 |
| Pelatiah Pierce, Judgment of Court | 17 15*s* 2*d* |
| Wm. Pitkin, Esq. Ballance on Adjustment of Capn. Ingraham Note | 27 |
| Thos. Porter Account | |
| Timo. Bartholmew | |
| Nath. Hewes | |
| Grand total | 1144 15*s* |

*Source:* "A List of Claims of several Creditors to the Estate of Alexa Phelps, late of Lime," Phelps Testamentary Documents.

a. Dartmouth College, Thomas Gilbert, John [Pirshallon], Dr. A. W. Cutler, Dr. John Warterous, Dr. John Crane, Dr. Elkanah Billings, Richard [Kammys?], Nath. Hewes, Jr., Steel Smith, Adonijah Gilbert, Jonathan Sawyer, John Wood, Aarpm [Stprs?], Benj. Grant, Walter Fairfield, [Tebeder?] Howard, Uriah Curtis, John Strong, other illegible names.

b. Ob Nobles, Dr. Saml Carey, Benj. Chamberlain, Tomo. Bartholomew, John Seargeant, Nath. Loomis, Capn. Wm. Bell, Saml Phelps, John Parker, and [ ] Boot, Esq.

were still extensive lands to be sold that ten years later would cause Davenport to seek English buyers.[125]

John Young was an early settler in Haverhill (the site that Alexander had chosen for Dartmouth), and a widower. Theodora and he were married in 1776. They may have lived in Lyme until 1781, when they moved to Hanover.[126] Theodora was left a widow for the second time when John Young died there in 1786,[127] but then the children were grown up, and with the efforts of Young, herself, and Davenport she was apparently in comfortable circumstances. In the Grafton County register there are four deeds from John Young to Davenport Phelps, the sole stepchild to be so recognized. Theodora received the bulk of her second husband's estate.[128] She lived to be 74 and died in Philmont, New Hampshire, in 1810 or 1811.[129]

Eleazar Wheelock had died in Hanover in 1779 at age 68, his great work completed and the college functioning despite the strains caused by the Revolution. (His interests in the American invasion of Canada in 1775 are described in chapter 4.) He bequeathed to Theodora and her sister, Ruth Patten, his house in Lebanon Crank (North Parish) and smaller items. His will included a bequest to a Patten grandchild but none to the Phelps grandchildren.[130]

The firstborn son, Davenport Phelps, and the third, Eleazar Wheelock Phelps, were energetic men whose careers and families are described in subsequent chapters. Young Alexander Phelps is stated in the family history to have returned to Hebron, where he was a physician, but there is no verification of this in the local or federal census records.[131] Ralph

---

[125] "Note signed by John Young, 13 May 1778, certifying that he will meet the unsatisfied claims on the estate of Alexander Phelps. Signed Sealed and Delds. In presence of Davenport Phelps," Phelps Testamentary Documents.

[126] Dexter, *Biographical Sketches,* 1:765–66.

[127] McCallum, *Eleazer Wheelock,* 63n.

[128] Grafton County [N.H.] Register of Deeds.

[129] A card in the Dartmouth College Library reads "Major John Young, Sr., Haverhill, Mass. 1715, d. 1785 Hanover, N.H.," and states that Theodora (Wheelock) (Phelps) Young "d. c. 1811, Piermont, N.H." Theodora "was living in Hanover in 1811." Dexter, *Biographical Sketches*, 1:765–66: McCallum, *Eleazer Wheelock,* states she died in 1810, 63n.

[130] McCallum, *Eleazer Wheelock,* 209–11.

[131] In the Hanover town records there is one reference to an Alexander Phelps: on 12 March 1799 a man of that name was sworn as a hog reeve. Records of the Town and Selectmen of the Hanover, N.H, 16. No Alexander Phelps is listed in the U.S. census for New Hampshire or Connecticut from 1790 to 1810.

Rodolphus Phelps, the large baby, was the longest-lived of the sons. He studied law at Dartmouth and in 1796 moved to western New York, where he became a lawyer. He was closely associated with his brother Davenport, and his career is also described in chapter 3. Sadly this writer has not been able to find any record of the later lives of the daughters, Sarah, Theodora, and Emelia.

"Lawyer or merchant are the fairest titles our town affords," wrote Hector St. John Crevecoeur of the colonial American society he observed in the 1760s and 1770s. Alexander Phelps bore one such title, and his career reflects the opening of opportunity for this generation of the descendants of the Puritan emigration. In his lifetime there came to be increasing ability to make choices of religion, profession, and dwelling place. We can see the growing social mobility of the time in his movements within the colony, Bermuda, Boston, and Portsmouth and the family's move to New Hampshire. "Land! Land!" continued to be the cry, as in Increase Mather's day.[132] There is also, and unmistakably, the energetic pursuit of gain: in land speculation, products for market, legal work. With this came risk, "affairs" in disarray. At the end Alexander played a "main chance" to recoup and lost. Theodora managed the settlement of the estate, found a second husband, and launched the children into mature life.

---

[132] Increase Mather, *An Earnest Exhortation to the Inhabitants of New England* (Boston: John Foster, 1676), 9, quoted in Stilgoe, *Common Landscape*, 43.

# III

## A REBEL PASTOR IN NOVA SCOTIA

*It is a land of promise where they have provision for soul as well as for body . . . When God wraps us in with his ordinances, and warms us with the life and power of them as with wings, there is a land of promise.*

—John Cotton, "God's Promise to His Plantation"

### The Rev. Benajah Phelps

"Things are in a Sorrowful Situation here," wrote the Rev. Benajah Phelps from Nova Scotia in the summer of 1769 to Eleazar Wheelock. "[A] Number of Episcopalians who used to be very friendly & ginerous to me," he told his mentor, have become "[violent] in their Endeavours to brake up the Disenting Cause, & in order to accomplish their designs they level all their rage & malice at me . . ."[1] Nine years later, in the midst of the American Revolution, whose cause he supported, he fled Nova Scotia alone for fear of arrest. Attempting to return to bring away his wife and children, "[H]e was taken by the *Albany* Man of War & after having been detained by her a number of Days was with the other Prisoners put unto an open Boat fourteen miles out at sea & left to the mercy [of the] Ocean which at that time was very Tempestuous & after having [been] exposed to momentary Death for about Twelve Hours were cast on Shore at Naskeag in uninhabited Wilderness about one hundred miles beyond Penobscot."[2]

Benajah Phelps was one of the Yankee Congregationalists who had been transplanted to a unique corner of the North Atlantic world—the township of Cornwallis on Minas Basin on the peninsula of Nova Scotia. It was there that the New England Planters, as they came to be called, gradually acquired a social identity distinct from their Yankee counter-

[1] Benajah Phelps, in Cornwallis, N.S., to Eleazar Wheelock, in Lebanon, 10 Aug. 1769, DCA MS 769460.4. The full text is given below. Dr. Allen B. Robertson, of Halifax, and Judith Plummer, of Westbrook, Maine, provided research assistance in preparation of this chapter, an abridged version of which was presented by the author at "Planter Links," a conference sponsored by The Planters Study Center, Acadia Univ., Wolfville, N.S., 26–28 Sept. 1997.

[2] Memorial to the Connecticut General Assembly, Ecclesiastical Affairs, 1st ser., vol. 15, 60a–60b, Conn. Arch., box 434, roll 82-75.

parts.[3] This chapter recounts the transformation of Phelps's defeat into the honor that comes with being on the "right" side of history. In his native Connecticut he enjoyed the sobriquet the "Uncompromising Whig."[4]

Phelps served his congregation in what was, and still is, an open and spacious land. From their fields and houses the Planters could see low-lying hills to the east separating them from the interior of the peninsula and, to the west, the rise of the bluffs that border the Bay of Fundy. The waters of the Minas Basin and its tributary rivers are nearby, reflecting light, ebbing and flowing with the great tides. Much of the land was reclaimed from marshland and is protected from salt inflow by a system of earthen barriers, many of which remain. This land, known now as the Annapolis Valley, has been a land of orchards since the eighteenth century. It produces apples, pears, and other fruits for a national market. The soil is good, not at all like the stony hardpan of the southern New England from which the Planters came or the scrubby highlands between the valley and the Atlantic coast. The weather is warmer and more temperate than that of foggy Halifax to the east. To this day it conveys a biblical sense of God's bounty.

Though the Planters found a green and productive land, the winters were severe—more so in the eighteenth century than today. Roads then were paths, which were impassable at some times of the year. The settlements on the Bay of Fundy side were isolated from the capital, and it was usual to go around the peninsula by sea rather than to traverse the rough

---

[3] The recent considerable literature on the New England Planters and on colonial Nova Scotian history has been invaluable in providing context for Benajah Phelps's experience. These include two volumes edited by Margaret Conrad—*The Planted Well: New England Planters in Maritime Canada* (Fredericton, N.B.: Acadiensis Press, 1988), and *Intimate Relations: Family and Community in Planter Nova Scotia, 1759–1800* (Fredericton, N.B.: Acadiensis Press, 1995); and Judith Norton, compiler, *New England Planters in the Maritime Provinces of Canada, 1759–1800* (Toronto: Univ. of Toronto Press, 1993).

[4] The name "Benajah" appears frequently repeated in the Old Testament; he was one of Solomon's advisers. In Hebrew "Jah" means intelligent; the name is variously referred to as meaning "God has built" and "God is intelligent." In the Old Testament, a community is judged by its faithfulness to the destiny laid out for it by God, and the "intelligent of God" show the way. In Phelps 1899 and in his Yale biography, the name is spelled "Benijah." The birth record and the gravestone inscription use "Benajah," the spelling used here. Arthur Hamilton Wentworth Eaton, *The History of Kings County, Nova Scotia, Heart of the Acadian Land* (Salem, Mass.: Salem Press, 1920), provides the most extensive account of Benajah Phelps's Nova Scotia ministry based on local sources. Dexter, *Biographical Sketches*, 2:713–14, includes a short biography of Benajah Phelps.

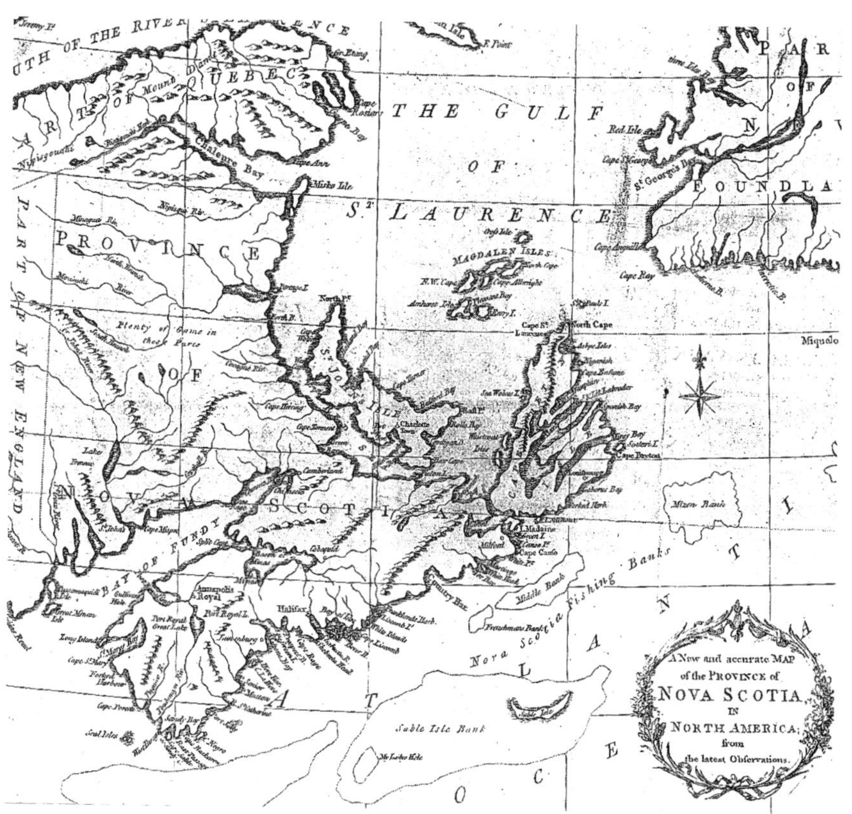


11.“A New and Accurate Map of the Province of Nova Scotia in North America from the Latest Observations,” 1781

The “Bason of Minas” lies on the western coastline of the peninsula, an inlet of the Bay of Fundy.

*Map Division, The New York Public Library, Astor, Lenox and Tilden Foundations*

interior lands to get to the capital at Halifax.[5] For all that, the soil was better, and there were similar challenges to survival as in New England, requiring close attention to the household economy. There was a shorter growing season for crops, and markets for surplus were remote. For the early Planters, including the Rev. Benajah and his family, waking hours were devoted largely to tending crops and animals, making clothes and other necessary items, and preparing food for the long winter months.

[5] John Bartlett Brebner, *The Neutral Yankees of Nova Scotia: A Marginal Colony during the Revolutionary Years* (New York: Columbia Univ. Press, 1937), 9.

Nova Scotia is situated on the major water route to northern North America from Europe. It was the ideal place for bases from which ships could be dispatched to defend or attack the entrance to the St. Lawrence estuary or other strategic locations from the Chesapeake to Machias, Maine.[6] A prize contested between the French and English, it was divided up at the treaties ending their several eighteenth-century wars, until the final British victory. By the Treaty of Paris in 1763, which settled the French and Indian War, it became wholly British.

In 1749, several years before the resolution of the struggle with the French, the British established a naval base on a deep-water harbor on the Atlantic coast. From its founding, Halifax, as it was called, was the Crown's most important North Atlantic base. The population of Nova Scotia at the time was composed largely of French-speaking Acadians, most settled on the Bay of Fundy side. Their forebears had made the land productive. Families thrived, and there were over 10,000 Acadians in the province by the mid-eighteenth century. As the war with the French intensified in the late 1750s, the British authorities came to suspect the French-speaking and Roman Catholic Acadians of collusion with their rivals and their Indian allies. They took the drastic step of deporting whole settlements, the pathos of which was commemorated by Longfellow in *Evangeline*. About 7,000 Acadians were forced from their homes between 1755 and 1758, loaded on transports, and carried to ports along the eastern seaboard.[7]

The colonial government then chose to encourage immigration to fill the vacant farms and villages with English-speaking, "non-papist" subjects, whose loyalty would presumably not be suspect. On 12 October 1758, Gov. Charles Lawrence issued a proclamation offering land to New England families. It was an enticing prospect for many in towns where several generations of large families had made farm land scarce for the younger sons. The governor's proclamation told of "interval Plow-Lands, producing, Wheat, Rye, Barley, Oats, Hemp, Flax . . . cultivated for more than a Hundred Years past, and never full of Crops, nor need manuring . . . Upland, clear'd and stoc'd with English Grass, planted with Orchards, Gardens . . . wild and unimproved Lands . . . well timber'd and

---

[6] Since Acadia "stretches into the Atlantic far to the east of Massachusetts . . . it also provided ideal bases from which to defend or harass the maritime commerce of New England"—as would be true in the American Revolution and War of 1812. Arthur Quinn, *A New World: An Epic of Colonial America from the Founding of Jamestown to the Fall of Quebec* (New York: Berkley Books, 1995), 386.

[7] N. E. S. Griffiths, "The Acadians," *DCB*, vol. 4, xxiii, xxvii. Quinn, *New World*, 412–26.

wooded, with Beach, Black-birch, Ash, Oak, Pine, Fir."[8] The governor exaggerated, but the announcement had the intended effect and attracted interest from southern New England farmers.[9] Mindful that the population the Crown wished to attract was entirely from Congregational southern New England, the governor, in a second proclamation, issued on 11 January 1759, assured the potential emigrants that they would be permitted "full liberty of conscience . . . Dissenters [would be] excused from any rates or taxes . . . for the support of the Established Church in England."[10] To ensure that grantees would actually settle (and to avoid speculation), the governor promised that the "quantities of land granted will be in proportion to the abilities of the planter to settle, cultivate, and enclose the same—[and] no one person can possess more than one thousand acres by grant."[11]

In April 1759 the governor invited a delegation of eastern Connecticut men to look at the Nova Scotia lands being made available. Robert Denison, the senior delegate, was a Connecticut-born veteran of the struggle for ascendancy in North America. In 1745 he commanded one of the eight companies of Walcott's Connecticut Brigade at the successful siege of Louisbourg on Cape Breton, where he was commissioned major. He was an elder of the North Society of New London (present-day Montville), which his father had founded when he moved to land purchased from the Mohegan sachem Oweneco.[12] He was three times married, with 18 children, and, at the advanced age of 60, was about to immigrate to new lands in British North America. Denison was Horton's first judge of common pleas and its representative to the assembly from his arrival in 1761 to his

---

[8] Quoted in George A. Rawlyk, *Nova Scotia's Massachusetts: A Study of Massachusetts-Nova Scotia Relations, 1630 to 1784* (Montreal: McGill-Queen's Univ. Press, 1973), 217–18; Brebner, *Neutral Yankees*, 7.

[9] Brebner, loc. cit., 9.

[10] Ibid., 26–27. Brebner believes that the governor "disingenuously" implied that Nova Scotia offered the same justice and local government as the New England colonies.

[11] Rawlyk, *Nova Scotia's Massachusetts*, 217–18. NSARM, 301, No. 3.

[12] *DCB*, vol. 3, s.v. "Denison, Robert"; E. Glenn Denison with Josephine Middleton Peck, and Donald Lines Jacobus, *Denison Genealogy: Ancestors and Descendants of Captain George Denison* (Baltimore, Md.: Gateway Press, 1978), 4, 12. See "Denison" in the Genealogical & Biographical Notes. A Denison genealogy is also available in Fred E. Crowell, *New Englanders in Nova Scotia* (Boston: NEHGS, 1979), no. 534. See also Francis Manwaring Caulkins, *History of New London* (New London, Conn.: privately published, 1852), 231–32. There are references to Denison as a Planter in Francis A. Norred, "Before They Were Planters: Economic Conditions in Eastern Connecticut, 1740–1760," in Conrad, ed., *Intimate Relations*, 66–77; in R. S. Longley, "The Coming of the New England Planters to the Annapolis Valley"; in Conrad, ed., *The Planted Well*, 14–28. Documents relating to Denison are cited in Norton, *New England Planters*.

12. Nova Scotia, near Port William

A view of the area near the former settlement of Cornwallis.

*Author's photograph, 1997*

death in 1765. His fourteenth child would marry Benajah Phelps seven years later.

The delegates traveled around the peninsula by ship from Halifax to reach the Minas Basin, where they saw that there was fertile soil on the banks of the seven rivers that flow into the bay—"the apple trees planted by the Acadians were ready to bud." They were "delighted" with the prospects, and their return spread the news to their fellow townsmen in New England.[13]

Several hundred families from eastern Connecticut, Rhode Island, and southeastern Massachusetts committed themselves to the terms of the grant. They traveled in family groups in ships that carried about 50 people and up to two tons of possessions per family. All told, several thousand people left their homes to make new ones.[14]

The replacement of the Acadians by these families from southern New England (and others from the British Isles) meant that

> Nova Scotia had been reorganized and essentially remade in twenty years. It was doubled in size by the amalgamation of French Acadia . . . nearly doubled in population, and, more important, had been drastically altered in character and cultural geography. In 1755, Halifax was a new English capital imposed on an old French colony. By 1775 it was still very much an imperial outpost, the obvious English and Anglican center, but was the capital of a peculiarly American colony, composed very largely of new communities of Yankees and Acadian returnees, two of the oldest European peoples in North America.[15]

The Yankees brought with them the Puritan culture, with its emphasis on education, religion, and the family, and its building styles and farming practices.

The authorities divided the expropriated lands into townships and gave them English names. Cornwallis, where Benajah Phelps would serve as pastor, and its neighbor, Horton, were among those known as "little Connecticut" because of the origins of the settlers.[16] The two townships were laid out to contain 100,000 acres each and were initially occupied by 200

---

[13] R. S. Longley, "The Coming of the New England Planters," 20–21.

[14] The best estimate is that about 8,000 New Englanders emigrated to the province. Ibid.; Eaton, *History of Kings County*, 63; Rawlyk, *Nova Scotia's Massachusetts*, 222. Personal communication from Margaret Conrad, 16 April 1998.

[15] D. W. Meinig, *The Shaping of America: Atlantic America, 1492–1800* (New Haven: Yale Univ. Press, 1986), 274.

and 150 families respectively. The first to arrive "liked the lands far better than expected," as reported in the *Boston Gazette* in the summer of 1760, when 800 settlers landed at Horton and Cornwallis. Some were so enthusiastic they returned to Connecticut with the transports to get more stock.[17]

Cornwallis was located on the southern shore of the Minas Basin at the eastern end of the Bay of Fundy. Minas is a great tidal inlet, penetrating 66 miles inland, and is the drainage of several rivers. A basin of the Bay of Fundy, its diurnal tides have an enormous range, sometimes over 50 feet. (By contrast at Halifax harbor on the Atlantic side, the spring tides rarely exceed seven or eight feet.) It was separated from Horton by the Cornwallis River, which flows into the bay, a modest barrier easily crossed by boat under most conditions. There were landings on each bank on high ground, where boats could discharge goods and passengers at high tide. The terrain of Cornwallis (now several towns, of which Port William contains the site of the first New England Planters' landing) gently rolls from the river westward to a ridge that separates it from the Bay of Fundy.

In this settlement the forests had been cleared and the good soil worked by the Acadians. The cleared land, then as later, created a spacious landscape with long views; the ridges to the west and in Horton (now Wolfville) to the east are features visible from nearly every point. The waters and, at low tide, sand flats of Minas Basin are edged by bluffs.

At the edge of the basin were expanses of low land that had once been flooded by the diurnal tides; it was "very good manure, [which] help greatly to enrich the Soil," according to a contemporary account. The Acadians had developed a system of earth dikes ("dykes," as the Planters referred to them) to prevent inundation by the sea. An observer at the time wrote that the land "with a Little Labour, yields fine Crops of Corn the second year after it is drained, and in a few years more, will produce both Scotch, and several other kinds of Seed Grass. Thus the Farmer is furnished with both Corn and Grazing Land in the marshes and a small part of Upland supplies him with Garden Stuff."[18] The earthen dikes were

---

[16] The township was named for Edward Cornwallis (1712/3–1776), the military officer who founded the port of Halifax. He was uncle to the Lord Cornwallis who commanded the British troops at Yorktown. *DCB,* vol. 4.

[17] *Boston Gazette*, 14 July 1760, summarized in Norton, *New England Planters*, no. 1390.

[18] *A Geographical History of Nova Scotia* (London: Otis Little, 1749), 22–23, quoted in J. M. Bumsted, *Henry Alline, 1748–1784,* Canadian Biographical Studies (Toronto: Univ. of Toronto Press, 1971), 6.

pierced with ingeniously controlled conduits to allow the fresh water to flow out while preventing salt water from flowing in. The merits of this system were at once apparent to the Yankee Planters, but a great storm in the year before they arrived had broken several of the dikes. As they did not know how to build or manage their drainage systems, they hired Acadians who had escaped the deportation to maintain them.[19] Many of these dikes remain in use today, and the great expanses of marsh are striking features of the local landscape.

Crown surveyors laid out a town plot for both Cornwallis and Horton. In the New England manner these consisted of lots of an acre or two laid out along streets in a grid pattern, some reserved for the town office, the meetinghouse, and adjacent minister's glebe.[20] The rest of the land in the townships was

> Divided according to its character, dyked marsh, cleared Acadian farmland, salt marsh, beach, cleared and uncleared upland, woodlots, and mill sites. These divisions were then subdivided, once more on the per share basis. Thus a single householder might have four or five different original pieces and was likely to acquire control of more through his family and servants or subsequent trading.[21]

Houses and farms were scattered about, and there were no built-up town centers in the seventeenth-century New England manner. In the early years there was no route suitable for wheeled vehicles between the Minas Basin towns and Halifax. Even travel between the towns on the western shore was usually by sea, in the treacherous tides and winds of the Bay of Fundy. Fences were few, livestock strayed. The "towns were redeemed by their gardens and orchards."[22] Early in the immigration period, Cornwallis and Horton were considered the most prosperous of the several plantation settlements.[23]

---

[19] Brebner, *Neutral Yankees,* 33, 42–43.

[20] "Nova Scotia" in *Encyclopaedia Britannica,* 11th ed. (London, 1911).

[21] Brebner, *Neutral Yankees*, 174.

[22] Ibid.

[23] John V. Duncanson, *Falmouth—A New England Township in Nova Scotia, 1760–1865* (Windsor, Ont.: privately printed, 1965), 2–11; Brebner, *Neutral Yankees*, 58–59.

Because the Acadians had cut most timber when they cleared their farms, the Yankees imported lumber from ports in Maine to replace the decayed or burnt houses that they found. The characteristic dwelling was the square house of their native New England. In 1775 two English visitors described the Planters' houses in favorable terms:

> Their houses are generally built square and chiefly of wood, with chimneys of brick in the centre, so contrived as to convey the smoke from all the different fire places. The windows are all sash'd, and they pay no duty for them, they are very numerous, and render their houses light and pleasant. They all build with post and pan; when they get about three yards high they take it in a little; above two yards higher they fix their chamber windows, and above them their roofs; some build a storey higher. After being boarded they appear very neat and compleat houses. They board the outside up to the roof with what they call clapboard . . . They wainscot the inside and make it very neat . . . Their roofs are covered with planks, on those they fix what they call shingles . . . All their houses have cellars under them, and are in general very convenient.[24]

The barns were also of wood, "some of them with clapboards and shingles in the manner of their houses. They contain different apartments for their horses, cows and sheep; and have a floor above for their hay and corn, which is for the most part deposited in their barns, as they do not seem fond of stacking. The entrance of their barns is so large as to admit a loaded wagon."

## Seeking a Pastor

The new residents of Cornwallis were Congregationalists from eastern Connecticut, where the New Lights were strong. They had not moved as congregations as in earlier Puritan migrations, and no pastors accompanied them. They did, however, form ecclesiastical societies soon after they arrived and met on the Sabbath in houses and barns.

To be without a pastor was a serious deficiency in an otherwise happy settlement. In the first December after their migration, in 1760, the heads of 54 of the Cornwallis families wrote a letter to the Reverends Eleazar Wheelock, Solomon Williams in Lebanon, and two others with the good news of their favorable circumstances and a request to help them find a

---

[24] Robinson and Rispit, quoted in Brebner, *Neutral Yankees*, 175.

pastor. It is a remarkable cultural document, which reveals the centrality of religion in the lives of people otherwise engaged in securing their physical well-being in the face of winter. The rough-hewn language is eloquent. "[W]e have had but a few occatianel Sermons sence we came into this government," they told their "Spiritual Fathers"—"[W]e are Left as Sheep without a Sheaperd, many find business enough on the Sabeth without attending on any Religious meeting, mean time they that have a wish for a preaching gosple Long for the time when they may be Satisfy$^{d}$." The prospects were good for "a comfortable Subsistence in temperery enjoyments yet we find vacency one thing needfull the gosple and the ordenances of it without which we can neither be happy nor Content but trusting you will Commit our Case to god Beging his assistence and direction, and that you will use Your utmost indeavours that a wise and faithfull gosple—ministry may be Settled in all vacant Societys." To these families the gospel was as important as the "comfortable Subsistence in temperery enjoyments" of life in the new place. And so, in the evening of the Lord's Day they wrote out and signed their petition for assistance to the "Reverend & Honoured Gentlemen."[25]

The Cornwallis Planters stated that they had recently learned that Dr. Wheelock "hath some reason to hope that he should soon send us a minister." Wheelock may have had in mind the candidacy of young Benajah Phelps, half nephew of his son-in-law, at the time a senior at Yale College.[26] Benajah Phelps was the fifth child of Alexander Phelps's half brother, Nathaniel Phelps [Jr.], and Mary Curtice of Hebron.[27] Yale was the young man's patrimony; in his will of 1781 his father provided that "As I have Given my Son Benajah a Liberal Education I Give him Nothing more than his Donation."[28]

The atmosphere at Yale in 1761 was far different from when Alexander attended. It was student drinking, not charges that he and the faculty were

---

[25] People of Cornwallis, N.S., to Rev. Solomon Williams, Eleazar Wheelock, Benjamin Lord, and Benjamin Throop, 5 Dec. 1760, DCA MS 760651.1. On the envelope is "March 1, 1761," probably the date of receipt. In another hand there are calculations and "Nevves Center, Joseph Nevves."

[26] Dexter, *Biographical Sketches,* 2:713–14.

[27] Nathaniel Phelps [Jr.] was born in 1703, early in the settlement of Hebron. See "Phelps I" in the Genealogical & Biographical Notes.

[28] Will of Nathaniel Phelps [Jr.], 2 June 1781, Colchester Probate District, CSL, box 139, packet 2417 (FHL film 1,015,791).

## The People of Cornwallis Seek a Pastor, 1760

*Former kindnesses and faithfull Instructions So freely bestoed on many of us embolden us to Address you dear Sirs. Not only as friends but as our Spiritual fathers Hoping & trusting that your Zeal for Christ his Gospel and Religeon will incline you to use your utmost endaeavours that a wise and faithfull gosple—ministry may be Settled in all vacant Societys,—we have latly heard by Lettors from Lebanon that M$^{r}$ Whelock hath sum reason to hope that he Should Soon Send us a minister would to god his kind endeavours may be Succeeded,*

*Dear Sirs give us leave to inform you of our Circumstances, we have had but a few occatianel Sermons sence we came into this government we are Left as Sheep without a Sheaperd many find besiness enough on the Sabeth without attending on any Religious meetings mean time they that have a wish [?] for a preached gosple Long for the time when they may be Satisfy$^{d}$,*

*Our Township Settles very fast and we Supose that had their not ben a Reserve made for Sum that we expect in the Spring it mite have ben near Completed, we think we have a good Country and shall probably soon be under precule advantages for a Comfortable Living and that their is as good provision made in this government for the maintanence of the gosple as in any that we know of, but dear Sirs notwithstanding our Raised expectations of a comfortable Subsistence in temperery enjoyments yet we find, vacency one thing needfull the gosple and the ordenances of it without which we can neither be happy nor Content but trusting you will Commit our Case to god Beging his assistence and direction, and that you will use your utmost indeavours in the thing Requested we Subscribe our Selves Your well wishing friends and serve$^{nts}$*

*John Newcomb*
*John Newcomb Jun$^{r}$*
*Hezekiah Coggesell*
*W$^{m}$ Woodworth*
*Moses Dewey*
*Stephen West*
*Calub Wheaton*
*Ezra Downes*
*Amasa Woodworth*
*Simeon Portor*
*Nathaniel Curtice*
*Sam$^{ll}$ Braston*
*Petter Wickwire*
*Nathan Stiles*
*Eliakim Tupper Jun$^{r}$*
*Ruben Cone*
*Calub Hide*
*John Tery*

*Benj$^{a}$ Killborn*
*Jonathan Wood*
*Peris Anderson*
*Benj$^{a}$ Woodworth*
*Je[remiah?] Bordman*
*Robert Parker*
*Benj$^{a}$ Newcomb*
*W$^{m}$ West*
*John Beckwith*
*Jonathan Rockwell*
*W$^{m}$ Newcomb*
*Daniel Parker*
*Elisha Parker*
*Lawrence Johnston*
*Sam$^{ll}$ Starr*
*Sol Parrish*
*Ephraim Loomis*
*Oliver Thorp*

*Ben$^{j}$ Kingman*
*Jabez Chappell Jun$^{r}$*
*Stephen Strong*
*Ebeneezer Bill*
*Silas Woodworth*
*Jehial Rast*
*[Egb] Newcomb*
*Ezekiel Huntington*
*Sam$^{ll}$ Portor [?]*
*David Bentlee*
*Elisha Porter*
*Ezekiel Colkin*
*Edward Ball*
*John Bartlett*
*John Deans*
*David Barnum*
*James Johnson*
*Widow Abigel English*

*P. S.: it is and has been a general time of helth Senc we Came in to this government and their has nothing extrordinery hapned amongst us.*

unconverted, that then challenged President Clap. The 1760 commencement was disturbed when several students violated oaths to limit the intake of liquor and had to make a public confession of sin before being awarded degrees.[29]

Five years passed between Benajah's graduation and his arrival in Nova Scotia as a "specially ordained" pastor. First there was an institutional hurdle to surmount. Congregationalism, as handed down from the first generation of the Puritan migration, was based on the covenants with God made by individuals on their admittance to the congregation.[30] It was the congregation that called and ordained the pastor; he was not sent or endorsed by a presbytery or other higher authority.

In Connecticut an agreement made among clergy early in the century (the Saybrook Platform of 1708) permitted "consociations" of pastors with limited supervisory and consultative roles. Even though they had no direct authority over individual congregations, these consociations were opposed by traditionalists in Connecticut and not permitted in Rhode Island and Massachusetts. As far as we know, Phelps was ordained by one of these, the South Hartford Association, of which Wheelock was probably a member.[31] The Congregationalists had no missionary tradition, and this was an innovation to deal with the problem of maintaining the denomination under the new circumstances of migration.

Wheelock and other Connecticut Congregational leaders sought to maintain in the outland the heritage of the faith that had brought them to the New World. They suspected the influence of the missionaries of the Anglican Society for the Propagation of the Gospel in Foreign Parts (SPG) and sought to buttress their co-religionists. The invitation from the Cornwallis Planters gave the Connecticut pastors cause to send them a spiritual leader. However, some of the difficulties Benajah Phelps faced in later years arose from the "unorthodox" manner of his ordination, for

---

[29] The spirit of rebellion continued; in 1766 the students sacked the president's house, and the college nearly ceased to function as only one third of students and one of the tutors returned after spring vacation. Dexter, *Biographical Sketches*, 2:682.

[30] Taylor, *Colonial Connecticut*, 119–20, 136–37.

[31] There are no records of Phelps's ordination or of the South Hartford Association. In Handley Chipman's letter of 1779 (below), he is described as specially trained. In the 1769 letter from the congregation to the Rev. Eliot in Boston (also below), Benajah Phelps is said to have been sent by "an association."

some members of the ecclesiastical society charged that he was not a genuine Congregationalist.

There was to be another bone of contention. In Connecticut, where Congregationalism was the established church, the assessments for the support of a pastor had the sanction of law. In the Anglican colony, the sums to support a pastor could have the sanction only of the ecclesiastical societies, and within those there were elders who opposed mandatory or "sworn" assessments. The result was an uncertain flow of funds for the annual stipend. This was a persistent difficulty throughout Phelps's ten-year pastorate. Most of our knowledge of his tenure comes from correspondence on these matters. It is well to remember, however, that the stipend only assisted a pastor in maintaining his family. Like most eighteenth-century ministers, Benajah kept a farm, which provided most of the family subsistence.

A principal source of information about Phelps's tenure in Cornwallis and church life in the village is a letter of ten densely-penned foolscap pages written in June 1777 by Handley Chipman. From Newport, Rhode Island, Chipman became influential in church and public affairs in the "little Connecticut" of Cornwallis, where he served as magistrate and judge of probate. Eaton, the Kings County historian, considered him "a man of strong character and great intelligence, who left more literary remains than any of the other New England Planters." He lived to be 82 and survived most of the early Planters.[32]

Chipman clearly relished taking on the role of chronicler and interpreter of events and was keen to justify his role in them. His letter, directed to the Rev. Daniel Cock, Presbyterian minister in nearby Truro, sought to explain the Cornwallis religious controversies.[33] The garrulous and perspicacious account vividly brings personalities and issues to life.

Chipman recalled that "in the year 1761 or 2 We Subscribed to Send to N. E. for a Congregational Minister," and that one of the elders insisted that "Congregational" be underlined to ensure against any suggestion of

---

[32] Handley Chipman to the Rev. Daniel Cock, 30 June 1777, Acadia Univ. Baptist Collection, A 286M .P C44341c, QCM, MG-1-136. The letter is preserved in the collection established by his family. The account of Benajah Phelps's relations with the congregation in Eaton, *History of Kings County*, 272 et seq., was based on this letter, which is quoted directly, though without attribution. See also Eaton's assessment of Chipman, ibid., 600. Handley Chipman was born at Sandwich, Mass., on 31 Aug. 1717 and died at Cornwallis, N.S., on 27 May 1799. He emigrated in 1761.

[33] The Rev. Daniel Cock (1717–1805) arrived with Scottish Planters of Truro in 1770.

presbyterianism.[34] According to Chipman "this matter was in Agitation" for several years. To bring things to a head, he had once offered to travel to Boston to seek a pastor—presumably a Harvard graduate—and another elder agreed to go to Connecticut to find a Yale graduate. These trips were rendered unnecessary when, in 1766, "Mr. Phelps came to Halifax, Sent down from a formation of ministers in Connecticut . . . ordained especially for this field."

Chipman met Phelps at Halifax and "waited upon him up" to Cornwallis. There "the People . . . Seem'd in General Extremely fond of him, & even contrary to mine & some others Inclination, Settled him, without his declaring his principles as to Church Government."

One of the early issues of his pastorate was whether the £80 yearly stipend he was promised was to be raised by binding (sworn) pledges or by voluntary contributions. Chipman, from Rhode Island, where support of the ministry was not law, favored the latter. He gave the new minister only conditional approval, "because it did not appear to me that the Ministry was his delight." Chipman "did not join in Settleing of him, altho' as I Subscrib'd 6 dollars a year towards the Support of a Minister I always paid it to him." Phelps thus began service in the new community with less than full support from one of its most influential residents.

Another participant in the religious life of the Minas Basin towns at the time was the Rev. Joseph Bennett, an Anglican missionary sponsored by the SPG. Unlike Phelps, he enjoyed an assured stipend from London of £70 per year. There were only five Anglican families in Horton when he arrived, and no minister for the majority Dissenters. Later, in 1765, he reported that "Two young gentlemen, ordained in New England want to come." (One of those was probably Phelps.) Referring to what would bedevil Phelps's pastorate (and what the Anglicans considered to be in their favor, requiring no local stipend), he commented that "the people cannot pay them and would much rather attend a church whose Minister would be no expense to them, than a Dissenter whom they must support."[35]

---

[34] This and subsequent quotations are from the previously cited letter from Handley Chipman to the Rev. Daniel Cock, 30 June 1777.

[35] The Rev. Joseph Bennett to the SPG in London, *Index, Calendar of Correspondence, Society for the Propagation of the Gospel in Foreign Parts*, NSARM, reel 15: letter 29, Kings County, 4 June 1763; letter 30, Horton, 28 July 1764; letter 66, Halifax, 14 June 1765; letter 76, Kings County, 2 Jan. 1766; letter 106, Windsor, 21 Feb. 1767.

According to Bennett, soon after Phelps arrived he was conducting services on alternate Sabbaths with an Anglican, Mr. Fuller. However, this cooperation did not last. "[O]wing to Mr. Phelps insistence on sitting during prayers rather than standing," the shared services ended. The Congregational practice of remaining seated during the service conflicted with the instructions in the *Book of Common Prayer*. Phelps is said to have thought it "a matter of indifference," but, in Bennett's view, he "could not take a more effectual step to forward the growth of the Church of England, than that which he took in order to prevent it."

Within months of his arrival in Nova Scotia the new pastor found a wife from a prominent family. She was Phebe Denison, daughter of the recently deceased Colonel Robert Denison and his third wife, Prudence Sherman, of the Connecticut family. Denison was one of the original grantees in Horton, a formidable figure who had been with those who looked over the lands before the migration. The old warrior's estate included a "Cape Breton gun and silver-hilted sword [and] the gun bought from Lake George."[36]

Phebe was experienced in the tasks of setting up a household in a new place. She was 14 when the family emigrated and would have assisted her mother and siblings in the journey and in the settlement. She was 19 when she married, ten years younger than her husband.[37] The couple exchanged vows on 19 November 1766. The Anglican Rev. Joseph Bennett officiated. It was not surprising that a Church of England priest should officiate. It was the established religion in the province, and while a Dissenting minister was allowed to officiate, there was probably none near Cornwallis at the time.[38] If it followed New England practice, the exchange of vows took place in the house of the bride's family.

---

[36] Crowell, *New Englanders in Nova Scotia*, no. 534.

[37] Phebe Denison was born in North Parish, New London (Montville), on 1 Jan. 1747. See the Genealogical & Biographical Notes. Phoebe or Phebe in Greek is "the shining one, an epithet of Artemis. St. Paul in *Romans* recommends 'Phebe our sister' and the name came into use in England after the Reformation." D. G. Withycombe, *The Oxford Dictionary of English Christian Names*, 2d ed. (Oxford: Clarendon Press, 1959).

[38] Eaton states that the Rev. Bennett officiated at this marriage, *History of Kings County*, 278. The issue of whether Dissenting ministers could preside at weddings was a contentious one at the time and involved consideration of who was due the fee. Personal communication from Barry Moody.

Phebe bore her first three children at two-year intervals: Elizabeth, 30 August 1768; Phebe, 7 October 1770; and Denison (who died shortly thereafter), 25 September 1772. Sherman, who died young, was born a year later, and Eunice (b. 1776), who survived to adulthood, are listed in a family history but not recorded in local records.[39] The three survivors made up the "Nova Scotia family"; Phebe bore two more children in Connecticut in the next decade.

The meetinghouse had yet to be built when Phelps arrived, and its location and size were controversial (as was frequently the case in New England). The final choice displeased some and led to long-term resentment of Phelps. According to Chipman, "a Number of people was of the Mind to have Two Small ones built, as the town was of very Large Extent, of which I was one, altho where it now stands accommodates me & most of mine best but it was carried otherwise. . . . " This led to a shrinking of the already limited contributions for the support of the minister, as "many over Canar & Habitant Rivers would never give one farthing to the Meeting house, & caus'd Some to be backward towards Mr. Phelps Support, & caused uneasiness that has subsisted ever since." By 1763 there were about 650 people in Cornwallis and 656 in neighboring Horton.[40]

The frame of the meetinghouse was brought from New England, "probably from Machias, Maine." It was completed in 1767 or 1768 at an intersection of roads that came to be called Chipman's Corner. A "little house" for Phelps was built next to it. Inside the large building were "high-backed pews, and a lofty pulpit arched by a canopy or sounding board."[41]

Another controversy involving Phelps concerned a grant of land by the Crown. In October 1769 Gov. William Campbell deeded Phelps 666 acres in Cornwallis Township, with conditions as to its cultivation and settlement. This was the first grant given to any minister and larger than that given to settlers, and as a result, according to Eaton, many resented it.[42]

---

[39] The Cornwallis Town Book records marriages and births. See Lorna Woodman Evans, comp., *Township Books, Kings County, Nova Scotia, Ayelsford, Cornwallis, Horton* (Kentville, N.S.: Family History Committee of the Kings Historical Society, 1996), 27. Phelps 1899 includes the first three births and records that the boy, Denison, died in 1773; it cites Eunice, born in 1776. *Denison Genealogy*, 32, lists Sherman, born Oct. 1773, died May 1774. The latter two are not listed in the Cornwallis or Horton Town Books.

[40] 1763 population after Isaac Deschamps in Brebner, *Neutral Yankees*, 59; Eaton, *History of Kings County*, 277.

[41] Eaton, *History of Kings County*, 267. The building stood until 1859.

When Phelps sold a portion of it five years later to John Robinson for £45, "the people believed that the land had been intended for the continual benefit of the church and they regarded the minister as having committed a moral wrong in treating it as his own." However, Eaton points out that the "grant . . . was made out in Mr. Phelps' own name, and he therefore evidently had a legal right to sell it."[43]

There were poor harvests in the late 1760s, meaning inadequate support for ministers. In April 1769, Governor Campbell addressed the plight of Phelps and the six other Dissenting clergy in the province in an effort to raise funds in Europe. The difficulties the Planters were experiencing explained their inability to support their ministers:

> This Province being yet in its Infancy and most of the Inhabitants being in Low Circumstances when they came hither and having Houses to build and New lands to clear and Cultivate, they have yet been scarcely able to raise bread corn to support their families. Nor have their stocks of Cattle increas'd to any considerable degree and notwithstanding many are people of great industry and frugality, yet such is their present situation that they can get but a bare subsistence for their Familys, partly owing to the breaches made in their Dykes from time to time by High Tides, the repairing which has been very expensive and possibly owing to heavy rains—especially the last year whereby the crops of Corn fell so far Short, that many suffer'd for want of Bread; and as the people are Low it renders them unable to perform the Contracts with their Ministers for although they are willing and desirous to support the Gospel among them, they have it not in their power.[44]

---

[42] Registry of Deeds, Kings County, N.S., Cornwallis Town Book, 1: 66, 76–77, issued Halifax 4 Oct. 1769, registered Cornwallis 26 Feb. 1770. Lord William Campbell (ca. 1730–1778), governor of Nova Scotia 1766–1773, was faced with a depressed economy and a lack of support from Whitehall. *DCB*, vol. 4.

[43] For the transfer to Robinson see Registry of Deeds, Kings County, N.S., Cornwallis Town Book, 1:282, 242–43. 1 July 1775. The indenture was signed by Benajah Phelps. Eaton notes that the offended parishioners later appealed to the South Hartford Association to take some action toward reclaiming the money, but that the request was "ignored." *History of Kings County*, 263, 268. The date of the transfer was after Lexington and Concord and almost two weeks after the successful rebel stand at Bunker Hill. Phelps could have made his pro-rebel views known, which could have added to the resentment in some circles. It is curious that Chipman does not mention the Crown grant.

[44] "A Brief State of the Circumstances of the Protestant Dissenters in Nova Scotia," 18 April 1769, NSARM, Record Group 1, vol. 284, no. 18, "Various Papers in conjunction with the Position of Dissenters in Nova Scotia, one, in the holograph and the others to the dictation of Governor," Add. MS 19.071 (micro. reel 15,370).

The governor noted that "95 out of 100 in the country towns" in the province were Dissenters whose pastors were impoverished while the SPG support meant comfortable stipends for the Anglican missionaries. He "earnestly recommended to all who are well wishers to Religion in general and the Dissenting Interest in particular, and who are Advocates for Liberty of Conscience and the right of private judgment," that they provide support to these pastors. This remarkably tolerant policy on the part of the governor could have been a means of mollifying the Yankee Dissenters in Nova Scotia during a period in which colonists to the south had been agitating against the Crown-imposed customs duties that followed the abortive Stamp Act of 1765.[45]

It was a wretched time for the Cornwallis pastor. In the summer of 1769, Phelps wrote to Eleazar Wheelock in Lebanon, Connecticut. "Things are in a sorrowful situation here," he confided to his mentor. The formerly friendly Anglicans had turned against him ("[A] Number of Episcopalians who used to be very friendly & ginerous to me . . . are riotin in their Endeavours to brake up the Disenting Cause"). He lamented that "A Surprising carelessness & stupidity seems to have fallen on those in gineral, who, I charitably believe are the real Children of god, others in gineral appear to be in an entire state of Carnal Ease & Security, neither the terrors of the Law alarm nor the Charms of of [sic] the gospel Alarms in the least." The situation was made worse by Phelps's indebtedness. Of his enemies, "the principle instrument they use for my disturbance & destruction, is this, I$^{ve}$ the unhappiness to be in debt to a Considerable Sum, to one of the most fierce & cruel of them all; & this he managed with Somuch art & Subtlty to my disadvantage, that I dont see but he will Entirely brake me up." Chipman notes in his letter that he had loaned Phelps £150, and it is possible that it was he to whom Phelps referred. This seems unlikely, though, as the Rev. Benajah later presided at Chipman family weddings and the funeral for his wife. Phelps's consolation was that he had "a god to go to to unbosom all my sorrows, to account all my woes, to tell all my sufferings, to seek counsel of, to receive comfort from, & to commune with."[46] The letter is a potent testament of a clergyman at a

---

45 It is possible that the award of the land grant to Phelps in October of the same year was part of an effort to assist the Dissenters.

46 Wheelock was involved at the time in planning what would soon be Dartmouth College and was shortly to dispatch Alexander Phelps to secure a charter from the royal colony of New Hampshire. There is no record of a reply to this letter.

### BENAJAH PHELPS TO ELEAZAR WHEELOCK, 10 AUGUST 1769

*Rev*[d] *Sir—*

*I again use the freedom to wright to you; tho I*[ve] *sometimes been fearful that it was disagreeable; as I have received no answer to any I have wrote; however I begg the indulgence of manifesting my highest affection to you, firmly believing you are a Lover of god of Jesus & divine truth; & knowing you are willing to give your assistance to the meaness of your fellow labourers, I therefore make application for your advice; which mortal never needed more; Things are in a Sorrowful Situation here, espitiialy with regard to the interest of real religion; a Surprising carelessness & stupidity seems to have fallen on those in gineral, who, I charitably believe are the real Children of god, others in gineral appear to be in an entire state of Carnal Ease & Security, neither the terrors of the Law alarm nor the Charms of of [sic] the gospel Alarms in the least. Another Discouraging Sircumstance is this a Number of Episcopalians who used to be very friendly & ginerous to me (tho always dissatisfied with the Essential doctrines of the gospel; regineration, repentance & faith) have [?] got a teacher after their own hearts; & are [violent?] in their Endeavours to brake up the Disenting Cause, & in order to accomplish their designs they level all their rage & malice at me, & the worst of reproach & slander is the best thing I*[ve] *had from several of them for some months past; & no paine is is [sic] spaired to disaffect my people to me; which in a few instances they have done; the principle instrument they use for my disturbance & destruction, is this, I*[ve] *the unhappiness to be in debt to a Considerable Sum, to one of the most fierce & cruel of them all; & this he managed with Somuch art & Subtlty to my disadvantage, that I dont see but he will Entirely brake me up.*

*—however I*[ve] *this for my consolation under all my trials; —I have a god to go to to [sic] unbosom all my Sorrows, to vent all my woes, to tell all my sufferings, to ask Counsel of, to receive comfort from, & to comune with; & to whom, thro the merits of his incarnate Son, I trust I have free access ——— I shall conclude only asking your prayers of me mine & & [sic] the people of my Charge; & intreat such Counsel as you shall be able to give from those broken Sketches; —to give a just & full account of the State of things here would have taken Sheets, for a more full account I refer you to Mr. Woodworth the bearer— this Is from your most obd*[t] *hum*[l] *Sev*[t]

*Benh Phelps*
*Cornwallis*
*August 10, 1769*

moment of crisis, reaching out for advice, and perhaps solace, to a distant but, he hoped, sympathetic reader.[47]

[47] Benajah Phelps, in Cornwallis, N.S., to Eleazer Wheelock, in Lebanon, Conn., 10 Aug. 1769, DCA MS 769460.4.

Phelps's salary continued to be in arrears, and although he was rich in land, money was short. Poor harvests made it unlikely that the funds to pay his salary could be raised locally. In November 1769 the Cornwallis Society elders requested support for Phelps's maintenance from the Rev. Andrew Eliot and his parishioners in the North Church of Boston, appealing to their "Christian Brethren of the Several Dissenting Churches in Boston in the Massachusetts-Bay in New England." This group of parishioners supported Phelps and wrote approvingly of how he "Came to us ordain'd to the work of the ministry, and well Recommended (by Said Association) who after one year's Continuance with us on probation took the pastoral Charge of us to our General Satisfaction. At which time we were in Circumstances to Afford him A Comfortable Maintenance, being a time of prosperity with us."[48] Five of the six signatories to this letter were among those who signed the request to the Connecticut pastors that first winter.

In Cornwallis at the time there were "133 familys (Not 10 of which of the Establish'd Church) And between Eight & Nine hundred Souls." The poor harvest of the previous year meant that much of what should have been saved for seed had been consumed: "the produce of our Village being much Cut Short, which occasions So Great A Scarcity Among us, that we had not last Spring a Sufficiency of grain in town to Seed our Lands."[49] The Planters had no cash to purchase seed, but the dire situation was saved by help from Halifax donors: "our Straits had Necessarily Increast to Extremeity through our Inability to purchase Seed had not god Inclined the ears of Some of our Father-like Friends at Halifax to Relive us. By procureing us Seed at a Neighboring Town, the produce of which hath well Answer'd our Expectations.

There had been "Extraordinary Expense on our Dikes," and the congregation was still paying for the meetinghouse. What funds were available had to be used for "Our necessary Expense For Clothing before we Could put our Selves in a way to make Any Proficiency in Manufacturing

---

[48] Letter from Samuel Beckwith, et al. (members of the Cornwallis Congregational Church) to the Rev. Mr. Andrew Eliot in Boston, 8 Nov. 1769, in Massachusetts Historical Society, *Proceedings*, ser. 2, 4 (Feb. 1888), 67–68. The signatories of the letter were Samuel Beckwith, Caleb Huntington, Isaac Bigalow, John Newcomb, Hezekiah Cogswell [Coggesell in a 1760 document], Elkanah Morton, Jr. Of these, all but Bigalow were signers of the 1760 appeal to the Rev. Solomon Williams, et al., to send a pastor. Supra.

[49] Ibid.

our Wooling, hath Involved us as far In Debt to our traders . . . that but very fue of us have Any produce By which we Can Relive our minister Under his present needy Circumstances, And Without Some Relief from Some other Quarter, Our Said Minister Cannot Continue much Longer with us."

Handley Chipman was scathing in his recollection of this effort by the elders "to beg Money;" and he accused them of having made the appeal "without ever calling a Vote of the Congregation therefor." He attributed Dr. Eliot's cool reply to the wheedling quality of the appeal. The historian George Rawlyk has seen this appeal by the Cornwallis elders in 1769 as an example of the "Nova Scotian Yankees' religious colonial relationship with their mother country." Chipman's criticism of the appeal would bear out this later view. The American Revolution would put an end to this vestige of a dependent relationship.[50]

The Boston churches did raise £100 and sent it to the Halifax merchant Benjamin Gerrish to be divided among the seven Dissenting ministers in the colony. In acknowledging the donation, Gerrish suggested that "if the Collection could be laid out in necessary provisions for the Use of their families, such as *Pork, flour, Meal, Chocolate, Coffee, Tea, Sugar* &c. it might be more advantageous than if *Money* was given."[51] This would have allowed the merchant to keep the scarce cash and send the commodities from his account, a "typical merchant strategy," according to a modern commentator.[52] Phelps, in his debt-ridden condition, could hardly have welcomed the alternative of foodstuffs.

Thus divided, the amount given to the individual Cornwallis Society was far less than expected. The elders, Chipman reports, then requested funds from the Rev. Solomon Williams in Lebanon.[53] Chipman vented his ire on one of the elders involved, calling him the "the Snake in the Grass."[54] Once again the elders had acted without a vote from the congregation: "God knows that the Church was never Call'd together, pass'd no Such vote for the Memorial."

---

[50] Rawlyk, *Nova Scotia's Massachusetts*, 223.

[51] B^n^. Gerrish to Revds. Eliott and Cooper, 10 May 1770, in Massachusetts Historical Society, *Proceedings*, ser. 2, 4 (Feb. 1888): 72. Benjamin Gerrish (1717–72) was Boston-born and bred and moved to Halifax in 1751. There he became a prominent merchant with considerable political influence. He was a leading Congregational layman, a member of Mather's Church in Halifax, and had used his influence with Boston church leaders in the 1770 appeal. *DCB*, vol. 4.

[52] Personal communication from Margaret Conrad, 16 April 1998.

Chipman's disdain for this appeal of the elders prompted him to write letters to a number of influential persons in Connecticut, including the governor. He quotes approvingly the reply from a "Gentleman in Norwich [who] Said if that Memorial was true he would not Contribute one farthing to keep them there, but he would contribute to bring them back again to Connecticut." Chipman approved the Rev. Williams's comment that "we must not Expect a Minister here until we had more money to Maintain him with."

Meanwhile Phelps was without adequate compensation. Two months later, in January 1770, the situation appeared desperate enough for Congregationalists in Halifax to address the situation of all the Dissenting ministers in the province. Their letter to the Boston churches singled out the Rev. Mr. Phelps in Cornwallis as particularly needy. "He says his People are not able to make good their Contract, and are of course very much in arrears. This Gentleman has purchas'd a farm, built an House and made other considerable improvements, which has much embarrass'd him, and we believe he at present struggles hard for a subsistence . . . " However, these Halifax men did not excuse the Cornwallis congregation, and pointed out that the town is "one of the most thriving settlements in the Province."[55]

The details of this controversy were fresh to Chipman eight years after the fact. The elders who had written for funds had attacked him for not supporting the pastor and alleged that he told them "Mr. Phelps is not a Congregational, & this obligation is for a Congregational." To Chipman this was a slur that he had never put right: "these Gentlemen have never given me any Christian Satisfaction for their abuses, & private abuses." Years later the disagreement was still a live issue in Cornwallis; E. Morton ("the Snake") "has Lately spoken on that Subject."

---

[53] The Rev. Solomon Williams, pastor in Lebanon from 1722 to his death in 1777, was one of the most prominent of the Congregational clergy in the colony. George Milne, *Lebanon, Three Centuries in a Connecticut Hilltop Town* (Lebanon, Conn.: Lebanon Historical Society, 1986), 15. Eleazar Wheelock was pastor in the North Parish in Lebanon. The appeal was supported by the Connecticut Colony Council in New Haven, which on 11 Oct. 1771 approved that the Rev. Solomon Williams should make an appeal to religious societies in New London, Norwich, Windham, Colchester, Canterbury and Lyme. Eaton, *History of Kings County*, 275.

[54] The elder so described was E[lkanah] Morton.

[55] Benjamin Gerrish and Malachy Slater, in Halifax, to the Revd. Messrs. Andrew Eliott and Samuel Cooper, 18 Jan. 1770, in Massachusetts Historical Society, *Proceedings*, ser. 2, 4 (Feb. 1888): 69–71.

In what must have been a satisfying occasion, the next summer Phelps and the other Dissenting ministers in Nova Scotia were "formed into an *ad hoc* presbytery" to ordain Bruin Romkes Comingo. The latter was a self-educated fisherman of Lunenburg on the Atlantic coast who was called to be their minister by the congregation of Lunenberg's German Reformed Church.[56] "A great occasion was made of the ceremony," held at Mather's Church (later St. Michael's) in Halifax July 1770, attended by Gov. William Campbell and members of the council—further evidence of the relaxed relations between the established church of the colony and Dissenters. Phelps spoke the words that concluded the service to extend the "Right Hand of Fellowship" to the newly ordained. This was published in Halifax a few days later with the sermon by the Rev. John Seccombe.[57]

In 1771 the Cornwallis Ecclesiastical Society requested Chipman and others to "swear" to subscribe. He and like-minded others refused, standing on the Rhode Island principle that contributions for the support of a pastor should be voluntary. (In that year Phelps's salary was agreed to be £75, increasing to £80, but it was not fully paid.) "Some of them [who proposed the sworn payment] were much offended with me," Chipman recalled, "Charging me with being an Enemy to Mr. Phelps." "I told them I was not," he adds, and the final proposal for raising the compensation by subscription "was much in the form I first advised them to." He then and later warned them that "if they went on as they did they might depend on it Mr. Phelps and they would break with each other." They would not listen, "some Scoffed, Some Laughed, & Some told me they was of my mind." Phelps had then recovered from smallpox and was preaching "pretty constantly." Resentment in the congregation "came to pass sooner than I expected . . . To my Sorrow." Reflecting on the controversy,

---

[56] Bruin Romkes Comingo (1723–1820) was a Netherlands-born woolcomber who immigrated to Nova Scotia in 1751 and became a fisherman. He was chosen from among fellow parishioners of the German Reformed Church to be their minister out of respect "for his piety and integrity." *DCB*, vol. 5.

[57] John Seccombe (1736/7–1792), *A Sermon Preached in Halifax*, 3 July 1770 (Halifax, N.S.: A. Henry, 1770), with appendix. Another participant in the ceremony was the Rev. James Lyon (1735–94), who left Nova Scotia during the Revolution and was known for his strong rebel sympathies in Machias, Maine, where he was pastor in 1771. For biographical sketches of Seccombe and Lyon see *DCB*, vol. 4. In his exhortation to the ordinand in this service Lyon urged him to "Meddle not with Politicks any further than is necessary to preserve the Peace of your own Mind; avoid a Party Spirit." Quoted in *DCB*, vol. 5, s.v. "Comingo, Bruinn Romkes," referring to United Church of Canada, *Committee on Archives Bulletin* (Toronto) 11 (1958): 19–32.

Chipman gave Phelps more credit than he did the elders: "It appears to me that he has Shewn a better Spirit than they, tho far from blame."

Sometime before the spring of 1775 the Rev. Benajah was dismissed or resigned the pastorate at Cornwallis. We know this from the title page of the published sermon he gave at the interment of Chipman's wife, Jane, on the Sabbath following her death in April 1775. His introduction describes him as a "minister of the Gospel, and late Pastor of the Church in Cornwallis." It was probably smallpox that led to the "sickness and infirmity" that "for a long time past [made him] unable to follow his study, or perform the duties of his Function." Discouragement and weakness evidently made him unable to resist his "opposers" and led to his departure from the pastorate. Phelps published the sermon reluctantly and only because "the request of the mourners and many of the auditory, has prevailed on the Author to give his consent that the following sermon should be made publick."[58]

The sermon itself shows no signs of flagging energy. It consists of 15 quarto pages in small type, and it must have taken an hour or more to read. In the manner of the sermons that Whitefield had so criticized thirty-five years before, it lists premises by number, explains each one, and offers proofs. The lesson was from *John* 20:23, the account of Thomas's doubting. The premise of the sermon was "[t]hat faith in Jesus Christ is abundantly sufficient to carry the believer far above the terrors of death, the horror of the grave, and to free him from all the curses of the law against sin." The preacher then listed, in numbered outline form, the reasons why faith will triumph over the terrors of death. In the body of the sermon he explained each in detail in sub-numbered paragraphs, defining what faith is, how it is expressed, its fruits and its sufficiency.

In his peroration, Phelps held up Jane Chipman as an exemplar of faith. "She lay under the extreme torture of a fractured leg, together with a fever, and many other distressing infirmities for three months and a half, during which time she manifested a resignation to God's will, rarely to be found in mortals. She bore with surprising fortitude, calmness and submission the strokes of her Father's rod . . . In a word she gave the most satisfying evidence of a real acquaintance with God." Turning to the

---

[58] Benajah Phelps, "Death: the Way to the Believer's compleat Happiness. Illustrated and Improved In a Sermon, occasioned by the DEATH of Mrs. Jane Chipman, Comfort to Handley Chipman, Esq., and delivered, the Sabbath She was enter'd, by Benajah Phelps, A. B., Minister of the Gospel, and late Pastor of the Church at Cornwallis" (Halifax, N.S.: A. Henry, 1776). Copy at Houghton Library, Harvard Univ. Norton, *New England Planters*, no. 1607.

DEATH:
The Way to the Believer's compleat Happineſs.
ILUSTRATED and IMPROVED,
In a SERMON, occaſioned
By the
DEATH
OF
Mrs. JANE CHIPMAN,
Conſort to *Hardley Chipman*, *Eſq*;
And delivered, the Sabbath She was enter'd, April 9th, 1775.

By BENAJAH PHELPS, A. B.
Miniſter of the Goſpel, and late Paſtor of the Church in CORNWALLIS.

HALIFAX: Printed by A. HENRY.
(1775)

13. Title Page of Benajah Phelps's Sermon on the Death of Jane Chipman, 1775

*By permission of the Houghton Library, Harvard University*

congregation, the preacher urged them to follow the example of the faith of the deceased. He concluded with a solemn warning. "Oh! unbeliever . . . be wise in time for eternity, that you may escape that wrath which is threatened to every transgressor, but especially to all despisers of God's Grace."

This was a sermon of a well-educated man, spoken to those who were also educated, able to follow the arguments and informed on the central questions of religion. It is clearly written and closely argued, and there are no references that might have made less educated listeners feel uncomfortable. This preacher appealed to the intelligence; his emotion was contained. The rare pamphlet gives us an example of the sermons that the Cornwallis Planters heard on the Sabbath. It is not hard to imagine the attraction of an evangelical, impromptu preaching style in comparison to this learned approach. It was soon to come to the Planter settlements.

The publication and the choice of the Rev. Benajah to honor his wife show the respect that Handley Chipman had for Phelps. He probably preached before the body in the family house. We know by the date of the sermon that he left the pastorate before the outbreak of the rebellion at Lexington and Concord and thus probably not for views that were to later identify him as the Uncompromising Whig.

## Little Connecticut in Nova Scotia

News of the political furor in their native New England over the imposition of the Stamp Tax in 1765 and the subsequent Townshend Decrees would have reached the Yankee outsettlements in Nova Scotia fairly quickly by letters and word of mouth. There were no newspapers in the Minas Basin townships, however, to leave a record of local responses, and there is a dearth of archival evidence that would reveal local attitudes.

Unlike the southern New England colonies, Nova Scotia had no charter to be used as the basis to appeal for legitimate rights. Its governor was appointed in London; the Crown-appointed council and even the elected assembly were dominated by the Halifax merchants who, in 1775, appealed to London, not to the Continental Congress in Philadelphia, to remove a governor who antagonized their interests.[59] Autonomy at the local level, with election of town officials, a key and strong element in the New

[59] Francis Legge, governor of Nova Scotia 1773–75, *DCB*, vol. 4.

England polity, had not been fully introduced in Nova Scotia. The only newspaper, then published only intermittently, was in Halifax. The Planters' settlements were still relatively young, and the settlers worked hard to maintain subsistence. Political agitation was a luxury they could not easily afford.

In southern New England in these years Congregational pastors preached against the impositions of the mother country, giving a political cast to Dissent. The inhabitants of "little Connecticut" in Cornwallis doubtless learned by letter and travelers' reports of the agitation in Boston and Hebron and other eastern Connecticut towns in the late 1760s. In this outland, however, Congregational and Presbyterian pastors arrived several years after the settlement, and by the 1770s there were only seven of them to serve a population of at least eight thousand. They did not command the authority of the pastors in the home communities, as the Rev. Benajah's experience confirms.

The seeds of rebellion did not grow in Nova Scotia for several reasons. First, in this Yankee outpost the networks of support and communication that stirred their native towns through committees of correspondence and newspapers were absent.[60] Second, the New England Planters were dependent on the government for their land; they may not have had the same feeling of heroic, Biblical possession as their forebears, who carved New England from "the howling wilderness." Finally, there were few, if any, incidents that could fan dissatisfaction and serve as *casus belli*. Nova Scotians were not outraged by the presence of troops as New Englanders were by General Gage's occupation of Boston; Halifax was, after all, a navy base.

There was much to lose from resistance to the Crown. The Planters had created a productive, pleasant, and well-settled land, not willingly to be risked by its owners. The Anglican Rev. Jacob Bailey, Loyalist exile from Connecticut, when journeying from Halifax to Cornwallis at the end of the 1770s, praised the "richness and fertility" of the country. "I was much pleased with the road and the fine farms through which we rode," he noted, referring to "plantations," "groves," and "public houses" for refreshment that he encountered on his journey to the Minas Basin. Near Cornwallis he celebrated the "Fine prospect of the dyked lands covered

---

[60] This and following paragraphs include points made in part 1 of Gordon Stewart and George A. Rawlyk, *A People Highly Favored of God: The Nova Scotia Yankees and the American Revolution* (Hamden, Conn.: Archon Press, 1972) .

with grain and english grass, with a large number of buildings intermixed with beautiful groves on the rising grounds—beyond at the distance of five or six miles the blowmedown mountains heave their lofty summits into the regions of the atmosphere and separate the Bay of Fundy from this fertile and delightful country."[61] From documentary evidence (albeit far scantier than that available in the longer-settled southern communities), a recent study concluded that the Yankee Nova Scotians were in a state of confusion after the outbreak of the rebellion in New England. They were in a time warp, and the harsh political realities that emerged were perplexing. According to George Rawlyk and Gordon Stewart:

> By missing the critical decade of ideological and political development in New England, the Yankees found themselves locked into the pre-1765 conceptual framework they had left behind. Their world at the beginning of hostilities had suddenly assumed an unfamiliar shape . . . they were using old words and phrases in a radically new and strange manner. Bitter civil strife pitting New Englander against New Englander and Briton had engulfed their former homeland. American privateers and British press gangs introduced further elements of instability into an already chaotic situation.[62]

"It was impossible to feel and remain convinced of being bound up in the same fateful train of events," wrote J. Bartlett Brebner, the first modern historian to analyze the reasons for Nova Scotian neutrality. There was not even a sense of solidarity among the local settlements. He warned against a single explanation and pointed to the complexity of behavior. But the "principal clue" is Nova Scotia's isolation from the rest of North America.[63]

When the news of the fighting at Lexington and Concord reached Nova Scotia in late April 1775, the governor, with few troops on hand, was near panic. He issued a proclamation requiring the population to take an oath of allegiance to the Crown, "Forbidding Aiding Rebellion." This, additional taxes, and a partial militia call-up prompted protests in several of the town

---

[61] The "lofty summits" are a few hundred feet high, but they are notable physical features of the valley. "Rev. Jacob Bailey's Journal of Part of Journey to Cornwallis," 13–16 Aug. 1779, NSARM, MG 100, vol. 30, no. 22.

[62] Stewart and Rawlyk, *A People Highly Favored,* 75. The same point was made in Rawlyk's earlier work, *Nova Scotia's Massachusetts*, 224.

[63] Brebner, *Neutral Yankees*, 298–300.

meetings in the Yankee areas. The inhabitants may have been initially favorable to the rebellion by virtue of their New England roots, but they soon became aware of the impracticality of revolt in their small and isolated communities. Any prospect of support from Massachusetts vanished early in the struggle.[64] The provincial government moved against spoken expressions of pro-rebel sympathy. In one instance, the Crown charged the Rev. J. Seccombe, the Dissenting pastor in Chester (who gave the sermon at the ordination of the Rev. Comingo), with praying for the rebels. He was forbidden to preach until he signed a loyalty oath and was required to post a £500 bond.[65]

The sole uprising in the colony of Nova Scotia by supporters of the mainland rebels was to the north, in what is now Cumberland County. The "Eddy Rebellion," named for its leader, involved an abortive attempt to seize Fort Cumberland in 1776. Despite belligerent words, no effort was made by Massachusetts or the Continental Congress to assist them, a sign not lost on the Yankee Planters and the Halifax elite.[66]

Benajah Phelps came from a long line of Dissenters, who were antagonistic to the exercise of royal authority from the seventeenth century on. He was a graduate of the "seminary of sedition," whose graduates were overwhelmingly allied with the patriot cause. (Of the 1,000 Yale graduates alive in 1776, only about 25 were Loyalists.) His father was an ardent patriot who, at age 69, with his oldest son rushed to support their fellows in Massachusetts in the Lexington alarm.[67] Presumably Benajah made his views known early in the conflict and earned the sobriquet the Uncompromising Whig.

---

[64] Rawlyk, *Nova Scotia's Massachusetts*, 232; Norton, *New England Planters*, no. 84 (Proclamation of Oaths of Allegiance, 1775/06/03, NSARM, Record Group 1, vol. 170, 366–67); no. 87 (Proclamation Forbidding Aiding Rebellion, ibid., 169–70); no. 151 *(Nova Scotia Gazette*, 5 Dec. 1775); and no. 152 (Dispatch to Whitehall, Need for troops in Nova Scotia, Gov. Legge, NSARM, Record Group 1, vol. 44, no. 86). See also *DCB*, vol. 4, s.v. "Seccombe, John."

[65] Executive Council Minutes, 6 Jan. 1777, NSARM, Record Group 1, vol. 189, 421 (micro. reel 15,289). Seccombe's summons before the Nova Scotia Council on charges of preaching a seditious sermon "locates him clearly within the New England Congregationalist tradition but tells more about government fears and the proximity of Chester to the capital." He preached at Halifax in 1777, and there is no record of the formal recantation he was required to make. He was one of only three American clergymen in Nova Scotia after the Revolution. *DCB*, vol. 4.

[66] Ernest Clarke, *The Siege of Fort Cumberland 1776: An Episode in the American Revolution* (Montreal: McGill-Queen's Univ. Press, 1995).

## The Great Awakening in Nova Scotia

Contemporaneous with the outbreak of the Revolution, a young, self-educated man in Falmouth, on Minas Basin, experienced a religious conversion, which led him to preach his message of spiritual rebirth in open meetings. Henry Alline (1748–1784) rose "prophet-like" to preach repentance and conversion to the transplanted Yankees in a troubling time in which the allegiances of many were confused. The revival he stimulated was akin to the Great Awakening in New England and would help transform the allegiances of the Planters. Benajah Phelps's ministry was passed by.

Alline had come with his family as a child of twelve from Newport, Rhode Island. He was 27 when, in March 1775, he experienced his conversion. He later described this in his spiritual diary as a three-step progression from intellectual understanding of good and evil, to recognition of human dependence and depravity, to an ultimate awareness of God's grace. Grace gave him the will and desire to believe and endowed him with the faith that "the saint will triumph." He was by all accounts an ardent speaker, and his journals reveal an eloquent and deeply spiritual sensibility.[68]

This remarkable man took up itinerant preaching in Cornwallis and Horton, at first in gatherings out of doors and in homes. His emotional, impromptu style, similar to that of the Rev. George Whitefield, was antithetical to traditionalists. One result of Alline's preaching was the splinter-

---

[67] Nathaniel Phelps [Jr.] served 21 days in the Lexington alarm and as sergeant from 9 July through 17 Dec. 1775 in the regiment of Col. Jebidiah Huntington from Norwich, 6th Company, Abijah Rowley, Captain. *Connecticut Military Record, 1775–1848* (Hartford: Connecticut General Assembly, 1889). The news of the action at Lexington and Concord is said to have reached Hebron in the midst of the Sabbath meeting. The men rushed out for their arms and travel kits to join the Massachusetts rebels, followed by their wives, who prepared food for the journey. Marcy Crofut, *Guide to the History and the Historic Sites of Connecticut*, 802. Tucker, *Connecticut's Seminary of Sedition*, 21; see also Alice M. Baldwin, *The New England Clergy and the American Revolution* (Durham, N.C.: Duke Univ. Press, 1928). The description of Phelps as an "uncompromising Whig" is found in the short biography of Phelps in Dexter, *Biographical Sketches*, 2:713–14.

[68] *The Journal of Henry Alline*, ed. James Beverley and Barry Moody (Hantsport, N.S.: Lancelot Press, 1982), 11; Bumsted, *Henry Alline*, 31 ff., 66–67; Duncanson, *Falmouth*, 35; Brebner, *Neutral Yankees*, 193; Peter L. McCreath and John G. Leete, *History of Early Nova Scotia*, 3d ed. (Tantallon, N.S.: Four East Publications, 1990), 308; Maurice Armstrong, *The Great Awakening in Nova Scotia* (Hartford, 1948); *DCB*, vol. 4.

14. Imaginative Portrait of the Rev. Henry Alline (1748–1784) on Itinerancy
Eva Scott, 1983.

*Courtesy of Acadia Divinity College, Acadia University, Wolfville, Nova Scotia*

ing of churches into "New Light" and "Old Light" and the establishment of Baptist churches in Cornwallis and Horton.[69]

The Congregational meetings were weak in 1776, with several of the pastors seen as rebel sympathizers and commanding doubtful (or controversial) support. As news of the Revolution came to Nova Scotia, Alline denounced the war of independence and told the Yankee Planters that they were blessed to have been "called away from the approaching storm that was hanging over your native land, and sheltered here from the calamities of the sweeping deluge." Consider "the miseries you have been extricated from, what dangers you have escaped, what kindness received, what hours enjoyed." This message deepened in the course of the Revolution to the

[69] The New Light Congregational Church of Horton and Cornwallis was formed 13 July 1778, Acadia Univ. Archives (AUA), Baptist Collection, Cornwallis Church Records, 1; the Horton Baptist Church was founded 28 Oct. 1778. Beverley and Moody, *Journal of Henry Alline*, 248.

charge that America was in the hands of the Antichrist and that "heaven's indulgent hand" had converted Nova Scotians into a "People highly favoured of God."[70]

Listening to Alline, Nova Scotians, according a modern scholar, began "to see their place in the world." Through Alline's vision, the Planters at this critical period learned they could attain an identity different from that of their Yankee forebears. He encouraged them to establish the pure society of which the Bible spoke. This had been an impetus for the Puritan migration to America in the 1630s, but the "New Jerusalem" in New England had been soiled, and the project had to begin again on Nova Scotian lands. This outlook took his hearers in the direction of separation from New England.[71]

In November 1776 Alline preached to gatherings in Cornwallis Township. "[T]he Lord began to set the word home with power on some of the hearers," he noted in his journal, adding with a humorous deprecation that people were attracted by word "that there was a wild youth lately converted and turned preacher." Benajah Phelps was among them and spoke against him. "The standing minister of, and then at the place came to hear," Alline wrote, "and seemed determined to dash me, but he and all the rest were to me then as worms of the dust like myself. He had been the minister of the town, but on account of some division between him and his people he was dismissed and did not seem pleased with my coming into the town."[72] We are faced with a poignant image of a frustrated and angry man, rejected by the congregation and now outshone by a magnetic preacher. Phelps's ten years' work in Cornwallis was at an end. He was isolated for his views, had no position, had been seriously ill, and now saw a more potent religious leader attract the townspeople.

---

[70] Stewart and Rawlyk, *A People Highly Favored*, 161. Part 2 of this book is devoted to the Rev. Henry Alline and his influence on Nova Scotian sense of identity. Rawlyk, *Nova Scotia's Massachusetts*, 250.

[71] Stewart and Rawlyk, *A People Highly Favored*, 176, 192. Henry Alline (Newport, R.I., 1748–North Hampton, N.H., 1784) rose "prophet-like out of Horton, traveled about the province to spread the New Light movement. This thundering preacher consistently interpreted the war as God's retribution exacted upon the wicked and corrupt societies of London and America, a conflict which those who wished to follow the good life would do well to avoid." McCreath and Leete, *History of Early Nova Scotia*, 308; *DCB*, vol. 4.

[72] Beverley and Moody, *Journal of Henry Alline*, 78. Alline's entry is dated 29 Nov. 1776. I am indebted to Professor Barry Moody for this reference.

Chipman, writing a year later, criticized the "hard and cruel disposition" of those who had driven Phelps from the pulpit and had not helped him in his financial distress ("poor Gentleman in his distress, a Spending as I suppose, fast, on what Little he had"). "We ought to have shewn a better tender to him," Chipman concludes, adding the qualifier, "tho it is well known I was never fond of his preaching."

The Rev. Benajah apparently continued performing clerical functions and was respected by the Chipman family. The last marriage performed by him was that of Handley Chipman's son, William Allen, and Ann Osborn, on 20 November 1777. Eaton states that this is "the latest that we can be sure of his having performed any clerical function in the county."[73] It may be that the "schism" (Eaton's phrase) in the Cornwallis church was such that Phelps had been dismissed by one faction but continued carrying on clerical functions for others. The Chipman family also evidently supported him; the November marriage date was three months after the long letter. However, Alline's preaching had put Phelps in the shade. "I like him very much," Chipman wrote of the new preacher; at gatherings on the Sabbath, "I never saw so many Sin Sick Souls Since I liv'd here as there now is."

In April of 1778 Benajah and Phebe Phelps bought a half-acre lot in the town plot of Horton.[74] In July of that year the New Light, Allinite Church of Cornwallis was founded by members of Benajah's former congregation.[75] Benajah was to suffer worse than dismissal. It was wartime. Rebel privateers operating out of Machias, Boston, and Rhode Island ports swarmed in Nova Scotian waters. The seizure of over 250 cargoes was recorded in the New England admiralty courts between 1775 and 1779. The effect was devastating on intra-coastal shipping in the Bay of Fundy and on the Atlantic coast. Local shipowners suffered, and trade was interrupted. A modern study of the activity concludes that the depredations of

---

[73] Eaton, *History of Kings County*, 278, 284.

[74] Benajah Phelps purchased a one-half acre lot in Horton from John Whitney, 1 April 1778. Book 3, 144 [1778 Horton Town Plot Deed]. Phelps, Phebe, his wife, and Eunice Denison, Spinster, of Horton [Phebe's sister] sold a lot to Joseph Allison (Book 3, 173 [1778 *Horton Town Book*]). Phelps purchased a lot from Cyprian Fitch, executed 10 April 1778, Book 3, 133 [1778 Town Plot, Horton]. Registry of Deeds, Kings County, index (micro. reel 18,263). The fourth transaction was recorded on 28 Jan. 1782, when Benajah Phelps "of East Hartford" sold two half-acre lots to his brother-in-law Samuel Denison for £10. Book 3, 577 [1784 Town Plot, Horton].

[75] The first meeting of the New Light congregation was 11 July 1778 at the home of Samuel Fitch. Eaton, *History of Kings County*, 285–86.

the privateers turned the sympathies of the Yankee Planters away from the rebels.[76]

There was a large, well-organized, and targeted raid on Cornwallis in August 1778, which resulted in a substantial theft. A prominent local resident described the incident in a memorial to the lieutenant governor:

> In the night between the 9th and 10th Inst August at Cornwallis in said County some whale-boats came up Cornwallis River with between thirty and forty Armed men, Invested and plundered the House of William Best Esqr. In said Township of every thing valuable and of Easey Carriage, they took in Cash and other Effects in the Amounts of one thousand pounds and upward & carried the same off unmolested, before any Aid or Assistance could be had; the Villains said they belong'd to two brigantines in the Bay; and supposed to be two Rebel privateers—[77]

Cornwallis was an important supplier of produce and had to be protected. The farms "are so very Beneficial to the publick in furnishing much the greatest part of the fresh provisions and other necessarys for the market at Halifax." If such depredations were to continue, the families would be obliged to leave.

William Best, whose house was sacked, was an English-born settler and a sometime member of the colony's assembly. Best was also closely connected to the Loyalist Halifax oligarchy.[78] Thus the privateers had raided the house of one of the richest and most loyal of Cornwallis's inhabitants. Some years before, Best had purchased land in Cornwallis on Starr's Point (near the present Port William) and made his residence there from 1769. He was the father-in-law of the daughter of a well-to-do Yankee Planter named Samuel Starr, who, according to Eaton, was a principal antagonist

---

[76] John Dewar Fairbisy, "Privateering and Piracy: The Effects of New England Raiding upon Nova Scotia during the American Revolution, 1775–1783" (master's thesis, Univ. of Massachusetts, Feb., 1972). On Machias, the home base of many of the privateers, see J. H. Ahlin, *Maine Rubicon: Downeast Settlers during the American Revolution* (Calais, Maine: Calais Advertiser Press, 1966), 11–43.

[77] Memorial of John Burbidge [& others], Kings County, 20 August 1778, re Aug. 9–10, NSARM, Record Group 1, vol. 222, no. 71 (micro. reel 15,329).

[78] Among the English residents in Halifax in 1749 was William Best. He was a representative in the first assembly in the colony in 1758, and in the third and fourth assemblies. On 15 March 1769 William Best, "master mason," was living in Cornwallis. He died in Halifax 17 Nov. 1782, aged 75. His son John, "gentleman," in April 1773 bought land in Cornwallis from Samuel Starr 29 Jan. 1774. Eaton, *History of Kings County*, 564–65.

of Benajah Phelps in the controversies discussed above.[79] Starr owned land on a point where the Cornwallis River meets Minas Basin, an advantageous spot, with high ground for a boat landing.

The English-born John Burbidge (ca. 1718–1812), who brought the raid to the attention of the governor and successfully urged military support in Cornwallis, had been an influential early settler in Halifax, prominent in its business and official life. He moved to Cornwallis in 1764, shortly after the Planters' arrival. His holdings grew to 300 acres, and on them he began the apple and fruit-growing that continues in the Annapolis Valley to this day. He held numerous offices—justice of the peace, collector of customs, judge, major in the militia, and the county's first registrar of deeds. Burbidge was an "active and devout member of the Church of England," and founded St. John's church in Cornwallis.[80]

The raid had hurt the most eminent and loyal of the Cornwallis inhabitants. Anyone suspected of support for the rebels would have powerful enemies. Phelps was one of these and was forced to flee for fear of arrest.[81] The governor dispatched a unit of the 84th Regiment of Foot (Royal Highland Emigrants) who established Fort Hughes on Starr's Point.[82] They occupied a wood-frame building, which came to be called the Planters Barracks. With the knowledge of the raid and the influential people affected, it is not surprising that Benajah Phelps should later recall that in August 1778 feelings in Cornwallis about "the Dispute between Great Britain and America had arisen to the highest degree." This Phelps reported to the Connecticut General Assembly six years later in the course of appealing for compensation in the form of confiscated Tory lands for his losses in Nova Scotia.[83] He had "Absolutely Refused" to take "an oath to take up

[79] Major Samuel Starr was born at Norwich, Conn., 1728, and buried at Starr's Point, 26 Aug. 1799. Eaton, *History of Kings County*, 823.

[80] *DCB*, vol. 5. Eaton calls him "one of the most conspicuous persons the county has ever had." *History of Kings County*, 561.

[81] There is an intriguing field for study to determine the relationship between the Yankee Planters and these (and other) Halifax men in Cornwallis in the early years of settlement. Study of the land and probate records would reveal ownership and trading patterns that could help establish wealth and social position.

[82] Personal communication from John V. Duncanson, Falmouth, N.S., 18 Oct. 1997.

[83] There are two versions of Phelps's memorial, one submitted May 1784 and a second, more detailed and polished version, submitted in October of the same year. The narrative was submitted under oath to and accepted by the Connecticut General Assembly. Ecclesiastical Affairs, 1st ser., vol. 15, 59a–59c (26 May 1784), 60a–60c (1 Oct. 1784), Conn. Arch., box 34, roll 82-75. The assembly's recognition of this memorial is found in *PRSC*, 5:474–75. The only reference to the dramatic escape in the secondary literature is that in *One Hundredth Anniversary of the Organization of the First Church of Christ in Manchester, Connecticut* . . . (Hartford: Lockwood and Brainard, 1880), 12–15.

### John Burbidge's Memorial to the Lt. Governor of Nova Scotia, 20 August 1778

*To the Honorable Richard Hughes, Esq., Lieutenant Governor and Commander in Chief and over His Majesty's Province of Nova Scotia, The Memorial of John Burbidge for and on behalf of himself and many of the principal inhabitants of Kings County.*

*Most humbly Sheweth*

*That in the night between the 9th and 10th Inst August at Cornwallis in said County some whale-boats came up Cornwallis River with between thirty and forty Armed men, Invested and plundered the House of William Best Esqr. In said Township of every thing valuable and of Easey Carriage, they took in Cash and other Effects in the Amounts of one thousand pounds and upward & carried the same off unmolested, before any Aid or Assistance could be had; the Villains said they belong'd to two brigantines in the Bay; and supposed to be two Rebel privateers—*

*From which violent and audacious Robery your Memorialist and many of the principal Inhabitants do Apprehend themselves, both lives and property in Imminent Danger and will be induced to remove with their familys from their Settlements unless some protection can be had for their future Security—*

*Your memorialist therefore most Humbly prays that some Measures may be taken by Government to Secure the Settlements in the Bay Fundy, which are so much Exposed, and are so very Beneficial to the publick in furnishing much the greatest part of the fresh provisions and other necessarys for the market at Halifax, your memorialist will not presume to point out what Steps may be taken for the purposes aforesaid, but as he is perfectly Acquainted with the Bay Fundy, and every Avenue leading to the Settlements there, he will readily give his Opinion on the Subject if required, and desires to refer the above to your Honours Consideration, to grant such Relief in these premises as in your wisdom may Seem meet, and your memorialist as in Duty Bound shall ever pray, &c, &c, &c*

*John Burbidge*

*Halifax 20th Augt 1778*

---

arms and fight against his Native Country." As a result he "was Treated by the officers of British government with the Greatest Insult and threatened to be Carried to England to Suffer Death as a Rebel." As it was then "impossible to reside among the aroused & open Enemies of his Native Country . . . [he] & in a secret manner came over to the United States," taking with him "a Share of his Property." Exaggerating considerably the value of land in the province, Phelps claimed that "about 600 hundred Pounds worth of his Property" remained in Nova Scotia."

The Rev. Benajah's precipitate flight left Phebe and the three living children, Elizabeth, then ten, Phebe, eight, and Eunice, two, on their own in Horton. There were Denison relatives close by—the house and lot were later sold to Samuel Denison, Phebe's brother—and her sister, Eunice, was co-owner of one of the two lots that Phelps owned in Horton.[84] With whatever family support she had, however, Phebe (Denison) Phelps was one of the many women with young families left on their own in the Revolution when their husbands went off to war or were separated by civil action. Phebe must have been short of money, and she had the care of young children. She and the children were on their own for about 18 months until Benajah arranged passage for them to Boston. After they were reunited Phebe had once again to establish a household. A consequence of the separation of husband and wife is the six-year interval (from 1776 to 1784) between the birth of Eunice in Nova Scotia and Sally, the first of the two children born in Connecticut.

Benajah Phelps's adventures were like those in the Shakespearean romances: flight from enemies; separation from loved ones; perils on sea and land; money that vanishes; guidance by strangers; perseverance; and the reward for loyalty and steadfastness—a reunion with loved ones. With the "secret flight" these adventures had only begun. In Boston he sold the tangible property (unspecified) he had brought with him and deposited a portion of the proceeds with a friend. (The cash was in Continental Paper, whose value later evaporated.) He secured permission to return to Nova Scotia "to bring his Family and Effects into any of the United States" and took passage. Five days into this voyage began an epic which he describes using the third person:

> [H]e was taken by the *Albany* Man of War & after having been detained by her a number of Days was with the other Prisoners put into an open Boat fourteen miles out at sea & left to the mercy [of the] Ocean which at that time was very Tempestuous & and after having [been] exposed to momentary Death for about Twelve Hours were cast on Shore at Naskeag in uninhabited Wilderness about one hundred miles beyond Penobscot, from which [he] proceeded to Machias in order to get a Passage from thence to Cornwallis with a view to get his family & Effects but upon his arrival at Machias he found his Plan impracticable & still persisting in the Idea of getting his family from their unhappy situation he went from Machias on Foot under the Direction of six Indians to an Island called Passamaquady, when he arrived there he received Letters from his Friends at Cornwallis informing him that

[84] See preceding references to B. Phelps's land transactions in Horton.

> his Enemies there had received intelligence of his having been taken & [were] resolved to attach him & [secure] him the Moment he arrived there.
>
> He then returned to Machias & it now being the Middle of Winter, he was detained till the Spring of the year [1779] & then returned to Boston at which time he found the Money he had left greatly depreciated but being by his Fiends in Boston [aroused?] with an Idea that Continental Money would be made better (which was then the Phrase) he suffered it to lie dormant.[85]

In 1778–79, by this account, Phelps had traveled through a hundred miles of rugged, heavily forested country in Maine, from Naskeag on Penobscot Bay, to Machias, and further north to Pasamaquoddy, in present-day New Brunswick, where he had hoped to get passage to return to Cornwallis for his family before he was warned off. In Machias that winter Phelps was among patriots, the most prominent of whom was the Presbyterian Rev. James Lyon. He had been one of the participants in the 1770 ordination of the Rev. Comingo. Lyon was formerly pastor in Onslow, Nova Scotia, and had been settled in the church in Machias since 1771. From the outbreak of hostilities he had been chairman of the local Committee of Public Safety. From his pulpit he thundered against the Crown and urged the Continental Congress to annex Nova Scotia.[86]

When the weather permitted in 1779, Phelps returned to Connecticut, after a 13-year absence. He was soon called to a small parish near Hartford. From there he worked to bring Phebe and the three daughters to join

---

[85] PRO, ADM52/1553, ADM51/23, reported by T. J. Hughes, March 1998. If the seizure of the ship on which Phelps was traveling occurred in the latter part of 1778, as his narrative seems to indicate, there is no confirmation from the records of the *Albany* as to the incident. The seizure could have occurred at another time, and it is possible that it is not one that would have been recorded in the official record. The muster lists of prisoners on the *H.M.S. Albany* in the period Aug. 1778–April 1779 show that apart from a group of long-term prisoners who had agreed to serve as crew, she carried one prisoner during August, and a group of thirty captured between the end of September and the beginning of December. None of these was named Phelps, and the group of thirty was discharged at Halifax. The movements of the ship during 1778/9 can be followed from the logs kept by the officers and give a picture of the naval presence at Nova Scotia at the time and its relation to naval movements involved in the war. The locations were: 17 July–22 Oct. 1778, moored in the river near St Johns; 24–27 Oct., moored at Annapolis; 1–6 Nov. 1778, moored at Manawagonish; 8–10 and 13–19 Nov. 1778, moored at Annapolis; the *Albany* had reached Long Island by 30 Nov. and linked up with *HMS Dispatch* to move a convoy of prize ships back to Halifax, where she arrived on 13 Dec. The vessel left Halifax, again in convoy, on 1 Jan., and arrived at New York on 13 Jan. 1779.

[86] Rawlyk, *Nova Scotia's Massachusetts*, 230. *Military Operations in Eastern Maine and Nova Scotia during the Revolution, Chiefly Compiled from the Journals and Letters of Colonel John Allen, with notes and a memoir*, Frederick Kidder, comp. (1867; reprint, New York: Kraus Reprint, 1971), 40. The Rev. Lyon is remembered by posterity primarily as an early composer of musical settings of psalms.

him. There was enough value in the depreciated Continental dollars to pay for the passage of Phebe and the children from Nova Scotia to Boston, and the family was reunited in 1780. According to his account, this used up his funds, and all his Nova Scotia property had been "seised & confiscated by the Government." He estimated his total losses of property and the costs of travel and of bringing his family from Nova Scotia to be £1,500, certainly exaggerated, but he had lost the land he had farmed and other land and presumably all or most of the family possessions.[87]

An era in the church life of the Minas Basin Yankee Planters had closed with this abrupt and angry departure. Benajah Phelps, who by all accounts was earnest and well-meaning, can be seen in retrospect to have been in a difficult, even false, position from the very outset of his pastorate. He had not been wholeheartedly supported either in the moral or the practical sense. His religious message seems not to have stirred the congregation either, judging by the turn to Alline with his appearance on the scene. The controversies around him escalated to open confrontation in the Revolution; his position became insupportable. He evidently had supporters ("friends"), but his views transgressed the law and local opinion, which bitterly resented the privateer raids.

Phelps was on the losing side in the history of that community in political and religious terms. Indeed, for the transplanted Yankees, the Congregationalism of their forebears had not translated effectively to the outlying colony. From then on, the community would be served by religious leaders of its own choosing, no longer dependent on "supply" from New England.

---

[87] "Memorials Submitted by Benajah Phelps to the Connecticut General Assembly . . . 1784," Ecclesiastical Affairs, 1st ser., vol. 15, 59a–59c, 60a–60b, Conn. Arch., box 434, roll 82-75, transcribed by Judith Plummer. The General Assembly did not approve the first request for compensation, but the second resulted in the award of confiscated Tory lands.

## BENAJAH PHELPS'S MEMORIAL TO THE CONNECTICUT GENERAL ASSEMBLY, MAY 1784

*To the Hon'l Gen'l assembly of the State of Connecticut now sitting in Hartford*

*The memorial of Benajah Phelps of the Society of Orford in East Hartford Humbly Sheweth that in the year 1766 your Memorialist was Settled in the Work of the Ministry at Cornwallis in Nova Scotia where he Continued untill August 1778 and had obtained a good Living at which Time the Dispute between Great Britain and America had arisen to the highest Degree and your Memorialist being a fast Friend of this Country was put to the alternative of leaving that Country or taking an oath to take up arms and fight against his Native Country, the latter of which he Absolutely Refused upon which he was Treated by the officers of British Government with the Greatest insult and threatened to be Carried to England to Suffer Death as a Rebel—That your Memorialist found means to Escape with about £(350).0 0 Value in Effects leaving about £500 0 0 to be forfeited to the King and came to Boston leaving his Family in Nova Scotia That he obtained a Permit to go back to Nova Scotia for his Family but was taken up by a british Man of War and after Some Time was with a Number of others put on Board a Boat about 14 miles from the Land in very Rough weather and left to the Mercy of the Seas but arrived at Machias and never Returned to Nova ScotiaThat your Memorialist Sold his said Effects in Boston for about £2000.0.0 Continental Bills That in the year 1780 his family came to him at Boston and it Cost him about the Whole of his Continental Money to bear his Expenses of transporting himself and Family to this State at which Time he was totally Reduced unable to Labour and without the Means of Support That in the Year 1781 your Memorialist was Settled in the Work of the Ministry where he now Dwells—That his Parish is new and the People not only under the Common Burthen of Public Expense but have been building a Meeting house and though they treat him with kindness and do all in their Power for his Support and assistance yet they Cannot at Present give him the assistance he Needs That your Memorialist has attempted to build him an house for Shelter & by that means in debt and not able to make his house comfortable And by means of his Loses and Sufferings aforesaid for his love to this County and to the Rights of Mankind is Reduced to Great Distress That Could he obtain Relief at Present he flatters himself he might in [ ] with the Common Blessing of Providence gain his Support and Continue in the Ministry with his People, but otherwise his Case must be exceeding unhappy Wherefore your Memorialist Prays your Honors to take his Pitiable Case into Consideration and Grant him Such Relief out of the Confiscated estates or otherwise as your honors Shall Please See [ ] as a Charitable Compensation for his Loses aforesaid or in Some other way Grant him such Relief as your honors in your Goodness shall Please and as in Duty bound Shall Ever Pray, Dated at Hartford the 26th Day of May 1784. Bena$^{j}$ Phelps*

## BENAJAH'S MEMORIAL TO THE CONNECTICUT GENERAL ASSEMBLY, OCTOBER 1784

*To the Honorable General Assembly of the State of Connecticut now sitting The Memorial of Benajah Phelps of East Hartford in the County of Hartford humbly Sheweth That your Memorialist was born at Hebron in this State & having had an Academic Education entered into the Work of the Ministry & in the year 1766 was regularly settled in the Work of the Gospel Ministry in the Town of Cornwallis in the Province of Nova Scotia where he continued till some time in the Summer of the year 1778 when finding it exceedingly irksome if not impossible for him to reside among the aroused & open Enemies of his native Country, he collected together a Share of his Property & in a secret manner came over to the United States, leaving about six hundred Pounds worth of his Property and his family at NovaScotia; that soon after his arrival in the State of Massachusetts he sold & disposed of his Property that he brought with him for Continental Money & having procured Liberty from the Assembly of that State to bring his Family & effects into any of the United States, he deposited the Money he had raised out of the Property which he had already bro't over in the Hands of a Friend & Set out for NovaScotia, but the fifth Day after he had left land he was taken by the Albany Man of War & after having been detained by her a number of Days was with the other Prisoners put unto an open Boat fourteen miles out at sea & left to the mercy of the Ocean which at that time was very Tempestuous & after having exposed to momentary Death for about twelve Hours were cast on Shore at Nas(k)eag in uninhabited Wilderness about one hundred miles beyond Penobscot, from whence your Mem'st proceeded to Machias in order to get a Passage from thence to Cornwallis with a view to get his family & Effects but upon his arrival at Machias he found his Plan impracticable & still persisting in the idea of getting his family from their unhappy situation he went from Machias on foot under the Direction of six Indians to an Island called Passamaquady, when he arrived there he received Letters from his Friends at Cornwallis informing him that his Enemies there had received intelligence of his having been taken & (were) resolved to attack him & (secure) him the Moment he arrived there he then returned to Machias & it now being the Middle of Winter, he was detained till the Spring of the year & then returned to Boston at which time he found the Money he had left greatly depreciated but being by his Friends in Boston [ ] with an idea that Continental Money would be made better (which was then the Phrase) he suffered it to lie dormant That in this interim of time his Estate at Nova Scotia was seised & confiscated by the Government of NovaScotia and in the Event by Confiscation there & depreciation here he has [?sonk?] & totally lost his whole Estate amounting to more than £1500 lawful Money, that he is now advanced in life has a family of small Children & is in an infirm state of Health & exposed to want & and the Horrors of Poverty*

*And your Mem's would most respect fully further suggest that there are confiscated Estates in this State taken from the Adherents of the King of Great Britain he therefore humbly prays your Honors to compassionate his (service) & to grant him some small*
*Recompense for his great losses in such Way & Manner as the Wisdom of this House shall think best & he as in Duty bound will ever pray 1 Oct 1784*
*Benajah Phelps*
*In the Lower House*
*On this Memorial Granted One Hundred Pounds Lawful money to the Memorialist out of the Confiscated Estate of Col. Brown and liberty of a (Bill) in (Favor) thereon*
*Test. James Hillhouse*
*Concurred in the upper House with Addition of the Words and fifty next after the Word hundred in the 3d line of the above Grant of the lower House*
*Test. George Wyllys*

In the summer following Phelps's departure, the Rev. Jacob Bailey found Nova Scotians congenial and their society a welcome contrast to the Yankees who had driven him from New England. His scornful opinion of the rebels was undoubtedly shared by the prominent residents of the Yankee communities he visited. It characterizes at least in part the conservative reaction to Phelps's "uncompromising" stance. In one anecdote, Bailey encountered "a fellow refugee" at an inn between Halifax and the Minas Basin. This man had been "mobbed, imprisoned, and expelled" from Phelps's native Hebron for his loyalty. "The madness of the present age," Bailey reflected, "is certainly beyond all example in the history of mankind . . . a passion for licentiousness . . . a spirit that can endure no legal controul . . . an utter contempt for all of the sanctions of authority."[88]

Bailey saw around him on his journey "visible and striking contrast between this and the regions from which I emigrated. In the latter poverty, nakedness, and famine appeared in all their horrors." He had a low opinion of New Englanders, characterized by "humble cunning, creeping artifice and smiling hypocrisy." Like Henry Alline, Bailey assured the former Yankees that they were better off where they were and that their character was superior to that of the population of their native land.

[88] Bailey, *Journey*. The identity of the refugee is unknown. The most prominent Loyalist in Hebron, the Rev. Samuel Peters, was in London in 1779.

## Safe Harbor

The safe harbor found by the Rev. Benajah was in a newly founded parish in Connecticut in what was then called Five Miles, a lightly populated agricultural settlement east of the Connecticut River across from Hartford, named for its distance from the river. It would become part of Manchester, when that town was established in 1823. At that time it was within the limits of what was then East Hartford, the address given in Phelps's legal documents.[89]

When Phebe (Denison) Phelps rejoined her husband in 1780 she was 34, and three children survived of the five she had borne: Elizabeth (Betsey), aged 12; Phebe, 10; and Eunice, 5. Mother and children had to establish a new household, make new friends, and maintain this growing family. In February 1784, Phebe bore Sally, a fourth daughter, in Orford. Three years later, Ralph Rodolphus, the last child and only son who survived to adulthood, was born. He was named for Eleazar Wheelock's father and great-grandfather, the latter the Wheelock immigrant ancestor. Alexander and Theodora Phelps's last child also shared this name.[90]

The Orford Parish Ecclesiastical Society was organized in Five Miles in 1772 "when sixteen men and two women met in a re-modeled dwelling which served as the first meeting house." Because of their lack of money, the distraction of the war, and disagreements over the site of the meetinghouse, it was not until 1781 that they were able to call a pastor. The Rev. Benajah Phelps was settled as their first. He was then in his early forties, a survivor of extraordinary adventures, now reunited with his wife and family. He surely welcomed the settlement given him of £150 and the promise of a salary of £100 "payable in money or in product according to the late regulation act; namely, wheat at 6*s* per bushel, rye at 4*s*, corn at 3*s*, and all other articles agreeable."[91] This compensation was supplemented in 1784 with the successful resolution of Phelps's appeal for compensation for damages suffered in Nova Scotia. The General Assembly awarded him 83 1/3 acres of confiscated Tory land, in Lyme, Connecticut, valued at £150

---

[89] In 1780 Benajah Phelps signed a petition by inhabitants of "the Two Societies of Town of Hartford on the East Side of the Great River" requesting that the town be divided so that the increasing population need not travel across the river to "Transact the Business of Said Town." This led to the establishment of East Hartford. Orford Parish was at the eastern edge of this new town. Travel, 1st ser., vol. 9, 281a, Conn. Arch.

[90] For children of Benajah Phelps and Phebe Denison see the Genealogical & Biographical Notes.

(at the mouth of the Connecticut River). He wasted no time in selling it and realized £135 in cash a few days after the award. In the same year he was able to convey the lot in Horton Township he had purchased in 1778 to his wife's brother, Samuel Denison.[92] Phelps returned to Yale to receive his M.A. degree in 1784.[93] In January of that year his second eldest child and daughter, Phebe, married Alexander Phelps's son, Eleazar Wheelock Phelps, in Stafford, Connecticut, the subject of chapter 5.[94]

Orford Parish was a safe harbor, but it was not a quiet one. Members of the congregation in the eastern part of town (who had to travel farthest to get to meeting) charged that it was "in a very inconvenient and very disgusting place." The issue must have smoldered during the Rev. Benajah's tenure, for the meetinghouse was not completed until his departure. In 1791 the church council greatly lamented "the [difficulties] that have long subsisted between the Pastor and the people in this place." They agreed to pay £100 to "Mr. Phelps for damage arising from his dismissal," and £128.6.9 in back pay to be paid over two years with the hope that this would resolve the "pastoral situation" and that God would bring them a new pastor.[95] There must have been respect for the Rev. Benajah, as the congregation allowed him to continue to live in the house they provided.[96]

The years of Phelps's pastorate coincided with a decline in Connecticut Congregationalism and a waning interest in religion characterized by preachers at the time as "infidelity" and the influence of deism. It was not until the turn of the nineteenth century, after his pastorate, that there came to be a revival in religion leading to the Second Great Awakening, marked

---

[91] William E. Buckley, *A New England Pattern: The History of Manchester, Connecticut* (Clinton, Conn.: Pequot Press, 1979), 48, 345–46; "Manchester" by Rev. S. W. Robbins, in *The Memorial History of Hartford County, Connecticut, 1633–1884*, Hammond Trumbull, ed. (Boston: Edward L. Osgood, 1886), 2:259–61. The Orford Ecclesiastical Society later became the First Congregational Church of Manchester.

[92] The confiscated lands had belonged to William Browne, Esq., and were transferred by act of the General Assembly to the Rev. Benajah Phelps on 20 May 1785. Revolutionary War Records, 1st ser., vol. 34, 376–77, Conn. Arch. Lyme [Conn.] Land Records, 17:114. Benajah Phelps of East Hartford, Hartford County grantor, Samuel Morgan of Colchester Connecticut grantee, 10 June 1785.

[93] Dexter, *Biographical Sketches*, 2:713–14.

[94] Buckley, *A New England Pattern*, 48, 345, 346; Robbins, "Manchester," 259–61.

[95] Manchester First Congregational Church, Church Records, no. 105 (June 1[9], 1791), Conn. Arch., vol. 3, 13.

[96] Robbins, "Manchester," 261.

by the proliferation of sects. Benajah Phelps's profession, stimulated by the embers of the first Great Awakening in eastern Connecticut, had been sorely beset among offshore New Englanders. It was less spectrally unsuccessful in Connecticut. When he retired from the ministry, he followed the family tradition and served in government.[97]

By this time, a great transformation in the Connecticut economy was under way. In 1794 the first cotton mill was built within Orford Parish, incorporating the more efficient machinery just then coming into use, and was the precursor of the cotton and silk mills that were to flourish in the next century. Hartford County, of which Orford was a part, had 5 cotton mills in 1800, and 13 in 1818. Their presence would later inspire the inhabitants to rename their parish Manchester, after the great textile-manufacturing center in Lancashire.[98] By the end of the first decade of the new century, there was a turnpike and post road north to Boston through Stafford, where Benajah's daughter, Phebe, lived, and to Boston via Worcester.

In retirement the Rev. Benajah is reported to have "preached occasionally." He became part of the Connecticut Congregational-Federalist establishment and represented East Hartford in the General Assembly from 1800 to 1803 and served as justice of peace in that town from 1801 to 1811.[99] He undoubtedly enjoyed his reputation as the "uncompromising Whig" and would have had many tales to tell of his family's adventures in the land that was no longer New England. His land transactions show that he continued to be hard-pressed for money, as he had been all his life. In 1809 he mortgaged land and buildings (presumably his house) for $1,000 to secure a note from the Hartford Bank.[100] He left no will and there is no inventory of his estate, suggesting that his assets may have been dissipated.[101]

Phebe (Denison) Phelps died in 1816 at the age of 69. Benajah Phelps died a year later, a few months before his eightieth birthday. This couple had lived through the two wars that established the independence of the

---

[97] Purcell, *Connecticut in Transition*, 23ff.

[98] John C. Pease and John M. Niles, *Gazette of Connecticut and Rhode Island* (Hartford, 1819), 66; Purcell, *Connecticut in Transition*, 63.

[99] *PRSC*, 10:182; 11:9, 190; 12:13, 191; 13:204; 14:10, 104; 15:14.

[100] East Hartford Land Records, 9:249.

[101] There is no record of a will or inventory in the Hartford Probate Records, which included East Hartford in 1818. Nor is there an entry in the statewide listing in the CSL.

United States from Britain, they had painfully lived through a major event in Nova Scotian history, and, in their late age, they had seen the beginnings of the social transformations that accompanied the emergence of a manufacturing economy. Their marriage had withstood an extraordinary separation and reunion after successful passage through dangers by sea and land. Both were buried in what became the first Manchester cemetery. Their unmarried daughter, Sally, and son Ralph Rodolphus and his wife, Mary Stephenson, were buried beside them at the end of their long lives.[102]

Though his twelve years in Nova Scotia ended in frustration and anger, Phelps had the satisfaction of being honored in the country whose independence he had supported and to whose future he had committed himself. He was on the "right" side of history in the United States. In Nova Scotia, where he was on the "wrong" side, he is a transitional figure in politics and religion, tied to New England and out of tune with its future.

As Americans, Benajah and Phebe and the children suffered the dislocations that affected hundreds of thousands of others during the Revolution. They were not as uprooted as the Loyalists who fled north, or those who lived in the seats of war. There were no wounds or deaths. They had the good fortune to have returned home from exile rather than the other way around.

---

[102] Connecticut Headstones, Charles R. Hale Collection, vol. 6, Manchester [E. Cemetery], 399, CSL, Record Group 72:1 [hereinafter cited as Hale Headstone Collection].

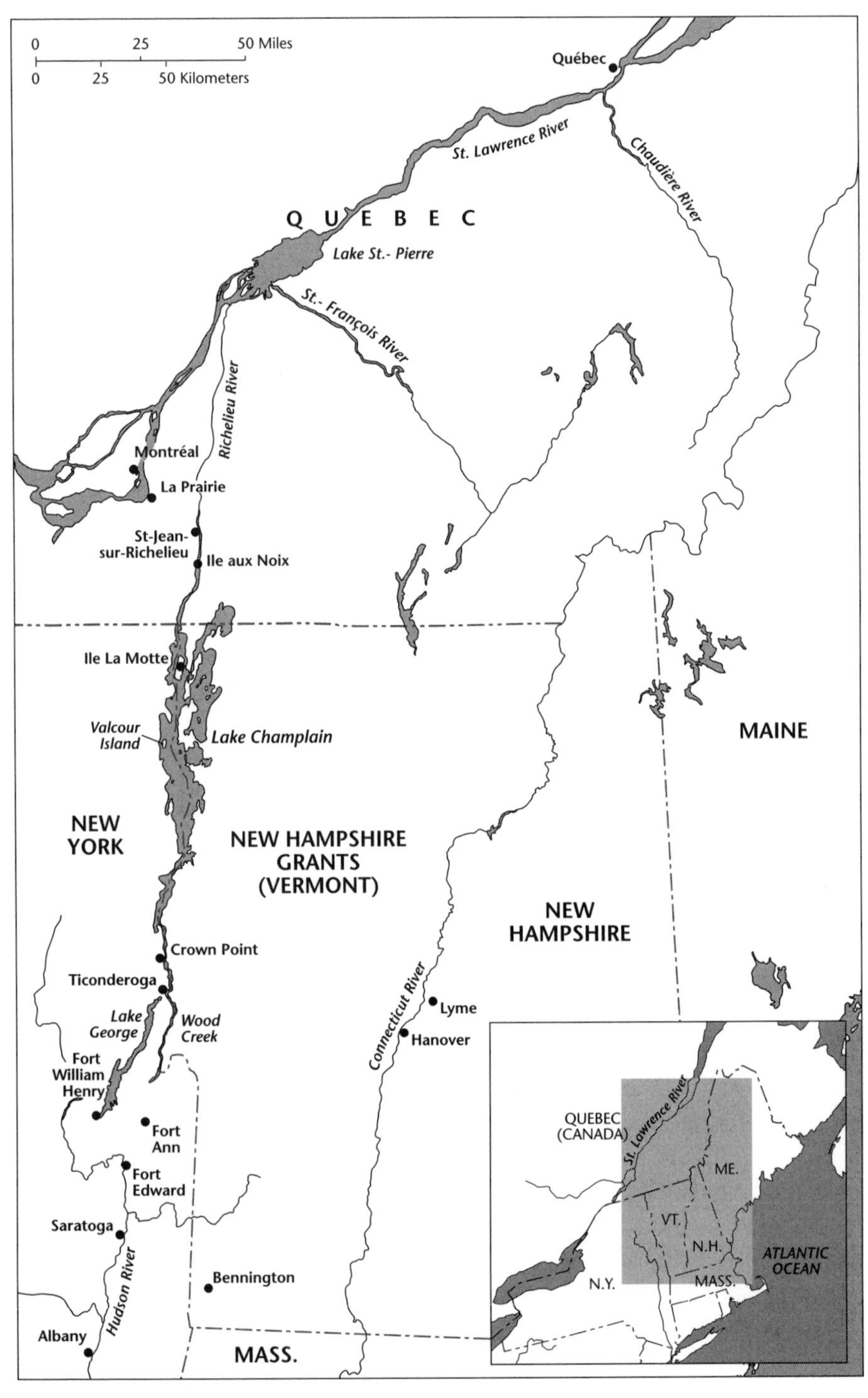


15. The Champlain Corridor and Quebec

# IV

## MAKING THE WILDERNESS BUD AND BLOSSOM

> *Go forth, every man that goeth, with a public spirit, looking not on your own things only, but on the things of others.*
>
> —John Cotton, "God's Promise to His Plantation"

### Davenport Phelps

Not quite 20 years after Davenport Phelps completed his life's work, young Alexis de Tocqueville journeyed west from Albany. The road, familiar to Phelps from his many journeys, was "detestable," but the Frenchman and his companion were

> Altogether given over to curiosity at the novel spectacle which struck our eyes . . . the whole country is still nothing but one vast forest, in the middle of which they have carved out some clearings . . . When by a fearful trail through a land of wilderness you have succeeded in reaching a dwelling, you are astonished to meet with a civilization more advanced than in any of our villages. The proprietor is carefully dressed, his house is perfectly clean, usually he has his newspaper beside him, and his first concern is to talk politics with you.[1]

The most prominent feature of the townscape was the church; from its steeple Tocqueville could "perceive only the tops of trees, which the wind is agitating like the waves of the sea." Davenport Phelps had a role in the creation of the civilized communities—"more advanced" than those in France—that appealed to Tocqueville in 1831. Indeed, he founded several of the churches on that route.

This Phelps's journey is a variant on the experience of those who came of age in the new republic. Like many others, he dabbled in one or two unsuccessful ventures, migrated from east to west, acquired land, and made a homestead. The speculators and entrepreneurs of his time shared such experiences. He pursued his goals vigorously, but his quest seems to

---

[1] George Wilson Pierson, *Tocqueville and Beaumont in America* (New York: Oxford Univ. Press, 1938), 189.

be of a different order. His letters reveal a questioning, a searching for order and a government he could respect. His views ran counter to what we might expect from a veteran of a regiment that fought at Bennington. For a time he embraced the post-Loyalist experiment of Upper Canada, preferring it to the republic created by the Revolution. There was something more, though. His mature life was animated by the cause of religion. He believed in the Episcopalian experience of faith based on formal observance and reason. Here too, he went against the grain, positioning himself far from the evangelical and revivalist strains generally characteristic of American religious life. He was successful in the endeavors of the latter part of his life and motivated many to lay the foundations for enduring institutions in western New York. His pioneering Anglican mission provides a counterpoint to the revivals that characterized the Second Great Awakening in the region after the 1820s. It is fascinating that a man once so dissatisfied with the temper of the United States polity should have accomplished so much of his life's work in democratic and socially mobile western New York State.

Davenport's was a journey that could only have occurred in North America at that particular time in history. It is American in the broadest sense, an example of the "second chance" theme that is so characteristic of careers on this continent.

There are few references to Davenport Phelps in the Phelps family history and in the Dartmouth archive. Other archives have proven more fruitful, and he was even the subject of a mid-nineteenth-century biography. Unfortunately, there is little record of Davenport's wife, Catharine Tiffany, aside from the vital records. She bore eleven children, only one of whom died in childhood. During her husband's frequent absences she was busy raising children and managing the household and farm. The family had meager finances, and one of Davenport's absences lasted for almost two years. At her husband's death, Catharine, who survived her spouse by 23 years, was left with five minor children. All the children were part of the great New England diaspora and ended their days in points west.

Davenport was born in Hebron on 12 August 1755, the first son and second child of Alexander and Theodora (Wheelock) Phelps.[2] His mother's maternal descent was commemorated in his naming, an early example of

---

[2] Hebron VRs, 2:223.

honoring family rather than a biblical figure.[3] He briefly attended Yale, but when his father moved to New Hampshire in 1771, he entered Dartmouth College, founded in that year by his grandfather, Eleazar Wheelock. He was among the first to be enrolled in a student body numbering 50, including 6 Native Americans and 20 English charity scholars.[4]

Davenport was 18 and an undergraduate when his father died in 1773 leaving him the man of the family. His older sister was 20, and his four younger siblings ranged in age from 1 year to 16. Theodora, his mother, was the executrix of a land-rich but heavily indebted estate. Davenport's first biographer says his mother saw him through to the completion of his studies, which is born out by the expenses incurred by the estate to maintain him there in comfort.[5] He graduated from Dartmouth with an A.B. in 1775.[6]

## The Invasion of Canada

The summer of 1775 was a fateful season to have entered to man's estate. New England men had been mobilized since the outbreak of fighting at Lexington and Concord in April. Rebels from Massachusetts had seized Portsmouth and forced Gov. John Wentworth, the supporter and friend to Dartmouth, into exile. By early summer the effective New Hampshire government was the Committee of Safety meeting in Exeter, soon to be superseded by a provisional congress. Members of the Dartmouth senior class petitioned President Wheelock that year not to have a public commencement as the "distressing State of public Affairs seems to render it necessary to retrench every Expense, as much as may be."[7]

---

[3] "The fashion was confined to the nobility and the landed gentry until the nineteenth century when it was imitated by the middle classes." D. G. Withycombe, *The Oxford Dictionary of English Christian Names,* xi.

[4] By 1774 there were 100 students, including 29 Native Americans. Chase, *History of Dartmouth College*, 1:295. By 1782, however, there were no Native Americans at the college, as the experiment had proved a great disappointment and was discontinued soon after Wheelock's death in 1779. Ibid., 1:528.

[5] Norton, *Pioneer Missionaries*, 21.

[6] *General Catalog, Dartmouth College*.

[7] "Senior Class with Sam'l Collins and James Hutchinson as committee to E. Wheelock, June 6 1775," DCA MS 775256. The seniors pointed out that a public commencement might cause some to consider that Wheelock favored the British in the current struggle.

In late June, emboldened by the strong showing made against the British at Bunker Hill, the Continental Congress approved an invasion of Canada. New Hampshire men, excited by the prospect that a "fourteenth colony" could be added to the rebel cause, joined regiments being formed by local leaders under the auspices of the Provincial Convention. By August these units were on their way through the largely unoccupied land of the Hampshire Grants (later Vermont) to join the Continental army under Philip Schuyler. He commanded a hastily assembled, raw, and ill-equipped band of New Yorkers and New Englanders who headed for Montreal along the traditional invasion route via the Champlain Valley.[8]

Davenport joined the army near the fortified approaches to Montreal in August or September. He remained with it through the winter and until the army's retreat in June 1776; there are no records of service with one of the units, but that he was present throughout the ill-fated campaign is verified by his and other's letters. Part of his time was spent looking out for his grandfather's and Dartmouth's interest in finding ways to recruit from the northern tribes. False hopes were raised by this nearly forgotten campaign of the Revolution, which was militarily, politically, and, for Dartmouth, institutionally disappointing.[9]

Northern New Hampshire expected that Canada would rally to the cause of the rebellion and help end the campaign quickly. Davenport's father's friend, Israel Morey (probate judge of his estate), conveyed the excitement and optimism of the time in mid-September. He reported that Col. Timothy Bedel and the volunteers in his regiment were "in high spirits," and that "Major Israel Curtis [who figures in later correspondence from Davenport] raised a Company of Volunteers in three days and marched on Sunday from Orford, in company with Captain Osgood. It is

---

[8] The most detailed account of the 1775 invasion of Canada and the 1776 retreat is found in Justin H. Smith, *Our Struggle for the Fourteenth Colony: Canada and the American Revolution* (New York: G. P. Putnam's Sons, 1907).

[9] Chase, *History of Dartmouth College*, 1:344, states that Phelps was in Bedel's regiment in 1775, but there is no record of this service in the National Archives. There are records of his commission as quartermaster in Bedel's regiment from 15 Dec. 1777 to 31 March 1778. He also served in Col. David Hobart's Regiment in 1777 at the Battle of Bennington (see below). "Staff Roll of Col. David Hobart's Regiment in Genl. Stark's Brigade of New Hampshire Militia . . . July 1777, Quartermaster, New Hampshire Militia"; "Muster Roll of the Officers and Soldiers enlisted in Capt. Davenport Phelps Co. in a Regiment of Volunteers, whereof Col. Timo. Bedel, Esq., is Commander . . . March 1778," War Department Collection of Revolutionary War Records, Record Group 93, National Archives and Records Administration, Washington, D.C.

expected that a number more will soon follow his example—a most noble spirit this—a number of which from Dartmouth College . . . Lieutenant [Ethan] Allen of the Green Mountain Boys, brought express orders for Col. Bedel to march immediately. I think he has acted himself much in his honour in pushing the Companies forward."[10]

Bedel had "a sort of power more promptly recognized . . . by dogs, horses and Indians," according to one account.[11] By September this rough-cut citizen soldier had led his men to the Isle aux Noix, a fortified post on the Richelieu River that flows from Lake Champlain to the St. Lawrence. Montreal was 25 miles away. If the small British force could hold it, the invasion would be stymied for the winter.

The New Hampshire men joined volunteers from Connecticut, Massachusetts, and New York under Gen. Richard Montgomery, a former British officer who had joined the patriot cause. Montgomery, in command owing to Schuyler's illness, was a dashing and intelligent man, popular with the men. (The New Englanders despised Schuyler as a New York aristocrat.) He had recently married Janet Livingston, the daughter of Robert R. Livingston of the family that owned large tracts on the eastern bank of the Hudson.[12] He was able and seemingly well favored by fortune, but the hastily assembled army that he led was composed of inexperienced and often unwilling soldiers. To his wife he wrote, "Such a set of pusillanimous wretches never were enlisted."[13] Later he reported to her that "the troops have hitherto gone home sick, almost as fast as they came. We have been like half-drowned rats crawling thro' the swamp."[14]

The news of the advance—"Providence appears so encouraging" is how he put it—prompted Wheelock to suggest to General Washington

---

[10] Morey had used his own funds to equip the troops: "I have helped to fix them out, and hope the Committee and Congress will think I did what was right, though at my own risk at present." Col. Israel Morey, in Orford, to New-Hampshire Committee of Safety, 12 Sept. 1775, Force 4, 2:697.

[11] Smith, *Our Struggle for the Fourteenth Colony*, 1:365.

[12] Robert R. Livingston (1718–75) married Mary Beekman; their daughter Janet (1743–1828) married Richard Montgomery (1738–75) in July 1773; she did not remarry after his death and lived a widow for another 53 years. *DAB.*

[13] Richard Montgomery, at Isle aux Noix, to Janet Montgomery, 12 Sept. 1775, in *Biographical Notes concerning General Richard Montgomery together with hitherto unpublished letters* (Poughkeepsie, N.Y.: "News" Book and Publishing Company, 1876), 11. References to fortifications on the approach to Montreal from Alan Gallay, ed., *Colonial Wars of North America, 1512–1763, an Encyclopedia* (New York: Garland, 1996).

[14] *Biographical Notes concerning General Richard Montgomery*, 12–13.

that a missionary to the Indians could be helpful. If the northern Indian tribes turned hostile, the consequences would be terrifying to the small northern Connecticut Valley communities. Wheelock's aim as soon as he moved to Hanover had been to develop relations with the northern Indians to secure a flow of children and youths for the school and college. He had previously sent emissaries north "to open and prepare a way for communication, commerce and intercourse between Canada and Dartmouth College," instructing them "to find if a door be open for missionaries and schoolmasters among them and the best way for affecting the same—to obtain a number of likely Indian boys to receive an education . . . "[15] On the eve of the invasion, Wheelock offered his support to the New Hampshire Committee of Safety.[16]

Wheelock told Washington that if a missionary to the Indians were assigned as chaplain to the army, it would "facilitate and effect the union of this Colony [Canada] with the other Colonies; and in case this design of your forces there should be successful, make it yet more extensive, by the union of Indian tribes therein, [and] confirm their friendship to these colonies . . . " Dartmouth would benefit, as the Indians would have "fresh assurance of the well-being of their children with me, and bringing a number more from these and (if it may be) from remotest tribes to this school, &c, &c."[17] During the winter he enlisted his son-in-law, son, and grandson in this effort.

The ragtag army was successful against the ill-led British. Israel Curtis, a captain in Bedel's regiment, probably Phelps's superior, wrote Wheelock about the capture of the British fort at St. Johns, which assured easy access to Montreal. It was a triumph, "500 Regular Troops Made Prison[r] of War with upwards of Two hundred Women and Children."[18]

---

[15] A letter of 1772, quoted without attribution in McCallum, *Eleazer Wheelock*, 191.

[16] Eleazar Wheelock to the New-Hampshire Congress, 28 June 1775, Force 4, 2:1051.

[17] Wheelock suggested his son-in-law, the Rev. Sylvanus Ripley, for the post, "now a tutor of this college, and [who] has been employed in several missions, is well acquainted with and is high in the affection and esteem of several of these tribes, and is the most suitable man I know . . . " Eleazar Wheelock to General Washington, 15 Oct. 1775, Force 4, 3:1070. Wheelock at this time was desperate for financial support since he had used up the considerable sum raised by Lord Dartmouth in England, and no further support from the mother country could be expected after the outbreak of hostilities. Eventually he was to gain modest support from the Congress to support Indian education, but by 1782, as pointed out above, there were no Indians enrolled in the college.

[18] Israel Curtis, at St. Johns, to Eleazar Wheelock, in Hanover, 3 Nov. 1775, DCA MS 775603. The surname is spelled Curtiss in this letter. Smith, *Our Struggle for the Fourteenth Colony*, 1:469.

Davenport at the time was ill with what Curtis described as "a Little poor Frothing uncommon for him."[19]

The army marched the next day with little opposition, as most of the British force in the province had surrendered. Curtis confidently expected to be home in two weeks. The small city of Montreal fell without a fight in November. Curtis wrote Wheelock of the potential opening up for the college with this new field for mission and recruitment. General Montgomery had sent for him and "Told me of the advantage [that] would Accrue to Dartmouth College by this Conquest and the advantage would Accrue to the Colonies by the means of your College Connection with the Indians and said all his Influence should be in favour of that Seminary. He said God in Providence had now opened a door for me with my company to do service."[20]

Montgomery intended to keep himself and the army in Montreal for the winter. "His men were in rags and his provisions exhausted," his widow recalled. "He had written repeatedly for more troops and none were sent. Twice he had sent in his resignation and twice it was refused." What forced his hand was the arrival before Quebec in early December of a force of 600 men from New England under the Connecticut merchant, Benedict Arnold, having hacked their way through the Maine wilderness. They drove the defenders across the river and lay siege to the fortress. "The wild march of Arnold up the Kennebec altered all the plans, and obliged Montgomery to sacrifice himself," the latter's widow wrote.[21] He joined Arnold with 300 men (leaving 500 in Montreal). Congress pressured Montgomery to attack to seize the stores in the fortress; moreover, the army was shrinking because the enlistment terms of many of the New England troops were up on New Year's Day. Against good military judgment, Montgomery ordered an attack on the night of December 30–31. Despite a heavy snowstorm, the attackers were anticipated, and Montgomery himself was killed. The remaining Americans kept up the siege until British reinforcements arrived by sea in May.[22]

---

[19] There was sickness of all sorts in the army, and Davenport's ailment, it seems, was short-lived.

[20] Israel Curtis, in Montreal, to Eleazar Wheelock, 19 Nov. 1775, Benedict Arnold Collection, NYHS. Sylvanus Ripley reported to Eleazar Wheelock the death of "our dear friend Major Curtis" on 10 Feb. 1776 in Montreal after a short illness. Sylvanus Ripley, in Montreal, to Eleazar Wheelock [at Dartmouth], 15 April 1776, DCA MS 776265.

[21] *Biographical Notes concerning General Richard Montgomery*, 8.

[22] An excellent account of the ill-fated invasion of Canada may be found in *DCB*, vol. 4, s.v. "Montgomery, Richard." The Americans both in Montreal and Quebec received food and other support from the populace when they first arrived.

On New Year's Day, unaware of the defeat at Quebec, Davenport wrote his grandfather ("Rev$^{d}$ and ever hon$^{d}$ Patron") of his efforts to recruit Indian children for the school. It is a respectful and fond letter to the venerable Wheelock, signed by his "sincere and dutifull Grandson." [23]

The "Capt. Lewie" he refers to in this letter was Atiatoharongwen, also known as "Louis A.," "Louis Cook," and "Colonel Louis." The son of a black man and a Saint-Francis Abnaki woman, he became a Mohawk chief later in life. He had served with the French in the French and Indian War and was "strongly attached to the American cause" during the Revolution, unlike most of the Caughnawagas, who remained neutral. When Phelps wrote his letter to Wheelock, Atiatoharongwen was serving as a messenger and scout for the forces under Gen. Montgomery. He had returned to Canada from Cambridge, where he had met with General Washington the previous August, assuring him of his support for the Americans. Later in the war he commanded a contingent of Indians on the American side in the Mohawk Valley. He died from a fall from his horse while fighting for the Americans against the British on the Niagara frontier in 1814. Like Brant, he was an able and articulate man, of two worlds, with a store of knowledge and connections that must have been fascinating to young Davenport.[24]

The city from which Davenport wrote was a small, provincial place. The New Englanders and later visitors found the Roman Catholic religion and its monuments foreign. Four years later a visitor from New York described it as having

> Nothing remarkable to distinguish it except a beautiful mountain behind the Town, from which the name is derived. The summit of which is covered with dark woods . . . The architecture of this place, like that of Quebec, is in a rude and heavy style. There are here several convents, which are spacious but inelegant, though not without that venerable gloom that inspires religious awe; the churches are built of rough stone plastered on the outside but greatly embellished within, especially about the altar, with tawdry monuments; the devotion of the people, though little connected with morality, leads them often to these places, which are for that reason mostly open to access.[25]

---

[23] DCA MS 1019LL; also transcribed in Chase, *History of Dartmouth College,* 1:344–45. The date in Phelps's writing on the letter is 1775, an understandable error for a letter written on New Year's Day.

[24] *DCB*, vol. 5, s.v. "Atiatoharongwen."

### Davenport's Letter to His Grandfather, 1776

*Had it not been for my being unwell, and the inconveniences of writing I should have transmitted a time before this; as in duty bound.*

*My situation in this place is Now very agreeable on many accts thro' the goodness of a mercifull Protector, am favoured with my health, and am in a capacity to pursue my Studies to pretty good advantage—I was with Gen*[l]*. [David] Wooster [Commander in Montreal in Montgomery's absence] yester*[d]*. and he informed me of the application a particular tribe of Indians made to him, a few days since—the Chiefs of the Tribe came, and presented him with a fat Deer. He returned them a present of a cask of rum, provisions &c—they had a long conference and they desired he should procure them a minister, and school master, as they professed to be Christians they want to be instructed in religion, and have their children educated— The Gen*[l]*. told them as it was late in the year, he could not promise them any this winter; but said he would send to y*[e]* Rev*[d]* Doct*[r]*. Wheelock from whom he expected they would be supplied in the Spring, upon which the Indians return*[d]*—The name of the Tribe I could not learn, but they are about 20 miles distance, and were [ ] from the Cahnawagas [Caughnawagas allied with the Six Nations]—Since the visit of the above Tribe, the Cahnawaga Tribe made y*[e]* Gen*[l]*. a visit they profess much friendship and [ ]—the prospect there, is better known to yourself [ ] than I can inform—*

*The prospect of procuring children to receive an Education at the school, I believe is [ ] great. One Capt. Lewie [ ], altho' an Indian from Cahnawaga, with whom I have had considerable acquaintance [ ] desired me to take his son of about 12 years [ ] to the School; which I promised him upon [ ] advice when at Crown Pt.—Lewie tells me there are numbers, he believes will be grac*[d]*. to send their children.*

*The state of affairs in this Province are as favorable as can be expected—particular as to the taking of Montreal. I suppose you have heard—The siege of Quebec still continues—we are informed by Maj*[r]*. Lockwood that the Gen*[l]*. determines soon to storm it, if the Enemy do not capitulate.*

*I shall be careful to inform of Indian affairs in particular, so long as I continue in this Province.*

In mid-February Wheelock sent his son-in-law, Sylvanus Ripley, and two others experienced in Indian affairs to assist Wooster by informing the

[25] Hannah Lawrence (1758–1838), of New York, married Jacob Schieffelin (1757–1835), of the New York merchant family of German origin. Shortly after their marriage in 1780, they left occupied New York to travel via the St. Lawrence and Lakes Ontario and Erie to Detroit, where Jacob was to set up a trading post. Hannah kept a journal of this rigorous journey, from which this description of what she saw in late 1780 is taken. Schieffelin Family Papers, box 7, NYPL Mss. Div.

tribes "of the goodness of our Cause, and the Sincerity of the Friendship of the Colonies towards the Indians, &c." The letter went with his youngest son, James, then 16, whom he sent to Montreal "to learn the French Language & whatever else may be useful to fit him for a position in some future Time into the Province of Quebec."[26] Here was another member of the family sent to do the business of recruiting students. He was younger than his nephew Davenport and would be closely associated with him on a commercial venture after the war and in Upper Canada in the 1790s.

Davenport wrote his grandfather again in February, reporting that General Wooster was soon to leave for Quebec "to take it himself," and "both Soldiers & officers . . . eagerly wait the command of an old and experienced Gen^l."[27] On his grandfather's business he had been to the Caughnawaga Indian settlement "in order to sound the Disposition of the Indians there." He found them "very friendly to y^e Americans," but he held back from making any proposals regarding the recruitment of their children for the school. One Indian village petitioned to General Wooster, and "He told'em he would apply to y^e Revd. Doctor Wheelock in N. England, who undoubtedly Could supply them by the Spring." Davenport reported that Israel Curtis was recovering from the smallpox, which was ravaging the army (in fact he died a few days later).[28] Amid all the illness of the army "I enjoy a better state of health than ever."

Wheelock replied to his grandson when he had learned the news that he and James were to be inoculated for smallpox. It was a risky procedure, deliberately infecting a mild case of the disease; at best this was temporarily disabling, and it could cause death. With evident fondness for the young men, he wrote as their spiritual mentor, signing it "your affectionate grandfather":

---

[26] Eleazar Wheelock to Gen. Wooster, 6 Feb. 1776, postscript dated 13 Feb., DCA MS 776156. In April Sylvanus Ripley reported to his father-in-law that he had found "one Dr. Holmes" who would take in "brother Jimmy" in an arrangement in which Holmes's son would live with the Wheelocks in exchange. However, the British shortly relieved the siege of Quebec, and by June the Americans were forced from Canada. Sylvanus Ripley, in Montreal, to Eleazar Wheelock [at Dartmouth], 15 April 1776, DCA MS 776265.

[27] Davenport Phelps, in Montreal, to Eleazar Wheelock, in Hanover, 24 Feb. 1776, Benedict Arnold Papers, NYHS; also transcribed in Stelter, "Davenport Phelps," 53.

[28] Sylvanus Ripley, in Montreal, to Eleazar Wheelock [at Dartmouth], 15 April 1776, DCA MS 776265.

> Your letters are very welcome, and acceptable to me. I thank you heartily for them, and have the pleasure to inform you that my family and your mother are well as usual of late. I have been for several months in a very poor state of health. You are amidst many and great temptations, and have special need to have on the whole armor of God, and to stand daily with your loins girt and your lamp trimmed and turning, in order to escape the deadly power of your spiritual enemies. Oh, my dear child, fear the great and dreadful God, and keep yourself poor, let the consequence to your name and outward comfort be what they will. The fear of God, and the peace of your own conscience will a thousand-fold compensate for all you can suffer here by it. By Mrs. Ripley, we are informed that you and James are about to take the small-pox by inoculation. The almighty preserve you through the dangers of it and may we soon hear of your better health. I have nothing new to inform you of, excepting what I have written to J. [James Wheelock] concerning the state of the college.[29]

A more complete view of Montreal under American occupation was sent to Wheelock by his son-in-law, Sylvanus Ripley. His letter conveys both what the Wheelocks and other Americans sought to achieve in Montreal and their view of the intractable cultural conflict between the Catholic inhabitants and the Protestant Yankees with their view of Rome as the "Whore of Babylon." He is prescient about the troubles that soon would engulf the invading force and sends best wishes from Davenport.[30]

By May 1776 there were as many as 7,000 American troops in Canada, but most were disabled by smallpox, dysentery, and other illnesses. A British counterattack from Quebec forced a retreat, a disorderly, humiliating affair by an army in a state of dissolution. Davenport Phelps returned from this debacle to Hanover in late June, but brought "no material intelligence."[31]

One of the factors that contributed to the hasty departure of the Americans from Canada was concern over the intentions of the Indians. In New York, Guy Johnson, Superintendent of Indian Affairs, encouraged the Indians to fight the rebels, a policy that soon led to engagements in the

---

[29] Eleazar Wheelock, at Dartmouth, to Davenport Phelps, in Montreal, 19 March 1776, transcribed in Norton, *Pioneer Missionaries*, 24–25.

[30] Sylvanus Ripley, in Montreal, to John Wheelock [at Dartmouth], 7 March 1776, DCA MS 776156.

[31] Sylvanus Ripley to Wheelock, then in Connecticut, 19 June 1776, Chase, *History of Dartmouth*, 1:357. Norton states that Phelps was taken prisoner and held in Montreal. However, his return to Hanover just at the end of the American retreat with no reference to the circumstance of imprisonment indicates that this was not so. Norton, *Pioneer Missionaries*, 26.

## Sylvanus Ripley to Eleazar Wheelock, 15 April 1776

*As for me I am mired with the din of battle, and have my ears saluted not only with a jargon of language and with the Gibberish of barbarous French, English, Scotch, Irish Dutch &c but with the infernal [ ] of oaths & curses issuing forth from almost any quarter. The civil state of this Province is very bad—Martial Laws only are now in force, for the French system never yet took place, soon as ever the war is over there will be a great necessity of Politicians of good heads & hearts to lay the foundations of civil Government in this Province. If you want to shine like a northern constellation, you may come here when you will have but a few lights to eclipse you—secret cowardly Tories I find very plenty here; but they live like Woodchucks under ground, & are not fond of the light—Many of the ignorant Canadians dont know what they are themselves—their Ideas of Liberty are very ill digested, their timidity very excessive, they are like meteors suspended in the Air, that hang in doubt & uncertainty. Every thing depends on our conquest of Quebec which I hope God for his own Glory will graciously give into our hands; for I am sure our Army are at the greatest remove from any kind of [ ] to found our hopes upon;—If Quebec is not taken, all is gone. We shall doubtless lose the acquisitions we have gained already and our frontiers will be incessantly exposed. I fear the consequences of the small Pox which begins to rage in our Army, and bids fair to have a general spread, several have already died with it; but tis to be hoped divine Providence will overrule it for good, and secure a victory to us in such a way as to hide all pride from Man.*

*One thing is attended here with some difficulty, and that is the Continental Paper currency which the French in general absolutely refuse to take. This seems some to impede the progress of affairs, & very much [inconveniences] Trade & commerce—The French at the conclusion of the last war suffered such extreme loss by Paper money as renders them extremely cautious. They are like Burnt Children that dread the fire—But upon the whole I think affairs look encouraging in the Province. The divisions between the Romish Priests and the People seems to forebode bad consequences to their religion. Those who have joined with the Colonies are refused absolutions. So that I can but hope that the Whore of Babylon is sick with a malady that may prove her death. The Priests are very jealous that their religion is in a declining state. I hope in God that the beams of learning & of the pure Gospel may shine with such strength & lustre into this dark Corner, as to discover the all the fooleries & fopperies of Antichrist in such a convincing light as to make all his Professors confounded & ashamed. But unless your patience is very good natured; I believe it will complain. I enjoy my health well hitherto—M$^{r}$ Phelps desires to be remembered to you—I have destroyed almost a sheet of Paper by writing. I demand two sheets in return; you wont deny me the favor a long Epistle. I shall trouble the Doctor with a letter soon wishing you all health & happiness am as ever your very &c*
*Sil. Ripley*

Mohawk Valley and other frontier settlements.[32] New Hampshire people feared such invasion by the Canadian Indians. Johnson had spent the winter of 1775–76 in London with the Mohawk chief Joseph Brant, alumnus of Moor's Charity School, and future patron and friend of Davenport Phelps. Brant became a formidable opponent of the rebels in the war. During the Revolution he led destructive expeditions for the British against frontier settlements in western New York, contrary to Wheelock's expectation that education under his auspices would produce Indians who supported the Revolution. It is ironic that Davenport should later take up his grandfather's mission work with the fervent support of Brant, whose activities in the war did much to enliven fears of Indian violence.

Wheelock's ideal for Dartmouth foundered in the course of the Revolution as the defeat in Canada and warfare in the west (and the resulting rancor on both sides) dried up the sources of Indian students.[33]

## Bennington

In the summer of 1777 the British army under Burgoyne moved down the Champlain Valley headed for Albany. There was an immediate threat to northern New England, and Davenport and others joined regiments formed for the campaign against the British. He was commissioned quartermaster in Col. David Hobart's Regiment of General Stark's Brigade of New Hampshire Militia (a force of about 1,500 men) on July 25.[34]

The British operation to end the rebellion in 1777 employed a two-pronged attack: the army under Burgoyne from Montreal was supposed to meet a force following the Hudson from New York City. Control of the river valley would cut the colonies in two and isolate the New England "hotheads" from the rest of the rebels. This grand plan promised success, but it was poorly executed. Sir William Howe, the commander of the troops occupying New York City, instead of advancing north in force,

---

[32] Smith, *Our Struggle for the Fourteenth Colony*, 2:362; Col. Moses Hazen, in Montreal, to Philip Schuyler, at Ticonderoga, 1 April 1776, Force 4, 5:869.

[33] Chase, *History of Dartmouth College* 1:528.

[34] Revolutionary War Records, National Archives and Records Administration. Phelps was discharged 26 Sept. 1777. Col. Hobart commanded the Twelfth Regiment, New Hampshire Militia, part of the Second Brigade commanded by Brig. Gen. John Stark. George C. Gilmore, *Roll of the New Hampshire Soldiers at the Battle of Bennington, August 16, 1777* (Manchester, N.H.: J. B. Clarke, 1891); Boatner, *Encyclopedia of the American Revolution.*

took his army by sea to take Philadelphia in the summer and made only forays up the Hudson. Burgoyne's army moved ponderously, slowed by its large baggage train. After taking Ticonderoga in early July, a victory for him and a major defeat for the rebels, Burgoyne made the disastrous decision to move the army through a trackless wilderness south of Lake Champlain to reach the Hudson rather than to use the longer route by Lake George. Slowed to an advance of one mile a day and harried by patriot rangers, the army's supplies dwindled.[35]

By mid-August Brig. Gen. John Stark, who had distinguished himself at Bunker Hill, assembled the New Hampshire men, including Hobart's Regiment with which Davenport was quartermaster, near the village of Bennington (then "consisting of a meetinghouse and twelve or fourteen dwellings") a few miles to the east of the Hudson.[36]

Burgoyne learned of horses and supplies at Bennington and dispatched a column to seize them. This force was composed largely of Brunswicker troops under the command of an officer who spoke only German. Stark's men surprised them using irregular, Indian-style tactics to break up the advancing column as they neared Bennington. The invaders regrouped and set up defensive positions. On 16 August Stark divided his forces into three columns, which attacked across the redoubts set up by the Brunswickers and a Tory force that had gathered to support them.

Davenport's regiment, under Col. Hobart, attacked the redoubt at the center, which was manned by the Tories. One of them was John Peters, nephew to the Rev. Samuel, colonel of the recently formed Queens Loyal Rangers. Davenport must have known him from his childhood and early youth. The patriot forces, hidden by a rise in the ground until they were close to the redoubt, surprised the Tories, who were able to fire only one volley. Then the former neighbors and acquaintances fought hand-to-hand.[37] This part of the battle was the bitterest kind of struggle—civil war.[38]

---

[35] A recent and lively account of the campaign is Richard M. Ketchum, *Saratoga: Turning Point of America's Revolutionary War* (New York: Henry Holt, 1997).

[36] Ibid., 290.

[37] Ibid., 312; Philip Lord, Jr., comp., *War over Walloomscoick: Land Use and Settlement Pattern on the Bennington Battlefield–1777*, New York State Museum Bulletin 473 (Albany, N.Y.: Univ. of the State of New York, State Education Department, 1989), 53–58.

Stark and most of his men remained near Bennington for several weeks after the battle and did not join the Continental Army awaiting Burgoyne's attack near Saratoga, for their terms of enlistments were about to run out. "Despite the appeals of Stark when he arrived, and an offer by [the commander, Gen. Horatio] Gates of ten dollars per man, these veterans of Bennington marched off punctually at midnight on their severance date of September 18." Thus Davenport did not take part in the actions near Saratoga that began at Freeman's farm the next day.[39]

Bennington was one of the most decisive actions of the war and established the conditions for the British defeat at Saratoga. The news of the humiliation of their ancient enemy by the colonials brought the French into the struggle. It was the turning point of the Revolution.

Horatio Gates, the commander at Saratoga, intended to invade Canada after the victory. When troops were raised for this invasion later in 1777, Phelps was commissioned quartermaster in Col. Timothy Bedel's Vermont Regiment. Washington did not approve Gates's plan though, which he viewed as self-serving and an unnecessary diversion of his limited resources. Davenport was discharged in May 1778, his military service at an end at the age of 22.[40]

---

[38] Dexter, *Biographical Sketches,* 2:607. John Peters (Hebron, 1740–London, 1788), nephew to the Rev. Samuel, A.M. Yale 1759. Peters recalled that "an old schoolmate and playfellow" bayoneted him with the words "Peters, you damned Tory, I have got you!" Peters was able to reload and shot the man dead, commenting after, "though his bayonet was in my body I felt regret at being obliged to destroy him." His account was published in the Toronto *Daily Globe*, 16 July 1877. Phelps likely knew of this Peters, fifteen years older, who was born in Hebron and had left for the northern Connecticut Valley lands in 1765. He was a prominent pioneer in northern New Hampshire, settling first in Piermont and commissioned in the militia by Governor Wentworth. As tensions grew with Britain, he was forced to flee to Canada for his Loyalist opinions, and he raised there and in northern New England the Tories who fought with Burgoyne. *Peters of New England: A Genealogy and Family History*, comp. Edmond Frank Peters and Eleanor Bradley Peters (New York: Knickerbocker Press, 1903), 186–87.

[39] Max M. Mintz, *The Generals at Saratoga: John Burgoyne & Horatio Gates* (New Haven: Yale Univ. Press, 1990), 190; Hoffman Nickerson, *The Turning Point of the Revolution or Burgoyne in America* (Boston: Houghton Mifflin, 1928), 302–3; Ketchum, *Saratoga*, 353. Phelps's enlistment expired on 25 Sept., just as the Saratoga engagements were under way.

[40] Revolutionary War Records, National Archives and Records Administration; F. B. Heitman, *Historical Register and Dictionary of the US Army from its Organization September 29, 1789 to September 29, 1880* (Washington, D.C.: National Tribune, 1890); Stelter, "Davenport Phelps," 54.

## New Hampshire under the Confederation

In the late 1770s Davenport became involved in a short-lived attempt by Hanover and other upper Connecticut Valley towns to form a state separate from seacoast New Hampshire. The proposed state was to be composed of the lands east and west of the Connecticut River, including the Hampshire Grants territory then contested by New Hampshire and New York. Phelps was Orford's representative at a meeting of delegates from the sixteen towns who shared this aim. That the freemen of Orford selected him at such a young age is evidence that he was already part of the local establishment.

The leader of the movement was his father's friend, Gen. Israel Morey, at that time the most prominent citizen of Orford. He was the owner of a sawmill and an ardent supporter of the New Hampshire revolutionary cause. The issue was the legislature's refusal to allow a delegate from each town rather than one representing several towns. It seems likely that the older man was a mentor to the young son of his friend. Morey's advocacy for the separate state earned him censure by the legislature and loss of his militia appointment, and for some years he was forced to live across the river in Vermont.[41]

There was no lack of family associations and acquaintance for Davenport in Orford. The town's first permanent resident was John Mann, who arrived from Hebron in 1765 and had a large family by the time Davenport lived there.[42] Mann had been married in Hebron by his uncle, the Rev. Samuel Peters. Daniel Tillotson and his family, formerly of Hebron, were established in Orford; Alexander Phelps had loaned him £150 in 1763, not repaid at the time of his death and one of the few credits to the estate.[43] Samuel Phelps, a Hebron-born relative, whose wife was Israel Morey's

---

[41] Hodgson, *Thanks to the Past*, 376–79. Chase, *History of Dartmouth College*, 1:469. The Hampshire Grants was territory in what later became Vermont, claimed by both New Hampshire and New York. Controversy intensified in 1777 when Ethan Allen's boys declared the territory the independent republic of Vermont. The New York–New Hampshire claims were settled by commission after the Revolution, and Vermont became the fourteenth state in 1792, the first admitted after the federal constitution. Hodgson, 361–79, discusses Morey's role in the Revolution and his prominence in Orford. His book also contains transcripts of Morey's correspondence and reminiscences of those who had known him.

[42] On Mann (Hebron, Conn., 1743–Orford, N.H., 1828) and his family see Hodgson, *Thanks to the Past*, 93–96, 431.

[43] Creditors to the estate of Alexander Phelps are listed above, in chapter 2, table 4.

sister, had been settled in Orford with his family since before 1771.[44] Davenport, although not yet married, on Christmas eve 1779 bought a house, barn, two river lots, and "range land" in Orford for £300 from a physician, Dr. Aaron Stiles, who is said to have sold the house at a great loss eight months after building it. The young man obviously had substantial funds available, indicating that his father's estate had at least partially been liquidated. He sold it for £400 seven years later when he moved to Piermont.[45]

In this transplanted Connecticut community of Orford, Davenport followed his father's career in the law and local elective office. In April 1781 he represented the town in the New Hampshire Assembly and served as magistrate and clerk of the court in Orange County.[46]

In 1785 Davenport married 16-year-old Catharine Tiffany (1769–1836). She was the fifth child of Dr. Gideon Tiffany (d. 1837), a Hanover physician, from a Puritan family that had first settled in southeastern Massachusetts Bay Colony.[47] Davenport was 30, considerably older than the average age of marriage at the time (the early 20s), but just slightly older than his father's age at his second marriage. The 14 years' difference in their ages may explain some of Davenport's later restlessness. His association with the Tiffany family was strong; all four of Catharine's brothers immigrated to Upper Canada in the 1790s after Davenport's move there.

In the year of his marriage, Davenport and his uncles, James and Eleazar Wheelock, left New Hampshire, three young men in pursuit of gainful employment, to establish a "mercantile business" in Hartford.[48] It was an unpropitious time to start a business; economic activity was depressed after the war and there was no national currency under the Confederation. The Phelps–Wheelock venture failed in about a year's time. Phelps later

---

[44] Hodgson, *Thanks to the Past*, 360, 400–401. In the Orford town census of 1771, Samuel Phelps and wife Lydia (Morey) Phelps were listed with four children; Joel Phelps, son, listed separately. Ibid., 424.

[45] The house is still standing in a village of handsome houses, many dating from the late eighteenth century. Ibid., 143.

[46] Stelter, "Davenport Phelps," 54.

[47] Norton, *Pioneer Missionaries*, 30; Phelps 1899, 1:267; Nelson Otis Tiffany, *The Tiffanys of America, History and Genealogy* (Privately printed, 1903), 41, according to which Gideon Tiffany married Sarah Dean Farrar in Norton, Mass., on 9 Feb. 1759. Sarah bore ten children, the last born in 1786. There are no birth or death dates for Dr. Gideon Tiffany in this account. Biographies of sons Silvester and Gideon are in *DCB,* vols. 5, 8, resp. Catharine's sister, Lucy, was married to James Wheelock. She died probably in childbirth the year of the Phelps marriage.

[48] Norton, *Pioneer Missionaries*, 30.

noted that his uncles had accumulated debts to the huge amount of £3,000.[49]

The first child of the Phelps marriage was born in New Haven on 21 October 1786, named Lucy for her mother's recently deceased sister.[50] Thereafter the family returned to New Hampshire, where Davenport resumed the practice of law in Piermont.[51] As a prominent citizen, he was appointed to the Third Regiment of Light Horse, New Hampshire Militia. He was made a major in 1786–87, and a colonel (like his father) in 1788.

## Freemasonry

Davenport began a lifelong association with the Masons when he participated in the formation of the Grand Lodge of New Hampshire on 18 December 1788. Its sponsor was the Grand Lodge of Massachusetts, and Paul Revere, one of its members and a future grand master, was at the gathering at the Bunch of Grapes Tavern in Hanover.[52] Like Revere and Phelps, many of the participants were Revolutionary War veterans.

The ideals of Freemasonry, which came to prominence in Europe and America in the eighteenth century, deeply attracted the leaders of the American Revolution and of the new republic. The Masonic affiliation of the recently inaugurated President Washington was well known. The order's cultivation of virtue and personal enlightenment appealed to many as suited to the task of creating the republic won by the veterans. "Masonry's great success . . . reflected its ability to fit new standards of honor, to balance Revolutionary demands for inclusiveness and exclusivity—for inclusive love and exclusive honor."[53] As at Hanover, lodges were established in outlying communities throughout the new nation: "The fraternity's ability to unite men in the bonds of brotherhood, so important for the Revolutionary officers, provided a legacy of continuing

[49] Davenport Phelps to Samuel Andrew Peters, 19 May 1787, *Peters Coll.*

[50] *AGC*, 2:8.

[51] Norton, *Pioneer Missionaries*, 30; 1790 U.S. census, New Hampshire.

[52] Stelter, "Davenport Phelps," 55, referring to *Proceedings, Grand Lodge of Massachusetts, 1769–1792*, 353.

[53] Steven C. Bullock, *Revolutionary Brotherhood: Freemasonry and the Transformation of the American Social Order, 1790–1840* (Chapel Hill: Univ. of North Carolina Press; published for the Institute of Early American History and Culture, Williamsburg, Virginia, 1996), 131.

significance in post-Revolutionary society as fluid and confusing as the officers' wartime experiences."[54] Freemasonry was a manifestation of the Enlightenment, emphasizing natural (rather than sectarian) religion, tolerance, and personal development through reason and understanding.[55] To the brothers like Phelps who gathered into lodges in these years the practice of Masonry was equated with the establishment of a new order of civilization based on the principles of the Enlightenment, of which the American Revolution was an expression. The role of the Mason was to guide a society so that it would reflect the ideals of the good and just:

> [T]he new vision of the fraternity fitted into the widely shared desire to reconceive the character of American society as it emerged from the Revolution. By celebrating morality and individual merit, Masonry seemed to exemplify the ideals necessary to build a society on virtue and liberty . . . taught [adherents] in new and successful ways, to be the teachers of the new order . . . Masonry offered participation in both the great classical tradition of civilization and the task of building a new nation. Just as important, the fraternity seemed to provide the leadership for these enterprises.[56]

Davenport became a member of Masonic lodges wherever he resided, and the order's moral teachings complemented his evolving commitment to the religious life. The order also brought him into close association with those who shared these ideals in New Hampshire, with the political leaders of Upper Canada in the 1790s, and with prominent citizens in the growing town of Geneva, New York, in the early 1800s.[57] He later sought to fulfill the Masonic ideal in a religious role, to bring civilization to the Indians and settlers in the raw new communities of western New York.

In April 1786 Davenport began what was to be a significant correspondence with the Rev. Samuel Peters, the former rector of St. Peter's Church in Hebron, then in London. As a child and youth in Hebron, Davenport

---

[54] Ibid., 132.

[55] Edith J. Steblecki, *Paul Revere and Freemasonry* ([Boston]: Paul Revere Memorial Association, 1985), 1–8; Bobby J. Demott, *Freemasonry in American Culture and Society* (Lanham, Md.: Univ. Press of America, 1986), 1–18. "Freemasonry," in *Encyclopedia of Religion* (New York: Macmillan, 1987).

[56] Bullock, *Revolutionary Brotherhood*, 237–38.

[57] It is interesting that in the very different ideological air of Upper Canada under Tory leadership in the 1790s all the leading government officials belonged, as did Davenport, to the local lodge.

Piermont N Hampr April 22d 1786

Reverend & very dear Sir,

The perusal of your very friendly favor by Mr Wheelock afforded me a satisfaction I had little expectation of— It was in truth a cordial tho it brought to mind a number of affecting considerations— The loss of a Father by death— the loss of a Friend our heavenly Guide and the loss of a Constitution— Your letter is not now by me but I remember you observe "multi magniq. morbi curantur abstinentia" I am apprehensive that for us there must be some ingredient beside abstinence— God grant there may be some one effectual—

It will be unentertaining I presume for me to write of affairs here— You know Sir the temper of this country too well to wish it— we are in statu quo— or rather worse— without commerce— without encouragement of manufactures, literature, & almost every thing else necessary to the wellbeing of Society—

Revd. Mr Peters. It

16. Davenport Phelps's Letter to the Rev. Samuel Peters, 22 April 1786

*Reprinted with the permission of the Archives of the Episcopal Church*

had certainly known Peters, but this was the first time they had communicated as adults, twelve years after the rector's exile. Phelps responded to a letter that Peters had sent him ("a very friendly favor" by "Mr. Wheelock").[58] Evidently he respected the Loyalist priest who had been ousted from Hebron and who railed against the Revolution from London, regretting "the loss of a Friend & our heavenly Guide." Word from Peters "was in truth a cordial 'tho it brought to mind a number of affecting consider-

[58] Probably referring to young Eleazar, who was in Europe on the ill-fated "mercantile business."

ations—The loss of a Father by death." Showing the sympathy this veteran of the winning side in the rebellion had for the past, he adds his regret for the passing of the former order, which he terms the "the loss of a constitution."[59] He was discouraged by the disorder of society and government under the Confederation: "[W]e are in status quo, or rather worse—without conscience, without encouragement of manufactures, Literature & almost any thing else necessary to the wellbeing of society . . . " The depressing conditions were causing people to consider joining the Loyalists in Canada: "Emigrations are talked of here to Nova Scotia & Cape Breton—whether any but Bankrupts will go I can't say—that last, however, makes a very numerous body in NEngland & is daily increasing." Peters would have found here confirmation of his disdainful views of the Revolution and his expectation that Canada would soon receive an influx of disappointed Americans.[60]

Davenport concluded with a reference to "Your former friendship to my Father & affectionate attention to his family merit my sincerest gratitude," and "best compliments" to Hannah, Peters's beloved only daughter. Later that year Hannah married William Jarvis (1756–1817), a Loyalist born at a Stamford, Connecticut, who had fought for the British in western New York and with whom Davenport would be associated in Upper Canada.[61]

Davenport Phelps, like many others at the time, was dismayed by the apparent despoiling of the ideals of the Revolution by civil disorder, and the weakness of the government under the Confederation to provide leadership and exercise authority. The struggle seemed to have produced drift and anarchy rather than purpose. As a Mason, Davenport had a clear sense of the virtues he sought in his fellow citizens, and this new society did not meet his standard. A longing for the order of his father's colonial Connecticut seems to have been beneath this disappointment. Whatever his deeper feelings, they impelled him to share his views with the rabid Tory who in

---

[59] Davenport Phelps, in Piermont, N.H., to Samuel Peters, in London, via "Mr. Mann in Hebron," 22 April 1786, *Peters Coll.* His use of the term "heavenly guide" confirms his father's attachment to "the English Church."

[60] For Peters's candidacy for the bishop of Nova Scotia and later of Upper Canada see below.

[61] Hannah Delvena Peters was born at Hebron, 2 Jan. 1762, and died at Queenston, on 20 Sept. 1845. She married in England, on 12 December 1786, William Jarvis. *DCB,* vol. 7; Peters, *Peters of New England,* 257.

exile filled his correspondence book with "I told you so" reminders of the consequences of "mob" rule.

The Rev. Peters was hyperactive among exiled Loyalists in London. His letters encouraged dissatisfaction in America, prophesied the break-up of the Confederation, and inflated his influence with English officials by exaggerating Loyalist sympathies among those remaining in America. In 1786–87 he put himself forward to be appointed to the newly created See of Nova Scotia, which, it was understood, would go to a Loyalist. His cousin, Joseph Peters (1729–1800), lobbied on his behalf in Nova Scotia, but to the Rev. Samuel's bitter disappointment, he was not chosen.[62] Later he put himself forward for bishop of Quebec and for bishop of Vermont. "In these fruitless efforts," writes his biographer, "the parson was motivated by both his enormous pride and his desire to confront his old enemies."[63]

In writing Peters in this vein Davenport seems to have put himself virtually in the Loyalist camp, paradoxical as that may seem for a veteran of the rebel army. What comes out strongly in his letters is his respect for order and hierarchy. In 1787 Davenport wrote again, asking for "answers to a question or two."[64] One matter had to do with the land inherited from his father in that heavily indebted estate. He sought a purchaser in London of "a tract of land belonging to my fatherless brothers & self . . . [of] about twelve thousand acres & perhaps 24." This was, of course, the legacy of Alexander's estate, which had come to the sons 15 years before. Davenport promised one hundred guineas to the person who could arrange the sale in London and suggested using the proceeds to pay off the debts of his Wheelock uncles, presumably accrued during the "mercantile venture" he and they had been associated with earlier. He reports that "Mesr$^{s}$ E & J. Whe." [young Eleazar and James Wheelock] owe £3,000 to London merchants, the payment "of which will not likely take place in a long time—some of the circumstances of which I can't now relate." If it is possible "by making payment or security . . . to procure an assignmen$^{t}$ of those debts—it would gratify me exceedingly to have the collecting of them—." Davenport was evidently willing to bail out his relatives from the enormous debt they had run up in the short-lived business. He offers to come to

62 On Joseph Peters see *DCB,* vol. 7.

63 Cohen, *Connecticut's Loyalist Gadfly,* 41–42.

64 Davenport Phelps, in Boston, to Samuel Peters, in London, 19 May 1787, *Peters Coll.*

England immediately should a potential purchaser come forth. This would not, in the event, be necessary, as in the next letter he reported the land was sold. A debt of such magnitude in the family from a failed business goes part of the way toward explaining his dissatisfaction with the Confederation and its stagnant economy.

The American scene seemed more troubled than previously, owing to "the late great commotions in America . . . particularly in Massachusetts" [Shays's Rebellion].[65] "The people in general are restless beyond discription—A great part publicly wish for the good things of Egypt." Like the Children of Israel in exile, the Americans were losing their sense of purpose in immediate gratification.

Davenport wrote Peters again in April 1791. This time he made no observations about American society. Perhaps with a federal government firmly established under the Constitution and Washington at the end of his first term there was less to be critical of. Davenport was in the midst of a personal crisis. His present circumstances were not sufficiently challenging, and he sought a wider field of endeavor. "I am now past 35," he wrote, "Living 200 miles up the Connecticut River . . . away from much society and books" on a farm with "my family consisting of a wife, three children, a Sister & two young servants . . . My time is taken up with no public business excepting what little arises from my being in the commissions of the Peace in the area, small concerns of society—." Like his father and grandfather, he wanted to be involved in public affairs and was not pleased to be in a backwater.

There was something more dramatic and important to discuss with Peters. He announced his intention to seek ordination in the Anglican Church. "I have been in contemplation to offer myself for episcopal orders," he wrote. He would come to England if necessary, but preferred to remain closer to home. "[S]ome of the Southern parts of Canada would by my choice, soil, climate, the present & probable future population of the country determine it." He had read that a bishop was soon to be

---

[65] On Shays's Rebellion see Mark Mayo Boatner, *Encyclopedia of the American Revolution*, 3d ed. (Mechanicsburg, Pa.: Stackpole Books, 1994). Shays's Rebellion was named for one of its leaders, Daniel Shays, a western Massachusetts farmer and Continental Army veteran. Bankrupt and foreclosed farmers between Worcester and Springfield had demonstrated since August of the previous year, and outright rebellion had broken out in December against the Springfield Armory. This impelled the Congress to raise troops to put down the revolt, effectively accomplished by Feb. 1787.

appointed in Canada, meaning it would be possible to be ordained without crossing the Atlantic.[66] He may have learned of the (false) report printed in a Boston newspaper early in the year that Peters had been appointed to a new see in Canada and, without saying so, was appealing for his support.[67]

Davenport's interest in the ministry was not entirely new. The fall he returned from Montreal in 1776 he had been interested in studying with the Rev. Benjamin Pomeroy of the Hebron Congregational Church. Pomeroy was then serving with Connecticut troops as a chaplain, and the plan came to nothing.[68] Almost 15 years later he had his mind set on the Anglican Communion.

## To Upper Canada

Davenport Phelps chose Upper Canada as a place to develop a more challenging life's work. There was land to be had in the newly created province, whose governor encouraged settlement. He would be part of what he considered a well-governed society, where the Church of England was the established church. The bulk of its population, centered along the eastern section of the northern shore of Lake Ontario, were Loyalists.

In 1792 he and James Wheelock made the arduous journey from New Hampshire to Albany and west to the small town of Newark at the far western end of the lake. It was 600 miles on horseback. Phelps was 37 when he made this move, Wheelock 33. Left behind were his wife, Catharine, the unnamed sister who had been living with them, and the two young serving girls. Catharine then had four young children to mind:

---

[66] Davenport Phelps, in Piermont, N.H., to Samuel Andrew Peters, in London, 4 April 1792. *Peters Coll.* The letter is stained and largely illegible.

[67] Peters was encouraged by the (inaccurate) report and unsuccessfully lobbied for the position. Cohen, *Connecticut's Loyalist Gadfly*, 42–44; *Columbian Centinel* (Boston), 9 Feb. 1791. Peters urged his case to John Graves Simcoe (1752–1806), who in 1791 was appointed governor of the newly created province of Upper Canada and whose chief secretary was Peters's son-in-law, William Jarvis. Although Simcoe supported him, once again, his designs came to nothing, and a year later the appointment of Jacob Mountain, 1748–1825, to the See of Quebec was announced, to Peters's fury. *DCB*, vol. 5.

[68] From Sylvester Gilbert, in Hebron, Conn., to Davenport Phelps [in New Hampshire], 22 Sept. 1776. Transcribed in Norton, *Pioneer Missionaries*, 28. Gilbert was interested in studying "divinity" with Pomeroy as well, which the "state of public affair" did not permit, as the reverend was serving as a chaplain with Connecticut troops.

Lucy, six, Sylvester Oliver, four, George Davenport, two, and William Alexander, born that February. It is sobering to realize that Davenport's venture to the west meant that his wife and these small children were left for almost two years with what support the sister and the serving girls offered in Piermont. Like a wartime wife, she was compelled to take responsibility for the household.

Conditions on the route west were primitive. A traveler in February of that year recalled that the portion from Albany to the future Utica (then Fort Schuyler) "was made possible for wagons," but further west the way was "little better than an Indian path, just sufficiently open to let a sled pass." There were "only a few straggling huts scattered along the paths at a distance of ten to twenty miles . . . and they afforded nothing but the convenience of fire and a kind of shelter from the snow . . ."[69]

Geneva, at the head of Seneca Lake, where Phelps and his family were to settle fifteen years later, then consisted of only a few huts. From there to Canandaigua "the road is only the Indian path, a little improved . . ." That county seat "consisted of only two small farm houses and a few huts . . . from [there] to the Genesee River 26 miles is almost totally uninhabited."[70]

About 1,500 of the Iroquois who had fought for the Crown in the Revolution had been settled across the Niagara River in Canadian territory. Others resettled in Buffalo Creek or on the Allegheny. Gen. John Sullivan and his army in 1779 had destroyed the villages and crops of the tribes of the Six Nations as far west as Genesee. It was a devastation from which they never recovered: "Their organization was destroyed, their empire gone."[71]

Some of the tribes that remained east of the river still considered King George their sovereign, and many resented the progress of American settlement. Now powerless, these Indians suffered the ills of unhealthy contact with white traders—alcoholism and disease. Their unhappy fate was

---

[69] An account by Capt. Charles Williamson describing a journey in 1792, quoted in George S. Conover, *Kanadesaga and Geneva* (Geneva, N.Y.: *The Geneva Courier*, March 1879), 34, from a text reprinted in *Documentary History of New York*, 2:1126. Charles Williamson was the agent for the English-owned Pulteney estates, a large tract of western New York land.

[70] Ibid.

[71] Boatner, *Encyclopedia of the American Revolution*, 1076, quoting Sydney George Fisher, *The Struggle For American Independence*, (Philadelphia, 1908), 2:265. John Sullivan (1740–95) was born in New Hampshire and served as a general in the Continental Army. *DAB*.

clear to any traveler, and Davenport must have been deeply impressed when he later befriended the Indians who had resettled in British territory.[72]

This was the first of Phelps's several traversals of western New York by horse and his first sight of the white settlements on the route, which he would later find the field for his missionary work.

## Another Chance for Imperial Policy

Upper Canada, established by Act of Parliament as a province in 1791, was a huge territory east of the province of Quebec. It extended from the entrance to the St. Lawrence River along the north shores of Lakes Ontario and Erie to the east shore of Lake Huron and included the lands to the north—roughly the limits of present-day Ontario. It was thinly settled, with about 6,000 persons there in 1784 and 10,000 at the time of the establishment of the province in 1791.[73] The rapid growth during this short span was due to the settlement of Loyalists on the northern shore of Lake Ontario from Kingston to York (later Toronto).

The largest westernmost settlement was Fort Niagara on the Niagara River at its junction with Lake Ontario, contested between the French and the British and until 1794 flying the Union Jack. It dominated the entrance to the river on the east bank; on the western bank were a barracks and a small trading settlement. The first governor, who had plans for western expansion, made this the provincial capital and named it Newark, after the New Jersey town where he had served for a time in the British army during the Revolution. (Sometimes called Niagara, this is the present Niagara-on-the-Lake.)

To prepare the settlement as a capital, the government ordered a survey of land on the east bank, where the military installation called Butler's Bar-

---

[72] The tribes who made up the Six Nations or Iroquois Confederation were the Mohawks, Oneidas, Onondagas, Cayugas, Senecas, and Tuscaroras. David M. Ellis, James A. Frost, Harold C. Syrett, Harry J. Carman, *A Short History of New York State* (Ithaca, N.Y.: Cornell Univ. Press, for The New York State Historical Association, 1957), 18. The British refusal to evacuate the forts in the Northwest (including Fort Niagara on the east bank of the River at Lake Ontario) after the Peace of Paris in 1783 was not resolved until Jay's Treaty in 1794, and it took two more years for the troops to withdraw.

[73] Frederic H. Armstrong, *Handbook of Upper Canadian Chronology* (Toronto: Dundurn Press, 1985), 265.

17. Niagara Falls
Elizabeth Simcoe, watercolor on paper, 30 July 1792.

*Simcoe Family fonds (F 47-11-1-0-71), Archives of Ontario*

racks—named for the commander of Loyalist troops in western New York during the war—and Navy Hall were located. The surveyors laid out a village, half-acre lots, and streets in a grid pattern. In 1792 there were 50 buildings, almost all of them log huts in what was then a raw, straggling village not yet reorganized into an orderly grid. Despite the severe winters and the hard life, Newark's population grew steadily. The military and governmental presence bolstered its economy, but Newark's prosperity derived from its strategic position between the lakes, which made it an ideal trading center.[74]

Col. John Graves Simcoe was named lieutenant governor of the newly established province. He had served in the British forces throughout the entire Revolutionary War, from Bunker Hill to Yorktown, and had commanded a force of Rangers active in New Jersey and in the southern campaigns. He despised the rebels and the Continental Congress, but admired the energy and enterprise of Americans. In England he made elaborate plans for the province, reflecting the lessons he had learned from the larger failure of imperial rule in America. In his view, colonial government had to be authoritarian and limit dissent in religion and politics; society should be hierarchically organized and regulated by the aristocracy and an established church. Simcoe was an enthusiast, fairly bubbling over with ideas for the development of the province in manufactures, trade, and the

---

[74] David Fleming, *A History of the Town of Niagara-on-the-Lake (1791–1970)*, typescript ([Ottawa]: National Historic Sites Service, 1971), 12–16; I am indebted to Linda Gula, Research Librarian, Niagara-on-the-Lake Public Library, for providing me with a copy of this useful work, Dec. 1997.

arts. Of his official correspondence on the subject, one scholar has commented that he "did not write dispatches, he wrote exhortations."[75]

Simcoe's ambitious strategy for the province was based on his expectation that the American government (which he persisted in terming "the Congress" three years after Washington's inauguration) would founder from weakness in the face of democratic pressures. Able Yankees then would relocate in Canada, where a government was able to maintain order. "I mean to prepare for whatever Convulsions may happen in the United States and the Method I propose is by establishing a free, bountiful British Government and a pure Administration of Laws, which shall hold out to the solitary Emigrant and to the several states Advantages that the present government doth not and can not permit them to enjoy." So Simcoe put it in a letter to Sir Joseph Banks, the noted naturalist, then the president of the Royal Society for the Advancement of Science.[76]

Simcoe was particularly interested in attracting New Englanders, who had a reputation for enterprise and steadiness. He harbored a curious misconception, for he told Banks that the "true New England Americans have as strong an Aristocratical spirit as is to be found in Great Britain nor are they anti-monarchical. I hope to have a Hereditary Council with some mark of Nobility." He proposed a See of Upper Canada as a keystone of this hierarchical society. With such governance, Upper Canada would attract the "best" Americans, have loyal subjects to resist aggression from the United States, and be a glory to the Sovereign, to make up in part for the humiliating loss of the Thirteen Colonies.

The new governor's plan was to attract the unhappy Loyalists ("enemies to Congress") who had remained in Connecticut and Vermont. An Anglican bishop in the province would keep the "sectaries" (the Dissenters, whose sermons Simcoe knew had stirred up the rebellion in the

---

[75] S. R. Mealing, "The Enthusiasm of John Graves Simcoe," in *Historical Essays on Upper Canada*, ed. J. K. Johnson, 302–16 (Toronto: McClelland and Stewart, 1975), 302. His contemporaries observed of him that he had "a benevolent heart . . . without much discrimination" and a manner "simple, plain, obliging." Ibid., 307. Among his expectations was that Vermont would break away from the union and join Upper Canada, and that he could make an alliance with "the unprincipled state of New York." Ibid., 304.

[76] Simcoe to Sir Joseph Banks, 8 Jan. 1791, in E. A. Cruikshank, ed., *The Correspondence of Lieut. Governor John Graves Simcoe*, vol. 2: 1793–1794 (Toronto: Ontario Historical Society, 1923), 17. Sir Joseph Banks (1743–1820) was president of the Royal Society from 1778 to his death, a "munificent patron of science." See also *DNB*. He wrote Banks because other parts of his plans dealt with the development of arts and letters and science in the education system he envisaged.

Thirteen) in line and preserve hierarchy: "The State Proprietary of some form of public Worship, politically considered, arises from the necessity there is of preventing enthuisastick & fanatatick Teachers from acquiring that superstitious hold of the minds of the multitude which Persons of such a description may prevent & are generally inclined to pervert to the Establishment of their own undue consequence in the State . . ."[77]

Little or nothing of Simcoe's grand plan was realized. There was no hereditary council, no bishopric (under Simcoe's regime), no great influx of disaffected New Englanders; the thinly populated territory could not yet support major educational institutions, and far from collapsing, the United States prospered under a stable government. Where did Simcoe's misjudged views come from? They were those of a veteran still smarting from the rebuff the Empire had suffered, and it is likely that the Rev. Samuel Peters, who sought and received Simcoe's support to be appointed bishop, contributed to the notion that there would be substantial defections of New Englanders.

Peters supplied Simcoe with a list of 51 Connecticut families likely to immigrate to Upper Canada, interpreting conditions in his native land through the tinted spectacles of the exile. He convinced the governor that his appointment as bishop would draw them to the province. He was not made bishop, though, and there were not enough other immigrants to create anything like the movement of people in western New York.[78] Phelps and his Tiffany in-laws were exceptions.

Davenport Phelps expressed to Peters that he was dissatisfied with the way the new country was developing. Some of the ideas floated by Simcoe for a different and more orderly North American society must have attracted him. It seemed an experiment to create a society with loftier standards, and he wished to take part. There was also an inviting material incentive. A key part of Simcoe's plan was to offer township-sized grants of land to settlers in the expectation they would attract others, and Daven-

---

[77] Simcoe to Henry Dundas, Treasurer of the Navy, 19 June 1791, Cruikshank, *Correspondence of Lieut. Governor John Graves Simcoe*, 2:31.

[78] Cruikshank, *Correspondence of Lieut. Governor John Graves Simcoe*, 2:31, 33. The list of names is included in Samuel Peters to Mr. Davison, 16 Jan. 1793, Great Britain, Colonial Office Records, CO 42, 316:229, NA, Manuscript Group 11, microfilm reel B-280 (Arch. Ont.). The letter is paraphrased in *Public Archives of Canada, U.C.Q.*, ser. 1791–1818, Arch. Ont. Library, 971.PAG STAT UC v.1 c.1 (annotated), 7. See also William Renwick Riddell, *The Life of John Graves Simcoe, First Lieutenant-Governor of the Province of Upper Canada, 1792–96* (Toronto: McClelland and Steward, 1926), 122.

port soon successfully applied for one. He probably also knew of the support Simcoe gave to Peters's candidacy for bishop of the putative See of Upper Canada.

Davenport arrived at the beginning of these apparently promising governmental initiatives and was in Newark in the year it was made the capital of the province. Simcoe opened the first government session in Newark in June 1792.[79]

Davenport spent the winter of 1792–93 in Newark. He stayed for a time in the house of Robert Kerr (1755–1824), also a Mason, surgeon to the Indian Department. Kerr had been with Burgoyne in 1777 and was married to Elizabeth Brant, daughter of Joseph Brant. He was "tall, well-built, enjoyed sports" and must have made Phelps welcome, as he was remembered on his tombstone for his "social habits and kindness of heart." He and Phelps were exact contemporaries and could tell each other of the military events they had shared from opposite sides.[80]

Davenport soon bought one of the half-acre lots, where he presumably built a log house, as others had. He lived there without his family for two years.[81] He became active in the life of the place and was appointed to positions that suggest he took an oath to uphold the sovereign, George III. In July 1794 the newspaper of the rapidly growing town announced that "His Excellency the Lieutenant Governor has been pleased to appoint DAVENPORT PHELPS, Esq. to be an Attorney and Advocate in his Majesty's Courts of Justice in this Province." Two weeks later the paper listed him as one of those commissioned in the militia, in his familiar role of quartermaster.[82] He was also in the "mercantile business." One of the few advertisements in the paper that summer read:

---

[79] The more centrally located York (Toronto) became the provincial capital after Simcoe's departure in 1796. *DCB*, vol. 5.

[80] Stelter, "Davenport Phelps," 56; *DCB*, vol. 5.

[81] We know this from a later document. In a petition of 9 July 1802 Phelps stated that in the first settlement and survey of the Township of Niagara he applied for Lot 5, consisting of half an acre, and as his name was omitted on the plan "there are now several Buildings on the said lot and pray[ed] that a Patent may be issued for said Lot"; his title was affirmed. National Archives of Canada, Executive Council records, Record Group 1, L 1, vol. 23, Upper Canada Land Minute Book E, 27–30, 10 July 1802, microfilm reel C-101 (Arch. Ont.).

[82] *Upper Canada Gazette or American Oracle*, 10 July, 31 July 1794.

> TO BE SOLD A quantity of Rum, Brandy, Geneva [Dutch gin], Wine &c. with a small Assortment of English Goods, Green and Bohea Tea. The whole of which will be sold together very low and prompt payment. They are now opened for Retailing at the House of D. PHELPS in Newark, 'till disposed of in the above way.[83]

Phelps was well connected to the small governing circle of the province through William Jarvis, Chief Secretary. Jarvis, a Loyalist from a Stamford, Connecticut, family, served under Simcoe in the Queen's Rangers in Virginia and had been in London since the end of the war. At Simcoe's request Jarvis was appointed to the "prestigious and lucrative" position in the new province, and he was with him when he inaugurated the government in 1792. (The bulk of his income came from fees from the registration of legal instruments.) Before his departure for the new province he married the Rev. Peters's sole and much-beloved daughter, Hannah.[84] Their first dwelling was a one-room log hut, and Jarvis referred to Newark as "a spot on the globe that appears to me as if it had been deserted in consequence of a plague." He criticized Simcoe for designating it as the capital instead of Kingston and was delighted with the later move to York. Despite the hardships, Hannah bore three children in Newark and another in York. Phelps was a nearly exact contemporary of Jarvis and a brother in the Masonic lodge established virtually on the arrival of the administration party. He would almost certainly have known Hannah when she was a small child in Hebron; she was eight when his family left.

Hannah (Peters) Jarvis had a good share of her father's asperity and epistolary habit, and her letters give a tart view of the tight and quarrelsome society that governed the province in the years of Phelps's residency. The British-born in the provincial government held themselves superior to the Loyalists (an early social burr) because "they think an American knows not how to speak." The small circle around Simcoe, in her view, was composed of "a lot of *Pimps*, Sycophants, and Lyars." The governor's lady (to whom we owe other descriptions of life in the province and charming drawings) was "a little stuttering vixen."

---

[83] Ibid., 2 June 1794.

[84] For William Jarvis (1756–1817) and Hannah (Peters) Jarvis (1763–1845) see *DCB,* vols. 5, 7, resp., from which the quotations are taken. Some letters of Hannah and William Jarvis were published in *Transactions of the Women's Historical Society of Toronto* 23 (1922–23), 20.

18. Navy Hall, Niagara

Elizabeth Simcoe, watercolor on paper, June–July 1793 [?]. The caption reads "Navy Hall, the light part is the canvas house by the fort at Niagara."

*Simcoe Family fonds (47-11-1-0-99 [70b]), Archives of Ontario*

There were 620 people living in 50 houses in Newark in 1794, making it considerably larger than the settlements Phelps had passed through in western New York.[85] It was a garrison town, and about 200 of the residents were soldiers. The site of government was Navy Hall, the military headquarters—"The Simcoes spend most of their time in canvas tents due to the dampness of their residence at Navy Hall."[86] It was the largest western outpost of the British army, protecting communications and trade to and from the western Great Lakes. The limited social life revolved around the military and civil hierarchy and consisted of occasional balls and the celebration of the king's birthday in June.

Mrs. Simcoe recorded excursions to the country and charming vistas. "Our marquees," she wrote of the tents pitched above Navy Hall, "command a beautiful view of the [Niagara] River and the garrison at the opposite side [Fort Niagara], which from its being situated on the point, has a fine effect, and the poorness of the building is not remarked at this dis-

[85] Personal communication from Linda Gula, Research Librarian, Niagara-on-the-Lake Public Library, 22 Nov. 1997.

[86] Fleming, *History of Niagara-on-the-Lake*, 15–16.

19. Fort Niagara and Newark
Elizabeth Simcoe, pencil sketch on paper, 26 July 1792–29 July.

*Simcoe Family fonds (47-11-1-0-75 [57]), Archives of Ontario*

tance, from whence a fine picture might be made." The mists from the great falls could be seen from miles away. On the boat bringing the governor's party Mrs. Simcoe saw the mists "rising like a cloud . . . 40 miles distant."[87]

The settlement was a boomtown in its first years. "Few places in north America can boast of a more rapid rise than the little town of Niagara [Newark]. Nearly every one of its houses having been built within the last five years," reported Isaac Weld, who visited there in 1796. "So sudden and so great has the influx of people into the town of Niagara and its vicinity been, that town lots, houses, provisions, and every necessary of life have risen, within the last three years, nearly fifty percent in value." At that time there were about 70 houses, "a court house, gaol, and a building intended for the accommodation of the legislative bodies. The houses,

[87] Entry of Wednesday, 25 July 1792, *The Diary of Mrs. John Graves Simcoe, wife of the First Lieutenant-Governor of the Province of Upper Canada, 1802–6*, with notes and a biography by J. Ross Robertson (Toronto: William Briggs, 1913), 120. The Simcoes came ashore at Navy Hall, Newark, the next day. An exhibit of Mrs. Simcoe's charming drawings took place at the London Regional Art and Historical Museums, London, Ontario, in 1993: *Elizabeth Simcoe: The Canadian Years, 1791–1796.*

with a few exceptions, are built of wood; those next the lake are rather poor, but at the upper end of the town there are several very excellent dwellings inhabited by the principal officers of government."[88]

The first building completed for public assembly was the Freemasons' Hall, used also for the early meetings of the council. Simcoe was a member, as was Joseph Brant, the exiled Mohawk leader, a great supporter of Davenport Phelps.[89]At the organization of the Grand Lodge of Upper Canada in 1796 Jarvis was Provincial Grand Master, Phelps the first Provincial Grand Secretary.[90] The Masonic brotherhood was the center of the social life of the small elite of the province, and Phelps was in the midst of it.[91]

Newark and its newspaper-reading elite were by no means isolated from knowledge of world events. The news in the *Upper Canada Gazette or American Oracle*, as in other newspapers of the time, consisted of articles that had appeared elsewhere. There was almost no local news save for government announcements. In the issue of 2 July 1794 that included the advertisement for "D. PHELPS," there were items that would have confirmed the provincial government's instinct to keep a tight grip. An article from Albany described planned fortifications on New York's western and northern frontiers intended to restrain the "restless British."[92] (Simcoe and the administration feared an American invasion.) In the same issue there was an account of the trial and execution of Danton in Paris, which doubtless fueled the local administration's fears of the democratic mob. There was also a report of a potentially positive development: Washington's appointment of John Jay as special minister to negotiate differences with Britain, which was to result in the treaty that soon reduced tensions on the frontier.

---

[88] Isaac Weld, *Travels through the States of North America and the Province of Upper and Lower Canada, 1795, 1796, 1797* (London, 1800), 2:83, quoted in Fleming, *A History of Niagara-on-the-Lake*, 22.

[89] There are references to Phelps's activities in the provincial Grand Lodge in J. Ross Robertson, *The History of Freemasonry in Upper Canada* (Toronto: George N. Morang, 1900), 1:473, 559, 632.

[90] Stelter, "Davenport Phelps," 6.

[91] Ibid.; Robertson, *Freemasonry;* D. B. Read, *The Life and Times of Gen. John Graves Simcoe* (Toronto: George Virtue, 1890), 145.

[92] This reflected the raids by hostile Indians allied to the British on settlements in the American Northwest Territory. The tribes were defeated at Fallen Timbers by the Americans under Anthony Wayne in Aug. 1794.

In the spring of 1793 Phelps and Wheelock petitioned for and received a grant of 84,000 acres, a township (designated by lines on the survey map) of about 10 miles square. It was Simcoe's policy to attract new settlers as "rapidly as possible in order to develop a strong defense against an expected invasion from the former colonies."[93] Except for fees, which could be onerous and probably account for Phelps's spending two years working in Newark before attending to his new grant, the land was free on condition that possessors agreed to settle on the land, divide it, and sell lots to other homesteaders.[94] The grantees were expected to sell lots in parcels of 188 or 200 acres covering the bulk of the tract and keep only a portion for themselves; "a township grant did not become the personal property of the grantee."[95] Glanford, which was what Phelps called his tract, was near the present-day city of Hamilton, at the western end of Lake Ontario.

In January 1794 Davenport made the 1,200-mile round trip to the upper Connecticut valley to fetch his wife Catharine and the four children from the farm in Piermont. Travel during the dead of winter had the advantage of firm, snow-packed ground on which a sled could ride—easier than wagon travel on rutted and muddy tracks. Nevertheless, it was a long and arduous journey, which he did not complete until March.

On the return journey, Davenport wrote the Rev. Peters from Albany in March. His letter reveals his vision of the future of Upper Canada and his commitment to taking holy orders.[96] Like Simcoe, Phelps expected that

---

[93] Leo A. Johnson, "Land Policy, Population Growth and Social Structure in the Home District. 1793–1851," in J. K. Johnson, *Historical Essays on Upper Canada*, 32–57 (Toronto: McClelland and Stewart, 1975), 34.

[94] "Petition of Davenport Phelps and Others," *Ontario Historical Society, Papers and Records*, vol. 24, ed. E. A. Cruikshank (Toronto, 1927), 104–5. Signed by: "Davenport Phelps & James Wheelock, Esqr. For themselves and David Curtis, Andrew S. Crocker and other Associates: 22 May 1793." The lands for which the petition was offered were described as "beginning nine miles from Lake Ontario on the west boundary of the tenth township—thence twenty degrees east nine miles & thence southerly twelve miles carrying the full breadth of nine miles." The petition was granted on 25 May 1793. Ibid., 106. Four years later the government acknowledged that this grant had been less than the standard ten miles square and granted additional lands. "Davenport Phelps claims for 97 square miles 1796," *Report Book*, Crown Lands Department, 1795–1799, 41, Arch. Ont., MS 2696.

[95] Stelter, "Davenport Phelps," 57, referring to personal communication from Mr. T. Roy Woodhouse, Hamilton, Canada, member of the Head-of-Lake Historical Society, 1972.

[96] There are two letters of this date. One gives a detailed description based on Jarvis's account of the failed effort to promote Peters's candidacy for bishop of Vermont in that state's diocesan convention. In the postscript to that letter Phelps states that he is returning to Newark bringing his family. The quotations are from a second letter of the same date, in which Phelps laments Peters's failure to be appointed bishop in Canada (the See of Quebec). Davenport Phelps, in Albany, to Samuel Peters, in London, 1 March 1794, *Peters Coll.*

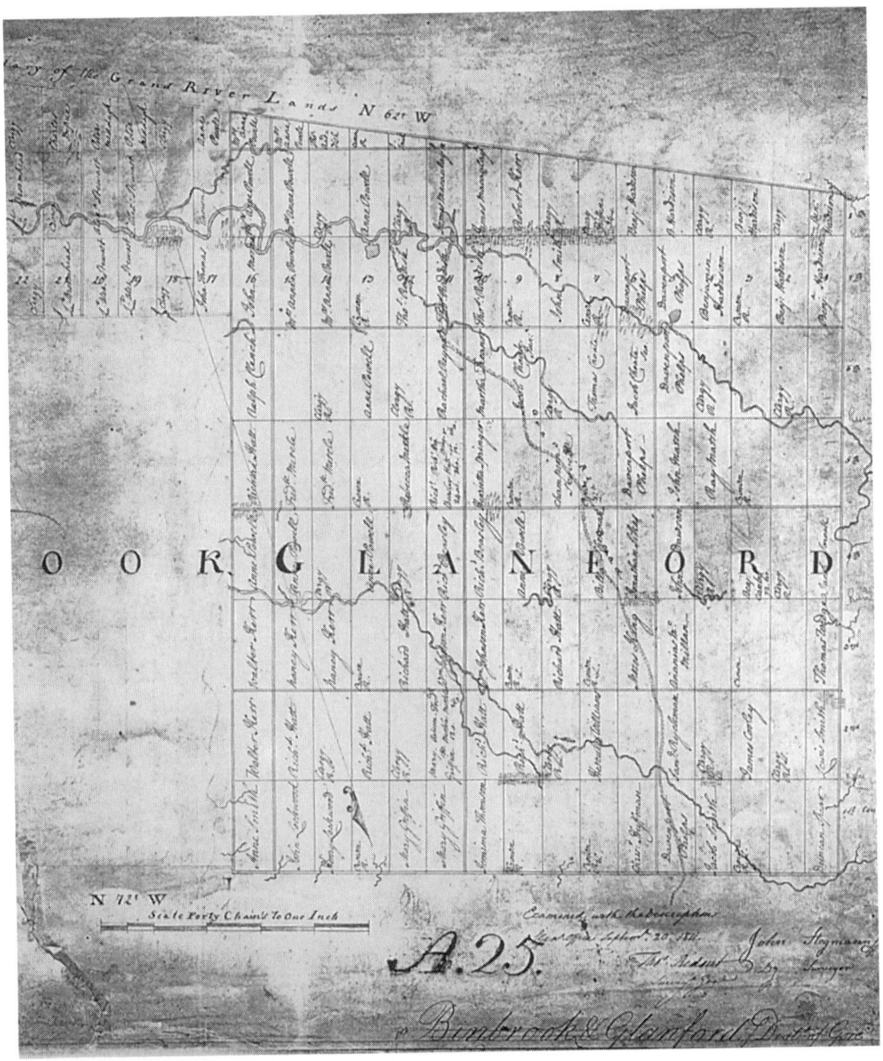


20. A Portion of Glanford Township

Davenport Phelps received the township as a grant in 1794 but was unable to sell lots. Three years later he relinquished rights to the township, retaining only the lots shown here, which were sold after his death. The lots are marked out in a rectangular grid pattern with no conformity to topographical features, though streams and ponds are indicated.

*Ontario Ministry of Natural Resources, Plan of Survey, Glanford Township, SR 1092 [1799]*

the contentious Yankee-born Anglican, if appointed bishop, would have pulled like-minded settlers to the promising soil of Upper Canada. "From a consideration of the inviting soil and climate of the upper province an attachment to the government with the prospect of your residence there as Bishop, many of your former acquaintances & others of their connections had earnestly and seriously calculated to remove themselves and families as soon as they should have been ascertained of your arrival."[97] (However, as happened repeatedly, Peters failed of appointment to the newly created see.)

Phelps continued: "If among other things it has been an object in government to promote the population of this province with useful inhabitants such as in America, are esteemed the best husbandmen, I mean Newenglanders, and with some of more than ordinary abilities, it is thought that in the appointment of a Bp. the object is in some manner lost." The province needs pastoral care, and though he is referring to what Peters could have done, we may read there his own aims as a minister. "The inhabitants are like sheep scattered upon the mountains—The field for usefulness there is rapidly and extensively increasing . . . "[98]

Catharine (Tiffany) Phelps's siblings moved virtually en masse to Upper Canada. A sister and four brothers emigrated. They proved to be typically "energetic Newenglanders" in the province. But they were also independent, and some were not as loyal to the established order as the government had hoped they would be. Oliver, a physician, and Gideon Tiffany arrived in Upper Canada in the same year as their sister (1794). Gideon (1774–1854) was soon appointed king's printer by Lieutenant Governor Simcoe and took over as publisher of the *Upper Canada Gazette or American Oracle*, in effect an official organ of the government. Their oldest brother, Silvester (1759–1811), moved to Newark about a year later and joined his brother as the official printer.[99] Both were Masons and mem-

[97] Jacob Mountain was named bishop of Quebec. (The Crown had not approved the creation of a separate bishopric for Upper Canada.) Phelps wrote Peters that he had "ardently expected your arrival in this country . . . the pleasing expectation of your coming out in the character of the Bishop of the Canadas."

[98] The failure to be appointed to Quebec was only one of Peters's many postwar disappointments. He had also campaigned to become the Episcopal bishop of Vermont. Phelps learned of this from Jarvis, whom he had met "at the head of the Mohawk on the way to Vermont" in January. In three and a half closely written pages in his letter from Albany that March, Phelps gave Peters an account of the jockeying that went on among the clergy of the Diocese of Vermont, in which Peters's candidacy was narrowly defeated.

[99] An engaging account of the brothers' tangles with the administration along with references to brothers Oliver and George is in W. Stewart Wallace, "The First Journalists in Canada," *Canadian Historical Review* 26 (1945), 372–81.

bers of the lodge—Silvester succeeded Phelps as Grand Secretary.[100] A fourth brother, George Tiffany, a surveyor, lived in Ancaster.[101] All of the Tiffany siblings who lived to maturity emigrated from New Hampshire, five to Upper Canada and three to western New York.

In 1795 or 1796 Davenport moved his family to Glanford township.[102] A private grantee such as Phelps was required by the grant to "build a house 16 feet by 20, to clear half the roadway in front of his lot and to clear and fence 5 acres of land—all within twelve months."[103] Phelps's lots were covered with hickory, oak, beech, and some pine, and there was a creek and a pond.[104]

Catharine entered on this pioneering life with an infant in arms. Theodora, named for the grandmother they left in New Hampshire, was born in January 1795. There were three other small children to attend as well. It was indeed pioneering, far from the shops of Newark. The forest had to be cleared, a house built, crops planted, animals tended. From Davenport's point of view, their proximity to Brant's settlement was an advantage.

---

[100] For Silvester ("Sylvester" elsewhere) Tiffany see *DCB*, vol. 5. Silvester later published satirical items and other material not sanctioned by the administration. This earned him the reputation of being pro-American and republican, for which he was removed from his position at the *Gazette*. He and Gideon started the first independent newspaper in Upper Canada in 1799, the short-lived *Canada Constellation*. Gideon later gave up the newspaper business and acquired 2,200 acres of land in Delaware Co. He operated sawmills and engaged in fur trading, In his 60s he was jailed for his leadership of a reform movement. Oliver practiced medicine in Ancaster Township. The account of Gideon in *DCB*, vol. 8, refers to Oliver Tiffany as a "well-to-do older brother" living in Ancaster. Oliver Tiffany (physician) was born in 1763 and died unmarried at Ancaster. George Tiffany was born in 1765 and died at Ancaster. Lucinda (Tiffany) Brigham was born in 1761 and died in Canada on 14 August 1814. See Tiffany, *Tiffanys of America*, 41.

[101] Stelter, "Davenport Phelps," 57.

[102] There is no present-day Glanford; the location of Phelps's tract is about two miles from the center of Hamilton, Ontario.

[103] Johnson, "Land Policy," 34, referring to Lilian F. Gates, *Land Policies of Upper Canada* (Toronto, 1968), 125. "Original Plan of Survey, Glanford Township [1 Jan. 1794; 1799]," Ontario Ministry of Natural Resources, SR 1092, SR 1093. A survey signed by Phelps, dated Jan. 1794, shows Glanford Township as Number 11, with the Township of Salfleet on one boundary and "Grand River Indian Lands" on the other. Fig. 20 reproduces a portion of John Stegmann's survey of the lot lines of Binbrook and Glanford Townships [No. 11], District of Gore, A25.

[104] Field Book of Glanford Township, by Davenport Phelps, 1797, 11 (15 Jan. 1798), Arch. Ont., Record Group 1, A I 1, vol. 55, Letters received by Surveyors General, October 1797 to June 1798, microfilm ser. 626, reel 3.

The government efforts to promote settlement had not produced the hoped-for emigrants, and Phelps was in no position (and probably had no inclination) to promote the sale of land. On 5 June 1797 the Crown repossessed the grant. Phelps did not challenge and was left with 1,200 acres of his own.[105]

## Joseph Brant

The farm was near the Iroquois settlements on the Grand River, and from there Davenport began a lay ministry to the Indians, preaching and leading prayers. Here was a man who, in middle life, was clearing land, raising crops, and building a homestead, and was driven to undertake this lay ministry at the same time. He was encouraged by one of the most remarkable figures in the history of the relations between native North American Indians and the Europeans, the Mohawk chief, Joseph Brant, or Thayendanegea (1742–1807).[106] Brant was a brother Freemason. That and his youthful association with Wheelock bound the men together. Their friendship and mutual respect flourished in part because of Davenport's gifts for instruction and spiritual counsel. Davenport's ministry began a chain of events that would eventually lead to his ordination, in New York, not Canada, and ultimately to his departure for what would be a successful mission in the towns of western New York.

Removed to British Canada after the peace, Brant was a well-known figure in North America and England, notorious for his military exploits on behalf of the Crown in western New York, fascinating to cultivated Britons as the best-known example of the "savage" who had become "civilized." A few days after their arrival, the Simcoes entertained him at dinner. Mrs. Simcoe reported in her diary, "He has a countenance expressive

---

[105] Stelter, "Davenport Phelps," 59.

[106] William E. Stone, *Life of Joseph Brant-Thayendanegea* (New York: George Dearborn, 1838), includes transcripts of several of his letters on behalf of Davenport Phelps; see also the biography by Isabel Thompson Kelsey, *Joseph Brant 1743–1807: Man of Two Worlds* (Syracuse, N.Y.: Syracuse Univ. Press, 1994). *DCB*, vol. 5, s.v. "'Thayendanegea." Gloria Lesser has comprehensively surveyed and analyzed the representations of Brant in "Iconography of Joseph Brant" (master's thesis, Concordia Univ., Quebec, 1983). Lois M. Huey and Bonnie Plis, *Molly Brant, A Legacy of Her Own* (Youngstown, N.Y.: Old Fort Niagara Association, 1997), has interesting material on the Brant family. Molly Brant was the mother of several children by Sir William Johnson, the British trader, landowner, and superintendent of the Indians in western New York until his death in 1773.

21. Joseph Brant
Oil on canvas by Ezra Ames, 1806.

*New York State Historical Association, Cooperstown*

of art or cunning. He wore an English coat, with a handsome crimson silk blanket, lined with black and trimmed with a gold fringe, and wore a fur cap; round his neck he had a string of plaited sweet hay."[107] His appearance was well known in prints from portraits by distinguished painters of the day.

As a youth in the 1760s (when Davenport Phelps was a child) Brant attended Wheelock's Moor's Charity School for a few months. He knew several Indian tongues and spoke English proficiently. He became an

[107] Entry of 9 Dec. 1792. *The Diary of Mrs. John Graves Simcoe, Wife of the First Lieutenant-Governor of the Province of Upper Canada, 1802–6*, with notes and a biography by J. Ross Robertson (Toronto: William Briggs, 1913), 141.

Anglican and translated the *Book of Common Prayer* into Mohawk. His first visit to England with Guy Johnson in the winter of 1775–76 attracted interest in social and intellectual circles.

While in London he was initiated into the order of Masons, to which he was devoted throughout his life, an important bond between him and Phelps. He was also interviewed by James Boswell and painted by George Romney. To Boswell (and presumably his readers), he was the sought-for noble savage, keen to learn "civilized" ways:

> The chief has not the ferocious dignity of a savage leader, nor does he discover any extraordinary force either of mind or body . . . [the] portrait of him in the dress of his nation . . . gives him a more striking appearance; for when he wore his European habit, there did not seem to be any thing about him that marked preeminence. Upon his tomahawk is carved the first letter of Christian name, Joseph, and his Mohawk appellation Thayendanegea. His manners are gentle and quiet, and to those who study human nature, he affords a very convincing proof of the tameness which education can produce upon the wildest race.[108]

During the Revolution the Mohawks and all but the Oneidas of the Six Nations sided with the British. Brant proved himself a valiant soldier in extensive campaigns in New York from 1777 to 1781, his name striking terror into the patriot settlers of the Mohawk Valley. (He was known, however, to have saved noncombatants at the Cherry Valley massacre in November 1778.)

At the end of the hostilities he journeyed again to London, and during this visit he secured from the Crown the grant of lands on either side of the Grand River in recognition of the Mohawks' wartime service.[109] Brant again attracted a major portraitist, Gilbert Stuart (1755–1828), whose representation reflected the experience of war, defeat, and exile "in which the traits of the vulnerability of the 'noble savage' adapting to change is the dominating moral. Brant is championed as a beaten but unvanquished foe."[110]

---

[108] James Boswell, "Account of the Chief of the Mohawk Indians lately visited England," *London Magazine* 45, July 1776, quoted in Lester, "Iconography," 21; Frank Grady, *James Boswell, The Later Years 1769–1795* (New York: McGraw Hill, 1984), 126.

[109] Charles M. Johnston, "An Outline of Early Settlement in the Grand River Valley," in *Historical Essays on Upper Canada*, ed. J. K. Johnson, 1–31 (Toronto: McClelland and Stewart, 1975), 36.

[110] Lesser, *Iconography*, 34; *DAB*.

On the Grand River he established "Mohawk Village," later called Brant's Ford (the present Brantford, 20 miles west of Hamilton and about 70 miles from Newark). When Lieut. Governor Simcoe arrived on the first official visit in winter 1793 "the Indians hoisted their flags and trophies of war, and fired a *feu de joi* in compliment to His Excellency, the representative of the King, their Father." One of his staff described the settlement: "The place is particularly striking when seen from the highland above it, extensive meadows, the Grand River near it, with a termination of Forests. Here is a well built wooden church with a steeple, a school house, and an excellent house of Captain Brant's . . . We heard Divine Service performed by an Indian. The devout behaviour of the women (Squaws), the melody of their voices, and the excellent time they kept in singing."[111]

Brant devoted himself to improving the lot of the Indian refugees: he strove unsuccessfully for intertribal unity and advocated acquisition of European skills. His welcoming attitude toward whites was not shared by all, and there were perpetual disagreements—the young war chiefs could not be controlled by their elders.[112]

His one-time American enemies respected him; President Washington received him in Philadelphia in 1792 in the course of negotiations with the Six Nations and other tribes. Brant was feted and sat for his portrait by Charles Willson Peale, an attractive portrait showing a "face full of sympathy and hope."[113]

The British remained in control of the western forts of Oswego and Niagara at the peace in 1783, and Brant looked to them to protect the tribes against the push of westward-moving Americans. When the British relinquished the forts in 1794 under Jay's Treaty, without security for the Indians, Brant felt betrayed. He and Simcoe fell out soon after the latter's taking office when Brant insisted that the Mohawks could sell the granted

---

[111] E. B. Littlehales's Journal, 7 Feb. 1793, in Cruikshank, *Correspondence of John Graves Simcoe*, 2:288–89. In 1800 Brant completed a manor house called Wellington Place, where he lived like an English gentleman with liveried servants.

[112] For a recent account of the relations between the Indians and the whites on the Northwest Frontier in which Brant figures as only one of many see Richard White, *The Middle Ground: Indians, Empires and Republics in the Great Lakes Region, 1690–1815* (New York: Cambridge Univ. Press, 1991).

[113] Lesser, *Iconography*, 43.

lands to support themselves (which he himself did).[114] The relationship foundered on mutual suspicion.[115]

Brant persisted in living in two cultures. He was present on 31 January 1796 at Barton Lodge (near Glanford) at a Masonic meeting that Phelps chaired.[116] He sent two sons to Hanover to be educated in 1800, witness to his respect for Wheelock's legacy and commitment to European languages and skills. Davenport Phelps shared Brant's view of the civilizing mission of religion. Brant saw in him the ideal candidate to serve the Indians as an Anglican missionary.

In 1797 Brant wrote the bishops of London and of Quebec in support of Phelps's candidacy for ordination. He described him as "one with whose character and family he had long been acquainted, who had ample testimonials respecting his literary and moral qualifications and who would consent to devote his life to the service of the Church among the Mohawks . . . Their choice was fixed on him in preference to any other . . . and [the Indians] regarded him with particular respect and even reverence."[117] The letter was sent under cover of one from Sir John Johnson, the prominent Loyalist exile, son of Sir William, then superintendent of Indian Affairs in the province.[118]

Bishop Jacob Mountain in far-off Montreal had not met Phelps or visited Newark. He was cautious, and referred the matter of Phelps's ordination to the political authorities, explaining that "[t]here is some degree of irregularity in the application which places me under considerable difficulty." There had been no "Testimonials," and he had not interviewed the candidate. He was reluctant to invite him to Montreal "without holding out to him, and to the Chiefs, a greater degree of encouragement than in the present stage of the business I am authorized to do." The Anglican bishop of the vast territory—Roman Catholic Quebec and Upper Canada—had only six active priests in the diocese at the time and by inclination as well as the constitutional nature of the Church of England, deferred

---

114 Ibid., 7. Johnston, "An Outline of Early Settlement in the Grand River Valley," 9–10.

115 Simcoe to Lord Dorchester, 16 Nov. 1798, Cruikshank, *Correspondence of John Graves Simcoe*, 2:102–5.

116 Robertson, *Freemasonry*, 1:73.

117 Quoted in biographical sketch of Phelps in *AGC*, 3:4.

118 *DCB*, vol. 5.

to the civil ministers. It was they who would have to come up with the stipend if a clergyman was to be assigned to the Six Nations.[119]

Simcoe had left the province on a leave from which he was not to return. Peter Russell (1733–1808), administrator in the absence of a governor, responded by denigrating Phelps's abilities, motivation, and background, and suggesting he was potentially disloyal:[120]

> What Mr. Phelps's literary qualifications may be I am ignorant, as the only knowledge I have of him arises from my having sometimes seen him before the Council Board as a Petitioner for land, and in the Courts of Law as an Advocate and Attorney. But if he is not more competent to execute the Functions of a Clergyman than he appeared to have been those of a Lawyer, I am persuaded your Lordship will not judge him a fit subject for Ordination.[121]

The secretary goes on to distrust Phelps's loyalty to the Crown and impugn his motives by suggesting it was the stipend he was after as a priest:

> Mr. Phelps is a Native of the United States and was (I understand) a Colonel in their Militia—He appears to be a shrewd sensible man; and to have the manner and address of good Company, but I apprehend the largeness of his family and the narrowness of his circumstances had more share than his fitness for the office in inducing Capt. Brant to recommend him for Orders, and the stipend of a Missionary for the five Nations—

While Davenport would surely have welcomed a cash stipend for his family, the course of his later career shows that he was not interested in ordination for the money.

There was also the delicate nature of relations with the Indians to be considered. A missionary had to be unswervingly loyal to the government, and Russell was unsure of Phelps's politics: "I have besides reason to doubt the propriety of placing Mr. Phelps as a Missionary among any Indians of this Province—As I hold it my duty to guard against the introduction of Persons to situations of that nature (wherein they may do mischief)

---

[119] Jacob Mountain to Peter Russell, 11 Jan. 1798, in *The Correspondence of the Honourable Peter Russell*, ed. E. A. Cruikshank (Toronto: Ontario Historical Society, 1935), 2:62–63. *DCB*, vol. 5.

[120] To the sharp-tongued Hannah (Peters) Jarvis, ever watchful for slights to Americans, the British-born Russell was "the old Rogue."

[121] Peter Russell to Jacob Mountain, 22 Feb. 1793, in Cruikshank, *Correspondence of the Honourable Peter Russell*, 2:98–99. *DCB*.

whose attachment to the British Constitution, I have the slightest cause to suspect. . . ." Russell concludes his thunderous negative with a charge that Phelps was more than unreliable, he was a trouble-maker, an agitator—an accusation he wanted kept from Brant:

> I deem it right to mention the cause of my doubt with respect to Mr. Phelps, which I beg leave to do in confidence that I may not be hereafter exposed to the necessity of further explanations to Capt. Brant—your Lordship will therefore be pleased to keep this communication to yourself.
>
> About two years since the Attorney General had filed an Information against a Person for Seditious Practices, and this Mr. Phelps (as I was told) was seen in his Barristers Gown at the head of a concourse of Farmers marching to the Court House with the professed intention of supporting the accused on the day of Trial—They had the prudence however to disperse in time, and the man was Convicted, but it was the Attorney General's intention to have made a motion in consequence for removing Mr. Phelps from the Bar had he not been prevented by his absenting himself from it almost ever since.

Regardless of what we know of Phelps's reasons for choosing the conservative regime of Upper Canada, there does seem to be something revolutionary in the spectacle of the barrister leading a crowd of farmers to protest one of their own brought in on a charge of sedition. Russell's views tell more of the uneasiness of the administration in the face of the threat of Indian discontent and American republicanism than they do about Phelps's qualifications for a religious vocation.

Russell evidently hoped the matter would go away, but Brant forced a response some months later with another letter urging Phelps's candidacy. Russell disingenuously replied that the matter was up to the bishop and that "my Ignorance of Mr. Phelps political or religious principles puts it out of my power to pass any opinion on the propriety of your choice, but it is of the utmost moment to the welfare of this Province that no person should be admitted to this situation, of whose attachment to the British Constitution there can be the smallest doubt."[122] The bishop, relieved to have the matter handled for him, concurred with Russell's views:

> I am clearly convinced of the importance of your observations upon the caution which is necessary to be used where persons are to be introduced into situations in which they will naturally have many opportunities of influencing

---

[122] Joseph Brant to Peter Russell, 8 May 1798; Peter Russell to Joseph Brant, 14 May 1798, ibid., 2:152–53, 233.

> the political sentiments of the people. And sure I am that he is least of all fit to be their Spiritual instructor who would be disposed to unsettle their notions of loyalty & obedience & weaken their attachment to the Governments under which it is their happiness to live. [123]

The civil and religious authorities acted as though they were seated on a powder keg and must have thought they handled a delicate matter with due caution.

To Brant this denial of his request was humiliating, the latest in many defeats at the hands of colonial officials. His life's work was coming to an unfulfilled, tragic conclusion. As Barbara Graymont concluded, "His major failure was his inability to understand the nature of British imperialism and to comprehend the fact that the British would not permit two sovereignties to exist in Upper Canada."[124] When he died in 1807, the tribes were divided, poor, and dependent.

Despite rejection, Brant persevered, and Phelps remained intent on becoming a missionary to the Indians. They turned their efforts toward ordination by the Episcopal bishop of New York. Davenport placed this effort in relation to his grandfather's life's work in a letter to John Wheelock: "I am fully persuaded that the labors of your venerable predecessor under God, have been the cause. Col. Brant greatly encourages civilization and Christianity . . . strong hopes may be entertained that we may yet see the wilderness bud and blossom like the rose."[125]

Brant wrote his "long standing friend" Col. Aaron Burr (Vice-President of the United States and in the midst of his campaign for the presidency in 1800), requesting him to recommend Phelps to the bishop of New York and sending a pair of moccasins for his daughter. Burr, grandson of Jonathan Edwards, son of the president of the Presbyterian College of New Jersey (Princeton), had an entirely Calvinist background, but he was prominent in Federalist circles, which included many Episcopalians.[126] Burr forwarded the letter to his daughter, Theodosia, who had left on her honeymoon and was later to stay with Brant at Wellington Place with her

---

[123] Jacob Mountain to Peter Russell, 12 June 1798, ibid., 2:166.

[124] *DCB*, vol. 5, s.v. "Thayendanegea."

[125] Davenport Phelps, in Glanford, Upper Canada, to John Wheelock, in Hanover, 1 Nov. 1800, quoted in McClure and Parish, *Memoirs of the Rev. Eleazar Wheelock, D. D.*, 99.

[126] In 1800, in a three-cornered presidential contest, Burr and Jefferson were candidates in opposition to the incumbent, President John Adams. *DAB*.

new husband after a visit to Niagara Falls.[127] There is a charming story of Brant's being invited to dinner with Burr in the city—in the unexpected absence of the host, his daughter, Theodosia, then 14, served as hostess.

The welcome that Davenport Phelps found in the Episcopal Church in New York instigated his return to his native country, where his mission in life would take a different course from the one he and Brant intended.

## Episcopal Mission

The church to which Brant and Phelps appealed was emerging from a low point of membership and institutional strength. After the Revolution many of the clergy and parishioners had gone to Canada or England. Those who remained acted decisively to make it an American church and incorporated it as the Protestant Episcopal Church in America in 1787. The *Book of Common Prayer* was revised, with references to the British sovereign eliminated.

In New York, Trinity Church grew in membership during the 1790s, in part because of increasing sympathy for things English as news of the French Revolution shocked propertied New Yorkers. Because of its ownership of land in lower Manhattan, Trinity parish financed the diocese. For generations after the Revolution the rector of Trinity also served as the bishop of a diocese that then covered the entire state. Outside of the city there were Episcopal churches in Westchester, Poughkeepsie and the other Hudson port towns, and in Albany and nearby Schenectady. Missions west of Albany were just beginning.[128] In 1800 the Diocese of New York was emerging from what its historian calls the "slumbering period."[129] Phelps's subsequent activities should be seen as part of an awakening institution that grew to play a more influential role in its communities than its numbers suggest.

---

[127] Aaron Burr, in New York, to Theodosia Burr (Mrs. Joseph Alston), in South Carolina, quoted in *AGC* 2:8, from *Memoirs of Aaron Burr*, ed. Mathew L. Davis, 2:163. Among the guests at the party overseen by Theodosia was the Episcopal bishop of New York. Milton Lomask, *Aaron Burr: The Years from Princeton to Vice-President 1756–1805* (New York: Farrar, Strauss, Giroux, 1979), 327–28.

[128] James Elliott Lindsley, *This Planted Vine: A Narrative History of the Episcopal Diocese of New York* (New York: Harper and Row, 1984), 78–91.

[129] E. Michael Allen, "Mitred Leaders of Evangelism" (master's thesis, The General Theological Seminary, 1991), 143.

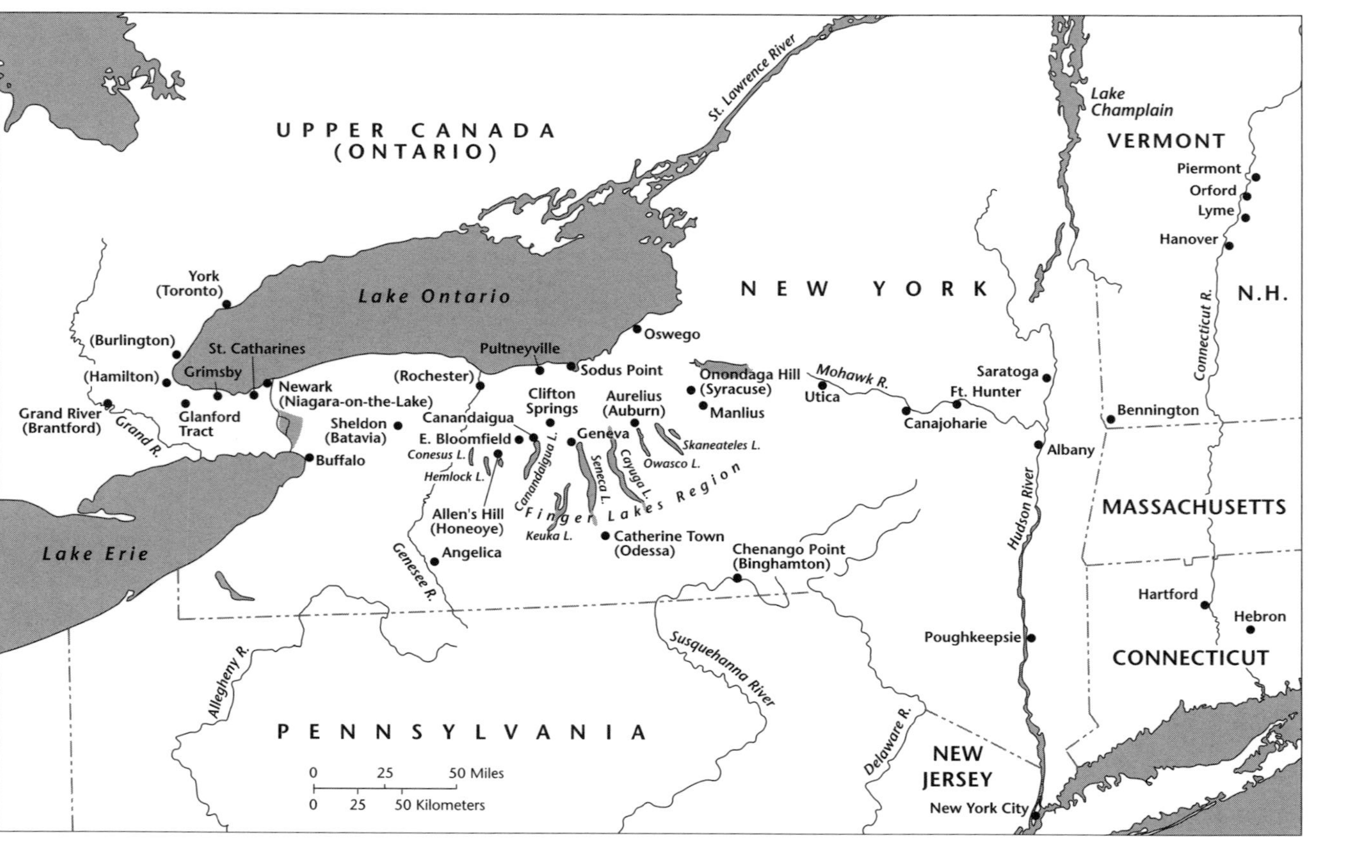


22. The Connecticut River Valley, New York State, and Upper Canada

In the new republic the Episcopalians were greatly outnumbered by Congregationalists and Presbyterians, who had agreed to a union in New York state in 1801 and whose ranks were swelled by the Connecticut families migrating into New York. The Baptists and the Methodists also grew rapidly after the turn of the century, led by evangelical itinerant preachers. The Episcopalians continued to have a tiny membership, only a small percentage of all church affiliates, with 3 percent in the United States as a whole in 1850.[130] The congregations in many places were composed of locally influential families, giving the church prominence disproportionate to its numbers.

There was little popular religious fervor in New York State until the revivals of the 1820s and 1830s, the local expression of the "Second Great Awakening" that swept much of the United States. The Methodists, a tiny sect in the 1780s, became the largest denomination in the state by 1860. Other sects emerged as well, notably the Mormons, who originated on western New York soil in the decades after 1820. The exuberant religious revival of the 1820s–40s was led by itinerant preachers, often uneducated men, and sects that, like the Mormons, denounced the established churches as of the rich.[131]

The Yankee emigration to New York State reached flood tide in the mid-1790s when former Indian lands, secured by treaty and subterfuge, were granted to Revolutionary War veterans. The sale of these lands (often by veterans who had never seen their properties) and lots held by speculative development companies stimulated migration from Connecticut and the rest of New England. Between 1800 and 1820 the population of New York doubled while that of Connecticut increased by only 10 percent.[132] The well-organized Presbyterian Church, sometimes coopera-

---

[130] Michael Barkun, *New York of the Millenium: the Burned-over District of New York in the 1840s* (Syracuse: Syracuse Univ. Press, 1986), 23ff.; Sydney E. Ahlstrom, *A Religious History of the American People* (New Haven: Yale Univ. Press, 1972), 387; Christopher Adamson, "God's Continent Divided: Politics and Religion in Upper Canada and the Northern and Western United States, 1775–1841," *Comparative Studies in Society and History* 36 (3) (July 1994), 417–46. Methodists, who had been negligible at the time of the Revolution, grew to be the largest denomination by the Civil War. By 1850 among American churchgoers affiliations among the older denominations were Methodists 34 percent, Baptists 20, Congregationalists 4, and Episcopalians 3. Adamson, "God's Continent Divided," 423, referring to Roger Finke and Rodney Stark, "How the Upstart Sects Won America, 1776–1850," *Journal of the Scientific Study of Religion* 28, no. 1 (1989), 31; Ellis et al., *Short History of New York State*, 195–96.

[131] Nathan O. Hatch, *The Democratization of American Religion* (New Haven: Yale Univ. Press, 1989), celebrates the proliferation of the anti-establishment sects, the revival preaching, and the mass participation in camp meetings as the yeast of American democracy.

[132] Dixon Ryan Fox, *Yankees and Yorkers* (New York: Univ. Press, 1940), 182–92.

tively with its Calvinist brethren, the Congregationalists, was, at an early stage, the most successful in following the westward movement of its people with clergy.[133]

The Episcopalians were only beginning to be active in the new communities in the late 1790s. One priest with experience in western New York early in his career was the Rev. Philander Chase (1775–1850), later an ardent missionary himself, and best known as the founder of Kenyon College in Ohio. Chase in his 20s had founded the first Episcopal church in Canandaigua in 1797, and was rector of Christ Church, Poughkeepsie, four years later when still in his 20s he gave Davenport Phelps useful support on his quest for ordination.[134]

In September 1801, following the installation of Bishop Benjamin Moore in New York City, Chase preached a sermon advocating mission, probably intending to stir the new leadership as well his parishioners.[135] He equated the spread of religion with the progress of civilization, arguing that the introduction of institutional religion was essential to counter the lawlessness and incivility that characterized the frontier communities. Such views were also held by Brant and Eleazar Wheelock before him and are consistent with the ideals of the Masonic brotherhood. Religion in this sense is necessary for public order and for personal decency:

"[M]ost of the settlements in the west have been made with a rapidity scarcely equaled in the peopling of any country," Chase told his hearers, and "every man does right in his own eyes with impunity." As a consequence "weeds of error, of sin, and of bad habits are sure to vegetate where the salutary seeds of religion, morality, and good order have not been cultivated."[136]

"Where could be found the proper person to go among them, to take care of [the western communities] and feed them with the bread of life?"

---

[133] John Allen Krout and Dixon Ryan Fox, "The Completion of Independence," in Arthur M. Schlesinger Sr. and Dixon Ryan Fox, *A History of American Life* [abridged ed.] (New York: Scribner, 1996), 443–44.

[134] *AGC*, 3:17.

[135] Philander Chase, *Bishop Chase's Reminiscences, an Autobiography*, 2d ed. (Boston: James B. Dow, 1848), 1:42; Ahlstrom, *A Religious History of the American People*, 624–25.

[136] Chase, *Bishop Chase's Reminiscences*, 1:38–39. The sermon was preached at Poughkeepsie on 21 Sept. 1801. Chase supported the call for a formal commitment to mission in the New York Diocesan Convention of 1800. He had urged such support to be adopted in the previously scheduled convention in 1797, which was canceled because of an outbreak of yellow fever in New York.

Chase asked that Sunday. He had the answer to his rhetorical question a few days later when, as he was "sitting quietly in his little dwelling on Canon Street, a loud tap was heard, and the name of Davenport Phelps announced." Chase's father (a resident of Cornish, New Hampshire, south of Hanover) had known him, and he was "much esteemed in the neighborhood of Dartmouth College."

Phelps told Chase that he had "long been attached to the Church" and loved her doctrines and esteemed her discipline. After hearing guidance from Chase concerning the procedures for ordination, he left for New York with a warm testimonial to the bishop. In his memoir Chase commended Phelps's "suavity of manners, his more than ordinary abilities, and very respectable acquirements, and, above all, his character for true piety of heart and holiness of life [which] seemed to constitute him a God-send to the Church."[137] Phelps also carried an endorsement from Gen. Israel Chapin of Canandaigua, the most prominent Indian agent in western New York. Brant had written him that the mission would be "most important and interesting to the present and future well being of the Indians *on both sides* of the lakes."[138]

Phelps was ordained to the deaconate, the order preliminary to the priesthood, by Bishop Benjamin Moore on 13 December 1801 at Trinity Church. The bishop gave him an extensive charge, articulating the purpose of the mission and the church's expectations for its servant. This document sets forth the conduct of the first official missionary of the American Episcopal Church. It was honored years later in a memorial panel placed in the choir of Trinity Church, Geneva, showing Phelps, head bowed, attending to the Bishop's charge (fig. 23).

The foundation of the mission was "the belief of the existence of an Almighty Creator and wise Governor of the Universe." "This will naturally open the way for the doctrine of atonement thro' a redeemer," the bishop continued, "and sanctification by the influence of the Holy Spirit, and you may then prompt them forward to religious obedience, from a principle of Love to their Creator, Redeemer and Sanctifier."[139]

In keeping with Episcopalian practice, the bishop instructed the new missionary to follow the forms of worship set forth in *The Book of Common Prayer*. "In the celebration of public worship you are to confine yourself to

---

[137] Ibid.

[138] Joseph Brant, in Grand River, Upper Canada, to Aaron Burr, in New York City, 7 May 1800, *AGC* 3:6–7.

[139] *AGC* 2:239.

23. Memorial Panel at Trinity Church, Geneva, New York
Phelps is charged with his mission by Bishop Benjamin Moore. Woodcarving, Trinity Church, Geneva, New York, ca. 1930s.

the established Liturgy." "Never," the Bishop warned, "indulge in extemporaneous effusions." The approach emphasized formality in service, set prayers, and theological doctrine (e.g., the doctrines of the Trinity, the atonement). Absent are appeals to self-scrutiny, rebirth, confessions, prayers spun out of the feelings of the moment. This mission would not rely on the evangelical appeal for spiritual rebirth of Phelps's grandfather's time, perpetuated by the Methodists and others.[140]

---

[140] "Episcopalians have been so much in the habit of praying in the Prayer Book that they cannot make bad prayers." John Henry Hobart, quoted in Lindlsley, *Planted Vine*, 115. The newly installed Bishop Moore is called "the benign bishop" by the diocesan historian, and in his tenure the church steadily grew in numbers of parishes and communicants. For most of the years he was assisted by John Henry Hobart (1775–1830), who succeeded him. Many of Phelps's later reports were to Hobart, who in his tenure as bishop was to greatly extend what Phelps started by planting Episcopal churches in the flourishing towns of western New York after the opening of the Erie Canal. Hobart was "probably the greatest religious leader the American Episcopal Church ever produced" in the judgment of the author of a recent history of American religion. Ahlstrom, *A Religious History of the American People*, 830. The spadework for this effort was done in part by Davenport Phelps.

Bishop Moore enjoined Phelps to keep a journal and send it to him every three months. In the first he reported from Hudson that contrary winds and ice had delayed his return upriver so that he did not reach there (just south of Albany) until after Christmas. In the new year he waited for snow in Schoharie, north of the Catskills, so he could load his supply of prayer books onto a sleigh; a fever further delayed him.

The sleigh at Schoharie was furnished by his youngest brother, Ralph Rodolphus, who had moved there from New Hampshire. He was the last-born of the family, a baby when his father died and 17 years younger than Davenport, who most likely served as a father figure to him. At the time of this visit he was in his late 20s, an example of the New England migrant seeking opportunity in New York. He later moved to the growing town of Manlius, New York, on the main path to the west, where he practiced law. The brothers saw each other regularly in later years, and the first Episcopal Church in Manlius was founded by Davenport.[141]

En route west Phelps stopped at Herkimer in the Mohawk Valley, where he found no Episcopalians (and where he could have learned of the hostility of the residents to Brant and the Mohawks, who had been the scourge of the valley in the Revolution). At Canandaigua he found "a handsome, flourishing Town—Several respectable and influential characters in it are firm episcopalians, and manifest their earnest wishes to be favored with a clergyman." He rejoined his family at the end of February, two months after the ordination.[142]

Phelps had seen a fruitful field. As he reported to the bishop, "in this part of the country, there is no Clergyman within fifty miles, I have applications from the Inhabitants of several Townships, distant from each other to visit and preach among them." He remained on course for the Indian mission, but the white communities also drew him:

> I intend—as soon as the Indians shall have returned to their villages on Buffaloe creek [near the future Buffalo, on the American side of the Niagara], to visit them. This will be a journey of between sixty & seventy miles. And, as a number of the inhabitants on the Genesee River and in Canandaigue, have

[141] See "Phelps I" in the Genealogical & Biographical Notes for a biographical sketch of Ralph Rodolphus Phelps. Manlius was an important way station on the east–west route until the opening of the Erie Canal in the 1820s, when Syracuse, to the north, became a major station on the canal route. Onondaga, the future Syracuse, was a small settlement in the 1790s and early 1800s.

[142] Davenport Phelps, in Glanford, Upper Canada, to Benjamin Moore, 17 March 1802, *AGC* 3:10–12.

> manifested their earnest desire, that I should return to them the ensuing summer, I shall, with the leave of providence, comply with their request.[143]

In the next several months, Phelps rode out from Glanford to Grimsby and other white settlements on the Upper Canada side of the river. He also rode to Indian camps there and across the river to Buffalo Creek, where he sought an encounter others might have avoided, by inviting Red Jacket (ca. 1758–1830), a "Chief Sachem" of the Senecas, to visit him. This chief was a formidable figure, an "intellectual, walking oracle, with encyclopedic knowledge of the affairs of the Indians." He was an avowed and implacable enemy of Brant and sought to sever his people from the influence of Christianity, schooling, and European culture. Phelps told him of his instruction from the bishop and was surprised by the courtesy of the response, but Red Jacket did not accept the invitation to return for another conversation. That the meeting took place at all is a tribute to Phelps's diplomatic skills.[144]

Of the exiled tribes, the Tuscaroras showed the most interest in Christianity, according to Phelps. His account of a meeting with them in 1802 gives a view on his approach to proselytizing as well as the Indian response at the time:

> In about two hours after our arrival, the natives who were at home (about forty in number, many of them being out, making preparations for hunting) assembled. The meeting commenced by reading a selection of collects both in English & Indian, then a lecture to direct and establish their belief in one Almighty Creator and Governor of the Universe; which, after reading prayers in Indian, was closed with some observations on the fallen nature of man, & an intimation that at our next meeting should be explained to them, the recovery of man by Jesus Christ. After service they seemed inclined to sit & remain awhile; when I made some remarks to them on the bad effects of the use of ardent spirits, and expressed my sorrow for the murder of two squaws, which had been a few weeks before dictated by a woman of their nation, about forty miles distant, who of late professes the art of divination. After finishing my observations, one of the Indians present, seemed to be much affected, advanced to me & by my interpreter told me "he was heartily sorry he had

[143] Phelps, in Glanford, to Benjamin Moore, *AGC* 3:284.

[144] Phelps, in Glanford, to Moore, 12 June 1802, *AGC* 3:40; Stelter "Davenport Phelps," 73, n. 64, referring to William E. Stone, *The Life and Times of Red-Jacket*, 184–87, 207. See also Merton M. Wilner, *Niagara Frontier: A Narrative and Documentary History* (Chicago: S. J. Clarke Publishing, 1931), 1:129.

> been concerned in the murder & hoped (poor creature) I would forgive him." I told him if he heartily repented, and would lead a new life, God Would forgive him; and added such further observations as I thought were suitable on the occasion. These people then formally returned thanks for my visit (which by the way was the first they had ever received from a clergyman) said they very much approved my advice, and earnestly requested me to visit them again. I ought here to mention, that some of these people, having heard of baptism, requested that it might then be administered to them, which I thought at that time proper to postpone, that they might be further instructed respecting that ordinance, previously to their receiving it.[145]

In a letter earlier that year Davenport reported that "unhappy animosity subsisted between the deputy Superintendent, who resides at Niagara, and Cap$^{t}$ Brant." It was the first indication of what would bring his mission to the Mohawks to an end.[146]

In early fall 1803 Davenport Phelps once again crossed New York State to Albany on horseback. (His faithful horse is prominent in the memorial plaque [fig. 23].) There, on 5 October, at St. Peter's, the strongest church outside of New York City in that era, Bishop Moore ordained Phelps to the priesthood. Davenport's ambition had been fulfilled in one of the diocese's oldest churches. His direction was sure, and the course of the remaining years of his vigorous life was set, though surprises lay ahead.

When he returned to Upper Canada Phelps found the conflict between Brant and the government had worsened. "Indeed, from information to which I must give credit, it has assumed so serious a complexion that I am apprehensive it would be imprudent in me to comply with the invitations of the Mohawks to visit them."[147] His service to the Indians west of the Niagara had effectively come to an end.

This failure let Davenport develop the work for which he has been remembered. He saw promise for mission in the settlements he had come to know so well on his traverses of New York State. "[A] greater field of usefulness is opening on the frontiers of New York," he wrote the bishop early in 1804; "there is in my view a high degree of probability, with pecuniary aid, that a few churches might be organized in that quarter, which

---

145 Davenport Phelps, in Grimsby, Upper Canada, to Benjamin Moore, 12 Dec. 1802, *AGC* 3:123.

146 Davenport Phelps, in Grand River, to Benjamin Moore, *AGC* 3:66.

147 Benjamin Phelps, in New Amsterdam, Buffalo Creek, to Benjamin Moore, 27 Jan. 1803, *AGC* 3:141.

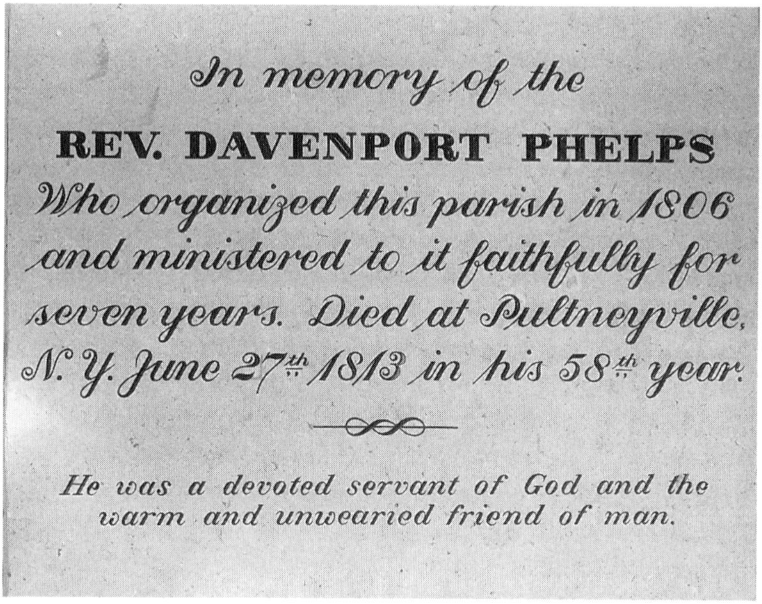

In memory of the
REV. DAVENPORT PHELPS
Who organized this parish in 1806
and ministered to it faithfully for
seven years. Died at Pultneyville,
N. Y. June 27th 1813 in his 58th year.

He was a devoted servant of God and the
warm and unwearied friend of man.

24. Memorial Tablet for Davenport Phelps at Trinity Church, Geneva, New York

after a few years would become respectable." Not willing to entirely give up the mission to Indians, he added, that a missionary "might occasionally visit the poor natives on y^e frontiers."[148] However, the white settlements would in fact demand his full attention for the rest of his life.[149]

## Mission Among the Lakes

Phelps spent the last nine years of his life among the villages in central New York, generally along what had come to be called the "Western," or "Genesee," Road that extended from Utica to the Genesee country. (Nowadays this would be termed the Finger Lakes region.) The villages he regularly visited stretched from Manlius in the east to Sheldon (later Batavia)

---

[148] Davenport Phelps, in Grimsby. Upper Canada, to Benjamin Moore, 15 Dec. 1802, *AGC* 3:125–26.

[149] Phelps was unable to sell all his land in Upper Canada upon his departure, and some remained in his estate (see below). There is the record of a sale of a 94-acre parcel in Glanford to Bela Hibard of the Town of Glanford, 1 Dec. 1804, Land Registry Office, Lincoln Co., *Memorial Book A*, 1795–1801.

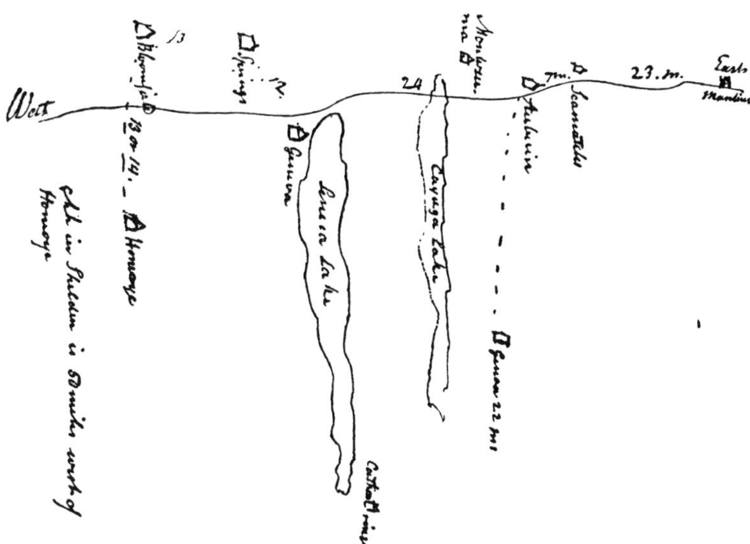


25. "Rough sketch of y$^{e}$ relative situation of our churches"
Davenport Phelps made this sketch of his mission circuit in a letter to Bishop John Henry Hobart, 4 January 1811.

in the west. The most prominent were Geneva, where the family came to live, and Canandaigua, both in the center of his east–west circuit, where the land development companies had their sales offices, with stores and inns catering to the traveler and settler. The long, narrow lakes that characterize this part of New York extend southward from these villages, making it relatively easy in the warm months to reach settlements along the shores and to the south by boat. Phelps's sketch of the circuit for the bishop conveys the extent of his mission (fig. 26).

The east–west highway had greatly improved by the new century, and a turnpike west to Genesee country had been opened in 1804.[150] By 1810 Timothy Dwight, traveling to Niagara, found the Western Road "excellent; the surface, smooth." He noted that the population of Manlius, where Phelps's youngest brother practiced law, had tripled in the decade of 1800 (from 1,000 to nearly 3,000). There was also amenity. Dwight thought the rising ground on which Geneva at the northwest corner of Seneca Lake was built gave it "the most beautiful eminence . . . for the site of a town

[150] Conover, *History of Ontario County, New York*, 202.

which I ever beheld." Geneva's spacious main street afforded a fine view of the lake and was "about a mile in length, and from 150 to 200 feet in breadth."[151] A hotel with a colonnaded front had been in operation since 1796. In 1804 there were only 35 houses in Geneva and 325 people.[152] Although Dwight considered the situation of Canandaigua "inferior in beauty to that of Geneva," the town itself was "greatly superior. The houses are remarkably good, in a better style than that of most older settlements, and at the same time are not defaced by any appearances of decay."[153] In fact, Canandaigua had the most energetic business of any town Dwight encountered west of Utica.[154] Bloomfield, a village of farms in Genesee County, had three churches, one of which Dwight considered "the handsomest I met with westward of Albany."[155] (Phelps founded St. Peter's in the village in 1811, after Dwight's visit.)

The long lakes of the region led to settlements to the south and served as water highways for lumber and wheat. A steamboat was launched at Geneva in 1806 to ply Seneca Lake.[156] Dwight foresaw trade flowing north to Oswego to be shipped on Lake Ontario down the St. Lawrence to Montreal. As it developed, however, the Erie Canal in the 1820s transformed this possibility by opening up access to markets for the fruit and grains from this land to the Hudson and the Port of New York. The countryside of Phelps's circuit was undulating, with no striking relief, but views of "about twenty miles on each side of the road . . . with no mountains to be seen," according to Dwight. Dwight added, "When you ascend from a valley to the top, you behold a vast plain spread before you and on both hands, where the view is uninterrupted except by forests . . . The traveler passes over them with sensations differing very little from those which are

---

[151] Timothy Dwight, *Travels in New England and New York*, ed. Barbara Miller Solomon, with the assistance of Patricia M. King (Cambridge, Mass.: Harvard Univ. Press, Belknap Press, 1969), 4:29.

[152] Conover, *History of Ontario County, New York*, 266.

[153] The town had been established as the center for land sales of the Pulteney estates. English investors, through their agent, Charles Williamson, had sunk $1 million in the development of roads, stores, and mills between 1792 and 1801, a colossal sum at the time. It had not attracted equivalent land sales, which led to the dismissal of Williamson, but by Dwight's account was doing well nine years later. Ellis et al., *Short History of New York State*, 135.

[154] Dwight, *Travels in New England and New York*, 4:30.

[155] Ibid., 32.

[156] Ibid., 267.

excited by a surface absolutely level, and they often extend from six or eight to twelve or fourteen miles."[157]

The pattern of Phelps's mission was set in his early visits. He would seek out any Episcopalians to be the nucleus of a parish and encourage them to build a church to focus their commitment and be an inspiration to others. "From a persuasion that the building of even small churches was a measure of real importance to the welfare and increase of the church I have been indefatigable in promoting the design," he wrote from Onondaga in 1806. Timing and circumstances were important. From Manlius, he wrote, "the prospect is good of their putting up and inclosing one of at least 30 by 45 feet," the "circumstances" of the parishioners made it unlikely they could complete it "without aid"—some small grants came from Trinity Church in this period, but most support was local, in money or in labor. Until there was a church building, other space had to do. In Onondaga, for example, "the court house, the principal room of which is now finished, must at present answer—Divine Service was performed there on Christmas and the Holy Communion administered to only 8 or 9 persons."[158]

Phelps appears to have met the first parishioners in their houses, and he reported no preaching out of doors. Typical of the modest support he sought from the diocese (or Trinity) was this request for prayer books and instructional materials: "a few doz[en] catechisms, Clergymans Advice, Treatise on y^e^ nature & const^n^ of y^e^ chh &c [which] might be extremely useful."[159]

Phelps's missionary emphasis was on liturgy and education. In his later tribute to Phelps, Bishop Hobart praised "the devotion and the decency with which the [congregations organized by Phelps] performed their parts of the public service . . . whatever prejudices our Liturgy may have at first to encounter among those who are unacquainted with it, a minister who will be diligent in explaining it, and enforcing its excellencies . . . will finally succeed, by the Divine blessing, in leading many to value it as their best help in the exercises of devotion, and, next to the Bible, their best guide to heaven."[160]

---

[157] Ibid., 19.

[158] Davenport Phelps, in Onondaga, to Benjamin Moore, 29 Jan. 1806, *AGC* 5:6.

[159] Davenport Phelps, in Onondaga, to John Henry Hobart, 6 April 1806, *AGC* 5:128–29.

[160] *Journals of the Convention, Diocese of New York*, 13 Oct. 1813, 256.

Phelps had personal trials of a mundane nature. His letters to the bishop refer repeatedly to serious financial difficulties caused by his inability to sell the Glanford property and to his and his wife's illnesses, which kept him from his rounds. And like the clergymen of his forebears' generations Phelps had to teach school to make ends meet; his having to teach also cut down on his circuit riding. Furthermore, he was concerned about educating his own children, which was difficult in remote Glanford. Indeed, one reason for his return to New York State was the possibility of better schooling. Joseph Augustus was the last child to be born in Upper Canada, in 1804; the youngest two children, Henry Rodolphus and Edward Lewis, were born in New York. The boy, Dean Wheelock, born in 1800, died four years later, the only one of the 11 children to die before maturity.

In a letter of 1805 he describes the effort required to satisfy circuit riding, instruct the children, and cope with illness:

> I visit the several churches as nearly in rotation as possible, but to provide those of my own house, in a country tho' new yet is nearly as expensive as any of our old settlements; and to attend to the instruction of my children, who by my absence for several years past have been neglected (& who must still be neglected were I not so to do) have thought it my duty to sit down as an instructor of youth in this neighborhood for three or four months, at liberty however, to be so much absent as may be requisite to visit these churches. The one however at Aurelius I have not been with since November. Were I not thus engaged in a school the bad state of the roads, with my infirm health would at any rate have rendered my going so far at least very inconvenient. But I hope soon to be there again."[161]

Davenport remained an indefatigable missionary despite occasional illness and had the satisfaction of seeing his chosen work bear fruit in the form of established church communities. He wrote from his brother's house in Manlius in 1805, full of enthusiasm for the prospects of his mission:

> So late as December ult$^{e}$ I came to this county, and have, with great satisfaction, found the newly organized churches laudably engaged to be built up in the order of the Gospel . . . Upon my arrival in this town a vestry meeting was notified & a subscription set on foot for building a Church, which bids fair to

[161] Davenport Phelps, in Onondaga, to Benjamin Moore, 29 Jan. 1806, *AGC* 5:96.

> meet with success. Indeed Sir I cannot but anticipate Churches rising in all the principal towns in this flourishing western hemisphere."[162]

Later that year, although a fever prevented his traveling for some months, he wrote of the founding of a church in Aurelius (later Auburn), at the northern end of Owasco Lake (between Manlius and Geneva, on his circuit). Aurelius had been part of the Military Tract where lots had been given to Revolutionary War veterans in the 1790s. At the turn of the century it had been little more than an enlarged clearing with log buildings and a mill.[163] Four years later Phelps found there "the prospect of perseverance & growth . . . respecting which, and appearances elsewhere, when fav$^{d}$ with suitable health, I will write more particularly."[164]

After a visit to Oswego on Lake Ontario in 1807, well north of his regular circuit, where he had found "16 or 18 families five of whom are episcopal," Phelps reflected on the purpose of his mission and echoed the theme which animated his Puritan forebears. "I flatter myself . . . that the light of the church will before many years shine in that long desolate quarter. Tho I am at times in some measure discouraged, yet I can but feel again animated with the consoling hope that a foundation is laying for the future establishment of the government and doctrines of our truly apostolic church this late howling wilderness."[165] Later that same year his sense of accomplishment grew. St. Peter's in Aurelius had been built and "was animating & agreeable beyond my former expectations—Thro divine favr I have been able thro y$^{e}$ Spring & Summer past, to pay an almost uninterrupted attention to y$^{e}$ duties of my mission, & have the unspeakable satisfaction of hoping that my labours are crowned with some success. I am now y$^{e}$ second time on my way to y$^{e}$ county of Ontario."[166]

In that county he found "an unusual degree of unanimity" among some of the inhabitants of Geneva for establishing a church.[167] Phelps's January letter to the bishop in 1807 tells of these efforts and his visits to other

---

[162] Davenport Phelps, in Manlius, Onondaga Co., to Benjamin Moore, 4 Feb. 1805, *AGC* 3:384.

[163] Henry Hall, *The History of Auburn* (Auburn, N.Y.: Dennis Bro's., 1869), 42–50.

[164] Davenport Phelps, in Onondaga, to Benjamin Moore, 19 July 1805, *AGC* 3:509.

[165] Davenport Phelps, in Onondaga, to John Henry Hobart, 6 April 1806, *AGC* 5:128–29.

[166] Davenport Phelps, in Aurelius, to Benjamin Moore, 7 July 1806, *AGC* 5:154.

[167] Davenport Phelps, in Onondaga, to Benjamin Moore, 28 Aug. 1806 *AGC* 5:175.

26. View of Geneva, New York, 1807

Baroness Hyde de Neuville, watercolor on paper.

*©Collection of The New-York Historical Society*

churches: "their engagedness & devotion greatly refresh & encourage me—"[168] With this promise, he chose Geneva as the base for his circuit.

The first Episcopal services in Geneva were held in 1806 in a school building shared with the Presbyterians; Phelps officiated on alternate Sundays. Trinity Church was organized the next year, assisted by a gift of $2,500 from Trinity Church in New York City, which also contributed $250 per year toward Phelps's salary.

Geneva was an active place on the east–west route. In 1810 there were 385 inhabitants living in 68 houses. Phelps moved his family there in 1807 to what was called Mile-Point House, one mile south of the village on the west shore of Seneca Lake.[169] He maintained his association with Freemasons in the local lodge. From Geneva, Phelps informed the bishop that

[168] Davenport Phelps, in Geneva, to Benjamin Moore, 25 Jan. 1807, *AGC* 5:262–63.

[169] The house is no longer standing. Stelter, "Davenport Phelps," 63. Davenport Phelps is listed in the 1810 U.S. census, Ontario Co., New York, 236; the household consisted of three males under 10, one between 6–25; one between 26–45; and 6 females 10–16, one 24–45. There are no listings for servants or slaves.

27. The First Trinity Church Building, Geneva, New York
Sketch by Henry Lawrence deZeng, 1809.

*Samuel H. Edsall,* Historical Sketches and Guide to Trinity Church, Geneva, New York *(Canandaigua, N.Y.: W. F. Humphrey, 1947)*

among the western churches there was "a gradual progress towards respectability." The vision of Philander Chase was being realized. Echoing his Puritan forebears, he adds: "And I hope & trust, it may in truth be ere said, with respect of this late howling desert, that y$^{e}$ wilderness buds & blossoms like y$^{e}$ rose."[170] Later he reported that the church at Geneva was in "a state of forwardness & will doubtless be finished before Christmas."[171]

Construction of the first church building in Geneva had began on All Saints' 1808 and was completed a year later. "The congregation gave

---

[170] Davenport Phelps, in Geneva, to John Henry Hobart, 2 May 1808, *AGC* 51:3.

[171] Davenport Phelps, in New York [City], to John Henry Hobart, 5 Oct. 1809, *AGC* 6:297.

$1,387 for an organ, bells, and stoves. Bishop Benjamin Moore consecrated the building during his first visit to western New York, June 9, 1810."

From 1806 to 1812 Phelps organized no less than twelve parishes, including those at Onondaga, Manlius, and Auburn. He was the first rector of Trinity Church, Geneva. The circuit and journeys to New York City on diocesan business required hard traveling on horseback. In late middle age, this man had found his vocation after many frustrations and a long search. The energy and perseverance he showed in its pursuit are astounding.

Table 5
Episcopal Parishes Organized by Davenport Phelps in New York State

| Year | Location |
|---|---|
| 1803 | St. John's Church, Onondaga Hill (now Syracuse, New York) |
| 1804 | Trinity Church, Manlius |
| 1805 | St. Peter's Church, Aurelius (now Auburn) |
| 1806 | Trinity Church, Geneva (sixth western New York parish) |
| 1807 | St. John's Church, Clifton Springs |
| 1808 | St. Peter's Church, Pultneyville |
| 1808 | St. Paul's Church, Allen's Hill (near Homeoye, New York) |
| 1809 | St. Paul's Church, Angelica, Allegany County |
| 1809 | St. John's Church, Catherine Town (now Odessa, New York) |
| 1810 | Christ Church, Chenango Point (now Binghamton, New York) |
| 1811 | St. John's Church, Sheldon (now Batavia, New York) |
| 1811 | St. Peter's Church, East Bloomfield |

*Source: Stelter,* "Davenport Phelps," 65.

In 1812, at age 57, Phelps became seriously ill. Bishop Hobart, who succeeded Benjamin Moore, had recently visited Geneva and other western parishes. Shortly thereafter Phelps informed him with his customary measured language of what he knew was a fatal illness:

> Since the first Sunday in the last month I have been providentially disabled from performing the duties of my mission, having been from that time confined with a painful infirmity, from which, it is hardly probable (as you must, I presume, be sensible, from your personal knowledge when you honoured me with an interview in your late visitation) that I shall soon, if ever, be so far

> recovered as to be again able to undergo the fatigue of attending statedly so many distant churches as are already in this county and its vicinity.[172]

It was September 1812, and, although he did not refer to it in his letter, the second war with Britain had begun, and troops were streaming through Geneva on the way to the Niagara frontier on what was to be an abortive invasion of Upper Canada. The sight of them must have stimulated strong feelings in the veteran of the 1775 invasion and the former resident of Upper Canada who had expected much from its polity. In the next year the familiar town of Niagara (the former Newark) would be occupied by American troops and disgracefully burned on their retreat.

In early 1813, Phelps retired with his family to the village of Pultneyville on the shore of Lake Ontario north of Geneva. He died there on 27 June 1813 in his fifty-eighth year. At the time his youngest child was 5, his eldest 27. His widow, Catharine, lived another 23 years.[173] The hard-working minister died without a will. His sons George Davenport and William Alexander and son-in-law, Iddo Ellis (husband to the first-born Lucy), were appointed administrators of the estate. The inventory drawn up by William and George showed a value of $1,163.92, including a $300 debt from Phelps's brother-in-law, Oliver Tiffany, in Upper Canada. The family had kept an active farm, and the inventory included a yoke of oxen, 2 cows, 26 sheep, 2 hogs as well as a horse, and farm implements, including pitchforks, corn baskets, and a grindstone. There was also a horse buggy, portmanteau, and two large trunks. Household items listed are silver spoons and forks, a candle mold, cupboards, chairs, a table, a writing desk, and ink stands. There were many books, most of those listed as religious and "sundry."[174] There was no real property, house, or land, only the wheat and grass of two fields. Eight years after Phelps's death, his remaining assets in Upper Canada were placed in charge of administrators there.[175]

---

[172] Davenport Phelps, in Geneva, to John Henry Hobart, 25 Sept. 1812, *Journals of the Conventions, Diocese of New York*, 528–29.

[173] See the Genealogical & Biographical Notes for a listing of the family.

[174] Ontario Co. [N.Y.] Surrogate Court Book 7, 18, 25. The inventory was filed on 22 July 1813.

[175] Wentworth County Surrogate Court Estate Files, Arch. Ont., Record Group 22-205, file 26, 1821, microfilm ser. 638, reel 1, 26ff.; Letters Administration, Lib.:AE, 17 (23 June 1821), Wentworth County Surrogate Court Registers, Arch. Ont., Record Group 22-204, microfilm GS 2, reel 224, 97–98. The court appointed Richard Beasley administrator, "joined by Oliver Tiffany, Physician of Ancaster, and Samuel Rice, Yeoman of Barton." Tiffany was Phelps's brother-in-law. Beasley filed, but there is no inventory. It is likely that some parcels of land remaining from the original grant were involved since a copy of that register entry is attached.

The first item in the Phelps inventory lists "1 Black woman & one child for about six years, $75.00." Though this indicates the mother was a slave, it is more likely that her status was that of a bond servant. The importation of slaves into New York State had been prohibited in 1785, when an active manumission movement began, and there were legal provisions for freeing slaves. All children born to slaves in New York State after 4 July 1799, by act of the legislature, were to have the status of bond servants to be freed (males at 25, females at 28). It was not until 1817 that slavery was entirely prohibited in New York, with all slaves to be freed within ten years.[176] Like his grandfather, this Phelps saw no contradiction between his religious teaching and the keeping of a slave in the role of a house servant.

In 1813 Davenport's brother, Eleazar Wheelock, was in Europe in the midst of his commercial, entrepreneurial career. There is no record of their relationship in their mature years. Davenport was also outlived by the Rev. Benajah Phelps, whose religious vocation in a different church and era had not been as intensely successful as his relative. Ralph Rodolphus survived Davenport by 35 years.

At the diocesan convention in the October of Phelps's death, Bishop Hobart paid tribute to him with words that reveal the affection and respect in which this latecomer to the priesthood was held:

> You have doubtless already anticipated me in the painful remark, that we no longer perceive in his place in this Convention, our venerable brother the Rev. Davenport Phelps has gone to his rest. For many years he has been employed as a missionary in the western parts of the State. Having visited the extensive district in which he officiated, I am able to bear testimony to the high estimation in which he was held for his pious and exemplary character, and for the fidelity and prudent zeal with which he discharged his arduous and laborious duties. He is justly revered as the founder of the congregations in the most western counties of the state; whom he attached, not merely to his personal ministrations, but to the doctrines, the ministry, and the Liturgy of our Church.[177]

---

[176] Ellis et al., *Short History of New York State*, 185–86.

[177] *Journals of the Convention*, 256 (6 Oct. 1813).

On his tombstone in Pultneyville Davenport Phelps was remembered as "The devoted servant of God, and the warm and unwearied friend to man."[178]

The Episcopal Church was the smallest of the venerable denominations in this land, and after the 1820s, when western New York experienced a proliferation of new sects, such as the Millerites and Mormons, among others, it was even smaller as a denominational percentage. However, with a different approach from the revival-style of the Methodists and other sects, the Episcopalians maintained and expanded an absolute presence and were notable for creating substantial church buildings and parishes in the cities that grew up along the Erie Canal. At the time of Phelps's death there were only two Episcopalian missionaries in the state. By 1830 there were 50 under Bishop Hobart.[179]

The years of sustained achievement were the last in Phelps's life. He may have seen them as some personal compensation for the failure of his pursuit of an ideal of white–Indian relations that he had acquired from his grandfather and shared with Joseph Brant. The catastrophic fate of the eastern Indians was evident to Brant before his death in 1807, and Phelps must have been equally aware of it.

---

[178] The full inscription reads: "Sacred to the memory of the Rev. Davenport Phelps who departed this life on the 27th of June, 1813, aged 57 years. He was for many years a Missionary of the Protestant Episcopal Church for the western part of the state of New York, and by his indefatigable exertions in the discharge of all the duties of the pastoral office, succeed in diffusing much religious knowledge and in forming many churches." Stelter, "Davenport Phelps," 67.

[179] There were about 6,000 communicants in the 1820s, 33,000 by 1859. Ellis et al., *Short History of New York State*, 195, 303.

Havana Septr 25th

My dear wife

We arrived here yesterday
all well. You will see by the
public papers ~~that~~ a Misfortune
occurred on our passage which
I hope will afford no uneasiness
to you ~~and~~ our dear family, and
I assure you ~~that~~ my health
was never better than at this
moment. The climate & the present
health of this place are excellent
and prospects good as can be expected.
shall write again by the first
opportunity & return as soon as
possible. Love to our dear children.

Yours Most Affectionately
E W Phelps

You may expect
another letter in about
one week after the arrival
of this

28. Eleazar Wheelock Phelps's letter to His Wife, 25 September 1818

# V

# OPPORTUNITY IN THE NEW REPUBLIC

*Some remove for merchandise and gain-sake:*
*Daily bread may be sought from far.*
—John Cotton, "God's Promise to His Plantation" [Proverbs 31:34]

## Eleazar Wheelock Phelps and His Family

"We arrived here yestr all well. You will see by the public papers that a Misfortune occurred on our passage which I hope will afford no uneasiness to you and our dear family, since I assure you that my health was never better than at this moment. The climate and the present health of this place are excellent and prospects good as can be expected." So wrote Eleazar Wheelock Phelps in September 1818 from Havana to his wife, Phebe (the Rev. Benajah's daughter), at their house on Greenwich Street, New York City.[1] The "Misfortune" he referred to was a pirate raid on the vessel that took him on an ill-fated trip to Havana.

Seven years before, when this Phelps family was well established in the town of Stafford, Connecticut, where Eleazar was an attorney and judge, there was an incident that belied the reputation of the "land of steady habits." As the husband and father deposed to the court, intruders who were known to him

> Did with force & Arms break & enter the dwelling house of the Plaintiff through a Window & through an outer door while the family of the plaintiff were asleep & did with great noise, tumult & hollowing continue in said house through the whole of said night & did threaten to pull the Plaintiff's Wife and Children out of bed & other great personal injury whereby the plaintiff's Wife & Children were much disturbed and put in great fear & disquiet.[2]

---

[1] Eleazar Wheelock Phelps, in Havana, to Phebe Phelps, in New York, 30 Sept. 1818, manuscript in possession of the author.

[2] *E. W. Phelps vs. B. Mann, L. Lyon, et al.*, re 4 Nov. 1811 trespass, Tolland County Superior Court Files, CSL, Record Group 3, box 7; Sept. 1811, Superior Court Files, CSL, Record Group 3, box 7.

In between this vandalism in Connecticut and the ill-fated trip to Havana during the years of the War of 1812, the family traveled in Europe. When the war ended, they returned to settle in New York City, just when it was becoming the most important port on the eastern Atlantic. In Stafford, Connecticut, known for its mineral springs and ironworks, Eleazar, a member of the establishment, left the practice of law and exchanged the accumulation of capital in land transactions for investment in a turnpike, whose construction he supervised. In New York the family entered into a world of commercial, impersonal relationships, where the prospect of gain attracted the adventurous.

The contrast between their origins and their new home was extreme. Eleazar was from colonial Hebron, Phebe from 1770s Nova Scotia. New York City had just entered on the age of steam. Their story is one of two worlds: the town with the mineral springs and the iron smelter and foundry in rural Connecticut, and that of New York City, where Eleazar's son in the fullness of the nineteenth century would become the merchant his father aspired to be. This family's journey took them to the cusp of the modern era.[3]

Eleazar Wheelock Phelps was seven when his father died, soon after the family removed to Lyme, New Hampshire. The child undoubtedly remembered the venerable grandfather for whom he was named more vividly than his father, as he was 13 when Eleazar Wheelock died.[4] The boy was one of the five dependent children left in their mother's care after her husband's death. Davenport, 11 years older, was probably an example for this younger brother. When Theodora remarried in 1776, the family again had a male head of the household. Eleazar was a child during the war years, and his awareness of the Revolution was limited to his brother's accounts and the news as it reached the northern valley.

The family emphasis on education extended to the younger sons. At age 19 Eleazar enrolled at Dartmouth, then led by his uncle, John

---

[3] There is a short biographical note on E. W. Phelps in Phelps 1899. A biographical sketch was made by his great-granddaughter, Julia Phelps (Haring) White in 1913, manuscript in possession of the author. The author's "An Interrupted Journey" appeared in *Seaport*, published by the South Street Seaport, New York City, Fall 1997; it includes a description of the voyage to Havana and Phelps's death there.

[4] Eleazar ("God has helped" in Hebrew) Wheelock Phelps was born at Hebron on 16 Oct. 1766, the tenth child of Alexander and Theodora Wheelock Phelps, Hebron VRs: 2:230.

Wheelock. He was there during the troubled and economically depressed years under the Confederation and left without a degree two years later.[5] He returned to his native Connecticut a short time after his departure from Dartmouth in 1787. He may have been with Davenport and his two Wheelock uncles when they began their short-lived and unsuccessful mercantile venture in Hartford. It was near there that he found through the family connection the bride he married in January 1793.

## Federal Connecticut

"Of all the different sections of the United States, Connecticut is I believe that of which the inhabitants are most orderly, and in which the laws are most easily enforced." So observed Augustus John Foster, an English visitor in the early 1800s. To him it seemed an ideal republic: "I never met with a single instance of disorderly conduct among the people, nor did I hear an oath or see a man drunk."[6] (At the end of his time in Stafford, Eleazer was to suffer many oaths as well as assault and battery.) Foster described the state's residents much as they, no doubt, would have described themselves. They were "a hardy race, very thickly located for America, and the country, which is full of hills and valleys and granite rocks, abounds in beautiful villages with neat little churches, while there is a cleanliness and an English air about everything, even to the laborers who take over their hats in passing you, which one meets with nowhere else on the American side of the Atlantic."[7]

From the 1760s on, the burgeoning population from several generations of large families put pressure on the land, as we have already seen. Connecticut men and women seized on opportunities to acquire land elsewhere, settling in Nova Scotia, New Hampshire, and New York. As the average population density increased, prices rose. Less land was available in the state, and it was more expensive.[8] This would have been a political

---

[5] *General Catalog, Dartmouth College.*

[6] Augustus John Foster, *Jeffersonian America: Notes on the United States of America Collected in the Years 1805–6–7 and 11–12 by Sir Augustus John Foster Bart.*, ed. Richard Beale Davies (San Marino, Calif.: Huntington Library, 1954), 31.

[7] Ibid., 306.

[8] Maximum densities for mixed agricultural economies are about 62 persons per square mile; Connecticut's had reached that by the 1760s. Personal communication from Christopher Collier, Connecticut State Historian, Dec. 1987.

and social pressure-cooker had emigration not provided relief. In a great diaspora, Connecticut men and women migrated north and east by the thousands. About 20 percent of the state's population left each decade, and by 1820 there were more Connecticut-born people outside the state than within it. There was thus only a modest population growth of 10 percent in the state from 1790 to 1810 (from 237,946 to 261,942), and by contrast, New England's population as a whole increased by 45 percent (led by New Hampshire and Vermont). New York's population increased by 182 percent in the same 20-year period.[9]

That there was an attractive outlet for people who would otherwise have been constrained within shrinking opportunities contributed to the stability of Connecticut society in these years. It helped a conservative and moneyed elite to remain in power and contributed to the often-remarked orderliness of its communal life.[10]

A native of Connecticut returning to his state after an absence of twenty years would have found much that was still recognizable in 1810. The farms were still entirely family-owned and largely family-operated; almost all the inhabitants were descended from the original English immigrants. The roads were slightly better, and the landscape was more open than before: forested inland areas were cut over, and there were more fields for grazing cattle and sheep. Merchants and tradesmen continued to do business almost exclusively with people they knew.

The towns, still relatively uncrowded, were largely self-sufficient, with local mills for lumber and grains, and local carpenters, blacksmiths, and other artisans. Water powered the mills, and oxen did the work of plowing and moving goods. Most houses were small and unpainted; there were few furnishings, and families lived, worked, and slept in close proximity, as they had done in colonial days. Since most families kept animals and did some farming, there was equipment lying about the trodden, muddy, or dusty ground—little or no attention to neatness. It was a rude landscape on land occupied by Europeans and their descendants for almost 175 years.[11]

---

[9] *Historical Statistics of the United States, Colonial Times to 1957* (Washington, D.C.: Government Printing Office, 1960), 13.

[10] Grossbart, "The Revolutionary Transition," 2.

[11] Kent McCallum, *Old Sturbridge Village* (New York: Harry N. Abrams, 1996), 12, 16, 20–21, 26.

There were, however, some differences that would have been obvious to our hypothetical revenant. In the cities and the river and port towns there were large painted houses that displayed the wealth of their owners. There were office buildings called banks that did not exist before; the metalworking shops in the towns were larger; there were a few textile mills, and some of the laborers in the commercial centers appeared to be living apart from their families. There was also a sense of movement—news circulated of people having migrated west and of the excellent prospects for getting land and making money elsewhere. In Connecticut itself there were more ways to make money, more people making money, and far better ways to save or transfer it around than in 1790. There were also more effective legal means to enforce contracts and collect debts. The state suffered from economic depression in the early years of the peace but was on the threshold of a period of prosperity, which Eleazar would share. In this period the economy was steadily transforming itself from a barter system into a commercial market system.

During the Revolution, Connecticut earned the sobriquet "the Provision State," as its farms and workshops supplied the Continental army. The steep postwar slump was not relieved until the new federal government assumed the debts of the states and introduced a national currency. This brought a standard of value that increased the reliability of exchange and thereby aided the circulation of money. The first banks and insurance companies, used by entrepreneurs to accumulate and invest capital, were started in the state in the 1790s. Merchants still employed barter as a form of exchange, but money in the form of notes issued by the banks was increasingly in circulation. The greater amounts of capital generated in the quickening economy were invested in metal shops, the first textile mills, and, by the end of the 1790s, turnpikes, one of which would occupy Eleazar in the 1800s.[12]

The transformation of Connecticut from a largely self-sufficient economy to a commercial, trading-based economy in the half century from 1750 has been called an "economic revolution": "[C]ommercially-minded farmers . . . produced large surpluses of grain, flaxseed, and especially livestock and meat and dairy products, and in so doing more fully exploited Connecticut's inland regions . . . The desire to produce for markets also affected manufactures so that manufacturing became a major sector of the economy."[13]

---

[12] This summary is based on Saladino, "Economic Revolution."

[13] Ibid., 1.

The "dominant figures of the economic revolution" were the merchants, according to the business historian Alfred D. Chandler, Jr. Following the example of his mentor in Stafford, John Phelps, Eleazar would become one such figure.

> Acting in tightly knit groups, they encouraged expansion by taking risks, mobilizing capital, and institutionalizing economic activities. In the 1790s, for instance, merchants (along with some farmers) formed turnpikes and river improvement companies in order to get goods to and from market towns—the *foci* of economic life. To promote trade and commerce, they organized banks and marine insurance companies. Influenced by businessmen, the state government in the 1790s emerged as a positive force for economic growth, incorporating a multitude of banks, turnpikes, and insurance companies.[14]

The merchants of the early national period performed functions similar to those of their colonial predecessors:

> The resident merchant acted as the community's financier and was responsible for the transportation as well as the distribution of goods. He provided short-term loans to finance staple crops and manufactured goods when they were in transit, and he made long term loans to planters, farmers and artisans to enable them to clear land or improve their facilities . . . he insured ships and cargoes . . . and by himself and with others built distilleries, candle works, ropewalks [or an iron works in John Phelps's case] . . . In all these activities, the colonial merchant knew personally most of the individuals involved.[15]

The incorporated cities of Hartford, Middletown, New London, Norwich, and New Haven were the hubs of trade and transportation. Else-

---

[14] Ibid.

[15] Alfred D. Chandler, Jr., *The Visible Hand: The Managerial Revolution in American Business* (Cambridge, Mass., and London: Harvard Univ. Press, Belknap Press, 1977), 17–18. See also Glenn Porter and Harold C. Livesay, *Merchants and Manufacturers: Studies in the Changing Structure of Nineteenth-Century Marketing* (Baltimore, Md.: Johns Hopkins Univ. Press, 1971), chapter 1. While changes were under way, they were less drastic than what was to come with the full-scale industrialization of the mid-nineteenth century. The turnpikes of the early 1800s facilitated the movement of goods but added only marginally to the speed of transfer and not at all to the carrying capacity. While Eli Whitney's cotton gin (1793) prepared raw cotton so it could be converted to thread in quantity, it was only after 1815 that the full effect of this was felt in the New England textile industry. In the 1790s firearms and buttons in Connecticut shops had begun to be made of uniform, machined parts using a division of labor. Early factories were beginning to replace the craft shops of colonial days. Real industrialization was to come later. In commercial life "the general merchant" still ruled, trading a variety of goods and using notes as the primary medium of exchange.

where most people lived on farms in rural towns. Men like John Phelps and Eleazar Wheelock Phelps in Stafford, who had other occupations, also kept animals and grew crops. The disparity of population between town and city was far less than it became. In 1790, for example, Hebron with its 2,304 people was more than half the size of Hartford with its 4,090. Stafford in the same year had a population of 1,885. The political and social culture remained centered largely on the towns as it had been in colonial times.[16]

The basic economic and social unit in Connecticut, as in the nation, remained the family.[17] The "family, not the conjugal unit, and certainly not the individual, stood at the center of economic and social existence . . . even as the wider economic structure was undergoing a massive transformation."[18] This generation of the Phelps family were living midway in change; the household economy was not so different from that of late colonial days (although there were more goods available for purchase), but Eleazar's business life was becoming increasingly subject to larger economic forces. In New York City the family would become part of commercial society, living in a populous and impersonal place, engaged in increasingly impersonal transactions.

## Marriage

Young Eleazar settled in the rocky town of Stafford, on the Massachusetts border. At some point after his return to the state in the late 1780s, he met up with the Rev. Benajah Phelps, his father's half-blood first cousin. It was an eastward journey of only about 20 miles from Hartford across the river to Orford Parish, where this cousin was pastor. He doubtless heard from him the story of the Nova Scotian escape years before. It was Phebe, Benajah's second eldest, named for her mother, who attracted him. In January 1793, at age 27, he married this half-blood first cousin once removed.

---

[16] A re-creation of that world is found today in Old Sturbridge Village in Worcester County, Mass., on the Connecticut border, less than 20 miles east of the Stafford where this Phelps family lived many years. The buildings and other exhibits and reenactments in the village show the life of New England from 1790 to 1840, the first two decades of which are those of this Phelps family's life in Stafford. McCallum, *Old Sturbridge Village*, 9.

[17] "Only 202,000 of the 3.9 million Americans lived in towns and villages of more than 2,500." Chandler, *Visible Hand*, 27.

[18] James Henretta et al., eds. *The Transformation of Early American History: Society, Authority, Ideology* (New York: Alfred A. Knopf, 1991), 32.

Phebe was then 23, a woman who had already experienced considerable difficulties in her short life.[19] She was eight when her father fled Cornwallis. For two years her mother was one of those wives separated from husbands during the war who had "to make crucial decisions involving not only household and family, but also the 'outdoor affairs'" from which women were excluded when the husband was present.[20] Phebe was then old enough to help her mother with the household and with the care of her two-year-old younger sister. With her mother and her two sisters, young Phebe crossed the waters from Nova Scotia, probably to Boston, and thence to Connecticut. The disruption of wartime brought challenges that, when successfully met, developed confidence and ability to deal with change. In that sense Phebe was one of the young "Liberty's Daughters."[21] This experience and a strong character stood her in good stead as she established a household in a growing town, mothered six children over fourteen years, accompanied her family to Europe, established a household in New York, and, as a widow, managed her own affairs there and, later, in Fairfield, Connecticut. She lived to the eve of the Civil War.

Eleazar and Phebe's marriage vows were recorded at the First Society in Stafford on 12 January 1793.[22] They remained in Stafford for the next eighteen years, and all their children were born there. Benajah Phelps's Orford Parish church was a day's ride from Stafford. Land and court records show that in later years he was occasionally involved in his son-in-law's affairs. Both he and his wife Phebe were alive throughout almost all of the 27 years of their daughter's marriage.[23] Benajah's only son, Ralph Rodolphus, became a lawyer and represented his brother-in-law in litigation in the early 1800s.[24]

---

[19] Phebe, daughter of Rev. Benajah and Phebe (Denison) Phelps, was born at Cornwallis, N.S., 7 Oct. 1770, *Cornwallis Town Book*. See the Genealogical & Biographical Notes.

[20] Norton, *Liberty's Daughters*, 195.

[21] Ibid.

[22] Stafford VRs. See the Genealogical & Biographical Notes.

[23] Phebe and Eleazar Wheelock Phelps were admitted to the Stafford Ecclesiastical Society on 23 Nov. 1794. Stafford First Congregational Church, Stafford, Conn., Church Records Collection, CSL, LBG:87 [hereinafter cited as Stafford Church Records].

[24] E. W. Phelps sold Ralph Rodolphus Phelps one half acre of land in Stafford for $250, recorded 15 May 1809. In May 1811 he paid pew rent to the Stafford Society. Stafford Land Records 10:177. Stafford First Congregational Church, Society Meetings 1803–37, minutes of 21 May 1811, 2:17.

As for the paternal in-laws, there seems to have been little further direct contact. Eleazar's mother was living in New Hampshire, where she remained until her death in 1810.[25] His oldest brother, Davenport, as we have seen, was in Upper Canada in 1792, and there is no record of his meeting up with Eleazar in later life. Similarly, there is no record of the other siblings having contact with the Stafford family.

## Stafford

Stafford (the present-day Stafford Springs) borders Massachusetts east of the Connecticut River; it was named for the northern English town. There were 315 families living there in 1790, with an average of slightly over three persons per household (thus small, probably mostly young families).[26] Because it was so far inland, Stafford was settled slowly and rather late in the eighteenth century. In 1718 the General Assembly approved the division of the land into allotments essentially within the later limits of the town, but it was nearly forty years before Stafford was large enough to send delegates to Assembly meetings.[27]

The most distinguishing geographic feature of the place is the Willimantic River, which flows south through a long valley. Its narrowness prevented the usual New England cluster of buildings around a common or green, and the main street stretched north to south, parallel to the river. In 1771 John Adams observed this "fine spacious Road laid out very wide, and of great Length and quite strait . . . with the Meeting House in the middle of it."[28] Twenty years later a visitor described "the spacious Stafford street, extending two miles in length, within parallel lines fifteen rods apart, with here and there a house on each side." Its "magnificence" faded, however, "when viewed in parts as . . . each side of the narrow road was full of rocks and bushes, except such spaces as afforded a common

---

[25] See the Genealogical & Biographical Notes.

[26] 1790 U.S. census, Connecticut.

[27] Hughes and Allen, *Connecticut Place Names*; Pease and Niles, *Gazette of Connecticut and Rhode Island* (Hartford, 1819), 297; J. R. Cole, *History of Tolland County* (New York: W. W. Preson, 1888), 2:485.

[28] John Adams, *Diary and Autobiography of John Adams*, ed. L. H. Butterfield (Cambridge, Mass.: Harvard Univ. Press, Belknap Press, 1961), 2:24.

pasture for cows, swine, sheep, and geese."[29] In the early 1800s Timothy Dwight described a "loosely built village upon a street running north and south, over elevated ground, and having a church without a steeple."[30]

Two routes provided access to the town, a west–east road from the Connecticut River valley through Suffield and Somers and a south–north road from the county seat of Tolland. Both connected to a post road to Boston, the first in Killingly in the eastern corner of Connecticut, and the second to Worcester in the north.[31] Stafford was "on the map" and better known because of its springs than many other towns at the time, making it attractive to an ambitious young man.

The religious life of Connecticut townspeople in the last decades of the eighteenth century had settled down somewhat after the excitement of the Great Awakening of only thirty years before. The pastor of the Stafford First Society was a scholarly, dedicated man serving during an era of tepid religious feeling. Adams visited the Rev. John Willard, a Harvard classmate, whose parsonage beside the meetinghouse he pronounced a "little, mean looking Hutt." Adams lamented that like him, "many of my Contemporaries at College . . . worthy Men live in poor and low Circumstances!" (Willard, whose brother became the president of Harvard and sent his son to prepare for college with him, was pastor for 36 years, and it was he who heard the Phelps's marriage vows. Samuel, his son, became the town doctor and proprietor of the springs and was closely associated with Phelps in the early 1800s.)

Interest in religion and support for the established church declined as the century advanced; the Enlightenment's faith in rationality and a deist God had pulled attention away from established Congregationalism. "Infidelity" became a frequent topic of sermons. After the Revolution,

---

[29] Sidney Willard, *Memories of Youth and Manhood* (Cambridge, Mass.: John Bartlett, 1853), 1:231, also 131, 242, 244; J. R. Cole, *History of Tolland County*, 2:492–95; Kenneth Grobel, *History of the First Church of Stafford, Connecticut, known as "The Stafford Street Congregational Church": from its Birth 1723 to its Death 1892* (Stafford Springs, Conn.: 1942), 41 ff.; *Willard Genealogy*, compiled by Joseph Willard and Charles Wilkes Walker, edited and completed by Charles Henry Pope (Boston: privately printed, 1915), 1:91.

[30] Dwight, quoted in *The History of the Town of Stafford* (Stafford, Conn.: Stafford Library Association, 1935), 10.

[31] Isabel S. Mitchell, *Roads and Road-Making in Colonial Connecticut* (New Haven: Yale Univ. Press, Tercentenary Commission of the State of Connecticut, 1934), vol. 15, map: "Connecticut at the End of the Colonial Period."

competing sects, principally Baptists and Methodists, who had more democratic governance and greater emotional appeal, pulled membership from the Congregational churches. Stafford is an example: its 315 families in 1790 divided their allegiances between the Congregationalists, the Baptists, and one of the first Universalist congregations in the state. The First Society, of which Willard was pastor, was riven by conflicts, and the congregation was unable to decide on a new meetinghouse for years and continued to support its learned parson on a pittance. After the secession of a part of the congregation, the finances of the church were so poor that a committee, including E. W. Phelps, sought aid from the lottery under the control of the General Assembly. He was also on a committee three years later that requested the aged Rev. Willard to "desist" from preaching, as the Society was so "few in number" that they were unable to pay him.[32]

## Water and Iron

In the 1760s news of a cure from the Stafford waters attracted health seekers from Boston and elsewhere, and it became the first American spa. (The Indians had been aware of the healing properties of the waters for years before this "discovery.") It continued to be a well-frequented center for "taking the waters" into the next century. A regular stage service from Boston ("for the middling sort") even allowed baggage to be sent ahead.[33] Visitors to the springs stimulated the economy of the town, and in the early 1800s prompted Phelps and others to finance a turnpike to improve access.

John Adams, then a Boston attorney, visited the springs in 1771 and wrote in his diary, in characteristically vivid terms, what has become the best-known description of them.[34] The spring "arises at the Foot of a Steep, high hill, between a Cluster of Rocks, very near the Side of a River. The Water is very Clear, limpid and transparent, the Rocks and Stones and Earth at the Bottom are tinged with a reddish yellow Colour, and so is the little Wooden Gutter that is placed at the Mouth of the Spring to carry the

---

[32] Stafford First Congregational Church, Society Meetings 1803–37, minutes of 29 April 1806, 19 Sept. 1806, 2:9, 10.

[33] Carl Bridenbaugh, "Baths and Watering Places of Colonial America," *William and Mary Quarterly*, 3rd ser., vol. 3, no. 2 (April 1946): 151–81.

[34] *Diary and Autobiography of John Adams*, 2:15–27. Adams was in Stafford 2–7 June 1771.

Water off—indeed, the Water communicates that Colour which resembles that of the Rust of Iron, to whatever object it washes." Its taste was that of "Fair water with an Infusion of some preparation of Steel in it."

The other natural resource that gave rise to industry in Stafford was iron. With his sharp ear for developments, Adams had learned of men "who are about erecting Iron Mills here, Furnaces, etc." One of these was Col. Abijah Willard, a distant relative of the reverend, who had started an iron foundry. Four years later he lost what he had developed when the local Sons of Liberty ran him out of town for his Loyalist sympathies. This may have cleared the way for John Phelps to develop the furnace that bore his name, which was in operation in 1777 to supply cannon shot to the patriot cause.[35]

John Phelps (ca. 1728–1804) was an entrepreneur, who became the leading citizen of Stafford after the Revolution; the "Major Phelps House," by the meetinghouse, was the most prominent in the village. Its owner was the "superintendent and principal proprietor of the furnace for casting hollow iron ware," recalled Sydney Willard, who prepared for Harvard with the Reverend John in the 1790s. "There was but one chaise in Stafford," but as John Phelps was a man of simple tastes, "it was seldom used, and . . . he and his wife generally preferred the saddle and the pinion."[36]

John Phelps is likely to have attracted his distant cousin Eleazar to Stafford. They shared descent from William Phelps of Windsor, but there were no common intervening forebears. John had come to Stafford as a young man in the late 1750s from his birthplace, the river town of Suffield. His father was an early purchaser of land in Stafford.[37] When the opportunity came during the Revolution, he started the Phelps foundry. This was the earliest and most prominent industry in Stafford and, along with his trading interests, made John Phelps a well-to-do man. Eleazar, who became his attorney, was involved in many of the same enterprises.[38]

---

[35] *Diary and Autobiography of John Adams,* 2:24; *Willard Genealogy,* 1:58–59.

[36] Willard, *Memories of Youth and Manhood,* 2:239.

[37] An 1801 deed that includes the furnace that was developed by John Phelps refers to it as on land formerly of Timothy Phelps, presumably John's father of Suffield. Stafford Land Records 8:407.

[38] John Phelps's first land purchase in Stafford was an 86-acre piece with dwelling house for £275 in 1757. In 1770 he purchased from Abijah Willard and William Brown, the proponents of the iron furnace noted by Adams, a quitclaim deed for 25 acres, executed in Worcester, Mass. Stafford Land Records, 3:80, 166. John Phelps and his wife, Mary (Richardson), were admitted to the First Society in 1770. See "Phelps II" in the Genealogical & Biographical Notes.

John Phelps's local eminence led to political office. The Council of the General Assembly in 1785 commissioned him major in the Connecticut militia and appointed him justice of peace for the first time (and reappointed him annually until his death in 1804). In 1793 the assembly awarded him the more influential and lucrative position of judge of probate, also renewed in succeeding years.[39]

The Stafford freemen chose John Phelps as a delegate to the Connecticut convention to ratify the federal Constitution, held in Hartford in January 1788. He voted with the large majority in favor, following the Federalist position under the leadership of Oliver Ellsworth, the influential Connecticut delegate to the Constitutional Convention in Philadelphia. He thereby supported Ellsworth's appeal to support "a more energetic system" of union, which would enable a common defense and lead to a stronger economy. The federation was important to Connecticut, as it would protect it from "the ambition and rapacity of New-York" and thus preserve "peace among ourselves."[40] In the same issue of the *Connecticut Courant* that recorded his affirmative vote, John Phelps advertised his furnace and its products.

The economic benefit of federation to Connecticut was fulfilled when the new federal government, under Secretary of the Treasury Alexander Hamilton's advocacy, assumed the debts of the states. This relieved the potential tax burden on the state's well-to-do and enabled them to invest in land and productive enterprises, which quickened the local economy.

The federal Constitution was widely supported in Connecticut, and not just by the moneyed establishment. Delegates from most rural towns joined delegates from the five incorporated cities in affirmative votes; there was no distinct pattern to the negative votes. John Phelps and Stafford, with its ironworks and springs, supported what one scholar has called the "cosmopolitan" position.[41]

While the little-used chaise was a luxury and a sign of wealth, the possessions listed in John Phelps's estate after his death show more closely the mixture of elegance and simplicity of this man of modest wealth. In the house there were "Silver flatware, china, carpet, beds and coverings," revealing the elegant items a man of his station could purchase. But there

---

[39] See "Phelps II" in the Genealogical & Biographical Notes.

[40] *PRSC*, 6:554; *Connecticut Courant* 7, 14 Jan. 1788.

[41] Personal communication from Christopher Collier, Dec. 1997; the term "cosmopolitan" is used by Grossbart, *Revolutionary Transition*, 13, 270.

was still farming to be done, and his estate also included "harrow teeth, ox cart, and plow." His library comprised the Bible, *Pilgrim's Progress,* and law books. He owned half a pew in the meetinghouse.[42]

## John Phelps and the "Standing Order"

The so-called Federalist Era in Connecticut lasted until the calling of a state constitutional convention in 1817. Until the new state constitution, Connecticut government continued with much the same blend of executive, judicial, and legislative powers as there had been in late colonial days, and Congregationalism remained the established church. State and most local governments were dominated by the "standing order" as they had been in colonial days, composed of men representing "family, wealth, talents . . . the bulwark of the church, the state and of law and order." Their wealth was based on trade, real estate, and—beginning in the 1790s—banks, insurance companies, and manufactures. John Phelps and Eleazar after him fit squarely into this mold. The executive branch of state government was the council, composed of the governor and members of the assembly. Its appointing power "allowed it to control every judge and Justice of the Peace."[43] Unlike states to the south and west, Connecticut voters did not take part in the movement that put the Jeffersonian-Republicans in power across the country in 1800.

The Federalist establishment shared an aversion to democracy, viewing its spread as a prelude to anarchy, with ominous comparisons to ancient Rome. The intensity of their fear of the opposition increased over the course of the 1790s, fueled by the news of the French Revolution's Terror of 1793. As the Jeffersonian victory in 1800 appeared to threaten private property, the "standing order" vigorously and frequently suppressed opposition.[44] This opposition supported tax and economic reform, increased democratization, and disestablishment of Congregationalism as the religion of the state—views that attracted the "state's yeomen, urban and rural artisans, and the growing number of dissenting church mem-

---

[42] John Phelps survived two wives and was buried by a third. Estate of John Phelps and Executor's Account of Expenses, Town of Stafford, Stafford Probate District, CSL, box 1372, packet 1705 (FHL film 1,018,463).

[43] *PRSC*, 9–15; Purcell, *Connecticut in Transition*, 126, 128, 193.

[44] Grossbart, *Revolutionary Transition*, 275.

bers," whose influence, however, was not decisive until the 1817 convention.[45]

John Phelps was elected to the General Assembly for the first time in 1786 and re-elected through the 1790s. We have a view of these legislators from Henry Wansey, an English visitor who attended a session of the General Assembly in Hartford in 1794 and found them, "plain in their dress, plain in their manners; with no other qualifications than good common-sense, actuated by the love of their country." These men "were very temperate, not sitting long after dinner—we sat down to dinner at one and by a quarter after two they adjourned to the house . . . out of 177 members, there was but six absent." A "Mr. Phelps" was among those who "made as good speeches as many I have heard in our own House of Commons."[46]

John Phelps was a merchant and trader as well as the guiding force behind the Phelps furnace. The Tolland County Court records have clues to activities at the time, which came to involve the services of Eleazar. Traders in the name of "John Phelps & Co." were plaintiffs in a number of proceedings in the 1790s, and "John Phelps, Esq. of Stafford" and his son "Timothy Phelps of New Haven" are cited in all the references to the company.[47] In one proceeding "Elijah Austin and Jeremiah Atwater of New Haven" and "Benjamin Gale & Sam'l Gale of Killingworth, New London County merchants and traders" are listed in an action to reclaim £12 owed.[48] (In 1795 John Phelps acted as administrator of Austin's estate.[49]) "Daniel Phelps, Lebanon, Grafton Co., New Hampshire" is mentioned in connection with several cases; this is probably John Phelps's son of that name.[50]

Most of the Phelps & Co. cases were actions on debt, often for small amounts. For example, the partners secured £12 from Amaziah Weston of Norwich in 1792[51] and £9 14*s* from Benajah Holcomb of Granby (an

---

[45] Ibid., 17.

[46] As there were three Phelps in the Assembly at that time, this may not refer to John, but it gives a sense of the quality of the deliberations in which he was involved. Henry Wansey, *Journal of an Excursion to the United States of America, 1794* (Salisbury, England, 1796), 40.

[47] Timothy Phelps, b. 1757 (Phelps 1899), was John Phelps's second child and first son.

[48] Tolland County Court Files, CSL, Record Group 3, box 89, case 30029.

[49] Ibid., box 92, case 28625 (Feb. 1795).

[50] See "Phelps II" in the Genealogical & Biographical Notes.

[51] Tolland County Court Files, CSL, Record Group 3, box 89, case 29626 (Feb. 1792).

example of old currency still in use). In 1797 Phelps brought action against Ebeneezer Thresher of Stafford for £15 ("Now converted to $70").[52] The actions with the largest sums at stake were against vendors of "coal" (as charcoal was termed locally) for failure to deliver it to the furnace; in 1797 the amounts said to be in default were large—2,110 and 2,104 bushels.[53] John Phelps and his partners also traded in other commodities. In one case the company sued a Norwich man for failure to deliver "Neat Cattle, Bulls & Staggs at the Connecticut River."[54]

In 1797, four years after his marriage, Eleazar Wheelock Phelps is listed as John Phelps's clerk of probate.[55] He wrote the judgment meting out a harsh action against Ebeneezer Thresher for failure to pay an award of $52.75 plus $5.42 costs. "On 4 April 1797," he reported the seizure of property to make up the fine, which "was levied on one horse & two oxen . . . delivered to the constable at the sign post neer the meeting house in the first society in s^d Stafford on 24 April." The sheriff had also attached "two cows of a reddish color" for payment of this debt.[56] Thresher and his brother James had earlier mounted up a debt of $372.94 for failure to deliver charcoal to the furnace.[57]

These cases show how the courts supported the merchants even for what seems to be quite minor indebtedness. The seizure of Thresher's horse, oxen, and "cows of a reddish color" seems harsh at this distance, and an action that cannot have endeared young Phelps to the general populace. He was never listed as a partner in John Phelps & Co., but as a justice of the peace he participated in several of later actions. Other court records show him as the clerk of the probate court presided over by John Phelps.

John Phelps, his company, and partners were engaged not only in the furnace but in trade involving merchants in the port towns of New Haven and Killingworth. The involvement of Daniel Phelps of New Hampshire indicates trade up the river as well. John Phelps's activities fit the description of a general merchant: he traded in a variety of goods and with individuals whom he personally knew.

---

52 Ibid., box 94, case 27843.

53 Ibid., box 95, case 27717; box 89, case 278845; case 27846.

54 Ibid., case 296526.

55 Ibid., box 89, case 827845 (Feb. 1797).

56 Ibid., box 96, case 27676 (Sept. 1797).

57 Ibid., box 94, case 27847 (Feb. 1797).

According to the 1797 assessment record, John Phelps owned "a grist mill, 1 horse, 2 oxen, 3 cows (3 yrs old), 2 neat cattle (2 yrs old), 14 acres Tillage land, 40 acres English Mowing & Clear Pasture, 3 acres Bog Meadow, 30 acres Bush Pasture, 56 acres 2nd Rate unimproved land." He also had the possessions of a gentleman: "1 silver watch, 4 wooden clocks, 1 Fin Pl [fine plate]"; and "John Phelps & Compy" had 3 acres of "Ist Rate unimproved land, 3 acres of 2nd rate unimproved land."[58]

Phelps's furnace sold cannon shot and cannon to the Continental army, giving rise to an industrial operation that lasted for over 50 years. The furnace produced hollowware, cast-iron kettles, Franklin stoves, potash kettles, tea kettles, skillets, hammers, and anvils. The local bog iron was considered particularly suitable for the casting of the hollowware that was the specialty of the Phelps Furnace. The Willimantic River powered the bellows for the furnace and later provided the power for the hammers when the foundry was built.

The organization of the furnace provided a perfect example of the industrialization of the Connecticut economy. In this era the "largest business unit either in mining or manufacturing [were] iron plantations," according to Alfred D. Chandler, Jr., and "with their rural setting, the seasonal nature of their work . . . [they] operated in many ways like the rice and tobacco plantations of the southern colonies."

Such an operation required entrepreneurial initiative, capital, and the management skills to coordinate the various labor and marketing. Two men or two men and a boy could produce from two to five tons of iron a week from a foundry of this type in the late eighteenth century. Eight to nine men were needed for the operation of the furnace and the forge. In addition there were woodcutters, charcoal burners, carters, and common laborers.[59]

---

[58] In the 1797 poll tax "John Phelps & Compy Gristmill" was assessed $50. List of the Polls, Estate, and Assessments of the First Society in the Town of Stafford in 1797, East Parish, Office of Town Clerk, Stafford, Conn.

[59] For early iron smelting and foundry technologies see Zelotes W. Coombs, "Early Blast Furnace Operations in Worcester County," *The Worcester Historical Society Publications*, n.s., 2, no. 3 (Sept. 1938), 138–52; George Winterhalter Schultz, "Antique Iron Works and Machines of the Water Power Age," *Bulletin of the Historical Society of Montgomery County, Pennsylvania* 5, no. 4 (April 1947): 291–310; W. H. C. Pynchon, "Iron Mining in Connecticut," *Connecticut Magazine* 5 (1899), 20–26, 232–38, 277–85.

A smelter of this type was 20–30 feet high and built of stone or brick. The fuel in this period was commonly charcoal, burned in a hearth in a pit at its base. In Stafford this was lined with the white fire-resistant stone that was abundant in the northern part of the town. The air "blast" to keep the fire ignited came from bellows powered by a water wheel. Once the fire was built, it was maintained for an entire season. This required a 24-hour watch to replenish the fuel, feed the ore, and separate the molten iron from the silicon and other impurities released by the heat. The "bog iron" feedstock, brought by wagon from surface excavations, was dumped from a ramp into the top of the chimney.

In a furnace of this size about eight tons of iron were smelted per week, which required 24 80-bushel loads of fuel. One load of "mine," as it was called (18 bushels of mixed ore that was broken and already roasted), was added to each load of fuel. The blast was at its height in about ten weeks, and a hearth of good stone would last forty "foundays," or weeks.

Cast iron is brittle. To prepare the more useful "wrought" iron, two large movable arms with iron sledges powered by the river were used to hammer the molten iron. These hammered a mass of molten metal weighing about 75 pounds and placed on an iron plate.

The furnace and forge remained in operation throughout John Phelps's lifetime and continued under other ownership until 1837. In 1796 another forge was built by Nathaniel Hyde, who was later associated with E. W. Phelps in the turnpike project.[60]

As the ultimate grace note for a successful man of property, John Phelps sat for a portrait in 1794. The artist was Ralph Earl, then the most prominent portraitist in Connecticut, who made a specialty of prosperous Federalists in the river towns. Earl characteristically painted a landscape in the background of his portraits to display the house and park of the sitter. For John Phelps, the ironmaker, he showed the furnace, and made its fire the most striking element of the painting. Phelps is shown seated in full side view, a tall man of substantial build in uniform in a pose evocative of Washington.[61]

---

[60] Cole, *History of Tolland County*, 2:503.

[61] A photograph of the portrait was included in Phelps 1899. Ralph Earl (1751–1801) painted Roger Sherman, Oliver Wolcott, and Chief Justice and Mrs. Oliver Ellsworth among other eminent sitters in Connecticut in the late 1780s and 1790s. See Elizabeth Mankin Kornhauser et al., *Ralph Earl: The Face of the Young Republic* (Hartford: Wadsworth Atheneum, 1991). On 23 May 1996 the John Phelps portrait was consigned by the William Lyon Phelps Foundation and sold to a private buyer at an auction conducted by Christie's New York (Sale 8,408, lot 3). The buyer did not reply to the author's request through Christie's to identify its present location.

## Eleazar Wheelock Phelps in Stafford

The births of the eight children of Phebe and Eleazar Wheelock Phelps came at roughly two-year intervals in the sixteen years between 1794 and1810; four of the six girls and the two boys survived childhood. The relatively small number of children over a shorter span, compared to eighteenth-century patterns, conforms to the demographic trends of the period.

This generation of the family no longer used Old Testament names. Eliza (1794–?), perhaps named for her mother's older sister, was born the year after the marriage. Harriet (1796–1876) was next, then Phebe (1799–1883), named for her mother and grandmother. The short-lived Emelia (1801–1805) followed her. George Alexander (1803–1880) was the first boy, perhaps named for the late president, as there was no George on either side in this family; his middle name honored the grandfather whom his own father had barely known. Julia Maria (1805) died in infancy, and Mary Amelia (1807–?) was the last born of the daughters. There seems to be no family origin for the first name of the last child, Henry Davenport (1810–1875), but his middle name perpetuated the Davenport line through his long-deceased great-grandmother. The two who died young, Emelia and Julia Maria, were buried in the First Society graveyard.[62]

In the United States census of 1800, the listing for E. W. Phelps included only one person (probably a servant) other than the immediate family. Eleven years later, an inventory of the household property revealed a well-to-do household, with home occupations for Phebe and her four daughters.

The law was Eleazar's route to local eminence. Four years after his marriage, the Council of the General Assembly appointed him justice of peace in Stafford in 1797. (Concurrently it reappointed John Phelps to the same office—there were several in each of the counties.) "The law being in this state the high-road to popular favor," wrote an English visitor to Connecticut in 1808, "the persons usually elected are lawyers."[63] As we have seen, it did not take long for the two distantly related Phelpses to become close colleagues; in 1797 E. W. Phelps served as clerk of the probate court of which the elder Phelps was the judge.[64] In the 1797 poll

---

[62] See "Phelps I" in the Genealogical & Biographical Notes.

[63] Foster, *Jeffersonian America*, 306.

[64] Purcell, *Connecticut in Transition*, 126, 128, 193; *PRSC*, 9; Tolland County Court Files, CSL, Record Group 3, box 94, packet 27845, Feb. 1797.

"E. W. Phelps Atty at Law" had the highest assessment of any listed, $167, twice that of "Willard & Alden traders," who were the next highest. His property was listed as "1 horse, 1 cow (3 yrs old), 2 acres Tillage Land, 3 acres English Mowing & Clear Pasture, 10 acres Bush pasture and 5 acres 2nd Rate unimproved land."[65]

By the time he was in his early 30s, the younger Phelps had been accepted by the governing establishment of the state and was linked to the leading citizen of Stafford. He was annually reappointed as justice of the peace until his departure in 1811 and was identified with the "Esq." that signified his office. As a lawyer, he followed in his father's footsteps and was a member of a profession growing in numbers and influence. There were more lawyers in Connecticut after the Revolution, with more work available to them, and it was common for each town to have one or two. Many Connecticut lawyers in this period were Yale graduates or had been trained by Tapping Reeve in his Litchfield academy. Phelps must have learned his law as an apprentice and trained himself, as had his father.[66]

He was not litigious on his own behalf, as there is only one such case in the available court records (some appear to be missing). His action of debt for $36 against Paul Blodgett and Samuel Trask of Stafford led the attachment of "one chaise" at the order of the court. This could be an indication of a harsh quality that could be resented by fellow townsmen. As we have seen, he was also associated with John Phelps in pursuit of similarly small debts. The pinnacle of his legal career came at the end of Eleazar's years in Stafford when, in 1810 and 1811, he was appointed to the prestigious and lucrative position of judge of probate and became known as Judge Phelps.[67]

E. W. Phelps was well placed to participate in the trading of property. The land records of Stafford reveal that he bought and sold land in prominent locations—and for substantial amounts—throughout his almost 18 years' residency in the town. There were 21 transactions in all. In these transactions he was often associated with John Phelps and in the 1800s

---

[65] List of the Polls, Estate and Assessments of the First Society in the Town of Stafford in 1797, East Parish.

[66] E. W. Phelps was not among the 1,000 students recorded as having attended the Tapping Reeve Academy. Personal communication from Cathie Fields, Director, Litchfield [Conn.] Historical Society, 24 Aug. 1996.

[67] Appointed May 1810 and May 1811 for the year ensuing. *PRSC*, 15:13, 158.

with Dr. Samuel Willard, the owner of the springs and advocate of their medical benefits. He followed the way of his father and other enterprising Connecticut men from the earliest days of European settlement by using land transactions as a means to build wealth.

In 1800 Phelps bought three pieces of land for $700, one a farm of 40 acres, which he sold the next year for $200, another for $450 (this included a mortgage deed with a provision for repayment "in iron hollow ware"). In 1801 with Samuel Willard, John Phelps, and others, he purchased for $800 one fourth of an interest in land on which the furnace lay. This site included "one gristmill, one furnace & coal house . . . the Cook house & Store." (This deed was witnessed by his father-in-law, Benajah Phelps.) In 1803 E. W. Phelps, John Phelps, and Samuel Willard and the other joint tenants of the ironworks property sold it for $2,000 to John Taylor Greene of Stafford. This apparently ended the family connection with the furnace 24 years after it was first put into operation. (John Phelps died the following year.)

In 1802 Phelps, with five others as joint tenants in common, purchased for $1,700 from Samuel Willard, four parcels, on one of which was a sawmill. Phelps used a note for $600 from the Hartford Bank for his purchase, an example of the increased availability of bank financing at the time. This was an extensive transaction consisting of: (1) 40 acres with buildings, (2) 55 acres "with one quarter of the sawmill lately owned by Solomon Moulton," (3) a "parcel of 60 acres with buildings thereon standing," (4) a parcel of 12½ acres, and (5) two others containing 14 ½ acres.

In 1806 Eleazar and three associates sold to Samuel Willard a piece "containing 105 acres known by the name of the mineral spring estate."[68] Dr. Samuel Willard, an exact contemporary of young Phelps, succeeded John Phelps in the early 1800s as the most prominent of Stafford citizens. Like his father, he was a Harvard graduate. He opened a medical practice in the town in 1791 and was the town druggist and owner of a general merchandise shop. In the early 1800s he built the Springs Hotel for visitors to the waters and used his medical knowledge to promote the springs.[69]

The younger Phelps was John Phelps's personal lawyer and was entrusted with the execution of his will in January 1804, a few months before the elder Phelps's death, his faint signature showing he was seri-

---

[68] Stafford Land Records, 9:298.

[69] Samuel Willard, Stafford, Conn. 1766–Cincinnati, Ohio 1820. *Willard Genealogy* 176–77; Cole, *History of Tolland County*, 2:502.

ously ill. The will contained detailed instructions in connection with Elizabeth, his widow, and the children, all from the first of his three marriages. The estate inventory was valued at $5,471 and took years to settle. In a curious twist, in 1809 the probate court, determining that the co-executor, John's son Timothy, "has absconded and gone to parts unknown," appointed E. W. Phelps the sole executor. Phelps received $801 for his administration.[70]

The Jeffersonian Republican sweep of 1800 did not include Connecticut, and the Federalist establishment remained in control of the state government and most of the towns until the end of the next decade. There were challenges, however, and local rank and influence could be attacked. In 1802 E. W. Phelps and another Stafford attorney, Jesse Cady (whose name appears as witness on several land transactions involving Phelps), were the targets of a bitter attack in the spring session of the General Assembly. The vehemently pro-establishment *Connecticut Courant* reported that they were the victims of a "democratic persecution," that is, by the Jeffersonian Republicans. One of the first things "which engrossed the attention of the legislature" in the recently completed session was, according to the paper,

> A remonstrance from a number of persons in the town of Stafford; in the county of Tolland, against the election of Jesse Cady, Esq. one of the representatives of the town; and also against Eleazer W. Phelps, Esq., a Justice of the Peace in the same town. The prosecution against Mr. Cady was dropped; but Mr. Phelps appeared before the House of Representatives and was heard upon the charges against him. The charges were numerous, and some of them *sounded* sufficiently heinous. When they came to be heard, they proved to be not only utterly unfounded but malicious in the extreme. The vote of the house was apparently unanimous in declaring the charges not supported. Though the whole was well known to be a democratic persecution, Mr. Phelps' proof was so complete, and irrefutable, that some of the democratic members spoke, and nearly all of them voted, in his favour. The result, which was so honorable to Mr. Phelps, stamped mortification and shame upon the faces of his adversaries; and they retreated from the scene with deep marks of disappointment and guilt.[71]

---

[70] In Phelps 1899 this Timothy Phelps is described as a businessman in New Haven. Estate of John Phelps and Executor's Account of Expenses, Town of Stafford, Stafford Probate District, CSL, box 1372, packet 1705 (FHL film 1,018,463).

[71] *Connecticut Courant*, 14 June 1802; Connecticut Official Records, 11:5.

It is possible that the dispute had to do with the proposal to build a turnpike, which Phelps and other partners were planning and proposed to the assembly in 1803.[72] The Jesse Cady mentioned in the matter was a witness to a Stafford land transaction in April of the same year in which Phelps and three partners bought from Samuel Willard a sawmill and four parcels of land.[73] There is no record of the charges brought by his opponents against Phelps in the *Courant* or in public documents.

## A Turnpike

In 1802 E. W. Phelps, Dr. Samuel Willard, and others submitted their first petition to the General Assembly to secure a charter for a turnpike corporation. They proposed to build "The Stafford Pool Turnpike" on a south-north route through the town to connect with a future turnpike at the Massachusetts line that would meet the main road to Boston at Worcester. The improved access to Stafford was meant to encourage visits to the springs and stays at Willard's hotel.

The late 1790s and early 1800s were the years of the turnpike era in the United States. The existing roads were poor, maintained by part-time and often reluctant townsmen paying off the poll tax. The quickened economy of early-nineteenth-century Connecticut by 1800 "gave zest to the construction of good roads which would shorten the distance to market."[74] As the state grew, new settlements were out of reach of sea- and river-based transport; older inland towns like Stafford were producing and buying more goods and needed readier access to markets.

Improvement was made a matter of business. Connecticut and other states chartered corporations to improve roads in exchange for the right to charge tolls and exclusive use of the right of way. Despite abuses and some corruption, historians of the subject agree that the toll roads enabled more rapid schedules for stages. Likewise, there came to be shorter and less arduous trips for the horse- and oxen-drawn wagons, which were the

[72] Travel, Highways, Ferries, Bridges and Taverns, 1737–1820, ser. 2, Conn. Arch.

[73] Stafford Land Records 8:373.

[74] Purcell, *Connecticut in Transition*, 107.

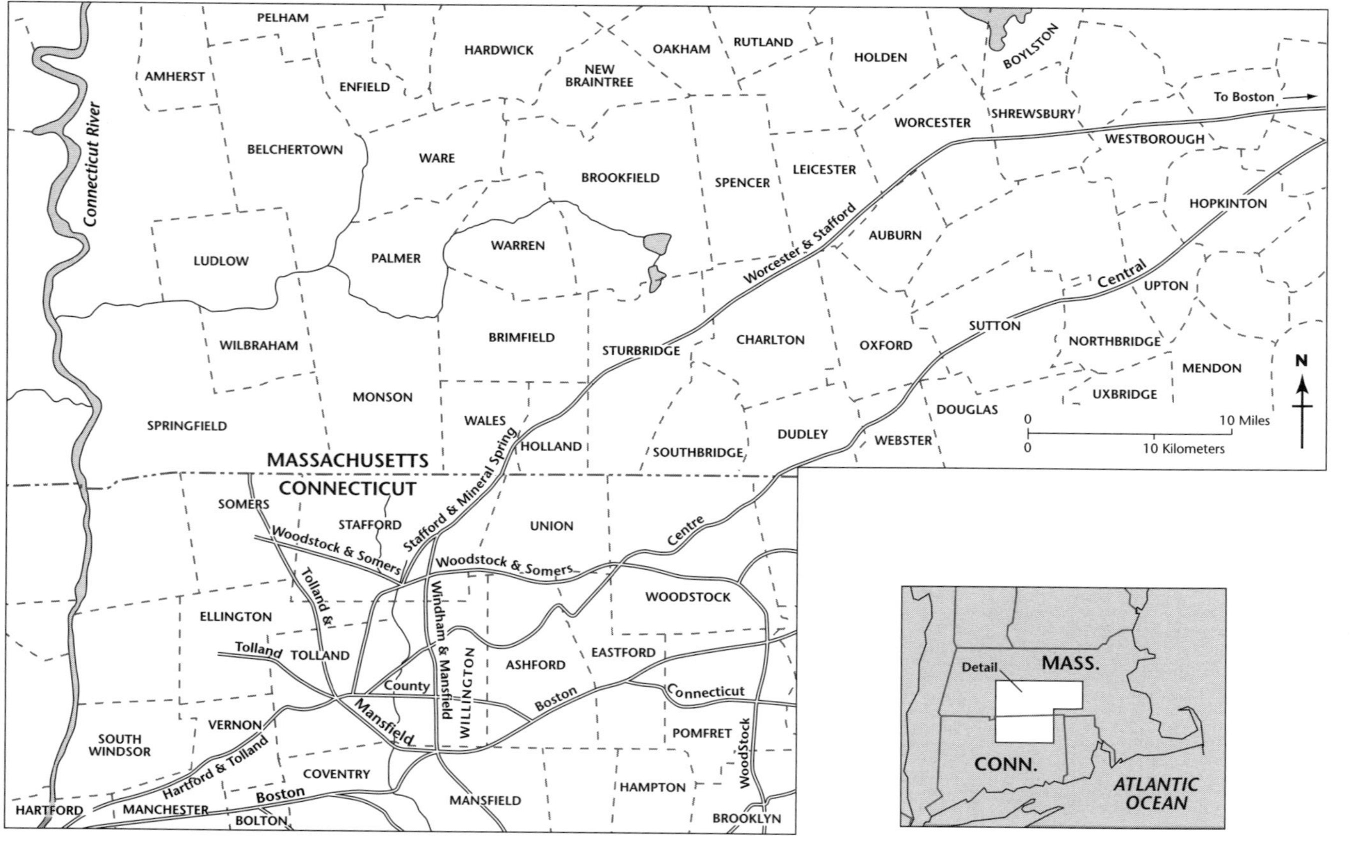


29. Major Turnpikes Linking Stafford to Points in Massachusetts and Connecticut

*Adapted from Frederic J. Wood,* The Turnpikes of New England *(Boston: Marshall Jones Company, 1919)*

principal means of transport for goods on land. By 1820 there were 70 turnpike corporations in Connecticut.[75]

Turnpikes became a favorite investment for Connecticut's wealthy and were supported by the Federalist-dominated General Assembly. The exclusivity of the charter did not go entirely unchallenged, however. A writer in a Jeffersonian Republican newspaper in 1802 charged Governor Trumbull with a "gross imposition" and referred to "people oppressed" by the granting of the turnpike charters.[76] The practice was attacked in a play—perhaps the first written in Connecticut—the subtitle of which was "*The Turnpike Road to a Fortune, A Comic Opera, or Political Farce in Six Acts.*" It may be opposition on these grounds that led to the challenge to Phelps in the 1802 General Assembly session.[77]

Phelps, Samuel Willard, and Nathaniel Hyde (an innkeeper and the owner of the second furnace and forge in Stafford, built in 1796) and other partners petitioned the General Assembly for a charter for the "Stafford Mineral Springs Turnpike Company." (They had changed "Pool" to "Springs" on the grounds it was more "elegant.") Their plan was to lay out and establish "a public highway from Tolland courthouse [due south] to the Massachusetts line in Stafford [heading northeast] . . . land leading by the mineral spring." There were to be "turnpike gates, one at or near the dwelling house of Benjamin Norris in said Tolland, the other at or near the dwelling house of Elisha Fisk in said Stafford." (These men also petitioned the General Assembly for approval of the turnpike.) The first meeting was to be held in Willard's house in January 1804.[78]

Clearly the turnpike and the springs were closely related. Samuel Willard promoted the benefits of the springs with the full authority of his

---

[75] Ibid., 107–8; Frederic J. Wood, *The Turnpikes of New England* (Boston: Marshall Jones, 1911); Joseph Austin Durrenberger, *Turnpikes: A Study of the Toll Road Movement in the Middle Atlantic States and Maryland* (Valdosta, Ga., 1931); U. Waldo Cutler, "Trail and Pike," *The Worcester Historical Society Publications, New Series*, vol. 1, no. 2, April 1929, Worcester Historical Society, Worcester Mass., 21-34; H. C. Warren, "Thoroughfares in the Early Republic Controlled by Corporations," *Connecticut Magazine* 5 (1904), 721–29; Pease and Niles, *Gazette*, 10, 66.

[76] Jonathan Trumbull, 1740–1809, governor of Connecticut from 1797 to his death. *DAB.*

[77] The play was *Federalism Triumphant in the Steady Habits of Connecticut Alone*, 1801, by Leonard Chester, a Wethersfield merchant. *PRSC*, 15:xiv. The route and chartering of the Stafford–Worcester Turnpike under its different names are described in Wood, *Turnpikes of New England*, 372.

[78] Travel, Highways, Ferries, Bridges, and Taverns, 1737–1820, ser. 2, vol. 16, 8a (1803), Conn. Arch.

medical credentials. In a long article in the *Connecticut Courant* in 1809 he related a history of the springs and his analysis of the properties of its waters, which could cure "ulcers, dropsical affections, glandular swellings, rheumatism, gout, piles, Salt Rheum and almost all other cutaneous diseases."[79] Accommodations "for the reception of visitors at this Spring," Willard wrote (in the third person), "are at this time more complete than they have ever been—a small but well chosen circulating Library has been furnished him by some friends in Boston which afford a mental repast to his sentimental guests. Some remedies for the *comfortably sick*, under the general head of rational amusements, are about to be compounded, which when innocently and rationally used are supposed to be better calculated for their particular complaints, than the most elaborate pharmaceutical preparations."

A testimonial from a "frequent visitor" to the springs that year supported the proprietor's claim of its salutary effects:

> The Principal Spring has within three months past, been newly enclosed in a plain, but neat and cleanly manner. A number of ornamental things have been done on the grounds around the House. The Table is furnished daily with well served viands, and with as great a variety as is obtainable in a country town. The House is well supplied with excellent wines and there are a variety of other refreshments of the best quality. The domestics are cleanly in their appearance, and obliging and attentive to their duty. In a word, the establishment may truly be said to be improved in every particular. The Mineral water of Stafford is unquestionably an excellent Chalybeate [impregnated or flavored with iron] . . . Much credit is due to Dr. WILLARD, the proprietor of the establishment for his unremitted exertions in bettering the situation.[80]

In 1808 a Massachusetts corporation was chartered "to locate & make a turnpike road through the towns from Worcester" to meet the Stafford Turnpike. This evolved into the Worcester & Stafford Turnpike Corporation.[81] Phelps owned 175 shares of this corporation, and he and Eliab and

---

[79] *Connecticut Courant*, 16 Aug. 1809.

[80] Ibid., 28 Aug. 1809.

[81] William Lincoln, *History of Worcester, Massachusetts* (Worcester, Mass.: Moses D. Phillips, 1837), 338. The Massachusetts towns through which the connection to Stafford passed were: "Leicester-Charlton-Sturbridge-Holland in Worcester County & Brimfield in Hampshire County." The dates for completion, standards, etc., are found in *Worcester & Stafford Turnpike Co. vs. Eliab Alden & Others*, Tolland County Superior Court Files, CSL, Record Group 3, box 7.

Joseph Alden of Stafford (associates of Phelps in a number of land transactions, whose land abutted the route) formed the committee responsible to complete the road. They were to provide compensation (subject to court settlement) to owners over whose property it passed. Phelps, as principal, and the Aldens, as surety, provided a bond on 24 February 1808 to the treasurer of the company, Israel Waters, Esq., of the town of Charlton, Massachusetts, through which the road was to pass. Phelps bound himself and the Aldens to complete the road "so that the gates shall be erected thereon" the following November. The agreement provided that "all water courses and sluice ways on s$^{d}$ road not more than 3½ feet wide . . . be done in a workmanlike manner well covered with stone." The partners agreed to "pay all damages which already have been or shall be assessed for the location of s$^{d}$ road which are not and shall not be relinquished to the corporation." Apparently some compensation was to be in the form of company stock, for Phelps was bound to "not suffer the capital stock of s$^{d}$ Corporation to surmount 400 shares at $75 each." The bond was set at $40,000, an astonishing sum for the time.[82]

Turnpike roads were built with shovels, hoes, and axes, with the aid of oxen-drawn carts. The usual specifications provided for widths from 18 to 28 feet and grading that would allow drainage from a hump in the middle. (This contour had the undesirable effect of concentrating traffic in the center of the road.) The most usual surface was earth. The construction included drainage ditches and bridges. "Directness was the singular feature" of these turnpike roads, and despite the rock and grades, the route from Tolland to Stafford and into Massachusetts appears generally straight on the map.[83]

The turnpike was in use in April 1811, judging by an advertisement by a Hartford stage service. The newly completed turnpike was "several miles shorter [than the route through Springfield] . . . less hilly and mountainous, and the road is better than any other from Boston to Hartford; and

---

[82] Israel Waters, Esq., was probably the son of Capt. Israel Waters, a tanner in Charlton, whom the first historian of Worcester County singled out in 1793 for his entrepreneurial spirit. Peter Whitney, *The History of the County of Worcester in the Commonwealth of Massachusetts* (Worcester, Mass., 1793; reprint, Worcester, Mass.: Isaiah Thomas Books and Prints, 1993). The Aldens were associated with Phelps as co-owners in the following transactions: Stafford Land Records, 8:247, 373, 378, 546; 9:33, 37, 292–93, 298; 10:177. In a deed not involving Phelps, their land was described as abutting that reserved for a highway "through the land leading from the Meeting House in the First Society in said Stafford to South Brimfield." Ibid., 8:247.

[83] Durrenberger, *Turnpikes: A Study of the Toll Road Movement*, 85–86.

will be performed in less time, and will be more easy and agreeable to the traveler." Passengers could leave Hartford or Boston on three days of the week at 3 A.M. and arrive at their destination by 8 P.M. Travelers from Boston could "take breakfast at Wheeler's in Framingham and dine at Stafford Springs." The proprietors pledged "the best of horses and carriages, good and obliging drivers, and [to] do every thing in their power to render the traveling pleasant and agreeable."[84]

While there may have been some success for the road in its early days, its route was lightly populated, and it was among the many turnpikes that did not yield a benefit to shareholders. In the 1830s it (and many like it) reverted to the states.[85]

## Violent Confrontations

The seven years between the petition for a charter for the Stafford leg and the opening of the full turnpike connections to Hartford and Worcester through Stafford must have been a financial trial for the investors. A dispute with the men contracted to construct the road had more dire consequences.

Phelps and his associates in 1810 sued Liakim Lyon, a Stafford resident, who had contracted to build the road, to recover the performance bond of $5,000 that he had posted. They charged that the specifications had not been followed, and detailed the particulars, which illuminate construction practices at the time:

> did not remove all stumps & stones to be seen above ground beyond the ditches before the ground was ploughed
> did not plough up the ground & form the same into a road by 15 November then next
> did not clear the ditches from stumps & stones
> did not make s^d road gradually ascending from the middle of each ditch to the middle of the traveled part
> did not make s^d road to contain as many sluice ways as the Directors of the Corporation or s^d Phelps or either of them directed

[84] Advertisement, *Connecticut Courant*, 24 April 1811.

[85] "Turnpikes that long-extended through-routes traversing unproductive districts were not remunerative was well demonstrated by the experience of those roads which 'gave up the ghost' at the time when other turnpikes were thriving. The Massachusetts road ceased efforts in 1835 and the Stafford Mineral Springs Turnpike was abandoned about that time." Wood, *Turnpikes of New England*, 372.

did not do all the sluice ways & water courses not more than 3½ feet wide in a workmanlike manner & cover them well with stones
did not [construct] all bridges over all streams of water & elsewhere of greater width than 3½ feet with chestnut plank at least 4 inches thick
did not well guard sd Bridges with every part of road where it was necessary with railings
did not make where said road ran on the side of a hill, make the same lowest on the side next to the hill
did not sufficiently raise all low grounds & meadows on s$^{d}$ portions nor well secure the same against floods.[86]

The defective construction led the Worcester & Stafford Turnpike Company in turn to claim the forfeit of the $40,000 bond Phelps and his partners had posted. This worked its way through the courts to a settlement. However, Phelps's calling in of the construction bond prompted a violent and personal response. In January 1811, E. W. Phelps's "action of debt on bond" against Liakim Lyon (father), Samuel C. Lyon and Lyman Lyon (sons) was successful, and the court ordered that $5,000 was due to Phelps for their failure to meet the performance for which the bond was surety.[87] Lyons reacted with two acts of violence that belied the state's reputation for orderly conduct.

Phelps submitted to the court that on the night of 30 March 1811, "Liakim and Samuel C. Lyon, accompanied by Samuel Strong and Samuel Jones,"

> Did with force & arms break and enter the dwelling house of the plaintiff . . . in Stafford and did in a noisy and tumultuous manner continue in said house about 4 hours and with rude insolent Profane and obscene Words and with threats greatly disturb and terrify the Plaintiff's family and did break open [the] inner doors two Cupboard doors tare up the garret and cellar floors and destroy one chimney board and did on their shoes carry such large quantities of mud and dirt into said house and did break open the plaintiff's trunk chests, boxes and casks in said house and did violently shake and tumble about the plaintiffs casks of Cider whereby said cider was greatly injured and many other Enormaties.[88]

---

[86] Ibid.

[87] Action of debt on bond, *Phelps vs. Lyon*, Sept. 1811–Sept. 1812, Tolland County Superior Court Files 1810–1817, Man-Z, CSL, Record Group 3, box 7.

[88] *Eleazar W. Phelps, Esqr., vs. Lyakim Lyon*, Sept. 1811, Dec. 1811, Sept. 1812, Tolland County Superior Court Files 1810–1817, Man-Z, CSL, Record Group 3, box 7. Pease and Niles, *Gazette*, 10.

The presence of the casks of cider suggests that Phelps was in the purveying business. Cider was used to make cider brandy, which with gin was "the first value of exportation" in early nineteenth-century Connecticut. For some reason the court found in this claim "that the Declaration is insufficient & therefore find for the defendants to recover of the Plaintiff their cost."

Phelps's antagonists were not mollified and returned for another trespass, this time armed and more abusive. On 4 November 1811, Liakim and Samuel C. Lyon and Samuel Strong of the first incident, with Nehemiah Lyon, and, surprisingly, an attorney, Benning Mann, Esq., forced themselves into the Phelps house. The resonant language of Phelps's statement gives a vivid picture of what happened. The intruders

> Did with force & Arms break & enter the dwelling house of the Plaintiff through a Window & through an outer door while the family of the plaintiff were asleep & did with great noise, tumult & hollowing continue in said house through the whole of said night & did threaten to pull the Plaintiff's Wife and Children out of bed & other great personal injury whereby the plaintiff's Wife & Children were much disturbed and put in great fear & disquiet; did break open the inner doors of said house; & did break open cupboards, chests, Trunks & Desks, examining, reading & destroying the Plaintiffs letters, Deeds, Notes, & other papers of Great value to the Plaintiff & did tear out & destroy the underpinning of the Plaintiffs said House in sundry places.[89]

The marauders made off with a large quantity of goods, listed in detail in Phelps's claim against his attackers. They stripped the family of its possessions: clothing, blankets, a "feather," linen, chairs and table, kitchen utensils, plates and serving dishes, tools, a carpet, furniture, the contents of the kitchen cupboard, cloth and materials used for making dresses, and household fabrics. When their wagon pulled away the Phelps house was not only structurally damaged, but the family had little or nothing to carry on daily living. The looting was thorough and systematic and certainly would have stirred the town of 300 families. This time the court awarded Phelps $1,000 and costs, an amount that exceeded the estimated value of the goods stolen. (Phebe's younger brother, Ralph Rodolphus Phelps, represented him, as the family had left the country by the time of the settlement.) The court documents do not say whether the goods were returned.[90]

---

[89] *E. W. Phelps action vs. B. Mann, L. Lyon, et al.*, re 4 Nov. 1811 trespass, Tolland County Superior Court Files, CSL, Record Group 3, box 7.

The inventory of the stolen goods tells us much about the Phelps family at the time.[91] The several purchased items show modest wealth and a household still linked to the land. Most striking is the evidence of female industry. Phebe Phelps's four daughters were aged 16, 14, 12, and 4 in 1811; the older girls and their mother would have used the quantities of different types of cloth in the house for making clothing for themselves and the other children, sheets, napkins, and curtains. There were a variety of fabrics and threads for different purposes, including lutestring, a shiny silky fabric, used for decoration.

The 3,500 yards of straw braid taken from the house indicates that the women had taken up what by then had become a home industry, the braiding of straw hats and baskets. After following models imported in the eighteenth century, American women developed styles and weaving techniques of their own.[92] By the 1800s there was a market for these American designs, and weaving and bonnet making became a popular home industry. A prospering straw braid manufacture was a "a source of pride" in Stafford in these years, and the Pease & Niles *Gazette* of 1819 states that there were $8,000 to $9,000 of sales per year of straw braid in the town.[93]

The women of the Phelps household doubtless had some farm work to do, as most town families at this date still grew produce and kept animals, but there was time enough to make things to sell for cash. The *Gazette*, reflecting on the potential for disorder in the changing conditions that gave women more leisure, sanctimoniously pointed out the home industry's social and moral utility as "a means of promoting female industry and habits of attention to business and a consequent abstraction from light and frivolous occupations or the more unwarrantable employment of local detraction." Within a generation young farm women would be going out to work in textile mills.

The family lived comfortably, if not luxuriously, with table napkins, a cherrywood table, a Turkish carpet, calico bed curtains, three looking

---

[90] The attorneys for the plaintiff are listed in one document as R. Phelps and William Perkins and in a second as "Phelps & Perkins."

[91] *E. W. Phelps action vs. B. Mann, L. Lyon, et al.*, re 4 Nov. 1811 trespass, loc. cit.

[92] The first patent issued by the United States to a woman was for straw braiding. Alice Morse Earle, *Home Life in Colonial Days* (1898; Stockbridge, Mass.: Berkshire House, 1993), 258–61.

[93] Pease and Niles, *Gazette*, 298.

### INVENTORY OF FURNISHINGS AND GOODS TAKEN FROM PHELPS'S STAFFORD HOUSE, NOVEMBER 1811

On 4 November 1811 Lyon and his accomplices "did then & there with like force take & carry away from the said house & from the Plaintiffs possession the following articles of household furniture & other property the proper Estate of the Plaintiff . . . All of the value of $700."

*40 yds of Callico*
*8 yds of Cotton Cambric*
*3500 yds of straw braid*
*5 pieces of linnen tape*
*6 pairs of white cotton hose*
*1 pair of mixed coloured cotton hose*
*30 yds of Gingham*
*4 papers of pins, 3 oz of line thread*
*7 Cambrick Handkerchiefs*
*3 diaper table cloths*
*2 diaper towels*
*1 new feather*
*1 brass warming pan*
*50 yds India Cotton*
*bolster & pillows*
*1 brass headed shovel & tongs*
*1 Martin muff & tippet*
*1 keg & 3 gallons of molasses*
*6 dining chairs*
*2 linen sheets*
*1 keg & 8 gallons of rum*
*1 keg & 3 gallons of cherry rum*
*1 1/2 yds Lutestring*
*30 yds quality binding*
*cotton sheets*
*1 Ca[stor?] hat*
*1 black coat*
*1 Turene*
*1 large cotton shawl*
*3 plaid woolen blankets*
*12 skeins black sewing silk*
*1 India cotton bed spread*
*1 calico bed spread*
*1 Turkey floor carpet*
*12 yds blue & white striped cotton ticking*
*8 yds book muslin*
*1 woolen bed quilt*
*2 suits calico bed curtains*
*1 round cherry tea table*
*1 wash bowl*
*2 flowered pint bowls*
*6 white pint bowls*
*1 soup plate*
*1 blue-edged dish*
*3 white dishes*
*1 silver mounted whip*
*8 pounds of brown sugar*
*1 sugar box*
*3 large looking glasses*
*1 large tea waiter*
*1 cherry candle stand*
*1 draft chain*
*1 set of horse chains*
*2 trunks*
*1 pair of snuffers*

glasses, and a "large tea waiter"(tray). There is modest luxury in the silver-mounted whip and the brass warming pan. The "draft chain" indicates that a horse was used for both riding and working in the field. There is rum (probably varieties made from sugar and cherries)—perhaps grown and fermented locally. The first raid had emptied barrels of cider, probably pressed in the home for family use and, perhaps, sale.

The household economy as we read it from this inventory is one of modest prosperity and certainly not one dependent on servants. Much was made within the family, but the fabric, the carpet, and the furniture would probably have been purchased with the cash that E. W. Phelps realized from his legal and judicial work. The round cherry tea table, the six chairs, the cherry candle stand encourage us to imagine the family at early supper or tea, the parents and the older children seated at the table, the tea and meal served on the "large tray." These were signs of gentility and status, the beginnings of what a recent study has called "the refinement of America," that would be advanced dramatically in Eleazar's children's generation.[94]

The vandalism and personal abuse that characterized the incidents in Phelps's account pose a mystery. In a community in which everyone knew one another these assaults on a prominent resident and his family would have been scandalous. While the precipitating cause was his calling of the bond because of poor construction, a mystery remains. There are no references to the incident or the trial to be found in the regional newspapers that might have carried such a story, the *Connecticut Courant*, the *American Mercury* (the Federalist newspaper, published in Litchfield), or the Worcester *Massachusetts Spy*.

What of the men involved? Lyman Lyon was an active member of the Ecclesiastical Society and served as moderator in its meetings from 1806 to 1812. In 1806 he was moderator in a meeting that approved Phelps's rent of "pew No. 2 opposite" at $5, the most expensive; the rent of his father, Liakim Lyon, was $1.20 in that year. The same meeting appointed Phelps to assist in securing aid from the General Assembly.[95] The Lyons were as active in the Ecclesiastical Society, as was Phelps.

The attorney, Benning Mann, Esq., accompanied the Lyons on the second and more severe raid. He was then a justice of the peace in neighboring Somers. In May 1811, between the two incidents, he rented a pew (for $1.05) in the meetinghouse for the first time.[96] It is astonishing that someone in his position should have taken part in the action. He was 29 in 1811, the son of a Hebron-born father, who was one of the first to settle

---

[94] Richard L. Bushman, *The Refinement of America: Persons, Houses, Cities* (New York: Alfred A. Knopf, 1992).

[95] Stafford First Congregational Church, Society Meetings 1803–37, 26 June 1806, 2:10.

[96] Ibid., 2:11.

Orford, New Hampshire. Like E. W. Phelps years before, he moved to Connecticut in his 20s. From their shared Hebron and Orford background, his family certainly knew the Phelps family. (A relative, Nathaniel Mann, was the caretaker of Samuel Peters's property in Hebron after his forced departure.)

Mann began aggressively purchasing land in 1812, shortly after his arrival in Stafford. Samuel Willard, the eminent doctor who promoted the springs and invested in the turnpike with Phelps, witnessed the early transactions. One of these transactions involved land on Main Street abutting the "Stafford Pool Turnpike."[97] Mann became unpopular in Stafford; in 1820 a number of local citizens petitioned to remove him from his position of postmaster.[98] The surnames on the petition included Hyde and Cady, families who had been associated with Eleazar Phelps. Mann later became a judge in Hartford and was honored by the Bar Association after his death in 1863.[99] There are no debts listed for Phelps to any of these men; there were no debts to any Mann in Alexander Phelps's estate. Except for apparent aggressiveness as a "new man in town," it is not possible to assign a motive for his involvement in the raid.

If there is a meaning to the assaults of 1811 that goes beyond the response to Phelps's calling of the bond, it has not yielded its secret up to extensive research. It remains a mystery why and how apparently respectable citizens carried out raids that by their description could have been the acts of drunken brawlers. Perhaps another explanation will come to light. What is certain is that in the "land of steady habits" there was an eruption of violence in Stafford in 1811 and that an establishment family was the

---

[97] Stafford Land Records, 10:594, 744–45.

[98] Jasper Hyde et al. to the Hon. John M. Niles, Post-Master, Hartford, 28 Jan. 1820, Niles Collection, CHS. The author is indebted to Martha H. Smart of the CHS Library for this reference.

[99] Benning Mann (1781–1863) was the son of John Mann (1743–1828) and Lydia Porter (1747–1805), both born in Hebron and married by the Rev. Samuel Peters. They moved to Orford, N.H., in 1765, where they became the first permanent residents. Benning was their seventh child. He became "Judge of Tolland County Court, United States Marshal for Connecticut, Senator in the State Legislature and Justice of the Police Court of Hartford for thirty years. In 1863 the Hartford Bar honored his memory. He was credited with such qualities as genial kindness, unvarying sympathy, sterling sense, unbending integrity . . . equable disposition." Hodgson, *Thanks to the Past: The Story of Orford N.H.*, 163, 431. Hodgson states that Mann attended Dartmouth College and graduated in 1794, but there is no record of his attendance. Personal communication from Barbara Krieger, DCA, 6 June 1998. Mann was buried in Hartford on 4 Feb. 1863. Hartford Christ Church records 2:307, CSL. References following the Hodgson account are in George Sumner Mann, *Mann Memorial, A Record of the Mann Family in America* (Boston: D. Clapp, 1884).

victim. It led to Phelps's departure from the place where he made his career.

The claim by the Turnpike Company in connection with its call of the $40,000 bond (which triggered Phelps's calling of the Lyons' bond) was resolved by seizure of property owned by Phelps and his Alden partners, but the amount was a small fraction of the bond's face value. The court awarded the Worcester & Stafford Turnpike Company $3,755 plus costs against Phelps, Eliab Alden, and the other partners.

In January 1813, the sheriff "went to the homes of the debtors, but found no one." (Phelps was out of the country and was represented by his nephew.) An execution was levied against Phelps's property in neighboring Somers, containing a dwelling house and barn. Because the debtors did not appear and "refused to choose an appriser," the sheriff applied to the justice of the peace, who appointed "apprisers." They valued the Phelps land in Somers at $1,053.09, and three mills plus fees and a 40-acre piece in Stafford that Phelps had earlier deeded to Eliab and Joseph Alden at $330 plus fees. The combined sums amounted to a small fraction of the 1808 bond. This was a humiliating episode, but doubtless less so than the Lyons' raids.

## To Europe

Phelps was not at home to receive the sheriff because he and the family had left for Europe. It is not surprising that E. W. Phelps chose to leave Stafford with his family after the incidents and the troublesome Turnpike Corporation claim, but it is remarkable that he and the family went so far and had the resources to do so. In his great-granddaughter's account, Phelps "visited England shortly before the War of 1812, where he remained until after the War, residing most of the time in London. He visited many of the cities of Old World including those of Italy and Spain." The Phelps family history adds that Phelps "resigned his judgeship, closed his law business, and with his family visited England."[100] As they do not mention the raids or the Turnpike involvement, these references make it seem that the move was an affluent man's impulse to enjoy travel with his

---

[100] Notebook containing a genealogical record for her granddaughter, Elizabeth Wade White, by Julia Phelps (Haring) White, 8 June 1919, JHW MSS. Phelps 1899; *General Catalog, Dartmouth College*.

family. Why he left Stafford seems clear enough, but judging by his later career, Phelps was also in search of opportunity abroad.

He was well recommended. John Wheelock provided him with an introduction to Congressman Josiah Bartlett (1768–1838). "The bearer, E. W. Phelps, Esq.," he wrote, "proposes to travel to the continent; and, as he is not particularly acquainted in that quarter, I took the liberty of introducing him to your notice, as a gentleman of good moral character, and propriety and may recommend him to any personal civilities, that you may please to show." Bartlett, then representing New Hampshire in the House of Representatives, was a well-known physician in the state, the son of a signer of the Declaration of Independence.

If the entire family traveled to Europe, there were eight in the group: Eleazar Wheelock Phelps, 46 in 1811, Phebe, 42, and six children ranging in age from Henry Davenport, 2 to Eliza, 17. Phelps's land transactions in the years leading to 1811 were principally sales, which could have furnished him funds for the journey. There is no record of where the family went in these years and how they traveled. There is no E. W. Phelps or a company that might have been his in the London city directory.[101] A search of the consular reports from Naples, Palermo, Bordeaux, and London from 1811 to 1814 reveals few references to visiting Americans (none to Phelps) other than those who had engaged the host country's authorities.[102] The later career of George Alexander Phelps as a fruit merchant in the Mediterranean trade suggests, however, that some of his father's business interests may have been along those shores.

It was not a propitious moment in international affairs for personal or business travel by an American. The war between Britain and Napoleon's France was at its apogee; relations between Britain and the United States broke into a declared war in June 1812. In the late spring and summer of that year, Napoleon led the French armies across Europe to penetrate Russia and occupy Moscow. The retreat that winter resulted in the death of half a million men, but the French continued to support the emperor in

---

[101] Holden's *Annual London and County Directory of the United Kingdom and Wales* (London, 1811–16). There is a "Phelps & Co." listed for 1811 and not thereafter, but E. W. Phelps was in Stafford that year.

[102] Bartlett Collection, DCA MS 743900.1. The letter is not dated, but the address to "His Excellency" indicates it was sent between 1810 and 1812, when Bartlett was a representative. Levi Bartlett, *Sketches of the Bartlett Family in England and America* (Lawrence, Mass., 1876), 67. John Wheelock was president of Dartmouth 1779–1815.

further campaigns against the coalition led by England and Prussia on the Continent until the final defeat at Waterloo in June 1814. The interrupted Congress of Vienna concluded its work later that year, establishing a peace between the great European powers that was to last 100 years and bring prosperity to countries on both shores of the North Atlantic.

Negotiations in Ghent between the British and the Americans to resolve their conflict concluded on Christmas Eve, 1814. When the news arrived in New York on 11 February 1815, people took to the streets to celebrate the return of prosperity to the port. No matter their hopes, the coming reality was to exceed them.[103] What brought prosperity to the port of New York, however, caused a steep depression in Connecticut. The cheap British manufactured goods that flooded into New York auction houses undercut those of the native manufacturers. Connecticut's maritime trade suffered a further shrinkage when the British West Indies became restricted to British ships as an article of the peace.

## New York City

After the peace, Eleazar Wheelock Phelps "returned with his family and settled in New York City, and entered into the mercantile and shipping business." Longworth's *New York City Directory* for 1817–18 corroborates the note in the family history and the Dartmouth records and shows "Phelps, E. W." at 166 Greenwich Street. (We do know the family returned to Stafford at some point, as the three oldest girls were admitted there to the First Society in 1815 and 1816.[104])

It was a good address in a newly built and attractive part of Manhattan, showing that Phelps had the means to support it from his European sojourn or from what he had accumulated in Connecticut. Greenwich Street ran from the Battery north to Greenwich Village. It was parallel to and west of Broadway—in the seventeenth century it had been at the edge of the North River; since then landfill had been added. The slips that

---

[103] Robert Greenhalgh Albion, *The Rise of New York Port* (New York: C. Scribner's Sons, 1939), 9.

[104] Harriet was admitted on 15 Jan. 1815 at age 16, Eliza on 16 May 1815 at age 19, and Phebe on 6 June 1816 at age 17. Stafford, Conn., First Congregational Church Records.

30. At the Corner of Greenwich Street
Watercolor and pencil on paper by Baroness Hyde de Neuville, 1810.

*I. N. Phelps–Stokes Collection, Miriam and Ira D. Wallach Division of Art, Prints, and Photographs, The New York Public Library, Astor, Lenox and Tilden Foundations*

served North River shipping in 1817 led from the new south-to-north Washington Street.

The house at 166 was three blocks due west from the handsome new City Hall; Columbia College on Park Place was nearby. Since the successful run of the *Claremont* in 1807, there had been scheduled steamboat service to Albany from the bottom of nearby Fulton Street, and a steam ferry to Paulus Hook in New Jersey had been in operation since 1812. The clang and whistles of the steamboats were another daily reminder that what was going on in the city was thoroughly new and modern.

*Blunt's Strangers' Guide* informed new arrivals like the Phelps family that there were 17,000 "dwelling houses" in the city and a population of 100,000, "6 persons per house," and improvements were under way:

> The houses were formerly built of wood with shingle roofs, but these are fast disappearing and substantial brick houses with slated roofs rising in their place. In the principal streets they are generally three stories high besides the attics and ground floor, which is [sic] used as kitchens and shelters—in their internal construction and conveniences, the dwelling houses of New York are not surpassed by any country. The street surface (the "causeway") is firm and neat, and the foot pavement, which was formerly constructed of reddish brick, is now giving way to durable, vault stones, from the quarries of Con-

> necticut; the crossings from one street to another are also generally laid with these stones . . . [there is] a regular night watch.[105]

*Blunt's* also praises the trees planted on the streets, which gave the impression of an orderly and well-cared-for residential neighborhood.

Nearby Broadway, "the Bond St. of New York," was the location of shops with elegant goods. Wall Street was "a handsome airy street" where there were offices for banking, insurance, the Customs House, and "the office of Exchange brokers." The Tontine Coffee House on Wall Street was the site of the many auctions in 1817 for the goods flooding in from England after the war years.[106]

Greenwich Street in 1817 according to *Blunt's* was an "extensive incline on the Hudson side of the city . . . [and] a place of considerable retail trade." Joseph T. Jacobs, tailor, was at 221 offering "his most sincere thanks to his friends and the public for their encouragement—and with a large assortment of Clothing of the latest fashion and highest quality." J. C. Morrison, druggist, was closer to the Phelps's at 188, offering "an extensive assortment of genuine Drugs, Medicines, Dyer's and Fuller's articles, Surgeon's instruments, Paints, and Painter's articles, English patent medicines, Apothecaries Glassware of Every Description."[107]

To the New Yorker of the late 1810s, "Pearl Street" meant all the mercantile establishments, notably auction houses, where goods were bought and sold. "South Street" referred to the importers and shippers by the East River slips, where the schooners and brigs for the Atlantic and coastal routes loaded and unloaded, sheltered from the winds of the North River. It was with South Street connections that Eleazar would plan the business venture that would take him to Cuba in 1818.

Phelps arrived in New York in a critical year. The great historian of the nineteenth-century port, Robert Greenhalgh Albion, termed 1817 "the *annus mirabilis* when the all-important innovations were decided upon." This is when the port achieved preeminence over its rivals on the Eastern

---

[105] *Blunt's Stranger's Guide to the City of New York* (New York, 1817), 35–36.

[106] Ibid., 36–38.

[107] Ibid., 37. Up to the 1760s Greenwich Street had been at the water's edge. By 1817 the steady filling in of the shoreline had expanded the land to the west. Washington Street was built on fill and ran parallel to Greenwich, providing several more blocks for development. *Historical Guide to the City of New York*, Tercentenary Ed. (New York:: n.d. [1924?]), 59; Advertisements from *New-York Spectator*, 13 and 20 Oct. 1818.

31. "Plan of the City of New York"

A portion of the "Plan of the City of New York, Drawn from Actual Survey by Casimir Rh. Goerck and Joseph Fr. Mangin, City Surveyor," published by R. D. Cooke in 1803. At this time Broadway was the principal avenue. Docks used by most ocean-going vessels were on the East River, which was sheltered from the prevailing westerly winds. The Hudson (or "North") River piers handled much of the upriver trade, which brought supplies into the city.

*Map Division, The New York Public Library, Astor, Lenox and Tilden Foundations*

seaboard. An orderly auction procedure was put in place in that year to handle the flood of textiles and manufactured goods coming in from England after the war, and scheduled shipping service across the Atlantic began.

The auction houses facilitated the distribution of goods and attracted buyers from the hinterland, greatly expanding the city's role as a center of finance and trade. Advertisements for scheduled shipping service to Liverpool appeared in late 1817, and in January of the next year the first packet boat sailed as scheduled (in a snowstorm) for Liverpool, introducing regular service that shippers could rely on. Thus began the era of the famous square-rigged packets of the Black Ball Line (replaced by steam in the 1830s). The schedule provided for crossings of 30 to 40 days on average, primarily to and from Liverpool.

Regular service had a direct benefit to the auction houses and dry goods merchants on Pearl Street, assuring them (and their bidders) of a reliable supply. The city became a magnet for up-country buyers, strengthening its role as an *entrepot*, and serving a far wider geographic area than in colonial times. The brisk pace of trade meant more ships were needed, and New York's shipbuilding yards on the East River expanded to meet the demand. This is a classic example of innovation in transportation strengthening a city's economy by bolstering a related manufacturing sector in which imports could be processed and recombined for resale, thus adding to the growth of the city's economy and employment.[108]

What was evident to anyone arriving in the city after the peace was the tempo of trade. It was obvious by a look at the harbor and the wharves, crowded with ships and swarming with purchasers for the goods flowing in from England. The port was growing rapidly. There was a 50 percent population increase between 1800 and 1810. In the latter year the census reported 96,373, and by 1820 the population in Manhattan rose to 123,000, an increase of 28 percent.[109] It was a bustling, disorderly place. A visitor in 1818 termed it an

> Overgrown sea-port village . . . the slips run up a considerable way in the center of the buildings, as it were in the middle of streets; and being built or faced up with logs of trees cut to the requisite length, allow free ingress and

---

[108] Albion, *Rise of New York Port*, 1, 9–13.

[109] Ira Rosenwaike, *Population History of New York City* (Syracuse, N.Y.: Syracuse Univ. Press, 1972).

> egress to the water, and being completely out of the current of the stream or tide, are little else than stagnant receptacles of city filth; while the top of the wharves exhibits one continuous mass of clotted nuisance, composed of dust, tea, oil, molasses, &c, where revel countless flies.[110]

With all this there were innovators, men seeking new ways of doing things, moving to open new markets to take advantage of the transformation in world trade. There was peace on the oceans, enforced by the Royal Navy. There were also new business methods and the promise of technical developments such as steam power for shipping.

The pulse of enterprise and innovation in New York City drew country boys to seek their fortunes. The pull was felt particularly strongly in Connecticut. In this era it was trade, not religion, that inspired able and intelligent young men. "Typical of the Connecticut boys who made good," writes Albion, was Anson Greene Phelps, who became a merchant in metals and dry goods and the founder of what became the Phelps-Dodge copper company. He was "left an orphan while young and learned saddlery under his elder brother. He established his own business in saddlery in Hartford and began to sell his products in the south . . . [and] in 1812 moved to N.Y. and went into partnership with Elisha Peck." This Phelps, from Simsbury, was a fifth or sixth cousin of Eleazar Wheelock Phelps, and there is no evidence that the latter (or his son in later years) knew the man who became the most noted of the family in New York. But E. W. Phelps came for the same reasons, albeit in middle age—to find opportunity for gain.[111]

In 1817 there was a short and novel episode in Phelps's career. He was appointed "steward unto the Mess house at West Point on the 1st of May 1817 . . . to provide board and sustenance for the cadets." The appointment was made by the then acting superintendent, Alden Partridge (1785–1854).[112] Partridge had attended Dartmouth before becoming one of the first cadets to enroll at the military academy. When he appointed Phelps, Partridge was under a cloud, charged with nepotism because of an earlier appointment of an uncle as steward. (Phelps could have been this person's replacement.) Col. Sylvanus Thayer (1785–1872) succeeded Partridge on 28 July 1817 as superintendent of a West Point "in chaotic

---

[110] Albion, *Rise of New York Port*, 221.

[111] Ibid., 248.

[112] 17 Congress 1 Petition, 133, 20 Feb. 1822, National Archives and Records Administration.

condition." A few weeks later Partridge was court-martialed.[113] The new superintendent doubtless appointed a steward of his own choosing.

Phelps's appointment probably lasted less than three months. The position had an intrinsic drawback in any case. The steward's compensation came from the difference between the fees paid by the cadets and the cost of the food and its preparation. At the time, there were about 100 cadets, who were supposed to pay $10 per month directly to the steward for their board. There was a built-in incentive on the one hand to provide cheap or inadequate rations; on the other there was the prospect of the cadets, withholding fees or not being able to pay them, with no redress to the academy paymaster. If the family stayed at West Point, it was in an apartment at one end of the two-story Mess Hall that had been completed two years before.

In this inherently troublesome arrangement, Phelps went unpaid. When he later requested compensation, a War Department aide wrote him that "[b]efore any arrangement can be made, with us purst. to the money due You from the Cadets it will be necessary for You to report the names of those cadets who are in debt to you, together with the amount due from each one, to this Department."[114] Phelps did not supply such a list, or at least not one that would satisfy this official. In 1822 Phebe petitioned

---

[113] *DAB*. The Partridge Papers at Norwich University, Vermont, contain no correspondence to or from E. W. Phelps. Personal communication from Julie Bresser, Research Librarian, Oct. 1996.

[114] George L. Blaney, Aide to Engineer Department, Engineer Department, Washington, to Mr. E. W. Phelps, New York, 18 June 1818, *Records Relating to the United States Military Academy, 1812–1867, Military Academy Letters*, vol. 1, 21 Dec. 1812–30 Dec. 1826, Microcopies of Records in the National Archives, no. 91, roll 1. National Archives, U.S. Military Academy at West Point. George S. Pappas, *To the Point: the United States Military Academy, 1802–1902* (Westport, Conn., and London: Praeger, 1993), 78–79, 82, 100ff.; Edward C. Boynton, *History of West Point* (New York: D. Van Nostrand, 1864), 256; *Regulations of the United States Military Academy at West Point* (New York, 1823), 31–32; United States Military Academy, Board of Visitors, *Annual Report*, 1820, "Of Feed," transcript; Roswell Park, *A Sketch of the History and Topography of West Point and the US Military Academy* (Philadelphia, 1840), 77; Stephen E. Ambrose, *Duty, Honor, Country: A History of West Point* (Baltimore, Md.: Johns Hopkins Press, 1966), 62ff. There were 17 graduates in the class of 1817; the four classes were of like size, this meant there was a total of less than 100 cadets in residence at the time. Personal communication with Mrs. Judith Sibley, Assistant Archivist, U.S. Military Academy, 24 Aug. 1996.

Congress for the payment; the decision was there was "no basis" for government to make up the payment.[115]

What soon caught Eleazar's interest was the possibility of trade with the old Spanish colonies of the Caribbean. The British West Indies was closed to American ships, and the once thriving trade with Jamaica and the other British islands virtually disappeared. The Spanish islands of Cuba and Puerto Rico were attractive prospects for New Yorkers who sought to sell flour and manufactured goods and buy sugar and coffee. Albion recounts that "New Yorkers, backed by South Street and Wall Street, settled as commission merchants at Havana, Matanzas . . . Pledging their coming crop to the commission merchants, the planters were advanced credit wherewith to buy slaves, land, New York-made steam-sugar machinery, and the wide variety of articles 'selected for the Spanish market.'"[116] An enthusiastic report from Havana in the *New-York Spectator* in September 1818 gives the flavor of the expectations in the air: "Business is getting a little brisker with us," wrote the correspondent; "[t]he prospect of the coming crop of Coffee is such as to exhilarate all those who are engaged in the culture of it. It boasts a price which surpasses anything of the kind ever known here—white Coffee at 28 dollars [per hundredweight], green at 30 dollars—and what is more wonderful, it is *purchased at these prices* . . . Brown Sugars have risen rapidly." The correspondent's optimism abounded: "few cases of Fever have occurred lately, and our city is becoming more healthy."[117] The goods shipped from American ports listed by this correspondent were: flour, beef, lard, hams, codfish, rice, candies, spermaceti, soap, castille, shelled almonds, whale oil, pitch, tar, catalonia wine, French brandy, saffron (fresh and dry), sheathing paper, Virginia tobacco, boards "plenty and dull, Scantling [small pieces of timber]."

---

[115] "The contract mentioned by the Petition has not been addressed, nor is it acknowledged that the United States had stipulated to guarantee the payment of the demands which might accrue for the board of the Cadets; and until the contrary be shown, the transaction must be regarded as of a [ ] for which the United States are not responsible." *Phebe Phelps, Report of the Committee of Claims on her Petition*, 20 July 1822, recorded, 177, U.S. House of Representatives, National Archives; *Digested Summary and Alphabetical List of Private Claims which have been presented to the House of Representatives from the First to the Thirty-First Congress* (Baltimore, Md.: Genealogical Publishing Company, 1970), 3:67.

[116] Albion, *Rise of New York Port*, 173, 181–82.

[117] *The New-York Spectator*, 3 Nov. 1818, with a report from Havana via Charleston dated 30 Sept.

Phelps sought to tap the Cuban market in September 1818, when he sailed for Havana on the schooner *Piper*. It was a fourteen-day journey on a route noted for its storms (then as now) and pirates. This husband and father of six minor children was taking a risk. The U.S. frigate *Macedonian*, sailing in the same waters the week before the *Piper*, was "dismasted in a severe gale . . . she had her mizzen mast carried away by the board; her fore and main-masts sprung, and . . . cut away, three of her boats lost. She returned to port for complete refitting."[118] (The *Piper* could not have endured such a storm; on its return from Havana, the "Shipping News" reported that "after being out 3 days [she] was obliged to put back in a leaky state, and was condemned as unseaworthy."[119])

What Shylock calls "water rats, water thieves, I mean pirates" did attack the *Piper* and its occupants. Phelps wrote Phebe when he arrived in Havana, a letter received four weeks later, on 24 October.

> We arrived here yestr all well. You will see by the public papers that a Misfortune occurred on our passage which I hope will afford no uneasiness to you and our dear family, since I assure you that my health was never better than at this moment. The climate and the present health of this place are excellent and prospects good as can be expected. Shall write again by the first opportunity & return as soon a possible. Love to our dear children
> Yours Most Affectionately
> E. W. Phelps
> You may expect another letter in about one week after the arrival of this.[120]

This letter is all that survives of Eleazar's words to his family. It is spare, affectionate, and tender. The "Misfortune" he referred to was an act of piracy, reported in the New York papers, from news relayed by ship captains who "bespoke" others with the news on the seas. News of it had appeared two weeks before Phebe received the reassuring letter. The Shipping News column in the *New-York Spectator* reported that a "New York Schr. with passengers, arrived Havana on the 25$^{th}$ Inst. from New York, after being plundered by a piratical schr. and the passengers shamefully abused."[121]

---

[118] *The New-York Spectator*, 20 Oct. 1818, with a report from Norfolk dated Oct. 12. The account quotes the ship's log describing in detail the storm and its damage.

[119] *The New-York Spectator*, 27 Nov. 1818.

[120] Eleazar Wheelock Phelps, in Havana, to Phebe Phelps, at 166 Greenwich Street, New York, 25 Sept. 1818, manuscript in possession of the author.

[121] *New-York Spectator*, 13 Oct. 1818.

Several such raids were reported in the papers in those weeks. A few days later there was a report of an attack that may have been by the same pirates that attacked the *Piper.* The brig *Edward Foster,* "40 days from Gibraltar," had arrived "at Havana—and reported that she had been robbed of a considerable amount of specie, by a boat of 10 men armed with cutlasses, pistols, etc. There was a schr. [possibly the *Piper*] robbed at the same time by the same boat."[122]

The perils of trading with the Caribbean were considerable. Piracy was rife. In the same news there was another account of the violent interruption of trade:

> The schooner, *Venus* . . . on the 14th of October was boarded by a small sloop, the crew consisting of twenty men, all black excepting the captain, armed with muskets, swords and pistols, who proceeded immediately to plunder the vessel of goods and her cabin and ship stores, also depriving the crew of the cloths which they had on. The remonstrances of capt. Samson against this piratical conduct were answered by threatening to assassinate him. The schr. was finally liberated, after a detention of four hours.

Phelps's optimism about his health was not fulfilled. He was dead of a fever 17 days after he wrote Phebe. An American businessman in Havana, Samuel DeForest, conveyed the solemn news to the widow in a letter dated 14 October:

> Dear Madam
>
> It falls to my to lot to communicate to you the melancholy misfortune of the death of your husband who departed this life on the 12th instant at about midnight, and was buried the following day at one o'clock. PM. His complaint was the fever which is peculiar to a southern climate.
>
> Mr. Phelps arrived here about three weeks ago in the Schooner Piper from New York, which vessel was robbed on her passage and Mr. P as well as others on board lost most of his wearing apparel, &c, &c.
>
> On the 5 instant while here he was attacked with fever & immediately a Physician was call'd, after which a consultation, but he continues gradually to grow worse till his last moments.
>
> The very best attention was paid him during the whole of his sickness. I was with him myself most of the time, and whatever his situation required was immediately procured.
>
> When all things were ready for the funeral ceremony, about eight American Gentlemen besides myself with carriages followed his coffin to the grave

[122] Ibid., 30 Oct. 1818.

where he was interred with all the decency, ceremony and respect the place could afford.

I shall send you at first opportunity all his things, which I found me his physician at the time of his death together with expenses, &c, &c.

I am most respectfully, yours,

Samuel DeForest

PS Most of the time for the last two days Mr. Phelps appeared in a state of mental derangement—said but little, and from every appearance was almost free from pain.

Yours, &c, &c.

S. D. F.[123]

Samuel DeForest was of the Connecticut family who at that time had opened up trade with Buenos Aires and the Plata region: manufactured goods shipped out, hides and skins for New York leatherworking shops on the return passage. The office of Lockwood DeForest and the L. & C. DeForest Company was at 48 Peck Slip in 1818.[124]

Phebe would have received DeForest's letter about four weeks after it was sent. The cause of death was probably yellow fever, then endemic in tropical ports; it has a short incubation period and "usually starts with languor, chilliness, headache and muscular pains" and can develop into "temperatures as high as 110 F and is often fatal."[125]

At her husband's death Phebe had the responsibility of five minor children; only Eliza, at 22, had passed her majority. Daughter Phebe was 19, George Alexander 15, Mary Amelia 12, Henry Davenport 8. There is no will recorded in New York City or Connecticut for this man who had been both an attorney and a judge of probate. The death of her husband followed closely her parents' deaths. The Rev. Benajah had died 10 March 1817, her mother the year before.[126] The family must have left New York

---

[123] Samuel DeForest, in Havana, to Phebe Phelps, in New York, 14 Oct. 1818, manuscript in possession of the author.

[124] Longworth's *New York City Directory*, 1817–18; no Samuel DeForest is listed in the city directory in this or nearby years. There is reference to the South American trade of the DeForests as opened up by Henry C. DeForest in Albion, *Rise of New York Port*, 188. Also see J. W. DeForest, *The DeForests of Vesnes (and of New Netherland), 1494 to the Present Time* (New Haven, 1900). There is no Samuel DeForest in that family history noted as being in New York or in the Caribbean or in South American trade. However, this Samuel DeForest's letter was sent via the *Garonne* to Peck Slip, where the family offices then were, indicating that he was of that family and firm.

[125] *Encyclopaedia Britannica*, 1911.

[126] Hale Headstone Collection, Manchester.

for a time. There is no listing for Phebe, Eleazar's widow, in the city directory for 1818–19 and subsequent years.[127]

In February 1822, three-and-a-half years after her husband's death, "Phelps, widow of Eleazer" made the claim to the United States Congress for what her husband had been owed by the cadets, but her address is not cited.[128] Three years later, in 1825, the city directory lists George Alexander Phelps ("Phelps, George A.") as a "fruiter" at Fulton Street, home on Gold Street. Both were close to the East River piers, where he would make his living and fortune in succeeding years.[129] It was only in 1836–37 (and in two subsequent editions) that Phebe Phelps, "wid. of Eleazar," was listed. (The "wid. of Eleazar" was used apparently to differentiate her from a widow of the same name listed earlier.) Her address was 176 Walker, a street opened up in 1810, west of Broadway and several blocks north of where the family had resided on Greenwich Street.[130]

After these years in the city and throughout her long old age, Phebe Phelps lived with her two unmarried daughters, Harriet and Phebe, in a house owned by George Alexander in Fairfield. A photograph of her as an elderly woman, captured by an instrument that must have seemed magical to her, shows an impassive face, its structure marred by an apparent absence of teeth. It is hard to imagine from it the extraordinary experience of the woman who observed the effects of the Revolution in Nova Scotia and after half a lifetime in Connecticut made a household in New York City. She lived from the age of wood and sail to that of iron and steam, the telegraph, and the railroad. Phebe Phelps died 17 January 1861 in a nation awaiting Lincoln, and a Fairfield illuminated with gaslight and served by steam trains and steamships. She was in her ninetieth year.

Phebe and four of her children are buried in the plot in the East Cemetery, Fairfield, which George Alexander purchased for the family. Phebe's marker bears the inscription, "Our Mother."[131] Her two sons and Harriet

---

[127] There is a "Phelps, Phebe, widow" listed in *Longworth's* from 1817 to 1825 on Division Street, in some years identified as "milliner." This could not be the widow of Eleazar because (a) she is identified as a widow before his death, and (b) care was taken years later to identify "Phelps, Phebe, widow of Eleazer," which is how the 1836–37 listing appears.

[128] 17, Congress 1, Petition 133, Claims, 20 Feb. 1822, National Archives.

[129] Mercein, Longworth, Trow: *New York City Directory*, 1817–1880.

[130] Walker Street was opened 10 July 1810: I. N. Phelps Stokes, *The Iconography of Manhattan Island, 1498–1909* (New York: Robert H. Dodd, 1915–1928), 6:index.

[131] Phelps family plot, East Cemetery, Fairfield, Conn., survey manuscript in possession of the author [hereinafter cited as Phelps family plot]. See "Phelps I" in the Genealogical & Biographical Notes.

32. Phebe (Phelps) Phelps (1770–1861)
This photo was probably taken in the 1850s, when, as the widow of Eleazar Wheelock Phelps, Phebe lived near the country house of her son George Alexander Phelps, in Fairfield, Connecticut.

and Phebe, the unmarried companions of their mother in her old age, survived her.[132] They too were buried in the Fairfield plot.

Of Phebe's four siblings who had survived to adulthood, three lived to great age. Ralph Rodolphus Phelps, who as a young lawyer had represented Eleazar Wheelock Phelps in the claims arising from the turnpike litigation, died on 26 February 1874 at the age of 87. Eunice died in 1850 at the age of 74, and the unmarried sister, Sally, died on 15 October 1875 in her 91st year. All three were buried in Manchester, Connecticut, next to the Rev. Benajah and the first Phebe.[133]

---

[132] Six of Phebe and Eleazar Wheelock Phelps's children survived to maturity. The two whose death dates are not known are Eliza, who married Billings Grant, and Mary Amelia, who married Richard Connell in New York City in 1827. See the Genealogical & Biographical Notes.

[133] Elizabeth, the eldest child, died at the age of 36. See the Genealogical & Biographical Notes.

Eleazar, born in Hebron, Connecticut, ten years before the Revolution ended his life in Havana in the midst of the sort of commercial venture that brought the port of New York to predominance. A family from a Connecticut town in the 1790s and 1800s experienced New York in the time of its emergence as the great port of the western Atlantic and ended their days in a rural retreat of successful New York merchants.

Consider the experiences of place and society and the geographic reach that this family lived through. For Eleazar the journey began in colonial Hebron, then to the upper Connecticut River valley in the early years of settlement, manhood in Federalist Connecticut, Europe, the port of New York, and the Havana venture. For Phebe there was a Nova Scotia childhood and commercial antebellum New York and the early, romantic suburb of Fairfield on Long Island Sound.

Eleazar seized the day in the reviving economy of Connecticut in its Federal period. He rose to the top social and economic level in Stafford. When the turnpike, the latest opportunity for investment, came along, he plunged into entrepreneurship. His was a thorough experience of life at the frontier of the Connecticut economy of the day. This energy and search for opportunity carried him in middle age to include both sides of the Atlantic. What stimulated Eleazar's vigorous life was the potential for gain from the new ways to make money that he found in Connecticut and the Atlantic seaboard.

Eleazar died less than 90 years after his forebears were swept up by the emotional upsurge in religion that displaced the Puritan-Calvinist orthodoxy of the previous century. Trade supplanted religion in this man's strivings—a counterpoint to the life journey of his older brother, Davenport. Eleazar opened new pathways for his progeny. It was his first son, George Alexander, who would follow them and become the successful merchant his father had aspired to be.

# VI

## LEANING ON THE LEVER OF ARCHIMEDES

*Yea our Savior approveth travail for merchants, Matthew 13:45–46, when he compareth a Christian to a merchantman seeking pearls, for he never fetched a comparison from any unlawful thing to illustrate a thing lawful.*

—John Cotton, "God's Promise to His Plantation"

### A Yankee Merchant in New York

George Alexander is another in the line of ambitious and able Phelps men. He seized opportunity in an era that offered material benefits in abundance. He was skillful and steady enough that his gains did not disappear in the downs of New York's nineteenth-century economy. His was not a rags-to-riches story but rather one of application and business acumen.

The fruits of this labor can be seen in a family photograph from 1872 (fig. 33). The retired merchant is seated on the veranda of the majestic house he bought in rural Fairfield on Long Island Sound. His wicker chair is placed by one of the pillars that made the house look like a Greek temple. Eliza, his wife, who bore eleven children and buried five, is seated by him in a voluminous black dress. Henry Davenport, who joined his brother in retirement, appears somewhat diffident, partly obscured by a column. The couple's eldest daughter and three grandchildren are there too. It must have been summer, to judge by their dress. Through the open door you can sense the light inside the house, filtered by curtains and half-drawn shades. The elderly couple was married almost 50 years before in a New York City that had since transformed itself several times over. In their retirement they are in comfort and elegance, accompanied by family. Their pursuit of happiness was realized.

Father of the New York Bar, Samuel Jones (1734–1818), "black letter lawyer" and the first controller of New York State, learned his craft before the Revolution. After the war he became a leading Federalist in New York. He gave advice to a grandson who had expressed his intention to become a merchant. The elderly Jones wrote from Oyster Bay in 1816; he may well have realized it was the dawn of a new era:

> Mercantile business is so various and complicated that it can only be learned by experience in a counting house. There are, however, many branches of learning taught in school that are useful to merchants as well as to others . . . Mercantile Business of every kind is always attended with some risk and therefore if ever you should be engaged in it you should never enter large and expensive speculations. They are always hazardous and frequently occasion bankruptcy instead of providing large Profit. To be content with moderate Profits in the ordinary course of Business is much safer, more conducive to Happiness, and generally to Health.[1]

One age was talking to another. The grandson was on the right course if he wanted to become a prosperous and influential New Yorker in his prime. His generation released an astonishing burst of entrepreneurial energy that made New York the leading port on the Atlantic coast—first in population, trade, and manufacturing—in less than a generation. His grandfather, intimately involved in the life of the city before and after the Revolution, had a clear-sighted view of the risk in the dynamic economy that was emerging. It would have periods of ruin as well as fortune, bust as well as boom. Many were destroyed in ruinous financial panics in 1819, 1837, and 1857. "[T]he merchant is constantly exposed to all the chances of a most capricious life," wrote one commentator in the middle of the century, and examination of the city's business directories shows that "an entire change of names takes place, and a generation passes off every five years."[2]

George Alexander Phelps's career in New York City from 1826 to the 1860s evolved from "fruiter" to "importer" to "commission merchant" to "merchant" and was impeded neither by the financial panics and depressions it traversed nor, apparently, by reversals in trade. He became a specialist in fruits, importing the dried varieties and Sicilian oranges and lemons from Mediterranean ports. For most of the 45 years he was in business (with various partners) he kept an office close to the other fruit merchants on Front Street, near the East River. His home addresses moved

---

[1] Samuel Jones to Samuel Jackson Jones (grandson), from Oyster Bay West Neck, 22 March 1816, Samuel Jones Papers, NYHS.

[2] Attributed to "Philip Hone's brother" in Stephen Girard, *The Merchant's Sketch Book and Guide to New York City* (New York, 1844), quoted in Edward Pessen, "The Business Elite of Ante-bellum New York City: Diversity, Continuity, Standing," in Joseph R. Frese, S. J. and Jacob Judd, *Business Enterprises in Early New York* (Tarrytown, N.Y.: Sleepy Hollow Press, 1977), 166.

33. The Phelps House in Fairfield, Connecticut, 1872

*Seated behind pillar on the left,* George Alexander and Eliza Phelps; *right,* probably Henry Davenport Phelps; *front left,* Julia Phelps Haring *(rear)* and Eliza Phelps Winter *(fore); seated right front,* probably Julia Maria (Phelps) Winter; the child may be Eliza's sister Emma.

uptown with those of the city's elite, from the crowded streets concentrated at the tip of Manhattan to Prince Street and—in the 1850s and 1860s—to a brownstone on West Fourteenth Street. With early prosperity, he bought a rural retreat in Fairfield, Connecticut, reached in those early years by steamer. There was even a connection with the venerable Samuel Jones who had advised his grandson on the perils of the mercantile career: Phelps's second daughter married his maternal grandnephew by marriage.[3]

[3] Cornelia (Herring) Jones (1741–1820), wife of Samuel, was the sister of Mary (Herring) Haring (1751–1825), the grandmother of James Demarest Haring, who married Caroline Eliza Phelps. See the Genealogical & Biographical Notes.

This Phelps was one of the many Connecticut young men who were instrumental in creating the prosperity of the port of New York as it evolved into the prime seaport of North America. In the family story, he fulfilled his father's dreams of commercial success. As one who "seized the time by the Top" in the Shakespearean sense, he worked with dominant energies of his age. In the larger picture of the era that might be called "mercantile New York," between the Peace of Ghent and the firing on Fort Sumter, this account of his career adds a thread to our understanding of the city tapestry of that period. New York was inventing itself as it went along. The city was fueled by a vast increase in wealth, accessible to more people than ever before. New opportunities for entry into the upper classes sprang up seemingly by the week, part of the same economic and social phenomena transforming the lands on either coast of the North Atlantic.

In the larger context, this story is a piece of the transformation of the world by capitalist entrepreneurs of Phelps's ilk. Freeman Hunt, editor of New York's *Merchants Magazine,* proclaimed the role of such men and celebrated the transformation of the world by free trade. "Commerce," he wrote, "is now the lever of Archimedes, and the fulcrum which he wanted to move the world is found in the intelligence, enterprise, and wealth of the merchants and bankers, who now determine the questions of peace and war, and deduce the destinies of nations."[4]

A perceptive French visitor to New York in the years when Phelps began his career observed that "the American people is . . . a *merchant* people . . . they appear to have but one single thought here, but one single purpose, that of getting rich." But there was an attractive other side: "you meet only happy households . . . everything in the last analysis comes down to family life."[5] The pursuit of wealth and the maintenance of family life are the two great themes of this account of George Alexander Phelps's life.

---

[4] Freeman Hunt (1804–1858) published a celebratory work on the New York merchants, *Lives of American Merchants* (New York: Office of Hunt's *Merchants Magazine*, 1856). This quotation is in Edward K. Spann, *The New Metropolis: New York City 1840–1857* (New York: Columbia Univ. Press, 1981), 7.

[5] From a letter from Gustave de Beaumont, who accompanied Alexis de Tocqueville to America, to his father in 1831. Pierson, *Tocqueville and Beaumont in America*, 71.

## In Trade

George Alexander was 15 years old when his father died in 1818. Where the family lived after they left their Greenwich Street house in 1818 or 1819 is not known.[6] The family reappears on the record when George is listed for the first time in the city directory in 1825. He was described as a "fruiter" with a business at 20 Fulton Street and home at 32 Gold Street.[7] Both addresses were convenient to the East River slips used by the ocean-going ships of the port. This listing would be repeated in all but one of the next 47 annual directories. The young man had begun to establish himself and was on course for a career that steadily advanced in material success.

A "fruiter"—the term dates back to the fifteenth century[8]—was the specialist grocer of the time, who dealt in dried fruits such as dates, figs, and raisins, sometimes in fresh lemons and oranges. The produce had to be imported from the Mediterranean, and it is probable that George started out as a wholesale grocer offering for resale what he had purchased from ships from Sicilian and Levantine ports. The business may well have stemmed from connections made during the family's travels ten years before.

A fruit merchant's advertisement of about 30 years later lists the delicacies available to the clientele when there were few if any fresh fruits available out of season.[9] There was a wide range of products in the barrels of this grocer, all imported, including many specialties no longer common, and nuts and spices were also in the fruit merchant's stock:

Lemons and Oranges
Raisins: Bunch, Muscatel, Bloom, Malaga, Smyrna, Zaine Currangs
Dates in frails [a basket made of rushes]
Figs in boxes, drums, frails
Prunes in boxes and jars
Madeira Citron

---

[6] There is no listing for Phebe Phelps in the U.S. census in either New York or Connecticut for 1820. In 1823, as noted in the previous chapter, Phebe unsuccessfully claimed settlement of her husband's compensation due from the West Point cadets to Congress, but no address was cited.

[7] *Longworth's American Almanac, New York Register and City Directory, New York*, 1825 [hereinafter cited as *New York City Directory*]. Longworth's was published 1822–1836; subsequent editions were published variously by Doggett, Trow, and others.

[8] 1483, *OED.*

[9] Advertisement of Messrs. Pendleton, Jr., 21 Fulton Street in T. Morehead, *The New-York Mercantile Register for 1848–49, Containing the Cards of the Principal Business Establishments including Hotels and Public Institutions* (New York, 1848), 166.

Italian do
Almonds: Princess or paper shell
Bordeaux
Marseilles
Malaga soft and hard shell
Jordan
Bitter
Nuts: Brazil, Madeira, Pecan, Filberts, Hickory Nuts, Cocao Nuts, Chestnuts, Peanuts
Spices: Mace, Nutmegs, Cloves, Cassia, Pimento, Black Pepper, Race Ginger, Ground Ginger, Cel
Salad Oil in boxes, 30 betties do in banksets
Seeds: Rape, Canary, Hemp, Yellow Mustard, Millet
Mustard: English Mustard, French, American
Sauces, etc.: India soy, quin, hervey, essence anchovies, reddin, cavis, shrimp
Capers, Olives and others

Like many New Yorkers at the time, George Alexander changed his home address several times during his early years, but his business address remained remarkably consistent throughout his lifetime, always by the East River piers. In 1826 Phelps was listed as a "fruiterer" at 196 Front Street with a home at 55 Ann Street, a few crowded blocks up the incline toward Broadway.

Front Street was to be the location of Phelps's office for all but a few years of his career and remained so when his sons took over until late in the century. It was an important street for trade, as the merchants could keep their counting houses within a few yards of the East River slips, where cargoes were loaded and unloaded. As early as the British departure from New York in 1783, Front Street was termed "the emporium of foreign commerce" because of its convenience to the East River slips, favored because of the shelter from the prevailing west winds. Built up on land filled with rubble and excavated soil, with Little Water Street and various wharves it was joined to form a continuous street from Whitehall to Beekman Slip in 1794; five years later it was considered one of the principal streets of the city. Like much of New York in the years of wood beam construction and inadequate fire-fighting equipment, its buildings had been swept by destructive fires and rebuilt several times and would be again during Phelps's lifetime.[10]

---

[10] Phelps-Stokes, *The Iconography of Manhattan Island*, 6:1304–305; Kenneth Holcomb Dunshee, *As You Pass By* (New York: Hastings House, 1952); John W. Ludwig, *Alphabet of Greatness: Manhattan's Street Names* (typescript, 1961; NYPL), 120–21.

The fruit traders were clustered in and around Phelps's office at 196. It was an impressive address for one starting out in business, for it was in one of the new buildings erected by Simon Schermerhorn in 1816–1817, which came to be called Schermerhorn Row. Phelps had placed himself in one of the best complexes of commercial buildings on the East River.[11] The 1826 city directory lists John Wait, grocer and fruiter at 199, and in later editions other fruiters and grocers are cited at the address. The office of his distant relative, Anson G. Phelps, one of the leading merchants of the time in the metals and cotton trade, was then at 181 Front Street at the corner of Burling Slip.[12] (Although the Schermerhorn block was destroyed, the neighboring buildings survived and are now part of South Street Seaport.)

A contemporary guidebook described the commercial complex by the East River in the 1820s:

> Front-street, and Water-street, together with the various slips intersecting them from South-street, are occupied by wholesale grocers and commission merchants, iron dealers, or as warehouses for the storage of merchandise and produce of every description . . . South-street, in its whole extent, is exclusively occupied by the merchants owning the shipping, and by those connected with that line of business, and it forms a range of warehouses, four and five stories in height, extending from the Battery to Roosevelt-street, facing the East river.[13]

The seaport city was ringed with wharves of virtually improvised construction at that time. "A frame-work of hewn logs is filled with loose stone, and covered with a surface of trodden earth," was how James Fenimore Cooper described them. He continued, "[T]he whole of the seven miles of water which fronts the city is lined with similar construction, if we except the public mall called 'The Battery,' which is protected from the waves of the bay by a wall of stone."[14]

---

[11] 196 Front Street discussed in "Historic Background Study of Block 74W," prepared for (N.Y.C.) Office of Economic Development, by Wendy Harris, 10 Oct. 1980; see also "Proposed Brooklyn Bridge Southeast LEA, Showing Construction Dates" (New York City Landmarks Preservation Commission, 1 May 1963), South Street Seaport Library. The Prudential-Bache building at the corner of Water Street occupies the Schermerhorn Row site today, adjacent to the principal entrance to the South Street Seaport.

[12] Richard Lowitt, *A Merchant Prince of the Nineteenth Century: William E. Dodge* (New York: Columbia Univ. Press, 1954), 14.

[13] Andrew T. Goodrich, *The Picture of New-York and Stranger's Guide to the Commercial Metropolis of the United States*, 1828, quoted in Phelps-Stokes, *Iconography*, 1673.

[14] Quoted in Albion, *Rise of New York Port*, 220.

Phelps's young manhood coincided with a burst of new activity in the port. The market for imported fruits was dependent on the wealth of New Yorkers, and the number enjoying such luxuries was expanding briskly.

One of the great celebrations in New York City history occurred on 4 November 1824, when the *Seneca Chief* arrived at the seaport after its traversal of the nearly completed Erie Canal and descent of the Hudson. The canal, whose last link was opened the next year, was an instant success. As Albion pointed out, although the elements that made New York port the center of shipping, finance, and manufacturing were in place before it was opened, the traffic generated by the canal greatly expanded the activity of the port. This led to an increase in the number of people gainfully involved in trade, from brokers to laborers, which in turn boosted the economy in general and the purchasing power of city residents. Thus opportunities abounded for the exchange of goods, all to the benefit of aspiring merchants such as Phelps.

The grains that arrived via the canal from the new fields of western New York soon became a major export crop. Grain and flour were to be shipped to southern ports, which sent back cotton in the same bottoms. Cotton went to Liverpool for the Manchester mills in ships that returned with metals, manufactured goods, and (later) immigrants. New York money flowed to the interior to purchase the commodities; it returned when the upstate storekeepers purchased goods from city agents. Soon commodity brokers learned to place advance payments against a contract with the farmer for the crop expected at the harvest; these contracts came to be fungible themselves, and a market in commodity futures emerged. The city's role as a financial center grew as trade increased in volume and type and new modes of exchange developed.

The burgeoning activities of the port required more and more commission agents, brokers, and factors, who bought and sold commodities, warehousemen, bankers, and insurance agents. Commodity specialists dealing in iron, copper, cotton, and flour replaced general merchants. The opportunities for gain pulled in the Yankee youths and before long, European immigrants as well.[15]

New Yorkers also had a way of adding value to the commodities they imported. This meant growth of supporting services: sugar had been refined in the city throughout the eighteenth century; hides and skins imported from Argentina after 1815 were made into boots and shoes;

[15] Ibid., 87–88.

wheat from upstate was processed into flour; Manchester textiles were converted into fashionable garments, which required ever more material and workmanship. The fashion trend was an astounding phenomenon: "the average dress of 1855 required some thirty yards of material, while the petticoats and other garments underneath brought the total close to 100 yards. This was about eight times the amount needed for all purposes in 1800."[16] Such manufacturing operations (and the financing and sales operations that accompanied them) added value to the imported cloth and required labor, fasteners, and other devices, all of which added to basic and middlemen jobs and thus had a multiplier effect on employment and on the financial markets. "By 1840," writes Edward K. Spann, the leading recent historian of the antebellum city, "New York's advantages had attracted the business talents and energies required to make it an international center of exchange—a wealth of outside skill and ambition infused into what had once been the sleepiest of the Atlantic ports."[17]

These New York mercantile families expanded and refined the financial instruments of trade that had been used by their colonial and European predecessors—double-entry bookkeeping, bills of exchange, and credit

---

[16] Ibid., 55. Albion cited Lucy Barton, who supplied him with the estimate for the astonishing quantities of material then used. Her *Historic Costume for the Stage*, illustrated by David Sarvis (1935; reprint, Boston: Walter H. Baker, 1961), is still a standard reference work. The styles in the early 1800s were virtually polar opposites. The thin, revealing Empire, or Republican, style for women was later displaced by an opulent style that used a great quantity of material, made possible by the sewing machine and the increase in wealth and purchasing power: "By 1855 . . . materials were heavy, colors were either somber or garish, chenille fringe and had cast their respectable blight on decoration. The sewing machine with its inviting possibilities for rapid and intricate stitching induced an orgy of braiding pleating, puffing, and tucking. The skirt grew wider and wider, more and more ornately trimmed. Just when women had reached a point where one would have said they could carry no more weight suspended from their waits, and therefore the style must surely change, behold the steel-wire hoop-skirt, which weighed only half a pound and could balance enormously wide side skirts with comparatively little discomfort to the wearer. As a result skirts expanded still further. . . . by the mid-1850s a skirt measured a minimum of ten yards around and sometimes ran into twenty or twenty-five if the goods were very thin . . . underpinnings until 1857 or '56 consisted of a multiplication of petticoats. In 1856: chemise, corset: long underdrawers trimmed with embroidery or lace . . . a couple of under-petticoats, one probably flannel; then the principal stiff petticoat, about three and a half yards around, heavily quilted and even wadded to the knee and stiffened with insert roundups of whalebone; under this another petticoat with three flounces of crinoline or heavily starched muslin, and on top of that more muslin petticoats, prettily decorated, over which a lady sometimes looped her skirt to take it from the ground." Barton, op. cit., 425, 440. See also Milla Davenport, *The Book of Costume* (New York: Crown Publishers, 1948), 376–78.

[17] Spann, *New Metropolis,* 6.

systems of trade were still indispensable tools of business. By midcentury, though, New York businessmen could also depend on banks for loans and deposits and on insurance companies for some degree of security. Business continued to be the pursuit of individuals until after the Civil War, when corporations became the dominant business force.

The merchant of the 1820s, unlike his colonial forebear, was a specialist. Alfred D. Chandler, Jr., writes of the colonial merchant that he "bought and sold all types of products and carried out all the basic commercial functions. He was an exporter, wholesaler, importer, retailer, shipowner, banker, and insurer." By the 1840s, however, in Chandler's analysis, such tasks were being carried out by different types of specialized enterprises. Numerous and readily accessible banks, insurance companies, and common carriers had appeared. Merchants had begun to specialize in one or two lines of goods, cotton, provision, wheat, dry goods, hardware, or drugs. They concentrated more and more on a single function, retailing, wholesale, importing, or exporting.[18] (The term "merchant" remained in wide use until after the Civil War.)

The society of businessmen in antebellum New York came to have fairly well defined roles for its members, and certain terms identified one man's entrepreneurial function to another.[19] A "merchant," in the colonial and early national periods was a general trader,[20] not a specialist in a single commodity. A "broker" or "factor," on the other hand, never sold directly to the public but brought buyers and sellers together and received a commission on his sales. He was entirely a middleman. A broker was also more of a specialist than the merchant; he dealt in a single line of goods, such as groceries, dry goods, drugs, iron, or hardware. The "commission merchant," like the broker, was a specialist, but unlike the broker, he sold

---

[18] "Doggett's 1846 *Directory* shows that the number of specialized business enterprises was highest in dry goods and groceries, with 318 in the first, 221 in the second. China, glass, and earthenware came next with 146, hardware with 91, drugs with 83, wines and spirits with 82, silks and fancy goods with 74, watches with 40 . . . [there were] more jobbers than importers in dry goods, groceries, china, glass and earthenware, and about the same number in drugs and wines and spirits. On the other hand, importers continued to dominate the hardware, fancy dry goods, and clothing trades. All 40 watch dealers were importers." Alfred D. Chandler, Jr., *Visible Hand*, 26.

[19] Porter and Livesay, *Merchants and Manufacturers*, 5.

[20] Sometimes referred to in the scholarly literature as "merchant capitalists," "colonial merchants," or "sedentary merchants."

partly on his own account. Finally there was the "jobber," who was a wholesaler who bought and sold on his own account, distributing purchases to other jobbers or to retailers.

A merchant house typically maintained accounts with factors in other ports and merchant houses abroad. A merchant would buy goods or commodities on account and balance that against expenditures for what he shipped back. (The charge to the purchaser of textiles sent from Manchester and Liverpool would be, for example, debited against the charge for the cotton or other goods sent eastward, with reckonings to be made at regular intervals.) In the Phelps–Dodge Collection in the New York Public Library this process is revealed in the correspondence between William E. Dodge in the New York office and factors and merchants in the southern North American ports and in Liverpool and London. Twice a year they compared accounts and made a reckoning, and the balance due would be paid by bank draft. This system depended greatly on credit and a large measure of trust. Like their colonial predecessors, these pre–Civil War merchants had to know well those with whom they dealt.[21]

The growth at New York was accompanied by the industrialization of the entire North Atlantic world. In the museum of Derby, England, there is a portrait of a large man in a bursting waistcoast. His commanding presence dwarfs a small table at his side on which there is a miniature machine. The man is Sir Richard Arkwright (1732–92), the machine is the spinning frame he invented, which made it possible for one person to spin twenty cotton threads. The hand-operated looms then in use soon became obsolete. With the mass-production of textiles, cotton cloth, once a luxury item, became common and inexpensive.[22]

Entrepreneurs built factories and marketed the textiles: "the great maw" of Manchester became the center of the new industry and drew laborers from the country. A few miles to the west was Liverpool, which in the early 1800s supplanted Bristol in the English Atlantic trade as the

---

[21] Phelps–Dodge Collection, box 5, letters, 1843, NYPL Mss. Div.

[22] The first application, using water power, was in Derbyshire in 1771, where two years later, the first wholly cotton cloth in England was produced. The application of this invention led to the cotton economy of the nineteenth century, which entailed supply through the slave plantations of the American south, commercial expansion in New York and Liverpool, and expansion of the factory system in Britain, all with far-reaching social implications.

prime destination of New York shipping. Manufactures, the factory system, and the trade they engendered transformed land and society.

Eli Whitney (1765–1825), of Connecticut, invented the cotton gin in 1793. His invention made it possible for cotton to be carded in large quantities and prepared for conversion into thread. It was not until after 1815, however, that the cotton trade significantly affected the port of New York. In the following years the cotton trade became the leading engine for the expansion of the economy of the port and city. There was no geographic determinant for this; cotton could have been shipped from Savannah, Charleston, Mobile, and New Orleans directly to Liverpool and thence to the mills of Manchester. That New York became the conduit for the cotton industry may be attributed entirely to the drive of the New York merchants, whose agents bought up the crops of the southern planters.[23]

Cotton was by no means the only commodity ensnared in the web of exchange. Flour, long a staple export from the Hudson Valley, arrived in increasingly larger quantities as the western fields opened up. Flaxseed, too, had been an export since colonial times. Naval stores, staves, and other wood products flowed into the city. Liverpool and New York City achieved economic preeminence together, inextricably linked through the cotton trade and the myriad other exchanges between the two ports that lasted from the 1820s to the end of the century.[24] The most prominent New York merchant and import houses had offices in Liverpool, invariably headed by a member of the family, a position the Phelps sons would assume after the Civil War.

---

[23] Albion, *Rise of New York Port*, 100ff.

[24] On Liverpool and the Atlantic trade in this period see Francis E. Hyde, *Liverpool and the Mersey: An Economic History of a Port 1700–1970* (Newton Abbot: David and Charles, 1971); David M. Williams, "Bulk Trade and the Development of the Port of Liverpool in the First Half of the Nineteenth Century," in Valerie Burton, ed., *Liverpool Shipping, Trade and Industry: Essays on the Maritime History of Merseyside 1780–1860* (Liverpool: National Museums and Galleries on Merseyside, 1989); Norman Sydney Buck, *The Development of the Organization of Anglo-American Trade, 1800–1850* (New Haven: Yale Univ. Press, 1925); John Crosby Brown, *A Hundred Years of Merchant Banking: A History of Brown Brothers and Company, Brown, Shipley & Company and the Allied Firms* (New York: Brown, Shipley, privately printed, 1909); Braithwaite Poole, *Commerce of Liverpool* (London and Liverpool, 1854); Thomas Baines, *History of the Commerce and Town of Liverpool and of the Rise of Manufacturing Industry in the Adjoining Counties* (London and Liverpool, 1852).

## The Yankees

Newly minted New Yorkers dominated New York's trade after Ghent; these were New Englanders, most of whom, like George Alexander Phelps, were from Connecticut. By the 1820s these Yankees became the famous "Codfish Aristocracy," looked at askance for their sharp and energetic ways by the Knickerbockers from the old Dutch families.

The best known in later times of the Connecticut boys who made good was Anson Greene Phelps (1781–1853), mentioned in the previous chapter. He and his partner, Elisha Peck, saw the opportunities in the metals trade—he bought and resold the sheaths of copper removed from the hulls of ships being broken up. He soon took advantage of the cotton trade, and his partner opened an office in Liverpool. Later he joined with his Hartford-born son-in-law, William E. Dodge (1804–83), who expanded the cotton and metals trade and added other commodities to the business.[25]

How did these Yankees do it? The midcentury chronicler of the merchants of New York City, Joseph A. Scoville, gave a fanciful account, often quoted for its color and, perhaps, insight into the poetic truth of the experience. The Yankee boy, he wrote,

> Gets a place somewhere in a "store," its all store to him. He hardly comprehends the difference between the business of the great South Street house that sends ships over the world, and the Bowery dry goods shop with three or four spruce clerks. He rather thinks the Bowery or Canal streets store the gigots, as they make more show. But wherever the boy strikes, he fastens. He is honest, determined and intelligent. From the word "go" he begins to learn, to compare, and no matter what the commercial business he is engaged in, he will not rest until he knows all about it, its details—in fact as much as the principals . . . no sooner has he got a foothold, than the New England boy begins to look for standing room for others.[26]

George Alexander, unlike the boy in Scoville's story, had come to the city in comfortable circumstances with his father, and his apprenticeship probably did not begin so humbly. The long and successful span of his

[25] This was the precursor of the Phelps Dodge Corporation. Dodge, known as a "merchant prince," was another Connecticut-born contemporary of George Alexander who was at the pinnacle of mercantile success. Lowitt, *A Merchant Prince of the Nineteenth Century*; Albion, *Rise of New York Port*, 248; Porter and Livesay, *Merchants and Manufacturers*, 20.

[26] Walter Barrett [Joseph A. Scoville], *The Old Merchants of New York City* (New York: Carlton, 1866), quoted in Albion, *Rise of New York Port*, 244.

career, however, indicates he observed, thought ahead, and moved as fast as Scoville's New England boy.

The successful Connecticut or Massachusetts man became a recognized type, caricatured and sometimes resented. Scoville described a merchant who "was the personification a Yankee—if there is such a race—long legs, hatchet face, skin and bones, slight[ly] pokey, and keen as a briar."[27] In Spann's more sober account, the Yankees were "only the most conspicuous element in a cosmos of talents and skills which had concentrated in New York. Collectively, this cosmopolitan merchant community formed the great system of knowledge required to manage the exchange of goods in both the national and international economies."[28]

George Alexander Phelps married Eliza Ayres in New York City on 8 September 1825, the year the Erie Canal was fully open. They began their married life at the 55 Ann Street address given in the directory for that year. The portrait made at the time of her marriage conveys the striking person of 17-year-old Eliza Ayres. It shows a titian-haired young woman seated with her left hand prominently placed to show her wedding ring. She is well dressed, and her expression is that of an astute and genteel young woman. The fact that there was a portrait and the quality of her clothing and jewelry indicate that her family was prosperous; the young couple appear to have had resources at the beginning of their married life.

Five years younger than George, Eliza Ayres was born on 6 November 1808, the daughter of John and Elizabeth (Pancoast) Ayres, who (according to a family record) had come to New York from Virginia.[29] From 1818 to 1823–24 "Ayres & Pancoast, silverplaters" are listed at 89 Maiden Lane; in 1821 John Ayres, "silver plater," is listed at that address. Since Pancoast was the maiden name of Ayres's wife, it is likely that his colleague in business was his brother-in-law or possibly his father-in-law.[30]

Julia Maria, their first child, was born 13 July 1826 in New York City, probably at the Ann Street address. The baby was named for her father's

---

[27] Albion, ibid., 242.

[28] Spann, *New Metropolis*, 7.

[29] Julia Phelps (Haring) White recorded that Eliza Ayres (her grandmother, who was alive until Julia was nearly 30) was born in Williamsport, Pennsylvania; this is repeated in Phelps 1899, which possibly used her as a source. JHW MSS. There are no church or other records from this time confirming the birth. There are no references to Ayres or Pancoast in J. F. Meginnes, *Biographical Annals of Deceased Residents of the West Branch Valley of the Susquehanna from the Earliest Times to the Present* (Williamsport, Penn.: Gazette and Bulletin Printing House, 1889).

younger sister, who had died at five months in 1805, when George was two years old.

The next year, while George's business remained at 196 Front Street, the family home was at 44 Roosevelt Street, which led up the hill from the East River. New York leases typically expired by the beginning of May, and as the city expanded there were new residences to move to and often more reasons to move away from commercial establishments in once residential streets. Philip Hone, the former mayor and diarist, recorded in May 1831, the "usual annual metamorphosis; many stores and houses are being pulled down, and others altered, to make every inch of ground productive to its utmost extent."[31] By then George Alexander's home was at 5 Chestnut Street, and two more daughters had been born, Caroline Eliza Phelps, on 13 September 1828, and Harriet Augusta, on 6 October 1830.[32] They and Julia Maria lived to maturity.[33]

New Yorkers at the time were conscious of their extraordinary prosperity. In May 1831 Philip Hone observed with pride that:

> Our country at large, and particularly this city, is at this time prosperous beyond all former example, and somewhat remarkable that all different interests, usually considered opposed to each other, are equally successful. Foreign commerce is in a thriving condition; vessels are worth fifty percent more than they were two years since, and freights are nearly double; real estate, up and down town, equally high; houses in great demand, at advanced rents; the dealers in imported goods doing a safe and profitable business; the farmer

---

[30] Julia Phelps (Haring) White recorded that Elizabeth Pancoast and John Ayres were born in Virginia, and that Elizabeth Pancoast was the daughter of Elizabeth White, "daughter of Mary White whose father was with Washington during the Revolution and was one of the sufferers at Valley Forge." Of Elizabeth White she wrote that her "brother was the father of Charles S. Pancoast, a lawyer in Philadelphia." JHW MSS. The surname is spelled "Ayres" in the New York City directory listings and on grave markers in the Phelps family plot. A payment from John Ayres to "M. Mead, Dr." of $5.10 for "schooling," dated 31 Jan. 1822, is among mss. in the author's possession. If it was for Eliza's instruction, she would have been 14 in that year. Eliza's sister Sarah (Ayres) Peck and brother Henry W. Ayres received bequests in her estate in 1880 (see later reference). Silversmiths Samuel Ayres (1767–1824) and Samuel Pancoast (?–1785) advertised in Philadelphia in the 1790s, and their surnames suggest a family connection. Stephen Guerney Cook Ensko, *American Silversmiths and Their Marks*, vol. 4, rev. and enlarged ed., comp. by Dorothea Ensko Wyle (Boston: David R. Godine, 1989). Considerable work remains to be done to clarify this family line.

[31] Philip Hone, *The Diary of Philip Hone, 1828–1851*, ed. Allan Nevins (New York: Dodd, Mead, 1927), 1:41, 5 May 1831.

[32] Chestnut Street was not far from City Hall. It no longer exists.

[33] See the Genealogical & Biographical Notes for a listing of the children of George Alexander and Eliza (Ayres) Phelps and references.

> selling his wool at seventy-five cents per pound, and availing himself of the increased price of breadstuffs occasioned by the brisk foreign demand; the manufactures, both of woolen and cotton goods, fully employed, and doing better than at any former period; and the lawyers doing nothing. This a cause of great exultation to our citizens, and should inspire them with gratitude to the Dispenser of all good things.[34]

The Phelps family were enjoying that prosperity. They resided at 28 Vandam in 1831 and 1832, a street that ran west from Broadway to the North River slips. This was an upward move, close to the spine of the city and away from the crowded area near the East River docks. Number 28 was close to the elegant shops on Broadway, a better residential area than where they had previously lived. (The address was a few blocks from Greenwich Street, where George Alexander had lived briefly when his father was alive.) Emma Ayres, their fourth child, was born there, 19 September 1832; she died as a young adult.

Alexis de Tocqueville landed at the Courtlandt Street North River pier, not far from the foot of Vandam, in May 1831 and sent home his impressions. "One sees neither dome, nor bell tower, nor great edifice," he wrote,

> With the result that one has the constant impression of being in a suburb. In its center the city is built of brick, which gives it a most monotonous appearance. The houses have neither cornices, nor balustrades, nor *porte-cocheres*. The streets are very badly paved, but sidewalks for pedestrians are to be found in all of them. We had all the trouble in the world getting lodgings because at this time of year strangers abound; and we wanted to find a *pension* rather than an inn. At length we succeeded in establishing ourselves admirably in the most fashionable street, called Broadway."[35]

On the self-congratulatory spirit he found among the residents de Tocqueville had a tart comment:

> Thus far the Americans seem to us to carry national pride altogether too far. I doubt whether it is possible to draw from them the least truth unfavorable to their country. Most of them boast about it without discernment and with an assertiveness that is disagreeable to strangers and that shows but little intelligence. In general it seems to me that there is much of the *small town* in their attitude and that magnify objects like people who are not accustomed to seeing great things.[36]

---

[34] Hone, *Diary of Philip Hone*, 1:41, 5 May 1831.

[35] Ibid., 67.

[36] Ibid.

## The Expanding City

Urban development in the colonial and early federal city was essentially confined to the area below the Collect Pond and the fetid canal that drained the northern limits of the built-up city. By the 1820s and 1830s development burst these bounds, and the pond and its watercourses were filled in, the latter becoming Canal Street. A grid system imposed on a map of the undeveloped island in 1811 confined development in the form of uniform rectangular blocks, with streets running west to east, avenues south to north. The blocks were divided into lots of a standard size. Although there were variations in this pattern as the city developed, most notably Central Park after the Civil War, the grid of streets and avenues remained the basic form. In the 1820s and 30s buildings were filling in the gridiron-patterned streets north of Canal. The population grew as Yankees and other country folk were attracted by the beacon of prosperity. In 1820 there were 123,706 in the city (up about 27,000 over the previous decade), in 1830 there were 202,899 (up 80,000), and by 1840 there were 312,710 an increase of 110,000.[37]

The standard residential construction at the time for an affluent family such as the Phelpses was the two- or three-story Federal-style house covering the width of a city lot, which was conventionally 25 feet wide by 100 feet deep. In that period, over half of the rear of the lot was customarily left open for a garden and a privy. A limited and fallible service brought water from springs north of the canal to houses and businesses, initially through wooden pipes. The pressure at the receiving end was variable, and as the water flowed only a few hours a day, the supply was inconvenient and notorious for failing when needed to extinguish fires.[38] The houses connected to the service had a tap below ground level where the service pipe entered, and water was carried in jugs from there to basins and vessels within the house. Human wastes were disposed of in the privy or picked up by the "night soil" man, who came after dark with his buckets to take the waste to the river to be dumped. The poor lived in shanties or in row houses in no longer fashionable streets, where the water supply was a well pump or fountain on the street.

---

[37] Rosenwaike, *Population History of New York City*, 16.

[38] Peter H. Judd, *How Much is Enough? Controlling Water Demand in Apartment Buildings* (Denver, Colo.: American Water Works Association, 1993), 15–30.

The expanding city was a noxious place. The odors of horse manure, garbage on the streets, and the night soil being carted to the rivers were omnipresent. Wells and piped water soon became contaminated. No one at the time understood that disease spread through the water supply, and Manhattan continued to be swept by epidemics in the warm weather. There was a severe outbreak of cholera in 1832. There were yellow fever epidemics in 1796, 1798, and 1822, when everyone who could afford to leave fled to Greenwich Village to escape contagion. The city was then a far less healthy place than the Connecticut towns of the preceding century, as the mortality among Eliza (Ayres) Phelps's children showed: five of the eleven died in childhood or early maturity.

The pressure from crowding, increasing commercialization south of Canal Street, and the prospect of living in modern accommodations propelled the well-to-do further and further uptown throughout the century. The Phelps family moved to Prince Street in 1833. This was (and is) an east-west street confined to the center of the island, four blocks above Canal Street; it was then traversed by West Broadway, Broadway, and Lafayette Street, and its east end met the Bowery.

George Alexander was keeping with fashion. Like Henry James's Dr. Sloper, he had been living downtown "in an edifice of red brick, with granite copings and an enormous fanlight over the door, standing in a street within five minutes' walk of the City Hall." (The Phelps on Vandam Street were also close.) That neighborhood

> Saw its best days (from the social point of view) about 1820. After this the tide of fashion began to set steadily northward, as, indeed, in New York, thanks to the narrow channel in which it flows, it is obliged to do, and the great hum of traffic rolled farther to the right and left of Broadway. By the time the Doctor changed his residence the murmur of trade had become a mighty uproar, which was music in the ears of all good citizens interested in the commercial development, as they delighted to call it, of their fortunate isle . . . when most of his neighbours' dwellings (also ornamented with granite copings and large fanlights) had been converted into offices, warehouses, and shipping agencies, and otherwise applied to the base uses of commerce, he determined to look out for a quieter home.[39]

Dr. Sloper's "ideal of quiet and genteel retirement" when he made his move in 1835 was Washington Square, several blocks north and east of

---

[39] Henry James, *Washington Square* (1880; New York: Library of America, 1985), 11.

Prince Street. Like the fictional doctor, Phelps moved for similar reasons. So did Philip Hone, who moved uptown in the same year. "All the dwelling houses downtown are to be turned to stores," he wrote, "We are tempted with prices so exorbitantly high that none can resist, and the old downtown burgomasters, who have fixed to one spot all their lives, will be seen during the next summer in flocks, marching reluctantly north to pitch their tents in places which in their time were orchards, cornfields."[40]

The Prince Street address removed the genteel families for a time from the most crowded part of the city. It was far from the great fire of August 1835, which destroyed 679 buildings on and near Wall Street, including that temple of commerce known as the Merchants Exchange, the symbol of the booming city that Phelps doubtless frequented for his transactions with other merchants.[41] George Alexander's business address in these years was 103 Front Street, the home addresses were 113, 140, and 143 Prince Street, each in the vicinity of Broadway.[42]

The family on Prince Street was growing. The four girls, Julia Maria, Caroline Eliza, Harriet Augusta, and Emma Ayres, were joined by George Alexander Jr., born 24 July 1834. He too was a healthy child and lived into the next century. The four children born in the eight years from 1836 to 1844 died early, multiple devastations in the midst of Eliza's child-bearing years. It is a curious pattern: four healthy children, followed by the four ill-fated ones, followed by three healthy boys. Amelia Chamberlain lived only from May to January in 1836. Her middle name honored her father's business partner, William M. Chamberlain, who was to remain associated with him for many years.[43] Henry Demarest was born in 1837 and died at

---

[40] Hone, *Diary of Philip Hone*, 1:202–3, 9 March 1836. Hone bought a 29' x 30' lot from Samuel Ward for $15,000 at the corner of Broadway and Great Jones Street.

[41] Ibid., 186–91.

[42] It is one of these properties that "George Alexander Phelps of the town and Co. of Fairfield, Connecticut Merchant and Elisa [sic] his wife" sold in 1853. It was 20' x 71'3". *New York City Records of Conveyances*, lib. 634, 149, 5 March 1853, 1 April 1853.

[43] See the Genealogical & Biographical Notes. The firm Chamberlain & Phelps, Shipping & Importing is reported at 103 Front Street by R. G. Dun & Co. in 1850, the same address as shown for G. A. Phelps in the 1837 city directory. (In 1851 Dun recorded that the firm's "trade was judged to be increasing in wealth . . . as merchants they rank high in credit," New York City, Dun, 340:37, 24 Dec. 1851.) William Chamberlain (probably William M.) was associated with George Alexander Phelps in 1855. There are deeds of Shepherd Knapp to Wm. Chamberlain & George A. Phelps for land in N.Y.C. dated 30 March 1855 and a deed of Gideon Lee to Wm. Chamberlain & George A. Phelps for land in N.Y.C. of the same date. *New York City Records of Conveyances*. Phelps wrote to the son of William Chamberlain in 1872, inquiring about a business matter and reporting his father's ill health. George Alexander Phelps to William Chamberlain [Jr.], 28 August 1872, *Misc.* MSS., G. A. Phelps, NYHS.

age 16. This middle name was that of an old New Amsterdam family, many of whose members lived in what was then Rockland County (formerly Orange County, "south of the mountains"), where New York and New Jersey meet by the Tappan Zee. It recurs in the name of Phelps's future son-in-law, James Demarest Haring, who was to marry Caroline Eliza in 1846.[44]

## A Country Retreat

In the spring of 1836 George Alexander Phelps bought property in Fairfield, Connecticut, where he kept a house as a country retreat for the family. A steam ferry service from the East River connected to nearby Bridgeport in three and a half hours. The property was on what was then called Main Street, within one of the four original squares that had formed the colonial town. The Congregational Church was at a crossroads a few lots to the east. There was a house on the property said to have been built around 1800, which Phelps brought up to date in the romantic Gothic style "with surrounding verandahs, a center gable."[45]

A photograph shows a charming building, whose verandah with trellis columns would have provided shade and cool for the family during their summer stays. The house was by the street on a long, deep lot that allowed room for a stable, a carriage house, and other outbuildings. There were tradesmen, school, and church within easy walking distance on tree-lined streets. The tax record of 1840 shows that Phelps owned 20 acres assessed at $1,300 and a house assessed at $1,400; there were two horses, a carriage, two cows, and three timepieces.[46]

The growing family could spend summers in the country. By the 1840s Fairfield was a fashionable spot for affluent New Yorkers, providing a social life for Eliza Phelps and her daughters and a healthy retreat from the

---

[44] Phelps must have had an association with a Demarest, although there is no record of it. William Chamberlain was born in Fairfield on 28 May 1840 and died two years later; Sarah Allen was born there in 1842 and survived only three years.

[45] Charles S. Peden, "The Old Post Road," *Fairfield Citizen*, 3 April 1974, is an illustrated article about the house, which still stands, remodeled in a colonial style with a current address as 766 Old Post Road (opposite Penfield Road). Phelps purchased the property on 28 April 1836 from Rebecca Rogers. Fairfield [Conn.] Land Records, 44:134–35, 833, Office of the Town Clerk.

[46] Tax Records, Town of Fairfield, from notebooks in the collection of the Fairfield [Conn.] Historical Society.

34. The Phelps Family House in Fairfield, Connecticut, 1836–1870
The family spent summers and some winters here, maintaining their principal residence in New York. In the "Gingerbread" Gothic style, this house, though greatly altered, still stands at 766 Old Post Road.

infectious hazards of city life.[47] They occupied this first of the family's two houses on Main Street from 1836 to 1870. Phelps bought adjacent lots over the years, which expanded the property; he also bought and sold other lots in the vicinity.[48] One purchase was a house for his mother and two unmarried sisters. The 1840 census lists Phebe in a nearby house, and the next two decennials list her with her two daughters, Phebe and Harriet, and a maidservant (in 1860 this was Aletia Goranna, 21, born in Ireland).[49]

---

[47] Farnham, *Fairfield*, 156.

[48] There are 44 entries in the Fairfield Land Records for George A. Phelps as grantee or grantor.

[49] U.S. census, Fairfield, Conn., 22 Sept. 1840, 365; 18 Sept. 1850, 11, dwelling no. 175, family 186; 10 July 1860, 967, dwelling 529, family 588. George Alexander Phelps entries: 1840, 362; 1850, 12, dwelling 179, family 180. The G. A. Phelps house also had Irish servants; the three listed in 1850 were Ellen Drew, age 40, Ellen Neville, 18, Mary O'Neill, 55, all born in Ireland. There are no entries for the G. A. Phelps family in the censuses of 1860 and 1870, presumably because the family was out of town on the day of the survey. In 1880, after G. A. Phelps's death, the widow Eliza and her son, Charles Haring Phelps, and his family are listed on 22 June 1880, 22C.

Fairfield is about forty miles from New York City. It had several harbors used in the coastal trade from colonial times into the next century. In 1830 it was a village of about 3,600 inhabitants, fewer by 400 than it had been ten years before.[50] The colonial town had been badly damaged when the British troops under Tryon burned it in 1779, and several of the prosperous Loyalist families left at the peace. After the War of 1812 opportunity elsewhere drew its youth, but farms with a prosperous New York trade remained.

The city had attracted a number of local boys who, like Scoville's Connecticut youths, made themselves wealthy on South Street. They returned to build elaborate country retreats, "an acceptable way of demonstrating to friends and neighbors the extent of their success, and by constructing a home that reflected the latest trends in architecture, they could show that they possessed the good taste with which men of wealth surely ought to be endowed."[51] The Greek Revival style was fashionable in the 1820s (an outstanding example of which Phelps purchased after the Civil War). A local historian at the time termed the community created by the Yankee New Yorkers in the romantic styles of the time, "the loveliest of earthly paradises."[52]

## "The Volcano has Burst"

The financial crisis of the mid-1830s was a result of speculation in western lands and a worldwide overextension of credit. It began with signs of weakness in the economy, which prompted withdrawals from the banks during the spring of 1837; this escalated to a rush on the banks, then bank closings, and the collapse of credit. It was a full-scale financial panic.

In May 1837 Philip Hone wrote, "The volcano has burst and overwhelmed New York; the glory of her merchants is departed. After a day of unexampled excitement, and a ruthless run upon all the banks, which drew from their vaults $600,000 in Specie yesterday." The nearly complete col-

---

[50] U.S. census data for Fairfield, Conn., from La Voie, et al., *A Graphic Presentation of Population Data.*

[51] Thomas J. Farnham, *Fairfield: The Biography of a Community, 1639–1989* (Fairfield, Conn.: Fairfield Historical Society, 1988), 146.

[52] Ibid., 141, 147; D. Hamilton Hurd, *History of Fairfield County, Connecticut, with Illustrations and Biographical Sketches of its Prominent Men and Pioneers* (Philadelphia, Pa.: J. W. Lewis, 1881), 332.

lapse in credit meant no trading, freezing the transactions of the port. A few days later Hone reported that a "deadly calm pervades this lately flourishing city. No goods are selling, no business stirring, no boxes encumber the sidewalks of Pearl Street."[53] Hundreds of businesses closed, including some of the best known firms, their owners ruined.

George Alexander Phelps survived, as he would all of the panics of his lifetime; he retained his office address at 172 Front Street from 1826 to 1840. He was then in partnership with Charles H. Hill, and the firm is listed as Phelps & Hill. Trade revived a year later, an example of the resilience of the city's economy that it had shown in the past and would again in the future.

On 25 April 1838 the first Atlantic steam-powered ships, the *Sirus* and the *Great Western*, from Liverpool, arrived in the port. The transit time to and from Liverpool shrank from 40 or more days each way to two weeks, and the capacity of the ships became far larger. The new technology greatly expanded the triangular trade. The New York merchants bought cotton from the southern planters, shipped it to New York, where it was in turn shipped to Liverpool (often adding grains and wood products to the cargo); Liverpool merchants sent metals, manufactured goods, and people on the westward journey.[54] Steam ocean transportation had a direct effect on Phelps's business. The reduced transit time from the Mediterranean meant some fresh citrus could be imported.

From 1840 to 1842 George Phelps (no "A") is listed with a residence at 218 East Broadway, in 1843 and 1844 at 165 East Broadway. There is no listing for Phelps & Hill; Charles H. Hill, "merchant," lived at 100 Second Avenue with a business address at 20 South Street, suggesting Hill was then in the dry goods trade. George A. Phelps reappears as "comm. mer." (the first of his designations as merchant) in 1844 with a business address at 103 Front Street, the firm's office until the end of his active career 25 years later. Although the moves early in the 1840s may indicate some business strain, by mid-decade he was on a rising curve of prosperity.

From 1850 we can observe the firm through the chatty R. G. Dun & Co. reports on its credit standing.[55] In 1850 Dun found that the credit of "Chamberlain & Phelps, Shipping & Importing" (Phelps in partnership

---

53 Hone, *Diary of Philip Hone*, 1:257, 263 (10 and 26 May 1837).

54 Ibid., 317.

55 This firm preceded Dun & Bradstreet.

with William M. Chamberlain) was "Fair but paper not very saleable."[56] A year later, after the retirement of a partner named Robinson, the firm's "trade was judged to be increasing in wealth . . . as merchants they rank high in credit." In 1852 the partners "continue to do a favorable business . . . The firm is called rich & making money, with v. gd. Credit."[57] By 1854 it was even better: The partners "[a]re in the best of credit & thought to be a very strong, long and good standing, are engaged in shipping and do a good business . . . A first rate house and report worth $300,000. Doing a large & profitable business."

In 1855 George A. Phelps, Jr., was admitted a partner, "a son of the 'p' of the firm . . . was clerk. He is smart & energetic, & a young man of great promise. He puts in a Capital Comm. & his admission is considered an acquisition in every point of view. He has thitherto & will continue to sustain a good career." (George Jr. is listed as "clerk" in the firm at age 15 in the 1850 U.S. census listing for the Phelps family in Fairfield.[58]) The partners "are in good credit . . . considered quite wealthy . . . & can make a good note."

There was another devastating financial panic in 1857; this involved the first New York stock market crash and was followed by a far worse depression of trade than in 1837. The Phelps partners were not impaired: in July 1858 Dun reported that the partners are "supposed to have made $27,000 on the last cargoes of fruit from the Mediterranean." In 1859 they were a "well established mercantile exportation, best credit."[59]

In 1861 Howard and Frank Phelps entered the firm as clerks, "[r]egarded sound, responsible, reported worth about a million. Chamberlain pays very little attention to bus., they give out but little paper, reliant men and have an unquestioned credit." The business appears to have been undeterred by the Civil War: in June 1864 Dun wrote "Have large means & give out no paper, one doing a good trade and either partner can retire with ample property"—as George Alexander, Sr., was shortly to do. In July "Frank Phelps this day admitted as partner," and the transition to

---

[56] Dun 374:799, 374:800a86, 374:800a153.

[57] William M. Chamberlain is reported to have joined the firm that year as clerk, the traditional position for a son growing up in the business. This undoubtedly was the son of the partner who was G. A. Phelps's contemporary.

[58] 1850 U.S. census, Fairfield, Conn., M432.38, 190.

[59] In autumn 1859 Chamberlain bought one third of 103 Front Street from John C. Cruger. Dun, 340:37, Nov. 1858.

Phelps Brothers was ready. In the fall of 1866 Dun opines that they "Continue to do a very large business with unlimited credit. Pecuniary strength from 500,000 to 1 million."

On 1 October 1868 Dun reported an advertisement announcing that the two senior partners, William M. Chamberlain and George Alexander Phelps, had retired from the firm. Charles Haring Phelps was admitted as a partner. Six months later, according to Dun, Chamberlain left funds in the firm and the "three sons continue in the house in the old style, have over 200,000 in their own standing." July 1871 Howard Phelps was admitted as partner: "former clerk, no means to speak of . . . firm occupies a high position in the trade."[60]

The transition to Phelps Brothers was complete with the assumption to the partnership of the four Phelps sons and the departure of the Chamberlain interest. What Dun reports is an enviable record of success on the part of the senior Phelps, who could retire in his mid-60s with ample means and the knowledge that his sons were carrying on a highly successful business.

George Alexander Phelps prospered when the city's commercial establishment was dominated by traders whose interests were in low tariffs, sound money, and freedom of trade, and whose political and (often) social affiliations reflected these views. Most of the New York merchants opposed Andrew Jackson in the 1830s and, as Philip Hone bitterly recorded, blamed his destruction of the Bank of the United States for the financial panic of 1837. New York merchants opposed the tariffs pushed by neighboring New England to protect their manufactures from British competition. In this they were allied with southern planter interests. Thus when the fissures in the republic widened in the late 1840s and throughout the 1850s the New York merchants supported compromise to save the Union and generally did not welcome the influence of the Abolitionists. After Fort Sumter there was a split between the old Whig merchants, who did not favor the re-making of the Union by force, and the modernizing Republicans, who emerged as a party in the 1850s and supported the maintenance of the union.

While George Alexander may have shared the ethos of the free-trading Whig merchant of his times, there are no traces of his political or social affiliations in numerous records. He seems to have applied himself to business and family, and, of course, much of his interest was in the family's Connecticut retreat. He was not a member of the venerable New England Society, founded 1805, to demonstrate the rise of the Yankees in the busi-

---

[60] Dun 374:799.

### THE LOAD OF COMMERCE

*The* Commercial Advertiser *of 15 September 1854 cost a lofty six cents (the* Tribune *and* Evening Post *were one-cent papers). It is a huge bedsheet of a paper, four pages, 25" x 30", ten columns to a page, densely printed in small type. Most of it consists of advertisements. From it the merchant could gain information about ship arrivals and departures, commodity and stock prices, public sales, advertisements for schools, etc. The range of goods being advertised is revealed in the categories used to organize the classified advertisements:*

*Flour*[a]
*Hop Sacking*
*India Rubber*
*Negro Kerseys*
*choice state flour*
*Alsopp's India Pale Ale*
*Table Tea Kettles*
*For sale and To Let*
*Clover Seed*
*Manila Gum Opal*
*Beans*
*Wicking*
*Linseed Oil*
*Fancy Cassimeres*
*Peace Dale Shawls*
*Linings*
*Prime Pork*
*China Tin*
*White Sarsenets*[b]
*Negro Colored Cotton*
*Whiskey*
*Superfine Flour*
*Apron Checks*
*Rye Flour*
*Lard*
*Extra Genesee Flour*
*Rhine Wines*
*Water Pitchers and Coolers*
*Sheathing Felt*
*Fine Pen Knives*
*Cotton Cordage*

a. By place of origin.
b. From "saracen cloth," a very fine and soft silk material used for linings. *OED*.

ness establishment and active throughout the pre-war years.[61] He did not serve on committees of the chamber of commerce, which had a membership of several hundred.[62] The list goes on. His name does not appear on any of the petitions of the period on issues that impacted his fellow merchants and leading citizens. His was not among the names calling for order after the Macready riots of 1849 (in which supporters of the American actor DeForest fought with supporters of the English Macready, resulting

[61] Horace McK. Hatch, *The New England Society in the City of New York* (New York: privately printed, 1957).

[62] The list of the members for the period is not extant. Joseph Bucklin Bishop, *A Chronicle of One Hundred & Fifty Years: The Chamber of Commerce of the State of New York, 1768–1918* (New York: Charles Scribner's Sons, 1918).

in several deaths). Nor did he subscribe with other merchants to the farewell dinner for August Belmont in 1853; nor was he at the Pine Street meeting in December 1860, in which merchants urged a moderate course against the South after the election of Lincoln. Nor was he a member of the Century Association, Union Club, or the pro-Republican Union League Club.[63]

Neither was this Phelps recognized as one of New York's wealthy. The wealthy were publicized in guidebooks, the most famous of which were in the annual series put out by Moses Yale Beach, entitled *Wealth and Wealthy Citizens of New York City*. These gave the curious an estimate of an individual's net worth and included remarks such as "from a respectable family." G. A. Phelps appeared in neither the 1845 nor the 1855 edition. (Anson G. Phelps and his sons amply represented the surname, however.) If he had philanthropic or religious interests there is no record of them; he left neither church nor charity bequests.

## The Palermo Office

A family member in charge of an office in a trading port assured secure and honest dealings; with George Jr., now a partner in charge, the firm opened an office in Palermo in 1859. Sicilians grew oranges and lemons for export, and the island was well located in relation to the Levant ports. George Jr. may have been in Palermo in the midst of the overthrow of its government in May and June 1860 (he is shown with home address in "Europe" in the 1859 directory for the first time). It was then that an enthusiastic populace welcomed Garibaldi and his insurgents to Palermo. The royal forces surrendered virtually without a shot, and the rule of the Bourbons of Naples and the Kingdom of Two Sicilies came to an end. Following his seizure of the Neapolitan capital and the collapse of the monarchy, Sicily and southern Italy joined the newly created Kingdom of Italy.[64]

---

63 "List of Merchant Subscribers to Belmont Farewell Dinner," 9 Aug. 1853, in August Belmont, *Letters, Speeches and Addresses* (New York, 1890), 3–4; "List of Macready Petitioners," The Pine Street Meeting, 15 Dec. 1860 and Membership of the Union League Club of New York, 1863, from Union League Club, Articles of Assoc., by-laws, Officers and Members of the Union League Club, 1863, in Iver Bernstein, *The New York City Draft Riots: Their Significance for American Society and Politics in the Age of the Civil War* (New York: Oxford Univ. Press, 1990), 272–76; Century Association Yearbook, "Former Members," (New York, 1984 *et seq.*); Will Irwin, Earl Chapin May, Joseph Hotchkiss, *A History of the Union League Club of New York City* (New York,: Dodd, Mead, 1952).

64 "Naples, Kingdom of," *Encyclopaedia Britannica*, 11th ed., 1911.

The young Phelps was in Palermo for much of the 1860s.[65] In those years it was a fashionable place for vacations and had a "season" in the winter. George Jr.'s niece, Julia Phelps Haring, visited him in December 1869, when Palermo feted the bride of its crown prince. She saw "Uncle George and Aunt Helen Phelps dressed in the most gorgeous apparel starting off for one of the balls." The newly married Marguerite, later queen of Italy, was "a lovely, young bride not more than seventeen—my age—and with her husband and King Victor Emanuel—the prince's father—were receiving all the homage the people could shower on them."[66]

## City and Suburb

From 1844 to 1848 Phelps's residence is listed at 622 and 624 Broadway; from 1848 for the next ten years the home address is "Conn.," meaning Fairfield. The Broadway addresses were rooming houses, probably of quality, as it was then a fashionable part of the avenue near Bleecker Street. This would indicate that the family remained in Fairfield. However, Eliza gave birth in New York in March 1844 and December 1846. Her last child was born in Fairfield in September 1849, which seems to indicate that the family was in the city in the cold weather months. The directory in these years referred to Phelps variously as importer or merchant ("imp," "mer"). The family's dual residences in Fairfield and the city came after regular train service along the Connecticut shore had begun. By 1849 there were regular departures from stations at Canal Street and 34th Street in Manhattan to Connecticut shore points to New Haven. The trip to Fairfield took two hours and ten minutes from 34th Street.[67]

The three last-born of Eliza's twelve children were boys who lived to ripe ages and, with George Jr., formed Phelps Brothers to continue the business after their father's retirement. Frank, not given a middle name, was born in New York City on 24 March 1844 and died in 1937, the long-

---

[65] George Jr., 27 in 1861, was of age to serve in the Union Army, but spent most of the war years abroad. His daughter Helen was born in New York City in 1863, though his business address continued to be "Europe" in the directories. Phelps 1899.

[66] This trip can be traced through letters from Julia Phelps Haring to her paternal aunt, Catharine Teller (Haring) Kip, in 1868–69, manuscripts in possession of the author; Julia Phelps (Haring) White to Carol White Griggs, 19 Jan. 1926.

[67] Farnham, *Fairfield,* 150, 152. Lydia Maria Francis Child (1802–1880) was an author and abolitionist. *DAB.*

est-lived of the children. Like his older brother, he was of age to be drafted in 1863. According to a nephew, writing eighty years later, he "seems to have been drafted and supplied a sub who was killed, but Frank died in his 98th year on bought time."[68] He became a partner and a lawyer and administered the estate of his sister and Haring brother-in-law until the end of the century.

Charles Haring Phelps was born in New York City 10 December 1846. His middle name commemorated James Demarest Haring, of New York, who had married Caroline Eliza on 1 September of that year. He too became a partner and carried on in the business into the next century.[69] Howard, the last child, also with no middle name, was born in Fairfield on 6 September 1849, when Eliza was 41. He became a partner with his brothers and like them, was long-lived, dying at 75 in 1924.

## The Harings

The first of the children to be married was Caroline Eliza, the second born. Her marriage to James Demarest Haring united a family with New Amsterdam roots with the Connecticut Phelpses. There is symmetry in the connection through marriage of a family importing wheat from the hinterland, using the Erie Canal and the Hudson River for its transport, and a family with transatlantic interests. Between them they touched the major geographic areas of the port's activity. James and Caroline's family remained close to the senior Phelps's family, frequently sharing the Fairfield and New York City addresses. Eliza (Ayres) Phelps was pregnant with her next-to-last child at the time of the wedding, and bore her last after the first of the Haring children was born.

The wedding took place in Fairfield on 1 September 1846, when the bride was 18 and the groom 27.[70] The couple sat individually for their portraits (figs. 1 and 2); Caroline Eliza is shown with a sensitive, reserved expression. She wears a lace collar and a brooch pinning the collar of her

[68] Letter from Charles Haring Phelps [III] in New Milford to "George" 24 June 1942, mss. in Fairfield Historical Society. With the letter was enclosed a crayon drawing of George Alexander Phelps, and the writer queried if recipient, stated to have been "born in '61," would "remember it as a reasonable likeness." The author cannot identity "George"; there was no Phelps child of that name who survived born in the 1860s. Frank Phelps died 27 September 1937, aged 92 years. *NYT*, 30 Sept. 1937 23:4. The crayon portrait is reproduced in this text.

[69] There is no notice of his death in the *NYT*.

[70] The date of the wedding is cited in family manuscripts and in Phelps 1899. No church record has been found.

35. James Demarest Haring (1819–1868)
These photographs of James and John Samuel were probably taken in the 1850s

dark, possibly velvet dress. Her hair is parted in the middle, brought down tight on each side covering the ears. It is an indication of dress that a historian terms a "graceful ultra-feminine and tasteful style."[71] Photographs of Caroline Eliza in later years suggest delicacy, perhaps confirmed by the birth of only two children recorded to the couple in 22 years of marriage. James Demarest Haring was given an elegant, refined look by the portraitist; he wears a high collar, a black tie in a bowed knot—he is a gentleman in his best. In a photograph taken about a dozen years later (above) he is ruggedly handsome, with an expressive face that suggests a gusto for living in contrast to his wife's reserve.

James Demarest Haring was a flour broker, partner in a firm started by his brother. They were part of that new community of opportunity that had grown up since the Erie Canal opening, and as flour brokers they were directly involved in buying the crops from the western New York lands and selling them in the city. The Haring office (from 1843 to 1854, when the building was razed) was at 35 Peck Slip at the northwest corner with

[71] "The distinguishing features being: demurely parted hair (arranged either in glossy curls or in smooth puffs over the ears), over it a small poke bonnet or a shallow-crowned gypsy hat; a tight, smooth bodice with long, slim, pointed waist; sleeves revealing the shape of the arm, long, full skirts, held out in a moderate bell-shape." Barton, *Historic Costume for the Stage*, 424.

36. John Samuel Haring (1810–1860)

Front Street, a short distance from Phelps at 103 Front.[72] Both were in the heart of the teeming East River docks: carters by the hundreds trucked consignments to and from the ships, and brokers such as the Harings checked consignments.

The firm of John S. Haring & Co. was consistently in business through the ups and downs of the business cycle, as was Phelps's. James Demarest's older brother, John Samuel Haring (1810–1860), began business as a grocer at 75 Bowery in 1831, and he and the firm were listed in city directories for the next 29 years as a flour broker. The business moved about in the early years, from West Street (on the North River) and Ludlow (on the Lower East Side) until Haring came to an office at 35 Peck Slip in 1843, when he was joined by his brother James Demarest, nine years his junior. (The site is at the corner of Peck Slip, leading in from the piers and the south–north Front Street. A hotel stands there now within the South Street Seaport.) When the Peck Slip building was replaced, they moved to 47 Pearl Street (1854–55) and then to 121 Broad until John's death. Each of the addresses was close to the heart of the seaport's commercial activity.

[72] The building that replaced the one where the Harings had their office is still standing, and is a hotel now in the historic district near the South Street Seaport.

R. G. Dun gave the firm a good rating in 1854, in a report that has more of a gossipy character than the one Phelps received. John Samuel Haring had, the report went, "been in bus. several years, formerly at Front Street, corner Peck Slip where he is supposed to have accumulated several thousand besides which his wife [Mary Clark, first cousin, see below] is supposed to have 20,000 in her own right. James D. became interested in the business about 3 years ago [in fact 12 years before] . . . been a clerk before. JD thought not to have means. Last spring they removed to the present location where the bus. has improved. They have a gd. Custom with Bakers and are in good credit with the trade."[73]

In the midst of the 1857 panic, Dun stated that the Harings "[a]re doing a cautious bus mostly as a Jobbing bus; are smart active & cautious, understand their business & attend closely to it & in good credit & good credit for contracts."[74] They seem not to have been harmed by the ensuing depression, for in the next year Dun laconically commented that the partners "stand well w. houses in that line."[75] The next year Dun reported "various est. of worth highest 50,000, av. 30–40" and "considered reliable for purchases."[76] John Samuel had considerable money to invest, as he "bought the interest of various parties in Feb. & May 58 in lot 18, South Street with water rights for $20,000."[77] While not as wealthy as Phelps, the senior Haring had prospered in the port.

James Demarest Haring was one of three minor children left in his mother's guardianship at his father's death in the city in 1831; he was 12, a brother, Clinton, 14, and Sarah Elizabeth, 7. There were two married sisters in Albany, and the eldest brother, John Samuel, was already in business at 21. The widow, Sarah (Clark) Haring, saw to it that the minor children were educated and that James and his younger brother were launched on their careers.[78]

---

[73] Dun, 370:585, 2 Nov. 1855.

[74] Ibid., 4 April 1857.

[75] Ibid., 4 Aug. 1858.

[76] Ibid., 14 March 1859.

[77] Ibid., 25 March 1859. J. S. Haring also "bot in Jan 5 2 lots in 132nd Street, east of 6th Ave. and 2 lots in 133rd St. West of 5th Ave. of Clinton Haring for $9"[Clinton Haring, younger brother, died in 1855; the purchase was from the estate].

[78] Clinton became a lawyer with a Wall Street address but died of tuberculosis while still a young man in 1855. James Demarest, as we have seen, joined his brother's business in his early 20s and would live to be nearly 50 when he too died of tuberculosis. That scourge took Sarah Elizabeth at age 18. See the Genealogical & Biographical Notes.

James Demarest's father was Captain Samuel Haring (1776–1831), to use the title that was his for service with the 13th U.S. New York Regiment on Lake Ontario in the War of 1812. Samuel had been a grocer in the city in the early part of the century and moved to Albany in 1812. He joined the 13th before the outbreak of the war, and in the 1813 campaign along the southern shore of Lake Ontario became severely ill with "lake fever," which affected his health in the latter part of his life. He and his wife returned to the city a few months before his death in 1831. She lived for another ten years, and must have been largely responsible for giving James and his younger brother a solid start in life.

The first of the family in the New World was Jan Pietersen Haring (ca. 1633–83), who arrived as a child from Holland in the 1630s. He married Grietje Cosyns (1641–ca. 1724), who brought with her a farm in the Manhattan Out Ward (near the present Bowery). After the British conquest he joined with other farmers of modest means to buy a tract from the Indians near the west banks of the Hudson River by the Tappan Zee, about 30 miles north of the Battery. (It was then "south of the mountains" in Orange County, within the present-day limits of Rockland County.) Until the disruption of the Revolution a hundred years later, this "Tappan Patent" provided ample land for division among the children and grandchildren of the original patentees. Jan's son, Peter (1664–1750), and his grandson, Abraham (1704–71), were prominent local leaders, each elected by their Orange County neighbors to represent them in the Province of New York Assembly. These leaders thus provided a link between their Dutch yeoman farmer neighbors and the English-dominated government and economy of New York City.[79]

Abraham's son, John Haring (1739–1809), was the most eminent of these Haring men. With little schooling, he trained himself as a surveyor and lawyer and in both capacities served clients in Orange County and New York City. He was a leader in the movement within the Dutch Reformed Church to establish a seminary for ministers in America (the future Rutgers College) and was one of its founding trustees. As disputes over trade restrictions intensified in the mid-1770s he was active in opposition in Orange County and was elected a delegate to the Continental Congress in 1775. As someone who was equally known and respected in the

---

[79] For a study at the Haring family in eighteenth-century Orange County and the Manhattan "cousins" see Firth Haring Fabend, *A Dutch Family in the Middle Colonies, 1660–1800* (New Brunswick, N.J.: Rutgers Univ. Press, 1991).

city as in the county he was a member of the various revolutionary bodies formed in 1775 and 1776, and was president *pro tem* of the convention that effectively ruled the city in 1776 until the British occupation of Manhattan. He was a local leader consulted by Washington on three wartime encampments of the Continental Army at Tappan. In Tappan during the war he was the head of a large patriot family (including exiles from the city) living in a region that, in the early years, was in a state of civil war and foraged by both armies.

Before the Revolution John Haring married his first cousin, Mary (1751–1825), daughter of Elbert Herring (1706–73). Elbert was a "city cousin" of the Tappan Harings who had anglicized his name. He had expanded the family land holdings on Manhattan to be the second largest farm on the island at the time of his death. Other of Elbert's daughters married prominent men, among them Cornelia, who married the Samuel Jones quoted at the beginning of this chapter. There were Kip, Roosevelt, and Herring in-laws, whose descendants were part of James Demarest Haring's associations in the New York of seventy years later.

John Haring was a "Clintonite," a supporter of the first governor of the state, George Clinton. Like Haring, his origins were on the west bank of the Hudson and, he was of the "west banker" faction opposed in politics to the gentry with large land holdings on the east bank of the Hudson. From 1780–84 Haring served in the New York State Senate, and in 1786 and '87 he returned to the Continental Congress, then meeting in New York City. He opposed the federal constitution in the 1788 ratification convention (as had George Clinton until the final vote). He spent the remaining years of his life as a surveyor and lawyer in Bergen County, New Jersey, and Rockland County.[80] Samuel was his first son and second child, born in Tappan in one of the darkest periods of the war, November 1776, after Washington's defeats in Brooklyn and the army's retreat from Manhattan.

To James Demarest Haring this grandfather was only a distinguished family memory since he was born 11 years after John Haring's death. A part of the kinship he may have felt for his Phelps in-laws was that George Alexander too had not known his paternal grandfather, and he had lost his father as a youth, as James had done his. Another source of attachment was the symbiosis of their businesses. They were both involved in commodities, the one from internal U.S. sources, the other from transatlantic sources.[81]

---

[80] Franklyn Burdge, *A Notice of John Haring* (New York: privately printed, 1878).

James Demarest had many kin in New York and Rockland County. Through his marriage to Caroline Eliza the Phelps family came to be in touch with the Dutch and revolutionary past. His great aunt Maria Haring (1775–1868) was alive throughout his lifetime. She had sat on the lap of General Washington on one of his visits to Tappan and witnessed the execution of Major André, which she recounted to visitors.[82] Mary (Herring) Haring, his grandmother, who died when he was five, had sisters who married enterprising men of their day (Samuel Jones among them) and a brother, Abraham (1755–1837), who was a prominent merchant with an upstate trade, at his death remembered as "a most conspicuous representative of the ancient Dutch stock."[83] His daughter remembered from the 1850s that "[a]s a little girl I used to visit with my father the home on 22nd Street of the Roosevelts and (what seemed to me much finer) the large house at Tenth Street and Broadway. There was an Aunt Margaret (Peggy) Haring [Herring] Roosevelt, quite old, and of whom my father seemed fond. Also a baby boy I was allowed to hold on my lap, possibly, but not certainly, Teddy."[84]

James Demarest Haring's older sister, Catharine Teller Haring (1808–72), married her second cousin, Henry Kip, in 1859, when they both were in their fifties. It was the second marriage for both. Kate had married a younger fellow officer of her father in Albany and bore a child who died; separated from this husband, she came to the city. Henry and Catharine

---

[81] They apparently did not do business together. There is only one record of a transaction between them: in 1853 the senior Phelps sold to his son-in-law a 13,172-square-foot lot in Lowell, Mass. Deed dated 6 Nov. 1852 *Index of Conveyances Recorded in the Office of Register of the City and County of New York*, Grantors N, O, and Q. (New York, 1858). This property was not listed in the estate of James Demarest Haring in 1868.

[82] Budke, *Historical Miscellanies*, 1:149–51.

[83] "This morning Mr. Abraham Herring, aged 82 years. Born on an estate owned and cultivated before and for a long time afterwards as a farm by his father, extending from the Bowery across Broadway nearly to Hudson Street of which Bond Street was the garden plot and the site of the Univ., Washington Square and all the adjacent streets were enclosed either for tillage or pasture. He had lived to see the almost magical changes that the city has undergone and was a most conspicuous representative of the ancient Dutch stock, its original founders. His funeral will take place on Wednesday (tomorrow) afternoon at half-past three o'clock from his late residence, 45 Hudson Street, and the friends of the family are requested to attend without further invitation. He will be interred in the family vault Middle Dutch Church corner Nassau and Liberty streets." *New York Evening Post*, 3 Jan. 1837.

[84] JHW MSS. TR was born in 1858, when Julia Phelps Haring would have been old enough to hold a baby. For the family interconnections see the Genealogical & Biographical Notes.

Teller Kip in the early 1870s lived on Henry Street in Brooklyn Heights.[85] The letters of "Aunt Kate" to her niece, Julia Phelps Haring, from 1868 to her death in 1882 are prime sources for life in the family in those years.[86]

Through his mother, Sarah (Clark) Haring, James had Clark cousins in the city, one of whom (Mary Clark 1813–82) married John Samuel Haring. Her sister, Helen Clark (1834–?), married George Alexander Phelps, Jr.[87] The Dun report quoted earlier indicates that these Clark sisters had substantial means in their own right.

James Demarest Haring, the first son-in-law to enter George Alexander Phelps's family, thus brought to the family a web of associations with past and present New York. His business interests were similar to Phelps's, their offices were close together, and his Clark cousin became the wife of the senior Phelps son, who would lead the business after his father's retirement. Caroline Eliza and her husband and Julia Phelps Haring, their surviving child, lived close to the older Phelps—in many years under the same roofs in the city and in Fairfield.

The sole surviving child of this marriage preserved the memory of the family for her descendants. We will return to the Harings after recounting the other Phelps marriages, the move uptown, and the flowering of the Fairfield life.

## Family

The next marriage of the Phelps children took place seven years after that of Caroline Eliza when the eldest, Julia Maria, married Royal Winter on 5 January 1853 in Hartford, Connecticut, at the advanced age of 27. Winter had been born in Croydon, New Hampshire, and was then 35. She moved with him to Boston and later Newton, Massachusetts.[88] Julia Maria retained close ties with the family in Fairfield, and the first of her two chil-

---

[85] 1873–74 *Brooklyn City and Business Directory*, compiled by George T. Lain. In 1870 Trow's New York City directory shows Henry Kip at 116 Henry Street, the next year at 119 (one of which could be a typographical error).

[86] Letters from Catharine Teller (Haring) Kip, manuscripts in possession of the author.

[87] William Clark (1780–183?) of New York City, brother of Sarah Clark (wife of Samuel Haring), married (2) Mary Bogart (1793–1871) on 4 April 1813. Their first child, Mary (1813–82), married her first cousin, John Samuel Haring (1810–60), on 13 Sept. 1831. The sixth and last child of this marriage was Helen Clark, who married George Alexander Phelps, Jr., in 1855. JHW MSS.

[88] National Society of Daughters of the American Revolution, Washington, D.C., application of Dorothy Phelps Wetherald. See the Genealogical & Biographical Notes.

dren was born there in 1854. She and both her children are seated on the verandah of the Fairfield house with parents and grandparents in the photo whose description opened this chapter.

Harriet Augusta, at the age of 24, married Thomas Reese Brooke in New York City in 1854. A son, Thomas R. Brooke, was born there early the next year. There is contradictory information about her husband in the family history, one date of death indicating the son was posthumous.[89] There are no references to this husband in the family correspondence, and he is not buried in the Phelps plot. By the turn of the century this nearly lifelong widow lived near her sister in Boston.[90] She died at age 83 on 12 February 1913 and was buried in the Phelps family plot.[91]

The youngest of the daughters was Emma Ayres Phelps, named for her mother's family, two years younger than Harriet. There are two letters from her, written from "Clay Hall" in June 1852 to Julia Maria in Fairfield. She reports a stop in New York City on the way, recounts tea parties she has been to with a "humorous gentleman," and sends her love to "little Howie," her youngest brother, then almost three years old. She refers to "Miss Henderson," perhaps the sister of the man she was to marry. Again, a light-hearted tone reveals a happy household in what she affectionately calls "Old Fairfield."[92]

Emma married William Coleman Henderson of Lancaster County, Pennsylvania, but their marriage was short-lived, as she died at age 22 on 23 January 1855.[93] There was a son of the marriage, named for his grandfather. George Alexander Phelps's will in 1880 provided "George P. Henderson the sum of $7,500," with a provision indicating a possible dependent status; his grandfather added, "that if he shall prove incapable the executors may provide him support."[94]

---

[89] Thomas R. Brooke (probably the son born 1855) and an Anna M. Brooke witnessed the codicil to the will of Eliza (Ayres) Phelps in 1880. Anna could be his wife; there is no reference to someone of this name in any family documents. Codicil 24 May 1880, Will of Eliza Phelps, Fairfield, Conn., Probate Records, Inv. 44 613, Acct. 44 552.

[90] Harriet Augusta (Phelps) Brooke: "Born New York City October 6, 1830. Wife of Thomas R. Brooke died February 12, 1913," grave marker, Phelps family plot. Son Thomas R. Brooke was born at New York City on 4 Jan. 1855. Phelps 1899.

[91] Grave marker, Phelps family plot.

[92] Emma Ayres Phelps, at "Clay Hall," to Julia Maria Phelps, 12 and 30 June 1852, manuscript in possession of the author.

[93] Grave marker, Phelps family plot.

[94] Will of George Alexander Phelps, Office of the Fairfield [Conn.] Town Clerk, Will 44 414, Admin. Act 44 528, filed 30 April 1880.

James Demarest Haring and Royal Winter were the longest-lived sons-in-law in the family. Henderson was left a widower shortly after marriage, and there is no reference to Brooke after his marriage, perhaps because of early death. James, by virtue of his residence in New York City, was the closest to the family.

George Alexander, Jr., was married on 3 January 1855 to Helen Clark in New York City. (His sister Emma died three weeks later.) Helen was the daughter of William and Mary (Bogart) Clark of New York City. Her oldest sister, Mary (Clark) Haring, was the wife (and first cousin) of John Samuel Haring. Thus the Harings and the Phelps were interwoven through George Jr.'s marriage to a Haring cousin and in-law and Caroline Eliza's marriage to James Demarest Haring.[95]

All the children were married within their parents' lifetimes. The three younger sons married in the 1860s and 70s. Frank married Mary A. Bradley Curtiss of Fairfield in that town on 10 May 1866. Charles Haring married Annie Brown Coleman on 13 October 1868, and Howard married Jennie I. Bierne 12 April 1873.[96]

The satisfaction that the senior Phelpses must have felt at the marriage in their lifetimes of all the living children may have weighed against their sense of loss at the death of six before the fullness of life and the apparent early deaths of two of their daughters' husbands.

Caroline Eliza gives a glimpse of the life of the family in the mid-1850s, after the marriage of two of the daughters and the arrival of the first of the elder Phelpses' grandchildren. She was then nine years married and the mother of Julie (Julia Phelps Haring), then aged four. She wrote to Julia Maria, herself two years married with a one-year-old named Eliza. It is a "bread and butter" letter, as Caroline Eliza had just been with her sister in Boston and returned after "a long and dusty ride" (probably by stage and rail).[97] "I presume Hattie is at home and her baby has grown so much that I should never have known her; she sends heaps of love to you and wants to see you very much." (This is Harriet Augusta, pregnant with the child that would be her only son.) "She and Ma were both terribly disappointed

[95] See discussion of Clark–Haring relationships, above.

[96] Phelps 1899, 1:830–31. "Curtiss" is the spelling in probate documents; in Phelps 1899 it is "Curtis." See "Phelps I" in the Genealogical & Biographical Notes.

[97] Caroline Eliza (Phelps) Haring, in Fairfield, Conn., to Julia Maria (Phelps) Winter, in Boston, 11 Sept. 1855, manuscript in possession of the author.

that you did not come home with me. I delivered your message to Ma [ ] but she [ ] as you are coming home so soon she will not mind. Tell Royal [Winter, Julia Maria's husband] that I have not had a bit of codfish since I came home and we do not starve within as he seemed to think." There is news of engagements in Fairfield: "Emma Allen is engaged to be married to Mr. Mott. She is to wait 8 years, I hear. She is making a great flourish around Fairfield with her diamond. Don't you suppose that Mrs. Allen is perfectly happy, and Honora Hobart is going to be married too. Fairfield will get rid of all its old maids if it keeps on." Caroline Eliza is making a dress for her daughter Julie, and " they all think it is the prettiest one she ever had. It is just dinner time and I must close. I should like to hear from you if you can find time to write. Ma sends her love." Her innocuous words and evanescent style convey warmth and fondness. She signs it "Carrie."

There was also life in town. From 1854 to 1871 Phelps's home address is listed on West Fourteenth Street. The family had moved further uptown to a wide street of newly built row houses, keeping pace with the affluent and genteel.

In 1856 George Alexander Phelps, Jr., in business with the firm at 103 Front Street, was listed at home at his father's West Fourteenth Street address. (The next year and until 1859 he was nearby at 98 West Thirteenth, after which his address is listed as "Europe," the firm's office in Palermo.) Certainly the most solemn events in the family's occupancy of the West Fourteenth Street brownstone were the deaths there within the space of four months in 1868 of James Demarest and Caroline Eliza Haring, who also lived at the house for three years in the 1860s.

Manhattan real estate development accelerated with the introduction of Croton water in the early 1840s, and developers began to throw up rows of houses on what had been streets identified only by the gridlines on the map. Fourteenth Street east and west had been established as a river-to-river thoroughfare in the late 1820s, when it was extended, on paper at first, east from the Bowery. On the ground it was nothing but open fields until it was paved in 1836. With the development to the south of Washington Square and the departure of the well-to-do from the commercialized vicinity of city hall, it was to be expected that the developers would build to attract new residents. (The population of Manhattan leapt from 312,000 in 1840 to 518,000 in 1850 to 814,000 in 1860, an 160 percent increase in twenty years.)

The brownstone-faced row house, which became the standard style of residential construction in the 1850s and to which the Phelps family moved, was a taller version of the federal row house, in their case with five floors rather than the old three. These were builders' houses, usually constructed in groups lining a street with uniform exteriors and interiors and offered for sale. They were faced with a veneer of the soft, workable stone from which the name is derived. The standard lot remained 25' x 100', with the building in the early years occupying about one half of its extent. (Some had 18' widths, but Phelps's house was the full 25'.) On the ground floor, often partly below grade, there was an entrance for tradesmen and servants connecting to the kitchen pantries and storerooms. On the exterior, a flight of stairs led from the sidewalk to the formal entrance on what was called the parlor floor; these stairs were the successors to the modest stoops of Dutch and federal New York. The double main entrance doors led to a narrow hallway off which there were the parlor at the front and dining room at the rear. Stairs led up two or three floors to bedrooms, a sewing room perhaps, and on the topmost level, small rooms for servants. It was up-and-down living; functions were separated by room and by floor, a long way from the small spaces of colonial times with their multiple uses. These were not mansions for the very wealthy with striking exterior and grounds; they were meant for the greatly increased class of moderately wealthy. The row houses were essentially mass-produced for rapidly growing families like the Phelpses. Within the uniform exteriors the lady of the house expressed the family's taste, affluence, and "breeding" in the decoration and furnishing of the parlor, where relatives and friends were entertained.

It took four servants to run one of these buildings to a standard of gentility.[98] The lady of the house had much to supervise, even more so in a large family. Certainly the West Fourteenth Street address had status and neighbors of like means, but luxury in New York of this period was cramped. Edith Wharton remembered from her childhood in the 1860s and 70s the "narrow houses so lacking in external dignity, so crammed with smug and suffocating upholstery."[99] The Phelps family, of course, had Fairfield, where they could live more spaciously.

---

[98] Richard Plunz, *A History of Housing in New York City* (New York: Columbia Univ. Press, 1990), 59–60.

[99] Edith Wharton, *Looking Backward* (New York: Appleton-Century, 1934), 54. Edith [Newbold Jones] Wharton (1862–1937) was born at 14 West Twenty-third Street. *DAB*.

The Phelps house was number 129 until 1867, then changed to 209 when Fifth Avenue replaced Broadway as the division between east and west. It was a south-facing building six doors west from Seventh Avenue on a block that had thirty identical houses in the row. It was a good address, not quite as fashionable as one closer to Union Square, to the east, then graced by a fountain and the center of respectable society.

The house was new when the Phelps family moved there in 1854, as its first owner is recorded in that year. Phelps must have rented, as other owners' names appear on the record for these years.[100] The house and five of its neighbors were demolished in the mid-twentieth century to make way for a building used for social services. The adjoining brownstones to the west remain. They are in shabby condition, shorn of steps and with shop fronts extending onto the sidewalk, but something of the early appearance of the block can be glimpsed in their uniform, somber upper facades.[101]

## Liverpool

Liverpool was the most important transatlantic terminus of the port of New York for most of the nineteenth century. New York merchants purchased cotton from southern planters and shipped it to Liverpool for use in the Lancashire mills. From up the Hudson and along the Erie Canal they purchased grains, corn, apples, and other commodities to ship across

---

[100] 209 West Fourteenth Street was Lot 32, Block 764 in the city property record. The block originated with lands of Peter Warren. A tract including this parcel was conveyed to Charles, Lord Southampton, son-in-law of Peter Warren, and conveyed to Col. McGregor. The latter sold the tract containing the S.E. parcel to John Rogers, who began selling his property in city lots on 13 December 1838. A triangular parcel backed by Fitz Roy Road, Southampton Road, by West 15th Street, was sold by McGregor to William Bayard, who began selling his property in city lots in March 1854. The first entries listed on Lot 32 were from Stephen P. Mash to Thomas B. Coddington, 6 May 1854; from Coddington to John D. P. Townsend, Trustee 1866, Trustee 1879; from Townsend to Catharine L. Townsend, 1879; from Catharine L. Townsend to Jos. G. Taylor, 1886. It is curious that G. A. Phelps was not listed as owner in the property records, though he and family members are listed at the address in the city directories. There are letters addressed to members of the Phelps family at this address in 1869, and it is listed in the obituary notices for James Demarest and Caroline Eliza Haring in 1868. G. A. Phelps may, therefore, have rented the property.

[101] The street adjoins upscale Seventh Avenue and a Chelsea neighborhood much refurbished in modern times. The tops and lights of the once formal doors on the parlor floor peek out above garish signs. The present block is hodgepodge of much altered and shabby brownstones, nondescript, modern buildings and tenements on a street with low-priced shops.

37. Liverpool Commercial District: Walmsley's Map of Liverpool and Its Suburbs, 1884

Sea access to the city was by way of the Mersey River, whose draft at low tide was insufficient for the ships of the day. With the construction of docks equipped with hydraulic locks to maintain a constant depth—ships were released on the two daily high tides—Liverpool flourished in the nineteenth century, surpassing Bristol as the leading western English port. The Phelps Brothers office opened in the late 1860s. It was located on Preesons Row, a block from the waterfront and Canning Dock, by the Crescent.

*Map Division, The New York Public Library, Astor, Lenox, and Tilden Foundations*

the Atlantic. As trade developed in the middle years of the century, several New York houses established offices in Liverpool. These sold the commodities and bought metals and manufactured goods for the westward run. Before the Civil War the U.S. trade accounted for between 40 and 50 percent of Liverpool's traffic, and it revived briskly after the peace.[102] From the 1840s Liverpool was also a major port for emigration.

Phelps Brothers opened an office in Liverpool in the early 1870s about the time of George Alexander's retirement. (At the time, the New York office was headed by Howard and Frank Phelps.) George Alexander Phelps, Jr., and Charles Haring Phelps went to live abroad and are listed as resident "fruit merchants" in the 1873 Liverpool city directory. "Phelps Brothers & Co., merchants," were at the Old Castle Buildings, 26 Preesons Row West. This was amidst the warren of streets in the commercial heart of the city close to the docks and the customs house. The listing of the other occupants of the building at the time conveys the flavor of the buying and selling that was going on. There was Hugh Evans, merchant and shipowner; The Liverpool & Mamanlan Steamship Co.; T & S Dugeld, sample room; Williamson, Millgram, merchants; Smith, F. J. & Co., hardware merchants; Fayn Matthews, ship broker; The St. Helens Colliery Co. Ltd.; Rude & Co., shipbrokers; Thomas V. Bird, commercial merchants; "Dining Rooms"; and the Swedish and Norwegian Consulate. Phelps Brothers & Co. was listed at this address at least through 1879.[103]

Her Majesty's Customs in Liverpool published a daily printed sheet that listed arriving ships, their masters, consignees and the goods and the duties assigned to them. An entry in May 1874 shows that the steamer *Zadne* arrived on 12 May from Palermo carrying "69 boxes oranges and lemons" for this port and "234 boxes of same, in transit" with Phelps Brothers as the consignee. The brothers were also brokering the traditional west–east commodity as shown by a shipment of 194 bales of cotton for Phelps Brothers on board the *Oceanic* from New York on 6 May of the same year.[104]

---

102 David Williams, "Bulk Trade and the Development of the Port of Liverpool," 13–14.

103 Gore's *Directory of Liverpool and Its Environs*, 1873 (Liverpool, Central Library, microfilm).

104 Liverpool Customs Bill of Entry, 6, 12 May 1874 (Liverpool: H. M. Customs, 1874). This was published each weekday with a list of all ships that arrived in the port with a list of their dutiable cargo and to whom consigned. The bound copies are in the Central Library, Liverpool.

Nathaniel Hawthorne described the bustling, congested area where the Phelps office was located when he had an office near it twenty years before, as "the most detestable place as a residence that ever my lot was cast in—smoky, noisy, dirty, pestilential." From the window in his office he could see "a tall, dismal, smoke-blackened, ugly brick warehouse—uglier than any building I ever saw in America." He watched bags of salt "swinging and vibrating in the air" and adjusted himself to the "continued rumble of heavy wheels."[105]

By the 1870s it was possible to live graciously above the clamor and filth. The brothers' home addresses were in Princes Park, on high ground overlooking the city, where residential development was incorporated into a romantic park design. This was the first creation of Joseph Paxton, most famous for his creation of the Crystal Palace for the Great Exhibition of 1851. Paxton incorporated into his designs for the 90-acre site "ornamental lakes, artificially molded hills, curving paths along which the gentry could parade." His "subtly contrived views and vistas . . . established the pattern for all future Victorian park design in Britain, America and on the Continent." (Paxton's park designs influenced Frederick Law Olmsted's plans for Central Park.[106])

The park was lined with row houses on "elegant stucco and brick terraces," and there were also "individual classical houses of great merit and charm, and exuberant late Victorian villas with every degree of intricate detail imaginable."[107] George Jr. lived in a terrace house on Sunnyside, Devonshire Road, whose other addresses were those of merchants; Charles lived at 86 Princes Road, leading into the park.[108] It was a far more gracious setting, because of the greensward and the walks nearby, than Fourteenth Street. (The houses and the park are still intact, though somewhat down-at-heel; the romantic copses and follies of the park are long gone.)

---

[105] Quoted in Edwin Haviland Miller, *Salem is My Dwelling Place: A Life of Nathaniel Hawthorne* (Iowa City, Iowa: Univ. of Iowa Press, 1991), 398–99.

[106] Joseph Paxton, 1801–1865, *DNB*; Laura Woods Roper, *FLO: A Biography of Frederick Law Olmsted* (Baltimore, Md.: Johns Hopkins Univ. Press, 1973), 71.

[107] Note on modern reprint of "Liverpool (Princes Park) 1905," Old Ordnance Survey Maps, St. Dunston, Gatehead: Alan Godfrey, 1989.

[108] Gore's *Directory of Liverpool and Its Environs*, 1873.

## Julia

After their marriage in 1846 Caroline Eliza and her husband, James Demarest Haring, first resided in houses on the newly opened streets where the island bulges out into the East River. It was a short walk to the Haring offices on Peck Slip from 63 Pike Street, their first address, or from the nearby 75 Monroe Street. They were probably the three-story plain federal-style row houses characteristic of the 1820s and 1830s, replaced by tenements later in the century.

Unlike most couples at the time, they had only two children. Catharine, called Kate and named for her father's sister, lived only five years. Julia Phelps (1851–1928), born four years after her sister, was named for her mother's older sister and her family. Her parents called her "Julie." She grew up as an only child, much treasured in an era when the death of small children was commonplace.[109] "I saw many little girls and boys at the depots," her father wrote her when he returned from a trip north, "and I thought of the danger of children being there. I hope you will be very careful as you are my only Baby."[110]

In the first years of their marriage Caroline Eliza and her husband lived in lower New York, not far from the East River. For most of their 22 years together they lived near her parents, in Fairfield and in New York, in some years at the same address. By the mid-1850s the directory shows James D. Haring's home address in "Conn" in one year, at the Astor Place Hotel in other years, and by the end of the decade at the elder Phelps's Fourteenth Street house or at "Conn." (James Demarest probably traveled a good deal on business; there is the letter to his daughter after the train ride, and in his estate was port-side property in Buffalo, which by the 1850s and 1860s was a terminus for the boats carrying the flour and grains he traded.) Like their elders, they and Julie seem to have been at home in both town and country.

At age 14, when her mother was living in Fairfield and expecting to find a place in the city again soon, Julie entered a girls' boarding school in the city. In the back-and-forth life of the family, her grandmother Phelps was in the city, and the Harings were in Fairfield until they would come down "and find a place." It was her first real separation from parents, and

---

[109] Mary (Clark) and John Samuel lost ten of their twelve children in early childhood.

[110] James Demarest Haring, in New York, to Julia Phelps Haring, in Fairfield, Conn., 22 June 1859, manuscript in possession of the author.

the sensitive Caroline Eliza took it hard. "I was delighted to hear from you Saturday by Papa and to get such a cheerful letter," she wrote to Julia:

> I think it did me a great deal of good for I had a miserable day of it Saturday. I cried nearly the whole day, but suppose in time I shall be accustomed to be alone. I am glad that Papa bought you such a nice trunk and hope you will take good care of it and learn to keep your things in good order. I think I put a new pair of undersleeves in your things that have no buttons so you had better sew them on before you want to wear them. I was much obliged for the candy. It is very nice, I have a piece in my mouth now.[111]

Julie had written that she was sharing a room with other girls. "I hope they are all good girls," wrote her mother, "and if they are not do not be led astray by them and above all things do not neglect to read your Bible and say your prayers as it is an easy thing to learn to neglect them and you will always regret it. You can never be glad or happy without God's help." Religion was still important to the family, though its influence was far less pervasive than a century earlier.

Julie's Fairfield friends had been asking for her, but her mother warned her not to continue to write to a boy in Norwalk. With their home empty of a child, it was quiet: "Colonel and Mrs. Wetmore are gone so we have very quiet times at table. We miss you too for you used to do considerable of the talking." Her mother also advised her not to buy curls (as Julie's letter had evidently suggested): "I do not think you are quite old enough to dress your hair in that manner and it would take up a great deal of time which would better be devoted to something else. If you have not clothes or dresses enough, send one word and I will see that you have all you want." In her conclusion she warns of the dangers of infection: "I wish you would not ride in stages, any more than necessary as they say there is a great deal of sickness and you had better be on the safe side."[112]

Julie sat for her portrait when she was seven; it was a painted photograph applied to glass, placed in an oval the same size as those of her parents' marriage portraits.[113] She is seated, wearing a blue dress with short puffed-sleeves, slightly off the shoulders. From one of the hands folded in her lap

[111] Caroline Eliza (Phelps) Haring, in Fairfield, Conn., to Julia Phelps Haring, in New York, 27 Feb. 1865, manuscript in possession of the author.

[112] Ibid. The Civil War was at its apogee, though it is not mentioned in this domestic letter. Julia disobeyed her mother's request to destroy the letter, and it is one of the few that survive.

[113] Portrait of Julia Haring Phelps, 1859, in possession of the author.

38. Julia Phelps Haring (1851–1928)
This painted photograph was taken when Julia was 7 years old.

she holds a partly opened fan. Most striking is the face beneath tightly wound hair, parted in the middle. Her blue eyes look directly at the viewer, and she wears a forthright, confident expression. There is nothing of her mother's shyness about her. In her dress and bearing she is a cherished child, but in this likeness serious, sober, not "putting on airs."

This small, affectionate family was sundered only nine years later in a double blow. James died of tuberculosis in his father-in-law's West Fourteenth Street house in June 1868. According to the death certificate he had suffered from the disease for five years. Caroline Eliza died in the house that October after an attack of peritonitis that lasted a few days.[114] Their bodies were taken to the 34th Street and Park Avenue station; their family and friends accompanied the coffins to Fairfield, where they were interred in the plot that George Alexander had purchased.

Julia was 17 when these deaths occurred with such brutal symmetry. Her family life and the New York world of her father became a paradise she would lament forever. She was hardly bereft of support, however. She

[114] New York City Municipal Archives, Manhattan Deaths, Index 1868: 10864, 21197; grave markers, Phelps family plot.

had a modest inheritance and was in the midst of the large Phelps family.[115] At her grandfather's behest, his youngest son, her uncle Howard Phelps, only two years older, accompanied her on a nine-month trip to Europe to assuage her grief. Their first stop was Palermo, where they stayed with George Phelps, Jr., and his wife Helen.

On her return, Julia was an attractive and eligible young woman, but it was not in New York that she met her future husband. On visits to family friends in Minneapolis, the son of a Universalist minister there, George Montgomery Tuttle, was smitten with her and wrote passionate letters to his "dear Julie," full of references to concerts, plays, and lectures. He eventually became a distinguished New York City doctor, but he was only a prep school student when they met and then a Yale undergraduate, in no position to marry.[116] Another easterner in the good air of Minneapolis, George Luther White, proposed to her, and they were married at St. Paul's Church in Fairfield in 1874.[117] Her home for the rest of her long life was in Waterbury, Connecticut, where George was in business. It was the memory of that lost paradise of her upbringing by the handsome, dashing father and the delicate, sensitive mother that prompted her to save family documents and to construct a family history. (She is the author's great-grandmother, and as Julia Haring White [Mrs. George Luther] she prepared the first family genealogy and preserved the family documents and pictures. The story of the families in Waterbury requires another book.)

---

[115] James Demarest Haring's estate had an inventory value of $14,700 and was left with life interests to his wife and his sister, Catharine Teller (Haring) Kip. When Caroline Eliza (Phelps) Haring died, George Alexander Phelps petitioned to become guardian of Julia, the surviving daughter. With the death of Catharine Teller Kip in 1872, Julia Phelps Haring became Haring's sole heir. G. A. Phelps was succeeded by Frank Phelps as trustee of the estate, which continued to file reports until 1893. The initial inventory of the estate included shares of Corn Exchange Bank and Mechanics Bank stock and federal bonds. Later submissions by the trustees show that it also owned dockside property in Buffalo and the site of a lumber yard there. Haring, James D., Probate Proceedings, 1868ff. New York City Municipal Records, *Probate Procedures in the matter of the Estate of James D. Haring*, July 1868, lib. 178, 220 (will filed 8 Feb. 1869). New York City, Municipal Records, Probationary Documents, loc. 09-041719.

[116] George Montgomery Tuttle (1856–1912) obituary, *NYT*, 30 Oct. 1912. Letters from Tuttle to Julia Phelps Haring, manuscripts in possession of the author.

[117] George Luther White (1852–1914) married Julia Phelps Haring on 15 April 1874, at St. Paul's Church, Fairfield. See the Genealogical & Biographical Notes.

39. Julia Phelps Haring

Julia (*left*) with her uncle, Howard Phelps, and an unknown companion in London, England, 1869.

## The House

By the end of the 1860s, while his sons were expanding the business, George Alexander Phelps retired to Fairfield. His wealth had grown in the postwar prosperity, and he sought a more imposing retreat. He apparently looked at Hudson River property, as did other magnates of the day. "Heard your Grandpa was negotiating for a Country Seat up the North River but had not closed yet—terms not meeting his approval," Julia's Haring aunt informed her at the time.[118] The negotiation was evidently not satisfactory, and George Alexander stayed with Fairfield.

In October 1870 he bought a house on Main Street, just east of the one the family had enjoyed for the past 24 years. It was a magnificent creation,

---

[118] Catharine Teller (Haring) Kip to Julia Phelps Haring, 9 Aug. 1869, in the possession of the author.

a Greek Revival mansion with 17 rooms and six two-story Doric columns on its face. A handsome wrought iron fence separated it from the street. It was built in the 1820s on the site of a house that had been burned by the British in the Revolution. The house had ample room for the expanding family of in-laws and grandchildren. There were four servants listed in the 1880 census, one more than there had been in the first house. The purchase price was $16,000.[119]

The formal magnificence—not too exaggerated an adjective to describe the structure—is conveyed in a photograph made soon after the family moved in (fig. 40).[120] For the first time we can see a Phelps house and family. The image is so comprehensive and detailed that it could only have been taken by the large box camera of the time. The edge of the smooth earthen roadway is visible. The façade is framed by the trees on the street that tower above it. The wood finial atop the pediment, crowned with an urn, is carved with fluted shapes that suggest wings. While the mass is striking, the incidentals picked up by the camera in the original 11" x 13" image are equally impressive. The upper-story windows glimpsed behind the columns each have lace curtains bowed open; the glass reflects the greenery opposite. There is a gas street lamp by the gate and a large urn filled with a leafy plant on a pedestal within the gate. The shades are pulled halfway down the glass panes of the double front doors. The light from open doors at the back of the house glows beneath one of the shades. The family dwells within the soft darkness of the interior: the front parlor, the dining room with a view of the parklike "yard" behind, a staircase leading to the shaded bedrooms whose windows shine above.

Here we see people as they wanted to be seen, in a setting they chose to display. George Alexander is seated on the veranda just to the right of the door. He has a short, white beard on his chin, in the style of the 1870s, and holds a newspaper. Perhaps this is where he usually sat on warm summer

---

[119] Fairfield Land Records, vol. 58, 73, Warranty Deed, dated 31 Oct. 1870, grantors James Rowland and Mary Rowland, Fairfield Town Records. Marcia Peden Miner, "Metamorphosis par Excellence," *Fairfield Citizen News*, 27 Sept. 1995. The columns were removed when the house was remodeled, probably at the turn of the century. A response to an inquiry by Henry Wade White revealed that the columns had been purchased by the architect Stanford White and used for a pavilion on his estate at St. James, Long Island. The columns were apparently destroyed in the 1938 hurricane. The Society for the Preservation of Long Island Antiquities, *Preservation Notes* 10, no. 1 (Feb. 1974). H. Wade White (1909–1995) was the great-great grandson of George Alexander Phelps. His manuscript notes are in the possession of the author.

[120] Probably taken 1871 or 1872, judging by Julia's mourning attire.

40. George Alexander Phelps House, ca. 1871, Fairfield, Connecticut
The senior Phelpses are probably the figures within the portico; by the cast-iron fence are Julia Phelps Haring (in black), granddaughter, and possibly daughters-in-law. The house still stands, altered to the Colonial Revival style at the turn of the century, at 458 Old Post Road, Fairfield. The cast-iron fence of George Alexander's day remains in place over 130 years later.

days, greeting passers-by, all of whom would have recognized him as "old school." He is framed by Ionic pillars, which probably conveyed a sense of earlier decades in the republic, of the 1820s and 1830s. You would not imagine from the relaxed pose that this man spent his career in the counting house, though his house amply reveals his success. Eliza, his wife, is seated on a lower step, reading or sewing something white; she is wearing black with a white collar and a white head-covering. Standing behind her is another woman similarly dressed, but with a wider head kerchief. She could be one of George Alexander's sisters who lived nearby. Three young women are standing on the lawn, two in white blouses with full skirts of darker material, much in the post–Civil War style familiar from Winslow Homer watercolors and prints. Next to them is a figure in mourning, certainly Julia Phelps Haring, returned from her grand tour. She is with two contemporaries, possibly neighbors, paying a call the morning the photographer came.

One of the youthful figures is blurred, indicating that all the others remained still for the long exposure needed for the portrait. It seems like a moderate summer day; the trees are fully in leaf, but the ample clothing does not suggest midsummer. The older women are dressed for the house during the day, starched and full dresses, with white kerchiefs on their heads giving them an "at home" informality. Youth and age are apart, not bunched and peering at a camera as would be done in later years. The counting house and the hurly-burly of Front Street and the docks are far away.

The photograph betrays a carefully organized informality, which shows the family at home. There is no mistaking their refinement and discretion. The pillars and the entablature are those of a classical temple. In marble they would have revealed its interior and be a backdrop for oratory in the agora. Here they are products of the carpenter's craft, and lead to domesticity and comfort. To the passer-by it speaks wealth, the gentleman of the "old school" from a spare and noble time. It is a uniquely American ceremony that we see: domestic bliss within a temple in the reach of any successful man.

George Alexander and Eliza Phelps enjoyed ten years of retirement in this Fairfield house. The first of their grandchildren to be married was the orphaned Julia Phelps Haring. She married George Luther White (1852–1914) of Waterbury, Connecticut, in an evening service at St. Paul's Episcopal Church on 15 April 1874. It was only a few steps away from the house where the reception was held. George was the son of a self-made inventor and manufacturer, Luther Chapin White (1821–93). This marriage thus united a New York Yankee merchant's family with the then burgeoning copper and brass and wire-forming industry of the Naugatuck Valley.

George Alexander's only brother, Henry Davenport Phelps, died in 1875 at age 65 and was buried in the family plot. Harriet, the unmarried sister who had lived with her mother in the nearby Fairfield house, died six years later. The dusk was closing in on that generation. George Alexander Phelps died in Fairfield on 12 April 1880 "aged 76 years seven months 22 days."[121] The local paper mourned him as one of a vanishing breed:

---

[121] The cause on the certificate was diabetes. Fairfield, Conn., Office of the Town Clerk, Death Certificate Index.

41. Eliza (Ayres) Phelps (1808–1880)

42. George Alexander Phelps (1803–1880)

These portraits probably date from the 1860s.

> Crape shrouds the entrance of a familiar mansion, out of whose portals its late wonder will pass but once more. Mr. George A. Phelps, who for nearly half a century has been identified with the best associations of our village, died on the evening of Monday the 12th inst. In the 77th year of his age. Of the thoroughly trained, successful class of business men, he was a model type. Of those liberal and genial qualities which make up the good citizen and neighbor, he possessed an affluent share; in those Christian and kindly attributes which hallow home and endear relationship, he was richly endowed, and in his death the community mourn the passing away of another of that lessening race of old-time upright, courteous, single-minded gentlemen who honored and dignified all the walks of Life.[122]

His will ran to several pages, the bequests revealing careful provision for the family.[123] The four sons were the executors (George Jr. then stated as resident in Liverpool). Phelps, the shrewd businessman, who had made his will two years before his death, provided that the "property in the city of

[122] *Southport Times*, 16 April 1880.

[123] Will 44 414, filed 30 April 1880 (dated 1 May 1878), Fairfield [Conn.] Probate Records; Letter of Administration 44 528, filed 22 Oct. 1880.

New York be divided, but that it not be sold at a sacrifice unless absolutely necessary." (In the inventory this is valued at $150,000.) Since the sons kept Phelps Brothers ever more prosperous well into the next century there was doubtless no need for such sacrifice. The Fairfield property was valued at $15,000, and there was $110,000 in securities. The cost of opening the grave in the plot George Alexander had bought was $10, and it was $2 for "tolling of the bell."

The heirs were his widow, children, grandchildren, nephews, and nieces. Eliza was provided for with a $70,000 bequest "and the use of the house and all privileges thereof" (she died in the autumn of the same year). He left his unmarried and sole surviving sister, Phebe Phelps (1799–1883), a legacy of $6,000 per year, which she enjoyed for the remaining three years of her life. Nephews and nieces received $1,000 each.[124] The grandchildren mentioned were both orphaned. George P. Henderson, son of Emma Ayres, was awarded $7,500 with the provision that if he "should prove incapable" the executors should support him. Julia Phelps (Haring) White (by then a mother of three) received the same amount outright. The legatees for the remainder of the estate in equal shares were the six surviving children, Julia Maria Winter, Harriet Augusta Brooke, George Alexander Phelps, Jr., Frank Phelps, and Howard Phelps. There were no bequests to organizations or unrelated individuals.

The securities in the estate included stocks of two railroads, a canal, and two insurance companies and several bonds, none of which related to the international trade with which Phelps had been associated. A great deal of the wealth was in the family-owned partnership, Phelps Brothers, which had devolved to the sons as active partners.

Charles Haring Phelps and his wife and children returned from Liverpool to be with his widowed mother that summer. Of the five children who accompanied them, three had been born during their years in England.[125] Eliza (Ayres) Phelps died of heart disease at age 71, while visiting her eldest daughter, Julia Maria Winter, in Massachusetts, on

---

[124] These were Harry Cornell and Annie Cornell (children of G. A. Phelps's sister Maria Amelia [1807–?] and Richard Cornell), and Eliza P. Smiley. The "P" in the latter name may refer to Phelps, but the author has found no record of a Smiley among those marrying into the family.

[125] The census taker on 22 June 1880 listed the children of Charles H. Phelps (Eliza's grandchildren) as Charles H., white male, "age 16, at school, born N.Y. [in fact born 1870, making him 10]," Thomas P., age 9, "at school," Nina, age 7, "born England," Frank G., age 6, born England, Julia, age 3, born England. Their mother is mistakenly identified as Alice, not Annie, age 30.

Table 6
Securities in the George Alexander Phelps Estate, Valued at $110,000 in 1880

| Securities | Value |
|---|---|
| 360 Shares Mechanics Savings Bank | $9,620 |
| 100 Chicago & Rock Island RR | $18,787 |
| 100 New York Central | $12,800 |
| 40 Fourth State Bank bonds | $10,130 |
| U.S. Bonds of 81 5 | $10,100 |
| Tennessee bonds | $5,000 |
| Schleigh & Wilksbane Bonds | $4,800 |
| Michigan Centennial Bonds | [?] |
| Orient Insurance Co. | $453 |
| Empire Insurance Co. | $919 |
| Cash | $6,111 |
| Delaware & Hudson Canal Co. | $7,635 |
| Hawthorne Congress Bonds | [?] |

*Source:* Fairfield [Conn.] Probate Records, Letter of Administration 44 528, filed 22 Oct. 1880.

2 September 1880; she survived her husband by less than five months.[126] Her executors were Frank Phelps, whose address was listed as Stamford, and Charles Haring Phelps of Fairfield (who was to continue on in the house until it was sold). To her two surviving daughters, Julia M. Winter and Harriet A. Brooke, Eliza left "all my wearing apparel and all my silver, watches, clocks, diamonds and all my jewelry of every description to be divided equally between them." She left "my sister Sarah Peck during her life the income from two thousand dollar bonds of the Michigan Central Railroad Co. having an interest of 7% or $140 per annum." In a codicil made in May 1880, after her husband's death, she left her brother "Henry W. Ayres the income from seven one thousand-dollar bonds of the Michigan Central Railroad Co." The six children were to share equally the residue.[127] The themes of property and family are entwined in these final arrangements as they were in life.

[126] She died in Allston, Mass. Death Certificate Index, Fairfield Town Records, portions obscured by water damage, birthplace incorrectly stated as Fairfield.

[127] Will 44 509, Inv. 44 613, Acct 44 552; will dated 20 Jan. 1879, codicil 29 May 1880, witnessed by Annie B. Phelps [Annie Brown (Coleman), wife of Charles Haring Phelps], Thomas R. Brooke, the son of Harriet Augusta (Phelps) Brooke, and Anna M., possibly his wife. The probate documents were also filed in New York, loc. 08-026861, Phelps, April 1882; Surrogates Court, New York State, New York County.

Unlike his father, grandfather, and great-grandfather, George Alexander did not have a college education, nor did his sons. The religious impulses that were part of the lives of Eleazar Wheelock and Alexander, Benajah, and Davenport Phelps seem to have struck no sparks in him. The Great Awakening was a long way away, but its effects in terms of self-actualization and individualism were evident.

George Alexander's and Eliza's lines spanned a transformation. Steam power replaced sail, railroads the stagecoach, piped water and the water closet the bucket, pump and privy, the furnace the fireplace, gas light candles and kerosene lamps. In business there was vastly increased information, transmitted by telegraph and available daily in the newspapers. Stocks and bonds became common ways to invest. Transatlantic travel was reduced from weeks to days. There were more ways to acquire wealth and more people who could share it. The "lever of Archimedes" had indeed pried open the riches of the world.

# EPILOGUE

Research expands and enlivens family memory and broadens personal perspective. It also tears at the heart. It is an encounter with the finiteness of life, a humbling confrontation with what can never be fully recovered, the essential mystery of the passage of time and of individual fates. None of this should dull curiosity about family, which links the lives of those who enjoyed the world's benefits, those who strove and lost, the dead children. Family was there before and after individual lives, and it lives in the past, present, and future.

Now I know what questions I would ask Caroline Eliza, the pale lady with the tilted gaze in the oval frame above the horsehair sofa in grandmother's house. I would ask her what it was like as a child to live near City Hall Park in New York or what her father told her about his boyhood in Stafford or the family's wartime sojourn in Europe. What did her great-grandmother Phelps, whom she knew for more than 30 years, tell her about growing up in Nova Scotia before the Revolution, of the sea journey or the idiosyncrasies of her father, the "Uncompromising Whig"? The things she could tell me about her mother and her maternal aunts and uncles would take me beyond the sketchy Ayres and Pancoast background I know. I could learn what her mother, the elegant lady in the wedding portrait of 1826, was like in her youth.

James Demarest Haring, the handsome young man in the oval frame, would tell me about the Dutch New York past he brought to the New England Phelps family and the sturdy patriarchs that created farms on Manhattan and upriver. He would surely love to tell me of his Uncle Kip, who lived on Washington Square, of Aunt Peggy Roosevelt and the "baby boy . . . possibly, but not certainly, Teddy," of old Aunt Mary Haring in Rockland County, who told visitors how she had watched the hanging of Major André from the pommel of Captain Stagg's horse. James could pass on what he had heard about his grandfathers during the Revolution, both dead long before he was born. His many country and city cousins, part of the old Dutch population, well aware by his lifetime of its own dwindling, would have sought to capture the past with stories that he would know.

Any family researcher imagines such conversations. Some could be poignant with the helpless awareness of what might have been and what cannot be undone. Some could reveal what might better remain hidden. Others would be inspiring, all illuminating. We make do, of course, with records and letters and imagine the rest. In this way the shades lift from the past and the span of family memory extends.

So it has been for me in this journey through the archives. I can now see Hebron and the homesteads dotted about the cleared land; the simple houses in New Hampshire, where Hebron seemed to be re-created and the widowed Theodora managed the household; the dikelands in Cornwallis and the meeting at which the Rev. Benajah shook his fist at the new preacher; the open boat in which he was set off Passamaquoddy; Davenport and his horse on the rough roads of New York State in all weather; the Finger Lakes towns that Timothy Dwight so admired; the russet-tinged waters of the Stafford mineral springs; and Eleazar's house after the depredations of the Lyons and Benning Mann. I can see the tree-lined Greenwich Street in a New York City abuzz with the celebration of peace; the mortally ill Eleazar in his Havana room; the Phelps ladies entertaining visitors in "old Fairfield"; the handsome Haring men at their Peck Slip office; shrewd George Alexander in his counting house nearby; the family in mourning at the West Fourteenth Street house; Julia at the festivities for the future queen in Palermo; the young Phelps families in the elegant terrace houses above the smoke in Liverpool; the soft light filtering through the neatly arranged curtains of the pillared house in Fairfield and the old gentleman on the veranda looking up from his newspaper to acknowledge a greeting.

> There is a history in all men's lives
> Figuring the natures of the times deceased,
> The which observed, a man may prophesy,
> With a near aim, of the main chance of things
> As yet not come to life, who in their seeds
> And weak beginnings lie intreasurèd.
> Such things become the hatch and brood of time . . .

Are there patterns in these stories from which a man might prophesy? Of the personal characteristics of the husbands and wives in this narrative, what leaps out of the record is firmness of purpose and physical hardiness. These men and women were able to take hold of life and meet its challenges with advantage. A "man might prophesy" that the tradition of leadership in the family in colonial times would give the descendants the confidence to navigate in the hurly-burly of the young republic.

These hardy survivors began their lives influenced by the geography of New England. The Phelpses and the other immigrants found there a territory with weakened and quickly outnumbered natives, presenting them vast lands for the taking. There was abundant water and wood for warmth and shelter; its long river valley gave a level route deep into the interior. The severe winters could only be mastered by planning and hard work.

The success of the first settlements created a collective memory that imbued future generations with the confidence that difficulties could be overcome.

There was also a favorable political environment, and with all its downs, an expanding world economy. The colonials benefited from the prosperity of the eighteenth-century British empire, which promoted worldwide trade. They were on the winning side when that empire triumphed over the French, and this family was among those on the winning side again when the colonies broke with the empire.

The cultural determinants for taking hold of the opportunities of the times lay in the heritage of the immigrants. These English Puritans had cohesive social and political structures and were conditioned to organize, build, and cultivate, to "redeem the time" through work as the preachers urged. They were fitted to take advantage of the expanding fields for endeavor. This was evident in Alexander's day with the opening up of the upper Connecticut Valley, a second chance for him. By his sons' day, the field extended to Upper Canada, western New York, and the Caribbean. In his grandson's day, steamships and railroads transformed how the world's resources were used and transported. The fields of endeavor for accumulating wealth became far larger, making room for more to take part. The obtainable material abundance, religious freedom, absence of an established order of nobility or land tied up by primogeniture, and the vitality of town culture were unique to America.

I have noted the decline in religion, the growth in secular pursuits, the seizing upon the accoutrements of conspicuous gentility at the end of George Alexander's life. The seeds that there "lie intreasurèd" will sprout in the future. Social position came to be asserted by evidence of dwelling, manners, and dress. As the merchant world that George Alexander inherited faded, a new society emerged. Gentility and "family" became markers of difference in an economy driven by actions of corporations and financial markets.

Family memory can be expanded, and there is always room for more. But think of what can never be here—textures, the feel of clothes, of a face; sounds of voices, of the world inside and on the country road or the city street, the wave of a child as the horse passes by, the struggle with the sled on ice, the struggling of the oxen in mud, the darkness of the world, streets and country roads, the ever-present smell of wood smoke, later of coal, the accumulated real memories of these people. Just imagine!

PART TWO

# *GENEALOGICAL & BIOGRAPHICAL NOTES*

# PREFATORY REMARKS

The genealogical and biographical notes in this section have two principal purposes. First they present in summary the lines of descent from the immigrant ancestors of the family members who are the subjects of the preceding chapters down to, generally, the sixth and seventh generations, from the seventeenth to the mid-nineteenth century. These include information about children not in the direct line of descent and abbreviated references to collateral relationships.

Each entry begins with a single "paragraph" that presents vital statistics (birth, death, marriage, parents or line of descent) for the subject and his or her spouse. Biographical summaries follow. These sometimes repeat information from the narrative part of this book but often refer to persons and events in finer detail. Superscript numerals assigned to names indicate the generational level of individuals vis-à-vis his or her immigrant ancestor. A "+" preceding a name indicates that further information about that individual is to be found in the following text.

A second purpose of these notes is to provide revisions and additions to extant genealogies. Researchers in the seventeenth-, eighteenth-, and early-nineteenth-century histories of the Phelps, Wheelock, Haring, and Denison families should find here material that adds considerably to what has been previously published.

The Phelps two-volume genealogy and family history published in 1899 was a pioneering work in its day and remains an important resource—publication of the present book on its 100th anniversary may be considered an act of gratitude.[1] However, examination of records and other archival sources in connection with the present work revealed considerably greater sources of information about the families here considered and the need for numerous corrections and additions.

The Phelps notes are in two parts. The first includes the line of the family to the eighth generation, which is the subject of the preceding chapter. The second is concerned with the descent to John[5] Phelps of Stafford, Connecticut. He was, like the other Phelpses, a descendant of William[1] of Windsor, but he was a distant cousin of his contemporary Eleazar[5] Wheelock Phelps. Since he was a mentor of the latter and a locally prominent leader in his day, it seemed advisable to prepare a descent to him as well.

---

[1] Oliver Seymour Phelps and Andrew T. Servin, comps., *The Phelps Family of America and their English Ancestors, with Copies of Wills, Deeds, Letters and Other Interesting Papers, Coats of Arms, and Valuable Records*, 2 vols. (Pittsfield, Mass.: Eagle Publishing Company, 1899).

The Haring descent includes the history of one line of the New York family of Dutch origin, one of whose members, James[6] Demarest Haring, married Caroline[6] Eliza Phelps in 1846. These individuals take this study into New Amsterdam and from the Province of New York to the booming mercantile world of nineteenth-century Manhattan, a counterpoint to the Puritan-Yankee Phelpses. The sole genealogical guide to this family is Ackerman's 1952 typescript.[2] This is generally accurate for the earliest generations but gives little biographical detail. The seven-generation descent that follows incorporates primary source material that greatly amplifies any previous work on this line of the family.

Similarly, there is no genealogy setting out the descent to Eleazar[4] Wheelock, despite his prominence as the founder of Dartmouth College. The notes here compile records of that line from the originals and include information about his children and their spouses, who were so important to the early development of Dartmouth College.

The notes on the Denison family that conclude this section rely to some extent on published genealogies. William[1] and the second generation are treated in Anderson's *The Great Migration Begins*, and a family genealogy from George[2] was published in 1978.[3] Here again, however, original sources have been used for the bulk of references in generations four through six.

While every effort on the part of the author and the editor was exercised in the interest of accuracy, there undoubtedly will be errors. There will also be lacunae, which future researchers may fill. The author looks forward to comment on and expansion of this work.

---

[2] Herbert S. Ackerman, "Descendants of Jan Pieter Haring" (Ridgewood, N.J.: typescript, Oct. 1952), NYPL.

[3] Robert Charles Anderson, *The Great Migration Begins: Immigrants to New England*, vol. 3 (Boston: NEHGS, 1996); E. Glenn Denison, with Josephine Middleton Peck, and Donald L. Jacobus, *Denison Genealogy: Ancestors and Descendants of Captain George Denison* (Baltimore: Gateway Press, 1978).

# PHELPS I

WILLIAM[1] PHELPS,[1] b. say 1593, based on date of marriage, prob. at Crewkerne, Somerset;[2] d. 14 July 1672 at Windsor, Conn. ("ould m[r] william phelps dyed July 14. 1672");[3] m. (1) say 1617 MARY ______, bur. at Crewkerne 13 August 1626; m. (2) on 14 November 1626 at Crewkerne ANN DOVER, d. 30 August 1689 at Windsor.

The date for the death of "Mrs. Ann Phelps" was recorded in the Windsor Vital Records. Anderson, without comment, assigns this date to Ann Dover for the first time.[4] When Barbour compiled the Connecticut VRs, he added a note to this particular item, stating that it referred to "Mrs. Ann (Gaylord) Phelps," the wife of Isaac[2] Phelps, son of George[1] Phelps. According to Stiles, Isaac and Ann settled in Westfield, Massachusetts, and town records give her date of death as 29 September 1690.[5] However, this is also the date on which Frances, the second wife of George[1], died. Stiles was apparently unsure whether the mother-in-law and daughter-in-law died on the same day or if the death date for Frances was simply a mistake. Evidently he did not find another date for Frances and was unwilling to consider the possibility of the two women having died on the same day. He apparently solved the problem by assigning the death date of Mrs. Ann Phelps in the Windsor records to the wife of Isaac[2]. It is highly unlikely, though, that the death of a woman in Westfield would have been recorded in Windsor, as the towns did not cross-file records. Thus "Mrs. Ann Phelps" was probably Ann Dover, the widow of William[1], and Anderson's attribution is almost certainly correct.

---

[1] William[1] and his immediate descendants are included in Anderson, *Great Migration*, 3:1444–46. The first genealogy of the Phelps and other Windsor families was Henry R. Stiles, *The History and Genealogies of Ancient Windsor* (Hartford: Case, Lockwood, and Brainerd, 1892), 2:562ff. [hereinafter cited as *Ancient Windsor*]. See also Kent C. L. Avery, Donna Siemiatkoski, and Robert T. Silliman, *The Settlement of Windsor, Connecticut* (Windsor, Conn.: Windsor Historical Society, 1983, 1993). The author wishes to acknowledge the assistance of Donna Siemiatkoski, Windsor, Conn., and Judith Plummer of Woodbury, Conn., for their research on his behalf.

[2] Myrtle Stevens Hyde, "The English Origin of William[1] Phelps of Dorchester, Mass., and Windsor, Conn., with Notes on his Marriages," *TAG* 65 (1990): 161–66. This article summarized recent research into the English origins of William[1], whose birthplace was incorrectly asserted, in Phelps 1899, to be Tewskesbury, Gloucestershire. Hyde also established William's marriage dates and the identity of his second wife, Ann Dover. A discussion of English origins also appears in *Search for the Passengers of the Mary & John 1630* (Toledo, Ohio, 1985– ), 2:94, 3:68, 7:99.

[3] *Ancient Windsor*, 2:593.

[4] Anderson, *Great Migration*, 3:1445.

[5] *Ancient Windsor*, 2:593.

Hyde and all before her applied the date of 27 November 1675 to the death of Ann Dover, which is the recorded date of death of "wife of William Phelps."[6] To whom then does this date refer? It probably refers to Isabel Wilson, the wife of William². Since the latter's father was dead by 1675, the recorder would not have had to refer to him as "the younger" or "Jr." Neither Stiles nor Anderson gives a death date for her, but both note the marriage of William² to Sarah Pinney on 20 December 1676, indicating that his first wife had died before that time. Thus, two death dates, both long confused, have been sorted out.[7]

William Phelps was part of the Dorchester party organized under the Rev. John White.[8] He and Ann Dover and their five children sailed on the *Mary & John* from Plymouth on 20 March 1630. It has been asserted in all but the most recent histories of the family that they were accompanied by two unmarried, younger brothers, George and Richard; however, there is no record that confirms this relationship, and Richard is only mentioned once in the *Dorchester Records*.[9]

On 30 May 1630 the *Mary & John* made landfall at Nantasket, and the party formed the settlement of Dorchester in the Massachusetts Bay Colony. On 19 October 1630 William applied for freemanship in Dorchester, and in 1632 and 1635 he was its representative at the General Court of Massachusetts Bay. In 1634–35 he was a selectman for the settlement.

In 1636 William emigrated with other members of the Dorchester group to settle a site along the Connecticut River, now Windsor, north of present-day Hartford. He was one of the eight commissioners appointed by the Bay Colony General Court on 3 March 1636 to govern Connecticut and to hear and resolve disputes among the settlers of the Connecticut River valley. He was elected assistant (a position in the Governor's Council) for the Connecticut Colony eleven times from April 1636 to April 1642 and again five times from May 1658 to May 1662.[10] He was elected deputy

[6] *TAG* 65 (1990), 161, gives the date 21 Nov., which should read 27 Nov., as above. Personal communication from Myrtle Stevens Hyde, 14 Oct. 1998.

[7] Personal communication from Donna Holt Siemiatkoski, June 1998.

[8] With the exceptions noted, this paragraph is based on that on William¹ in Anderson, *Great Migration*, 3:1444–45.

[9] Hyde asserts that "further investigation is necessary to determine the origin of George¹ Phelps of Windsor and his possible relationship to William¹ Phelps." See "English Origin of William¹ Phelps," 165–66.

[10] Donald Lines Jacobus, comp., *List of Officials Civil, Military and Ecclesiastical of Connecticut Colony from March 1636 through 11 October 1677 and of New Haven Colony throughout its Separate Existence also Soldiers in the Pequot War* (New Haven: Roland Mather Hooker for the Connecticut Society of the Order of the Founders and Patriots of America, 1935), 43.

from Windsor to the Connecticut legislature 17 times between April 1645 and October 1657. In May 1653 and October 1654 he served on the War Committee for Windsor.[11] William left no will.

*Children of William[1] and Mary (—) Phelps:*[12]

- i. WILLIAM[2] PHELPS, bp. 9 September 1618 at Crewkerne, Somerset; d. 17 February 1681/2 at Windsor, Conn.;[13] m. (1) there on 4 June 1645 ISABEL WILSON,[14] d. 21 November 1675 at Windsor; m. (2) there on 20 December 1676 SARAH PINNEY.[15]
- ii. SAMUEL[2] PHELPS, bp. 5 August 1621 at Crewkerne, d. 15 May 1669 at Windsor; m. there on 10 November 1650 SARAH GRISWOLD.
- iii. [INFANT], bur. 8 January 1623/4 at Crewkerne.
- \+ iv. NATHANIEL[2] PHELPS, bp. 6 March 1624/5 at Crewkerne, d. 27 May 1702 at Northampton, Mass.;[16] m. on 17 September 1650 ELIZABETH COPLEY at Windsor,[17] widow, d. 6 December 1719 at Northampton. *See* Phelps II *in these Notes.*

*Children of William[1] and Ann (Dover) Phelps:*[18]

- v. CORNELIUS[2] PHELPS, bp. 13 October 1627 at Crewkerne; no further record found.
- vi. JOSEPH[2] PHELPS [twin], bp. 12 November 1628 at Crewkerne, d. bef. 5 March 1683/4 at Simsbury, Conn.; m. (1) on 20 September 1660 HANNAH NEWTON; m. (2) on 19 January 1676 at Northampton MARY (—) SALMON.

---

[11] Ibid.

[12] Hyde, "English Origin of William[1] Phelps," 163–64.

[13] Edwin Stanley Welles, ed. and trans., *Births, Marriages, and Deaths Returned from Hartford, Windsor, and Fairfield, and Entries in the Early Land Records of the Colony of Connecticut* (Hartford, 1898), 54 [hereinafter cited as Welles].

[14] *Ancient Windsor*, 2:564.

[15] Ibid.

[16] Hyde, "The English Origin of William[1] Phelps," citing James Buckman, comp., "Northampton Deaths," Forbes Library, Northampton, 13.

[17] Stiles, *Ancient Windsor*, 2:565; Louis Marinus Dewey, "Thomas Copley of Suffield, Conn., and Some of His Descendants," *Register* 64 (1910), 248n.

[18] Hyde, "English Origin of William[1] Phelps," 163–64.

vii. MARY[2] PHELPS [twin], bp. 13 [sic] November 1628 at Crewkerne; prob. d. y.

viii. MARY[2] PHELPS, bp. 6 December 1629 at Crewkerne; prob. d. y.

ix. SARAH[2] PHELPS, b. say mid-1630s, d. 10 July 1659 at Windsor; m. there on 9 June 1658 WILLIAM WADE of Middletown, Conn.[19]

\+ x. TIMOTHY[2] PHELPS, b. 1 September 1639 at Windsor.

xi. MARY[2] PHELPS, b. 2 March 1644;[20] prob. d. 13 February 1725/6 at Simsbury as "Marey Barber ye Eldest";[21] m. on 17 December 1663 at Windsor THOMAS BARBER.[22]

TIMOTHY[2] PHELPS (*William*[1]), b. August or 1 September 1639 at Windsor, Conn.;[23] d. there bet. 2 March 1716/7, when witnesses made oath to his signature, and 28 September 1719, when his will was executed;[24] m. there on 19 March 1661/2 MARY GRISWOLD,[25] dau. of Edward and Margaret (—) Griswold, b. ca. 1644.[26]

On 8 November 1663 Timothy Phelps owned the Halfway Covenant at the Windsor Church.[27] On 8 October 1663 he was proposed for freeman, which he became on 12 May 1664.[28]

About 1683 he was made sergeant in train band.[29] On 8 May 1690 Timothy was chosen by the train band as lieutenant,[30] and on 14 May 1696, as captain, he was assigned to the area "south of the rivulet" (Farmington River).[31] On 15 April 1698 he applied to the General Court "by

---

19 *Ancient Windsor*, 2:564.

20 Ibid.

21 Hyde, "English Origin of William[1] Phelps," 164, citing Albert C. Bates, *Simsbury, Connecticut, Births, Marriages, and Deaths* . . . (Hartford, 1898), 13.

22 *Ancient Windsor*, 2:564.

23 Windsor VRs, 1:39; Anderson, *Great Migration*, 3:1444.

24 Windsor Probate Record, 338-50-1, transcribed in Charles William Manwaring, *A Digest of the Early Connecticut Probate Records* (Hartford, 1904–6; reprint, Baltimore, Md.: Genealogical Publishing, 1995), 2:419–20.

25 Ibid.

26 Hyde, "English Origin of William[1] Phelps," 164.

27 *Ancient Windsor*, 2:565.

28 *PRCC*, 1:409–10, 425.

29 "Sergt. Timothy Phelps" is listed as the father of Hannah (1684) and her younger sisters in vital records.

30 *PRCC*, 4:26.

31 Ibid., 4:162.

way of complaint against a late act of the townsmen of Windsor concerning their common fence."[32] His military service outside the town was acknowledged on 6 February 1706/7, when the governor and council ordered that Timothy Phelps and others that "went up to the Great Falls in October last shall be allowed eight shillings apiece more than what is allowed them in the debenture given them by Capt. Mathew Allin."[33]

Timothy's will, dated 2 March 1716/17, was proved on 6 October 1719.[34] The executors of his estate, valued at £344 19*s* 06*d*, were sons William, Cornelius, and Samuel. The following bequests were made:

> Being very aged yet retaining good measure of understanding and memory . . . I give, devise and bequeath all my estate whatsoever, both real and personal to my three sons, William, Cornelius and Samuel, to have hold and improve the same in trust for the use of my wife during her natural life, and after her decease my will is, and I hereby do give and devise all my houseing and lands with the appurtenances to my sons Timothy Phelps, William Phelps, Cornelius Phelps, Samuel Phelps, and heirs of Joseph Phelps in the room of their father, to be equally divided into six equal parts . . . and it is my will, that they pay and make up to their sisters, Sarah, Hannah, Ann and Martha, my daughters or to their heirs and to the heirs of my daughter Abigail deceased, £48 as money apiece; and my will is that what they have already recd. as entered upon my book shall be reckoned as part of s^d^. summs, and y^t^ my s^d^. Sons and the heirs of my son Joseph shall pay their sisters and their heirs above mentioned in equal proportion except that the heirs of Joseph shall pay £4 more than an equal proportion, and my son Cornelius £4 less than an equal proportion. And my will further is, that my wife shall have the free disposal of all her wearing apparel at her decease, and that my grandson Samuel Fyler shall have half that bequeathed to the heirs of my daughter Abigail if he liveth with me so long as I live, or till he comes to the age of 18 years.

*Children of Timothy² and Mary (Griswold) Phelps, all born at Windsor:*

i. TIMOTHY³ PHELPS, b. 1 November 1663; bp. 8 November 1663.[35]

ii. JOSEPH³ PHELPS, b. 27 September 1666; d. bef. 1717.[36]

---

32 Ibid., 4:255–56.

33 Ibid., 5:16.

34 Windsor Probate Record, 338-50-51, transcribed in Manwaring, *A Digest of the Early Connecticut Probate Records*, vol. 1, 419–20.

35 Windsor VRs, col. 1, 54; records kept by Mathew Grant.

36 Ibid., Mathew Grant.

iii. WILLIAM[3] PHELPS, b. 4 February 1668.[37]
iv. CORNELIUS[3] PHELPS, b. 26 April 1671.[38]
v. MARY[3] PHELPS, b. 14 August 1673; d. 28 May 1690 at Windsor.[39]
vi. SAMUEL[3] PHELPS, b. 29 January 1675.[40]
\+ vii. NATHANIEL[3] PHELPS, b. 7 January 1677.
viii. SARAH[3] PHELPS, b. 27 December 1679;[41] m. DAVID MARSHALL.[42]
ix. ABIGAIL[3] PHELPS, b. 5 June 1682;[43] d. 28 January 1709 at Windsor;[44] m. on 19 November 1702 SAMUELL FILER [FYLER] of Hartford.[45]
x. HANNAH[3] PHELPS, b. 4 August 1684;[46] m., as his second wife, JAMES ENO.[47]
xi. ANN[3] PHELPS, b. 2 October 1686.[48]
xii. MARTHA[3] PHELPS, b. 12 November 1688;[49] m. SAMUEL HOLCOMB.[50]

NATHANIEL[3] PHELPS (*Timothy*[2] *William*[1]), b. 7 January 1677 at Windsor, Conn.; bp. 13 January 1677;[51] d. 23 September 1746 at Hebron, Conn.;[52] m. (1) on 20 March 1700 at Windsor HANNAH BISSELL,[53] b. 18 September 1682 at Windsor,[54] d. 24 February 1717 at Hebron;[55]

---

37 Ibid., 1:32.

38 Ibid., Mathew Grant.

39 Ibid., Mathew Grant.

40 Ibid., Mathew Grant.

41 Ibid., Mathew Grant.

42 Windsor VRs, 2:176.

43 Ibid., 1:29.

44 *Ancient Windsor*, 2:566.

45 Ibid.

46 Windsor VRs, 1:31.

47 *Ancient Windsor*, 2:566.

48 Windsor VRs, 1:31.

49 Ibid.

50 Ibid., 2:161.

51 Windsor VRs.

52 Hebron VRs, 1:44.

53 Windsor VRs, 2:185.

54 Ibid., 1:4.

55 Hebron VRs, 1:71.

m. (2) on 5 November 1719 at Hebron ABIGAIL PINNEY,[56] d. there 28 November 1761.[57]

About 1702 Nathaniel moved south from Windsor and east of the Connecticut River to become, with his brother Timothy, one of the original settlers of Hebron. He was the first town clerk, elected to other town offices, and was elected the town's first innkeeper in 1712.[58] In 1726 and 1731 he was elected by Hebron freemen as deputy to the Connecticut General Assembly.[59] In 1729 he was made captain of Hebron train band.[60] Known thenceforth as "Captain Nathaniel," he remained a prominent farmer and landowner in the town.[61]

His will, dated 8 September 1746 and proved on 7 October 1746, was witnessed by Joseph Phelps, Samuel Filer, and Joseph Phelps, Jr. "Nathanell Phelps" signed it with an *X*, "his mark." Abigail (Pinney) Phelps and Nathaniel Phelps [Jr.] were the executors of his estate. Bequests were made as follows:

> To my loving wife Abigail one half part of my dwelling house and one third part of my barn and the third part of all my Lands during her naturell life or widerwood [widowhood] and the third part of all my mare best [ ], one [ ] and one Cow [ ] . . . to my son Nathanell Phelps forty acres of my house lot whereon my house and Barn stands together with my said dwelling house or barn, said boundaries to be of equal Breadth through the Lott & the end west bounding North on said Nathanell's land . . . to Solomon Phelps what I have payed him toward his farm [near] onkefons pond which was five hundred pounds payed to oliver pinney . . . further I give him five acres of Land onto of my house lott & building north on said Nathanell's part . . . having given to my son Alexander Phelps twenty acres of Land bounding North on Joseph Phelps Land and also his College Learning and youth [and also?] my Cow Scale and [ ] . . . and to my three dahters hannah Abigail and Mehitabel to each of them ten acres of Land upon onto my house Lott . . . I further give to my wife the best Swine & [ ] goatt and ten Bushell of garden corn and [ ] Bushells of whete . . .[62]

---

[56] Ibid., 1:70.

[57] Ibid., 2:337.

[58] John Sibun, *Our Town's Heritage, 1708–1958, Hebron, Connecticut*, (Hebron, Conn.: Douglas Library, 1958; reprint, 1992), 16.

[59] *PRCC*, 7:2311.

[60] General Assembly, Society of Colonial Wars, *An Index of Ancestors and Roll of Members of the Society of Colonial Wars* (New York, 1922).

[61] Hebron Land Records, 3:211, 3:213, 3:175, 4:10 (partial listing).

[62] Will of Nathaniel Phelps, Colchester Probate District, CSL, box 139, packet 2417 (FHL film 1,015,791). The ink is partially faded.

*Children of Nathaniel[3] and Hannah (Bissell) Phelps, all but first child born at Hebron:*[63]

i. HANNAH[4] PHELPS, b. 12 January 1701/2 at Windsor;[64] m. on 30 March 1734 JACOB SHERWIN.[65]

\+ ii. NATHANIEL[4] PHELPS, JR., b. 19 September 1703.

iii. JOSHUA[4] PHELPS b. 19 September 1709; d. 1 January 1727/28 at Hebron.[66]

iv. SOLOMON[4] PHELPS, b. 29 July 1716; m. on 10 July 1738 at Hebron TEMPERANCE BARBUR [*or* BARBER].[67]

*Children of Nathaniel[3] and Abigail (Pinney) Phelps, all born at Hebron:*

v. ABIGAIL[4] PHELPS b. 18 April 1721;[68] m. _____ BARTHOLOMEW.[69]

\+ vi. ALEXANDER[4] PHELPS, b. 6 January 1723/4.

vii. MEHITABEL[4] PHELPS, b. 22 January 1726;[70] m. on 4 September 1746 at Hebron DANIEL INGHAM.[71]

NATHANIEL[4] PHELPS [JR.] (*Nathaniel*[3] *Timothy*[2] *William*[1]), b. 19 September 1703 at Hebron, Conn.; d. there August 1781; m. there on 26 May 1726 MARY CURTICE, dau. of Samuel and Mary (Parker) Curtice of Hebron, b. 3 March 1706 at Hebron,[72] d. after 1781.

Phelps 1899 includes a second wife, Rachel Sawyer, whom Nathaniel[4] supposedly married at Hebron on 26 March 1752.[73] The town VRs record

---

63 Unless otherwise noted, children found in Hebron VRs, 1:71.

64 Windsor VRs, 1:32.

65 *Ancient Windsor,* 2:569.

66 Ibid.

67 Hebron VRs, 1:29.

68 Ibid., 1:70.

69 *Ancient Windsor,* 2:569.

70 Hebron VRs, 1:70.

71 Hebron VRs, 1:55. "David Ingraham" in *Ancient Windsor,* 2:569; Phelps 1899, 1:111.

72 Hebron VRs, 1:77.

73 Phelps 1899, 1:152.

eight children for a "Nathaniel, Jr." and Rachel Sawyer; however, none of these children is mentioned in the will of Nathaniel. Furthermore, in that document he identifies Mary as his wife. He is also called "Lieut.," not "Jr.," in the death record. It appears, therefore, that the Nathaniel Jr. who married Rachel Sawyer is a different Phelps, whose birth and death records are not found in the Hebron VRs. In fact, another Nathaniel Phelps appears in the land records in 1748, where he is carefully identified as "Nathaniel Phelps of Lebanon."[74] It is possible that this is the Phelps who married Rachel Sawyer in 1752. The evidence does not warrant positing a second wife and a second set of children for Nathaniel[4] Phelps.

Nathaniel, like his father, was a landowner and farmer in Hebron. On 10 November 1726 the elder Nathaniel conveyed land to his son ("Nathaniel Jr.").[75] As this was later in the same year of the son's marriage, it may have been a nuptial gift. "Nathaniel Sr." again conveyed land to "Nathaniel, Jr." on 9 July 1746, a few months prior to his death.[76]At the age of 72, Nathaniel—"Lieut. Nathaniel"—was in the Lexington alarm in Jebidiah Huntington's Regiment.[77]Nathaniel Phelps signed his will on 2 June 1781.[78] It was witnessed by "Alex[r] Phelps, Theod[a] Phelps, Sarah Phelps." The executors of his estate were Joshua Phelps and Mary (Curtice) Phelps. The bequests were as follows:

> To my Loving Wife Mary after my Just Debts and funeral Charges are payd, I give one Third part of all my Real Estate, to use and improve During her Natural Life & I Give one Third part of all my movable Estate to her own Disposal. & one Good Cow & five Good Sheep,— to my Sons Joshua, Nathll., Samuel, Joel & Ephraim, I Give & Bequeath all my real & personal Estate except what [was] Given to my wife, to them their Heirs and Assigns forever to be Equally Divided between them; the one acre and half of Land I have given to Joel to be Considered, as a part of his proportion . . . to Each of my Daughters, viz. Mary & Elizabeth Eighteen pounds lawfull money & to Heirs of my Daughter Hannah Eighteen pounds lawfull money inclusive of that I have already or shall in my Life Time give them respectively— my P Sons [sic] also providing for my wife a sufficiency of fire wood to maintain one Good Fire for her, cut fit for y[e] fire place at y[e] Door During her Life; and as I have given my son Benajah a Liberal Education I Give him Nothing more than his Donation.

---

74 Hebron Land Records, 3:207, 214.

75 Ibid., 2:54–55.

76 Ibid., 3:186.

77 *Connecticut Military Records, 1775–1848* (Hartford, 1889).

78 Colchester Probate District, packet 2417, box 139, CSL (FHL film 1,015,791).

*Children of Nathaniel*[4] *and Mary (Curtice) Phelps, all born at Hebron:*[79]

- i. JOSHUA[5] PHELPS, b. 9 January 1729/30.
- ii. HANNAH[5] PHELPS, b. 7 August 1734; d. bef. 1781.
- \+ iii. BENAJAH[5] PHELPS, b. 30 March 1737.
- iv. ELISABETH[5] PHELPS, b. 18 October 1739.
- v. SAMUEL[5] PHELPS, b. 6 July 1742.
- vi. JOEL[5] PHELPS, b. 24 November 1746; m. on 21 February 1768 at Hebron MARY MORAY [MOREY?].[80]

ALEXANDER[4] PHELPS (*Nathaniel*[3] *Timothy*[2] *William*[1]),[81] b. 6 January 1723/4 at Hebron, Conn.;[82] d. 19 April 1773 at Lime [Lyme], N.H.;[83] m. (1) on 20 July 1749 at Hebron the widow ANNE (PHELPS) JONES,[84] dau. of John Phelps of Hebron and Anna Horsford,[85] b. 25 May 1729 at Hebron, d. there 18 April 1750, after giving birth to twins, who died within days;[86] m. (2) there 9 January 1751/2 THEODORA[5] WHEELOCK,[87] dau. of Eleazar[4] Wheelock and Sarah (Davenport) Maltby.[88] *See* Wheelock *in these Notes.*

Alexander Phelps received his A.B. from Yale College in 1744 and his M.A. in 1747.[89] He studied for the ministry but in 1746 did not accept a call from the congregation in Union, Connecticut.[90] According to Dexter,

[79] Hebron VRs, 1:15, 19, 23, 30, 35, 45, resp.

[80] Hebron VRs, 2:82.

[81] Short biographies of Alexander[4] Phelps appear in Dexter, *Biographical Sketches*, 1:765–66, and in Phelps 1899, 1:155–56. There are numerous references to him in Chase, *A History of Dartmouth College*, vol. 1, and in James Dow McCallum, *Eleazer Wheelock, Founder of Dartmouth College* (Hanover, N.H.: Dartmouth College Publications, 1939).

[82] Hebron VRs, 1:71.

[83] *New Hampshire Gazette*, 30 April 1773; Phelps Testamentary Documents (see chapter 2, n. 113).

[84] Phelps 1899, 1:228.

[85] Ibid.

[86] Hebron VRs, 1:53, 54.

[87] Ibid., 2:80.

[88] Lebanon VRs, 1:331.

[89] Dexter, *Biographical Sketches*, 1:765.

[90] Charles Hammond, *The History of Union Connecticut* (New Haven: Price, Lee, and Adkins, 1895), 65.

Phelps subsequently taught school for a time in Monson, Massachusetts, then a part of Brimfield.[91] Sometime prior to his first marriage in 1749 he returned to Hebron, where he became an attorney and served in town and colony offices. In 1757, and again each December from 1760 to 1765, he was elected town clerk. He was elected selectman in 1763.[92] In 1754 he was appointed justice of the peace for the first time in Hebron by the Governor's Council and reappointed annually until he left the Connecticut colony in 1771. In 1749 he was elected delegate to the Connecticut General Assembly from Hebron and was subsequently re-elected, serving 11 terms in the period 1749–1771.[93]

In 1744, with inheritance of land from his father, he began to acquire and exchange land in Hebron until his departure in 1771.[94] On 12 August 1761, with other Phelpses in Hebron, he was a signatory to the charter of the town of Thetford (in the New Hampshire Claims, later in Vermont), granted by the colony of New Hampshire.[95] In May 1766 he was appointed "Lieutenant Colonel of the 12th regiment in this colony."[96]

From 1763 Phelps felt the financial strains of the depressed Connecticut economy following the French and Indian War. In October 1766 he unsuccessfully proposed to the General Assembly that they support his project to grow a plant that could produce a tea comparable to that of bohea tea.[97] In September 1767 he visited Bermuda, where he investigated possibilities for trade and reported to his father-in-law, Eleazar Wheelock, that he had seen the latter's stepson, John Maltby.[98] Jonathan Mason of Boston successfully brought judgment for debt in the amount of £290 against Alexander and Obadiah Horsford in 1768. They were

---

[91] Dexter, *Biographical Sketches,* 1:765.

[92] Reference to these elections and to other offices of trust for which Alexander Phelps was chosen (to lay out a highway, as agent in the case of an idiot child, to represent the town in a Memorial to the General Assembly) are found in Hebron Town Meetings, vols. 1–4 , 1708–99, 184–92, 195, 226.

[93] The longest gap in the nonconsecutive terms was between 1762 and 1771. *PRCC,* 10–14.

[94] Hebron Land Records, 3:175, 204, 211, 213; 4:10, 26, 56, 59, 60, 71, 72, 213, 214, 233; 5:56, 64, 69–70, 119, 124–25, 140, 146, 235, 247, 269, 491, 494, 497–98, 552, 578, 634; 6:240; 7:101.

[95] Abby Maria Hemenway, ed., *The Vermont Historical Gazetteer: A Magazine* (Burlington, Vt.: privately printed, 1871), 2:1002.

[96] *PRCC,* 11:569.

[97] Industry, 1st ser., vol. 2, 123, Conn. Arch., box 71, roll 92-75.

[98] Alexander Phelps, in Bermuda, to Eleazar Wheelock, in Lebanon, 14 Sept. 1767, DCA MS 767514.1.

required to give up "a certain piece of land lying a little northward of the Meeting House in said Hebron."[99] Theodora Phelps wrote to her father in March 1769 requesting the loan of one of his slaves, noting, however, that she feared an "attachment" from litigation then in process against her husband.[100]

In the same month Alexander was one of 60 proprietors who received a royal grant of land in the township of Bath, N.H.[101] On 10 September 1770 Hebron freemen in town meeting selected Phelps to represent them in a meeting with representatives of other trading towns. He was charged with advocating the maintenance of non-importation agreements made to protest unfair British custom duties—support for these agreements had begun to wane among merchants of the coastal towns.[102]

In October 1769 Alexander began negotiations for a royal charter for Eleazar Wheelock's proposed college in New Hampshire. In December 1770 the charter for Dartmouth College was approved by Governor John Wentworth and the Council of New Hampshire.[103] From January to March 1770, under the assumption that he was Wheelock's agent with full powers, he negotiated with the town of Haverhill, N.H., to place the college there; however, Wheelock independently chose Hanover. This led to a misunderstanding between the men and, in 1771, to an apparently baseless charge by a Hanover resident that Alexander had accepted a bribe in his negotiations. On 23 March Alexander indicated in a letter to his father-in-law his sympathy with and possible membership in the Anglican Church.[104]

In late summer 1771 he removed with his family to Lime (later Lyme), N.H., north of Hanover, where he acquired extensive lands.[105] He died intestate, leaving a substantial list of creditors and extensive land holdings (see table 4). Theodora was appointed executrix.[106]

---

[99] Hebron Land Records, 5:498.

[100] Theodora Phelps, in Hebron, to Eleazar Wheelock, in Lebanon, March 1769, DCA MS 769240.1.

[101] Grafton County [N.H.] Probate Court, 3:334.

[102] Resolutions of 10 Sept. 1770, Hebron Town Meetings, 200.

[103] Letters from Alexander Phelps to Eleazar Wheelock, and from Wheelock to Phelps, 1769–70: DCA MSS 769568.3, 769575.3, 769619, 769620, 769669, 7701102, 770120, 770129.3, 77022.3.

[104] The charge of bribery is related in a copy in Phelps's hand of his letter of 22 March 1770, DCA MS 77022.1, which is enclosed in his letter, written in Hebron, to Wheelock, in Hanover, of 23 March 1771, DCA MS 771223.2.

[105] Grafton County [N.H.] Probate Court, 1:226, 275, 278, 281–83; 3:165; 9:710.

[106] Phelps Testamentary Documents.

*Children of Alexander[4] and Anne (Phelps) Phelps, born at Hebron:*[107]

i. THEODOTIA[5] PHELPS, b. 8 April 1750; d. 14 April 1750 at Hebron.

ii. ANNE[5] PHELPS, b. 9 April 1750; d. 15 April 1750 at Hebron.

*Children of Alexander[4] and Theodora (Wheelock) Phelps:*[108]

iii. SARAH[5] PHELPS, b. 15 July 1753 at Hebron; no further record found.

In her father's testamentary papers, she is reported as ill on a trip from New Hampshire to Connecticut in 1774.[109]

\+ iv. DAVENPORT[5] PHELPS, b. 12 August 1755 at Hebron.

v. THEODORA[5] PHELPS, b. 8 September 1757 at Hebron; no further record found.

vi. ALEXANDER[5] PHELPS, b. 2 September 1759 at Hebron.

According to Phelps 1899 he returned to Hebron and practiced as a physician, but there is no record of him there.[110]

vii. LUCEY[5] PHELPS, b. 17 March 1762 at Hebron; d. there 14 April 1767.

viii. EMELIA[5] PHELPS, b. 14 June 1764 at Hebron; no further record.

\+ ix. ELEAZAR WHEELOCK[5] PHELPS, b. 16 October 1766 at Hebron.

x. RALPH RODOLPHUS[5] PHELPS, b. 21 March 1772 at Orford, N.H.;[111] d. 23 March 1849 at Ellicottsville, N.Y.;[112] m. on 23 October 1799 ABIGAIL SLOAN of Schoharie, N.Y., d. 21 July 1826 at Ellicottsville, N.Y.[113] Ralph received his A.B. from Dartmouth College in 1794.[114] A biographical note reports that he

---

107 Hebron VRs, 1:53, 54, resp. The girls were probably twins; the discrepancy in birth dates may be a transcription error in Barbour's record.

108 Ibid., 1:25; 2:223, 225, 227, 237, 280.

109 "Account for Provisions and other necessary Family Articles for Col° Phelps Family since his death (exclusive of Clothing) under Adm. of Theod[a] Phelps)," Phelps Testamentary Documents.

110 Phelps 1899, 1:268.

111 The baby weighed 16 ½ pounds at birth. *Massachusetts Gazette*, 13 April 1772.

112 *ACG*, 2:300.

113 Ibid.

114 The biographical note is included in a publication of a portion of the Episcopal Diocese of New York archives, which contains correspondence from and references to his brother, Davenport. *General Catalog, Dartmouth College*.

Studied law, and after practicing a short time in his native town, removed, about 1796, to western New York, where members of the family had made extensive purchases of land. He settled in Manlius, Onondaga County, being the second lawyer in that town. He had a high reputation both as a citizen and member of the bar. It was at the home of this brother that the Rev. Davenport Phelps stayed on his missionary journeys in that region. Ralph Phelps was one of the two persons in Manlius who owned a Prayer Book. It is said that late in life he removed to Cattaraugus County, and made a new home at Ellicottsville.[115]

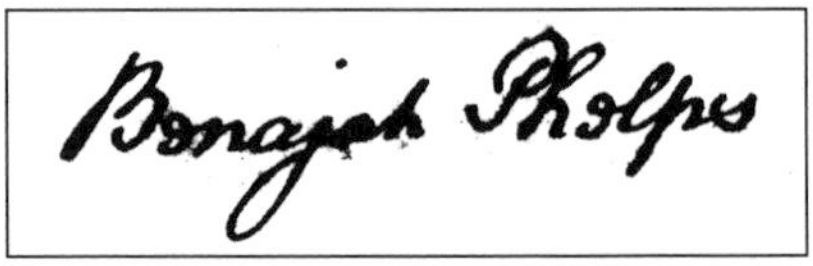

BENAJAH$^{5}$ PHELPS (*Nathaniel$^{4}$ Nathaniel$^{3}$ Timothy$^{2}$ William$^{1}$*), b. 30 March 1737 at Hebron, Conn.;[116] d. 10 February 1817 at Manchester, Conn.;[117] was m. on 19 November 1766 at Cornwallis, N.S., by the Anglican missionary Rev. Joseph Bennett,[118] to PHEBE$^{6}$ DENISON,[119] dau. of Robert Denison and Prudence Sherman, formerly of the North Society, New London (Montville), then of Horton, N.S.[120] *See* Denison *in these Notes.*

Benajah Phelps received his A.B. from Yale College in 1761 and his M.A. in 1784.[121] Prior to 1766 he was ordained a Congregational minister.[122] In 1766, probably sponsored by the South Hartford Association and probably under the guidance of Eleazar Wheelock, he was sent to the Minas Basin township of Cornwallis, Kings County, Nova Scotia. There he was elected minister of the Ecclesiastical Society in 1767.[123]

---

115 *AGC*, 2:300.

116 Hebron VRs, 1:23.

117 Hale Headstone Collection, Manchester.

118 Arthur Wentworth Hamilton Eaton, *The History of Kings County Nova Scotia, Heart of the Acadian Land* (Salem, Mass.: Salem Press, 1910), 278.

119 Cornwallis Town Book, in Lorna Woodman Evans, comp., *Township Books: Kings County, Nova Scotia: Aylesford, Cornwallis, and Horton* (Kentville, N.S.: Family History Committee of the Kings Historical Society, 1996), 67 [hereinafter cited as Cornwallis Town Book]. Denison et al., *Denison Genealogy*, 13, 32.

120 Horton Town Book in Evans, *Township Books, Kings County, Nova Scotia* [hereinafter cited as Horton Town Book].

121 Dexter, *Biographical Sketches*, 2:713–14.

122 No record of his ordination survives.

His pastorate was troubled by the inability of the congregation to pay the agreed-upon stipend and by questions of church governance involving tithing and the legitimacy of a pastor ordained elsewhere.[124] He was deeded a 666-acre tract of land—larger than that of other settlers—on 4 October 1769 by order of Gov. William Campbell.[125]

On 3 July 1770 he was one of the participants at the ordination of the Rev. Bruin Romkes Comingo at Mather's Church, in Halifax, and gave the concluding "Call to Fellowship."[126] Before April 1775 he suffered from smallpox and was dismissed as pastor of the Cornwallis Ecclesiastical Society.[127] In April 1775 he preached the funeral sermon on the death of Mrs. Jane Chipman, wife to Handley Chipman, a prominent resident of Cornwallis, which was subsequently published by A. Henry in Halifax.[128] On 1 July 1775 he purchased property in the adjoining town of Horton and probably moved there.[129] Following a raid by rebel privateers on Cornwallis on 9–10 August 1778, Benajah fled the province for fear of arrest. As he later (1784) memorialized to the Connecticut General Assembly, his attempted return for his wife and family later in 1778 resulted in his being captured by a British man-of-war and released in an open boat of the coast of Maine. He reached Machias on foot, where he spent the winter of 1778–79.[130] Returned to Connecticut, he was called to serve as the first pastor to the Ecclesiastical Society of Orford within East Hartford.[131] In 1782 his

---

[123]A letter from Handley Chipman, in Cornwallis, to the Rev. Daniel Cock, in Truro, N.S., 30 June 1777, is a principal source for the pastorate of Benajah Phelps. Acadia University Baptist Collection, A 286M .P C44341c, QCM, MG–1–136.

[124]Ibid.

[125] Registry of Deeds, Kings County, N.S., *Cornwallis Book* 1:66, 76–77, issued at Halifax 4 Oct. 1769, registered at Cornwallis 26 Feb. 1770; Eaton, *History of Kings County*, 268.

[126] John Seccombe, *A Sermon Preached in Halifax*, 3 July 1770 (Halifax, N.S.: A. Henry, 1770), Appendix.

[127] Noted in the introduction to his printed sermon.

[128] Benajah Phelps, "Death: the Way to the Believer's compleat Happiness. Illustrated and Improved In a Sermon, occasioned by the Death of Mrs. Jane Chipman, Comfort to Handley Chipman, Esq., and delivered, the Sabbath She was enter'd, by Benajah Phelps, A.B., Minister of the Gospel, and late Pastor of the Church at Cornwallis" (Halifax, N.S.: A. Henry, 1776).

[129] *Registry of Deeds*, Kings County, N.S.; Cornwallis Town Book, 1:242–43, 282, 1 July 1775; Horton Town Plot Deed. Book 1778, 3:133, 144; 173, 577.

[130] Ecclesiastical Affairs, ser. 1, vol. 15, 26, May 1784, 59a–c, 1 Oct. 1784, 60a–c, Conn. Arch., box 34, roll 82-75. *PRSC*, 5:474–75.

[131] Dexter, *Biographical Sketches*, 2:713–14; *One Hundredth Anniversary of the Organization of the First Church of Christ in Manchester, Connecticut . . .*, 13–15. Orford Parish was incorporated into Manchester when the latter was created in 1823. The Orford Ecclesiastical Society became the First Congregational Church of Manchester.

wife and children rejoined him from Nova Scotia. In 1784 the General Assembly awarded him forfeited Tory lands as compensation for expropriated property in Nova Scotia.[132] On 19 June 1793 he was dismissed as pastor after a "long-standing disagreement."[133] He represented East Hartford in the General Assembly from 1800 to 1803 and served as justice of peace in that town from 1801 to 1811.[134] In 1809 he mortgaged land and buildings (presumably his house) for $1,000 to secure a note from the Hartford Bank.[135] He left no will and no inventory of his estate was filed, suggesting that his assets may have been dissipated.[136]

*Children of Benajah[5] and Phebe (Denison) Phelps:*

i. ELIZABETH[6] PHELPS, b. 30 August 1768 at Cornwallis, N.S.;[137] d. 27 August 1804; m. _____ SAMSON.[138]

\+ ii. PHEBE[6] PHELPS, b. 7 October 1770 at Cornwallis;[139] d. 17 January 1861 at Fairfield, Conn.;[140] m. on 12 January 1793 at Stafford, Conn., ELEAZAR WHEELOCK[5] PHELPS *(see below)*.

iii. DENISON[6] PHELPS, b. 24 September 1772 at Cornwallis;[141] d. there August 1773.[142]

iv. SHERMAN[6] PHELPS, b. October 1773 probably at Cornwallis; d. there May 1774.[143]

---

[132] Revolutionary War Records, ser. 1, vol. 34, 376–77, Conn. Arch., Lyme [Conn.] Land Records, 17:114.

[133] Manchester First Congregational Church Records, Index of Church Records, 64:72, CSL.

[134] For his appointment as deputy from East Hartford see *PRSC*, 10:4, 94, 175, 412; 11:2. His appointments as justice of the peace are covered in 10:182; 11:9, 190; 12:13, 191; 13:204; 14:10, 104; 15:14.

[135] East Hartford Land Records, 9:249.

[136] There is no record of a will or inventory in the Hartford Probate Records, which included East Hartford in 1818, and no record in the statewide listing in CSL.

[137] Cornwallis Town Book, 46.

[138] Denison et al., *Denison Genealogy*, 32.

[139] Cornwallis Town Book, 46.

[140] Phelps family plot.

[141] Cornwallis Town Book, 46.

[142] Ibid.

[143] Denison et al., *Denison Genealogy*, 32. Neither his birth nor death appears in the Cornwallis or Horton Town Books.

v. EUNICE[6] PHELPS, b. April 1776; d. 29 May 1850 at Hartford; m. JAMES FOSTER, b. 3 August 1771 at Windsor; d. 31 December 1846; three children.[144]

vi. SALLY [SARAH][6] PHELPS, b. 15 February 1784 at Orford Parish, Conn.;[145] d. 15 October 1875 at Manchester, Conn.; unm.[146]

vii. RALPH RODOLPHUS[6] PHELPS, a lawyer, b. 1 March 1787 at Orford Parish;[147] d. 26 February 1874 at Manchester; bur. there in the E. Cemetery;[148] m. 1829 MARY STEPHENSON, b. ca. 1787, d. 21 February 1873 at Manchester "aged 90 years"; bur. in the E. Cemetery;[149] no children; one adopted dau.[150]

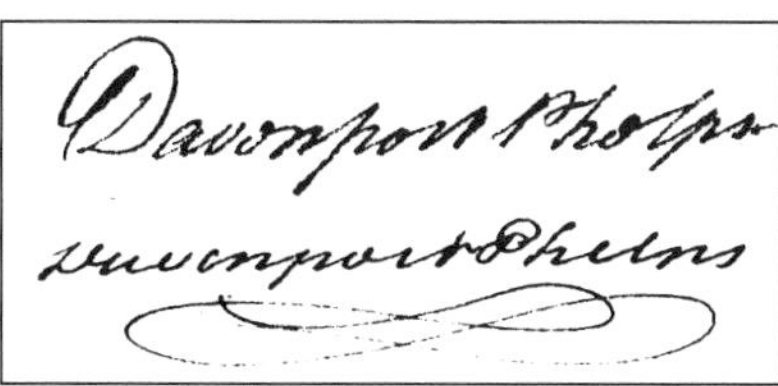

DAVENPORT[5] PHELPS (*Alexander*[4] *Nathaniel*[3] *Timothy*[2] *William*[1]),[151] b. 12 August 1755 at Hebron, Conn.;[152] d. 27 June 1813 at Pultneyville, N.Y.;[153] m. in 1785, prob. at Hanover, N.H., CATHARINE TIFFANY, dau.

---

[144] Ibid. No record of her birth appears in the Cornwallis or Horton Town Books.

[145] East Hartford VRs, 1:36.

[146] Hale Headstone Collection, vol. 6, Manchester, 399.

[147] East Hartford VRs, 1:36.

[148] Hale Headstone Collection, vol. 6, Manchester, 399.

[149] Ibid.

[150] Denison et al., *Denison Genealogy*, 32.

[151] Davenport Phelps was the subject of a biography by John N. Norton, *Pioneer Missionaries or the Lives of Phelps and Nash* (New York: General Protestant Episcopal & School Union and Church Book Society, 1858). A more recent study is John H. Stelter, "Rev. Davenport Phelps—Lawyer, Freemason, Missionary," in *Transactions of The American Lodge of Research: Free and Accepted Masons* 12, no. 1 (31 Jan. 1972–27 Dec. 1972), 51–74. There is a short account of Davenport Phelps in the *General Catalog, Dartmouth College,* and in Phelps 1899, 1:267. A short biographical note and transcript of letters written by Joseph Brant on Phelps's behalf are included in William E. Stone, *Life of Joseph Brant—Thayendanegea,* 2 vols. (New York: George Dearborn, 1838), 2:431 ff. Phelps's correspondence with Bishop Benjamin Moore and John Henry Hobart, later a bishop, has been reprinted in its entirety in *AGC.* These include a biographical sketch, a listing of Davenport and Catharine (Tiffany) Phelps's children, and notes on references to the people and places cited. There are frequent mentions of Phelps in the *Journals of the General Convention of the Episcopal Diocese of New York* from 1804 to 1814.

[152] Hebron VRs, 2:223.

[153] *Columbian Centinel* (Massachusetts), 13 July 1813.

of Dr. Gideon and Sarah Dean (Farrar) Tiffany,[154] b. ca. 1769 at Norton, Mass.,[155] d. 23 November 1836 at Pultneyville.[156]

In 1771 he was enrolled at Yale College,[157] but later that year when his family removed to Lime, N.H., he enrolled at Dartmouth College, founded by his grandfather, Eleazar Wheelock. He was graduated in 1775 with an A.B.[158] From October 1775 he was with the Continental Army as it invaded Quebec.[159] He was in Montreal from December 1775 to June 1776.[160]

He was back in Hanover by late June, after the American retreat (May–June 1776).[161] On 16 August 1777 he was commissioned quartermaster in Col. David Hobart's Twelfth Regiment, New Hampshire Militia, part of the Second Brigade, commanded by Brigadier Gen. John A. Stark.[162] On 17 August 1777 he participated in the Battle of Bennington.[163] He was discharged on 26 September 1777.[164] From 15 December 1777 to 31 March 1778 he served as captain in Col. Timothy Bedel's New Hampshire Regiment.[165] After the war, in 1786–88, he served as a major in the New Hampshire Militia, Third Regiment of Light Horse. In 1788 he was promoted to the rank of colonel.[166]

---

154 Tiffany, *The Tiffanys of America*, 41. Dr. Gideon Tiffany was a physician in Hanover.

155 Ibid.; *AGC*, 2:69–70.

156 *AGC*, 2:69–70.

157 Norton, *Pioneer Missionaries*, 21.

158 *General Catalog, Dartmouth College*.

159 His military status is uncertain. Chase, *History of Dartmouth College*, 1:344 states that Phelps was in Bedel's regiment in 1775, but there is no record of this service in the National Archives. Nevertheless, his presence with the troops is attested by a letter from Israel Curtis, at St. Johns, to Eleazar Wheelock, at Hanover, 3 Nov. 1775, DCA MS 7705603.

160 DCA MS 1019LL; also transcribed in Chase, *History of Dartmouth College* 1:344–5. Davenport Phelps, in Montreal, to Eleazar Wheelock, in Hanover, 24 Feb. 1776, Benedict Arnold Papers, NYHS, transcribed in Stelter, "Rev. Davenport Phelps," 53. Eleazar Wheelock, at Dartmouth, to Davenport Phelps, in Montreal, 19 Mar. 1776, transcribed in Norton, *Pioneer Missionaries*, 24–25.

161 Sylvanus Ripley to Eleazar Wheelock, in Connecticut, 9 June 1776. Chase, *History of Dartmouth*, 1:357.

162 Revolutionary War Records, National Archives and Records Administration, Washington, D.C.

163 George C. Gilmore, *Roll of the New Hampshire Soldiers at the Battle of Bennington, August 16, 1777* (Manchester, N.H: J. B. Clarke, 1891).

164 N.H. Militia, *Rev War Rec.*

165 Ibid.

166 Stelter, "Rev. Davenport Phelps," 55.

In 1778 he represented Orford in a joint effort with other towns to establish the upper Connecticut Valley as a separate state.[167] In 1779 he bought a house in Orford, which he owned for about 10 years.[168] He was in Hartford in 1785–86, engaged in a mercantile business with his mother's half-brothers, James and Eleazar Wheelock. He also resided in New Haven, as his first daughter was born there. After the failure of the business he returned to New Hampshire.[169]

On 12 December 1788 he assisted in the formation of Dartmouth Lodge (Masons), Hanover, New Hampshire.[170] By 1790 he resided in Piermont.[171] In 1786 he began a correspondence, continued until 1794, with the exiled Rev. Samuel Peters, formerly rector of St. Peter's, Hebron, Connecticut.[172] Peters was a Loyalist who left the colonies in 1775 for London.

In 1792 he journeyed 600 miles with James Wheelock to Newark, the recently established capital of Upper Canada on the west bank of the Niagara River near Lake Ontario.[173] By 1793 he owned a house and lot there.[174] In July of the following year he was appointed attorney and advocate in His Majesty's Courts of Justice in the Province of Upper Canada. At the same time he advertised a mercantile business in Newark.[175] He was active in Freemasonry soon after his arrival in Newark; he was a leader in the formation of the Grand Lodge of Upper Canada and was elected Grand Secretary at its organization on 26 August 1795.[176]

---

[167] Chase, *History of Dartmouth College*, 1:469.

[168] Alice Doan Hodgson, *Thanks to the Past: The Story of Orford, N.H.* (Orford, N.H.: Historical Fact Publications, 1965; reprint, 1992), 143.

[169] Norton, *Pioneer Missionaries*, 30.

[170] Ibid., citing *Proceedings, Grand Lodge of Massachusetts, 1769–1792*, 353.

[171] *Heads of Families at the First Census of the United States in the Year 1790, New Hampshire* (Washington, D.C.: United States Government Printing Office, 1907; reprint, Baltimore, Md.: Genealogical Publishing, 1966, 1973), 36.

[172] Davenport Phelps, in Albany, wrote the last of the five extant letters of this correspondence to Samuel Peters, in London, 1 March 1794, *Peters Coll.*

[173] Norton, *Pioneer Missionaries*, 32.

[174] Land Book E 1802–1804, Receipt of Petitions in Executive Council minutes, no. 439, 10 July 1802, Record Group 1 C102, Arch. Ont.

[175] *Upper Canada Gazette or American Oracle*, 10 and 31 July 1794.

[176] J. R. Robertson, *The History of Freemasonry in Upper Canada* (Toronto, Ont.: 1916), 1:473, 559, 632; Stelter, "Rev. Davenport Phelps," 56.

On 25 May 1793 he received a grant of land in Upper Canada, later called the Glanford Tract, consisting of 84,000 acres.[177] He returned to Piermont, New Hampshire, in January 1794 to bring wife and children to settle in Newark.[178] In 1797 the government repossessed the bulk of Glanford Township, leaving Phelps with only 1,200 acres.[179]

In 1797 Joseph Brant, Mohawk chief and Masonic lodge brother, urged Phelps to become an Anglican priest to minister to Indians.[180] The Upper Canada authorities refused to support his ordination in 1799.[181] On 13 December 1801 he was admitted to the Holy Order of Deacons by the Rt. Rev. Benjamin Moore, Bishop of New York, at Trinity Church, New York, and given a charge of particulars of conduct to govern his mission to the Indians in Upper Canada. His ordination was supported by Brant and by the Rev. Philander Chase, of Poughkeepsie.[182] On 5 October 1803 he was ordained to the priesthood by Bishop Moore at St. Peter's Church, Albany.[183]

The distrust by officials in Upper Canada resulted in his transfer to mission in western New York, where he conducted an active mission from 1804 to 1813. His territory was roughly 100 miles in the east-west section of western New York along the northern shores of the Finger Lakes, where he was responsible for founding 12 parishes.[184] From 1807 to 1812 he resided with family in Geneva, New York, where he was the first rector of Trinity Church.[185] On 25 September 1812 he informed Bishop

---

[177] E. A. Cruikshank, ed., "Petition of Davenport Phelps and Others," *Ontario Historical Society, Papers and Records* 24 (Toronto, Ont., 1927), 104–106. *Report Book*, Crown Land Dept., 1795–1799, "Davenport Phelps claims for 97 square miles 1796," 41, Arch. Ont., MS 2696.

[178] Davenport Phelps, in Albany, to Samuel Peters, in London, 1 March 1794, *Peters Coll.*

[179] Field Book of Glanford Township, by Davenport Phelps, 1797, Arch. Ont., Record Group 1, A I 1, vol. 55, Letters received by Surveyors General, October 1797 to June 1798, microfilm ser. 626, reel 3, 89.

[180] *DCB*, vol. 4. Stone, *Life of Joseph Brant—Thayendanegea*, 2:431 ff.

[181] Letter from Jacob Mountain to Peter Russell, 11 Jan. 1798, in *The Correspondence of the Honourable Peter Russell*, 2:62–63. Peter Russell to Jacob Mountain, 22 Feb. 1793, in ibid., 2:98–99.

[182] *AGC* 2:239; Philander Chase, *Bishop Chase's Reminiscences, an Autobiography*, 2d ed. (Boston: James B. Dow, 1848), 1:38–39.

[183] *AGC* 3:8.

[184] *AGC* 3, *passim.*

[185] *AGC* 5:262–63; Stelter, "Rev. Davenport Phelps," 64.

Hobart that illness prevented him from continuing his mission duties[186] and moved with family to Pultneyville, where he died and was buried.

Davenport Phelps died intestate.[187] The inventory of his estate showed a value of $1,163.92 and a $300 debt to his brother-in-law, Oliver Tiffany. Assets included "1 Black woman & one child for about six years, $75.00," a yoke of oxen, two cows, 26 sheep, two hogs as well as a horse, and farm implements (including pitchforks, corn baskets, and a grindstone), a horse buggy, portmanteau, two large trunks, silver spoons and forks, a candle mold, cupboards, chairs, a table, a writing desk, inkstands, and books. There was no real property, only the wheat and grass of two fields.[188] His sons George Davenport Phelps and William Alexander Phelps and son-in-law Iddo Ellis administered the estate. A memorial bas-relief showing Phelps, his horse, and Bishop Moore was installed in the choir of Trinity Church, Geneva, when it was rebuilt in 1932 under the direction of architect Hobart Upjohn, after the earlier building had been destroyed by fire.[189]

*Children of Davenport[5] and Catharine (Tiffany) Phelps:*

i. LUCY[6] PHELPS, b. 21 October 1786 at New Haven, Conn.; d. 22 August 1824 in Putnam Co., Ga.; m. 1809 Dr. IDDO ELLIS, son of _____ and _____ (Day) Ellis, b. in N.H., d. 1847 at Columbus, Ga., a physician who lived in New York until 1817, when he removed to Edenton, Putnam Co., Ga.; seven children.[190]

ii. SYLVESTER OLIVER[6] PHELPS, b. 27 September 1788, prob. at Orford, N.H.; d. 20 February 1843; unm.[191]

iii. GEORGE DAVENPORT[6] PHELPS, b. 16 August 1790, prob. at Orford, N.H.;[192] m. at Marion, N.Y., on 22 December 1823 SARAH MARIA REES, dau. of William and Abigail (Powell) Rees, b. New York City, d. 9 July 1846 at Pultneyville, N.Y.; six children.[193]

---

186 Phelps, in Geneva, N.Y., to John Henry Hobart, 25 Sept. 1812, *Journals of the Conventions, Diocese of New York*, 528–29.

187 Surrogate Register, Davenport Phelps Estate File, Archives of Ontario (N.Y.) G42-224–97–98.

188 Ontario Co. [N.Y.] Surrogate Court Book 7, 18, 25. The inventory was filed on 22 July 1813.

189 Samuel H. Edsall, *Historical Sketches and Guide to Trinity Church Geneva, New York* (Geneva, N.Y.: Trinity Church, 1947; rev. 1984), 28ff.

190 Phelps 1899, 1:476–77; *AGC* 3:9.

191 Phelps 1899, 1:268; *AGC* 3:9.

192 Ibid.

193 Phelps 1899, 1:477–78; *AGC* 3:9.

In 1863 George Davenport was a merchant in Milwaukee, Wisconsin.[194]

iv. WILLIAM ALEXANDER[6] PHELPS, b. 19 February 1792, prob. at Freemont, N.H.; d. 1 April 1862; unm.[195]

v. THEODORA[6] PHELPS, b. 22 January 1795, prob. at Newark, Upper Canada; d. 12 November 1816; "presumably unm."[196]

vi. AURELIA[6] PHELPS, b. 4 July 1798, prob. at Glanford, Upper Canada; d. 3 October 1862.[197]

vii. SARAH[6] PHELPS, b. 4 July 1798, prob. at Glanford, Upper Canada;[198] d. 1882 at Milwaukee, Wis.;[199] m. 1819 at Pultneyville, N.Y., BENNETT CHEW FITZHUGH, son of Peregrine and Elizabeth (Chew) Fitzhugh;[200] res. at Sodus Point, N.Y., and later at Milwaukee, Wis.; eleven children.[201]

viii. DEAN WHEELOCK[6] PHELPS, b. 15 October 1800, prob. at Glanford, Upper Canada; d. 18 October 1804.[202]

ix. JOSEPH AUGUSTUS[6] PHELPS, b. 16 April 1804, prob. in New York State; d. 23 March 1889; m. on 20 December 1833 SARAH ANN SELBY,[203] b. 26 June 1815, d. 6 September 1854; eight children.[204]

x. HENRY RODOLPHUS[6] PHELPS, b. 1 February 1806, prob. in New York State; d. 7 April 1887; m. (1) in 1831 JULIA EDUS; m. (2) ca. 1841 at Palmyra, N.Y., MARTHA MOSES, b. 10 December 1820, d. 30 November 1873; three children by first wife, six by second. [205]

xi. EDWARD LEWIS[6] PHELPS, b. 15 November 1807, prob. at Geneva, N.Y.; d. 7 October 1876; unm.[206]

---

194 Phelps 1899, 1:477–78.

195 Phelps 1899, 1:268; *AGC* 3:9.

196 Ibid.

197 Phelps 1899, 1:268; *AGC* 6:4

198 Phelps 1899, 1:268; *AGC* 3:9.

199 Phelps 1899, 1:477–78.

200 *AGC* 3:9.

201 Phelps 1899, 1:477–78.

202 Phelps 1899, 1:268; *AGC* 3:9.

203 Ibid.

204 Phelps 1899, 1:478– 79; *AGC* 3:9.

205 Phelps, 1899, 1:479; *AGC* 3:9.

206 Phelps 1899, 1:268; *AGC* 3:9.

ELEAZAR WHEELOCK[5] PHELPS (*Alexander*[4] *Nathaniel*[3] *Timothy*[2] *William*[1]), b. 10 October 1766 at Hebron, Conn.;[207] d. 12 October 1818 at Havana, Cuba;[208] bur. there; m. on 12 January 1793 at Stafford, Conn., his half first cousin once removed, PHEBE PHELPS,[209] dau. of Benajah and Phebe (Denison) Phelps *(see above)*.

In 1771 Eleazar Wheelock Phelps,[210] then a child, removed with his family to Lime, N.H. From 1785 to 1787 he attended Dartmouth College but did not receive a degree.[211] Between 1787 and 1792 he was probably in Connecticut, but there is no record. His marriage to Phebe established him as a resident of Stafford, where he and his wife remained until 1811. On 23 November 1794 he and Phebe Phelps were admitted to the Stafford Ecclesiastical Society.[212] He was closely associated with John[5] Phelps, a fifth cousin, who managed and owned the Phelps Iron Furnace and Foundry in Stafford.

In 1797 he was clerk of the probate court of which John[5] Phelps was the judge.[213] From 1793 to 1811 he acquired and sold land and buildings in Stafford.[214] He was annually appointed justice of peace from 1797 to 1811.[215] In 1802 he was the object of charges alleging unfitness to hold office, which were not sustained by the Connecticut General Assembly.[216] From 1804 he served as executor of estate of John[5] Phelps.[217]

In 1803 he joined with others in a successful proposal to the General Assembly to charter a turnpike from Stafford to the Massachusetts border.[218] In 1808 he was a stockholder in the Worcester & Stafford

---

207 Hebron VRs, 2:230.

208 Samuel De Forest, in Havana, to Phebe Phelps, in New York City, 14 Oct. 1818, manuscript in possession of the author.

209 Stafford VRs, 2:134.

210 There is a short biographical note on E. W. Phelps in Phelps 1899, and his enrollment at Dartmouth is cited in *General Catalog, Dartmouth College*. His great-granddaughter, Julia Phelps (Haring) White, wrote a biographical note in 1913, JHW MSS.

211 *General Catalog, Dartmouth College*.

212 Stafford Church Records, LBG:87.

213 Tolland County Court Files, CSL, Record Group 3, box 94, case 27845 (Feb. 1797).

214 Stafford Land Records, 7:344; 8:36, 239, 240, 247, 373, 378, 407, 546; 9:87, 293, 298, 315, 343, 418, 475; 10:177, 428, 430, 443, 571.

215 *PRSC*, vols. 9–15.

216 *Connecticut Courant*, 14 June 1802; *Connecticut Official Records*, 9:5.

217 Estate of John Phelps and Executor's Account of Expenses, Town of Stafford, Stafford Probate District, CSL, box 1372, case 1705 (FHL film 1,018,463).

218 Travel, Highways, Ferries, Bridges, and Taverns, 1737–1820, ser. 2, Conn. Arch.

Turnpike Corporation and in charge of construction of Stafford link that connected with a turnpike leading from Worcester.[219]

In 1810–11 he served as judge of the Stafford Probate Court.[220] In 1810 he successfully called the bond that had been placed in surety by individuals constructing the turnpike, on the grounds of failure to keep to specifications. On two occasions in 1811 those individuals, in apparent retaliation for the action on that bond, sacked his house, removing property and terrorizing the family.[221]

From late 1811 to about 1815, according to family record, he and the family traveled in Europe.[222] They returned to the United States in 1815. In 1817 he served as steward at the Military Academy at West Point.[223] In 1817–18 he resided at 166 Greenwich Street, New York City.[224]

In September 1818 he embarked on the schooner *Piper* on a business trip to Havana, Cuba. The schooner was attacked by pirates, and the passengers were robbed.[225] After arriving, he contracted "tropical fever" (possibly yellow fever) and died.[226] No will or estate inventory has been found in Connecticut or New York.

*Children of Eleazar[5] Wheelock and Phebe (Phelps) Phelps, all born and baptized at Stafford:*[227]

i. ELIZA[6] PHELPS, b. 2 September 1794;[228] bp. 23 November

---

[219] *Worcester & Stafford Turnpike Co. vs. Eliab Alden & Others*, Tolland County Superior Court Files, CSL, Record Group 3, box 7.

[220] Appointed May 1810 and May 1811 for the year ensuing. *PRSC*, 15:13, 158.

[221] Action of debt on bond: *Phelps vs. Lyon*, Sept. 1811–Sept. 1812, Tolland County Superior Court Files, 1810–1817, Man–Z. *Eleazar W. Phelps, Esqr., vs. Lyakim Lyon*, Sept. 1811, Dec. 1811, Sept. 1812, Tolland County Superior Court, Files 1810–17, Man–Z, CSL, Record Group 3, box 7. *E. W. Phelps action vs. B. Mann, L. Lyon, et al.*, re 4 November 1811 trespass, Tolland County Superior Court Files, Sep'r Sup'r Court 1812, CSL, Record Group 3, box 7.

[222] JHW MSS; Phelps 1899; *General Catalog, Dartmouth College.*

[223] George L. Blaney, Aid to Engineer Department, Engineer Department, Washington, 18 June 1818, to Mr. E. W. Phelps, New York, *Records Relating to the United States Military Academy, 1812–1867, Military Academy Letters*, vol. 1, December 21, 1812–December 30, 1826, File: Microcopies of Records in the National Archives, no. 91, roll 1, National Archives and Records Administration; U.S. Military Academy at West Point. 17 Congress 1 Petition, 133, 20 Feb. 1822, National Archives.

[224] Longworth's *New York City Directory*, 1817–18.

[225] Peter Haring Judd, "An Interrupted Journey," *Seaport*, South Street Seaport, New York City, Fall 1997, 36–39.

[226] Eleazar Wheelock Phelps, in Havana, to Phebe Phelps, in New York, 30 Sept. 1818, manuscript in possession of the author.

[227] Unless otherwise stated, birth dates are from grave markers.

1794;[229] was m. on 21 April 1830 at New York City by the Rev. William McMurry to BILLINGS GRANT.[230]

On 6 May 1815 Eliza was admitted as communicant to Stafford Congregational Church.[231]

ii. HARRIET$^6$ PHELPS, b. 7 August 1796; bp. 23 October 1796;[232] d. 28 June 1876 at Fairfield, Conn.;[233] unm.

On 15 January 1815 she was admitted as a communicant to Stafford Congregational Church.[234]

iii. PHEBE$^6$ PHELPS, b. 8 March 1799; bp. 23 June 1799;[235] d. 19 July 1883 at Fairfield;[236] unm.

She was admitted as a communicant to Stafford Congregational Church on 2 July 1816.[237]

iv. EMELIA$^6$ PHELPS, bp. 5 July 1801; d. 26 December 1805 at Stafford.[238]

\+ v. GEORGE ALEXANDER$^6$ PHELPS, b. 21 September 1803.

vi. JULIA MARIA$^6$ PHELPS, b. July 1805; d. 9 December 1805 at Stafford.[239]

vii. MARY AMELIA$^6$ PHELPS, b. 8 February 1807;[240] m. on 7 November 1827 RICHARD CONNELL [CORNELL] at New York City;[241] children HARRY CORNELL and ANNIE CORNELL, cited as "nephews and nieces" in the will of George$^6$ Alexander Phelps.[242]

viii. HENRY DAVENPORT$^6$ PHELPS, b. 12 March 1810; d. 5 August 1875 at Fairfield; [243] m. on 9 May 1840 at New York City SUSAN A.

---

228 Stafford VRs, 2:53.

229 Stafford Church Records, LBG:104.

230 Stafford VRs, 2-M:80.

231 Stafford Church Records, LBG:104.

232 Stafford Church Records, LBG:88.

233 Grave marker, Phelps family plot.

234 Stafford Church Records, LBG:104.

235 Stafford Church Records, LBG:94.

236 Grave marker, Phelps family plot.

237 Stafford Church Records, LBG:105.

238 Ibid., LBG:109.

239 Stafford Church Records, LBG:99, 109.

240 Phelps 1899, 1:269.

241 *N.Y. Evening Post*, 10 Nov. 1827.

242 Will of George A. Phelps, Fairfield Probate Records, 44:414–19.

243 Grave marker, Phelps family plot.

DEROSE;[244] poss. child ELIZA P[HELPS?] SMILEY, cited as "niece" in the will of George[6] Alexander Phelps.

GEORGE ALEXANDER[6] PHELPS (*Eleazar*[5] *Alexander*[4] *Nathaniel*[3] *Timothy*[2] *William*[1]), b. 21 September 1803 at Stafford, Conn.; bp. on 9 October 1803;[245] d. 12 April 1880 at Fairfield, Conn., of diabetes;[246] m. on 8 September 1825 at New York City ELIZA AYRES,[247] dau. of John Ayres and Elizabeth Pancoast, b. 6 November 1808 according to family record at Williamsport, Penn.,[248] d. 2 September 1880 at Allston, Mass., home of her oldest daughter, of heart disease.[249]

Julia Phelps (Haring) White, granddaughter of Eliza Ayres, recorded that Elizabeth Pancoast and John Ayres were born in Virginia and that Elizabeth Pancoast was the daughter of Elizabeth White, who was the "daughter of Mary White whose father was with Washington during the Revolution and was one of the sufferers at Valley Forge." Of Elizabeth White she wrote that her "brother was the father of Charles S. Pancoast, a lawyer in Philadelphia."

In the New York City directories from 1818 to 1823–24 "Ayers & Pancoast, silverplaters" are listed at 89 Maiden Lane (probable brothers-in-law). In 1821 John "Ayers," "silver plater," is listed at that address.[250] George Alexander Phelps was first listed in the New York City directory for 1825–6 as a "fruiter." In subsequent years, until 1867, he was listed as an importer and merchant. He and various partners imported fruits from Mediterranean ports. The firm was given positive reports as to credit and capital by R. G. Dun & Co.[251] His business addresses were

---

244 *N.Y. Evening Post*, 10 May 1840.

245 Stafford Church Records, LBG:99.

246 Grave marker, Phelps family plot; Fairfield Town Clerk, Death Certificate Index; Fairfield Probate Records, Will 44414, filed 30 April 1880 (dated 1 May 1878), Letter of Administration 44528, filed 22 Oct. 1880; obit., *Southport Times*, 16 April 1880.

247 JHW MSS.

248 JHW MSS. Neither Williamsport nor Lycoming County have church or vital records from this period.

249 Death Certificate Index, Fairfield Town Records, portions obscured by water damage, birthplace incorrectly stated as Fairfield. Will 44 509, Inv. 44 613, Acct. 44 552; will dated 20 Jan. 1879.

250 The surname is spelled "Ayers" in the directories, but it is "Ayres" in the Phelps family plot grave marker and in the estate papers.

251 Credit reports on G. A. Phelps and firm at annual/semiannual intervals 1850 to retirement of G. A. Phelps in 1867, R. G. Dun.

| Year | Address |
|---|---|
| 1825 | 20 Fulton Street |
| 1826–27 | 196 Front Street |
| 1830 | Burling Slip |
| 1832–36 | 103 Front Street |
| 1837–38 | 172 Front Street |
| 1840–41 | 218 East Broadway |
| 1844–69 | 102 Front Street |

*Source:* New York City directories, 1825–1869.

About 1858 the partnership opened an office in Palermo, Sicily, which was headed by George Alexander Phelps, Jr.[252] From 1825 to 1872 he maintained a residence in New York City at the following addresses:

| Year | Address |
|---|---|
| 1825 | 32 Gold |
| 1826 | 55 Ann |
| 1827 | 44 Roosevelt |
| 1830 | 5 Chestnut |
| 1832 | 28 Vandam |
| 1833 | 113 Prince |
| 1834 | 140 Prince |
| 1837–38 | no home address listed |
| 1839 | 122 Rivington[a] |
| 1848–53 | "Conn." |
| 1840–44 | no home address listed |
| 1846 | 622 Broadway |
| 1847 | 624 Broadway |
| 1854–67 | 129 West Fourteenth |
| 1870–72 | 209 [129] West Fourteenth[b] |

*Source:* New York City Directories.

a. As "George Phelps," no "A."
b. The change in numbering reflected Fifth Avenue as the division between east and west in place of Broadway.

In 1872, at his retirement, the ownership of the firm (renamed "Phelps Brothers & Co.") passed to his sons. From 1837 to 1870 he owned a house and property on Main Street (now 766 Old Post Road) in Fairfield, Connecticut, for summer and occasional use, and maintained a house nearby

[252] G. A. Phelps, Jr., listed in 1859–60 New York City directory with home "Europe" for the first time.

for his mother and two unmarried sisters, Harriet and Phebe.[253] From 1870 he owned a larger house on Main Street in Fairfield (now 458 Old Post Road), where he died.[254]

On 1 May 1878 George signed his will, which was proved on 29 April 1880. It contained the following bequests: his sister Phebe Phelps would receive $6,000 annually; "to each of my nephews and nieces e.g. Eliza Smiley, Harry Cornell and Annie Cornell, $1,000"; grandson George Henderson was to receive $7,500 (with provision that "if he should prove incapable" the executors could provide him support); to granddaughter Julia P. White $7,500; the will specified that the foregoing "bequests be made if the estate is $250,000 at least; if less than that it should be proportionately reduced"; to Eliza Phelps, widow, $70,000, and "the use of the house and all privileges thereof." The remainder was to be divided equally among the children. Property in the City of New York could be divided, but not "sold at a sacrifice unless absolutely necessary." The value of securities at the time was $109,975.50. Sons Charles H. Phelps, George A. Phelps, Jr., Frank Phelps, and Howard Phelps were executors.[255] Eliza's will, signed on 20 January 1879, with a codicil of 29 May 1880, was proved on 7 September 1880.[256] She bequeathed "to two daughters, Julia M. Winter and Harriet A. Brooke all my wearing apparel and all my silver, watches, clocks, diamonds and all my jewelry of every description to be divided equally between them . . . to my sister Sarah Peck during her life the income from two thousand dollar bonds of the Michigan Central Railroad Co. having an interest of 7% or $140 per annum . . . All rest and residue I give and bequeath to six living children, Julia P. Winter, Harriet A. Brooke, George A. Phelps, Jr., Frank Phelps, Charles H. Phelps and Howard Phelps." The codicil added "to my brother Henry W. Ayres the income from 7 one thousand dollar bonds of the Michigan Central Railroad Co." The codicil was witnessed by Annie B. Phelps (probably Annie Brown [Coleman], wife of Charles Haring Phelps), Anna M. Brooke, and Thomas R. Brooke.

---

253 Fairfield Land Records, 44:134–35, 833.

254 Ibid., 58:73, warranty deed, dated 31 Oct. 1870, James Rowland and Mary Rowland, grantors.

255 Will of George A. Phelps, Fairfield Probate Records, 44:414–19; Administrative Actions, 44:528.

256 Will filed in Fairfield and New York City. Fairfield Probate Records, 44:509, inventory 44:613, location 08-026861, Phelps April 1882; New York County Surrogates Court.

*Children of George Alexander[6] and Eliza (Ayres) Phelps:*

i. JULIA MARIA[7] PHELPS b. 13 July 1826 at New York City; d. 13 March 1899 at Newton, Mass.;[257] m. on 5 January 1853 at Hartford, Conn., ROYAL WINTER, b. 26 April 1818 at Croydon, N.H., d. 22 February 1888 at Newton, Mass.[258]

*Children of Royal and Julia Maria (Phelps)[7] Winter:*[259]

a. ELIZA PHELPS[8] WINTER, b. 8 May 1854 at Fairfield.; d. 6 February 1924 at Pasadena, Calif.; m. on 10 October 1889 at Grace Church, Boston, James Taylor Wetherald, b. 5 October 1858 at Richmond, Ind., d. 25 June 1927 at Pasadena, Calif.; two children.

b. EMMA[8] WINTER, b. 17 June 1864 at Boston.

\+ ii. CAROLINE ELIZA[7] PHELPS, b. 13 September 1828 at New York City.

iii. HARRIET AUGUSTA[7] PHELPS, b. 6 October 1830 at New York City;[260] d. 12 February 1913 at Boston;[261] m. on 3 February 1854 at New York City THOMAS REESE BROOKE;[262] child, THOMAS REESE BROOKE, b. 4 January 1855.[263]

With Anna B. Brooke, Harriet witnessed the 1880 codicil to the will of Eliza (Ayres) Phelps.[264]

iv. EMMA AYRES[7] PHELPS, b. 19 September 1832 at New York City;[265] d. 23 January 1855;[266] m. WILLIAM COLEMAN HENDERSON of Lancaster Co., Penn.;[267] prob. child, GEORGE P. HENDERSON, referred to as "grandson" in George Alexander Phelps's will.

v. GEORGE ALEXANDER[7] PHELPS, JR., b. 24 July 1834 at New York City;[268] d. 28 April 1914 in Fairfield County, Conn.;[269] m. on

---

257 Colonial Dames application of Dorothy Phelps Wetherald, admitted 9 Dec. 1963 by right of descent from John Davenport (granddaughter of Julia Maria [Phelps] Winter).

258 Ibid.

259 Ibid.

260 JHW MSS.

261 Grave marker, Phelps family plot.

262 JHW MSS.

263 Phelps 1899, 1:820.

264 Will of Eliza Phelps, Fairfield Probate Records, 44 509.

265 JHW MSS.

266 Grave marker, Phelps family plot.

267 Phelps 1899, 1:480.

268 JHW MSS; Phelps 1899, 1:481.

269 Grave marker, Phelps family plot.

3 January 1855 in New York City HELEN CLARK, dau. of William Clark and second wife, Mary Bogart, b. 28 May 1834.[270]

On 3 April 1855 George became a partner in Chamberlain & Phelps (predecessor to Phelps Brothers & Co.), New York.[271] He represented the firm in Palermo from about 1858 to about 1864 and in Liverpool from 1859 to after 1878. In 1872 the office was at the Old Castle Buildings, 26 Preesons Row W., and his residence, in 1873, at Sunnyside, Devonshire Road, Princes Park.[272] George's will required cremation without religious services. From his estate, valued at $80,000, his daughter, Mrs. Helen Ackerley of England, was bequeathed $40,000.[273]

*Children of George Alexander[7] and Helen (Clark) Phelps:*

a. GEORGE[8] PHELPS, b. ca. 1857, d. 5 September 1860, bur. Phelps family plot, Fairfield.[274]

b. HARLEY[8] PHELPS, b. 1861, d. 11 June 1861.[275]

c. HELEN[8] PHELPS, b. 24 July 1863 at New York City; m. _____ ACKERLEY, living in England in 1914, as noted in father's will.[276]

d. ALEXANDER[8] PHELPS, b. 12 July 1870 at Paris, France; res. at Liverpool, England, in 1888.[277]

vi. AMELIA CHAMBERLAIN[7] PHELPS, b. 22 May 1836 at New York City; d. there 13 January 1837.[278]

vii. HENRY DEMAREST[7] PHELPS, b. 14 October 1837; d. 2 September 1853.[279]

viii. WILLIAM CHAMBERLAIN[7] PHELPS, b. 28 May 1840; d. 16 December 1842.[280]

ix. SARAH ALLEN[7] PHELPS, b. 26 July 1842 at Fairfield; d. 15 December 1845.[281]

---

270 JHW MSS; John Albert Bogart, comp., *The Bogart Family* (Harrison, N.Y: privately printed, 1959), 196–97.

271 R. G. Dun 340:37.

272 S. Gore's *Directory of Liverpool and Its Environs* (alphabetical), 1872ff.

273 Notice of will filing. *NYT,* 15 June 1916, 9:2.

274 Ibid.

275 Ibid.

276 Notice of will filing names Helen Ackerley of England as sole heir to G. A. Phelps, Jr. *NYT,* 15 June 1916, 9:2.

277 Phelps 1899, 1:829; not mentioned in will.

278 Phelps 1899, 1:481; grave marker, Phelps family plot.

279 Grave marker, Phelps family plot.

280 Ibid.

281 Ibid.

x. FRANK[7] PHELPS, b. 24 March 1844 at New York City,[282] d. 27 September 1937 at Stamford, Conn.;[283] m. on 10 May 1866 at Fairfield MARY A. BRADLEY CURTISS [*sometimes* CURTIS], dau. of Henry Tomlinson and Mary Eliza Henderson (Beardsley) Curtiss,[284] b. 13 June 1848 at Fairfield, d. 5 June 1917 at Stamford.[285]

On 1 October 1865 Frank, also an attorney in New York City, was admitted partner in Phelps Brothers & Co.[286]

*Children of Frank[7] and Mary A. Bradley (Curtiss) Phelps:*

a. HENRY CURTIS[8] PHELPS, b. 4 August 1867 at Fairfield.[287]
b. GEORGE ALEXANDER[8] PHELPS, b. 16 November 1874; d. 30 October 1926.[288]
c. MARION BRADLEY[8] PHELPS, b. 26 September 1876.[289]
d. MARY[8] PHELPS, b. 27 January 1866; m. HORACE C. JONES.[290]

xi. CHARLES HARING[7] PHELPS, b. 10 December 1846 at New York City;[291] m. on 13 October 1868 ANNIE BROWN COLEMAN,[292] dau. of Thomas Jefferson and Sophia (Brown) Coleman, b. 14 September 1849 at New York City .[293]

On 1 October 1868 Charles became a partner at Phelps Brothers & Co.[294] From 1873 to 1878 he was resident partner of the firm in

---

282 JHW MSS; Phelps 1899, 1:481.

283 *NYT,* 30 Sept. 1937, 23:4.

284 Harlow Dunham Curtis, comp., *A Genealogy of the Curtiss–Curtis Family of Stratford, Connecticut: A Supplement to the 1903 edition* (Stratford, Conn.: Curtiss–Curtis Society, 1953), 98.

285 Spelling of Curtiss and date of marriage and death, Stamford Probate Records, 86:393. Phelps 1899, 1:829–30, has spelling of "Curtis."

286 R. G. Dun, 374/799.

287 Phelps 1899, 1:830. Henry does not appear in *Genealogy of the Curtiss–Curtis Family.*

288 Ibid.

289 Ibid.; *Genealogy of the Curtiss–Curtis Family,* 98.

290 *Genealogy of the Curtiss–Curtis Family,* 98.

291 JHW MSS; Phelps 1899, 1:481.

292 Ibid.

293 James Cash Coleman, *The Genealogy of William Coleman of Gloucester, Mass and Gravesend, England, 1619–1906* (Goshen, N.Y.: Independent Republican, 1906), 128 [hereinafter cited as *Coleman Genealogy*]. Phelps 1899 gives his middle name as Beach.

294 R. G. Dun, 374/799.

Liverpool with a home address at 86 Princes Road, Princes Park.[295] In 1899 his New York City residence was at 120 West 79th Street.[296]

*Children of Charles Haring[7] and Annie Brown (Coleman) Phelps:*[297]

a. CHARLES HARING[8] PHELPS, JR., b. 17 July 1869 at New York City; d. 1944; of New Milford, Conn., in 1940.[298]
b. THOMAS COLEMAN[8] PHELPS, b. 26 December 1870 at New York City; of Scotland, Conn., in 1944.[299]
c. NINA[8] PHELPS, b. 20 December 1872 at Liverpool, England; m. RICHARD PEASE of Pomfret, Conn., 1944.[300]
d. FRANK GEORGE[8] PHELPS, b. 7 October 1874 at Liverpool, England; of Saugerties, N.Y., in 1944.[301]
e. JULIE [GROSCHEN][8] PHELPS,[302] b. 7 October 1876 at Liverpool England; m. _____ LOMBARD; later of Wonalancet, N.H.[303]

xii. HOWARD[7] PHELPS, b. 6 September 1849 at Fairfield; d. 1 November 1924 at 601 West 113th Street, New York City;[304] m. on 12 April 1873 JENNIE I. BIERNE.[305] On 1 October 1871 Howard became a partner at Phelps Brothers & Co.[306]

*Children of Howard[7] and Jennie I. (Bierne) Phelps:*[307]

a. MABEL MARSTON[8] PHELPS, b. 12 May 1876 at New York City; d. ca March 1959; m. WILLIAM LAWTON.[308]

---

[295] Gore's *Directory of Liverpool and Its Environs* (1872).

[296] Phelps 1899, 1:830.

[297] Children's birth dates from Phelps 1899, 1:830.

[298] Obit., *NYT,* 20 Feb. 1944. Note pasted in copy of *Coleman Genealogy* at NYPL: "William Augustus Coleman [father of Thomas J.] was born in 1842, not 1840, according to the family Bible. Chas. H. Phelps, RFD 3, New Milford, Conn., 5 Dec. 1940."

[299] Phelps 1899, 1:830.

[300] Obit., Charles Haring Phelps, Jr., *NYT,* 20 Feb. 1944.

[301] *Coleman Genealogy,* 128.

[302] Ibid. (source of middle name).

[303] Personal recollection of the author.

[304] Obit., *NYT,* 3 Nov. 1924, 17.4.

[305] Phelps 1899, 1:830.

[306] R. G. Dun, 374/799.

[307] Children's birth dates from Phelps 1899, 1:831.

[308] Personal communication from Mrs. Charles H. Phelps, 1982, 22 Pryne St., Hamilton, N.Y., to John Edwards Phelps, 302 Laurelton Street, Springfield, Mass. 01109, copy supplied to the author by J. E. Phelps, 1997.

b. HOWARD[8] PHELPS, JR., b. 16 June 1886 at Newton, Mass.; d. 6 February 1920 at New York City; m. on 27 September 1912 ELIZABETH M—.[309]

CAROLINE ELIZA[7] PHELPS, b. 13 September 1828 at New York City;[310] d. there at 209 West Fourteenth Street on 21 October 1868 of peritonitis;[311] bur. in the Phelps family plot, Fairfield;[312] m. on 1 September 1846 at Fairfield, Conn., JAMES DEMAREST HARING, son of Samuel and Sarah (Clark) Haring. *See* Haring *in these Notes.*

*Children of James Demarest and Caroline Eliza (Phelps)[7] Haring:*

i. CATHERINE [KATE][8] HARING, b. 29 May 1849 prob. at New York City; d. 27 May 1851 at Fairfield, Conn.; bur. there.[313]

ii. JULIA PHELPS[8] HARING, b. 31 March 1851 at New York City,[314] perhaps at 73 Monroe Street;[315] d. 14 May 1928 at Waterbury, Conn.;[316] m. on 15 April 1874 in St. Paul's Church, Fairfield, Conn., GEORGE LUTHER WHITE, son of Luther Chapin White and Jane Amelia Moses of Waterbury.[317] *See* Haring *in these Notes.*

---

309 Stamford, Conn., Probate Court Records, 44/430/432.

310 JHW MSS.

311 New York City Municipal Archives, *Manhattan Deaths*, Index 1868, 21197; marker, Phelps family plot.

312 *Manhattan Deaths*, Index 1868:21197.

313 JHW MSS; Phelps family plot.

314 William Richard Cutter, et al., ed., *Genealogical and Family History of the State of Connecticut* (New York: Lewis Historical Publishing Company, 1911), 3:1567, where Julia's year of birth is given as 1852. The family copy of this publication contains a correction in her daughter's hand.

315 New York City directory, 1851–52.

316 Family record; *Waterbury American*, 14 May 1928.

317 JHW MSS.

RALPH[1] WHEELOCK,[318] b. say 1605 in Shropshire;[319] matriculated as a sizar at Clare Hall, Cambridge, Easter 1623; B.A. in 1626–27; M.A. in 1631;[320] on 6 May 1630 ordained as curate at Norwich;[321] emigrated with his family perhaps in 1637;[322] d. 11 January 1683/4 at Medfield, Mass.;[323] his will was proved on 1 May 1684;[324] m. on 17 May 1630 at Wramplingham, Norfolk, REBECCA CLARKE, third child and first dau. of Thomas[A] and Mary (Canne) Clarke,[325] b. 26 August 1610 at Banham, Norfolk, d. 1 January 1680/1 at Medfield, Mass.[326]

Ralph settled in the town of Dedham, Massachusetts, where he was made a freeman in 1639 and clerk of writs in 1642. In 1651 he became one of original proprietors of Medfield, created from Dedham. He was a selectman from 1651 to 1655 and, from 1655, schoolmaster.[327]

---

318 Data and references to Ralph[1] Wheelock, wife Rebecca Clarke, and children are based on Christopher Gleason Clark, "The English Ancestry of Joseph Clark (1623–80) of Dedham and Medfield, Massachusetts," *Register* 152 (1998), 18. Clark, in "Mr. Wheelock's Cure," *Register* 152 (1998), suggests that Ralph Wheelock's date of birth may be indicated by his matriculation date of 1623—at this time the average age for newly enrolled students was about 18.

319 William S. Tilden, *History of the Town of Medfield, Massachusetts, 1650–1886* (Boston: George H. Ellis, 1887), 506; Clark, "English Ancestry," 18.

320 John Venn, *Alumni Cantabrigienses* (Cambridge: Cambridge Univ. Press, 1927), 1:4:381. "Although age at matriculation was often listed, none is given for Ralph Wheelock." Venn identifies him as the possible brother of Abraham Wheelock, a Cambridge professor, b. ca. 1593, at Whitchurch in Shropshire. Clark, "English Ancestry," 18.

321 Clark, "Mr. Wheelock's Cure," 311.

322 "Peskett claims that Wheelock, with wife Rebecca and a daughter, appears on a passenger list for the *Transport* on a second voyage to New England in 1637, but we find no published passenger list." Clark, "English Ancestry,"18, citing Victor Peskett, *Wheelock "Founder of Medfield"* (Medfield, Mass.: privately printed, 1992), 2.

323 *Vital Records of Medfield, Massachusetts to the Year 1850* (Boston: NEHGS, 1903), 140 [hereinafter cited as *Medfield VRs*]; Clark, "English Ancestry," 18.

324 Suffolk County [Mass.] Probate File 1334; Clark, "English Ancestry," 18.

325 Clark, "English Ancestry," 14; Thomas, b. 7 March 1567/8 at Banham, Norfolk, bur. at Banham 10 May 1638, m. on 17 Oct. 1602 Mary Canne at Banham.

*Children of Ralph[1] and Rebecca (Clarke) Wheelock:*

- i. MARY[2] WHEELOCK, b. 2 September 1631 at Banham, "daughter of Ralph Wheelock cleric";[328] m. on 28 January 1662/3 JOSEPH MILES and removed to Shrewsbury.[329]
- ii. GERSHON [*or* GERSHOM][2] WHEELOCK, b. 3 January 1632/3 at Eccles, south of Banham;[330] d. 1684 at Medfield; m. in 1658 HANNAH STODDER, dau. of John Stodder of Hingham, by whom he had seven children.[331]
- iii. REBECCA[2] WHEELOCK, b. 24 August 1634 at Eccles;[332] m. in 1654 JOHN CRAFTS of Roxbury.[333]
- iv. PEREGRINA[2] WHEELOCK, b. say 1636–37 in England;[334] m. on 26 October 1672 JOHN WAKEFIELD.[335]
- v. RECORD[2] WHEELOCK, b. 15 December 1644 at Dedham; d. 1698; m. in 1678 at Rehoboth SARAH KENDRICK.[336]
- vi. EXPERIENCE[2] WHEELOCK, b. 3 September 1648 at Dedham;[337] m. on 23 May 1668 JOSEPH WARREN.[338]
- \+ vii. ELEAZAR[2] WHEELOCK, b. 3 May 1654 at Medfield.

ELEAZAR[2] WHEELOCK (*Ralph*[1]), b. 3 May 1654 at Medfield, Mass.;[339] d. ca. 1731 at Mendon, Mass.; m. (1) ca. 1679 ELIZABETH FULLER of

---

326 *Medfield VRs,* 24; Clark, "English Ancestry," 18; Robert Charles Anderson, "Clark, Hunting, and Wheelock Families of Dedham, Massachusetts: Some English Clues," *NGSQ* 74 (1986), 4–5.

327 Tilden, *History of the Town of Medfield,* 506.

328 Ibid.

329 *Medfield VRs,* 181.

330 Clark, "Mr. Wheelock's Cure," 111.

331 Tilden, *History of the Town of Medfield,* 506.

332 Clark, "Mr. Wheelock's Cure," 111.

333 Tilden, *History of the Town of Medfield,* 506.

334 Ibid., 507. "Not recorded at Dedham" according to Clark, "English Ancestry," 18.

335 Tilden, *History of the Town of Medfield,* 506; "Warfield" in *Medfield VRs,* 181.

336 Ibid.

337 Robert Bransen Hansen, ed., *The Vital Records of Dedham, Massachusetts* (Bowie, Md.: Heritage Books, 1997), 1:302, cited in Clark, "English Ancestry," 18.

338 *Medfield VRs,* 181

339 Clark, "Mr. Wheelock's Cure," 312.

Rehoboth, whose date of death is unknown;[340] m. (2) MARY CHENERY, d. ca. 1732.

According to Tilden, the "first notice of him in the town records is in 1676, when he killed four wolves. He removed to Mendon after his marriage. He was a surveyor of land here in 1681. He distinguished himself as a hunter of wild beasts while living in Mendon." On 27 June 1701 he received a proprietor's grant of a 10-acre lot in Mendon, which included land acquired in 1690 and in the later 1690s.[341] He apparently returned to Medfield about 1701, where he later purchased the lands of the "original Wheelock estate on the west corner of North Street."[342] He became a selectman in 1720.

*Children of Eleazar² and possibly Elizabeth (Fuller) Wheelock:*

i. ELIZABETH³ WHEELOCK, b. 2 January 1678/9 at Medfield.[343]
\+ ii. RALPH³ WHEELOCK, b. 1683.
iii. MARY³ WHEELOCK, b. 1686 at Mendon; m. in 1703 DAVID CLARK.[344]

*Children of Eleazar² and Mary (Chenery) Wheelock:*

iv. EPHRAIM³ WHEELOCK, b. 24 November 1690 at Mendon;[345] d. 1785 at Medfield; m. (1) in 1722 MIRIAM BULLEN, d. 1727; m. (2) PRISCILLA PLIMPTON, d. 1742; m. (3) EXPERIENCE BULLARD, d. 1755; m. (4) MARY ILIS, wid. of Samuel, d. 1762; m. (5) ELIZABETH COLBURN of Dedham, d. 1775. Nine children.[346]

---

340 *Medfield VRs,* 101. Tilden states she died in 1699, but a child was born to Wheelock's second wife in 1690.

341 *The Proprietors' Records of the Town of Mendon, Massachusetts* (Boston: Rockwell and Churchill Press, 1899), 300 [hereinafter cited as *Mendon VRs*].

342 Tilden, *History of the Town of Medfield,* 506.

343 Ibid.

344 *Mendon VRs,* 209.

345 Ibid., 208.

346 Tilden, *History of the Town of Medfield,* 508–9.

v. ELEAZAR$^{3}$ WHEELOCK, b. 24 November 1690 at Mendon;[347] d. 17 April 1705 at Medfield.[348]

vi. REBECCA$^{3}$ WHEELOCK b. 2 November 1692 at Mendon;[349] m. (1) JOHN FISHER; m. (2) in 1715 JOSEPH ADAMS of Medway, Mass.[350]

vii. ABIGAIL$^{3}$ WHEELOCK, b. 26 February 1698/9 at Medfield,[351] d. 1726; m. in 1723 PETER COOLEDGE.[352]

RALPH$^{3}$ WHEELOCK (*Eleazer*$^{2}$ *Ralph*$^{1}$), b. ca. 1683[353] presumably at Mendon, Mass.;[354] d. 15 October 1748, bur. at Old Cemetery, Hebron, Conn.;[355] m. (1) on 8 January 1707/8 at Windham, Conn., RUTH HUNTINGTON,[356] dau. of Christopher [Jr.] and Sarah (Adgate) Huntington,[357] b. ca. 1683, d. 31 August 1725 at Windham,[358] tombstone inscr: "Mrs. Ruth, late wife of Mr. Ralph Wheelock who died August y$^{e}$ 31$^{st}$ 1725 & in y$^{e}$ 43 year of her age";[359] m. (2) on 30 September 1725 at Windham, MERCY STANDISH,[360] dau. of Josiah Standish, of Preston, Conn., and Ann Allen, of Braintree, Mass.,[361] admitted to church at Preston on 30 May 1718,[362] admitted to church at Windham on 18 October 1726,[363] d. aft. 1748, as she is mentioned in her husband's will.

---

347 *Mendon VRs*, 209.

348 *Medfield VRs*, 240.

349 *Mendon VRs*, 209.

350 Ibid.

351 Tilden, *History of the Town of Medfield*, 506.

352 Ibid.

353 Ibid.; Merton Taylor Goodrich, "The Children and Grandchildren of Capt. Myles Standish," *Register* 87 (1933), 151.

354 Clark, "English Ancestry," 18.

355 "Ralph Wheelock, died 24 October 1748." Hale Headstone Collection, Old Cemetery, Hebron, Connecticut, 7. No date of death in Windham VRs.

356 Windham VRs, 1:27.

357 Ibid.

358 Hale Headstone Collection, Windham, Conn.

359 Joel N. Eno, "Connecticut Cemetery Inscriptions," *Register* 71 (1917), 337.

360 Windham VRs, 1:27.

361 Goodrich, "The Children and Grandchildren of Capt. Myles Standish," 151.

362 Ibid.

363 Windham Congregational Church Records, 1700–1852, Index of Church Records, 130:6, CSL.

Mercy Wheelock's tombstone at Windham is inscribed: "Sacred to the memory of Mrs. Mercy, wife of Deacon Ralph Wheelock ob Nov 4 A.D. 1746 [sic] Aetat 6 [ ]."[364] On 10 December 1700 Ralph owned the covenant at the First Congregational Church, Windham,[365] where he was a deacon and communicant in 1726.[366] In his will, dated 10 October 1748, he, "Weak of Body but of sound Mind and Memory," made the following bequests:

> To my Well Beloved Son Eleazar Wheelock all my farm lying on the west side of [Shebucket] River in Windham . . . to my Well Beloved daughters Elizabeth Handy the sum of five pounds & thirty shillings in silver pr. ounce that with what she hath already Receives as may approx by Record to be her portion . . . to Ruth Hibard the sum of five pounds in Bills of publick Credit old Honour at the [ ] of thirty shillings in Silver pr. Ounce that with what she hath already Received as may appear on record to be her portion, to Abigail Pumery [Pomeroy] all that neck of Land Lying in Windham Called the horse shore lying on the west side of the Nachoag River with about one acre of Land Lying on the East Side of sd. River . . . [to dau. Sarah Bingham] the one half of my House Lot and buildings wh. now Dwell Lying upon both [sides] of the highway Leading from Windham to Coventry [to] my daughter Mary, all my Sheep and one Cow and all my Household Stuff [the other half of the house lot, to] my well beloved wife mercy the whole [ ] and improvement of my House and Homehold upon both sides of the Highway . . . and all my Personal Affects. . . .

To son Eleazar he further bequeathed "all of my Wearing Apparel, my riding Horse and Horse furniture and my Books, namely the *Assembly of Divine Annotation*, *Mr. Perkins Book* in folio, a Concordance, Mr. *Willsons Dictionary* and my *Great Bible*." The remaining books were to be divided equally among the other children and his wife.[367]

*Children of Ralph$^3$ and Ruth (Huntington) Wheelock:*[368]

i. ELIZABETH$^4$ WHEELOCK, b. 25 May 1709 at Windham, m. _____ HANDY.[369]

---

[364] Eno, "Connecticut Cemetery Inscriptions," 237.

[365] Windham Congregational Church Records, 130:1.

[366] Ibid., 5.

[367] Windham, Conn., Probate District, CSL, box 1573, packet no. 4103 (FHL film 1,032,803).

[368] Windham VRs, 1:27.

[369] "Elizabeth Handy" (poss. "Hendy,") in will of Ralph$^3$.

\+ ii. ELEAZAR[4] WHEELOCK, b. 22 April 1711 at Windham.

iii. RUTH[4] WHEELOCK, b. 25 May 1713 at Windham; m. on 6 November 1730 ROBERT HEBARD, son of Robert Hebard and Mary Reed,[370] b. 30 April 1706, d. 19 April 1771.

Ruth was admitted to Windham church on 1 March 1730.[371]

iv. ABIGAIL[4] WHEELOCK, b. 3 March 1717 at Windham; d. 5 January 1803 at South Windsor, Conn.;[372] m. BENJAMIN POMEROY, b. 11 November 1704 at Suffield, Conn., d. 21 December 1784 at Hebron, bur. there; by whom Abigail had thirteen children.

Pomeroy received his A.B. from Yale in 1733 and his D.D. in 1774. He was minister in Hebron from 1734 to 1784, a trustee of Dartmouth College, chaplain in the army in the French and Indian War; and chaplain of the 3rd Regiment, Connecticut Line, from January 1777 to July 1778. His tombstone was inscribed:

> Here lies the body of the Rev. Benj. Pomeroy, D.D. minister of the First Church in Hebron, & a Trustee of Dartmouth College. Native of Suffield. Ob. Dec 21st 1784 aged 81. For 50 years a zealous Preacher of the gospel, and eminently successful about 1743. A Patron of learning, a firm and active Pastor, and a friend to the distressed.
> Along the gentle slope of life's decline
> He bent his gradual way,
> All full of years, he drops life's
> *Mellow fruit into the grave.*[373]

v. JOHN[4] WHEELOCK, b. 20 January 1719/20 at Windham; d. 29 January 1719/20.

vi. SARAH[4] WHEELOCK, b. 7 July 1725 at Windham; admitted to church at Windham on 30 August 1741;[374] m. on 21 December 1742 at Windham JOSEPH BINGHAM, JR.;[375] a son, Ralph Bingham, was b. on 17 February 1750/1 at Salisbury, Conn., and d. 15 September 1751.[376]

---

370 Hebard m. (2) Joanna Cleveland, b. 12 May 1708, d. 19 Apr 1771. *Register* 51 (1897), 319.

371 Windham Congregational Church Records, 130:7.

372 Dexter, *Biographical Sketches,* 1:488.

373 William Woodbridge Rodman, comp., "Eltweed Pomeroy of Dorchester, Mass., and Windsor, Conn., and Four Generations of his Descendants," *Register* 57 (1903), 270–71.

374 Windham Congregational Church Records, 130:31.

375 Windham VRs, 1:27. A second listing has 1 Dec. 1742.

376 Salisbury VRs, 1:225.

*Child of Ralph³ and Mercy (Standish) Wheelock:*

vii. MARY⁴ WHEELOCK, b. 26 November 1728 at Windham;[377] bp. on 12 January 1729 by Rev. Thomas Clap, Windham First Congregational Church;[378] m. 29 December 1746 at Windham JABEZ BINGHAM.[379]

Mary was admitted to Windham church on 11 October 1741.[380]

ELEAZAR⁴ WHEELOCK (*Ralph³ Eleazer² Ralph¹*), b. 22 April 1711 at Windham, Conn.;[381] d. 24 April 1779 at Hanover, N.H.;[382] bur. there in family plot; m. (1) on 29 April 1735 at Lebanon, Conn., SARAH (DAVENPORT) MALTBY, widow,[383] dau. of Rev. John² (1668–1731) and Martha (Gold) (Selleck) Davenport of Stamford, b. July 1702 at New Haven,[384] d. 13 November 1746 at Lebanon, bur. there; [385] m. (2) on 24 November 1747 at Lebanon MARY BRINSMAID,[386] b. ca 1714,[387] d. 1783 at Hanover, bur. there in the family plot.

Sarah was married on 12 February 1724 at New Haven, by the Rev. John² Davenport,[388] to Capt. William Maltby, who was born on 26 May

---

377 Windham VRs, 1:100.

378 Ibid., 1:11.

379 Ibid., 264.

380 Windham Congregational Church Records, 130:31.

381 Ibid.; "Eleazar" in Windham VRs, 1:27.

382 *DAB.*

383 Lebanon VRs, 1:331.

384 Dorothy (Maltby) Verrill, "Maltby-Maltbie-Molby," *Register* 111 (1957), 292; Robert Ralsey Davenport, *Davenport Genealogy* (privately printed, 1982), 50.

385 Sarah was the great-granddaughter of John¹ Davenport (1597–1670), founder of New Haven Colony, and Abigail Pierson.

386 Marriage record in Lebanon VRs, 1:331, appears to be "Brunsmead."

387 Calculated from age at death.

388 "Mr. William Maltbie of New Haven and mrs Sarah Davenport of Stamford were Joyned in Marriage to each other the 12th day of february 1723/4 [seal] the Rev. Mr John Davenport." *Vital Records of New Haven*, 134.

1700 at New Haven[389] and died before 1734.[390] Their children, baptized at the First Congregational Church in New Haven, were: [391]

i. Elizabeth Maltby, bp. 27 March 1726.
ii. John Maltby, bp. 30 July 1727.
iii. William Maltby, bp. 6 April 1729.
iv. Sarah Maltby, bp. 26 July 1730.
v. William Maltby, bp. 20 June 1731.

The second Maltby child, John, was graduated from Yale College in 1747 and married Susanna Hutchings on 7 November 1754. He was appointed the second Presbyterian minister at Bermuda in 1750 and served until about 1769. He died on 30 September 1771 at the house of his step-father, who had hoped he would succeed him as president of Dartmouth College.[392] According to his second cousin, the Rev. Jonathan Maltby, John left Bermuda to become minister to the Presbyterian Church at Wilton, South Carolina, after 1768, after which he "came to New Haven to my father's in Northford in 1771 from South Carolina on his way to Dartmouth College to succeed President Wheelock. In two weeks he was a corpse." Ezra Stiles described him as "the best Hebrewisher of the age."[393]

Sarah (Maltby) Wheelock's tombstone inscription reads, "Sacred to the Memory of Miss Sarah Wheelock, Who died Nov. 13 A.D., 1746, and in the 44th Year of her Age; and of a Character too Great and Good to have any thing said worthy to be inscribed here."[394] Mary (Brinsmaid) Wheelock's tombstone inscription reads:

> Consecrated to the memory of MARY of the family of Brinsmaid in Milford, Connecticut and consort of Eleazer Wheelock S.T.D., President of Dartmouth College. She lived in the fear of God, and in the lively exercise of

---

389 Ibid., 84.

390 Verrill, "Maltby-Maltbie-Molby," 292.

391 Donald Lines Jacobus, comp., *Families of Ancient New Haven* (reprint, Baltimore, Md.: Genealogical Publishing, 1974), 5:1136. Baptized First New Haven Congregational Church.

392 Verrill, "Maltby-Maltbie-Molby," 296.

393 Ibid.

394 Theodore Chase and Laurel K. Gabel, *Gravestone Chronicles II: More Eighteenth Century New England Carvers and an Exploration of Gravestone Heraldica* (Boston: NEHGS, 1997), 543, ill. 579.

> the Christian virtue till her departure in 1783, Anno aetatis 69. In testimony of filial reverence this monument was erected and inscribed by John Wheelock.[395]

On 13 August 1729 Eleazar was admitted to the Windham First Congregational Church. He received his A.B. in 1733 from Yale College and shared the Berkeley Prize with Benjamin Pomeroy.[396] On 24 February 1735 he was called to the Second or North Society of Lebanon, Connecticut (Lebanon Crank), where he was ordained pastor on June 1735.[397] In 1735–36 he was engaged in preaching "itinerancies" as part of the frontier revival. From 1741 to 1743 he preached in Massachusetts, Rhode Island, and Connecticut in the aftermath of the tour of the Rev. George Whitefield.[398]

Around 1740 he began to accept pupils for elementary instruction in Lebanon. The first Native American to attend, in 1743, was the Mohegan Samson Occum, and the school began to regularly recruit Native American children from 1754.[399] To publicize the work of his school, renamed "Moor's Charity School" in 1755, and to encourage charitable donations, Eleazar published the first of his *Narratives* in 1763.[400]

In the late 1760s he developed a proposal to establish a college for instruction of Native Americans in western New York State. On 13 December 1769 the charter for Dartmouth College was approved by the governor and council of the royal colony of New Hampshire after Alexander Phelps's successful negotiations.[401] In April 1770 his relationship with Lebanon Crank Church was dissolved.[402] In July of that year he moved to Hanover, N.H., to found Dartmouth College, which he served as president from 1771 to 1779.[403]

---

395 Marcus Warren Waite, *Eleazer Wheelock and Some of His Descendants* (Hanover, N.H., typescript, in DCA, no date).

396 McCallum, *Eleazer Wheelock*, 4.

397 Ibid., 8.

398 Ibid., 15.

399 Chase, *A History of Dartmouth College,* 1:67, 80.

400 Ibid., 1:33.

401 Ibid., 1:121.

402 Connecticut Church Records, Lebanon Crank; Chase, *A History of Dartmouth College*, 1:154.

403 *DAB.*

Eleazar's will, signed on 2 April 1779, was proved on 4 June 1779 in Grafton County, N.H., by Israel Morey, judge of probate. It contains the following bequests:

> To my loving wife, Mrs. Mary, the use of the house and barn, with a provision that she and the property should be looked after by son John; to my loving son Ralph or Radulphus Wheelock . . . for whom there is little or no prospect he will ever be able to get into any business . . . I give the sum of fifty pounds per annum so long as he shall live and be incapable of performing business for his own subsistence [to be paid to those] that take care of him; to my loving Daughters Theodora Young and Ruth Patten the house and lot of land lying in Lebanon Crank near the meeting house . . . and also my rights of Land in Bridgewater the whole to be equally divided between them[;] to my loving son-in-law the Rev$^{d}$. Sylvanus Ripley fifteen acres being equal to that which I gave to my son-in-law Beza$^{l}$. Woodward, Esq$^{r}$. of the lots which were given me by Mr. John House bounded westerly on the College farm, easterly on Connecticut River northerly on lands which my wife bought of Mr. House &c and this I do in consideration of his settling as tutor of Dartmouth College—and to my loving daughters Mary Woodward and Abigail Ripley, I give the [ ] of P Lotts to be equally divided between them; to my loving Son John Wheelock . . . the care and charge of my loving wife in her declining Life, I give and bequeath my dwelling house in which he now live, my barn & [barn house] and log house; and two hundred acres of land adjoining and remaining . . . I also give him for taking this charge of his Mother all my interests in, and rights to my servants, not to interfere or be inconsistent with any disposal I shall make of them hereafter in this will, viz. Brister, Archelaus, Selina, Anna and the infant Child; I also give him all my working oxen, and all my husbandry to it that he shall have occasion for, and also my horses and as many swine as he shall have occasion for—and whereas I have founded on my own Covenant and at my own expenses an Indian Charity school, now called Moor's Charity School which from small beginning has thro' much labor application and care for more than twenty years . . . by divine providence arrived at its present state of importance and appears to exhibit a fair prospect of great usefulness towards the Christianizing and civilizing the natives of our American Wilderness which is its object, and . . . perpetuating a firm and lasting friendship and peace between all those numerous tribes and the American Colonies as well as of great edification to the church of God among the English & is now incorporated by royal Charter and armed with all the powers, privileges and immensity of a University as by said Charter may fully appear; and whereas it appertains unto me as Founder and Proprietor thereof, as well as by grants in said Charter, to dispose of said School, and all donations and grants of lands and other interests and . . . for the benefit and uses of said School in the best manner for the well being of the same

> and [to] appoint to my successor in the office of President of said Seminary I do hereby nominate, constitute and appoint my said son John Wheelock to be my Successor said Office of President of my Indian Charity School and Dartmouth College, with, and into which said School is now incorporated. . . .[404]

Eleazar's gravestone inscription reads (in Latin): "By the Gospel, he subdued the ferocity of the savage, and to the civilized he opened new paths of science. Traveller Go if you can, and deserve the sublime reward of such merit."[405]

*Children of Eleazar[4] and Sarah (Davenport) (Maltby) Wheelock:*

i. MERCY[5] WHEELOCK, b. say 1737 at Lebanon, Conn.; d. 28 February 1738; bur. at the Old Cemetery, Hebron, Conn.[406]

ii. THEODORA[5] WHEELOCK, b. 23 May 1736 at Lebanon;[407] d. after 1811 at Piermont, N.H.,[408] m. (1) on 9 January 1751/2 at Hebron, ALEXANDER PHELPS, b. 6 January 1723/4 at Hebron,[409] d. 19 April 1773 at Lime (later Lyme), N.H.; m. (2) on 27 April 1777, prob. at Hanover, N.H., JOHN YOUNG of Lisbon, N.H.,[410] d. 1787,[411] who was poss. m. previously to Susannah Getchell,[412] with dau. Tryphena Young, who later m. Eleazar[5] Wheelock.[413] *See* Phelps I *in these Notes.*

iii. ELEAZAR[5] WHEELOCK, b. 14 August 1737 at Lebanon; d. there on 23 November 1737.[414]

---

[404] Grafton County [N.H.] Probate Court, 4 June 1779; copy provided author by DCA. The ink is much faded in this document, and portions are illegible.

[405] Transcription in Waite, *Eleazer Wheelock,* 3.

[406] "Daughter of Rev. Eleazar Wheelock, died 28 Feb. 1738." Immediately nearby are the graves of Benjamin and Abigail [Wheelock] Pomeroy (aunt), and Ralph Wheelock d. 1748 (grandfather). Hale Headstone Collection, 7.

[407] Lebanon VRs, 1:331.

[408] "She was living in Hanover in 1811," Dexter, *Biographical Sketches,* 1:766; McCallum, *Eleazer Wheelock*, 63n, states that she d. at Piermont, N.H.

[409] Hebron VRs, 1:71.

[410] Waite, *Eleazer Wheelock*, 4.

[411] Ibid., states that it was second marriage for John Young and that he had a child by a previous marriage, Polly Young.

[412] The reference occurs in J. Q. Bittinger, *History of Haverhill, N.H.* (Haverhill, N.H., 1888), 94, but which also incorrectly states that Tryphena Young became the wife of John Wheelock.

[413] Waite, *Eleazer Wheelock*, 6.

[414] Lebanon VRs, 1:331.

iv. RUTH[5] WHEELOCK, b. 12 January 1739/40 at Lebanon;[415] d. 6 December 1831 at Hartford, Conn.; bur. there;[416] m. on 9 June 1758 WILLIAM PATTEN, son of William and Mary Patten, b. 11 March 1738 at Billerica, Mass.,[417] d. 16 January 1774 at Roxbury, Mass., bur. in Halifax, Mass. [418]

In 1752 Patten earned his A.B. from Harvard College, to which he had been admitted at the age of 12, one of the youngest ever to be admitted. In 1759 he was awarded an honorary degree from Yale. On 2 February 1757 he was installed as pastor at Halifax, Mass., at age 19.[419] He was installed at South Church of Hartford on 23 September 1767. In 1772 the church council decided not to keep him "to supply a pulpit." On 20 January 1773 the council found "it is proved that Mr. Patten had used strong liquors in so unseasonable and intemperate a manner as did either cause these actions which the witnesses judged the Signs of Drunkenness, or did bring on, or increase Mr. Patten's natural disorder."[420]

His wife returned him to his father in Roxbury, Mass., where he died.[421] His tombstone inscription reads: "Rev. William Patten, who after a life of peculiar trials Died in great peace, At his father's house in Roxbury, Mass, Jany 16, 1774 in the 37th year of his age, and 18th of his ministry."[422]

Ruth (Wheelock) Patten remained in Hartford the rest of her life. There she became a well-known educator and adherent to the Congregational Church. From 1785 to 1807 she established a school with her three daughters. Over the years more than 2,000 young women from nearby and as far away as "Bermuda, Jamaica, Barbadoes, Demarara, Switzerland, England, France and Ireland" were educated there.[423] Another school, called the "Literary Institution,"

---

415 Ibid.

416 Clifford K. Shipton, *Sibley's Harvard Graduates*, vol. 13, *Biographical Sketches of Those who Attended Harvard College in the Classes 1751–1755* (Boston: Massachusetts Historical Society, 1965), 459.

417 Ibid.

418 Ibid.

419 Ibid., 460.

420 Ibid., 461, referring to Edwin Pond Parker, *History of the Second Church in Hartford* (Hartford, 1892), 140.

421 Ibid., 463.

422 Thomas W. Baldwin, *Patten Genealogy: William Patten of Cambridge, 1635 and his Descendants* (Boston: Thomas W. Baldwin, 1908), 77.

423 *Interesting Family Letters of the Late Mrs. Ruth Patten of Hartford, Conn.* (Hartford: D. B. Moseley, 1845), 18–20.

was taught by her son George Jaffrey Patten; here too about 2,000 young men were educated before it closed in 1825.[424] Her tombstone reads: "Madam Ruth Patten Relict of Rev. William Patten and daughter of Rev. Eleazer Wheelock D.D. Founder and first President of Dartmouth College, N.H. She fell asleep in Jesus Dec 5 1831 in the XCII year of her age. She was 78 years a member of the Church, was strong in faith, cheerful in trials, fervent in prayer, full of great works. A mother in Israel."[425]

*Children of William and Ruth (Wheelock)[5] Patten:*[426]

a. ELEAZAR WHEELOCK[6] PATTEN, b. 14 Mar 1759 at Halifax, Mass.; d. 24 March 1769 at Hartford.
b. SARAH[6] PATTEN, b. 1781 at Halifax; d. 11 Dec 1843 at Hartford.
c. WILLIAM B.[6] PATTEN, b. 1763 at Halifax; d. 9 May 1839 at Hartford; m. HANNAH HURLBURT, of New London.

   William earned his A.B. from Dartmouth in 1780, studied at Yale in 1785, and received his A.M. at Brown in 1787. In 1807 he was made D.D. He was a minister at Newport, R.I., from 1786 to 1833.[427]
d. RUTH[6] PATTEN, b. 1764 at Halifax; d. 9 March 1850 at Hartford.
e. CHARLOTTE[6] PATTEN, b. 1767 at Hartford; d. there 24 April 1775.
f. MARY[6] PATTEN, b. 1769 at Hartford; d. there 19 April 1850.
g. NATHANIEL WHEELOCK[6] PATTEN, b. October 1771 at Hartford; d. there 19 July 1773.
h. GEORGE JAFFREY[6] PATTEN, b. September 1775 at Hartford; d. there 17 February 1820.

v. RADULPHUS[5] [*also known as* RALPH RODOLPHUS *and* RALPH] WHEELOCK, b. 18 August 1742 at Lebanon;[428] d. 2 February 1817 at Hanover.

He earned his A.B. from Yale in 1765.[429] Dexter describes him as having spent his "first three years of college at Princeton"; after graduation from Yale he "served for nearly two years as preceptor in the Indian Charity Schools . . . [then] began to show the arbitrary

---

[424] Ibid., 20.

[425] Baldwin, *Patten Genealogy*, 77.

[426] Ibid.

[427] *General Catalog, Dartmouth College and Related Schools* (Hanover, N.H.: Dartmouth College, 1940).

[428] Lebanon VRs, 1:331.

[429] Dexter, *Biographical Sketches,* 3:59.

temper which was afterwards more conspicuous. . . ." He was sent by his father on a mission to the Six Nations in 1768 and "stirred up antagonism by his arrogant and domineering spirit. . . ." His father, "whose favorite child he was, uprooted him" and he went with the family to Hanover . . . in Jan 1774 he was appointed Major . . . but did not take up position . . . [as] disease [epilepsy] unsettled his mind, so that he had to be put under guardianship, and at times was subject to restraint."[430] In 1773 letters to his sister, Ruth Patten, he wrote of his "disorders";[431] in 1812 John Wheelock wrote her that "Our brother the Major, enjoys pretty good health—he lives at Capt. S's . . . [and] is well taken care of."[432] Eleazar Wheelock's will provided son Ralph, or Radulphus[5], with lifetime support.[433]

*Children of Eleazar[4] and Mary (Brinsmaid) Wheelock:*

vi. MARY[5] WHEELOCK, b. 28 August 1748 at Lebanon;[434] d. 26 March 1807 at Hanover,[435] m. on 6 February 1772, prob. at Hanover BEZALEEL WOODWARD, son of Deacon Israel and Mary (Sims) Woodward of Lebanon,[436] b. there 16 July 1745,[437] d. 25 August 1804 at Hanover,[438] bur. there in the Wheelock family plot;[439] nine children.[440] Woodward earned his A.B. from Yale in 1764, his A.M. in 1773, having prepared for college at Moor's Charity School, where he taught from November 1766.[441] In 1767–68 he acted as master, bookkeeper, and general assistant. In 1768 a collegiate branch was added to the school, and Woodward was appointed tutor. On 22 October 1770 he became the first tutor to be appointed

---

430 Ibid.

431 Letters of 2 and 11 May 1773 in *Interesting Family Letters of the Late Mrs. Ruth Patten*, 42, 50, 51.

432 John Wheelock, at Dartmouth College, to Ruth Patten, at Hartford, 28 Aug. 1812, ibid., 58–60.

433 Ibid.

434 Lebanon VRs, 1:331.

435 Dexter, *Biographical Sketches*, 2:91.

436 Ibid. 2:89. He was the grandson of Henry and Hannah (Burrows) Woodward, of Lebanon.

437 Ibid., 2:89.

438 Ibid., 2:91.

439 Waite, *Eleazer Wheelock*, 3.

440 Ibid.

441 This précis is based on Dexter, *Biographical Sketches*, 2:89 ff.

by the board of trustees. In June 1772 he was appointed justice of the peace in Hanover, and in May 1773 he became a justice of the county court, an office he held for the rest of his life.

He was elected a trustee of Dartmouth College in May 1773, a position he held until 1804. In March 1775, serving on the Committee of Correspondence for Hanover, he took a leading part in the opposition of the towns in Grafton County to the measures of the New Hampshire Provincial Congress that had denied these towns full representation. He was an advocate of an independent state for upper Connecticut River valley towns from 1778 to 1780. From 1782 to 1804 he was professor of mathematics and natural philosophy at Dartmouth. He was one of first petitioners for the establishment of Dartmouth Lodge, A.F. & A.M. When, in 1806, a new lodge was formed at Hanover, it was named "Bazaleel Lodge."[442] He acted as head of Dartmouth after Eleazar Wheelock's death in 1779, and again when John Wheelock was in Europe in 1783.

vii. ABIGAIL[5] WHEELOCK, b. 21 December 1751 at Lebanon;[443] d. 9 April 1818 at the home of her daughter at Fryeburg, Maine;[444] m. SYLVANUS RIPLEY, son of Jonathan and Hannah (Sturtevant) Ripley,[445] b. 29 September 1749 at Halifax, Mass., d. 5 February 1787 at Hanover, bur. there in the Wheelock family plot;[446] six children.[447]

Ripley studied divinity with the Rev. Pres. Eleazar Wheelock, D.D., at Hanover. He was ordained a missionary in 1772, and in this capacity he went to the Caughnawagas in Canada. He was tutor at Dartmouth from 1772 to 1782. He became a trustee of the college in 1776, pastor of the college church in 1779, and, in 1782, Phillips Professor of Theology. He held these three positions to the day of his death, which was caused by his being thrown from a sleigh "and instantly killed."[448]

---

442 Waite, *Eleazer Wheelock*, 3.

443 Lebanon VRs, 1:331.

444 "No gravestone found for her in Hanover." Waite, *Eleazer Wheelock*, 4.

445 *Genealogy of the Ripley Family*, H. W. Riley, comp. (Newark, N.J., 1867), 40.

446 George T. Chapman, *Sketches of the Alumni of Dartmouth College* (Cambridge: Riverside Press, 1867), 13.

447 *Genealogy of the Ripley Family*, 40.

448 Chapman, *Sketches of the Alumni of Dartmouth College,* 13.

viii. JOHN[5] WHEELOCK, b. 28 January 1754 at Lebanon,[449] d. 4 April 1817 at Hanover;[450] bur. there in the Wheelock family plot;[451] m. on 29 November 1786 MARIA MALLEVILLE SUHM, dau. of Christian and Maria (Malleville) Suhm, b. 20 January 1758 at St. Thomas, W.I., d. 16 February 1824, at Brunswick, Maine.[452]John Wheelock was a member of the first graduating class of Dartmouth College and received his A.B. in 1771. According to Waite, he was tutor at Dartmouth from 1772 to 1774 and represented Hanover in the legislature in 1776.[453] During the Revolution he commanded New Hampshire units and was appointed a lieutenant colonel in the Continental Army the same year.

Upon his father's death, and directed by the latter's will, he became president of Dartmouth in 1779. The most critical problem for the college's presidents in these early years was to secure financial support for the institution. In 1783 John Wheelock journeyed to France and Holland to raise funds and finally secured a grant from Scottish donors. Returning from this voyage, he suffered shipwreck on Cape Cod.[454] During the first 25 years of his presidency he established salaried professorships and added Dartmouth Hall and a chapel to the college. After 1800 he was in frequent conflict with the trustees, who eventually removed him from office in 1815. In that year the college was subject to action by the state legislature that transformed the institution into Dartmouth University and increased the number of trustees. Wheelock was appointed president again by trustees opposed to the state's move. He was ill by this time, however, and died before the resolution of the conflict in the famous case of *Trustees of Dartmouth College vs. Woodward*, which, argued by Daniel Webster before the Supreme Court, resulted in a victory for

---

449 Ibid.

450 *DAB.*

451 Waite, *Eleazer Wheelock*, 5.

452 *The Genealogist* 4 (1983): 19, 46–47 and from Kenneth C. Cramer, archivist of Dartmouth College; marriage probably took place in Morris Co., N.J., where Maria was living with her mother and stepfather, Lucas Van Beverhout. See Thomas B. Wilson, *Notices from New Jersey Newspapers 1781–1790* (1988). Personal communication from Henry B. Hoff, 28 May 1997.

453 Waite, *Eleazer Wheelock*, 5.

454 John Wheelock, in Plymouth, Mass., to Ruth Patten, in Hartford, 7 Jan. 1784, in *Interesting Family Letters of the Late Mrs. Ruth Patten*, 45.

the college.[455] His only child, Maria Malleville Wheelock, married Rev. Dr. William Allen, later president of Bowdoin College.[456]

ix. ELEAZER[5] WHEELOCK, b. 17 August 1756 at Lebanon;[457] d. 7 December 1811 at Boat Run, Ohio; A.B. Dartmouth College 1776;[458] m. (1) on 15 October 1784 at Hanover TRYPHENA YOUNG,[459] said to be dau. of Capt. John Young and Susannah Getchell of Lisbon, N.H., and Hanover[460] (the same John Young who m. Theodora [Wheelock] Phelps), d. 1 September 1790 at Hanover;[461] m. (2) THANKFUL PENNOCK;[462] Eleazer had nine children by his two wives.[463]

In 1785 Eleazer[4] joined with brother James and Davenport Phelps in a "mercantile venture" in Hartford.[464] He evidently became heavily indebted, as Phelps referred to a debt of £3,000 on the part of Wheelock in 1787.[465] Eleazer's brother John wrote on his death that he had been

> In former years unsteady and irregular, which reduced his property, but his unfavorable habits were concentrated in himself rather than injurious to others. . . . [he] removed with his family to country bordering on the Ohio, Boatrun, 16 miles above Cincinnati. There he was industrious, and after undergoing great hardships with his dear wife and family, found the prospect of a comfortable living more favorable . . . 7 Dec last while standing and cutting down a tree a few rods from his house, he was seized the third shock, and fell; his wife was there in sight—came and embraced him—medical assistance was obtained, but all in vain . . . left three dau by the first wife, and six children by his last.[466]

---

455 *DAB.*

456 Chapman, *Sketches of the Alumni of Dartmouth College*, 13–14.

457 Lebanon VRs, 1:331.

458 *General Catalog, Dartmouth College and Related Schools* (Hanover, N.H.: Dartmouth College, 1940).

459 Waite, *Eleazer Wheelock*, 6.

460 Bittinger, *History of Haverhill*, 94.

461 Ibid.

462 Chapman, *Sketches of the Alumni of Dartmouth College*, 20.

463 Waite, *Eleazer Wheelock*, 6.

464 Norton, *Pioneer Missionaries*, 30.

465 Davenport Phelps to Samuel Andrew Peters, 19 May 1787, *Peters Coll.*

466 From John Wheelock at Dartmouth College to Ruth Patten, 29 Aug. 1812, in *Interesting Family Letters of the Late Mrs. Ruth Patten*, 58–60.

x. JAMES[5] WHEELOCK, b. 6 May 1759 at Lebanon;[467] d. 14 January 1835 at Burlington, Vt.;[468] bur. there at Elmwood Cemetery;[469] m. 15 July 1784 at Hanover, LUCY TIFFANY, dau. of Dr. Gideon Tiffany and Sarah Dean Farrar, widow, of Norton, Mass., and Hanover,[470] b. 21 August 1767 at Norton, Mass.; d. 27 September 1785 at Hanover;[471] m. (2) ABIGAIL KINSMAN, dau. of Col. Aaron Kinsman and Rose Burnham of Hanover,[472] b. 1768,[473] d. 27 September 1842 at Montpelier, Vt., bur. there in Green Mountain Cemetery;[474] one child by Lucy, thirteen by Abigail.[475]

In 1792 James accompanied Davenport Phelps on horseback through New York State to take up claim for two townships in Upper Canada. Though he is said to have lived for a time in the province, he did not occupy granted land as did Phelps.[476] As Chapman states, "He was resident of the college vicinage the most of his life, and a magistrate in the County of Grafton, but eventually removed to Burlington where two daughters resided, successively the wives of the Rev. Dr. James Marsh, Dartmouth 1817."[477] James was made a Mason in Vermont Lodge No. 1 on 2 October 1782 and later was a petitioner for the founding of Dartmouth Lodge, A.F. & A.M. at Hanover. He became its first Worshipful Master. He was selectman in Hanover in 1787 and for several terms in later years.

---

467 Lebanon VRs, 1:331.

468 Chapman, *Sketches of the Alumni of Dartmouth College*, 20.

469 Waite, *Eleazer Wheelock*, 7.

470 Ibid. Lucy was the sister of Catherine Tiffany, wife of his step-nephew, Davenport Phelps.

471 Tiffany, *The Tiffanys of America*, 41.

472 Ibid.; Chapman, *Sketches of the Alumni of Dartmouth College*, 20.

473 Waite, *Eleazer Wheelock*, 7.

474 Ibid.

475 Ibid.

476 Norton, *Pioneer Missionaries*, 32. Petition of Davenport Phelps and Others, Ontario Historical Society, *Papers and Records*, 24, ed. E. A. Cruikshank (1927), 104–5 (Davenport Phelps & James Wheelock, Esqr.). For themselves and David Curtis, Andrew S. Crocker, and other associates see their petition to Simcoe of 22 May 1793.

477 Chapman, *Sketches of the Alumni of Dartmouth College*, 20. Marsh m. (1) on 14 Oct. 1824 Lucia Wheelock, (2) on 7 Jan. 1835 Laura Wheelock. Ibid., 188.

JAN PIETERSEN[1] HARING [*also* HARINGH, HEARINGH, HERIGH], first mentioned in New York City records on 2 May 1667, when his first daughter (his second child) was baptized at the New York Dutch Reformed Church [N.Y. Du. Ref. Ch.];[478] d. there intestate on 7 December 1683;[479] m. bef. 1667, perhaps on 18 May 1662,[480] at New Amsterdam (perhaps at the chapel on Peter Stuyvesant's farm) GRIETJE COSYNS, a widow,[481] dau. of Cosyn Gerritsen van Putten and wife Vroutje,[482] bp. on 5 May 1641 at N.Y. Du. Ref. Ch., d. ca. 1724 at Tappan, N.Y.[483]

Grietje Cosyns m. (1) on 19 April 1654 at New Amsterdam Harmen Theuniszen,[484] by whom she had one child, Vroutje, bp. 24 February 1658 at N.Y. Du. Ref.; m. (3) on 4 March 1686/7 at New York City Daniel De Clark (Klerck),[485] who became the successor to Jan Pietersen Haring as the unofficial leader of the Tappan patentees and one of the most prominent and affluent early settlers.

Jan Pietersen Haring's date and place of birth are unknown. Despite the assertions by Burdge, the nineteenth-century biographer of his great-grandson, and Ackerman, who compiled a Haring genealogy in the 1950s,

---

478 *Baptisms from 1639 to 1730 in the Reformed Dutch Church, New York,* (New York: NYGBS, 1902), 2:87 [hereinafter cited as *Bapt. Ref. Du. Ch.*]; Ackerman, *Descendants,* 1; Henry Pennington Toler, *The Harlem Register: A Genealogy of the Twenty-Three Original Patentees of the Town of New Harlem, New York* (New York: New Harlem Press, 1903), 138.

479 Franklyn Burdge, "A Notice of John Haring" (New York: privately printed, 1878), unpaginated, a biography of Jan Pietersen Haring's great-grandson, John Haring (1739–1809); Firth Haring Fabend, *A Dutch Family in the Middle Colonies, 1660–1800* (New Brunswick, N.J.: Rutgers Univ. Press, 1991), 257n. 3.

480 Whitsuntide, date cited without reference in George Olin Zabriskie, "Daniel De Clark (De Klerck) of Tappan and His Descendants," *Record* 67 (1965), 194.

481 Ibid. The Stuyvesant site reported in Ackerman and Fabend, *Dutch Family,* 3, cannot be substantiated by surviving records. Fabend states that the couple were married by Dominie Henricus Selyns, minister of the Dutch Reformed Church in New Amsterdam and the first pastor of Stuyvesant's new chapel on his farm in the Bowery and, with Ackerman, *Descendants,* 1, asserts that it was the first marriage in that chapel.

482 Cosyn Gerritsen owned land on Manhattan Island (Fabend, *Dutch Family,* 7) and claimed an inheritance from Susanna Elefersen, who died at Hoorn. On 12 August 1649 Gerritsen granted power of attorney to one Sibout Claessen to collect his legacy from Elefersen, deceased. See Arnold J. F. Van Laer, trans., *New York Historical Manuscripts: Dutch,* ed. Arnold J. F. van Laer, Kenneth Scott, and Kenn Stryker-Rodda, vol. 3, *Register of the Provincial Secretary* (Baltimore, Md.: Genealogical Publishing Company, 1974), 132–33. This record was probably the basis for Ackerman's positing a Hoorn origin for Jan Pietersen[1] Haring.

that he was born in Hoorn, North Holland, and arrived in New Amsterdam with his (unnamed) parents in the 1630s, no record of this has been found.[486]

Through his marriage, Jan Pietersen Haring acquired land in the Out-Ward of Manhattan, which he farmed. He was a member of the Dutch Reformed Church in 1673–74 and was elected *schepen* (public official).[487] On 17 March 1681/2 he and others, of whom he was considered the leader, purchased from the Tappaen, or Tappan, Indians a tract of land near the west bank of the Hudson River, about 20 miles from the southern tip of Manhattan, which became the Tappan Patent. He was an original patentee, as was his son Peter, but he died before the associated families moved to take up the land after 1683.[488]

*Children of Jan Pietersen[1] and Grietje (Cosyns) Haring, all born probably on Manhattan Island, all baptized at New York Dutch Reformed Church:*

\+ i. PETER[2] HARING, b. ca. 1664 at Manhattan.

---

483 Ackerman, *Descendants*, 1, states that she died in this year at age 90, but no record has been found.

484 Zabriskie, "Daniel De Clark," 194.

485 Daniel De Clark, widower of Marie De Mull at the time of his marriage to Grietje, was b. ca. 1654. Ibid. The administration of his estate was approved on 16 Nov. 1731 at Tappan. *Marriages from 1639 to 1801 in the Reformed Dutch Church, New Amsterdam–New York City*, Collections of the New York Genealogical and Biographical Society (New York: NYGBS, 1940), 9:56 [hereinafter cited as *Mar. Ref. Du. Ch.*]. His house, built in 1700, still stands. Fabend, *Dutch Family*, 59.

486 Fabend, *Dutch Family*, 253n. 1, discusses the lack of documentation for Burdge's association of J. P. Haring with the hero of the Dutch revolt against Spain, John Haring. She suggests that Burdge may have had access to a family Bible, now lost, which could have established the Hoorn origins. The Pieter Jantzen from Hoorn cited in some accounts as J. P. Haring's father died childless; there is no record in the Hoorn archives that identifies this child or his parents. The most comprehensive and generally accurate work on the early generations of Harings is Ackerman's genealogy. Although he does repeat the story of the Hoorn origins without comment, other relevant data cited here for the first four generations have been verified in the original records.

487 Fabend, *Dutch Family*, 10, referring to *The Records of New Amsterdam from 1653 to 1674*, comp. Berthold Fernow (New York, 1897), 7:127.

488 Fabend, *Dutch Family*, 10–22; George H. Budke, "The History of the Tappan Patent," in *The Rockland Record, Being the Proceedings and Historical Collection of the Rockland County Historical Society of the State of New York, Inc., for the Years 1931 and 1932*, (Nyack, N.Y.: Rockland County Historical Society of the State of New York, 1932), 35–50 [includes transcripts of documents].

ii. VROUTJE[2] HARING, b. 3 March 1667; bp. on 15 May 1667,[489] m. on 1 December 1689 at N.Y. Du. Ref. Ch. THEUNIS JACOBSEN QUICK,[490] whose will is dated 25 April 1739.[491]

On 26 February 1685 Vroutje became a member of the N.Y. Du. Ref. Ch. Theunis had interests in New Jersey and removed there late in life. The two-handled silver bowl made for Theunis and Vroutje Quick by Cornelius Kierstede, silversmith, is now at the Metropolitan Museum of Art.[492]

iii. COSYN[2] HARING, b. 3 February 1669; bp. on 3 March 1669;[493] d. 1743;[494] m. MARGRETSJE BLAUVELT, dau. of Gerrit Blauvelt, bp. on 26 March 1670 at N.Y. Du. Ref. Ch.;[495] eight children.[496]

Margretsje was the sister of Hubert Gerritsen (Blauvelt), a Tappan patentee.[497]

iv. CORNELIUS[2] HARING, b. 4 March 1672; bp. on 10 April 1672;[498] m. 1693 CATTRYN FLIERBOOM, dau. of Matthew Flierboom, a schepen of Albany.[499]

v. BRECHTJE[2] HARING, b. 4 July 1675; bp. on 14 July 1675;[500] d. 12 January 1709 at Tappan, after giving birth to a set of triplets;[501] m. 1694 TEUNIS TALMAN, son of Douwe Talman and Dirkje Teunis,[502] he the owner of a large portion of the northern tract of the Tappan Patent.[503]

---

489 *Bapt. Ref. Du. Ch.*, 2:87.

490 Arthur Craig Quick, *A Genealogy of the Quick Family in America (1625–1942)* (South Haven, Mich.: privately printed, ca. 1943), 22.

491 Ibid.

492 Ibid., 23.

493 *Bapt. Ref. Du. Ch.*, 2:94.

494 Ackerman, *Descendants*, 2.

495 *Bapt. Ref. Du. Ch.*, 2:98.

496 Ibid., 40.

497 List of Tappan patentees in George H. Budke, "The Division of the Tappan Patent," n.d., 30, Budke, BC-71.

498 *Bapt. Ref. Du. Ch.*, 2:105.

499 Ackerman, *Descendants*, 2. Matthew Flierboom with his brother, Abraham, was a purchaser of land in Kakiat, to the west of the Tappan patent. See Fabend, *Dutch Family*, 37.

500 *Bapt. Ref. Du. Ch.*, 2:119.

501 Fabend, *Dutch Family*, 44.

502 Ackerman, *Descendants*, 3.

503 Fabend, *Dutch Family*, 37.

vi. MARYTIE[2] HARING, b. 27 September 1679; bp. on 11 October 1679.[504]

vii. ABRAHAM[2] HARING, b. 24 November 1681; bp. on 3 December 1681;[505] m. on 25 June 1707 at Tappan DIRKJE TALMAN,[506] dau. of Harmen and Grietje (Minneus) Talman, d. 18 March 1772, bur. in Tappan.[507]

PETER[2] HARING (*Jan Pietersen*[1]), b. 13 August 1664 at Manhattan;[508] d. 1750 at Tappan, Orange County, N.Y.;[509] m. on 4 December 1687 in Haarlem GRIETJE BOGERT, dau. of Jan Louwe Bogert and Cornelia Everts of Haarlem, b. at Bedford, Brooklyn, after 1672.[510]

On 28 October 1694 Peter Haring and his wife were received by the Tappan Dutch Reformed Church and belonged to its original membership. In 1701 the freemen and householders of Orange County elected Peter to the General Assembly, Colony of New York, for the first time. He participated in the 8th (1701–2), 12th (1709), and 17th (1716–26) sessions.[511] The 1702 census of Orange County lists "Peter Hearingh, Grietje His Wife, 1 boy child, 5 Gerills, 1 man."[512]

---

504 *Bapt. Ref. Du. Ch.*, 2:138.

505 Ibid., 2:150.

506 Fabend, *Dutch Family*, 37, 40.

507 Ackerman, *Descendants*, 4.

508 No baptismal record found, but he is believed to be the first son of Jan Pietersen[1]. Ackerman, *Descendants*, 1, records 13 August 1664 as Peter's birth date, without citing a reference. On his career see Fabend, *Dutch Family*, 177–83.

509 Will of Peter Haring, 27 June 1750, *Abstracts of Wills on File in the Surrogates Office, City of New York, with Letters of Administration*, vol. 4, 1744–53, 209, Collections of the New-York Historical Society for the Year 1895 (New York: NYHS, 1900) [hereinafter cited as *Abstracts of Wills N.Y. Co.*]; New York County Wills, 17:180; Fabend, *Dutch Family*, 95.

510 *Mar. Ref. Du. Ch.*, 1:63; I. N. Phelps-Stokes, *The Iconography of Manhattan Island, 1398–1909* (New York: Robert H. Dodd, 1918–1928), 6:106; John A. Bogart, *The Seven Bogert-Bogart Families in Canada . . .* (Harrison, N.Y.: privately printed, 1962), 18. The marriage record states that the bridegroom was formerly of New York City but was then residing in Tappan. *Mar. Ref. Du. Ch.*, 63; Phelps-Stokes, 6:106.

511 *Journal of the Legislative Council of the Province of New York* (Albany, N.Y., n.d.), 379, 425, 433–36, 449, 453; Fabend, *Dutch Family*, 176.

512 Edmund Bailey O'Callaghan, *Lists of Inhabitants of Colonial New York: Excerpted from The Documentary History of the State of New-York* (Baltimore, Md.: Genealogical Publishing Company, 1979), 14–15.

Peter's will was probated in New York on 17 June 1750 ("Peter Haringh of Tappan in Orange County, yeoman"). He left bequests to wife Margaret, to son Abraham ("my great nether Dutch Bible for his right of first born"), to children Elbert, Margaret, Peterjie, Brechtje, Janetje, Catharina, and Classie, and grandchildren Peter and Richard Truman. To his son Theunis he left £100; "all the rest" he left to Elbert.[513]

*Children of Peter[2] and Grietje (Bogert) Haring:*

i. GRIETJE PIETERS[3] HARING, b. 8 September 1688; bp. on 7 October 1688 at N.Y. Du. Ref. Ch.; [514] m. on 13 October 1708 at Tappan CLAES VAN HOUTEN,[515] b. 1684, d. 2 January 1744, bur. in Orangeburg, N.Y.[516]

ii. CORNELIA[3] HARING, b. 24 February 1690; m. (1) on 26 November 1710 at N.Y. Du. Ref. Ch. RICHARD TRUMAN;[517] m. (2) GYSBERT CROM.[518]

iii. BRECHTJE[3] HARING, b. 19 June 1692 prob. at Tappan; m. on 11 October 1710 GERRIT SMITH,[519] son of Lambert and Margarietje (—) Smith, b. 1685.[520]

iv. [CHILD], b. 25 May 1695, prob. at Tappan; d. y.[521]

v. PIETERJE[3] HARING, b. 31 January 1696; bp. on 15 April 1696 at Tappan Ref. Du. Ch.;[522] m. on 15 December 1705 JACOB BLAUVELT,[523] son of Abraham and Grietje (More) Blauvelt, b. 30 May 1692.[524]

---

513 *Abstracts of Wills N.Y. Co.*, vol. 4, 1744–53, 289; New York County Wills, 17:180.

514 *Bapt. Ref. Du. Ch.*, 2:187.

515 David Cole, comp., "Marriage Record of the Reformed Dutch Church of Tappan, Clarkstown, Rockland County, N.Y., 1694–1831," rev. Walter K. Griffin (New York, 1909), 175 (NYPL microfilm) [hereinafter cited as *Tappan Mar. Rec.*].

516 Ackerman, *Descendants*, 4.

517 *Mar. Ref. Du. Ch.*, 113.

518 Ackerman, *Descendants*, 4,5; Toler, *Harlem Register*, 138.

519 *Tappan Mar. Rec.*, 159 (from Toler).

520 Ackerman, *Descendants*, 5.

521 Toler, *Harlem Register*, 138.

522 Tappan births and baptism dates from a numbered list in David Cole, *History of Rockland County . . . , Baptisms at Tappan and Clarkstown October 25, 1694 to January 10 1816* (New York: J. B. Beers, 1884) [hereinafter cited as *Tappan Baptisms*], 17.

523 *Tappan Mar. Rec.*, 85.

524 Ackerman, *Descendants*, 5.

vi. JANETJE[3] HARING, b. 24 January 1698; bp. on 14 April 1698 at Tappan Ref. Du. Ch.;[525] d. 1766; m. on 14 February 1714 CAREL DE BAAN.[526]

vii. JOHN[3] HARING, b. 15 April 1700; bp. on 17 April 1700 at Tappan Ref. Du. Ch.;[527] m. on 5 October 1723 at Tappan ELIZABETH BLAUVELT,[528] dau. of Abraham and Grietje (More) Blauvelt, bp. on 17 April 1700, sister to Jacob, who married Pieterje[3].

viii. CATHARINA[3] HARING, b. 5 April 1702 at Tappan; bp. on 5 April 1702 at Tappan Ref. Du. Ch.;[529] m. on 21 April 1722 ADOLPH MEYER,[530] son of Adolph and Maria (Verveelen) Meyer, bp. on 24 July 1692 at Tappan.[531]

\+ ix. ABRAHAM[3] HARING, b. 9 April 1704 at Tappan.

\+ x. ELBERT[3] HARING [HERRING], b. 3 March 1706.

xi. THEUNIS[3] HARING, b. 12 July 1708; bp. on 29 August 1708 at Hackensack;[532] m. SARAH BLAUVELT,[533] b. 6 May 1713, bp. on 22 June 1714 at Tappan.[534]

xii. KLAATJE[3] HARING, b. 21 April 1711; bp. on 3 June 1711 at Hackensack Du. Ref. Ch.; [535] m. ADOLPH LENT, son of Abraham and Anna Katrina (Meyer) van Lent,[536] b. 1703, d. at Nyack.[537]

ABRAHAM[3] HARING (*Peter*[2] *Jan Pietersen*[1]), b. 9 April 1704 at Tappan; bp. on 11 April 1704 at Tappan Ref. Du. Ch.,[538] d. 11 April 1771 at Tappan; m. on 27 March 1725 at Hackensack, New Jersey GRIETJE BOGERT, dau. of Jan Cornelisz and Maria (Bertholf) Bogert [*or* Bongaert

---

525 *Tappan Baptisms,* 32.

526 *Tappan Mar. Rec.*, 108.

527 *Tappan Baptisms,* 36.

528 *Tappan Mar. Rec.*, 126.

529 *Tappan Baptisms,* 63.

530 *Tappan Mar. Rec.*, 141.

531 Ackerman, *Descendants,* 6.

532 Bapt. Hackensack Du. Ref. Ch., in Toler, *Harlem Register,* 139.

533 Ackerman, *Descendants,* 7.

534 *Tappan Baptisms,* 213.

535 Recorded in ibid., 167.

536 Ibid.

537 Ackerman, *Descendants,* 7.

538 *Tappan Baptisms,* 83.

*or* Boomgaert], bp. on 17 March 1705 at Hackensack, d. 23 July 1783, her will proved on 26 March 1793.[539]

In 1740 Abraham was appointed judge of the Court of Common Pleas in Orange County. In 1745 the freemen and householders of Orange County elected him to the General Assembly of the Colony of New York. He served in the 20th (1745–47), 24th (1759–60), 28th (1759–60), and 29th (1761–68) sessions.[540] In 1740–45 he consistently voted against expenditures by the province in support of King George's War.[541] From 1748 onward he was an adherent of the Coetus party of the Dutch Reformed Church, which advocated the training of ministers in America and the use of English in the liturgy.[542] In 1752 Abraham became an elder of the Tappan Dutch Reformed Church.[543] In 1760 he was a colonel in the militia activated in the French and Indian War and was charged with defending the northern boundaries of Orange County against the Indians.[544]

On 6 October 1766 Abraham was elected treasurer of Orange County, and on 17 October that year he was elected supervisor.[545] On 10 November 1766 he became one of the signatories of the charter for Queens College (later Rutgers College) at New Brunswick, N.J.[546] In 1769, when the New York–New Jersey boundary dispute was settled, the farm of Abraham Haring was among those in changed jurisdiction within New Jersey,[547] and he "viewed it as unqualified abhorrence."[548]

Abraham's will, signed on 10 April 1771 at Orangetown, Orange County, and proved many years later on 16 March 1793 at Hackensack, Bergen County, makes the following bequests:

---

539 Ackerman, *Descendants,* 7; Toler, *Harlem Register,* 139 cites for the marriage Schraalenburg Du. Ref. Rec., 39.

540 Ibid.

541 Fabend, *Dutch Family,* 183.

542 Cole, *History of the Reformed Church in Tappan, N.Y.*, 29.

543 Ibid., 133ff.

544 "Men Inlisted of Coll. Abraham Haring's Regim't" (22 May 1760), *Report of the State Historian* (Albany, N.Y., 1896), 3:613–15; Fabend, *Dutch Family,* 187.

545 Budke, BC-9.

546 Hugh Hastings, supervisor, "Acts of the Coetus of New York," *Ecclesiastical Records of the State of New York* (Albany, N.Y.: State of New York, 1901–1905, 1926), 4085.

547 George L. Budke, "The Settlement of the Boundary Line Between the Province of New York and New Jersey 1769" (typescript), Budke BC-24.

548 Fabend, *Dutch Family,* 187.

Wife Martinjie [Grietje], 1 negro wench, mansion house and farm wheron I now live, and movable estate, during her widowhood. Oldest son, Peter, Dutch Bible and walking cane; also house and farm now in his possession, Son Abraham, home farm, after wife is married or deceased, he paying £200 for same. Son Cornelius already had his share. Sons, John and Abraham, 2 lots called the Church lots and each ½ of residue. Daughters, Mary, wife of Hendrick Zabriskie, and Margaret, wife of Isaac Blanch, each ½ of residue. Executors—sons, John and Abraham. Witnesses—Yon Nagel, Christian Campbell, Thomas Outwater.[549]

*Children of Abraham[3] and Grietje (Bogert) Haring:*

i. PETER[4] HARING, b. 1 September 1726; bp. on 4 October 1726 at Tappan Ref. Du. Ch.; d. y.[550]
ii. PETER[4] HARING, b. 30 September 1728; bp. on 27 October 1728 at Tappan Ref. Du. Ch.;[551] d. 25 July 1807; m. on 31 April 1757 CATHARINE BLAUVELT, dau. of David B. and Maria (De Clark) Blauvelt, b. 25 September 1738, bp. on 15 October 1738.[552]
iii. MARY[4] HARING, b. 12 July 1733; bp. on 15 July 1733 at Tappan Ref. Du. Ch.;[553] d. 29 August 1800;[554] m. on 31 August 1753 HENRY ZABRISKIE, son of Christian and Lea Hedridge (Hoppe) Zabriskie, b. April 1718, bp. on 15 May 1718 at Hackensack, m. first to Neesje Van Hoorn, d. 19 October 1800.[555]
iv. MARGARET[4] HARING, b. 28 February 1736; bp. 7 March 1736 at Tappan Ref. Du. Ch.;[556] m. in 1758 ISAAC BLANCH,[557] son of Richard and Klaatjie (—) Blanch, b. 7 December 1737, d. 14 February 1804.[558]

---

549 Elmer T. Hutchinson, ed., *Documents Relating to the Colonial, Revolutionary and Post-Revolutionary History of the State of New Jersey*, 1st ser. (Jersey City, N.J.: State of New Jersey, 1942), 37:163 [hereinafter cited as *N.J. Docs.*].

550 Cole, *Tappan Baptism*; 490.

551 Ibid., 553.

552 Ackerman, *Descendants,* 16.

553 *Tappan Baptisms,* 728.

554 Toler, *Harlem Register,* 139.

555 George Olin Zabriskie, comp., *The Zabriskie Family: A Three Hundred and One Year History of the descendants of Albrecht Zaborowski (ca. 1638–1711) of Bergen County, New Jersey*, 2 vols. (n.p.: privately printed, 1963), 1:23.

556 *Tappan Baptisms,* 856.

557 *Bapt. Ref. Du. Ch. N.Y.,* 2:240; Toler, *Harlem Register,* 139.

558 Ackerman, *Descendants,* 16.

\+ v. JAN [JOHN][4] HARING, b. 28 September 1739.

vi. ABRAHAM[4] HARING, b. 15 March 1742; bp. on 18 April 1742;[559] d. 25 February 1807;[560] m. SARAH NAGEL, dau. of Hendrick and Catharine (Blauvelt) Nagel,[561] b. 1 April 1747, bp. on 20 April 1747 at Tappan Ref. Du. Ch.[562]

vii. CORNELIUS[4] HARING, b. 14 July 1744; bp. on 22 July 1744 at Tappan Ref. Du. Ch.;[563] d. January 1823;[564] m. (1) LEA _____; m. (2) ANTJE AVRYANSEN, dau. of Aury and Elizabeth (—) Avryansen.[565]

viii. ELBERT[4] HARING, b. 24 May 1747; bp. on 7 June 1747 at Tappan Ref. Du. Ch.; d. y.[566]

ix. MARTYNTJE[4] HARING, b. 6 February 1750; bp. on 21 February 1750 at Tappan Ref. Du. Ch.;[567] d. 20 November 1770;[568] unm.[569]

ELBERT[3] HERRING (*Peter*[2] *Jan Pietersen*[1]), b. 3 March 1706; bp. on 31 March 1706 at N.Y. Du. Ref. Ch.;[570] d. 3 December 1773 "at his house in the Bowery, in the Outward of New York City, in his 68th year";[571] m. (1) on 14 December 1726 at N.Y. Du. Ref. Ch. CATHERINE LENT,[572] d. 1731; m. (2) on 17 September 1732 at N.Y. Du. Ref. Ch. ELISABETH BOGERT,[573] his first cousin, dau. of Nicholas and Margaret (Conselyea) Bogert,[574] b. September 1714, bp. on 19 September 1714 at N.Y. Du. Ref.

---

559 Ibid., 1184.

560 Ackerman, *Descendants,* 18.

561 Ibid.

562 *Tappan Baptisms,* 1469.

563 Ibid., 1309.

564 Ackerman, *Descendants,* 18.

565 Ibid.

566 *Tappan Baptisms,* 1475.

567 Ibid., 1565.

568 Ackerman, *Descendants,* 7.

569 Toler, *Harlem Register,* 139.

570 *Bapt. Ref. Du. Ch. N.Y.*, 2:315.

571 Kenneth Scott, comp., *Rivington's New York Newspaper: Excerpts from a Loyalist Press, 1773–1783* (New York: NYHS, 1973), 54.

572 *Mar. Ref. Du. Ch.*, 146

573 Ibid., 154.

574 Ackerman, *Descendants,* 7; John A. Bogart, *The Seven Bogert-Bogart Families in Canada*, 20–21. Nicholas Bogert was brother to Grietje Bogert, mother of Elbert[3].

Ch.,[575] d. 10 June 1787 at New York City.[576] Elbert Herring moved to New York City in his childhood or early youth and adopted an anglicized form of the family name. In 1732, as a baker, he applied for and was granted the trade privileges appertaining to a freeman of the City of New York.[577]

On 4 October 1738 he purchased of Jacob Brat, baker, a dwelling house and lot on Queen Street, adjoining the home of John Roosevelt.[578] He purchased an adjoining lot on the west side of his residence from the same Jacob Brat in 1743; the deed states that the said Brat had bought the property from the Bogert family in 1728.[579] On 29 July 1752 the Common Council directed that a common road (Amity Lane) be laid out for Elbert Herring, "for him to go to his Land, Lying to the Westward of Jacob Duyckman's House and Ground."[580] On 5 December 1755 he bought land from Hendrick and Catherine (Elias) Bogaert and Leah [?], "a parcel of Out Ward, Bowery Division, beginning at a maple tree marked with three notches; N of a run of water called Minetta . . . border land of Nicholas Bayard and Adam van de Bergh." Elbert continued to assemble property in the Ninth Ward (Bowery) and at the time of his death owned the second largest farm on Manhattan Island.[581] It amounted to more than 100 acres, "part of Worter van Twiller's bouwery, consisting of two tracts of land separated by the Minetta Water, connected by the old Negroes' causeway . . . [t]he map of the farm made in 1784, No. 105 in the Registrar's office, shows a vestige of this causeway. The Holmes Map of the farm, completed in 1869 [shows that it] crossed West Third Street west of Macdougal Street, Minetta Street between Bleecker Street, and Minetta Lane, called *the way to go out*, formed part of the old causeway."[582]

---

575 *Bapt. Ref. Du. Ch.*, 2:377.

576 "Record of Burials in the Dutch Church, New York," *Year Book of the Holland Society of New York*, 1899, 168.

577 John Roosevelt's son, Cornelius, married Margrietje Herring, dau. of Elbert[3], in 1751; Budke, *Historical Miscellanies*, 39:169.

578 Budke, *Historical Miscellanies*, 39:170.

579 Ibid.

580 *Minutes of the Common Council of the City of New York*, 1675–1776, 8 vols., *January 16, 1755 to December 28, 1765* (New York: City of New York, Dodd, Mead, 1905), 5:372 [hereinafter cited as *MCC*], referenced in Phelps-Stokes 4:634.

581 Fabend, *Dutch Family*, 94–99; Phelps-Stokes 6:106ff.; Budke, *Historical Miscellanies*.

582 Surveyed 1784, "A long hard day's work, One Pound 4*s*." Phelps-Stokes, 6:106ff.

In 1741 Elbert was made church master of the N.Y. Du. Ref. Ch.[583] On 11 March 1743 he was appointed by the church to the committee to "treat" with the freeholders of the Manor of Fordham.[584] In 1748–49 he was deacon of the N.Y. Du. Ref. Ch., and an elder in 1755–56. On 19 September 1753 he was appointed by the Assembly of the Coetus meeting in New York to "adjust matters" between "Dom. Muzelius and the Consistory and congregation of Tappan"—a dispute had arisen between adherents of the traditionalist Conferentie party of the church and the Coetus party.[585]

In 1750 he gave bond in the sum of £500 to administer his father's estate, he described as "of the City of New York, baker," and inherited his father's New York property.[586] The will of his childless uncle by marriage, Elbert Leverse, lime burner, of New York City, was proved on 15 June 1750. The nephew received "two bolting cloths and bolting chest" and "half of the estate."[587]

On 7 March 1755 he was appointed by the Common Council to serve on a committee to "Enquire into the Rights of this Corporation in the Out Ward" and also to lay out a road in the Out-Ward for "Mr. Albert Herring."[588] He was elected assistant alderman from the Montgomerie Ward on 29 September 1755 and sworn on 14 October 1755; he was re-elected from the Out-Ward on 29 September 1756 and again on the same date in 1757.[589]

On 17 June 1772 Elbert signed his will, which was proved on 13 December 1773.[590] He appointed as executors "my Elizabeth, and my

---

583 "Records of Reformed Dutch Church of New York," *Ecclesiastical Records of the State of New York*, 2100–101.

584 Ibid., 2793.

585 "Acts of the Coetus of New York, Sept. 11–20, 1753," *Ecclesiastical Records of New York State*, 3417.

586 Budke, *Historical Miscellanies*, unnumbered; Fabend, *Dutch Family*, 59.

587 *Abstracts of Wills N.Y. Co.*, 4:417; New York County Wills, 18:177, in Fabend, *Dutch Family*, 59.

588 *MCC*, 6:3, 5.

589 Ibid., 34, 58–60, 66, 99–102.

590 *Abstracts of Wills N.Y. Co.*, 8:150–52; New York County Wills, 29:27. The inventory of the estate, dated 13 December 1773, is in the NYHS manuscript collection. Fabend, *Dutch Family*, 175n. 28 states that a recent study considers "that the household's quantities of porcelain, silver, and 'food service equipage' suggest elegant entertainment and that the furnishings have an 'unexpected stylishness' for an urban farmhouse." Ruth Piwonka, "New York Colonial Inventories: Dutch Interiors as a Measure of Cultural Change," *New World Dutch Studies: Dutch Art and Culture in Colonial America, 1609–1776* (Albany, N.Y.: Albany Institute of History and Art, 1987), 67–68.

son Nicholas, and my son-in-law, Samuel Jones, and my brother in-law, Petrus Bogert [and by codicil] my sons-in-law John De Peyster, Jr., and John Haring." The will makes the following bequests:

> I leave to my son Peter £5 with which to bar him from any further claim as heir at law. I leave to my wife Elizabeth all my silver wrought plate. Whereas I have given to each of my children who are of age a deed to a lot of land 25 feet wide and 100 feet long, adjoining to the road that leads from the Bowery Lane to Greenwich, therefore, to make my under aged children equal, I leave to my son Abraham, all that certain lot of land hereafter to be called Lot No. 3, bounded east by said road, south by Lot No. 2, now belonging to my son Nicholas, north by Lot No. 4, now belonging to my daughter Catharine, and extending west 100 feet. I give to my daughter Mary the lot of land to be called Lot No. 9, bounded east by said road, south by Lot No. 8, now belonging to my daughter Anatje, and to extend along the road 25 feet, and west 100 feet. I leave to my daughter Sarah the Lot No. 10, bounded east by said road, south by Lot 9. I leave to my wife all the remainder of my personal estate, and the use of all my real estate, during so long a time as she remains my widow, subject to the payment of £100 to my son Abraham, and £100 to each of my daughters, Mary and Sarah, provided they have not their outsets before my decease. And my wife is to bring up, maintain, and educate my underaged children, and if the income of my lands is not sufficient, my executors may sell lands for that purpose. If my wife marries, I leave her £300. I leave to my niece, Elizabeth Bogert, who now lives in my family, £50 when she is married. After the death of my wife I leave all my estate, real and personal, as follows: Whereas my son Peter hath already had very considerable sums of money, I release him from all claims. And whereas my daughter, Catharine, wife of George Brinkerhoff, hath received all the estate and effects of her mother; in order to make my other children as near as may be equal, I leave to my sons, Nicholas and Abraham, and my daughters, Margaret, widow of Cornelius Roosevelt, Cornelia, wife of Samuel Jones, Elizabeth, wife of John De Peyster, Jr., Anatje, wife of Samuel Kipp, Mary, and Sarah, £450 each, and to my daughter Catharine £400, and to my son Peter £50, to be paid before any general division. All the rest of my estate, real and personal, I leave to all my children, and to their heirs and assigns forever.

On 23 December 1774 a newspaper notice reported that the deceased's "horses, cattle and household furniture are to be sold by Elizabeth Herring executrix, and Petrus Bogart, Samuel Jones, John De Peyster, Jr. and John Haring, executors."[591]

---

[591] *Rivington's New York Newspaper*, 56.

Elizabeth Herring's will, dated 12 January 1787, proved 30 June 1787, reads as follows:[592]

> To my six daughters, Margaret Roosevelt, Cornelia Jones, Elizabeth De Peyster, Ann Kip, Mary Haring, and Sarah Jones, to be equally divided among them, share and share alike, all my wearing apparel; all the remainder of my goods, chattels, to be sold, and the moneys arising from such sale, also all the money I die possessed of, and that what shall be owing to me at my death shall be put out at interest by my executors for and during the natural life of my son Peter; if my son Peter dies, the moneys so arising to go to my grandchildren, to Elbert Kip and Elizabeth Kip, children of my daughter, Ann Kip; Elizabeth and Elbert Roosevelt, children of my daughter, Margaret Roosevelt; Elbert and Elizabeth Haring, children of my daughter Mary Haring; Nicholas and Elizabeth Jones, children of my daughter, Sarah Jones; and Elbert and Elizabeth Herring, children of my son Abraham, each one equal sixteenth part; to Elbert Haring Jones, son of my daughter, Cornelia Jones, Elizabeth Schuyler De Peyster, daughter of my daughter, Elizabeth De Peyster, and Nicholas Herring, son of my son Nicholas, each one equal eighth part; if any or either of my above-named grandchildren shall die during the lifetime of my son Peter, then the respective parts of him so dying shall go to the respective representatives; if any of my grandchildren die under the age of twenty-one years, his share to go to his parents. I appoint my son Abraham, my son-in-law Gardner Jones, and my grandson, Cornelius C. Roosevelt, executors.

*Children of Elbert[3] and Catherine (Lent) Herring, all born at New York City and baptized at N.Y. Du. Ref. Ch.:*

i. CATHARINE[4] HERRING b. 2 October 1727; bp. on 4 October 1727;[593] d. 30 August 1728.[594]

ii. CATHARINE[4] HERRING, b. 26 May 1729; bp. on 1 June 1729,[595] d. 1807;[596] m. GEORGE BRINKERHOFF, b. 1726, d. 1797, son of Theunis Brinkerhoff and Elizabeth Ryder.[597]

iii. MARGARET[4] HERRING, b. 1 March 1731; d. 12 March 1731.[598]

---

592 *Abstracts of Wills N.Y. Co.*, 14:120–21; New York County Wills, 40:19.

593 *Bapt. Ref. Du. Ch. N.Y.*, 2:478.

594 Ackerman, *Descendants*, 7.

595 *Bapt. Ref. Du. Ch. N.Y.*, 2491.

596 Ackerman, *Descendants*, 7.

597 George Brinckerhoff and his wife, Catherine, conveyed her right in the Elbert Herring property to Nicholas Herring 1 July 1776. "Map of Two Lots," Jones Family Papers, 1801–19, NYPL Mss. Div.

598 *Bapt. Ref. Du. Ch. N.Y.*, 3:11.

*Children of Elbert[3] and Elizabeth (Bogert) Herring, all born at New York City and baptized at N.Y. Du. Ref. Ch.:*

iv. MARGARET[4] HERRING, b. 6 July 1733; bp. on 6 July 1733 at N.Y. Ref. Du. Ch.;[599] d. 6 February 1821;[600] m. 10 December 1751 at N.Y. Du. Ref. Ch. CORNELIUS ROOSEVELT,[601] son of Johannes and Hilletje (Sjoerts) Roosevelt, bp. on 11 July 1731 at N.Y. Du. Ref. Ch.,[602] d. 13 March 1772 at New York City.[603]

From 1759 to 1763 Cornelius was an assistant alderman of New York City, and in 1763–67 an alderman.[604] He left an undated will, proved 21 May 1772, in which he was described as "Cornelius Roosevelt of New York, chocolate maker." The will mentions wife Margaret, sons John (oldest), Cornelius, and Elbert, daughters Mary and Elizabeth, brother Jacobus Roosevelt, and brother-in-law Abraham Duryea.[605]

v. ELBERT[4] HERRING, b. 12 August 1735; bp. on 13 August 1735 at N.Y. Du. Ref. Ch.; d. 18 August 1736.[606]

vi. ELBERT[4] HERRING, b. 7 April 1737; bp. on 10 April 1737 at N.Y. Du. Ref. Ch.,[607] d. 8 December 1762.[608]An administration bond of 3 November 1763 was established for: "Harring, Elbert Jr., lieut in H. M.'s 42nd Regt of Foot," with administrators, by "Elbert Herring, father of dec'd," with guarantors "Elbert Herring father of dec'd of Outward of NYC, gent., Cornelius Roosevelt, of Outward of NYC, chocolate maker, and Cornelius Bogart of New York City, shopkeeper."[609]

---

599 Ibid., 2:27.

600 *Deaths . . . Taken from the New York Evening Post*, copied by Gertrude A. Barber, typescript, 4.58.

601 *Mar. Ref. Du. Ch. N.Y.*, 184.

602 *Bapt. N.Y. Ref. Du. Ch.*, 3:14.

603 *Deaths N.Y. Ref. Du. Ch.*, 188.

604 *MCC*, 4:390 *et seq.*

605 *Abstracts of Wills N.Y. Co.*, 8:40; New York City Surrogates Court Office, 28:253.

606 Ackerman, *Descendants*, 7.

607 As "Egbert" in *Bapt. Ref. Du. Ch. N.Y.*, 2:57.

608 Ackerman, *Descendants*, 7.

609 *Genealogical Data from New York Administration Bonds 1753–1799*, abstracted by Kenneth Scott, Collections of the NYGBS (New York: NYGBS, 1969), 9:67.

vii. PETER[4] HERRING, b. 27 December 1738; bp. on 31 December 1738 at N.Y. Du. Ref. Ch.;[610] removed to Tappan, where, disinherited by his father, he shot and killed himself in 1787, at age forty-nine; m. CATHARINE BLAUVELT.

Peter's suicide was reported in the *New Jersey Journal:* "About a fortnight since, at Tappan, Peter Haring shot himself—Desperate [man]! to arrogate to [himself] the prerogative of the Deity, and thus afront God, and the wrath of Heaven defy."[611]

viii. CORNELIA[4] HERRING, b. 15 February 1741; bp. on 18 February 1741 at N.Y. Ref. Du. Ch.[612]; d. 29 July 1821 at Oyster Bay, N.Y.;[613] m. on 7 July 1768 at N.Y. Ref. Du. Ch. SAMUEL JONES,[614] son of William and Phoebe (Jackson) Jones, b. 26 July 1734 at Oyster Bay, d. 21 October 1819 at Oyster Bay, m. (1) Ellen Turk;[615] six children.

Samuel studied law under William Smith, Jr., in New York City and became a prominent attorney before the Revolution. In 1764 he was listed as an attorney practicing before the Orange County Court of Common Pleas.[616] From 1765 he was among attorneys practicing before the Supreme Court of Judicature.[617] On 29 May 1769 he was appointed by the New York Assembly as member of the commission to settle the New York–New Jersey boundary.[618] In 1771–76 and again in 1788–96 he was treasurer of the New York Society Library.[619]

---

610 *Bapt. Ref. Du. Ch. N.Y.*, 3:269.

611 *New Jersey Journal*, Elizabethtown, 16 May 1787. Thomas B. Wilson, ed., *Notices from New Jersey Newspapers 1781–1790* (Lambertville, N.J.: Hunterdon House, 1988), 224; Fabend, *Dutch Family*, 233.

612 *Bapt. Ref. Du. Ch. N.Y.*, 3:2:85.

613 Ackerman, *Descendants*, 7.

614 *Mar. Ref. Du. Ch. N.Y.*, 2:229.

615 Ackerman, *Descendants;* John H. Jones, *The Jones Family of Long Island: Descendants of Major Thomas Jones (1665–1726) and Allied Families* (New York: Tobias A. Wright, 1907), 33 et. seq.

616 *The Origin of Orange County, New York and a List of Its People from 1683 to 1847, abstracted from Eagers History of Orange County New York*, comp. by Mildred F. Roberts (Orange, Calif., 1968, typescript), 13.

617 Herbert A. Johnson, *John Jay: Colonial Lawyer* (New York: Garland, 1989), Appendix A.

618 Cole, *History of Rockland County*, 139.

619 *Correspondence of the Van Cortlandt Family of Cortlandt Manor, 1748–1800*, compiled and edited by Jacob Judd (Tarrytown, N.Y.: Sleepy Hollow Restoration, 1977), 525.

In 1773, with other sons-in-law, he was appointed co-executor of estate of Elbert$^3$ Herring, not settled until after the Revolution.[620] On 16 March 1774 he became a member of the Committee of 100 in New York City, "the guardians of the rights and liberties of the Colonies," who protested the taxation policies of the mother country.[621] On 22 November 1775 he became a member of the more radical Committee of 60.[622] He spent the years of the Revolutionary War at the family estate at Oyster Bay.[623] In 1782 Samuel Jones and Richard Varick "were appointed to collect and reduce into proper form for legislative enactment all such statutes of Great Britain as were continued in force under the constitution of 1777."[624]

From 15 May 1785 to 2 February 1786 he served with his brother-in-law John Haring on the Cheesecocks Commission, which was to settle the lines of property boundaries in south Orange County.[625] On 9 June 1785 Alexander Hamilton and he were appointed "Counselors and Solicitors on the part of this State" to negotiate a settlement of the boundary dispute between New York State and Massachusetts; a year later, on 18 April 1786, he and others (including John) were appointed to the commission by action of the New York State legislature; the New York and Massachusetts commissioners met in Hartford 30 November 1786 and by 16 December had reached an agreement to resolve the dispute, accepted by New York in January 1787.[626] From 17 June to 23 July 1788 he served as a delegate to the New York State Ratifying Convention called to ratify the proposed Federal Constitution and meeting in Poughkeepsie. He initially supported rejection but made the final motion in favor of approval.[627] He represented Queens County as a Federalist in the

620 Transactions involved in the settlement of the estate are found in Samuel Jones Papers, 1764–1800, NYHS; Jones Family Papers.

621 Jones, *Jones Family of Long Island*, 105.

622 Carl Lotus Becker, "The History of Political Parties in the Province of New York, 1760–76," *Bulletin of the University of Wisconsin*, no. 286, History Series 2, no. 1, (1909), 167.

623 *DAB*.

624 "The revision of Jones and Varick became authoritative and may be regarded as the only comprehensive digest or revision of the laws of New York down to 1800." J. G. Wilson, *The Memorial History of the City of New York* (New York: New York History Company, 1892), 2:622; *Bench and Bar of New York*, David McAdam, ed. (New York: New York History Company, 1897), 1:106.

625 Transcripts in *Papers of Aaron Burr* (NYHS microfilm).

626 Julius Goebel, Jr., and Joseph H. Smith, eds., *Alexander Hamilton: Documents and Commentary* (New York: William Nelson Cromwell Foundation, Columbia Univ. Press, 1964), 1:572–78.

627 Stephen L. Schechter, ed., *The Reluctant Pillar: New York and the Adoption of the Federal Constitution* (Troy, N.Y.: Russell Sage College, 1985), 108–14.

New York State Assembly from 1786 to 1790.[628] From 1789 to 1796 he was the recorder of the City of New York.[629]

In 1790 Samuel Jones was listed in the U.S. census in Montgomery Ward with four males over 16 and three females.[630] He served in the state senate from 1791 to 1797.[631] He was the first comptroller of the state of New York, serving from 1797 to 1800, and drafted the laws governing that office.[632] Following 1800 he retired to Oyster Bay (Westneck, Long Island) for the remainder of his life, though he ran unsuccessfully in 1806 and 1807 as a Federalist for the State Senate.[633]

Samuel's will was recorded on 24 December 1819.[634] William A Duer, his contemporary, recalled that "[h]e was an old-fashioned, black-letter lawyer, and mistook his vocation when he became a politician. To the reputation of an orator, or any other distinction as an advocate, save that derived from laborious and faithful devotion to the causes of his clients, he never pretended . . . [his] most lucrative practice was chamber counsel and special pleader . . . specialized in family settlements."[635] According to another contemporary, Dr. David Hosack, who had attended Hamilton after the duel, "Common consent has assigned him the highest attainment in jurisprudence and the appellation of father of the New York bar."[636]

ix. ELIZABETH[4] HERRING, b. 21 February 1743; bp. on 27 February 1743;[637] d. 21 April 1821;[638] m. on 14 September 1769 at N.Y. Du. Ref. Ch., JOHN DE PEYSTER,[639] b. 16 February1731, bp. on 2 May 1731 at N.Y. Du. Ref. Ch.,[640] d. 7 June 1807 at New York;[641] four children.

---

628 DAB.

629 Ibid.

630 *Heads of Families at the First Census of the United States taken in the Year 1790, New York* (Baltimore, Md.: Genealogical Publishing Company, 1976).

631 Jones, *Jones Family of Long Island*, 107.

632 *DAB.*

633 Ibid.

634 Samuel Jones Papers, 1764–1800.

635 W. A. Duer, *Reminiscences of an Old New Yorker* (New York: W. L. Andrews, 1867), 24.

636 Quoted in *History of the Bench and Bar of New York*, 1:375.

637 *Bapt. Ref. Du. Ch.*, 3:100.

638 Waldron Phoenix Belknap, *The De Peyster Genealogy* (Baltimore, Md.: privately printed, 1956), 63.

639 *Mar. Ref. Du. Ch. N.Y.*, 230.

640 *Bapt. Ref. Du. Ch. N.Y.*, 3:13.

641 Belknap, *The De Peyster Genealogy*, 63.

On 23 November 1761 Elizabeth became a member of the N.Y. Du. Ref. Ch.;[642] John had become a member on 23 May 1753.[643] In 1773 he was a co-executor of estate of Elbert$^3$ Herring. During the Revolution the family removed from occupied New York to Tappan, where two of their children were born. In the 1790 census he was listed in Montgomery Ward with one male over 16, three females, and one other female.[644]

The family lived at 93 Liberty Street in New York at the time of John's death. His will, dated 22 February 1792 and proved on 14 August 1807, identifies him as "of New York, Gentleman" and mentions his wife, Elizabeth, and children John, Margaret, and Elizabeth Schuyler de Peyster. The executors were his wife, brothers-in-law Samuel Jones and John$^4$ Haring, nephew John B. de Peyster, and friend John Contine. A portrait of John and Elizabeth by Charles Willson Peale, dated 1798, is now in the collection of the New-York Historical Society.[645]

x. ANN [ANNATJIE]$^4$ HERRING, b. 31 December 1744; bp. on 6 January 1745 at N. Y. Ref. Du. Ch.;[646] d. 10 May 1801 at Kip's Bay, New York; m. on 7 June 1764 SAMUEL KIP,[647] son of Jacobus and Catharine Kip, b. 13 November 1731, bp. on 21 November 1731 at N.Y. Ref. Du. Ch.,[648] d. 14 February 1804 at Kip's Bay;[649] eight children.

During the Revolution the family left occupied New York City for Tappan, where one child was born. They returned to the city in 1783.[650] In the 1790 census Kip was listed in the Out-Ward with two males over 16, two under 16, six females, and slaves.[651]

---

642 *Record* (61) 268, cited in Belknap, *The De Peyster Genealogy.*

643 Ibid., 166.

644 *Heads of Families at the First Census of the United States taken in the Year 1790, New York.*

645 Belknap, *The De Peyster Genealogy*, 129.

646 *Bapt. Ref. Du. Ch.*, 3:114.

647 *Mar. Ref. Du. Ch. N.Y.*, 216; Frederic Ellsworth Kip, assisted by Mararrita Lansing Hawley, *History of the Kip Family in America* (Montclair, N.J.: privately printed, 1928), 410.

648 *Bapt. Ref. Du. Ch.*, 3:16.

649 Ackerman, *Descendants*, 20.

650 Kip, *The Kip Family in America*, 401.

651 *Heads of Families at the First Census of the United States taken in the Year 1790, New York.*

xi. NICHOLAS$^4$ HERRING, b. 28 July 1747; bp. on 2 August 1747 at N.Y. Du. Ref. Ch.; d. 13 August 1747.[652]

xii. NICHOLAS$^4$ HERRING, b. August 1748; bp. on 7 August 1749; d. 1 October 1798;[653] m. on 3 February 1777 at N.Y. Du. Ref. Ch. ANNE BOGERT,[654] dau. of Peter and Maria (Roome) Bogaert,[655] bp. on 24 April 1757 at N.Y. Du. Ref. Ch.,[656] d. 1 October 1798, m. (1) Jacob Phenix.

xiii. ABRAHAM$^4$ HERRING, b. 11 June 1750; d. y.[657]

xiv. MARY$^4$ HERRING, b. 13 July 1751; bp. on 14 July 1751 at N.Y. Du. Ref. Ch.;[658] d. 22 October 1825 in Rockland Co.; m. her first cousin JOHN$^4$ HARING *(see below)*.

xv. SARAH$^4$ HERRING, b. 5 May 1753; bp. on 9 May 1753 at N.Y. Du. Ref. Ch.;[659] d. August 1837;[660] m. on 14 March 1774 at N.Y. Du. Ref. Ch. GARDNER [GARDINER] JONES,[661] descendant of the Johnes family of Southampton, Long Island,[662] b. ca. 1744, d. 20 May 1823 at 79;[663] seven children.

Gardner was a physician. During the Revolution the family left occupied New York City for Tappan, where four children were born.[664] In the 1790 census he was listed in West Ward with three males over 16, five under 16, four females, and six slaves.[665]

xvi. ABRAHAM$^4$ HERRING, b. 16 April 1755; bp. on 20 April 1755;[666] d. 3 January 1837 at New York City;[667] m. say 1775 at the N.Y. Du.

---

652 *Bapt. Ref. Du. Ch. N.Y.*, 3:135.

653 Ibid., 2:144.

654 *Mar. Ref. Du. Ch. N.Y.*, 30.

655 Ackerman, *Descendants*, 20.

656 *Bapt. Ref. Du. Ch. N.Y.*, 3:219.

657 Ibid., 3:202.

658 Ibid., 3:168.

659 Ibid., 3:184.

660 Ackerman, *Descendants*, 7, 21.

661 *Mar. Ref. Du. Ch. N.Y.*, 243.

662 Not related except through marriage to Samuel Jones's family. Jones, *Jones Family of Long Island*, 102.

663 Ackerman, *Descendants*, 21.

664 *Tappan Baptisms*, 2490, 2595, 2691, 2760.

665 *Heads of Families at the First Census of the United States taken in the Year 1790, New York*.

666 *Bapt. Ref. Du. Ch. N.Y.*, 344.

667 Obituary, *New York Evening Post*, 3 Jan. 1837.

Ref. Ch. ELIZABETH IVERS, dau. of Thomas and _____ Ivers,[668] d. 22 October 1845; eight children.

In 1776 Abraham fled with his family to Stratford, Conn., where he spent the war years.[669] In 1790 he was a resident of the East Ward of New York City, where his household included three free males over 16, three under 16, three white females, and three slaves.[670] In the city he became a merchant with trading interests in Albany and points west, including the early settlement of Utica.[671] In the first New York City directory (1786) he was listed at 42 Water Street and was listed at other addresses on Water Street to 1798, when his office was at 192 Pearl to 1806, then at 44 Broadway. Later he entered into business with son Thomas.[672] In his last years he resided at 45 Hudson Street. The *New York Evening Post* wrote on the afternoon of his death that he had been

> [b]orn on an estate, owned and cultivated before and for a long time afterwards by his father, spreading from the Bowery across Broadway nearly to Hudson street of which Bond Street was the garden plot, and the site of the University, Washington Square and all the adjacent streets were enclosed fields for tillage and pasture. He had lived to see the almost magical changes the city has undergone, and was a most conspicuous representative of the old Dutch stock, its original founders.[673]

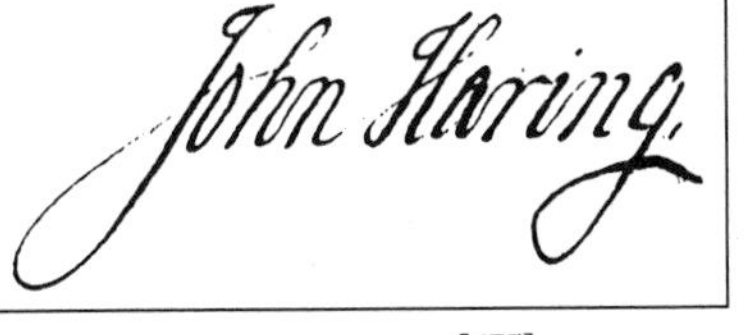


JOHN[4] HARING (*Abraham*[3] *Peter*[2] *Jan Pietersen*[1]), b. 28 September 1739 at Tappan, Orange County, N.Y.; bp. on 30 September 1739 at Tappan Ref. Du. Ch.;[674] d. 1 April 1809 at Blauveltville, Rockland Co., N.Y.; bur. in Tappan Church cemetery;[675] m. on

---

668 Ackerman, *Descendants*, 21.

669 Budke, BC-53, 153ff.; Frederick Gregory Mather, *The Refugees of 1776 from Long Island to Connecticut* (Albany, 1913), 671.

670 *Heads of Families at the First Census of the United States taken in the Year 1790, New York.*

671 T. Wood Clarke, *Utica for a Century and a Half* (Utica: N.Y.: Widtman Press, 1952), 14–15.

672 New York City directories, 1786 et seq.

673 *New York Evening Post*, 3 Jan. 1837.

674 *Tappan Baptisms*, 1037.

675 Personal inspection by the author, 1997; Burdge, "Notice of John Haring"; idem, "Notes," *Magazine of American History* 2 (1878), 429–40.

30 October 1773 at N.Y. Du. Ref. Ch. MARY$^4$ HERRING *(see above)*,[676] his first cousin, dau. of Elbert$^3$ Herring and Elisabeth Bogert;[677] ten children.

According to his nineteenth-century biographer, Franklyn Burdge, John Haring had only six weeks of schooling. The *Biographical Directory of the American Congress* states that he "attended school in New York City."[678] He probably learned the law with a practicing attorney; no record of his studies survives. He was executor of estates as early as 1770.[679] He practiced law in New York City and Rockland County, but there is no record of his admittance to the bar. In 1773 he was named co-executor of the estate of Elbert Herring, his father-in-law. In these pre-Revolutionary years he was also a surveyor.[680]

In 1769 he stood for his ailing father's seat in the Provincial Assembly and was defeated in an allegedly fraudulent election. His petition to have the vote reversed was denied, and he was fined petition costs by council on 6 April 1769.[681] Later in that year the readjustment of the New York–New Jersey boundary placed his residence and property (and those of other members of the Haring family) in New Jersey, an action bitterly resented as exposing them to "utter ruin."[682] By the next year, however, John Haring had established a house in Tappan, within New York, from which he conducted a merchant business.[683]

---

676 *Mar. Ref. Du. Ch.*, 9:240.

677 Fabend, *Dutch Family*, 201.

678 Burdge, "Notice of John Haring"; *Biographical Directory of the American Congress, 1774–1927* (Washington, D.C.: United States Government Printing Office, 1928); Fabend, *Dutch Family*, 200–201, citing "Records of the Supreme Court of New York County," Division of Old Records, 39 Chambers Street, New York; field book of John Haring and S. Metcalfe for a survey of Man of War Ridge (1771); Bayard-Campbell-Pearsall Papers, Orange County, box 3, NYPL Mss. Div.

679 Notice in *New-York Gazette and The Weekly Mercury*, 6 Aug. 1770, in *Genealogical Data from Colonial New York Newspapers: A Consolidation of Articles from the New York Genealogical and Biographical Record*, comp. Kenneth Scott (Baltimore, Md.: Genealogical Publishing Company, 1977), 143.

680 Fabend, *Dutch Family*, 200–201.

681 Ibid., 188–89; William Smith, *Historical Memoirs from 16 March 1763 to 25 July 1778*, ed. by William H. W. Sabine (New York: Arno Press, 1969), 65.

682 Fabend, *Dutch Family*, 187, quoting *New Jersey Archives, Newspaper Extracts*, 2nd ser. (Trenton, N.J.: State of New Jersey, 1916–1917), 7:518.

683 "The Settlement of the Boundary Line Between the Province of New York and New Jersey 1769," Exhibit 48, Budke BC-24; Burdge, "Notice of John Haring"; Fabend, *Dutch Family*, 187–88.

In 1770 he became one of the original trustees of Queens College (later Rutgers College), which had been established to train Dutch Reformed ministers. He was supported by the Coetus party of the Dutch Church, with which he and his father and the majority of members of the Tappan Church had been associated. One of their aims was the education and ordination of ministers in America. The opposing Conferentie party supported continued reliance on the Amsterdam Consistory.[684]

In April 1770 he advertised for his lost slave Tom.[685] He inherited property in Tappan from his father in 1771.[686] On 14 March 1772 he was elected treasurer of the board of supervisors for Orange County.[687] In October 1773 he was elected one of "Overseers of the High Wais" for Orange County.[688] In the same month he repurchased the house and farm he had sold to his brother, but continued "to live with Aged Mother."[689] On 12 December 1773 the will of the estate of his father-in-law, Elbert Herring, of which he was co-executor, was proved.[690]

On 21 March 1774, in order to qualify for appointment as a judge, he attested to Chief Justice Horsmanden that he resided in Orange County.[691] On 29 March 1774 he was appointed judge of the Court of Common Pleas for that county.[692] He also carried out a mercantile business and in 1774 purchased goods for the trade in New York City.[693]

John Haring contributed significantly to the patriot cause before and during the Revolutionary War. On 4 July 1774 he was one of the signatories of the Orangetown Resolutions to the Crown, which requested the removal of trade duties. (Orangetown was then the official, English name for the village of Tappan, location of the county seat.) He was also appointed to the Committee of Correspondence.[694] In 1774 he was

---

684 Burdge, "Notice of John Haring."

685 *New-York Gazette and The Weekly Mercury*, 1 April 1770, in Scott, *Genealogical Data from Colonial New York Newspapers*, 153.

686 Fabend, *Dutch Family*, 120.

687 Budke, BC-33:91.

688 Budke, BC-36, Record of the Board of Supervisors for Orange County.

689 Affidavit quoted in Smith, *Historical Memoirs*, 180.

690 *New York Gazette-Mercury*, 20 Dec. 1773, in Scott, *Genealogical Data from Colonial New York Newspapers*, 180.

691 Donald Clark Collection, NYHS.

692 Letters Patent, Budke, BC-25.

693 Budke, BC-33:101 ff.

694 Force 4, 1:566, also transcribed in Cole, *History of Rockland County*, 27.

elected as a delegate from Orange County to the Provincial Congress in New York.[695] In August of the same year he was elected as delegate from Orange County to the First Continental Congress, sitting in Philadelphia.[696] Before he took his seat on 14 September 1774 in Philadelphia,[697] he was made chairman of the Committee of Safety of the Provincial Congress in New York City.[698]

In October 1774 he was elected to the post of treasurer for the Orange County Board of Supervisors.[699] In 1775 he moved into the parsonage at Tappan.[700] He was re-elected by the Orangetown freeholders as delegate to the Provincial Congress on 15 April 1775 and took his seat at its meeting in New York City on 23 May 1775.[701] In August of that year the Provincial Congress elected him chairman of the committee formed to appoint officers in the militia.[702] On 16 September 1775 he was made a member of the Committee of Safety,[703] and on 16 December 1775 he was unanimously elected president *pro tem* of the Provincial Convention (briefly successor to the Congress). Thus he was, according to Fabend, for a time "in effect the head of the revolutionary government in New York."[704] Throughout May 1776 he participated in meetings of the Provincial Congress in New York,[705] and on 16 May 1776 was again formally admitted as a delegate from Orange County.[706] On 24 May 1776, with John Jay and John Morin Scott, he was appointed to a committee of the Provincial Congress to consider the Continental Congress Resolutions of 15 May supporting independence.[707] On 31 May the report of this committee

---

695 Cole, *History of Rockland County*, 30.

696 *Letters of Delegates to Congress, 1774–1789*, August 1774–August 1775, Paul H. Smith, ed. (Washington: Library of Congress, 1976), 1:xxix.

697 Ibid., xxx.

698 John Haring to Brigadier Gen. Wooster, In Committee of Safety for the Colony of New York, 16 Sept. 1775, Emmet Collection, reel 1:684, NYPL Mss. Div.

699 Records of the Supervisors, Orange County, in Budke, BC-36.

700 Budke, *Historical Miscellanies*, 1:149.

701 Cole, *History of Rockland County*, 27; Force 4, 1:1243.

702 Donald F. Clark Collection, NYHS, 530.

703 John Haring to Brigadier Gen. Wooster, 16 Sept. 1775. Emmet Collection, reel 1:684.

704 Force 4, 1:418; Cole, *History of Rockland County*, 31; Fabend, *Dutch Family*, 203.

705 Force 4, 1:1000ff.

706 Cole, *History of Rockland County*, 32.

707 Force 4, 1:1338.

supported the Resolutions and the intention "to adopt such Government as shall, in the opinion of the Representatives of the People, best conduce to the happiness and safety of their constituents in particular and America in general."[708] On 13 August 1776 he was appointed brigade major by the Provincial Congress[709] and continued as chairman of the Committee of Safety, which operated as the executive arm when the Congress was not in session.[710]

With the British seizure of the city of New York in September 1776, John Haring returned to Orangetown (Tappan), where he, his family, and the families of sisters Mary, Ann (Herring) Kip, Elizabeth (Herring) de Peyster, and Sarah (Herring) Jones from New York City spent most of the war years. This was territory known as "neutral ground," subject to foraging by armies of both sides and, in the early years of the war, a scene of conflict between Loyalists and supporters of the rebellion.[711] On 7 February 1777 he resigned his commission as brigade major.[712] As a civilian he remained an important local leader in the rebel cause throughout the war and continued to serve in local government.

On 21 January 1778 he was appointed the first judge of the Orange County Court of Common Pleas. He served from 1778 to 1788.[713] On 28 May 1778 he was appointed justice of the court of oyer and terminer by the New York State Council of Appointment.[714] On 3 April 1779 he was made responsible by Gov. George Clinton for supplying flour to the army in Orange County.[715] In April 1780 he was elected supervisor in Orange

---

708 Ibid., 1:1351.

709 *Calendar of Historical Manuscripts relating to the War of the Revolution in the Office of the Secretary of State* (Albany, N.Y.: State of New York, 1868), 628.

710 George Clinton, *Public Papers of George Clinton, first Governor of New York, 1777–1795–1801–1804* (Albany, N.Y.: State of New York, 1900), 4:44.

711 Ibid.; 1:444, 523–25, 539; 545, 555–57; Emmet Collection, reel 1:584; *Journals of the Provincial Congress, Provincial Convention, Committee of Safety and Council of Safety of the State of New-York, 1775–1776–1777*, 2 vols. (Albany, N.Y.: State of New York, 1842), 1:315; Adrian C. Leiby, *The Revolutionary War in the Hackensack Valley: The Jersey Dutch and the Neutral Ground, 1775–1783* (New Brunswick, N.J.: Rutgers Univ. Press, 1962).

712 *Calendar of Historical Manuscripts relating to the War of the Revolution*, 629.

713 *Biographical Directory of the American Congress* (Washington, D.C.: U.S. Government Printing Office, 1928), 200–201; S. C. Hutchins, *Civil List . . . New York* (Albany, N.Y., 1869), 102.

714 *Minutes of the Committee and of the First Commission for Detecting and Defeating Conspiracies in the State of New York, December 11, 1776–September 23, 1778 with collateral documents to which is added Minutes of the Council of Appointment, State of New York, April 2, 1778–May 3, 1779*, Collections of the New-York Historical Society for the Year 1925 (New York: NYHS, 1924), 20.

715 *Clinton Papers*, 4:686–87, 817.

County.[716] In August 1780 he was local leader and host when the Continental Army under General Washington encamped at Tappan (one of four such encampments during the war).[717] In October of that year he was present during the imprisonment and execution of Major John André.[718] In April 1781 he was re-elected supervisor in Orange County.[719]

On 24 October 1781, after election from Orange County, he took his seat for a first term as state senator in Poughkeepsie, an office he held until 1788.[720] In the senate, on 22 July 1782, he was appointed a member of Council of Appointment and of the Council of Revision.[721] On 4 February 1783 the senate appointed him to the Committee on Requisitions, responsible for fulfilling the requests for supplies from the Continental Congress.[722]

After the peace, John Haring lived in New York City in 1784 and was involved with other executors in the settlement of the estate of Elbert[3] Herring, including the division and distribution of portions of the Haring farm in the Bowery to the heirs.[723] In 1785 he built a house near the corner of Bleecker and Christopher Streets in New York City, which he occupied until 1788.[724] He was again elected to the Continental Congress on 11 April 1785 and took his seat as delegate from New York in its meetings in New York City, serving until the new constitution in 1788.[725] In 1785–86

---

716 Budke, BC-36.

717 *The Writings of George Washington from the Original Manuscript Sources, 1745–1799*, John C. Fitzpatrick, ed., June 12, 1780–September 5, 1780 (Washington, D.C.: United States Government Printing Office, 1937), 19:358–59.

718 Budke, *Historical Miscellanies*, 1:149–51.

719 Budke, BC-36.

720 Edward Countryman, *A People in Revolution: The American Revolution and Political Society in New York, 1760–1790* (New York: W. W. Norton, 1981), 245; Appendix 2, 318–25.

721 Hugh Hastings, comp. and ed., *Military Minutes of the Council of Appointment of the State of New York 1783–1821* (Albany, N.Y.: [State of New York], 1901), 1:62; Hutchins, *Civil List*, 79.

722 Don R. Gerlach, *Proud Patriot: Philip Schuyler and the War of Independence, 1775–1783* (Syracuse, N.Y.: Syracuse Univ. Press, 1987), 493.

723 Burdge, "Notice of John Haring"; folder 46, Miscellaneous Account Books, Jones Family Papers.

724 Budke BC-34:91 (includes receipts for materials).

725 *Biographical Directory of the American Congress*, 200, 201. H. James Henderson, *Party Politics in the Continental Congress* (New York: McGraw-Hill, 1974), 354–8, 395. *Journals of the Continental Congress, 1774–1789*, edited from the Original Records in the Library of Congress by Gaillard Hunt, 34 vols. (Washington: United States Government Printing Office, 1923; reprint, New York: Johnson, 1968), 1784 and 1785 entries in vols. 26 and 28.

he was one of the commissioners appointed to resolve the Cheesecocks boundary dispute in Orange County,[726] and in 1786–87 he served on the commission which settled the Massachusetts land claims.[727] (His brother-in-law, Samuel Jones, was a member of both commissions.) On 20 September 1787 he resigned as judge in Orange County.[728] On 12 February 1788 he was appointed as auditor to settle the accounts of the troops of the state of New York in the service of the United States.[729] In June 1788 he was a delegate from Orange County in the New York State Federal Constitution Ratifying Convention meeting in Poughkeepsie. He voted in the minority against acceptance of the United States Constitution.[730]

In 1788 Haring purchased land in and moved to Franklin Township, New Jersey.[731] In the same year he was elected to the Bergen County Board of Chosen Freeholders from the township.[732] He was also appointed agent for the General Proprietors of Eastern New Jersey to sell their Ramapo lands.[733] He was asked to undertake the sale of remaining lands on 20 May 1796.[734]

By 1791 he had returned to Tappan, where he practiced law and served as judge of the court of common pleas.[735] On 7 December 1791 he was the executor of the will of Abraham A. Haring.[736] On 26 December 1795 he sold slave Susan to her father.[737] As "friend," he acted as the executor of

---

726 *Papers of Aaron Burr*, 26:625ff (NYHS microfilm). *The Law Practice of Alexander Hamilton: Documents and Commentary*, Julius Goebel, Jr., Joseph H. Smith, eds. (New York: William Nelson Cromwell Foundation, Columbia Univ. Press, New York 1980), 3:450–67.

727 *The Law Practice of Alexander Hamilton*, 1:563–78; *Journal Continental Congress*, 32:231; Burdge, "Notice of John Haring."

728 Myers Collection, 98, NYPL Mss. Div.

729 *Albany Journal*, 4 Feb. 1788.

730 *The Debates in the Several State Conventions for the Adoption of the Federal Constitution as Recommended by the General Convention at Philadelphia of 1787*, Jonathan Elliot, ed. (Philadelphia: J. B. Lippincott, 1881), 412–13; Burdge, "Notice of John Haring."

731 Reginald McMahon, *Ramapo: Indian Trading Post to State College* (Mahwah, N.J.: Ramapo College of New Jersey, 1977), 24–27; Budke, BC-34:91.

732 Adrian C. Leiby, *The United Churches of Hackensack and Schraalenburgh New Jersey, 1686–1822* (River Edge, N.J.: Bergen County Historical Society, 1976).

733 Budke, BC-34:73.

734 Budke, BC-34-70ff.

735 "Oldest Book of Records in the Office of the Clarkstown Town Clerk at New City, New York," Budke, BC-33; Minnie Cowen, comp., *Abstracts of Wills of Rockland County, New York, 1766–1843* (New York, 1937–39), 1:27.

736 *N.J. Docs.*, 1st ser., 37:163–64.

737 Burdge, "Notice of John Haring."

the will of Stephen Terhune, yeoman of the precinct of New Barbadoes, Bergen County, on 2 March 1795.[738]

About 1796 he removed to Teaneck, New Jersey, where he was made an elder of the Schraalenburgh Church.[739] In 1801 and 1802 he corresponded with the Rev. Wilhelmus Eltinge on questions of polity and discipline in the church.[740] On 3 December 1803 he and Mary rejoined the Tappan Church.[741] In May 1804 he was elected to the assembly of New York State.[742] John Haring died of a paralytic stroke on 1 April 1809. His 19 December 1808 will, proved on 8 April 1809,[743] provided to his wife, Mary Haring: "One of my Bedsteads with the Beds, Bedclothes and their appurtenances; and my Negro woman slave named Abigail; also the sum of Eight hundred Dollars." He bequeathed $504 each to his three daughters and to his son Samuel, whom he had lent $3,154 on 20 June 1806 in advance of estate.[744] The remainder was to be divided among sons Samuel, Elbert, Nicholas Lansing and daughters Maria, Elizabeth, and Margaret. His sons Elbert and Nicholas Lansing received "real Estate in the County of Cayuga." His son John Bogert Haring received the "remainder of real Estate provided always that my wife Mary Haring shall be at liberty for and during the time she shall remain my widow personally to occupy and enjoy the two northerly rooms in my present dwelling house."[745] On 8 March 1810 executors Richard Blauvelt and Samuel G. Verbryck filed an inventory that valued the estate at $5,894.87 as of 8 April 1809.[746] A vendue of the inventory to divide household goods was agreed to the follow-

---

738 *N.J. Docs.*, 1st ser., 37:353–54.

739 Leiby, *The United Churches of Hackensack and Schraalenburgh*; Burdge, "Notice of John Haring."

740 From 1799 Rev. Eltinge (1778–1851) was the Dutch Reformed minister of the Paramus and Saddle River, N.J., churches. His correspondence with Haring was published posthumously in *The Little Horn, or Letters of Correspondence Between John Haring, Esq. late of the County of Rockland, N.Y. and Rev. Mr. Wilhelmus Eltinge, and others* (Hackensack, N.J.: John G. Spencer, 1822). There are four letters from John Haring in this compilation, 21 July 1800 to 2[4] May 1801. Communication from Firth Haring Fabend to the author, 16 Oct. 1998.

741 Cole, *History of the Reformed Church in Tappan, N.Y.*, 155.

742 Budke, BC-57:60; Clarkstown Records, 180.

743 Cowen, *Abstracts of Wills of Rockland County*, 1:34.

744 Budke, BC-34:108.

745 Transcript in Burdge, "Notice of John Haring," appendix; copy in Budke, BC-35.

746 *Index to Inventories (from 1798), Surrogates Court, Rockland County, New York*. A copy of the inventory was supplied to the author by Sally Dewey of the Tappan Historical Society, Jan. 1995.

ing month.[747] John's tombstone, in the Tappan Churchyard, was inscribed "Sacred to the memory of John Haring, Esq., who departed this life, April 1st, 1809, aged 69 years, 5 months and 22 days."[748]

*Children of John⁴ and Mary (Herring) Haring:*

i. MARIA[5] HARING, b. 20 January 1775; bp. on 26 February 1775 at Tappan Ref. Ch.;[749] d. 15 March 1868 at Closter, New Jersey;[750] m. on 24 June 1797 PETER D. HARING, son of Dirck Haring and Frytje Bogert of Closter, d. 28 January 1842 at Closter, his will dated 6 December 1841.[751] On 2 October 1780, at the age of five, Maria witnessed the execution of Major André in Tappan.[752]

\+ ii. SAMUEL[5] HARING, b. 10 October 1776 at Tappan.

iii. ELBERT[5] HARING, b. 28 May 1779 at Tappan; bp. on 20 June 1779 at Tappan Ref. Ch.;[753] d. 9 October 1845; m. on 17 June 1800 RACHEL ROSE; five children.[754]

iv. MARTYNTJE[5] HARING, b. 25 April 1781; bp. on 2 May 1781 at Tappan Ref. Ch.;[755] d. 1 July 1800;[756] m. on 29 October 1799 HENRY VAN DER BECK of Schraallenburgh.[757]

v. ELIZABETH[5] HARING, b. 11 April 1782; bp. on 20 April 1782 at Tappan Ref. Ch.;[758] d. 28 February 1879 at Monsey, New York;[759] m. on 15 May 1803 at Tappan the Rev. JAMES DEMAREST,[760] son of David and Hester (Brower) Demarest, b. 3 September 1780, d. 10 August 1869.

---

747 Manuscript copy provided to the author by Firth Haring Fabend.

748 Ibid.

749 *Tappan Baptisms,* 2398.

750 Budke, *Historical Miscellanies*, notes by Ambrose T. Secor, 1:149–51.

751 Howard J. Durie, *The Kakiat Patent in Bergen County New Jersey* (Woodcliff Lake, N.J.: privately printed, n.d.), 160.

752 Budke, *Historical Miscellanies*, 1:149–51.

753 Ibid., 2634.

754 Toler, *Harlem Register,* 138.

755 *Tappan Baptisms,* 2563.

756 Toler, *Harlem Register,* 138.

757 *Records of the Reformed Dutch Churches of Hackensack and Schraallenburgh, New Jersey* (New York: Holland Society of New York, 1891), 2:67.

758 *Tappan Baptisms,* 2717.

759 Ackerman, *Descendants,* 39.

760 Ibid.

On 18 August 1803 Elizabeth was admitted to the Tappan Ref. Ch.[761] James was pastor of Kakiat Ref. Ch. from 1824 to 1854.[762]

vi. MARGARET$^5$ HARING, b. 24 March 1786; bp. on 7 May 1786 at N.Y. Du. Ref. Ch.;[763] d. 6 September 1850; unm.[764]

vii. NICHOLAS LANSING$^5$ HARING, b. 18 April 1788; bp. on 14 May 1788 at Tappan;[765] d. 29 February 1789.[766]

viii. JOHN BOGERT$^5$ HARING, b. 27 March 1790; d. 24 March 1873; m. on 2 July 180[9] at Tappan Ref. Ch. CATHARINE HELMAN, b. 14 December 1792, d. 7 January 1857, bur. at Eskeath Ref. Ch. Cemetery, New York.[767]

ix. NICHOLAS LANSING$^5$ HARING, b. 19 April 1792 at Tappan; bp. on 19 June 1792, d. 24 May 1826;[768] m. on 16 June 1810 ELIZABETH SMITH, b. 6 August 1793, d. 1877.[769]

x. [SON], b. 23 February 1796; d. 12 days old.[770]

SAMUEL$^5$ HARING (*John$^4$ Abraham$^3$ Peter$^2$ Jan Pietersen$^1$*), b. 10 October 1776 at Tappan; bp. on 3 November 1776 at Tappan Ref. Du. Ch.;[771] d. 9 July 1831 at 53 Chrystie Street, New York City;[772] was m. on 8 October 1797 at Aurelius, New York (Military Tract), possibly by the Rev. Peter Labagh,[773] to SARAH CLARK, dau. of James Clark and Deborah

---

761 Cole, *History of the Reformed Church in Tappan*, 155.

762 *Records of the Reformed Dutch Church of Kakiat (Went New Hampstead), Rockland Co. N.Y., 1774–1864, including the marriage records of the Rev. George Brinkerhoff 1793–1806 and the Rev. James Demarest 1808–1824 and 1824–1864 (from their private registers, being in the most part, a copy of the translation of the records made by Rev. David Cole D.D.)*, with additions and corrections by Walter Kenneth Griffin (New York, 1909).

763 *Bapt. Ref. Du. Ch.*, 3:377.

764 Ackerman, *Descendants*, 17, where the marriage year provided is 1806.

765 Ibid.

766 Budke, BC-70:181.

767 Ackerman, *Descendants*, 17.

768 Ibid.

769 Budke, BC-70:181.

770 Ackerman, *Descendants*, 20.

771 *Tappan Baptisms*, 2489.

772 New York City Probate Court, probationary documents filed 21 July 1831.

773 Labagh was trained at Tappan, and at the date of the marriage on a mission to western New York. W. N. Dailey, *The History of Montgomery Classis R. C. A.* (Amsterdam, N.Y.: Recorder Press, 1916), 10; John A Todd, *Memoir of Rev. James Labagh, D. D., with Notes of the History of the Reformed Protestant Dutch Church in North America* (New York: House of Publications of the Reformed Protestant Dutch Church, 1860), 40.

Denton,[774] b. 9 July 1780 at New Windsor, New York,[775] d. 11 February 1841 at 98 Varick Street, New York City;[776] ten children.

After she was widowed, Sarah lived in New York City at 159 Washington (1831), 67 Franklin (1832), 7 Fourth Street (1833), and 180 Fourth Street (1834).[777] In 1833 by action of the Mayor's Court of Albany "Sarah Haring, Execr of the last will & Testament of Samuel Haring decd" was awarded damages against John W. Cushman, attorney, "by reason of not performing certain premises as for her costs and charges," resulting in a sheriff's seizure and sale of real property owned by Cushman.[778]

Before 1797 Samuel Haring became one of the original settlers at Hardenbergh Corners (the future Aurelius) in the Military Tract set aside by the New York State legislature for veterans of the Revolutionary War.[779] In 1798 he was made captain in Lt. Col. John L. Hardenbergh's militia regiment of Onondaga County.[780] There is a possible listing for Samuel as grocer in the Albany Mayor's Court jury list for 1798.[781] In 1799 the Albany annual city tax assessment roll listed "Samuel Herron" in the Second Ward, with a house lot on Pearl Street, valued at $504, and personal property valued at $162.[782]In 1801 he and his wife "Sally" became members of Schraalenburgh Church, New Jersey.[783]

---

774 Revolutionary War Pension Application W16907, National Archives, Washington, D.C.; Ackerman, *Descendants*, 39; JHW MSS.

775 Toler, *Harlem Register*, 139, JHW MSS has birthdate 1 Oct. 1780.

776 *New York Herald*, 12 Feb. 1841.

777 New York City directories.

778 Mayor's Court, Minutes 11 May 1833, Albany County Hall of Records; Albany Public Records, Grantee List, Property conveyed to Sarah Haring by Albert Gallup, Sheriff, 3 Feb. 1833, Grantee Book 48, 422, Albany County Hall of Records; Sheriff's Certificates, Book 1, 293, Office of the Albany City Clerk.

779 This settlement was established by John L. Hardenbergh. Joel H. Monroe, *Historical Records of a Hundred and Twenty Years, Auburn, N.Y.* (Geneva, N.Y., 1913), 29; *Collections of Cayuga Historical Society: The Journal of Lieut. John L. Hardenbergh* (sic) *of the Second New York Continental Regiment from May 1 to October 3, 1779 in General Sullivan's Campaign against the Western Indians*, Introduction by General John S. Clark, and Biographical Sketch by Rev. Charles Hawley (Auburn, N.Y., 1879), 1:15.

780 *Military Minutes of the Council of Appointment of the State of New York 1783–1821.*

781 Personal communication from Stefan Bielinski, Director, Colonial Albany Social History Project, Cultural Education Center, Albany, N.Y., 14 July 1994.

782 Ibid.

783 *Records of the Reformed Dutch Churches of Hackensack and Schraalenburgh*, 2:37.

Samuel was listed in New York City from 1802 to 1812 as follows:

| Year | Occupation | Address |
|---|---|---|
| 1803 | grocer | 74 Vesey-street |
| 1807–10 | grocer | 5 or 51 Cortlandt |
| 1811 | sugar refiner | 30 Leonard[a] |
| 1811–12 | | residence at 15 ½ John |

*Source: Longworth's New York Register and City Directory*, 1802 et seq.

a. This is the same address as his first cousin, Thomas Herring, son of Abraham.

On 20 June 1806 he received a loan of $3,154 from his father. On 10 December 1807 in New York City he gave conveyance releasing slaves Tom and Sarah.[784] On 12 March 1811 he was awarded $100 plus damages by the Mayor's Court in an action against Elizabeth Fine for her failure to pay for "divers quantities of goods, groceries, wares and other merchandizes."[785] Later that year, on 17 April, he was awarded $100 and $33.85 damages by the Mayor's Court in response to his claim that Charles I. Richardson, "Gentleman," had not paid him for "divers quantities of candles, Sugar, Teas, Spirituous Liquors. Groceries, goods, wares and merchandizes. . . ."[786]

The last listing for Samuel Haring in the New York City directory in this period is for 1811–12. Thereafter he returned to Albany, where he would remain until 1829. On 12 March 1812 he was commissioned a lieutenant in the Thirteenth U.S. New York Regiment; he was made captain on 1 April 1813.[787] After the declaration of war in June, the regiment proceeded from Greenbush (across the river from Albany) to the Niagara frontier, where some units took part in the Battle of Queenston Heights on 12 October 1812. There is no record of Samuel having participated in this action. In the summer of 1813 he was with the regiment as it took part in

---

[784] *Office of Register of the City and County of New York*, 78: 512.

[785] *Office of the New York County Clerk*, Samuel Haring vs. Elizabeth Fine, filed 12 March 1811, Mayor's Court Records, 1811:323.

[786] Ibid. Samuel Haring vs. Charles I. Richardson, filed 17 April 1811, Mayor's Court Records, 1811:310.

[787] F. B. Heitman, *Historical Register and Dictionary of the U.S. Army from Its Organization September 29, 1789 to September 29, 1880* (Washington, D.C.: National Tribune, 1890); *Pension Application Files, War of 1812 Death or Disability*, National Archives, Washington, D.C. "Old War" Invalid, File No. 27931, Veteran, Samuel Haring, Grade: Capt., Service, U.S. Infantry, bundle no. 34, can no. 129; Act Mil. Est., 2:170.

the (unopposed) seizure and occupation of Fort George (near Niagara). Samuel became ill with "lake fever" at that encampment and was sent to hospital at Henderson Harbor (near Sacketts Harbor) on Lake Ontario in the autumn. He rejoined the army in winter quarters at French Mills, New York, in late 1813. He was honorably discharged on 15 June 1815.[788]

In Albany he resided at 10 North Pearl in 1815. He was appointed justice of the peace and master in chancery, serving 1816–19. In 1816 he lived on Ferry Street, with an office at 2 South Pearl; in 1817–18 at 80 Lydius, with an office at 2 Green; in 1819 at 47 Hudson; in 1822–23 at 51 Hamilton, which was listed as a "boarding house"; in 1825 at 82 Lydius, a "boarding house"; in 1827–29 at 338 N. Market.[789] He was elected to the Common Council from Ward IV in 1817.[790] On 1 August 1819 he purchased Lot 11 at the N.W. corner of Johnson and Court Streets from John Willard.[791]

During this period he retained business interests in New York City, as shown by the Mayor's Court action of 26 June 1817 against John Sproull resulting in award of $100 plus $38.32 for the defendant's failure to pay for (unspecified) goods or services, an action repeated with additional damages awarded on 3 November 1817.[792] In 1830 the family returned to New York City, residing at 53 Chrystie Street;[793] they are listed in the census of that year in the 10th Ward.[794]Samuel Haring's will, dated 3 August 1827 and proved 22 July 1831,[795] was executed by Sarah Haring and Hubbell Knapp. It provided bequests to daughter Mary, wife of Hubbell Knapp; son Samuel; Catharine, wife of John Gates; sons John, Clinton, and James; and daughter Sarah Elizabeth. To his wife Sarah he left "five hundred dollars to be at her disposal for ever, also all my household furniture so long as she shall remain my Widow and no longer."

---

788 Ibid.

789 Albany city directories, 1812–30.

790 Cuyler Reynolds, comp., *Albany Chronicles: A History of the City Arranged Chronologically, from the Earliest Settlement to the Present Time, Illustrated with Many Historical Pictures of Rarity and Reproductions of the Robert C. Pruyn Collection of the Mayors of Albany, Owned by the Albany Institute and Historical and Art Society* (Albany, N.Y., 1906), 427.

791 *Albany Public Records*, Grantee Book 25, page 258, Albany County Hall of Records.

792 *Office of the New York County Clerk*, Samuel Haring vs. John Sproull, filed 26 June 1817 and 3 Nov. 1817, Mayor's Court Records, 1817:248.

793 New York City directory, 1830–31.

794 1830 U.S. census, New York.

795 *New York City Surrogates Court*, Wills 68:135.

*Children of Samuel$^5$ and Sarah (Clark) Haring:*

i. JOHN$^6$ HARING, b. 12 November 1798; d. 10 October 1809 in St. Bartholomew, West Indies.[796]

It is possible that his father took his son with him on a trading voyage during which the boy died; Samuel$^5$ was listed as a "sugar ref." in 1812 with his cousin, Thomas Herring, and he may have been involved with the trade before then.

ii. MARY$^6$ HARING, b. 27 April 1800, d. 22 January 1832 at Albany;[797] m. on 21 February 1816[798] in Albany to HUBBELL KNAPP, son of James and Mary (Hubbell) Knapp, Jr., b. 22 September 1788 at Stamford, Conn., d. 1 March 1862 at Albany; seven children.[799]From 1818 to 1823 Hubbell Knapp & Co. was listed in Albany directories at 67 and 71 Quay Street. On 24 January 1820 "Samuel and Sally Haring" transferred Lot 1, NW Corner Johnson and Court Streets to Knapp.[800] The Knapps resided at 51 Hamilton in Albany 1822–23, at the same address as Samuel Haring in those years. In 1827 Hubbell Knapp was listed as skipper or waterman; in 1837 as "master of sloop Syren."[801]

iii. JAMES CLARK$^6$ HARING, b. 11 March 1802, prob. at New York City; d. 30 September 1808.[802]

---

796 The place and date of death exist only in a family record. St. Bartholomew at the time was under Swedish administration, though the Royal Navy in its struggle with the French effectively controlled the island. Thomas Southey, *Chronological History of the West Indies*, 3 vols. (London: Longman, Rees, Orme, Brown, and Green, 1827), 2:241 ff. It was not acquired by France until 1876. There was considerable traffic between New York City and the island; the *New York Commercial Advertiser* in 1801 and 1812 randomly sampled shows notices of ships with shipments of flour to the island and those arriving with consignments of sugar. An extensive search in the secondary literature concerned with the West Indies at the time reveals no records. The U.S. consular reports from St. Bartholomew in 1809 go only through August (and resume in 1813). There are no references to a vessel or incident that could have involved the Harings. National Archives, Department of State, Consular Despatches, M72, "St. Bartholomew Consular Report."

797 Toler, *Harlem Register*, 170.

798 *Albany, New York, Records of First and Second Reformed Churches, Marriage Register*, Mss. NYGBS.

799 *Nicholas Knapp Genealogy*, Alfred Averill Knapp, comp. (Winter Park, Fla., privately printed, 1958), 289–90; Toler, *Harlem Register*, 170.

800 *Index of Public Records in the County of Albany: State of New York 1630–1894*, vol. 7, *Grantors* (Albany, N.Y., 1904), 290.

801 Albany city directories.

802 JHW MSS.

iv. SAMUEL KIP[6] HARING, b. 2 November 1804, prob. at New York City; d. September 1849; m. on 30 June 1830 MARTHA ANN LYDIA MANN.[803]

v. CATHARINE TELLER[6] HARING, b. January 1807 at New York City; bp. on 28 March 1807 at N.Y. Du. Ref. Ch.;[804] d. in infancy.[805]

vi. CATHARINE TELLER[6] HARING, b. 26 August 1808, prob. at New York City; d. 18 October 1872 at 143 Henry Street, Brooklyn;[806] bur. at Greenwood Cemetery, Brooklyn;[807] m. (1) on 27 January 1824 at Albany JOHN GATES, JR.,[808] son of John Gates,[809] b. 4 January 1794, prob. at Albany; one child, JOSEPH EGBERT GATES, b. 31 December 1825, prob. at Albany,[810] d. 17 July 1854 at Albany;[811] was m. (2) on 20 April 1859 at New York City, by the Rev. D. Hutton, to HENRY KIP,[812] her second cousin, son of Samuel and Elisa (Howell) Kip,[813] grandson of Samuel and Ann[4] (Herring) Kip, b. 26 July 1807 at New York City, bp. 31 August 1807 at N.Y. Ref. Du. Ch., d. after 1872, m. (1) Elizabeth Abbott, m. (3) Geraldine Gardiner.

On 12 March 1812 John Gates, Jr., enlisted as an ensign in the Thirteenth U.S. New York Regiment in which Samuel[5] Haring was lieutenant and later captain.[814]

---

803 JHW MSS.; Toler, *Harlem Register,* 139.

804 Toler, *Harlem Register,* 139, based on "Fam. Rec."

805 JHW MSS; Toler, *Harlem Register,* 139.

806 New York City directories; 143 Henry is specified as residence of Henry Kip in 1872 in *Brooklyn City and Business Directory for the Year Ending May 1st, 1872,* comp. George T. Lain (Brooklyn, N.Y.: privately printed); JHW MSS.

807 Lot 8494, Section 119.

808 *Albany, New York, First Reformed Church, Marriage Records.*

809 John Gates, a veteran of the attack on Quebec of 1775, d. 9 Sept. 1825 at Albany. Culver Reynolds, *Albany Chronicles, A History of the City Arranged Chronologically from the Earliest Settlement to the Present Time* (Albany, N.Y.: J. B. Lyon Company, 1906), 456.

810 Toler, *Harlem Register,* 139.

811 *New York Herald,* 18 July 1854.

812 *New York Herald,* 1 Sept. 1859; James P. Maher, comp., *Index to Marriages and Deaths in the New York Herald, 1856–1863* (Alexandria, Va.: privately printed, 1991), 2:63.

813 Emma Howell Ross, *Descendants of Edward Howell (1584–1655) of Westbury Manor, Marsh Gibbon, Buckinghamshire and Southampton, Long Island, New York,* rev. by David Faris (Baltimore, Md.: Gateway Press, 1985), 239–40; Kip, *Kip Family in America,* 424; JHW MSS.

814 *List of Officers of the Army of the United States,* 60; John Gates, Jr., served in various positions and resigned 5 June 1819. Heitman, *Historical Register.* No date of death for John Gates, Jr., found in Albany or New York City sources.

A Henry Kip (sometimes Kipp) is listed in New York City directories for the years 1851–54 as "harbourmaster" with addresses at 32 W. Twenty-fourth Street in 1851 and 38 South Street in the next three years. There is no entry for Kip in Manhattan for the years 1854–59. In 1859 Henry Kip is listed as a grocer at 576 Third Avenue. In 1860 and again in the years 1864–67 he is listed as a clerk at 67 Wall Street with a home address at 22 "Clermont Ave nr De Kalb Ave., Brooklyn." In 1870 he was listed as "sec" (secretary) at 12 Wall Street, residing at 119 Henry Street in Brooklyn. His home address for 1873–76 was 143 Henry Street.[815] In 1875 his profession was listed as "ins,"(insurance); in 1876 (the final entry with his name) as "asst. Sec."[816]

vii. JOHN SAMUEL[6] HARING, b. 13 April 1810 [at New York City]; d. 6 June 1860 at 108 East Thirty-ninth Street, New York City, of heart failure;[817] m. on 12 September 1831 at New York by Rev. Dr. McMurray to MARY CLARK,[818] dau. of William Clark and second wife Mary Bogart, b. 28 December 1813, d. 6 December 1882[819] at New York City;[820] fourteen children, of whom only the two mentioned in the will survived their father.

From 1830 to 1860 John Samuel Haring is listed as a grocer and flour broker in New York City and a senior partner in John S. Haring & Co. at 35 Peck Slip (1843–53), at 47 Pearl (1854–55), and at 151 Broad (1855–60).

Haring's will, signed on 3 May 1860 and proved on 30 June 1860 left "to my beloved wife Mary all my household furniture, books, pictures, and silver plate the use of all the rent, residence and remainder of my Real and Personal Estate during her natural life. After the decease of my said wife I give devise & bequeath all my said ~~real~~ [sic] unto my two children, to wit, George T. and Clinton, to be equally divided between them, share & share alike . . ."[821] Mary (Clark)

---

815 The Brooklyn Directory confirms this Henry St. address.

816 New York City and Brooklyn directories.

817 *New York Herald*, 6 June 1860.

818 In wedding announcement: "Mary Clark 'dau of Wm.,'" *New York Evening Post*, 15 Sept. 1831. Gertrude A Barber, comp., *Marriages Taken from the N.Y. Evening Post* (mimeograph, 1934), vol. 11.

819 JHW MSS.

820 Ibid.; John Albert Bogart, comp., *The Bogart Family* (Harrison, N.Y: privately printed, 1959), 196–97.

821 New York City Surrogates Office, Wills 138:491.

Haring was authorized as executrix to "make an advance to children as they embark on business."

viii. JAMES[6] HARING, b. 13 March 1812; d. y.[822]

ix. CLINTON[6] HARING, bp. on 9 March 1817 at Albany Second Ref. Ch.;[823] d. 8 January 1855 at 237 Broadway, New York City, of consumption;[824] m. on 14 August 1849 at New York City ROWENA HEYWOOD,[825] d. after 1873;[826] no children.

From 1844 to 1855 Clinton listed as a lawyer, New York City.[827]

\+ x. JAMES DEMAREST[6] HARING, b. 26 August 1819 at Albany.

xi. SARAH ELIZABETH[6] HARING, b. 2 April 1822, prob. at Albany;[828] d. 29 July 1839 at Albany of consumption.[829]

JAMES DEMAREST[6] HARING (*Samuel*[5] *John*[4] *Abraham*[3] *Peter*[2] *Jan Pietersen*[1]), b. 25 November[830] 1819 at Albany, N.Y.; bp. on 31 March [1820] at Albany Second Ref. Ch. (named for the husband of his father's sister, Elizabeth[5] (Haring) Demarest);[831] d. on 24 June 1868 at 209 West Fourteenth Street, New York City, of consumption;[832] bur. in Phelps family plot, Fairfield, Conn.;[833] m. on 1 September 1846 at Fairfield, Conn., CAROLINE ELIZA PHELPS, dau. of George Alexander and Eliza (Ayres) Phelps of New York City and Fairfield.[834] *See* Phelps I *in these Notes.*

---

822 JHW MSS.

823 *Albany, New York, Records of First and Second Reformed Churches, Register of Baptisms in Second Church*, manuscript, NYGB.

824 *New York Tribune*, 5 Jan. 1855.

825 *New York Evening Post*, 16 Aug. 1849.

826 Sometimes "Hayward." She is last listed in New York City directories in 1873.

827 New York City directories.

828 JHW MSS; Toler, *Harlem Register*, 170.

829 *The New Yorker*, 10 Aug. 1839, in Kenneth Scott, comp., *Marriages and Deaths from* The New Yorker, *Double Quarto Edition, 1836–1841* (Washington, D.C.: National Genealogical Society, 1980).

830 JHW MSS.

831 Albany, New York, Second Reformed Church, Baptism Records.

832 *Manhattan Deaths*, Index 1868, 10864. Marker, Phelps family plot.

833 New York City Municipal Archives, *Manhattan Deaths*, Index 1868:10864.

834 Judith Rush, comp., *Nation-Wide Marriage Notices as Gleaned from the New York Weekly Tribune 1843–1849* (Privately printed, 1978), 12 Sept. 1846.

James was a flour broker in New York City from 1843 to 1863, in partnership with his brother John Samuel Haring in "John S. Haring & Co." until his brother's death. He resided in New York and Fairfield, Connecticut. On 10 July 1868 his will was proved, his estate then valued at $20,000. George Alexander Phelps, his father-in-law, and Frank Phelps, his brother-in-law, were the executors. Life beneficiaries were his widow, sister Catharine Teller (Haring) (Gates) Kip, and his daughter. With the death of his widow four months later and his sister in 1872, the estate devolved on the sole surviving minor child.[835]

*Children of James[6] Demarest and Caroline Eliza (Phelps) Haring:*

i. CATHARINE [KATE][7] HARING, b. 27 May 1849 prob. at New York City; d. 27 May 1851 at Fairfield, Conn.; bur. there.[836]

ii. JULIA PHELPS[7] HARING, b. 31 March 1851 at New York City, perhaps at 73 Monroe Street;[837] d. 14 May 1928 at Waterbury, Conn.;[838] m. on 15 April 1874 at St. Paul's Church, Fairfield, Conn., GEORGE LUTHER WHITE, son of Luther Chapin and Jane Amelia (Moses) White of Waterbury, Conn.,[839] b. 15 July 1852 at Meriden, Conn.,[840] d. 1 December 1914 at Waterbury, Conn.;[841] three children.

---

835 New York City Municipal Records, Probate Procedures in the matter of the Estate of James D. Haring, July 1868, 178:220, Probate Proceedings File, Location 08026615, Circ. 0338950; New York City Municipal Records, Probationary Documents, loc. 09-041719.

836 JHW MSS; Phelps family plot.

837 New York City directory, 1851–2.

838 JHW MSS; *Waterbury American*, 14 May 1928.

839 JHW MSS.

840 Ibid.

841 JHW MSS; *Waterbury Republican*, 1 Dec. 1914.

NATHANIEL[2] PHELPS (*William*[1]), bp. 6 March 1624/5 at Crewkerne; d. 27 May 1702 at Northampton, Mass.;[842] m. on 17 September 1650 at Windsor, Conn., ELIZABETH (—) COPLEY, widow,[843] d. 6 December 1719 at Northampton.[844]

Nathaniel Phelps was one of the original settlers of Northampton. He signed the petition to the General Court on 18 March 1657/8 requesting (1) a settled minister and (2) assistance in reducing drunkenness.[845] On 6 January 1658/9 he contributed three acres of land for the use of the ministry.[846] He signed the covenant of the church on 18 April 1661[847] and was elected one of the first deacons.[848] In 1663 he was listed as owner of Home Lot 4, Meadowland 29.[849]

On 27 March 1676 the "wife of Nathaniel Phelps" was among 23 persons presented at the court in Northampton for "wearing silk in a flaunting manner and for long hair and other extravagance contrary to honest and sober order, and demeanor not becoming a wilderness state, at least the profession for Christianity and religion."[850] On 9 February 1679 Deacon Nathaniel, with sons Nathaniel and William, took the oath of allegiance before Worshipful Major Pynchon.[851] On 11 February 1679/80 he was sworn in as tithing-man.[852]

Nathaniel was sworn in as freeman by the General Court in Boston on 11 May 1681.[853] On the 21 May 1688 there was a town resolution "to

---

842 Myrtle Stevens Hyde, "The English Origin of William[1] Phelps," citing James Buckman, comp., "Northampton Deaths," in Forbes Library, Northampton, 13. For William[1] see Phelps I in these Notes.

843 Stiles, *Ancient Windsor,* 2:565; Louis Marinus Dewey, "Thomas Copley of Suffield, Conn., and Some of His Descendants," *Register* 64 (1910), 248n, referring to children Thomas and Elizabeth, children of Elizabeth Copley.

844 *Ancient Windsor*, 2:565.

845 James Russell Trumbull, *History of Northampton from Its Settlement in 1654* (Northampton, Mass.: Gazette Publishing Company, 1898), 1:58–59.

846 Ibid.

847 Trumbull, *History of Northampton*, 1:106–7.

848 *Ancient Windsor*, 2:565.

849 Trumbull, *History of Northampton*, 1:144–45.

850 Ibid., 1:290–91.

851 *Ancient Windsor*, 2:565.

852 Trumbull, *History of Northampton*, 1:274.

853 *Ancient Windsor*, 2:565.

Rectifie and Record that Highway that Goeth up to Mr. Stoddard's house: Between Deacon Phelps & goodman miller lots."[854] In the town record he is listed as having donated five pounds of flax for the support of Harvard College.[855] Elizabeth (Copley) Phelps's will, according to Stiles, divided "house and lands equally between her sons Nathaniel and William; to her dau. Abigail £30; to children of Matthew and Mary Clossen £5 each, to her son-in-law, Matthew Closson, 10*s*; to Thomas Copley £3, to Samuel and John Lankton 30*s* each."[856]

*Children of Nathaniel² and Elizabeth (Copley) Phelps:*

i. MARY³ PHELPS, b. 21 June 1651 at Windsor;[857] m. on 13 December 1670 at Northampton MATTHEW CLOSSON, an Irishman, servant of one of the early settlers of Northampton; removed to Deerfield about 1679;[858] ten children, of whom four lived to maturity.

ii. ABIGAIL³ PHELPS, b. 5 April 1655 at Windsor;[859] m. JOHN ALVORD.[860]

\+ iii. NATHANIEL³ PHELPS, b. 2 April 1653 at Windsor.

iv. WILLIAM³ PHELPS, b. 22 June 1657 at Northampton;[861] m. ABIGAIL STEBBINS.[862]

v. THOMAS³ PHELPS, b. 20 May 1661 at Northampton, d. y. [863]

vi. MERCY³ PHELPS, b. 16 May 1662, d. 15 July 1662.[864]

NATHANIEL³ PHELPS (*Nathaniel² William¹*), b. 2 April 1653 at Windsor,[865] d. 19 June 1719 at Northampton;[866] m. on 11 August 1676 at

---

854 Trumbull, *History of Northampton*, 1:391.

855 Ibid., 1:501.

856 *Ancient Windsor*, 2:565.

857 Windsor VRs.

858 *Ancient Windsor*, 2:565.

859 Windsor VRs.

860 *Ancient Windsor*, 2:565.

861 Windsor VRs ("at Northampton").

862 *Ancient Windsor*, 2:565.

863 Ibid.

864 Ibid.

865 Windsor VRs, col. 2:155.

Northampton, GRACE MARTIN, dau. of William Martin and Lydia Marsh,[867] b. 1656, d. 2 August 1727 at Northampton.[868] In his will, dated 1719, Nathaniel directed his sons Samuel and Nathaniel to help their brother Timothy to build a house if he settled in the town. The will also mentions daughters Lydia, Abigail, Sarah, Grace, and Elizabeth.[869]

*Children of Nathaniel*[3] *and Grace (Martin) Phelps, all born at Northampton:*[870]

i. GRACE[4] PHELPS, b. 11 November 1676; d. 1677.
ii. NATHANIEL[4] PHELPS, b. 1678; d. May 1690.
iii. SAMUEL[4] PHELPS, b. 9 December 1680; d. 9 December 1745; m. MARY EDWARDS, b. 1685, d. 20 November 1729.
iv. LYDIA[4] PHELPS, b. 7 January 1683; m. MARK WARNER.
v. GRACE[4] PHELPS, 10 November 1685, m. SAMUEL MARSHAL.
vi. ELIZABETH[4] PHELPS, b. 19 February 1688; m. JONATHAN WRIGHT.
vii. ABIGAIL[4] PHELPS, b. 8 November 1690; m. JOHN LANGTON [LANKTON].
viii. NATHANIEL[4] PHELPS, b. 13 February 1693, d. 14 October 1747 at Northampton; m. (1) 1716 ABIGAIL BURNHAM, b. 1697, d. 1724; m. (2) CATHARINE HICKOCK, widow.
\+ ix. TIMOTHY[4] PHELPS, b. 1697.

TIMOTHY[4] PHELPS (*Nathaniel*[3] *Nathaniel*[2] *William*[1]), b. 1697 at Northampton, Mass.;[871] d. 8 December 1788 at Suffield, Conn.;[872] m. in 1725 at Northampton ABIGAIL MERRICK, dau. of Capt. John and Mary

---

866 Myrtle Stevens Hyde, "Grace Martin, Wife of Nathaniel Phelps," *TAG* 58 (1982), 223. Grace Martin and Nathaniel Phelps are in the descent of U.S. President Rutherford Birchard Hayes. Gary Boyd Roberts, comp., *Ancestors of American Presidents* (Boston and Santa Clarita, Calif., NEHGS and Carl Boyer, 3rd ed., 1995), 39–45.

867 Hyde, loc. cit., citing Dwight Whitney Marsh, *Marsh Genealogy, Descendants of John Marsh of Hartford, Connecticut* (1895).

868 Ibid.

869 Ibid.

870 *Ancient Windsor*, 2:596.

871 Ibid.

872 Ibid., 2:589.

(Day) Merrick,[873] b. 5 April 1702 at Springfield, Mass., d. 16 August 1791 at Suffield.

On 18 December 1726 Timothy renewed his baptismal covenant at Suffield Church.[874] He and his wife were admitted as members to the church on 28 February 1730/1.[875] Later they were listed among the "names of those who to a Judgment of Charity have been Converted since y^e^ Mille of 2nd Day of March 1734/5."[876]

At a freeholders meeting on 11 March 1727/8 Timothy was allocated 24*s* 6*d* for "Repairing y^e^ Glass and Window Frames in y^e^ School House."[877] The meeting instructed him to attend to glaze at the school house again on 13 March 1731/2.[878] On 26 November 1736 he was instructed to mend the school house.[879] On 15 December 1741 he was given £1 18*s* ½*d* "for work he has done about the school house."[880] Timothy was appointed constable on 8 March 1730/1.[881] On 30 November 1732 he was awarded a portion of rates of people who had "absconded."[882] On 13 March 1737/8 he was given 2*s* back pay.[883]

On 14 March 1723/4 and 4 March 1741/2 the meeting appointed him a surveyor.[884] He was made surveyor of highways on 4 December 1749.[885]

No will has been found in Hartford or Suffield probate records.

---

873 Phelps 1899, 1:130; *Ancestors of American Presidents*, 41.

874 *Records of the Congregational Church in Suffield, Conn., 1710–1836* (Hartford: Connecticut Historical Society, 1941), 18; *Documentary History of Suffield in the Colony and Province of the Massachusetts Bay in New England, 1660–1749* (Springfield: Mass.: Clark W. Bryan, 1879), 270.

875 *Records of the Congregational Church in Suffield, Conn.*, 11.

876 Ibid., 22.

877 *Documentary History of Suffield*, 233.

878 Ibid., 252.

879 Ibid., 263.

880 Ibid., 285.

881 Ibid., 248.

882 Ibid., 254.

883 Ibid., 270.

884 Ibid., 289, 297.

885 Ibid., 309.

*Children of Timothy[4] and Abigail (Merrick) Phelps, all baptized at Suffield:*

i. TIMOTHY[5] PHELPS, bp. 18 December 1726;[886] d. 22 August 1759 at Fort Edward; unm.[887]Timothy was a quartermaster in General Lyman's Regiment in the French War.[888]

ii. GRACE[5] PHELPS, bp. 15 September 1728.[889]

\+ iii. JOHN[5] PHELPS, b. 1728 or 1729.[890]

iv. ABIGAIL[5] PHELPS, bp. 14 November 1731;[891] d. January 1816 at Wilmington, Vt.; m. on 28 December 1749 at Suffield, Conn., DANIEL AUSTIN, b. 28 April 1760 at Suffield, d. 24 June 1804 at Wilmington.[892]

v. AARON[5] PHELPS, bp. 5 May 1734;[893] d. 24 June 1804; m. on 3 April 1760, according to Warner, RUTH HATHAWAY or SUSANNAH WELLS.[894]

Aaron was an adjutant in General Lyman's Regiment during the French War.[895]

vi. MARY[5] PHELPS, bp. 22 May 1737.[896]

vii. SETH[5] PHELPS, bp. 3 December 1738;[897] unm.

Seth was graduated from Yale in 1760.[898]

ix. SAMUEL S.[5] PHELPS, bp. 13 November 1741;[899] m. on 20 October 1768 LUCY KENT.[900]

---

886 *Records of the Congregational Church in Suffield, Conn.*, 35.

887 Frederic Chester Warner, *The Ancestry of Samuel, Freda and John Warner* (Boston: typescript, 1949), 503.

888 *Documentary History of Suffield*, 270.

889 *Records of the Congregational Church in Suffield, Conn.*, 37.

890 The closeness of his year of birth to that of Grace[5] Phelps suggests that they were twins. Otherwise there would have been an unusually short interval between these children.

891 Ibid., 40.

892 Warner, *Warner*, 503; *Ancestors of American Presidents*, 41.

893 Ibid., 42.

894 Warner, *Warner*, 503.

895 *Documentary History of Suffield*, 270.

896 *Records of the Congregational Church in Suffield, Conn.*, 47.

897 Ibid., 49.

898 Warner, *Warner*, 503.

899 *Records of the Congregational Church in Suffield, Conn.*, 47.

900 Warner, *Warner*, 503.

JOHN[5] PHELPS (*Timothy*[4] *Nathaniel*[3] *Nathaniel*[2] *William*[1]), b. 1728 or 1729, as his Stafford, Conn., gravestone records that he died "in his 76th year";[901] d. 7 July 1804 at Stafford;[902] m. (1) bef. 1752, when her first child was born, MARY RICHARDSON,[903] b. ca. 1734, as she died 18 April 1776 in "y[e] 43rd year of her age" at Stafford, prob. due to complications from childbirth;[904] m. (2) on 5 December 1776 at Stafford, Mrs. RUTH BARNARD of Coventry,[905] b. ca. 1750, as she died d. 25 August 1800 at Stafford, aged 50;[906] m. (3) ELIZABETH _____, b. ca. 1744, d. 7 May 1817, aged 73, at Stafford.[907]

Mary and John were admitted to the Stafford Ecclesiastical Society on 18 November 1770.[908] Ruth and John were admitted on 1 June 1777.[909]

On 28 February 1757 John Phelps purchased an 86-acre piece with dwelling house in Stafford for £275.[910] On 10 September 1770 he purchased from Abijah Willard and William Brown, the proponents of the iron furnace whose plans were noted by John Adams in 1771, a quitclaim deed for 25 acres, executed in Worcester, Massachusetts.[911] An 1801 deed that includes the furnace refers to it as land formerly of Timothy Phelps, presumably John's father, of Suffield.[912]

John Phelps was manager and part owner of Phelps Furnace and Foundry from 1770 to about 1802. He was also a merchant and trader in his own right ("John Phelps & Co.").[913] In 1797 he was listed as the owner of

---

901 Joel N. Eno, comp., "Connecticut Cemetery Inscriptions, Stafford," *Register* 66 (1912), 39 [hereinafter cited as Eno]. There is no birth record in the Suffield VRs.

902 Ibid.; obit. in *Columbian Centinel*, 1 Aug. 1804.

903 In Phelps 1899, 1:185, she is said to be the daughter of Lady Abigail and William Richardson of Edinburgh, Scotland. It is asserted that she eloped with John Phelps over the opposition of her parents because he was poor. Unfortunately, this romantic story cannot be confirmed by documentary evidence.

904 Stafford Church Records, LBG:50; Eno, 39.

905 Stafford Church Records, LBG:53.

906 Ibid.; gravestone inscription: "y[e] wife to Mr. John Phelps died August 25[th], 1800 in ye 50[th] year of her age." Eno, 39.

907 "Mrs. Elizabeth, relict of John Phelps, died May 7, 1817 AE. 73." Eno, 39.

908 Stafford Church Records, LBG:29.

909 Ibid., LBG:81.

910 Stafford Land Records, 3:80.

911 Ibid. 3:166.

912 Ibid. 4:166.

913 Tolland County Court Files, CSL, Record Group 3, box 95, case 27717; box 89, case 278845; case 27846 and others, most concerning action on debt.

a grist mill in the Stafford poll, and his property included "1 Poll, 1 horse, 2 oxen, 3 cows (3 yrs old) 2 neat cattle (2 yrs old) 14 acres Tillage land, 40 acres English Mowing & Clear Pasture, 3 acres Bog Meadow, 30 acres Bush Pasture, 56 acres 2nd Rate unimproved land, 1 silver watch, 4 wooden clocks, I Fin . Pl[ate]." The record noted that "John Phelps & Compy had 3 acres of 1st Rate unimproved land, 3 acres of 2nd rate unimproved land."[914]From 1785 to 1803 he was annually reappointed justice of the peace for Stafford.[915] He was elected deputy to the General Assembly from Stafford from 1786 to 1796.[916] In 1787 he was elected by Stafford freemen as a delegate to the Ratifying Convention of the Federal Constitution—he voted in favor of ratification in January 1788.[917]

In 1792 his portrait was painted by Ralph Earl.[918] From 1788 to 1797 he was annually appointed probate judge for Tolland County by the General Assembly.[919] In 1788 he was appointed major of the 22nd Regiment of Militia, from which rank he resigned in 1792.[920]John's signature is faint but legible on his 10 January 1804 will, in which he left

> One third of estate to wife Elizabeth, for the rest of her natural life, except about 45 acres of the potash lot (so-called) on west side of town; one third of indoors moveables, my chaise and harnesses and one good chaise horse and one cow and one hundred collars to her forever . . . six hundred dollars to be aid to her within one year by my Executors . . . in lieu of her legacy from her late son, Oleg Lanford of New Haven, which I have received; my beloved daughter Eleanor Brace, support in sickness and health for the rest of her natural life. . . . she has equal share with my other three children . . . to my beloved daughter in law Roxana and son Josiah Phelps [property] . . . to Lucy B. Lanford, daughter-in-law, one hundred dollars . . . to grandson one hundred dollars . . . to children, Daniel Phelps, Timothy Phelps, Esther Lanford, widow of Peleg Lanford, Abigail Beers wife of Nathan Beers, Mary Mills wife of Isaac Mills the rest.[921]

---

914 *List of the Polls, Estate & Assessments of the First Society in the Town of Stafford in 1797, East Parish*, Office of the Town Clerk, Stafford.

915 *PRSC*, 6–9.

916 Ibid.

917 Ibid., 6:552, 570.

918 The portrait of John Phelps by Ralph Earl was sold at Christie's, N.Y., auction of 23 May 1996, Lot 3, Sale 8,408, consigned by William Lyon Phelps Foundation, purchaser not identified. Personal communication from Kim Kessler, Christie's American Painting Department, 27 July 1996.

919 *PRSC*, 6–9.

920 Ibid., 6–7.

921 Town of Stafford, Stafford Probate District, Estate of John Phelps and Executor's Account of Expenses, case 1705, box 1372, CSL (FHL 1,018,463).

His inventory, amounting to a total $5,471, included silver flatware, china, carpet, beds and coverings, Bible, law books, *On Regeneration*, *Pilgrim's Progress*, farm equipment: harrow teeth, ox cart, plow, old horse, mare and colt, cows, heifers, three swans, sow, small pig; the house frame and building were valued at $3,333; a potash lot containing 45 acres at $750; there were also five and a half acres of land "on the road from the old furnace to the village," "half of a pew in meeting house standing at the left of the last door." On 7 March 1805 was recorded "Additions to Inventory: One Likeness of John Phelps at $25, one do. of Ruth Phelps at $25." The first likeness is probably the portrait by Ralph Earl of ca. 1793, which has survived; it seems likely that the "likeness" of Ruth Phelps was also by Earl, although its present whereabouts is unknown.

Executors of the estate were son Timothy, of New Haven, and Eleazar W. Phelps, Esq., of Stafford. The total inventory was valued at $5,471. On 1 May 1809 the court determined that, as Timothy Phelps had "absconded and gone to parts unknown," E. W. Phelps would be sole executor.[922]

*Children of John$^5$ and Mary (Richardson) Phelps, all except first born at Stafford and baptized there at the Congregational Church:*[923]

i. JOHN$^6$ PHELPS, JR., d. 28 April 1770 at Stafford, aged 18 years.[924]

ii. DANIEL$^6$ PHELPS, no b. or bp. record at Stafford; m. on 28 July 1774 at Stafford ELISABETH GREENE of that town;[925] five children, the first b. 24 Sept. 1754, another, SAMUEL WARD PHELPS, "s. of Daniel Phelps of Lebanon, N.H. & grandchild of Maj. John Phelps," bp. 22 July 1787 at Stafford.[926]

iii. ESTHER$^6$ PHELPS, b. 23 October 1757 at Stafford;[927] bp. 30 October 1757; m. (1) on 6 November 1776, prob. at Stafford ELIJAH AUSTIN of New Haven;[928] m. poss. (2) PELEG LANFORD, as she is mentioned in her father's will as widow of Peleg.

922 Ibid.

923 Stafford Church Records.

924 Hale Headstone Inscriptions, Stafford.

925 Stafford Church Records, LBG:38; Stafford VRs, 2:130.

926 Stafford Church Records, LBG:72.

927 "Heta" in Stafford VRs, 2:7.

928 Stafford Church Records, LBG:58.

iv. TIMOTHY$^6$ PHELPS, b. 26 December 1759 at Stafford;[929] bp. 30 December 1759.

Phelps 1899 describes Timothy as a merchant in New Haven.[930] He was co-executor of John's estate. In 1809 the court noted that Timothy "has absconded and gone to parts unknown."[931]

v. MARY$^6$ PHELPS, b. 18 March 1763 at Stafford;[932] bp. 20 March 1763.[933]

vi. JOSIAH$^6$ PHELPS, b. 20 July 1765 at Stafford;[934] bp. 21 July 1765; m. on 31 January 1788 ROXEY [ROXANE] NEWCOMB of Somers, Conn.[935] "my beloved daughter-in-law Roxane" in the will of John$^5$.

vii. ELEANOR$^6$ PHELPS, bp. 13 October 1767; m. on 15 June 1786 at Stafford CONSIDER BASS [BRACE], mentioned in the will of John$^5$ as "Brace."

viii. DOROTHY$^6$ PHELPS, b. 15 October 1767 at Stafford.[936]

ix. ABIGAIL$^6$ PHELPS, b. 15 February 1770,[937] bp. 18 February 1770; m. NATHAN BEERS;[938] prob. m. (2) on 23 January 1790 ISAAC MILLS of Huntington, Conn.[939]

x. [INFANT], d. 6 April 1776 "near the time of its birth."[940]

---

929 Stafford VRs, 2:11.

930 Phelps 1899, 1:309.

931 Town of Stafford, Stafford Probate District, Estate of John Phelps and Executor's Account of Expenses, case 1705, box 1372, CSL (FHL 1,018,463); Phelps 1899, 1:304.

932 Stafford VRs, 2:14.

933 Stafford Church Records, LGB:9.

934 Stafford VRs, 2:17.

935 Stafford VRs, 2:133.

936 Ibid., 2:19.

937 Ibid., LBG:16.

938 "Abigail Beers wife of Nathan Beers," in the will of John$^5$.

939 Stafford Church Records, LBG:81.

940 Stafford Church Records, LBG:50.

WILLIAM[1] DENISON,[941] son of John and Agnes (Willie) Denison,[942] bp. on 3 February 1571 at Bishop's Stortford, Hertfordshire;[943] d. 25 January 1653/4 at Roxbury, Mass.;[944] m. on 7 November 1603 at Bishop's Stortford, MARGARET (CHANDLER) MONK, wid.,[945] d. 3 February 1645/6 at Roxbury.[946]

Margaret was married first, on 2 April 1600 at Albury, Hertfordshire, to Henry Monk, who was buried on 10 December 1602 at Bishop's Stortford.[947] She was admitted to Roxbury Church as member number 33: "Margret Dennison, the wife. of Willia[m] Dennison, It pleased God to work upon her heart & change it in her ancient years, after she came to this land; & joined to the church in the year 1632."[948]

William and his family immigrated to the Massachusetts Bay Colony in 1631 and settled in Roxbury. He was admitted to Roxbury Church when it was gathered in 1632, as member number 3: "William Dennison, he brought 3 children to N.E. all sons; Daniel, Edward, & George; Daniel married at Newtowne, & was joined to the church there, he afterwards removed to the church at Ipswich."[949]

A maltster by trade,[950] William was made a freeman on 3 July 1632.[951] On 4 March 1633/4 he was elected constable at Roxbury, and exactly one year later he was elected deputy to the General Court.[952] On the same date he was appointed to the committee for inspecting ships.[953]

---

941 Based on the entry for William[1] Denison in Anderson, *Great Migration*, 1:321–23.

942 Spencer Miller, "Willie, Denison and Abbott Families of Bishop's Stortford, Co. Herts, England," *Record* 67 (1936), 50–51.

943 Ibid., 47.

944 *Roxbury Land and Church Records*, Sixth Report of the Boston Record Commissioners (Boston, 1884), 175.

945 Ibid., 48.

946 Ibid., 172.

947 Peter Walne, "Emigrants from Hertfordshire 1630–1640: Some Corrections and Additions," *Register* 132 (1978), 19.

948 *Roxbury Land and Church Records*, 75.

949 Ibid., 73.

950 Walne, "Emigrants," *Register* 132 (1978), 20.

951 Nathaniel B. Shurtleff, ed., *Records of the Governor and Company of the Massachusetts Bay in New England, 1628–1686* (Boston: W. White, 1853–54), 1:367 [hereinafter cited as *MBCR*].

952 Ibid., 1:112, 135.

953 Ibid., 1:142.

An undated list of estates at Roxbury, compiled about 1642, shows William Denison, one of the five wealthiest men in Roxbury, with a personal estate worth £24 7*s* and real estate of seven acres valued at £1 6*s* 8*d*.[954] On 27 October 1647, William Denison was commissioned to "press any sufficient workman or workmen to repair defects of a certain bridge in Roxbury."[955]

William Denison left no will, and the inventory of the possessions of Roxbury residents, which was compiled at or just before the time of his death by his son Edward, contains no entry for William. The entry for Edward Denison includes land "given to him by his father, and purchased by him of his brother George Denison."[956]

*Children of William[1] and Margaret (Chandler) (Monk) Denison, all baptized at Bishop's Stortford, Hertfordshire:*[957]

i. JOHN[2] DENISON, bp. on 7 April 1605.

After studies at Cambridge, John Denison served as the vicar at Standon, Hertfordshire, from 1660 to 1670. At the time of the family's removal to New England, according to his brother Daniel, he was "married with a good portion . . . a minister . . . and lived about Pelham . . . not far from Stratford [i.e., (Bishop's) Stortford] where we were born."

ii. WILLIAM[2] DENISON, bp. on 5 October 1606.

According to his brother Daniel's memoir, he "would needs go a soldier into Holland in the year 1624 at the famous Seige of Breda when it was taken by Spinola and Count Mansfield had an army out of England, to have raised the seige, but the army miscarried and my brother William was never heard of since."

iii. GEORGE[2] DENISON, bp. on 15 October 1609; bur. on 18 June 1614.

---

954 Roxbury Town Records, 5.

955 *MBCR,* 2:198.

956 *Roxbury Book of Possessions,* in Sixth Report of the Boston Record Commissioners (Boston, 1884), 20.

957 Miller, "Willie, Denison and Abbott Families," *Record* 67 (1936), 48. The accounts of William's children are taken from Daniel Denison's memoir of 1672. See Daniel Denison Slade, "Autobiography of Major-General Daniel Denison," *Register* 46 (1892), 127–28. See also J. L. Glascocx, Jr, "Pedigree of Denison," *Register* 46 (1892), 352–54.

iv. DANIEL[2] DENISON, bp. on 18 October 1612; m. on 18 October 1632 at Cambridge PATIENCE DUDLEY, dau. of Gov. Thomas Dudley and Dorothy York, [958] d. 8 February 1689/90 at Ipswich, aged 90.[959] Daniel Denison left a remarkable record addressed to his grandchildren, which details the immigrant's family. In his own words,

> That you being left fatherless children might not be altogether ignorant of your ancestors, nor strangers to your near relations, I thought meet to acquaint you with your predecessors, and your descent from them.... Your great grandfather my dear father whose name was William, had by my dear Mother whose name was Chandler six sons, and one daughter, two of which (viz.) one son and the daughter died in their childhood ..., your grandfather [*sic—great*-great-grandfather] my father though very well seated in Stratford [*sic* (Stortford)], hearing of the then famous transplantation in New England, unsettled himself and recalling me from Cambridge removed himself and family in the year 1631 in New England, and brought over with him myself being about 19 years of age, and my two younger brothers, Edward, and George, leaving my eldest brother john behind him in England.... My father brought with him into New England a very good estate and settled himself at Roksbury and there lived (though somewhat weakening his estate) till the year 1653 in January when he died, having buried my mother about eight years before.[960]

v. SARAH[2] DENISON, bp. on 8 October 1615; bur. on 15 October 1615.

vi. EDWARD[2] DENISON, bp. on 3 November 1616; m. on 30 March 1641 at Roxbury ELIZABETH WELD.

According to Daniel, "Edward also was married about the same time with your uncle George about the beginning of the year 1641 and lived the rest of his days at Roxbury..."

\+ vii. GEORGE[2] DENISON, bp. on 10 December 1620.

---

958 "I was the eldest of the three brothers that were brought to New England ... on the 18th day of October [1632] I married your grandmother, who was the second daughter of Mr. Tho[ma]s Dudley." *Register* 46 (1892), 128.

959 *DAB*, s.v. "Dudley, Thomas."

960 Ibid.

GEORGE[2] DENISON (*William*[1]),[961] bp. on 10 December 1620 at Bishop's Stortford, Hertfordshire; d. 23 October 1684 at Hartford, Conn.;[962] bur. at Elm Grove Cemetery, Mystic, Conn.;[963] m. (1) on March 1640 at Roxbury BRIDGET THOMPSON, dau. of John and Alice (Freeman) Thompson of Preston, Northamptonshire;[964] m. (2) say 1645 in England ANN BORODELL,[965] d. 26 September 1712 at Stonington, Conn.[966]

According to Daniel Denison, "Brother George buried his first wife in the year 1643, went into England, was a soldier there above a year, was at the Battle of York or Marston Moor, where he did good service, was afterward taken prisoner, but got free and having married a second wife he returned to New England, the year before our mother died, and not long after removed himself to New London . . ."[967] According to the *Denison Genealogy* he had been wounded in the battle and was nursed at the home of John Borodell, a cordwainer, by his daughter Ann, who became George's second wife.[968]

George served as deputy to the Connecticut General Court from New London in September 1653, May 1654, and February 1657.[969] In 1652 the town of New London granted him 200 acres of land in the Pequot-se-pos valley at Mystic, where he built a house. This was razed in 1663, presumably on the removal of the family to Stonington.[970] He was deputy to the Connecticut General Court from Stonington in October 1671; October 1674; May 1678; October 1682; May and October 1683; May, July, and

---

961 With exceptions noted, this paragraph based on Anderson, *Great Migration*, 1:321–23.

962 Denison et al., *Denison Genealogy*, 1.

963 Richard Anson Wheeler, *History of the Town of Stonington* . . . (Stonington, Conn.: 1900; reprint, Mystic, Conn., 1966), 338.

964 *Note-book Kept by Thomas Lechford, Esq., Lawyer in Boston, Massachusetts Bay, from June 27, 1638, to July 29, 1641*, Edward Everett Hale, Jr., ed. (Cambridge: Mass., 1885; reprint, Camden, Maine, 1988), 381; *TAG* 13 (1936), 18.

965 Her identity derives from an agreement of 3 May 1662 in which George Denison names her and her brother. "[T]he text of this agreement is found in the history of Stonington with the citation to 'First Book of Connecticut State Records in Hartford, Conn., page 274'; but what exactly was meant by 'First Book' has not been determined." Anderson, *Great Migration*, 1:322; the history referred to is Wheeler, *History of the Town of Stonington*.

966 Ibid.

967 Slade, "Autobiography," *Register* 46 (1892), 127–28.

968 Denison et al., *Denison Genealogy*, 1.

969 Ibid.

970 Wheeler, *History of the Town of Stonington*, 338.

October 1684; May and October 1685; May 1686; May 1687; September 1689; May, September, and October 1693; and May 1694.[971]

When first mentioned in colonial Connecticut records he was called "captain," on account of his service and commission in England. He served on the War Commission for New London in 1653, when hostilities with the Dutch threatened.[972]

At the age of 55 he served under Maj. Robert Treat in the Great Swamp fight at the outset of King Philip's War, on 19 December 1675. In the next year he raised and commanded forces that pursued and defeated the remnants of the Narragansett and Wampanaug Indians, capturing the chief Camonachet, who was brought to Stonington and shot when he refused to make peace with the English.[973] George was appointed provost marshal in 1677.[974]

*Children of George² and Bridget (Thompson) Denison, born at Roxbury:*[975]

i. SARAH³ DENISON, bp. on 20 March 1641/2; d. 19 December 1701 at Stonington, Conn.; m. THOMAS STANTON, JR., b. ca 1638, d. 11 April 1718 at Stonington.[976]

ii. HANNAH³ DENISON, bp. on 21 May 1643; m. (1) in 1659 NATHANIEL CHEESBROUGH, bp. at Boston, Co. Lincoln, England; m. (2) Capt. JOSEPH SAXTON, son of Thomas and Ann (Copp) Saxton, b. 9 May 1656 at Boston, England, d. 18 July 1725 at Stonington.[977]

*Children of George² and Ann (Borodell) Denison:*[978]

\+ iii. JOHN³ DENISON, bp. on 14 June 1646 at Roxbury, Mass.

iv. ANN³ DENISON, bp. on 20 May 1649 at Roxbury; d. 1694 at Stonington; m. on 28 November 1667 GERSHOM PALMER.[979]

---

971 Denison et al., *Denison Genealogy*, 1.

972 Wheeler, *History of the Town of Stonington*, 338.

973 Ibid.

974 Denison et al., *Denison Genealogy*, 1.

975 Ibid., 1–2.

976 Ibid., 1.

977 Ibid, 2.

978 Ibid.

979 Ibid., 3.

v. BORODELL$^3$ DENISON, b. ca 1651; d. 11 January 1702, prob. at Stonington; m. SAMUEL STANTON.[980]

vi. GEORGE$^3$ DENISON, b. ca 1653; d. 27 December 1711 at Westerly, R.I.; m. MERCY GORHAM.[981]

vii. WILLIAM$^3$ DENISON, b. ca 1655; d. 26 March 1715 at Stonington; m. SARAH PRENTICE.[982]

viii. MARGARET$^3$ DENISON, b. ca 1657; d. May 5 1741 at Barrington (then Mass., now R.I.); m. JAMES BROWN, JR.[983]

ix. MERCY$^3$ DENISON, b. ca 1659; d. 10 March 1670/1.[984]

JOHN$^3$ DENISON (*George*$^2$ *William*$^1$), bp. on 14 June 1646 at Roxbury, Mass.; d. 1698 at Stonington, Conn.;[985] m. on 26 November 1667 PHEBE LAY, dau. of Robert Lay of Saybrook and Sarah (Fenny) Tully, widow,[986] b. 5 January 1651 at Saybrook, Conn., d. 1699.

In August 1673 John Denison was appointed ensign in the New London Co. Troop. In October 1694 and again a year later he was elected deputy from Stonington.

On 26 April 1698 he signed his will, which was proved on 10 June.[987]

*Children of John*$^3$ *and Phebe (Lay) Denison, all born at Stonington:*[988]

i. JOHN$^4$ DENISON, b. 1 January 1669; bp. on 14 October 1677; d. 1700 at Saybrook; m. ca. 1690 ANN MASON.

ii. GEORGE$^4$ DENISON, b. 28 March 1671; bp. on 14 October 1677; d. 20 January 1719/20 at New London; m. ca. 1694 MARY (WETHERELL) HARRIS.

\+ iii. ROBERT$^4$ DENISON, b. 17 September 1673.

iv. WILLIAM$^4$ DENISON, b. 7 April 1677; bp. on 14 October 1677; d. 13 February 1731/2 at Stonington; m. MARY AVERY.

---

980 Ibid.

981 Ibid.

982 Ibid.

983 Ibid.

984 Ibid.

985 Ibid., 2.

986 Wheeler, *History of Stonington*, 139.

987 Denison et al., *Denison Genealogy*, 2, 4, 5.

988 Ibid.

v. DANIEL[4] DENISON, b. 28 March 1680; d. 13 October 1747 at Stonington; m. (1) MARY STANTON; m. (2) JANE COGSWELL; m. (3) ABIGAIL ELDRIDGE.

vi. SAMUEL[4] DENISON, b. 23 February 1683; d. 12 May 1683.

vii. ANNA[4] DENISON, b. 3 October 1684; bp. on 13 February 1685; m. (1) on 7 April 1702 SAMUEL MINOR, son of Ephraim and Han[nah] (Avery) Minor, b. 26 August 1680, d. 8 December 1717; m. (2) her first cousin EDWARD DENISON; prob. m. (3) 16 July 1734 Lieut. JERE RIPLEY.

viii. PHEBE[4] DENISON, bp. on 6 April 1690; d. 30 December 1775; m. EBENEZER BILLINGS.

ix. SARAH[4] DENISON, b. July 1692; m. ISAAC WILLIAMS.

ROBERT[4] DENISON (*John*[3] *George*[2] *William*[1]), b. 17 September 1673 at Stonington;[989] bp. there 14 October 1677;[990] d. 1737 at North Parish, New London, Conn.;[991] m. (1) JOANNA STANTON, dau. of Robert and Joanna (Gardiner) Stanton, b. 5 January 1678/79,[992] d. ca. 1717;[993] m. (2) ca. 1718 his first cousin, DOROTHY (STANTON) FRINK, dau. of Thomas Jr. and Sarah[2] (Denison) Stanton, b. 5 June 1679.[994]

Robert was Dorothy's fourth husband. She married first, on 9 May 1696, Nicholas Lynde, Jr. (d. 1703), a graduate of Harvard College (1690). Her second husband was John Trerice, Sr., whom she married on 22 January 1707/8. Her third husband was Samuel Frink (d. 22 October 1713).[995]

In 1710 Robert Denison bought for £20 from Oweneco (sometimes "Owanco"), the Mohegan sachem, 500 acres of land on Mashipaug (Gardiner's) Lake, where the bounds of Norwich, New London, and Colchester adjoined. Around 1712 he settled in North Society (Mohegan, now Montville) of New London.

He was elected deputy for Stonington in October 1698, May 1708, and June 1711. In May 1714 he was made commanding captain of North Company, New London.[996] On 11 July 1723 the meeting house was raised in

[989] Montville, Congregational Church [formerly New London North Parish] Records, 1722–1904, CSL 1962, 3:2 [hereinafter cited as *Mont. Ch. Rec.*].

[990] Denison et al., *Denison Genealogy*, 4.

[991] Ibid.

[992] Ibid.

[993] Ibid.

[994] *Mont. Ch. Rec.*, 3:12.

[995] Ibid., 2.

[996] Ibid., 4.

the North Parish, and on 4 August 1723 special pews were established for Robert[4] and his family.[997]

In June 1720 he was made a member of the Governor's Council.[998] In January 1726/7 Robert and Capt. James Rogers complained to the council about a raucous town meeting held in New London on 26 December, so disorderly that proper elections could not be held.[999]

Both Robert[4] and his son Robert[5] seem to have participated in the General Assembly at the October session of 1731 in New Haven.[1000] In this session, one of them brought a petition against James Otis, also of New London, complaining of the Superior Court's judgement that awarded Otis one-fifth of 600 acres of land. The assembly resolved that Denison would have one more trial on the matter.[1001]

When the General Assembly meeting at Hartford in May 1737 approved the division of the western part of Norwich into a new society called New Concord, the "house & improvements" of Capt. Robert Denison were excluded and thus remained within the limits of the North Society of New London, of which he was a founder.[1002]

Among the many land records for Capt. Robert Denison, is a survey of tracts of land purchased from Oweneco by "Coll. John L[e]vinston, Mr. Robart Denison Mr. Samuel Rogers Junr and Mr. James Harris, Junr.," in 1725.[1003] Almost all of land both for himself and for his son Robert was in Stony Brook, or North Parish, or both. At least two deeds were for "ministry land" or "for building church."[1004]

In the October 1737 session of the General Assembly at New Haven,"On the memorial of Robert Denison of New London, shewing administration on the estate of Robert Denison, late of New London, deceas'd, was granted to him, and that on a true inventory of the moveable estate that could be found there appeared in the whole £60 4*s* 1*d*, whereupon there is wanting of the personal estate of said deceas'd, to satisfy the said debts, the sum of £485 0*s* 6*d*." The court granted permission to sell

---

997 Francis Manwaring Caulkins, *History of New London* (New London: privately printed, 1852), 433.

998 Ibid.

999 *PRCC*, 7:85–86.

1000 Ibid., 347.

1001 Ibid., 352.

1002 *PRCC*, 8:94.

1003 New London Land Records, 11:167.

1004 Ibid., 8:100.

and convey land to help pay that debt.[1005] The land records of New London show that Robert[5] Denison did sell land, specifically stating the reason for the sale was "raise money to pay 485 pounds debt of late Capt. Robart Denison of New London deceased."[1006]

*Children of Robert[4] and Joanna (Stanton) Denison, all born at North Society, New London (later Montville):*[1007]

+ i. ROBERT[5] DENISON, bp. on 27 March 1697.
 ii. JOHN[5] DENISON, b. 28 November 1698;[1008] d. 28 November 1776 at Lyme;[1009] m. on 5 November 1724 PATIENCE GRISWOLD.[1010]
 iii. JOANNA[5] DENISON, bp. on 27 August 1699; d. November 1733 at Saybrook; m. THOMAS MOREHOUSE of Fairfield.[1011]
 iv. NATHANIEL[5] DENISON, bp. on 19 April 1702;[1012] d. "at about 30."[1013]
 v. ANDREW[5] DENISON, bp. on 23 April 1704; d. "in 23rd year in West Indies."[1014]
 vi. SARAH[5] DENISON, bp. on 14 April 1706; d. 1714.[1015]
 vii. ANNA[5] DENISON, bp. on 21 March 1708; d. 1792;[1016] m. on 12 February 1727/8 JAMES FITCH.[1017]
 viii. THOMAS[5] DENISON, bp. on 20 1709;[1018] d. 24 October 1787; m. ELIZABETH BAGLEY [BAILEY].[1019]

---

1005 *PRCC*, 8:146.

1006 New London Land Records, 12:87–88.

1007 Wheeler, *History of Stonington*, 139.

1008 Denison et al., *Denison Genealogy*, 13; *Mont. Ch. Rec.*, 3:2.

1009 Wheeler, *History of Stonington*, 139.

1010 Denison et al., *Denison Genealogy*, 4.

1011 *Mont. Ch. Rec.*, 3:2.

1012 Denison et al., *Denison Genealogy*, 4.

1013 *Mont. Ch. Rec.*, 3:4.

1014 Ibid., 3:2.

1015 Denison et al., *Denison Genealogy*, 4; "d. aged about 11 years." *Mont. Ch. Rec.*, 3:2.

1016 "Ann" in Denison et al., *Denison Genealogy*, 4; "Anna" in *Mont. Ch. Rec.* 3:2; 1:37.

1017 *Mont. Ch. Rec.*, 1:37.

1018 Ibid., 3:2.

1019 Ibid.; "Bailey" in Denison et al., *Denison Genealogy*, 4.

ix. LUCY[5] DENISON, bp. on 12 August 1711; m. SAMUEL ROGERS.[1020]
x. ELIZABETH[5] DENISON, bp. on 1713; d. y.[1021]
xi. ABIGAIL[5] DENISON, bp. on 6 November 1715;[1022] m. WILLIAM WATTLES of Lebanon.[1023]
xii. GEORGE[5] DENISON, bp. on 13 October 1717; d. "an infant."[1024]

*Children of Robert[4] and Dorothy (Stanton) (Frink) Denison:*

xiii. GEORGE[5] DENISON, b. ca 1719;[1025] m. HANNAH DODGE.[1026]
xiv. DOROTHY[5] DENISON, bp. on 30 December 1722; m. (1) EBENEEZER ROGERS; m. (2) DAVID COPP; m. (3) JONATHAN AVERY of Norwich.[1027]

ROBERT[5] DENISON (*Robert[4] John[3] George[2] William[1]*), bp. on 27 March 1697 at North Society, New London, Conn.;[1028] d. 1766 at Horton, N.S.; m. (1) on 19 October 1721 DEBORAH GRISWOLD, dau. of Matthew Griswold and Phebe Hyde of Lyme, Conn., d. 24 December 1731, prob. at North Society, New London; m. (2) on 4 April 1733 PRUDENCE SHERMAN, dau. of Deacon David and Mercy (Wheeler) Sherman of Stratford,[1029] bp. on 20 October 1706 at Stratford, Conn., d. after 1766, prob. at Horton, N.S. She was one of the heirs of an estate valued at £9,429 1*s* at her father's death at Stratford on 1 January 1753.[1030]

---

1020 Denison et al., *Denison Genealogy*, 4.

1021 *Mont. Ch. Rec.*, 3:2.

1022 Denison et al., *Denison Genealogy*, 5.

1023 *Mont. Ch. Rec.*, 3:2.

1024 Ibid.

1025 Denison et al., *Denison Genealogy*, 5.

1026 *Mont. Ch. Rec.*, 3:2.

1027 Ibid.

1028 Denison et al., *Denison Genealogy*, 12.

1029 Records of the Bridgeport United Congregational Church [incorporating Stratfield Congregational Church], Bridgeport, Conn., United Congregational Church Records, 1695–1911, 1:15, CSL.

1030 Ibid., 1:95. The will is dated 1 Aug. 1748. Fairfield Probate District, packet 5263 [including will and inventory], CSL 342 (FHL film 1,018,779).

Like his father, Robert owned extensive property in North Society and served in local and colony office. On 10 October 1728 he was commissioned ensign in the North Company in New London and was promoted to the rank of captain in October 1731.[1031] He was elected to the Connecticut General Assembly in 1737 and 1742.[1032] In March 1745 he became captain of a company for the expedition against Ile Royale (Cape Breton Island) and participated in the capture of Louisbourg that June.[1033]

Robert was elected to the General Assembly again in 1751, and in March 1755 he was commissioned a major in the First Regiment of Connecticut. In August of that year he attended a war council held by Sir William Johnson near the south end of Lac Saint-Sacrement (Lake George) and early in September took part in the Battle of Lake George. He was discharged on 3 October 1755. The following year he served again in the General Assembly.[1034]

Robert was one of four agents from eastern Connecticut selected to inspect Nova Scotian lands being made available as grants to New England families. He and the others, including one agent from Rhode Island, met at Halifax, N.S., on 18 April 1759 with the Executive Council of the province under Lieutenant Governor Belcher.[1035] The agents, referred to in the official records as "Settlers or Planters," were sent by sea around Yarmouth into the Bay of Fundy to the Minas Basin, where, with a surveyor, they examined the region between Cape Biomidon and Piziquid, now Windsor, N.S. They selected land for a township of 100,000 acres to be called Horton.[1036] On their return to New England they recruited families to emigrate. Robert's family and 200 other families from southeastern New England arrived at Horton on 4 June 1760 in a fleet of 22 ships provided by the Provincial Council to transport them and their furnishings.[1037]

---

1031 *PRCC*, 7:198.

1032 *PRCC*, 8:119, 486.

1033 Colonial Wars, 1st ser., CSL, 4:231, 355.

1034 *DCB*, vol. 3; *PRCC*, 8:119, 486; 9:92, 97, 98, 236, 277, 343.

1035 Public Records for the Executive Council: Record Group 1, vol. 188 (17 Aug. 1757–21 Aug. 1766), 53, NSARM.

1036 Ibid., 59.

1037 *DCB*, vol. 3; R. S. Longley, "The Coming of the New England Planters to the Annapolis Valley," 14–28, 20–21, in Margaret Conrad, ed, *The Planted Well: New England Planters in Maritime Canada* (Fredericton, N.B.: Acadiensis Press, 1988).

Robert received a Crown grant of 750 acres in Horton. He was commissioned lieutenant colonel of the militia on the day of the landing. In that same year he was commissioned a justice of the peace for Kings County and became a justice of the Inferior Court of Common Pleas for Horton Township in 1761. From 1760 to May 1765 he participated in the Court of Quarter Sessions held at Horton, which administered the local government of the township and tried minor criminal offences. In 1762 he signed a protest by 63 "New Eng'd Settlers of King's county . . . the Magistrates Representatives and other principal inhabitants," blaming the lieutenant governor for breaking promises made by his predecessor, especially that the settlers would have their own township government "and all our civil and Religious Rights and Liberties, as we enjoyed them in the Governments from whence we came."[1038] He resigned from the assembly in April 1764, citing "age and infirmities."[1039]

Robert signed his will on 25 June 1765 and died shortly thereafter. To his eldest son, Andrew, he left his "Cape Breton Gun and silver Hilted S[word]"; to his son Samuel he left "the Gun I brought from Lake George." Other heirs were his wife, Prudence, daughters Deborah Manwaring, Elizabeth Huntington, Sarah, Phebe, and Eunice; and sons David Sherman and Gurdon.[1040]

*Children of Robert[5] and Deborah (Griswold) Denison:*

i. DEBORAH[6] DENISON, b. December 1722; bp. on 24 March 1723 at North Society, New London;[1041] d. 22 March 1816;[1042] m. CHRIS. MANWARING.[1043]

ii. ELIZABETH[6] DENISON, b. at North Society, New London; "lived but a few days."[1044]

iii. ROBERT[6] DENISON, b. 5 March 1724 at North Society, New London; d. 16 May 1724.[1045]

---

1038 *DCB*, vol. 3.

1039 Longley, "The Coming of the New England Planters," 19.

1040 Registry of Probate, Hampshire Co., N.S.: Will Book vol. 1: 1761–1824: 16–21.

1041 *Mont. Ch. Rec.*, 3:12

1042 Denison et al., *Denison Genealogy*, 13.

1043 *Mont. Ch. Rec.*, 3:12.

1044 Ibid.

1045 Denison et al., *Denison Genealogy*, 13.

iv. ELIZABETH[6] DENISON, b. 10 September 1726 at North Society, New London; m. NATHAN SMITH of Groton.[1046] The *Denison Genealogy* states that she married ELISHA HUNTINGTON, and she is so named in her father's will. [1047]

v. ANDREW[6] DENISON, b. 2 May 1728 at North Society, New London;[1048] d. 1803; m. MARY THOMPSON.[1049]

vi. MARY[6] DENISON, b. January 1730; d. 21 December 1743.[1050]

vii. ROBERT[6] DENISON, b. ca 1731; d. 1732.[1051]

*Children of Robert[5] and Prudence (Sherman) Denison, born in North Parish, New London:*[1052]

viii. DAVID SHERMAN[6] DENISON, b. 12 August 1734;[1053] d. 1796 at Horton, N.S.; m. SARAH FOX.[1054]

ix. MERCY[6] DENISON, b. 5 October 1736; d. 15 January 1743.[1055]

x. ROBERT[6] DENISON, b. 31 July 1739; d. 25 December 1743.[1056]

xi. PRUDENCE[6] DENISON, b. 31 March 1741; d. 20 December 1743.[1057]

xii. SAMUEL[6] DENISON, b. 8 February 1742/3;[1058] d. 1820; unm.[1059]

xiii. SARAH[6] DENISON, b. 11 November 1744; m. Capt. KENNEDY.

---

1046 *Mont. Ch. Rec.*, 3:12.

1047 Denison et al., *Denison Genealogy*, 13.

1048 *Mont. Ch. Rec.*, 3:12.

1049 Denison et al., *Denison Genealogy*, 13.

1050 Ibid.

1051 Ibid.

1052 Ibid.

1053 *Mont. Ch. Rec.*, 3:12.

1054 Denison et al., *Denison Genealogy*, 13.

1055 *Mont. Ch. Rec.*, 3:12.

1056 "But a Robt served as pvt 9th Co, 3d Regt, French and Indian War, d. 15 Aug 1758." Denison et al., *Denison Genealogy*, 13.

1057 *Mont. Ch. Rec.*, 3:12.

1058 Ibid.

1059 Denison et al., *Denison Genealogy*, 13.

xiv. PHEBE[6] DENISON, b. 1 January 1746/7;[1060] bp. 1 March 1746/7 at North Society;[1061] d. March 1816 at Manchester, Conn.;[1062] m. on 19 November 1766 at Cornwallis, N.S., by the Rev. Joseph Bennett, to BENAJAH PHELPS.[1063] *See* Phelps I *in these Notes.*

xv. GURDON[6] DENISON, b. ca 1749; d. 1807; m. CATHERINE FITZPATRICK.[1064]

xvi. EUNICE[6] DENISON m. JOHN LOTHROP.[1065]

---

1060 Ibid.; Crowell, *New Englanders in Nova Scotia*, no. 534.

1061 *Mont Ch. Rec.*, 3:12.

1062 Hale Headstone Collection, Manchester Cemetery, 1:5.

1063 Eaton, *History of Kings County*, 278.

1064 Denison et al., *Denison Genealogy*, 13; not listed in *Mont. Ch. Rec.*

1065 Ibid.; not listed in *Mont. Ch. Rec.*

# SELECT BIBLIOGRAPHY

## Archives and Manuscript Collections


Acadia University, Wolfville, Nova Scotia
  Baptist Collection
    Cornwallis Church Records
Archives of the General Convention, Episcopal Diocese of New York
  John Henry Hobart Correspondence
  Journals of the Convention
Archives of Ontario, Toronto
  Record Group 1—Crown Lands and Resource Administration Records
  Record Group 22—Surrogate Court Records
Baker Library, Harvard Business School, Cambridge, Massachusetts
  Historical Collections
    R. G. Dun & Co. Collection
Connecticut State Library, Hartford [CSL]
  Connecticut Archives [Conn. Arch.]
  Lucius B. Barbour Collection, Vital Records
  Bolton Church Records
  Charles R. Hale Collection
  Lyme Land Records
  Revolutionary War Records
  Stafford Church Records
  Stafford Probate District Records
  Tolland County, County Court Files
Dartmouth College Archives, Rauner Special Collections Library,
Dartmouth College Library, Hanover, New Hampshire [DCA]
  Josiah Bartlett Papers
  Eleazar Wheelock Papers
Fairfield [Connecticut] Historical Society
  Town of Fairfield, Tax Records
National Archives, Episcopal Church, Austin, Texas
  Samuel Andrew Peters Collection [Peters Collection]

National Archives and Records Administration, Washington, D.C.
Department of State, Consular Dispatches
Pension Application Files, Death or Disability, War of 1812
Records Relating to the United States Military Academy, 1812–1867
Revolutionary War Pension Applications
Revolutionary War Records, N.H. Militia

New York Public Library, Manuscripts Division, New York City [NYPL Mss. Div.]
Emmet Collection
Frederick C. Haacker Collection
George H. Budke Collection
Jones Family Papers
Phelps-Dodge Collection
Schieffelin Family Papers

New-York Historical Society Library, New York City [NYHS]
Benedict Arnold Collection
Donald F. Clark Collection
Aaron Burr Papers
Samuel Jones Papers

Nova Scotia Archives and Records Management, Halifax [NSARM]
Manuscript Group 1, vol. 742—Papers of Families and Individuals.
Manuscript Group 1, vol. 183—Chipman Family Papers, Kings County, Nova Scotia, 1760–1869.
Record Group 1, vol. 1—Provincial Secretary's Letter Book, 1760–1784.
Record Group 1, vol. 39A—Letter Book.
Record Group 1, vol. 189—Executive Council Minutes, 1766, 1777–1778.
Record Group 1, vol. 222—Report on State and Conditions of Nova Scotia, 1773; Memorial of John Burbidge [& others], Kings County, 20 August 1778.
Record Group 1, vol. 284—"A brief state of the circumstances of the Protestant Dissenters in Nova Scotia."
Record Group 34, ser. P, vol. 4—Kings County Proceedings of the Court of General Sessions of the Peace.
Record Group 39—Supreme Court of Nova Scotia: Halifax County, 1776–1779.

National Maritime Museum, Greenwich, United Kingdom
*HMS Albany*, 1776–1780, Lieutenant's logs

Public Record Office, Kew, Richmond, Surrey, United Kingdom [PRO]
*HMS Albany*, Master's log, 1778–79

## Newspapers

*Massachusetts Centinel* [*Columbian*] (Boston, Mass.)
*Connecticut Courant* (Hartford, Conn.)
*Fairfield Citizen News* (Fairfield, Conn.)
*Massachusetts Gazette* (Boston, Mass.)
*Merchants Magazine* (New York, N.Y.)
*New Hampshire Gazette* (Portsmouth, N.H.)
*New York Evening Post*
*New York Times*
*New-York Spectator*
*Southport Times* (Fairfield, Conn.)
*Upper Canada Gazette* or *American Oracle* (Newark, U.C.)

## Directories

*Doggett's New York City Directory*, 1842/43–1851/52.

*Elliot's Improved New-York Double-Directory*, 1812.

*Gore's Directory of Liverpool and Its Environs*, 1868–77.

*Holden's Annual London and County Directory of the United Kingdom and Wales*. London, 1811–16.

Lain, George T. *1873–74 Brooklyn City and Business Directory.*

*Longworth's American Almanac, New York Register and City Directory*, 1796–1842/43.

Morehead, T. *The New-York Mercantile Register for 1848–49, Containing the Cards of the Principal Business Establishments including Hotels and Public Institutions*. New York, 1848.

*The New-York Business Directory for 1844 & 1845*. New York: John Doggett, Jr.

*Rode's New York City Directory*, 1851/52–1852/3.

*Trow's New York City Directory*, 1852/53–1882/83.

## Records, Compilations, and Abstracts

Baldwin, Thomas W., comp. *Vital Records of Mendon, Massachusetts to the Year 1750*. Boston, Mass., 1920.

Barber, Gertrude A., comp. *Marriages Taken from the* New York Evening Post. Vol. 11. New York, 1934. Mimeograph.

*Biographical Directory of the American Congress, 1774–1927*. Washington, D.C.: United States Government Printing Office, 1928.

Boyd, Julian P., ed. *The Susquehannah Company Papers*. 11 vols. Ithaca, N.Y.: Cornell Univ. Press, published for Wyoming Historical and Genealogical Society, Wilkes-Barre, Pa., 1930. Reprint, 1962.

*Calendar of Historical Manuscripts Relating to the War of the Revolution in the Office of the Secretary of State*. Albany, N.Y.: State of New York, 1868.

Clinton, George. *Public Papers of George Clinton, First Governor of New York, 1777–1795, 1801–1804*. 10 vols. Albany, N.Y.: State of New York, 1900.

Connecticut Historical Society. *Records of the Congregational Church in Suffield, Conn., 1710–1836*. Hartford: Connecticut Historical Society, 1941.

Connecticut General Assembly. *Connecticut Military Record, 1775–1848*. Hartford: Connecticut General Assembly, 1889.

Cowen, Minnie, comp. *Abstracts of Wills of Rockland County, New York, 1766–1843*. Vols. 1–3. New York, 1937–39.

Cruikshank, E. A., ed. *Ontario Historical Society, Papers and Records*, 24. Toronto, 1927.

*Digested Summary and Alphabetical List of Private Claims which have been presented to the House of Representatives from the First to the Thirty-First Congress*. Baltimore, Md.: Genealogical Publishing Company, 1970.

*Documentary History of Suffield in the Colony and Province of the Massachusetts Bay in New England, 1660–1749*. Springfield, Mass.: Clark W. Bryan, 1879.

Eagles, Douglas E., comp. *Horton Township Records, Kings Co., Nova Scotia: Register of Births, Marriages and Deaths, 1751–1895*. Sarnia, Ontario: Compiler, 1974.

Elliot, Jonathan, ed. *The Debates in the Several State Conventions for the Adoption of the Federal Constitution as Recommended by the General Convention at Philadelphia of 1787*. Philadelphia: J. B. Lippincott, 1881.

Evans, Lorna Woodman, comp. *Township Books: Kings County, Nova Scotia: Aylesford, Cornwallis, and Horton*. Kentville, N.S.: Family History Committee of the Kings Historical Society, 1996.

Force, Peter. *American Archives, Fourth Series, Containing A Documentary History of the English Colonies in North America from the King's Message to Parliament of March 7, 1774 to The Declaration of Independence by the United States*. Washington, D.C.: St. Clair Clarke and Peter Force, 1843.

General Assembly, Society of Colonial Wars. *An Index of Ancestors and Roll of Members of the Society of Colonial Wars*. New York, 1922.

Hastings, Hugh, supervisor. *Ecclesiastical Records of the State of New York.* 7 vols. Albany, N.Y.: State of New York, 1901–1926.

———, ed. *Military Minutes of the Council of Appointment of the State of New York 1783–1821.* Albany, N.Y., 1901.

Heitman, F. B. *Historical Register and Dictionary of the U.S. Army from its Organization, September 29, 1789, to September 29, 1880.* Washington, D.C.: National Tribune, 1890.

Hunt, Gaillard, ed. *Journals of the Continental Congress, 1774–1789.* 34 vols. Washington: United States Government Printing Office, 1923. Reprint, New York: Johnson Reprint, 1968.

*Index of Conveyances Recorded in the Office of Register of the City and County of New York, 1800–1880.* New York, 1858.

Jacobus, Donald Lines, comp. *List of Officials Civil, Military and Ecclesiastical of Connecticut Colony from March 1636 through 11 October 1677 and of New Haven Colony throughout its Separate Existence, also Soldiers in the Pequot War.* New Haven: Roland Mather Hooker, for the Connecticut Society of the Order of the Founders and Patriots of America, 1935.

*Journal of the Legislative Council of the Colony of New York.* Albany, N.Y.: State of New York, 1861.

*Journals of the Provincial Congress, Provincial Convention, Committee of Safety and Council of Safety of the State of New-York, 1775–1776–1777.* 2 vols. Albany, N.Y.: State of New York, 1842.

*Liverpool Customs Bills of Entry.* HM Customs, 1859, 1867–1878.

Maher, James P., comp. *Index to Marriages and Deaths in the* New York Herald, *1856–1863.* Vol. 2. Alexandria, Va.: privately printed, 1991.

Manwaring, Charles William. *A Digest of the Early Connecticut Probate Records.* 3 vols. Hartford, Conn., 1904–1906. Reprint, Baltimore, Md.: Genealogical Publishing Company, 1995.

New York Genealogical and Biographical Society. *Baptisms from 1639 to 1730 in the Reformed Dutch Church, New York.* Vol. 2. New York: New York. Genealogical and Biographical Society, 1902. Reprint, Upper Saddle River, N.J.: Gregg Press, 1968.

New-York Historical Society. *Abstracts of Wills on File in the Surrogates Office, City of New York, with Letters of Administration, 1754–1782.* Vols. 4–8. Collections of the New-York Historical Society for the Year 1899. New York: New-York Historical Society, 1900.

New-York Historical Sociey. *Minutes of the Committee and of the First Commission for Detecting and Defeating Conspiracies in the State of New York, December 11, 1776–September 23, 1778 with collateral documents to which is added Minutes of the Council of Appointment, State of New York, April*

*2, 1778–May 3, 1779*. Collections of the New-York Historical Society for the Year 1924. New York: New-York Historical Society, 1925.

Norton, Judith, comp. *New England Planters in the Maritime Provinces of Canada, 1759–1800*. Toronto: Univ. of Toronto Press, 1993.

O'Callaghan, Edmund Bailey. *Lists of Inhabitants of Colonial New York: Excerpted from the Documentary History of the State of New-York*. Baltimore, Md.: Genealogical Publishing Company, 1979.

Powell, Wm. H., comp. *List of Officers of the Army of the United States from 1779 to 1900*. New York, 1900. Reprint, Detroit: Gale Research Company, 1967.

*The Proprietors' Records of the Town of Mendon, Massachusetts*. Boston: Rockwell and Churchill Press, 1899.

*The Public Records of the Colony of Connecticut*. Edited by J. Hammond Trumbull and Charles J. Hoadly. 15 vols. Hartford, Conn.: [State of Connecticut], 1850–90.

*The Public Records of the State of Connecticut*. Edited by Charles J. Hoadly, Leonard W. Labaree, Catherine Fennelly, Albert R. Van Dusen, Christopher Collier, Bonnie Bromberger, Dorothy Ann Lipson and Douglas M. Arnold. 15 vols. Hartford, Conn.: [State of Connecticut], 1894–.

*Records of the Reformed Dutch Churches of Hackensack and Schraalenburgh, New Jersey, with the Registers of Members, Marriages, Baptisms, and the Consistories to the Beginning of the Nineteenth Century*. New York, Holland Society, 1891.

*Records of the Town and Selectmen of Hanover N.H., 1761–1818*. Hanover, N.H, 1905.

*Roll of the New Hampshire Soldiers at the Battle of Bennington, August 16, 1777*. Manchester, N.H.: J. B. Clarke, 1891.

Scott, Kenneth, comp. *Genealogical Data from Colonial New York Newspapers: A Consolidation of Articles from the* New York Genealogical and Biographical Record. Baltimore, Md.: Genealogical Publishing Company, 1977.

———, ed. *Marriages and Deaths from* The New Yorker, *Double Quarto Edition, 1836–1841*. Washington, D.C.: National Genealogical Society, 1980.

*Vital Records of Medfield, Massachusetts to the Year 1850*. Boston: NEHGS, 1903.

Welles, Edwin Stanley, ed. *Births, Marriages, and Deaths Returned from Hartford, Windsor, and Fairfield, and Entries in the Early Land Records of the Colony of Connecticut*. Hartford, Conn., 1898.

## Memoirs, Journals, and Correspondence


Adams, John. *Diary and Autobiography of John Adams*. Edited by L. H. Butterfield. 4 vols. Cambridge, Mass.: Harvard Univ. Press, Belknap Press, 1961.

Alline, Henry. *The Journal of Henry Alline*. Edited by James Beverley and Barry Moody. Hantsport, N.S.: Lancelot Press, 1982.

Burr, Esther Edwards. *The Journal of Esther Edwards Burr, 1754–1757*. Edited by Carol F. Karlsen and Laurie Crumpacker. New Haven and London: Yale Univ. Press, 1984.

Cameron, Kenneth Walter, ed. *The Papers of Loyalist Samuel Peters: A Survey of the Contents of his Notebooks—Correspondence During His Flight to England, Exile, and the Last Years of His Life*. Hartford: Transcendental Books, 1972.

Chase, Philander. *Bishop Chase's Reminiscences: an Autobiography*. 2d ed. 2 vols. Boston: James B. Dow, 1848.

Cruikshank, E. A., ed. *The Correspondence of Lieut. Governor John Graves Simcoe*. Vol. 2, 1793–1794. Toronto: Ontario Historical Society, 1923.

———, ed. *The Correspondence of the Honourable Peter Russell*. 2 vols. Toronto: Ontario Historical Society, 1935.

De Crevecoeur, J. Hector St. John. *Letters from an American Farmer and Sketches of Eighteenth-Century America*. New York: Penguin Books, 1981.

DeForest, Louis Effingham. *Louisbourg Journals 1745*. New York: Society of Colonial Wars, 1932.

Denison, Daniel. "Autobiography of Major-General Daniel Denison." *Register* 46 (1892): 127–133.

Hamilton, Alexander. *Itinerarium*. 1744. St. Louis, Mo., 1907. Reprint, New York: Arno Press, 1971.

Hone, Philip. *The Diary of Philip Hone, 1828–1851*. Edited by Allan Nevins. 2 vols. New York: Dodd, Mead, 1927.

Kidder, Frederick, comp. *Military Operations in Eastern Maine and Nova Scotia during the Revolution, Chiefly Compiled from the Journals and Letters of Colonel John Allen*. Albany, N.Y.: Joel Munsell, 1867.

Montgomery, Richard. *Biographical Notes concerning General Richard Montgomery together with hitherto unpublished letters*. Poughkeepsie, N.Y.: "News" Book and Publishing Company, 1876.

Patten, Ruth. *Interesting Family Letters of the Late Mrs. Ruth Patten of Hartford, Conn.* Hartford: D. B. Moseley, 1845.

Simcoe, Elizabeth [Mrs. John Graves]. *The Diary of Mrs. John Graves Simcoe, wife of the First Lieutenant-Governor of the Province of Upper Canada, 1802–6*. Edited by J. Ross Robertson. Toronto: William Briggs, 1913.

Smith, Paul H., ed. *Letters of Delegates to Congress, 1774–1789*. Vol. 1, August 1774–August 1775. Washington, D.C.: Library of Congress, 1976.

Wansey, Henry. *Journal of an Excursion to the United States of America, 1794*. Salisbury, England, 1796.

Washington, George. *The Writings of George Washington from the Original Manuscript Sources, 1745–1799*. Edited by John C. Fitzpatrick. Vol. 19, *June 12, 1780–September 5, 1780*. Washington, D.C.: United States Government Printing Office, 1937.

Wheelock, Eleazar. *Memoirs of the Rev. Eleazar Wheelock, D. D.* Edited by David McClure and Elijah Parish. Newburyport, Mass.: Edu and Little, 1811.

Williams, William. *Journal Kept by William Williams of the Proceedings of the Lower House of the Connecticut General Assembly, May 1757 Session*. Edited by Sylvie J. Turner. Hartford: Connecticut Historical Society, 1975.

## Genealogies

Ackerman, Herbert S. *Descendants of Jan Pieter Haring*. Ridgewood, N.J., October 1952. Typescript at NYPL.

Baldwin, Thomas W. *Patten Genealogy: William Patten of Cambridge, 1635 and his Descendants*. Boston: Thomas W. Baldwin, 1908.

Bartlett, Levi. *Sketches of the Bartlett Family in England and America*. Lawrence, Mass., 1876.

Belknap, Waldron Phoenix. *The De Peyster Genealogy*. Baltimore, Md.: privately printed, 1956.

Crowell, Fred E. *New Englanders in Nova Scotia*. Boston: NEHGS, 1979.

Davenport, A. Benedict. *A History and Genealogy of the Davenport Family*. New York: S. W. Benedict, 1851.

Davenport, Robert Ralsey. *Davenport Genealogy*. Cambridge, Mass.: privately printed, 1982.

DeForest, J. W. *The DeForests of Avesnes (and of New Netherland), 1494 to the Present Time*. New Haven, 1900.

Denison, E. Glenn, with Josephine Middleton Peck, Donald L. Jacobus. *Denison Genealogy: Ancestors and Descendants of Captain George Denison*. Baltimore, Md., 1963. Reprint, Baltimore, Md.: Gateway Press, 1978.

Goodrich, Merton Taylor. "The Children and Grandchildren of Capt. Myles Standish." *Register* 87 (1933): 149–60.

Jacobus, Donald Lines, comp. *Families of Ancient New Haven*. Reprint, Baltimore, Md.: Genealogical Publishing Company, 1974.

Kip, Frederic Ellsworth, assisted by Mararrita Lansing Hawley. *History of the Kip Family in America*. Montclair, N.J.: privately printed, 1928.

Maltby, Georgia Lord (Morehouse). *Family Record of the Maltby–Morehouse Family*. N.p.: privately printed, 1895.

Mann, George Sumner. *Mann Memoria: A Record of the Mann Family in America*. Boston: D. Clapp, 1884.

Peters, Edmond Frank, and Eleanor Bradley Peters, comps. *Peters of New England: A Genealogy and Family History*. New York: Knickerbocker Press, 1903.

Phelps, Oliver Seymour and Andrew T. Servin, comps. *The Phelps Family of America and their English Ancestors with Copies of Wills, Deeds, Letters and Other Interesting Papers, Coats of Arms, and Valuable Records*. 2 vols. Pittsfield, Mass.: Eagle Publishing Company, 1899.

Quick, Arthur Craig. *A Genealogy of the Quick Family in America (1625–1942)*. South Haven and Palisades Park, Michigan: privately printed [ca. 1943].

Rodman, William Woodbridge, comp. "Eltweed Pomeroy of Dorchester, Mass. and Windsor, Conn., and Four Generations of his Descendants." *Register* 57 (1903): 268–73.

Ripley, H. W., comp. *Genealogy of the Ripley Family*. Newark, N.J.: A. Stephen Holbrook, 1867.

Tiffany, Nelson Otis. *The Tiffanys of America: History and Genealogy*. Privately printed, 1903.

Toler, Henry Pennington. *The Harlem Register: A Genealogy of the 23 Original Patentees of the Town of New Harlem, New York*. New York: New Harlem Press, 1903.

Waite, Marcus Warren. *Eleazer Wheelock and Some of His Descendants*. DCA, n.d. Typescript.

Willard, Joseph, and Charles Wilkes Walker, comps. *Willard Genealogy*. Edited and completed by Charles Henry Pope. 2 vols. Boston: privately printed, 1915.

## Books, Pamphlets, Dissertations, Theses, and Typescripts

Ahlin, J. H.. *Maine Rubicon: Downeast Settlers during the American Revolution*. Calais, Maine, 1966.

Ahlstrom, Sydney E. *A Religious History of the American People*. New Haven: Yale Univ. Press, 1972.

Albion, Robert Greenhalgh. *The Rise of New York Port*. New York: C. Scribner's Sons, 1939.

Allen, E. Michael. "Mitred Leaders of Evangelism." Master's thesis, The General Theological Seminary, 1991.

Ambrose, Stephen E. *Duty, Honor, Country: A History of West Point*. Baltimore, Md.: Johns Hopkins Univ. Press, 1966.

Anderson, Robert Charles. *The Great Migration Begins: Immigrants to New England*, 3 vols. Boston: NEHGS, 1996.

Armstrong, Frederic H. *Handbook of Upper Canadian Chronology*. Toronto, and London: Dundurn Press, 1985.

Baines, Thomas. *History of the Commerce and Town of Liverpool and of the Rise of Manufacturing Industry in the Adjoining Counties*. London and Liverpool, 1852.

Baldwin, Alice M. *The New England Clergy and the American Revolution*. Durham, N.C.: Duke Univ. Press, 1928.

Barkun, Michael. *New York of the Millenium: the Burned-over District of New York in the 1840s*. Syracuse, N.Y.: Syracuse Univ. Press, 1986.

Barrett, Walter [Joseph A. Scoville]. *The Old Merchants of New York City*. New York, 1865–66.

Barton, Lucy. *Historic Costume for the Stage*. Illustrated by David Sarvis. 1935. Reprint, Boston: Walter H. Baker, 1961.

Beardsley, E. Edwards. *The History of the Episcopal Church in Connecticut from the Settlement of the Colony to the Death of Bishop Seabury*. 2 vols. New York: Hurd and Houghton, 1874.

Bernstein, Iver. *The New York City Draft Riots: Their Significance for American Society and Politics in the Age of the Civil War*. New York: Oxford Univ. Press, 1990.

Bishop, Joseph Bucklin. *A Chronicle of One Hundred & Fifty Years: The Chamber of Commerce of the State of New York, 1768–1918*. New York: Charles Scribner's Sons, 1918.

Bittinger, J. Q. *History of Haverhill, N. H.* Haverhill, N. H., 1888.

*Blunt's Stranger's Guide to the City of New York*. New York, 1817.

Boatner, Mark Mayo III. *Encyclopedia of the American Revolution*. Bicentennial ed. New York: David McKay, 1974.

Boynton, Edward C. *History of West Point*. New York: D. Van Nostrand, 1864.

Brebner, John Bartlett. *The Neutral Yankees of Nova Scotia: A Marginal Colony during the Revolutionary Years*. New York: Columbia Univ. Press, 1937.

Brown, John Crosby. *A Hundred Years of Merchant Banking: A History of Brown Brothers and Company, Brown, Shipley & Company and the Allied Firms*. New York: Brown, Shipley, 1909.

Buck, Norman Sydney. *The Development of the Organization of Anglo-American Trade, 1800–1850*. New Haven: Yale Univ. Press, 1925.

Buckley, William E. *A New England Pattern: The History of Manchester, Connecticut*. Clinton, Conn.: Pequot Press, 1979.

Bullock, Steven C. *Revolutionary Brotherhood: Freemasonry and the Transformation of the American Social Order, 1790–1840*. Chapel Hill, N.C., and London: Univ. of North Carolina Press, published for the Institute of Early American History and Culture, Williamsburg, Va., 1996.

Bumsted, J. M.. *Henry Alline, 1748–1784*. Canadian Biographical Studies. Toronto: Univ. of Toronto Press, 1971.

Burdge, Franklyn. "A Notice of John Haring." New York: privately printed, 1878.

Bushman, Richard L. *The Refinement of America: Persons, Houses, Cities*. 2d ed. New York: Vintage Books, Random House, 1993.

———. *From Puritan to Yankee: Character and Social Order in Connecticut, 1690–1765*. Cambridge, Mass.: Harvard Univ. Press, 1967.

Caulkins, Francis Manwaring. *History of New London*. New London, Conn.: privately published, 1852.

Chandler, Alfred D., Jr. *The Visible Hand: The Managerial Revolution in American Business*. Cambridge, Mass., and London: Harvard Univ. Press, Belknap Press, 1977.

Chase, Frederick. *A History of Dartmouth College and The Town of Hanover, New Hampshire*. Edited by John K. Lord. 2 vols. Cambridge, Mass.: John Wilson and Son, 1892.

Chapman, George T. *Sketches of the Alumni of Dartmouth College*. Cambridge, Mass.: Riverside Press, 1867.

Child, Hamilton, comp. and ed., *Gazetteer of Grafton County, New Hampshire, 1709–1886*. Syracuse, N.Y., 1886.

Clarke, Ernest. *The Siege of Fort Cumberland 1776: An Episode in the American Revolution*. Montreal: McGill–Queen's Univ. Press, 1995.

Cole, David. *History of Rockland County, New York, with Biographical Sketches of Its Prominent Men*. New York: J. B. Beers, 1884.

———. *History of the Reformed Church in Tappan, N.Y.* New York: Stettiner, Lambert, 1894.

Cole, J. R. *History of Tolland County*. 2 vols. New York: W. W. Preson, 1888.

Collier, Christopher, with Bonnie B. Collier. *The Connecticut Scholar: The Literature of Connecticut History*. Middletown, Conn.: Wesleyan Univ. Press, 1983.

Conover, George S. *Kanadesaga and Geneva*. Geneva, N.Y.: *Geneva Courier*, 1879.

Conrad, Margaret, ed. *The Planted Well: New England Planters in Maritime Canada*. Fredericton, N.B.: Acadiensis Press, 1988.

———. *Intimate Relations: Family and Community in Planter Nova Scotia, 1759–1800*. Fredericton, N.B.: Acadiensis Press, 1995.

Countryman, Edward. *A People in Revolution: The American Revolution and Political Society in New York, 1760–1790*. New York: W. W. Norton, 1981.

Crofut, Florence S. Marcy. *Guide to the History and the Historic Sites of Connecticut*. 2 vols. New Haven: Yale Univ. Press, 1937.

Cronon, William, *Change in the Land: Indians, Colonists, and the Ecology of New England*. New York: Hill and Wang, 1983.

Cuthbertson, Brian C. *The Loyalist Governor: Biography of Sir John Wentworth*. Halifax, N.S.: Peteric Press, 1983.

Daniels, Bruce C., ed. *Power and Status: Office Holding in Colonial America*. Middletown, Conn.: Wesleyan Univ. Press, 1986.

———. *The Fragmentation of New England: Comparative Perspectives on Economic, Political and Social Divisions in the Eighteenth Century*. Westport, Conn.: Greenwood Press, 1988.

Davenport, Milla. *The Book of Costume*. New York: Crown Publishers, 1948.

Demott, Bobby J. *Freemasonry in American Culture and Society*. Lanham, Md.: Univ. Press of America, 1986.

Dexter, Franklin Bowditch. *Biographical Sketches of the Graduates of Yale College*. Vol. 1. New York: Henry Holt, 1896.

Duncanson, John V. *Falmouth: A New England Township in Nova Scotia, 1760–1865*. Windsor, Ont., 1965.

Durie, Howard J. *The Kakiat Patent in Bergen County New Jersey*. Pearl River, N.J.: privately printed, 1976.

Durrenberger, Joseph Austin., *Turnpikes: A Study of the Toll Road Movement in the Middle Atlantic States and Maryland.* Valdosta, Ga.: 1931.

Dwight, Timothy. *Travels in New England and New York.* Edited by Barbara Miller Solomon, with Patricia M. King. 4 vols. Cambridge, Mass.: Harvard Univ. Press, Belknap Press, 1969.

Earle, Alice Morse. *Home Life in Colonial Days.* 1898. Reprint, Stockbridge, Mass.: Berkshire House Publishers, 1993.

———. *Child Life in Colonial Days.* 1899. Reprint, Stockbridge, Mass.: Berkshire House Publishers, 1995.

Eaton, Arthur Hamilton Wentworth. *History of Kings County, Nova Scotia, Heart of the Acadian Land.* Salem, Mass.: Salem Press, 1920.

———. *The Church in Nova Scotia.* New York, Thomas Whittaker, 1891.

Edsall, Samuel H. *Historical Sketches and Guide to Trinity Church, Geneva, New York.* 1947. Reprint, Canandaigua, N.Y.: W. F. Humphrey Press, 1983.

Ellis, David M., James A. Frost, Harold C. Syrett, and Harry J. Carman. *A Short History of New York State.* Ithaca, N.Y.: Cornell Univ. Press, for The New York State Historical Association, 1957.

Fabend, Firth Haring. *A Dutch Family in the Middle Colonies, 1660–1800.* New Brunswick, N.J.: Rutgers Univ. Press, 1991.

Fairbisy, John Dewar. "Privateering and Piracy: The Effects of New England Raiding upon Nova Scotia during the American Revolution, 1775–1783." Master's thesis, Univ. of Massachusetts, 1972.

Farmer, John, "Sketches of Graduates of Dartmouth College." Dartmouth College Library. Typescript.

Farnham, Thomas J. *Fairfield: The Biography of a Community, 1639–1989* Fairfield, Conn.: Fairfield Historical Society, 1988.

Fischer, David Hackett. *Albion's Seed: Four British Folkways in America.* New York: Oxford Univ. Press, 1989.

Fisher, George. *The Struggle for American Independence.* 2 vols. Philadelphia, 1908.

Fleming, David. *A History of the Town of Niagara-on-the-Lake (1791–1970).* [Ottawa]: National Historic Sites Service, 1971. Typescript.

Flick, Alexander C. *History of the State of New York.* Vols. 3–4. New York: Columbia Univ. Press, 1933.

Foster, Augustus John. *Jeffersonian America: Notes on the United States of America Collected in the Years 1805–6–7 and 11–12 by Sir Augustus John Fraser Bart.* Edited by Richard Beale Davis. San Marino, Calf.: Huntington Library, 1954.

Fox, Dixon Ryan. *Yankees and Yorkers.* New York: Univ. Press, 1940.

Gallay, Alan, ed. *Colonial Wars of North America, 1512–1763: An Encyclopedia*. New York and London: Garland, 1996.

Gaustad, Edwin S. *The Great Awakening in New England*. New York: Harper, 1957.

*General Catalog, Dartmouth College and Related Schools*. Hanover, N.H.: Dartmouth College, 1940.

Gerlach, Don R. *Proud Patriot: Philip Schuyler and the War of Independence, 1775–1783*. Syracuse, N.Y.: Syracuse Univ. Press, 1987.

Grady, Frank. *James Boswell, The Later Years 1769–1795*. New York: McGraw Hill, 1984.

Greene, Evarts B., and Virginia D. Harrington. *American Population before the Federal Census of 1790*. New York, 1932.

Grobel, Kenneth. *History of the First Church of Stafford, Connecticut, known as "The Stafford Street Congregational Church": From its Birth 1723 to its Death 1892*. Stafford Springs, Conn.: 1942.

Grossbart, Stephen Reed. "The Revolutionary Transition: Politics, Religion and Economy in Eastern Connecticut, 1765–1800." Ph.D. diss., Univ. of Michigan, 1989.

Hall, Henry. *The History of Auburn*. Auburn, N.Y.: Dennis Bro's., 1869.

Hamilton, Alexander. *The Law Practice of Alexander Hamilton: Documents and Commentary*. Edited by Julius Goebel, Jr., and Joseph H. Smith. 4 vols. New York: Columbia Univ. Press, William Nelson Cromwell Foundation, 1980.

Hammond, Charles. *The History of Union Connecticut*. New Haven: Price, Lee, and Adkins, 1895.

Hatch, Horace McK. *The New England Society in the City of New York*. New York: privately printed, 1957.

Hatch, Nathan O. *The Democratization of American Religion*. New Haven: Yale Univ. Press, 1989.

Hayner, Carter Stone. "The Reaction of Yale to the Great Awakening, 1740–1766." Ph.D. diss., Univ. of Texas, 1977.

Heimert, Alan and Andrew Delbanco, eds. *The Puritans in America: A Narrative Anthology*. Cambridge, Mass.: Harvard Univ. Press, 1985.

Henretta, James, et al., eds. *The Transformation of Early American History: Society, Authority, Ideology*. New York: Alfred A. Knopf, 1991.

Hicks, Lewis W. *Mr. Ralph Wheelock, Puritan*. Hartford: Hartford Press, 1899.

*Historical Guide to the City of New York*. Tercentenary ed. New York, n.d.

*Historical Statistics of the United States, Colonial Times to 1957*. Washington, D.C.: United States Government Printing Office, 1960.

Hodgson, Alice Doan. *Thanks to the Past: The Story of Orford, N.H.* Orford, N.H.: Historical Fact Publications, 1965. Reprint, 1992.

Holcomb, Kenneth Dunshee. *As You Pass By.* New York: Hastings House, 1952.

Hotchkin, James H. *A History of the Purchase and Settlement of Western New York and of the Rise, Progress and Present State of the Presbyterian Church.* New York: M. W. Dodd, Brick Church Chapel, 1848.

Huey, Lois M., and Bonnie Plis. *Molly Brant, A Legacy of Her Own.* Youngstown, N.Y.: Old Fort Niagara Associatian, 1997.

Hughes, Arthur H., and Morse S. Allen. *Connecticut Place Names.* Hartford: Connecticut Historical Society, 1976.

Hunt, Freeman. *Lives of American Merchants.* New York: Office of Hunts' *Merchants Magazine*, 1856.

Hurd, D. Hamilton. *History of Fairfield County, Connecticut, with Illustrations and Biographical Sketches of its Prominent Men and Pioneers.* Philadelphia: J. W. Lewis, 1881.

Hyde, Francis E. *Liverpool and the Mersey: An Economic History of a Port 1700–1970.* Newton Abbot: David and Charles, 1971.

Irwin, Will, Earl Chapin May, and Joseph Hotchkiss. *A History of the Union League Club of New York City.* New York: Dodd, Mead, 1952.

James, Henry. *Washington Square.* New York: Harper and Brothers, 1880. [New York] Library of America, 1985.

Jones, Alice Hanson. *Wealth of a Nation to Be: The American Colonies on the Eve of the Revolution.* New York: Columbia Univ. Press, 1980.

Kelsey, Isabel Thompson. *Joseph Brant 1743–1807: Man of Two Worlds.* Syracuse, N.Y.: Syracuse Univ. Press, 1994.

Kerr, Wilfred Brenton. *Bermuda and the American Revolution: 1760–1783.* Princeton, N.J.: Princeton Univ. Press, 1936.

Ketchum, Richard M. *Saratoga: Turning Point of America's Revolutionary War.* New York: Henry Holt, 1997.

Kornhauser, Elizabeth Mankin, with Richard L. Bushman, Stephen H. Kornhauser, and Aileen Rubeiro. *Ralph Earl: The Face of the Young Republic.* Hartford: Wadsworth Atheneum, 1991.

Lambert, Frank. *"Pedlar in Divinity": George Whitefield and the Trans-atlantic Revivals, 1737–1770.* Princeton, N.J.: Princeton Univ. Press, 1994.

Leiby, Adrian C. *The United Churches of Hackensack and Schraalenburgh New Jersey, 1686–1822.* River Edge, N.J.: Bergen County Historical Society, 1976.

Lesser, Gloria. "Iconography of Joseph Brant." Master's thesis, Concordia Univ., Quebec, Canada, 1983.

Lincoln, William. *History of Worcester, Massachusetts*. Worcester, Mass.: Moses D. Phillips, 1837.

Lindsley, James Elliott. *This Planted Vine: A Narrative History of the Episcopal Diocese of New York*. New York: Harper and Row, 1984.

Lomask, Milton. *Aaron Burr: The Years from Princeton to Vice-President 1756–1805*. New York: Farrar, Straus, and Giroux, 1979.

London Regional Art & Historical Museums. Exhibition Catalogue, "Elizabeth Simcoe: The Canadian Years, 1791–1796." London, Ont.: London Regional Art and Historical Museums, 1993.

Lowitt, Richard. *A Merchant Prince of the Nineteenth Century: William E. Dodge*. New York: Columbia Univ. Press, 1954.

Ludwig, John W. *Alphabet of Greatness: Manhattan's Street Names* (1961). NYPL. Typescript.

Main, Jackson T. *Society and Economy in Colonial Connecticut*. Princeton, N.J.: Princeton Univ. Press, 1985.

McCallum, James Dow. *Eleazer Wheelock, Founder of Dartmouth College*. Hanover, N.H.: Dartmouth College Publications, 1939.

McCallum, Kent. *Old Sturbridge Village*. New York: Harry N. Abrams, 1996.

McCreath, Peter L., and John G. Leete. *History of Early Nova Scotia*. 3d ed. Tantallon, N.S.: Four East Publications, 1990.

McMahon, Reginald. *Ramapo: Indian Trading Post to State College*. Mahwah, N.J.: Ramapo College of New Jersey, 1977.

Meginnes, J. F. *Biographical Annals of Deceased Residents of the West Branch Valley of the Susquehanna from the Earliest Times to the Present*. Williamsport, Pa.: Gazette and Bulletin Printing House, 1889.

Miller, Edwin Haviland. *Salem is My Dwelling Place: A Life of Nathaniel Hawthorne*. Iowa City, Iowa: Univ. of Iowa Press, 1991.

Milne, George. *Lebanon, Three Centuries in a Connecticut Hilltop Town*. Lebanon, Conn.: Lebanon Historical Society, 1986.

Mitchell, Isabel S. *Roads and Road-Making in Colonial Connecticut*. New Haven: Tercentenary Commission of the State of Connecticut, Yale Univ. Press, 1934.

Morgan, Edmund S. *The Puritan Family*. New York: Harper and Row, 1966.

Nickerson, Hoffman. *The Turning Point of the Revolution, or Burgoyne in America*. Boston: Houghton Mifflin, 1928.

Norton, John N. *Pioneer Missionaries or the Lives of Phelps and Nash*. New York: General Protestant Episcopal & School Union and Church Book Society, 1859.

Norton, Mary Beth. *Liberty's Daughters: The Revolutionary Experience of American Women, 1750–1800*. Boston: Little, Brown, 1980.

*One Hundredth Anniversary of the Organization of the First Church of Christ in Manchester, Connecticut* . . . Hartford: Lockwood and Brainard, 1880.

Pappas, George S. *To the Point: The United States Military Academy, 1802–1902.* Westport, Conn.: Praeger, 1993.

Park, Roswell. *A Sketch of the History and Topography of West Point and the U.S. Military Academy.* Philadelphia, 1840.

Paulin, Charles O. *Atlas of the Historical Geography of the United States.* Washington, D.C.: Carnegie Institution of Washington, American Geographical Society, 1932.

Pease, John C., and John M. Niles. *Gazette of Connecticut and Rhode Island.* Hartford, Conn., 1819.

Peters, [Samuel Andrews]. *General History of Connecticut, by a Gentleman of the Province.* London, 1781. New Haven, 1829.

Phelps Stokes, I. N. *The Iconography of Manhattan Island, 1398–1909.* 6 vols. New York: Robert H. Dodd, 1918–1928.

Pierson, George Wilson. *Tocqueville and Beaumont in America.* New York: Oxford Univ. Press, 1938.

Plunz, Richard. *A History of Housing in New York City.* New York: Columbia Univ. Press, 1990.

Poole, Braithwaite. *Commerce of Liverpool.* London and Liverpool, 1854.

Poole, Edmund Duval. *Annals of Yarmouth & Barrington: Nova Scotia in the Revolutionary War.* Yarmouth, N.S., 1899.

Porter, Glenn, and Harold C. Livesay. *Merchants and Manufacturers: Studies in the Changing Structure of Nineteenth-Century Marketing.* Baltimore, Md.: Johns Hopkins Univ. Press, 1971.

Purcell, Richard J. *Connecticut in Transition 1775–1818.* 1918. Reprint, Middletown, Conn.: Wesleyan Univ. Press, 1963.

Quinn, Arthur. *A New World: An Epic of Colonial America from the Founding of Jamestown to the Fall of Quebec.* New York: Berkley Books, 1995.

Rawlyk, George A. *Nova Scotia's Massachusetts: A Study of Massachusetts–Nova Scotia Relations, 1630 to 1784.* Montreal: McGill-Queen's Univ. Press, 1973.

Read, D. B. *The Life and Times of Gen. John Graves Simcoe.* Toronto: George Virtue, 1890.

*Regulations of the United States Military Academy at West Point.* New York, 1823.

Richardson, Leon Burr. *History of Dartmouth College.* Hanover, N.H.: Dartmouth College Publications, 1932.

Riddell, William Renwick. *The Life of John Graves Simcoe, First Lieutenant-Governor of the Province of Upper Canada, 1792–96.* Toronto: McClelland and Steward, 1926.

Robertson, J. R. *The History of Freemasonry in Upper Canada*. 2 vols. Toronto: 1916.

Roper, Laura Woods. *FLO: A Biography of Frederick Law Olmsted*. Baltimore, Md.: Johns Hopkins Univ. Press, 1973.

Rosenwaike, Ira. *Population History of New York City*. Syracuse, N.Y.: Syracuse Univ. Press, 1972.

Sabine, Lorenzo. *Biographical Sketches of Loyalists of the American Revolution*. Boston, 1864. Reprint, Baltimore, Md.: Genealogical Publishing Company, 1979.

Saladino, Gaspare John. "The Economic Revolution in Late-Eighteenth-Century Connecticut." Ph.D. diss., Univ. of Wisconsin, 1964.

Seccombe, John. *A Sermon Preached in Halifax, July 3, 1770*. Halifax, N.S.: A. Henry, 1770.

Selesky, Harold E. *War and Society in Colonial Connecticut*. New Haven: Yale Univ. Press, 1990.

Shammas, Carole, Marylyn Salmon, and Michel Danin. *Inheritance in America from Colonial Times to the Present*. New Brunswick, N.J.: Rutgers Univ. Press, 1987.

Shipton, Clifford K. *Biographical Sketches of Those who Attended Harvard College in the Classes 1751–1755* (*Sibley's Harvard Graduates*). Boston: Massachusetts Historical Society, 1965.

Sibun, John. *Our Town's Heritage, 1708–1958, Hebron, Connecticut*. Hebron, Conn.: Douglas Library of Hebron, 1958. Reprint, 1992.

Smith, Justin H. *Our Struggle for the Fourteenth Colony: Canada and the American Revolution*. 2 vols. New York: G. P. Putnam's Sons, 1907.

Smith, William, Jr. *Historical Memoirs from 16 March 1763 to 25 July 1778*. Edited by William H. W. Sabine. New York: Arno Press, 1969.

Snyder, Charles M., ed. *Red and White on the New York Frontier: A Struggle for Survival: Insights from the Papers of Erastus Granger, Indian Agent, 1807–1819*. Harrison, N.Y.: Harbor Hill Books, 1978.

Spann, Edward K. *The New Metropolis: New York City 1840–1857*. New York: Columbia Univ. Press, 1981.

Stafford Library Association. *The History of the Town of Stafford*. Stafford, Conn.: Stafford Library Association, 1935.

Stark, Bruce Purinton. "Lebanon, Connecticut: A Study of Society and Politics in the Eighteenth Century," Ph.D. diss., Univ. of Connecticut. 1970.

Steblecki, Edith J. *Paul Revere and Freemasonry*. [Boston]: Paul Revere Memorial Association, 1985.

Stewart, Gordon, and George A. Rawlyk. *A People Highly Favored of God: The Nova Scotia Yankees and the American Revolution*. Hamden, Conn.: Archon Press, 1972.

Stiles, Henry R. *The History and Genealogies of Ancient Windsor*. 2 vols. Hartford: Case, Lockwood and Brainard, 1892.

Stilgoe, John R. *Common Landscape of America, 1580 to 1845*. New Haven: Yale Univ. Press, 1982.

Stone, William E. *Life of Joseph Brant-Thayanendegea*. 2 vols. New York: George Dearborn, 1838.

Taylor, Robert J. *Colonial Connecticut: A History*. Millwood, N.Y.: KTO Press, 1979.

Tilden, William S. *History of the Town of Medfield, Massachusetts, 1650–1886*. Boston: George H. Ellis, 1887.

Toler, Henry Pennington. *The Harlem Register: A Genealogy of the 23 Original Patentees of the Town of New Harlem, New York*. New York: New Harlem Press, 1903.

Trumbull, Benjamin. *A Complete History of Connecticut, Civil and Ecclesiastical, from the Emigration of its First Planters from England in the year 1650 and to the close of the Indian Wars*. 2 vols. New Haven: Maltby, Goldsmith, and Samuel Wadsworth [1797], 1818.

Trumbull, Hammond, ed. *Hartford County Connecticut, The Memorial History of Connecticut, 1633–1884*. 2 vols. Boston: Edward L. Osgood, 1886.

Trumbull, James Russell. *History of Northampton from Its Settlement in 1654*. Northampton, 1898.

Tucker, Louis Leonard. *Connecticut's Seminary of Sedition: Yale College*. Chester, Conn.: Pequot Press, A Publication of the American Revolution Bicentennial Commission of Connecticut, 1974.

Ulrich, Laurel Thatcher. *A Midwife's Tale: The Life of Martha Ballard, Based on Her Diary, 1785–1812*. New York: Vintage Books, 1991.

———. *Good Lives: Image and Reality in the Lives of Women in Northern New England 1650–1750*. New York: Vintage Books, 1991.

Van Dusen, Albert E. *Connecticut*. New York: Random House, 1961.

Warfle, Richard T. *Connecticut's Western Colony: The Susquehannah Company* Hartford: American Revolution Bicentennial Commission of Connecticut, 1979.

Weaver, Glenn. *Jonathan Trumbull: Connecticut's Merchant Magistrate (1710–1785)*. Hartford: Connecticut Historical Society, 1956.

Weld, Isaac. *Travels through the States of North America and the Province of Upper and Lower Canada, 1795, 1796, 1797*. 2 vols. London, 1800.

Wharton, Edith. *Looking Backward*. New York: Appleton-Century, 1934.

White, Richard. *The Middle Ground: Indians, Empires and Republics in the Great Lakes Region, 1690–1815.* New York: Cambridge Univ. Press, 1991.

Whitney, Peter. *The History of the County of Worcester in the Commonwealth of Massachusetts.* 1793. Reprint, Worcester: Isaiah Thomas Books and Prints, 1993.

Wilkinson, Henry C. *Bermuda in the Old Empire: A History of the Island from the Dissolution of the Somers Island Company until the End of the American Revolutionary War, 1684–1784.* London: Oxford Univ. Press, 1950.

Willard, Sidney. *Memories of Youth and Manhood.* 2 vols. Cambridge, Mass.: John Bartlett, 1853.

Wilner, Merton M. *Niagara Frontier: A Narrative and Documentary History.* Vol 1. Chicago: S. J. Clarke, 1931.

Withycombe, D. G. *The Oxford Dictionary of English Christian Names.* 2d ed. Oxford: Clarendon Press, 1959.

Wood, Frederic J. *The Turnpikes of New England.* Boston: Marshall Jones, 1911.

Wrong, George M. *Canada and the American Revolution: The Description of the First British Empire.* New York: Macmillan, 1935.

## Articles

Adamson, Christopher. "God's Continent Divided: Politics and Religion in Upper Canada and the Northern and Western United States, 1775–1841." *Comparative Studies in Society and History* 36, no. 3 (1994): 417–46.

Beard, Timothy Field, and Henry B. Hoff. "The Roosevelt Family in America: A Genealogy." *Theodore Roosevelt Society Journal* 16, no. 1 (1990).

Bridenbaugh, Carl. "Baths and Watering Places of Colonial America." *William and Mary Quarterly.* 3d ser., 3, no. 2 (1946): 151–81.

Bushman, Richard L. "Portraiture and Society in Late-Eighteenth-Century Connecticut." In *Ralph Earl: The Face of the Young Republic*, by Elizabeth Mankin Kornhauser, 69–82. Hartford: Wadsworth Atheneum, 1991.

Clark, Christopher Gleason. "The English Ancestry of Joseph Clark (1623–1680) of Dedham and Medfield, Massachusetts." *Register* 152 (1998): 3–23.

———. "Mr. Wheelock's Cure." *Register* 152 (1988): 311–12.

Cohen, Charles L. "The Post-Puritan Paradigm of Early American Religious History." *William and Mary Quarterly*, 3d ser., 54, no. 4 (1997): 695–722.

Coombs, Zelotes W. "Early Blast Furnace Operations in Worcester County." *The Worcester Historical Society Publications*, new ser., 2, no. 3, (1938): 138–52.

Cutler, U. Waldo. "Trail and Pike." *Worcester Historical Society Publications*, new ser., 1, no. 2 (1929): 21–34.

Daniels, Bruce C., "The Political Structure of Local Government in Colonial Connecticut." In *Town and Country: Essays on the Structure of Local Government in the American Colonies*, edited by Bruce C. Daniels, 44–71. Middletown, Conn.: Wesleyan Univ. Press, 1978.

Harris, Wendy. "Historic Background Study of Block 74W." Prepared for the Office of Economic Development [New York City], 10 October 1980.

Hyde, Myrtle Stevens. "The English Origins of William[1] Phelps of Dorchester, Mass., and Windsor, Conn., with Notes on His Marriages." *TAG* 65, no. 3 (1990): 161–66.

Johnson, Leo A. "Land Policy, Population Growth and Social Structure in the Home District. 1793-1851." In *Historical Essays on Upper Canada*, edited by J. K. Johnson, 32–57. Toronto: McClelland and Stewart, 1975.

Johnston, Charles M. "An Outline of Early Settlement in the Grand River Valley." In *Historical Essays on Upper Canada*, edited by J. K. Johnson, 1–31. Toronto: McClelland and Stewart, 1975.

Judd, Peter Haring. "An Interrupted Journey." *Seaport* 31, no. 2 (fall 1997): 36–39.

Krout, John Allen, and Dixon Ryan Fox. "The Completion of Independence." In *A History of American Life*, edited by Arthur M. Schlesinger, Sr., and Dixon Ryan Fox, 409–516. Abridged ed. New York: Scribners, 1996.

Maltby, Dorothy (Maltby) Verrill. "Maltby–Maltbie–Molby," *Register* 111 (1957): 291–99.

Mealing, S. R. "The Enthusiasm of John Graves Simcoe." In *Historical Essays on Upper Canada*, edited by J. K Johnson, 302–16. Toronto: McClelland and Stewart, 1975.

New York City Landmarks Preservation Commission. "Proposed Brooklyn Bridge Southeast LEA, Showing Construction Dates." 1 May 1963.

Pessen, Edward. "The Business Elite of Ante-bellum New York City: Diversity, Continuity, Standing." In *Business Enterprises in Early New York*, edited by Joseph R. Frese, S. J., and Jacob Judd, 163–70. Tarrytown, N.Y.: Sleepy Hollow Press, 1977.

Phipps, Frances, ed. "Joshua Hempsted's Journey to Maryland." Part 2. *Connecticut Antiquarian* (1971).

Pynchon, W. H. C. "Iron Mining in Connecticut." *Connecticut Magazine* 5 (1899): 20–26, 232–38, 277–85.

Stelter, John H. "Rev. Davenport Phelps—Lawyer, Freemason, Missionary." *Transactions of The American Lodge of Research: Free and Accepted Masons* 12, no. 1 (1972): 51–74.

United States Military Academy, Board of Visitors. "Of Feed." *Annual Report* 1820. Transcript.

Wallace, W. Stewart. "The First Journalists in Canada." *Canadian Historical Review* 26 (1945): 372–81.

Warren, H. C. "Thoroughfares in the Early Republic Controlled by Corporations." *Connecticut Magazine* 5 (1904): 721–29.

Williams, David M. "Bulk Trade and the Development of the Port of Liverpool in the First Half of the Nineteenth Century." In *Liverpool Shipping, Trade, and Industry: Essays on the Maritime History of Merseyside 1780–1860*, edited by Valerie Burton, 8–24. Liverpool: National Museums and Galleries on Merseyside, 1989.

Zabriskie, George Olin. "Daniel De Clark (De Klerck) of Tappan and His Descendants." *Record* 96 (1965): 194–217.0

# INDEX


A

Abbott, Elizabeth, 385
Acadia. *See* Nova Scotia
Acadians, 74, 77, 78, 79, 80
Ackerley, Helen (Phelps), 264 n. 65, 330
Ackerman, Herbert S., 352
Adams, John, 195, 196, 197–98, 394
Adams, Joseph, 337
Adams, Rebecca (Wheelock) (Fisher), 337
Adgate, Sarah, 337
Albany, New York, 37–38, 143, 165, 175, 224, 269, 271 n. 80, 320, 354, 371, 381, 382, 383, 384, 385, 387
*Albany* Man of War, 71, 108, 109 n. 85, 111, 112
Albion, Robert Greenhalgh, 225, 228, 230, 244
Albury, Hertfordshire, England, 398
Alden, Eliab, 212, 221
Alden, Joseph, 213
Allen, Ethan, 123
Allen, Ann, 337
Allen, Emma, 275
Allen, Maria Malleville (Wheelock), 350
Allen, William, 350
Allen's Hill, New York, 182
Allin, Mathew, 305
Alline, Henry, 101–3, 113; portrait, 102
Allison, Joseph, 104 n. 74
Allston, Massachusetts, 326
Alston, Theodosia (Burr), 164–65
Alvord, Abigail (Phelps), 390, 391, 397
Alvord, John, 390
Amherst, Lord Jeffrey, 39
Ancaster, Upper Canada, 156, 156 n. 100
Anderson, Peris, 82
André, John, 271, 376, 379
Angelica, Allegany County, New York, 182
Anglican Church: former Congregational members of, xiii, 20, 41, 50, 86, 86 n. 38; growth after Great Awakening, 44, 45 n. 75; proportion of town residents in, 45 n. 74; in Nova Scotia, 83, 85, 106; support of pastors, 84, 89; in Upper Canada, xvii, 142, 146–47, 161. *See also* Protestant Episcopal Church
Anglican–Congregational conflict, 20, 41, 50, 86, 86 n. 38
Annapolis Valley, 72, 106
Apthorp, New Hampshire, 67, 68
Arkwright, Richard, 247
Arnold, Benedict, 125
Atiatoharongwen, 126, 127
Atwater, Jeremiah, 201
Auburn, New York, 179, 182
Aurelius, New York, 179, 182, 380, 381
Austin, Abigail (Phelps), 393
Austin, Daniel, 393
Austin, Elijah, 201, 396
Austin, Esther (Phelps), 396
Avery, Dorothy (Denison) (Rogers) (Copp), 407
Avery, Hannah, 404
Avery, Jonathan, 407
Avery, Mary, 403
Avryansen, Antje, 360
Avryansen, Aury, 360
Avryansen, Elizabeth (—), 360
Ayres, Eliza. *See* Phelps, Eliza (Ayres)
Ayres, Elizabeth (Pancoast), 250, 251 n. 30, 326
Ayres, Emma, 252
Ayres, Henry W., 251 n. 30, 291
Ayres, John, 250, 251 n. 30, 326
Ayres, Samuel, 251 n. 30
Ayres, Sarah, 251 n. 30

B

Baan. *See* De Baan
Bagley [Bailey], Elizabeth, 406
Bailey, Jacob, 98, 113

Ball, Edward, 82
Banham, Norfolk, England, 334, 335
banking, 191, 207, 246
Banks, Joseph, 146, 146n. 76
Baptist Church, 102, 167, 197
Barbadoes, Bergen County, New Jersey, 378
Barber, Mary (Phelps), 304
Barber, Thomas, 304
Barbur [Barber], Temperance, 308
Barbut, David, 68
Barnard, Ruth, 394
Barnum, David, 82
Barrington, Rhode Island, 403
Bartholmew, Timothy, 68
Bartholomew, __, 308
Bartholomew, Abigail (Phelps), 307, 308
Bartholomew, Tomo., 68
Bartlett, John, 82
Bartlett, Josiah, 222
Bass, Consider, 397
Bass, Eleanor (Phelps), 397
Batavia, New York, 174, 182
Bath, New Hampshire, 48, 312
Bayard, William, 277n. 99
Bay of Fundy, 72, 73, 78, 79
Beach, Moses Yale, 263
Beardsley, Mary Eliza Henderson, 331
Beaumont, Gustave de, 240, 240n. 5
Beckwith, John, 82
Beckwith, Samuel, 91n. 48
Bedel, Timothy, 122, 123, 133
Bedford, Brooklyn, 355
Beekman, Mary, 123n. 12
Beers, Abigail (Phelps), 397
Beers, Nathan, 397
Belcher, Jonathan, 408
Bell, William, 68
Belmont, August, 263
Bennett, Joseph, 85, 86, 314, 411
Bennington, Vermont, xvi, 133, 318
Bentlee, David, 82
Bergen County, New Jersey, 270, 358, 377, 378
Bermuda, 40–41, 311, 341
Bertholf, Maria, 357–58
Best, John, 105n. 78
Best, William, 105, 105n. 78, 107
Bible, King James Version, 20
Bierne, Jennie I., 274, 332
Bigalow, Isaac, 91n. 48
Bill, Ebeneezer, 82
Billerica, Massachusetts, 345
Billings, Ebenezer, 404
Billings, Elkanah, 68
Billings, Phebe (Denison), 404
Bingham, Jabez, 340
Bingham, Joseph, Jr., 339
Bingham, Mary (Wheelock), 340
Bingham, Ralph, 339
Bingham, Sarah (Wheelock), 339
birthing pattern, in New England, 34
Bishop's Stortford, Hertfordshire, England, 398, 399, 400, 401, 402, 403
Bissell, Hannah, 306, 308
Blanch, Isaac, 359
Blauvelt, Abraham, 357, 358
Blauvelt, Catharine, 359, 360
Blauvelt, Catherine, 366
Blauvelt, David B., 359
Blauvelt, Elizabeth, 357
Blauvelt, Gerrit, 354
Blauvelt, Grietje (More), 357, 358
Blauvelt, Hubert Gerritsen, 354
Blauvelt, Jacob, 356, 357
Blauvelt, Klaatjie (—), 359
Blauvelt, Margaret (Haring), 359
Blauvelt, Margretsje, 354
Blauvelt, Maria (De Clark), 359
Blauvelt, Marretje, 354
Blauvelt, Pieterje (Haring), 356, 357
Blauvelt, Richard, 359, 378
Blauvelt, Sarah, 357
Blauveltville, Rockland County, New York, 371
Bliss, John, 44
Blodgett, Paul, 206
Bloomfield, New York, 176

Boat Run, Ohio, 350
Bogaert, Catherine (Elias), 361
Bogaert, Hendrick, 361
Bogaert, Maria (Roome), 370
Bogaert, Peter, 370
Bogart, Cornelius, 365
Bogart, Mary, 272n. 87, 274, 330, 386
Bogert, Anne, 370
Bogert, Cornelia (Everts), 355
Bogert, Elizabeth, 360, 362, 363–64, 365, 372
Bogert, Frytje, 379
Bogert, Grietje, 355, 356, 357–58, 359
Bogert, Jan Louwe, 355
Bogert, Margaret (Conselyea), 353, 360, 362
Bogert, Maria (Bertholf), 357–58
Bogert, Nicholas, 353, 360, 362
Bogert [Bongaert, Boomgaert], Jan Cornelisz, 357–58
Bohea Tea, 40, 149
Boot, ___, 68
Bordman, J., 82
Borodell, Ann, 401, 402
Borodell, John, 401
Boston, County Lincoln, England, 401, 402, 404
Boston, Massachusetts, xi, 98, 104, 272, 273, 311, 329, 401, 402, 404; travel to, 12, 37–38, 116, 196, 197, 213–14
Boswell, James, 159
Bowdoin College, 350
Brace, Consider, 397
Brace, Eleanor (Phelps), 395, 397
Brainerd, David, 25, 25n. 17, 32
Brainerd, John, 32
Braintree, Massachusetts, 337
Brant, Elizabeth, 148
Brant, Joseph, 34, 126, 131, 148, 152, 157–65, 168, 320; support of Davenport Phelps's ordination, xvii, 161–64, 169; portrait, 158; opponents of, 172, 173
Brant, Molly, 157n. 106
Brantford, Ontario, 160
Brant's Ford, Upper Canada, 160
Braston, Samuel, 82
Brat, Jacob, 361
Brebner, J. Bartlett, 99
Bridgeport, Connecticut, 256
Brigham, Lucinda (Tiffany), 156n. 100
Brimfield, Massachusetts, 311
Bringe, Isaac, 68
Brinkerhoff, Catharine (Herring), 363, 364
Brinkerhoff, Elizabeth (Ryder), 364
Brinkerhoff, George, 363, 364
Brinkerhoff, Theunis, 364
Brinsmaid, Mary, 340, 341–42, 343, 347
Bristol, England, 247
Britain. *See* Great Britain
broker, 246
Brooke, Anna M., 273n. 89, 291n. 127, 328, 329
Brooke, Harriet Augusta (Phelps), 251, 255, 273, 273n. 90, 274, 290, 291, 291n. 127, 328, 329
Brooke, Thomas R., 291n. 127
Brooke, Thomas Reese, 273, 273n. 90, 328, 329
Brooke, Thomas Reese [Jr.], 273, 329
Brower, Hester, 379
Brown, ___, estate confiscated, 113
Brown, James, Jr., 403
Brown, Margaret (Denison), 403
Brown, Sophia, 331
Brown, William, 198n. 38, 394
Brunswick, Maine, 349
Buffalo, New York, 281, 284n. 115
Buffalo Creek, New York, 171, 172
Bullard, Experience, 336
Bullen, Miriam, 336
Burbridge, John, 105n. 77, 106, 107
Burdge, Franklyn, 352, 372
Burgoyne, General John, 131–32, 133n. 38
Burlington, Vermont, 351
Burnham, Abigail, 391

Burnham, Rose, 351
Burr, Aaron, 164–65
Burr, Esther (Edwards), 31n. 34, 44n. 71
Burr, Theodosia, 164–65
Bushman, Richard L., 25

## C

Cady, Jesse, 208, 209
Cady family, 220
Cambridge, England, 334
Cambridge [Newtowne], Massachusetts, 398, 399, 400
Camonachet, 402
Campbell, Christian, 359
Campbell, William, 87, 88, 88n. 42, 89, 94, 315
Canada, invasion of, 121–31
*Canada Constellation*, 156n. 100
Canandaigua, New York, 168, 169, 171; description of, 143, 175, 176
Canne, Mary, 334
Carey, Samuel, 68
Caribbean: trade in, 11, 223, 230–32, 349, 384, 406
Catherine Town, New York, 182
Cattaraugus County, New York, 314
Caughnawaga Indians, 126, 127, 128, 348
Cayuga County, New York, 378
Chamberlain, Benjamin, 68
Chamberlain, William M., 255, 255n. 43, 260, 260n. 57, 260n. 59, 261
Chamberlain & Phelps, 330
Champlain Valley: map of, 118; military campaigns in, 122, 131–33
Chandler, Alfred D., Jr., 192, 203, 246
Chandler, Margaret, 398, 399
Chapin, Israel, 169
Chapman, George T., 351
Chappell, Jabez, Jr., 82
Charter of 1672, 36
Chase, Philander, 168–69, 181, 320
Cheesbrough, Hannah (Denison), 402
Cheesbrough, Nathaniel, 402
Cheesecocks Commission, 367, 377
Chenango Point, New York, 182
Chenery, Mary, 336
Chester, Nova Scotia, 100, 100n. 65
Chew, Elizabeth, 322
Child, Jonathan, 68
Chipman, Ann (Osborn), 104
Chipman, Handley, 84–85, 87, 89, 92, 93, 94, 97, 104, 315
Chipman, Jane (—), 315
Chipman, William Allen, 104
Church of England. *See* Anglican Church
Clap, Thomas, 22n. 7, 25, 83
Clark. *See also* De Clark
Clark, David, 336
Clark, Deborah (Denton), 380–81
Clark, Helen, 272, 272n. 87, 274, 284, 330
Clark, James, 380
Clark, Mary, 272, 272n. 87, 281n. 109, 386–87
Clark, Mary (Bogart), 272n. 87, 274, 330, 386
Clark, Mary (Wheelock), 336
Clark, Sarah, 268, 269, 272, 272n. 87, 333, 380–84
Clark, William, 272n. 87, 274, 330, 386
Clarke, Mary (Canne), 334
Clarke, Rebecca, 334, 335
Clarke, Thomas, 334
clergy: support of, 6, 80–81, 83–84, 89–97; authority of, 23; unconverted, doctrine of, 24–25; selection of, 80–81, 83–84, 94
Clifton Springs, New York, 182
Clinton, George, 270, 375
Closson, Mary (Phelps), 390
Closson, Matthew, 390
Closter, New Jersey, 379
Cock, Daniel, 84
Coddington, Thomas B., 277n. 100
Codfish Aristocracy, 249
Coetus party, 358, 362, 373

Coggesell, Hezekiah, 82, 91 n. 48
Cogswell, Hezekiah, 91 n. 48
Cogswell, Jane, 404
Colburn, Elizabeth, 336
Colchester, Connecticut, 12, 37, 404
Coleman, Annie Brown, 274, 331, 332
Coleman, Sophia (Brown), 331
Coleman, Thomas Jefferson, 331
Colkin, Ezekiel, 82
College of New Jersey. *See* Princeton University
Collins, Samuel, 121 n. 7
Columbia, Connecticut, 5
Columbus, Georgia, 321
Comingo, Bruin Romkes, 94, 94 n. 56, 315
commerce, impact of colonial wars on, 38–39, 40–41
commission merchant, 246–47
Cone, Ruben, 82
Confederation, 135, 189; New Hampshire under, 134–36; weakness of, 139, 141
Conferentie party, 373
Congregational Church: selection and support of pastor, 6, 83–84, 89–93, 94; state religion in New England, 6–8; rivalry with Anglican church, 20, 41, 50, 86, 86 n. 38; education of pastors, 22; move to Nova Scotia, 71, 75, 80; consociation of pastors in, 83; missionary tradition, 83. *See also* Dissenters
Congregational church: division into New and Old Lights, 14–15, 102; declining membership, 110, 115–16, 167, 196–97, 200; westward movement, 167–68
Connecticut: organization of colonial towns in, xii, xiv, 3–5, 7; standing order, xii, 200–5; during era of early republic, xx-xxi; economy of 4, 9–10, 11–12, 189–93, 207, 246; emigration from, 11, 48, 56, 59 n. 108, 75, 77–78, 80, 97–100, 108, 149, 167–68, 189–90; land-owning patterns in, 3–4, 12, 29–30; population in eighteenth century, 11 n. 25; case load of county courts, 27; government of, 35, 35 n. 48, 36, 200, 208; patterns of office-holding, 36–38; road network, 37–38, 209–11, 213–14; economic impact of colonial wars on, 38–39, 40, 189–93, 223; Dissenters in, 41, 43; economic depression in, 46–47, 48, 223; emergence of manufacturing economy, 116, 117; religious sects in, 196–97; support of Constitution, 199
Connecticut, General Assembly of: delegates, xiii, 19, 29 n. 28, 35, 35 n. 48, 58, 116, 201, 403, 404, 408; and settlement of Hebron, 4–5; tasks of, 30, 36; patent request for Bohea Tea, 40; B. Phelps's appeal for compensation to, 106–7, 110 n. 87, 111–13, 114–15; land division in Stafford, 195; attack against E. W. Phelps before, 208–9
Connecticut River Valley, map of, 6, 166
Connell [Cornell], Mary Amelia (Phelps), 205, 233, 235 n. 132, 290 n. 124, 325
Connell [Cornell], Richard, 235 n. 132, 290 n. 124, 325
Conselyea, Margaret, 353, 360, 362
Constitution, Federal, xviii, 199, 270, 367, 376, 377, 395
Contine, John, 369
Continental Congress, 100, 374–75, 376
Cook, Louis, 126, 127
Cooledge, Abigail (Wheelock), 337
Cooledge, Peter, 337
Copley, Elizabeth (—), 303, 389–90
Copley, Thomas, 390
Copp, David, 407
Copp, Dorothy (Denison) (Rogers), 407
corn, cultivation of, 9
Cornell: *See also* Connell [Cornell]
Cornell, Annie, 290 n. 124, 325, 328
Cornell, Harry, 290 n. 124, 325, 328

Cornwallis, Edward, 78n. 16
Cornwallis, Nova Scotia, xv, 194n. 19, 314, 315, 316, 411; Yankee settlement of, 71, 77–80.105, 106; physical layout of, 79; Congregational pastor and, 80–81, 89–97; controversy over meeting house site, 87; population, 87, 91; political opinions during Revolution, 98–100; preaching of H. Alline at, 101–3, 113; Baptist churches started at, 102; raided by privateers, 105–8
Cosyns, Grietje, 269, 352, 353
cotton, trade in, 244–45, 247–48, 279
Coventry, Connecticut, 394
Crafts, John, 335
Crafts, Rebecca (Wheelock), 335
Crane, John, 68
Crevecoeur, Hector St. John, 70
Crewkerne, Somerset, England, 301, 303, 304, 389
Critical Period, xviii
Crocker, Andrew S., 155n. 94
Crom, Cornelia (Haring) (Truman), 356
Crom, Gysbert, 356
Croton, William, 10
Croydon, New Hampshire, 272, 329
Cruger, John C., 260n. 59
Cumberland County, Nova Scotia, 100
currency: scarcity of, 11, 92; Continental paper, 108, 111, 112, 130; national, 135, 191
Curtice, Mary, 81, 308, 309, 310
Curtice, Nathaniel, 82
Curtis, David, 155n. 94
Curtis, Israel, 122, 123, 124–25, 125n. 20, 128
Curtis, Uriah, 68
Curtiss, Henry Tomlinson, 331
Curtiss, Mary Eliza Henderson (Beardsley), 331
Curtiss [Curtis], Mary A. Bradley, 274, 331
Cushman, John W., 381
Cutler, A. W., 68

D

Dartmouth, Lord, 49, 51, 124n. 17
Dartmouth College, 8; origins, xiii, 19, 32–33, 49–56; Native American students, 32, 33, 34, 123–24, 126, 127, 131; charter negotiations, 50, 53, 53n. 93, 312, 342; trustees, 50, 53, 53n. 93, 339, 348; first construction at, 54; Wheelock's plan for, 55–56, 123–24; creditor to estate of Alexander Phelps, 68; first class, 121; Supreme Court case, 349
Davenport, Abigail (Pierson), 31
Davenport, James, 24–25, 25n. 15, 26
Davenport, John, 31, 31n. 34
Davenport, Martha (Gould) (Selleck), 31
Davenport, Sarah, 30, 31, 310, 340, 341, 344
Day, ___, 321
Day, Mary, 391–92
Deane, Silas, 66, 68
Deans, John, 82
De Baan, Carel, 357
De Baan, Janetje (Haring), 356, 357
De Clark, Maria, 359
De Clark [Klerck], Daniel, 352
Dedham, Massachusetts, 334, 335, 336
Deerfield, Massachusetts, 390
DeForest, Lockwood, 233
DeForest, Samuel, 232, 233
Delaware County, New York, 156
Demarest, David, 379
Demarest, Elizabeth (Haring), 364, 378, 379–80, 387
Demarest, Hester (Brower), 379
Demarest, James, 379–80
democracy, opposition to, 200–1
Denison, Abigail, 407
Denison, Abigail (Eldridge), 404
Denison, Agnes (Willie), 398
Denison, Andrew, 406, 410
Denison, Ann, 402
Denison, Anna, 404, 406

Denison, Anna (Denison) (Minor), 404
Denison, Ann (Borodell), 401, 402
Denison, Ann (Mason), 403
Denison, Borodell, 403
Denison, Bridget (Thompson), 401, 402
Denison, Catherine (Fitzpatrick), 411
Denison, Daniel, 398, 399, 400, 401, 404
Denison, David Sherman, 409, 410
Denison, Deborah, 409
Denison, Deborah (Griswold), 407, 409
Denison, Dorothy, 407
Denison, Dorothy (Stanton) (Frink), 404, 407
Denison, Edward, 398, 399, 400, 404
Denison, Elizabeth, 407, 409, 410
Denison, Elizabeth (Bagley [Bailey]), 406
Denison, Elizabeth (Weld), 400
Denison, Eunice, 104n. 74, 409, 411
Denison, George, 398, 399, 400–2, 403, 407
Denison, Gurdon, 411
Denison, Hannah, 402
Denison, Hannah (Dodge), 407
Denison, Jane (Cogswell), 404
Denison, Joanna, 406
Denison, Joanna (Stanton), 404, 406
Denison, John, 398, 399, 402, 403, 406
Denison, John [Jr.], 403
Denison, Lucy, 407
Denison, Margaret, 403
Denison, Margaret (Chandler) (Monk), 398, 399
Denison, Mary, 410
Denison, Mary (Avery), 403
Denison, Mary (Stanton), 404
Denison, Mary (Thompson), 410
Denison, Mary (Wetherell) (Harris), 403
Denison, Mercy, 403, 410
Denison, Mercy (Gorham), 403
Denison, Nathaniel, 406
Denison, Patience (Dudley), 400
Denison, Patience (Griswold), 406
Denison, Phebe, 404. *See also* Phelps, Phebe (Denison)
Denison, Phebe (Lay), 403
Denison, Prudence, 409, 410
Denison, Prudence (Sherman), 86, 314, 407, 410
Denison, Robert, 75, 77, 86, 314, 403, 404–6, 407–9, 410
Denison, Robert [Jr.], 405, 406
Denison, Samuel, 104n. 74, 108, 115, 404, 409, 410
Denison, Sarah, 400, 402, 404, 406, 409, 410
Denison, Sarah (Fox), 410
Denison, Sarah (Prentice), 403
Denison, Thomas, 406
Denison, William, 398–99, 403
Dennis, John, 66
Denton, Deborah, 380–81
De Peyster, Elizabeth (Herring), 363, 364, 368, 369, 375
De Peyster, Elizabeth Schuyler, 364, 369
De Peyster, John, 363, 368–69, 369
De Peyster, John B., 369
De Peyster, Margaret, 369
DeRose, Susan A., 325–26
Detroit, Michigan, 127n. 25
Dewey, Moses, 82
Dexter, Franklin Bowditch, 346
Dissenters: financial difficulties, 88, 92, 93
Dodge, Hannah, 407
Dodge, William E., 249
Dover, Ann, 301–2, 303
Downes, Ezra, 82
dressmaking, changes in, 245, 245n. 16
Drew, Ellen, 257n. 49
Dudley, Dorothy (York), 400
Dudley, Patience, 400
Dudley, Thomas, 400
Duer, William A., 368
Dun, R. G., & Co.: reports on Phelps's businesses, 259–61; reports on John S. Haring & Co., 268
Duryea, Abraham, 365
Duyckman, Jacob, 361
Dwight, Timothy, 175–77

## E


Earl, Ralph, 204, 204n. 61, 395, 396
East Bloomfield, New York, 182
East Hartford, Connecticut, 11, 112, 113, 116, 315, 316
Eaton, Arthur Hamilton Wentworth, 84, 87, 88
Eccles, Norfolk, England, 335
Eddy Rebellion, 100
Edenton, Putnam County, Georgia, 321
education, in colonial New England, 8, 8n. 16, 20, 32
Edus, Julia, 322
Edwards, Esther, 31n. 34, 44n. 71
Edwards, Jonathan, 14, 16, 25n. 17, 164
Edwards, Mary, 391
Eldridge, Abigail, 404
Elias, Catherine, 361
Eliot, Andrew, 83n. 31, 91, 91n. 48, 92
Eliot, Jared, 10
Ellicottsville, New York, 313, 314
Ellis, __, 321
Ellis, __ (Day), 321
Ellis, Iddo, 183, 321
Ellis, Lucy (Phelps), 136, 143, 183, 321
Ellsworth, Oliver, 199
Eltinge, Wilhelmus, 378
English, Abigel, 82
Enlightenment, 15, 137, 196
Eno, Hannah (Phelps), 305, 306
Eno, James, 306
Episcopal Church. *See* Anglican Church; Protestant Episcopal Church
Erie Canal, 171n. 141, 244
Eskeath, New York, 380
Everts, Cornelia, 355


## F


Fabend, Firth Haring, 374
factor, 246
Fairfield, Connecticut, xxii, 234, 235, 237, 260, 265, 274, 275, 281, 283, 284, 291, 316, 325, 326, 327, 328, 329, 330, 331, 332, 333, 387, 388, 406; Phelps's residences in, 239, 257, 285–88; description of, 256, 258; steam ferry and train service to, 256, 264
Fairfield, Walter, 68
Fairfield County, Connecticut, 329
Falmouth, Nova Scotia, 101
Farrar, Sarah Dean, 135n. 47, 318, 351
Fenny, Sarah, 403
Filer [Fyler], Abigail (Phelps), 305, 306
Filer [Fyler], Samuell, 306, 307
Fine, Elizabeth, 382
Fischer, David Hackett, xxiv
Fisher, John, 337
Fisher, Rebecca (Wheelock), 337
Fisk, Elisha, 211
Fitch, Anna (Denison), 406
Fitch, Cyprian, 104n. 74
Fitch, James, 406
Fitch, Samuel, 104n. 75
Fitzhugh, Bennett Chew, 322
Fitzhugh, Elizabeth (Chew), 322
Fitzhugh, Peregrine, 322
Fitzhugh, Sarah (Phelps), 322
Fitzpatrick, Catherine, 411
Five Miles, Connecticut, 114
Flierboom, Cattryn, 354
Flierboom, Matthew, 354
Fort Cumberland, 100
Fort Edward, New York, 393
Fort Hughes, 106
Fort Niagara, 144, 144n. 72, 150–51, 160
Fort Oswego, 160
Fort St. Johns, 124
Fort Schuyler, 143
Foster, Augustus John, 189
Foster, Eunice (Phelps), 87, 108, 114, 235n. 133, 317
Foster, James, 235 n. 133, 317
Fox, Sarah, 410
Franklin, Benjamin, on Whitefield, 22–23, 23 n. 9
Franklin Township, New Jersey, 377
Freeman, Alice, 401

Freemasonry and Masons, xvii, 136–37, 148, 149, 152, 155–56, 157, 168, 180, 319, 320, 348, 351
freemen, rights and powers of, 35
Freemont, New Hampshire, 322
free trade, impact of, 240, 261
French and Indian War, 38, 74, 126, 339, 358, 393; military activities in, 133, 222
Frink, Dorothy (Stanton), 404, 407
Frink, Samuel, 404
fruiter, 241–42, 243
Fryeburgh, Maine, 348
Fuller, __, 86
Fuller, Elizabeth, 335–36

G

Gale, Benjamin, 201
Gale, Samuel, 201
Gardiner, Geraldine, 385
Gardiner, Joanna, 404
Gardiner's Lake, 404
garment industry, 245
Gates, Catharine Teller (Haring), 271–72, 284n. 114, 383, 385, 388
Gates, Horatio, 133
Gates, John, 385
Gates, John, Jr., 383, 385
Gates, Joseph Egbert, 385
Gaylord, Ann, 301
Geneva, New York, xviii, 143, 320, 321, 322; description of, 175, 176, 180; establishment of Episcopal Church in, 179–82
gentility, increase in, 13–14, 219
George III, King of England, 33, 48–49, 143
German mercenaries, 132
Gerrish, Benjamin, 92, 92n. 51
Gilbert, Adonijah, 68
Gilbert, Samuel, 47n. 79
Gilbert, Sylvester, 142n. 68
Gilbert, Thomas, 68
Glanford, Upper Canada, 153, 154, 156, 156n. 102, 172, 174n. 149, 178, 320, 322
Goranna, Aletia, 257
Gorham, Mercy, 403
Gould, Martha, 31
Grafton County, New Hampshire, 63, 343
grain, trade in, 244–45
Granby, Connecticut, 201
Grant, Benjamin, 68
Grant, Billings, 235n. 132, 325
Grant, Eliza (Phelps), 205, 222, 223n. 104, 233, 235n. 132, 324–25
Graymont, Barbara, 164
Great Awakening: impact on religion in New England, xiii, 13, 14, 15, 44, 45n. 75; Second, xvii, 115–16, 120; effect on career choices of young men, 19, 20, 25, 26; at Yale College, 22, 22n. 7, 24–25; in Nova Scotia, 101–13
Great Britain: military activities, 38, 39, 131–33, 183, 222; naval bases in Nova Scotia, 74; forts in Northwest, 144n. 72. *See also* Revolutionary War
Green, Ebeneezer, 61n. 112, 65, 67
Green, John, 68
Greene, Elisabeth, 396
Greene, John Taylor, 207
Gretchell, Susannah, 344, 350
Griswold, Deborah, 407, 409
Griswold, Edward, 304
Griswold, Margaret (—), 304
Griswold, Mary, 304, 305
Griswold, Matthew, 407
Griswold, Patience, 406
Griswold, Phebe (Hyde), 407
Griswold, Sarah, 303

H

Hackensack, New Jersey, 357, 358, 359
Halfway Covenant, 13

Halifax, Massachusetts, 345, 346, 348
Halifax, Nova Scotia, 72, 73, 74, 77, 78, 78n. 16, 91, 92n. 51, 94, 97, 98, 105n. 78, 106, 315, 408
Hamilton, Alexander, 199, 367, 368
Hamilton, Ontario, 153
Hampshire Grants, 118, 134, 134n. 41
Handley, Jane, 95–97
Handy, __, 338
Handy, Elizabeth (Wheelock), 338
Hanover, New Hampshire, xvii, 19, 48, 52, 53, 69, 135, 136, 312, 317, 318, 319, 340, 342, 344, 346, 347, 348, 349, 350; early town meetings, 48; site of Dartmouth College, 52, 53
Hardenbergh, John L., 381
Hardenbergh Corners, New York, 381
Haring: *See also* Herring
Haring, Abraham, 269, 355, 356, 357–59, 360
Haring, Abraham A., 377
Haring, Antje (Avryansen), 360
Haring, Brechtje, 354, 356
Haring, Caroline Eliza (Phelps): portrait, xxv, xxvi; lineage, xxvii-xviii; marriage, 239, 239n. 3, 256, 265–66, 271, 333, 387; childhood, 255, 329; correspondence, 274–75, 281–82; death, 275, 283, 388; children, 281, 333, 388
Haring, Catharina, 356, 357
Haring, Catharine (Blauvelt), 359, 360, 366
Haring, Catharine (Helman), 380
Haring, Catharine [Kate], 281, 333, 388
Haring, Catharine Teller, 271–72, 284n. 114, 383, 385
Haring, Cattryn (Flierboom), 354
Haring, Clinton, 268, 268n. 77, 383, 386, 387
Haring, Cornelia, 356
Haring, Cornelius, 354, 360
Haring, Cosyn, 354
Haring, Dirck, 379
Haring, Dirkje (Talman), 355
Haring, Elbert, 357, 360, 364, 378, 379. *See also* Herring, Elbert
Haring, Elizabeth, 364, 378, 379–80, 387
Haring, Elizabeth (Blauvelt), 357
Haring, Elizabeth (Smith), 380
Haring, Frytje (Bogert), 379
Haring, George Titus, 386
Haring, Grietje (Bogert), 355, 356, 357–58, 359
Haring, Grietje (Cosyns), 269, 352–53
Haring, Grietje Pieters, 356
Haring, James, 387
Haring, James Clark, 384
Haring, James Demarest: portrait, xxv, xxvii, 266; lineage and relatives, xxvii-xxviii, 239n. 3, 269–74, 281, 387–88; marriage, 256, 265–66, 271, 274; business career, 266–68, 268n. 78, 281, 388; childhood and education, 268; land transactions, 271n. 81; death, 275, 283, 387; residences in Fairfield and New York City, 281, 388; estate, 284n. 115, 388; inheritance, 383
Haring, Janetje, 356, 357
Haring, Jan [John], 359, 360
Haring, Jan Pietersen, 269, 352
Haring, John, 269–70, 357, 363, 367, 369, 370, 371–79, 384
Haring, John Bogert, 378, 380
Haring, John Samuel, 267–68, 272, 272n. 87, 281n. 109, 383, 386–87, 388; portrait, 267
Haring, Julia Phelps. *See* White, Julia Phelps (Haring)
Haring, Klaatje [Classie], 356, 357
Haring, Lea (—), 360
Haring, Margaret, 359, 378, 380
Haring, Maria, 271, 378, 379
Haring, Maria (Haring), 271, 378, 379
Haring, Marretje (Blauvelt), 354
Haring, Martha Ann Lydia (Mann), 385
Haring, Martyntje, 360

Haring, Martyntje [Margaret], 378, 379
Haring, Mary, 359, 383, 384
Haring, Mary (Clark), 272, 272n. 87, 281n. 109, 386–87
Haring, Mary (Herring), 239n. 3, 270, 271, 363, 364, 370, 375, 378, 379
Haring, Marytie, 355
Haring, Nicholas Lansing, 378, 380
Haring, Peter, 269, 353, 355–56, 359
Haring, Peter D., 379
Haring, Pieterje, 356, 357
Haring, Rachel (Rose), 379
Haring, Rowena (Heywood), 387
Haring, Samuel, 269, 270, 333, 378, 379, 380–84, 385
Haring, Samuel Jones, 369
Haring, Samuel Kip, 383, 385
Haring, Sarah (Blauvelt), 357
Haring, Sarah (Clark), 268, 269, 272, 272n. 87, 333, 380–84
Haring, Sarah Elizabeth, 268, 268n. 78, 383, 387
Haring, Sarah (Nagel), 360
Haring, Theunis, 356, 357
Haring, Vroutje, 354
Haringh. *See* Haring; Herring
Harris, James, Jr., 405
Harris, Mary (Wetherell), 403
Hartford, Connecticut, xix, 199, 306, 317, 319, 329, 345, 346, 367, 401, 405; travel to, 12, 37–38, 210, 213–14; economic importance, 192; population, 193
Hartford County, Connecticut, 116
Harvard College, 21, 48
Hathaway, Ruth, 393
Havana, Cuba, xx, 230, 231, 232, 323, 324
Haverhill, New Hampshire, 52, 53, 69, 312
Hawthorne, Nathaniel, 280
Hearingh. *See* Haring; Herring
Hebard, Mary (Reed), 339
Hebard, Robert, 339
Hebard [Hibard], Ruth (Wheelock), 338, 339
Hebron, Connecticut, 29, 30, 81, 139n. 61, 188n. 4, 306, 308, 309, 310, 313, 317, 323, 337, 339, 344; descriptions of, xii, xiii; founding, 4–5, 9–12, 19, 307; geography, 9; population, 11, 193; religious dissension in, 15, 20, 98; cultural and institutional characteristics, 19–20; Anglican church in, 20, 44–45; land transactions in, 28, 39, 41, 58–59, 66, 66n. 121, 311–12; office-holding patterns in, 37; importation resolution, 47; New Hampshire families from, 56, 59n. 108, 134; Loyalists from, 113, 113n. 88, 137, 138
Hebron, New Hampshire, 48
Helman, Catharine, 380
Henderson, Emma Ayres (Phelps), 255, 273, 274, 290, 329
Henderson, George Phelps, 273, 290, 328, 329
Henderson, William Coleman, 273, 329
Henry, A., 315
Herigh. *See* Haring; Herring
Herkimer, New York, 171
Herring: *See also* Haring
Herring, Abraham, 271, 271n. 83, 363, 370–71, 382
Herring, Ann [Annatjie], 363, 364, 369, 375
Herring, Anne (Bogert), 370
Herring, Catharine, 363, 364
Herring, Catharine (Blauvelt), 359, 360, 366
Herring, Catherine (Lent), 360, 364
Herring, Cornelia, 239n. 3, 270, 363, 364, 366
Herring, Elbert, 270, 357, 360–64, 365, 372, 373, 376
Herring, Elbert [Jr.], 365
Herring, Elizabeth, 363, 364, 368, 369, 375
Herring, Elizabeth (Bogert), 360, 362, 363–64, 365, 372
Herring, Elizabeth (Ivers), 371

Herring, Margaret, 271, 363, 364, 365
Herring, Mary, 239 n. 3, 270, 271, 363, 364, 370, 375, 378, 379
Herring, Nicholas, 363, 364, 370
Herring, Peter, 363, 364, 366
Herring, Sarah, 363, 364, 370, 375
Herring, Thomas, 371, 382, 384
Hewes, Nath., 68
Hewes, Nath., Jr., 68
Heywood, Rowena, 387
Hibard, Bela, 174 n. 149
Hickock, Catharine (—), 391
Hide, Calub, 82
Hill, Charles H., 259
Hillhouse, James, 113
Hingham, Massachusetts, 335
Hobart, David, 122 n. 9, 131, 132, 318
Hobart, Honora, 275
Hobart, John Henry, 170 n. 140, 175, 177, 184–85
Holcomb, Benajah, 201
Holcomb, Martha (Phelps), 305, 306
Holcomb, Samuel, 306
Homeoye, New York, 182
Hone, Philip, 251, 255, 258, 261
Hoorn, North Holland, 353
Hopkins, Stephen, 24 n. 14
Hoppe, Lea Hedridge, 359
Horsford, Alexander, 311
Horsford, Anna, 29 n. 28, 310
Horsford, Obadiah, 39, 39 n. 59, 41, 42, 66, 68, 311
Horsmanden, David, 373
Horton, Nova Scotia, xv, 314, 407, 408, 409, 410; Yankee settlement of, 75, 77, 78, 86; physical layout of, 79; religious sects in, 85; population, 87; preaching of H. Alline at, 101–3, 113; Baptist churches started at, 102; Phelps land transactions in, 104, 104 n. 74, 108
Hosack, David, 368
House, John, 343
Howard, Tebeder, 68
Howe, William, 131
Howell, Elisa, 385
Hubbard, Daniel, 39
Hubbard, William, 39
Hubbell, Mary, 384
Hudson, New York, 171
Hudson River Valley, 118, 131–33, 166
Hughes, Richard, 107
Hunt, Freeman, 240, 240 n. 4
Huntington, Caleb, 91 n. 48
Huntington, Christopher [Jr.], 337
Huntington, Connecticut, 397
Huntington, Elisha, 410
Huntington, Elizabeth (Denison) (Smith), 410
Huntington, Ezekiel, 82
Huntington, Jebidiah, 309
Huntington, Ruth, 337, 338
Huntington, Sarah (Adgate), 337
Hurlbut, Hannah, 346
Hutchings, Susanna, 341
Hutchinson, James, 121 n. 7
Hutton, D., 385
Hyde, Nathaniel, 204, 211
Hyde, Phebe, 407
Hyde family, 220

## I

Ilis, Mary (—), 336
Ilis, Samuel, 336
individualism, origins in Great Awakening, 25, 26
industrialization, 247
Ingham, Daniel, 307
Ingham, Mehitabel (Phelps), 307, 308
Ingraham, Daniel, 68
insurance companies, 191, 246
Intolerable Acts, 47
Ipswich, Massachusetts, 398, 400
iron manufacturing, 198, 203–4
Iroquois Indians, 32, 34, 143, 157–65
Isle aux Noix, 123
itinerant preachers, 20 n. 2
Ivers, Elizabeth, 371
Ivers, Thomas, 371

## J

Jackson, Andrew, 261
Jackson, Phoebe, 366
Jacobs, Joseph T., 225
James, Henry, 254
Jarvis, Hannah Delvena (Peters), 139, 139n. 61, 149, 149n. 84, 162n. 120
Jarvis, William, 139, 149, 149n. 84, 152
Jay, John, 152, 160, 374
Jay's Treaty (1794), 160
Jeffersonian-Republicans, 200, 208
jobber, 247
Johnes family, 370. *See also* Jones
Johnson, Guy, 129, 130, 159
Johnson, James, 82
Johnson, John, 161
Johnson, Samuel, on Whitefield, 22
Johnson, Tho., 68
Johnson, William, 49, 157n. 106, 161, 408
Johnston, Lawrence, 82
Jones, Anne (Phelps), xiii, 29, 29n. 28, 310
Jones, Cornelia (Herring), 239n. 3, 270, 363, 364, 366
Jones, Elbert Haring, 364
Jones, Elizabeth, 364
Jones, Ellen (Turk), 366
Jones, Gardner [Gardiner], 364, 370
Jones, Horace C., 331
Jones, Mary (Phelps), 331
Jones, Nicholas, 364
Jones, Phoebe (Jackson), 366
Jones, Samuel, 215, 237, 239, 239n. 3, 270, 271, 363, 366–68, 367, 377
Jones, Samuel Jackson, 238n. 1
Jones, Sarah (Herring), 363, 364, 370, 375
Jones, William, 366
Judd, Peter (Haring), xi, xii, xxvi
Justice of the Peace, duties of, 37n. 51

## K

Kakiat, Rockland Co., New York, 380
Kammys, Richard, 68
Kendrick, Sarah, 335
Kennedy, Sarah (Denison), 409, 410
Kent, Lucy, 393
Kenyon College, 168
Kerr, Elizabeth (Brant), 148
Kerr, Robert, 148
Kierstede, Cornelius, 354
Killborn, Benjamin, 82
Killingly, Connecticut, 37, 196
Killingworth, Connecticut, 10, 201, 202
King George's War, 75, 358
Kingman, Benjamin, 82
King Philip's War, 402
Kings County, Nova Scotia, 314
Kingston, Upper Canada, 144
Kinsman, Aaron, 351
Kinsman, Abigail, 351
Kinsman, Rose (Burnham), 351
Kip, Ann [Annatjie] (Herring), 363, 364, 369, 375
Kip, Catharine (—), 369
Kip, Catharine Teller (Haring) (Gates), 271–72, 284n. 114, 383, 385, 388
Kip, Elbert, 363
Kip, Elisa (Howell), 385
Kip, Elizabeth, 363
Kip, Elizabeth (Abbott), 385
Kip, Geraldine (Gardiner), 385
Kip, Henry, 271–72, 272n. 84, 385–86
Kip, Jacobus, 369
Kip, Samuel, 363, 369, 385
Kips Bay, New York, 369
Knapp, Hubbell, 383, 384
Knapp, James, 384
Knapp, Mary (Haring), 383, 384
Knapp, Mary (Hubbell), 384
Knapp, Shepherd, 255n. 43

## L

Labagh, Peter, 380
Lancaster County, Pennsylvania, 273, 329
land: desire for, 3–4; method of clearing, 9; speculation in, 29–30, 47–48; net worth of, 38–39
land grants: in eighteenth century, 4; in New Hampshire, 47, 48–49; in Upper Canada, 153, 154, 156, 157; in New York State, 167–68, 179, 380, 381; and development companies, 175; to veterans, 179, 381
Lanford, Esther (Phelps) (Austin), 396
Lanford, Oleg, 395
Lanford, Peleg, 396
Langton [Lankton], Abigail (Phelps), 391
Langton [Lankton], John, 390, 391
Lankton, Samuel, 390
Lawrence, Charles, 74
Lawrence, Hannah, 127n. 25
Lawton, Mabel Marston (Phelps), 332
Lawton, William, 332
Lay, Phebe, 403
Lay, Robert, 403
Lay, Sarah (Fenny) (Tully), 403
Lebanon, Connecticut, 12, 15, 20, 32, 37, 80, 93n. 53, 309, 340, 342, 344, 345, 346, 347, 348, 349, 350, 351, 407
Lebanon, New Hampshire, 48, 201, 397
Lebanon Crank [North Parish], Connecticut, 69, 342, 343, 404, 405, 406, 410
Lee, Gideon, 255n. 43
Legge, Francis [Governor of Nova Scotia], 99–100
Lent, Abraham van, 357
Lent, Adolph, 357
Lent, Anna Katrina (Meyer) van, 357
Lent, Catherine, 360, 364
Lent, Klaatje (Haring), 356, 357
Leverse, Elbert, 362
Levinston, John, 405
Lisbon, New Hampshire, 344, 350
Littleton, New Hampshire, 52
Liverpool, England, xxii, 247, 248, 259, 330, 332; and transatlantic trade, 227; description of, 277–79; 1884 map of, 278
Livingston, Janet, 123, 123n. 13
Livingston, Mary (Beekman), 123n. 12
Livingston, Robert R., 123, 123n. 12
Lockwood, __, Major, 127
Lombard, __, 332
Lombard, Julie [Groschen] (Phelps), 290n. 124, 332
London, England, 319; Loyalists exiled in, 44, 113n. 88, 137, 138, 140, 220
Loomis, Ephraim, 82
Loomis, Nath., 68
Lothrop, Eunice (Denison), 409, 411
Lothrop, John, 411
Louisbourg, Cape Breton Island, 75
Loyalists: military service of, xvi, 132, 133n. 38; in Connecticut, 12, 113, 113n. 88, 137, 138; exiled in London, 44, 113n. 88, 137, 138, 140, 220; exiled in Nova Scotia, 98, 113; among Yale graduates, 100; in Canada, 130, 133n. 38; in Upper Canada, 144, 146; confiscated property of, 198
Lunenberg, Nova Scotia, 94
Lyme [Lime], Connecticut, 114, 406, 407
Lyme [Lime], New Hampshire, xiii, 48, 60, 67, 69, 188, 310, 312, 318, 323, 344
Lynde, Nicholas, Jr., 404
Lyon, James, 94n. 56, 109
Lyon, Liakim, 215, 216, 219, 241
Lyon, Lyman, 215
Lyon, Nehemiah, 216
Lyon, Samuel C., 215, 216

## M

Machias, Maine, 87, 94n. 56, 104, 108, 109, 315
Macready riots of 1849, 262–63
Malleville, Maria, 349

Maltby, Elizabeth, 341
Maltby, John, 25, 31–32, 41, 311, 341
Maltby, Jonathan, 341
Maltby, Sarah (Davenport), 30, 31, 310, 340, 341, 344
Maltby, Susanna (Hutchings), 341
Maltby, William, 341
Manchester, Connecticut, 114, 115n. 91, 116, 235, 314, 317, 411
Manchester, England, 247
Manhattan, 269, 353, 355, 360, 361, 362, 365, 369. *See also* New York City
Manlius, New York, 171, 174, 175, 177, 178, 179, 182, 314
Mann, Benning, 216, 219–20, 220n. 99
Mann, John, 59n. 108, 134, 220n. 99
Mann, Lydia (Porter), 59n. 108, 220n. 99
Mann, Martha Ann Lydia, 385
Mann, Nathaniel, 220
Mansfield, Connecticut, 48
Manwaring, Chris., 409
Manwaring, Deborah (Denison), 409
Marlborough, Connecticut, 5
marriage, in colonial America, 7–8
Marsh, James, 351
Marsh, Lydia, 391
Marshal, Grace (Phelps), 391
Marshal, Samuel, 391
Marshall, David, 306
Marshall, Sarah (Phelps), 305, 306
Martin, Grace, 391
Martin, Lydia (Marsh), 391
Martin, William, 391
*Mary & John*, xi, 302
Mash, Stephen P., 277n. 99
Mashipaug Lake, 404
Mason, Ann, 403
Mason, Jonathan, 41, 41n. 67, 311
Massachusetts, mortality rates in, 3
*Massachusetts Gazette*, 60
Mather, Increase, 3, 70
McGregor, __, 277n. 99
McMurray, __, 386
McMurry, William, 325
Medfield, Massachusetts, 334, 335, 336, 337
Medway, Massachusetts, 337
Mendon, Massachusetts, 335, 336, 337
merchant, changing meaning of, 246
merchants: role in economic expansion, 192; in New York City, 225, 227, 243–48
Meriden, Connecticut, 388
Merrick, Abigail, 391, 393
Merrick, John, 391–92
Merrick, Mary (Day), 391–92
Methodist Church, 185; growth in New York State, 167, 167n. 130; increasing membership, 197
Meyer, Adolph, 357
Meyer, Anna Katrina, 357
Meyer, Catharina (Haring), 356, 357
Meyer, Maria (Verveelen), 357
Middletown, Connecticut, 37n. 53, 192, 304
Miles, Joseph, 335
Miles, Mary (Wheelock), 335
Military Tract [in New York State], 179, 380, 381
Millerites, 185
Mills, Abigail (Phelps) (Beers), 397
Mills, Isaac, 395, 397
Mills, Mary (—), 395
Milwaukee, Wisconsin, 322
Minas Basin, Nova Scotia, 97, 314, 408; settlement of, 71; geography, 72–73, 77, 78–79, 98–99
mineral springs, at Stafford, Connecticut, 197–98
Minneapolis, Minnesota, 284
Minneus, Grietje, 355
Minor, Anna (Denison), 404
Minor, Ephraim, 404
Minor, Hannah (Avery), 404
Minor, Samuel, 404
Mohawk Indians, 34, 157, 159. *See also* Brant, Joseph
Mohegan, Connecticut, 404

Mohegan Indians, 26, 75, 404
Monk, Henry, 398
Monk, Margaret (Chandler), 398, 399
Monsey, New York, 379
Monson, Massachusetts, 27, 311
Montgomery, Janet (Livingston), 123, 123n. 13
Montgomery, Richard, 123, 123n. 13, 125, 126
Montpelier, Vermont, 351
Montreal, Quebec, Canada, 318; military activities around, 122–31; descriptions of, 126; Tories in exile in, 130
Montville, Connecticut, 75, 314, 404
Moore, Benjamin, 168, 169–70, 170n. 140, 171, 173, 182, 320, 321
Moor's Charity School, 33–34, 49, 131, 158, 342, 343, 344, 346, 347
Moray [Morey], Mary, 310
More, Grietje, 357, 358
Morehouse, Joanna (Denison), 406
Morehouse, Thomas, 406
Morey, Israel, 39n. 59, 56, 56n. 100, 67, 122, 123n. 10, 343
Morey, Lydia, 134–35, 135n. 44
Morey, Martha (Palmer), 56n. 100
Morey, Samuel
Mormons, 185
Morrison, J. C., 225
Morton, Elkanah, 93, 93n. 54
Morton, Elkanah, Jr., 91 n. 48
Moses, Jane Amelia, 333, 388
Moses, Martha, 322
Mott, ___, 275
Mountain, Jacob, 155n. 97, 161, 162, 163–64
Mystic, Connecticut, 401

N

Nagel, Catharine (Blauvelt), 360
Nagel, Hendrick, 360
Nagel, Sarah, 360
Nagel, Yon, 359
Napoleon, 222–23
Narragansett Indians, 402
Native Americans: missionaries to, xvii, 49, 161–65, 172; education of, 32, 33, 34, 55–56, 123–24, 126, 127, 342, 343, 344, 346–47; role in colonial conflicts, 129–31, 143, 152, 152n. 92, 159, 358, 402; resettlement in Upper Canada, 143–44, 157–65, 172. *See also specific tribes*
Neville, Ellen, 257n. 49
New Amsterdam, 352, 353
Newark, New York, 183
Newark, Upper Canada, xvii, 322; settlement of, 142, 144–45, 148, 150–52, 319; watercolor painting of, 151; description of, 151–52
New Brunswick, New Jersey, 358
Newcomb, Benj., 82
Newcomb, E., 82
Newcomb, John, 82, 91n. 48
Newcomb, John, Jr., 82
Newcomb, Roxey [Roxane], 395, 397
Newcomb, William, 82
New Concord, Connecticut, 405
New England: community organization in, xiv, xx-xxi; desire for land in, 3–4; agricultural practices, 9–11; schooling in colonial, 8, 8n. 16, 20, 32; increasing refinement in, 13–14, 219; birthing patterns in, 34; naming patterns for children in, 35, 72n. 4, 86n. 37, 120–21, 121n. 3, 205, 255–56; patterns of office-holding in, 36–38; travel in, 37–38, 59, 116, 196, 212–14; net worth of land in, 38–39; inheritance laws in, 64–65
New England Planters: move to Nova Scotia, xv, 71–72, 75, 77–78; architectural style of houses, 80; impact of Revolution on, 98–100, 103, 104–5, 110, 113; shifting religious affiliations, 101–3, 110
*New England Primer, The,* 20

New Hampshire: site of Dartmouth College, 19, 49–56; settlement of, 40; land grants in, 47, 48–49, 118; under Confederation, 134–36
*New Hampshire Gazette*, 64
New Haven, Connecticut, 22, 136, 192, 201, 202, 319, 321, 340, 341, 395, 396; travel to, 12, 37–38; description of, 21; founders, 24, 31
New Jersey: missionaries in, 32; boundary dispute with New York, 366, 372
New Lights: in New England, xiii, xv, 14, 16, 20, 30, 44n. 71, 45n. 73; in Nova Scotia, 101–3, 103n. 71, 104, 104n. 75
New London, Connecticut, 11, 25n. 15, 40, 75, 86n. 37, 192, 314, 346, 401, 402, 404, 408
New Milford, Connecticut, 265n. 68, 332
Newport, Rhode Island, 22, 58n. 102, 84, 101, 346
Newton, Hannah, 303
Newton, Massachusetts, 272, 329, 333
Newtowne. *See* Massachusetts, Cambridge
New Windsor, New York, 381
New York: Brooklyn, 355, 385, 386; Haarlem, 355
New York City, 168, 269, 273, 320, 321, 324, 325, 326, 327, 329, 330, 331, 332, 333, 352, 353, 354, 356, 360, 361, 362, 364, 365, 366, 367, 368, 369, 370, 371, 372, 374, 375, 376, 380, 381, 382, 383, 384, 385, 386, 387, 388; mercantile business in, xx, xxi-xxii, 225, 227, 238, 240, 241–48, 259, 277, 279; travel to, 12, 224, 256, 264; during Revolution, 131; religious changes in, 165; trade connections to western New York, 171n. 141, 176, 244; Phelps's residences in, 187; descriptions of, 223–25, 227–28, 242–43, 252; housing styles, 224–25, 253, 276; maritime activities, 225, 227–28; 1803 map of, 226; population, 227, 275; prosperity of residents, 251–52, 263; water supply and sewage disposal, 253–54; expansion of, 253–56, 275–77; financial panics, 258–59, 260; Macready riots of 1849, 262–63
New York, General Assembly of, 355, 358
New York–Massachusetts boundary dispute, 367, 377
New York–New Jersey boundary dispute, 366, 372
New York State: settlement of, 11, 167–68; forts in, 118; map of, 118, 166; description of early nineteenth-century countryside, 119, 176–77; roads in, 175, 176–77, 224–25; prohibition of slavery in, 184
Niagara, New York, 183
Niagara Falls, watercolor of, 145
Niagara-on-the-Lake, 144
Niagara township, Upper Canada, 148n. 81
Nobles, Ob, 68
non-importation agreements, 47, 52
Norris, Benjamin, 211
Northampton, Massachusetts, 14, 303, 389, 390, 391
Northbury (later Plymouth), Connecticut, 45n. 73
North Church of Boston, 91
Northford, Connecticut, 341
North Parish [Lebanon Crank], New London, Connecticut, 69, 342, 343, 404, 405, 406, 410
North Society, New London, Connecticut, 75, 404, 405, 406, 407, 408, 409, 410, 411
Norton, Massachusetts, 135n. 47, 318, 351
Norwalk, Connecticut, 282
Norwich, Connecticut, 9, 11, 12, 192, 201, 404, 405, 407
Norwich, England, 334

Nova Scotia: settlement of, xv, 11, 39–40, 71–72, 74–78, 408; earthen dikes in, 19, 72, 78–79, 88, 98–99; Congregational Church in, 71, 75, 80–81, 87, 89–97, 110; Dissenters in, 71, 75, 85, 86, 89, 101–13; Little Connecticut in, 71–72, 75, 77–78, 80, 97–100; 1781 map of, 73; strategic military location, 74, 74n. 6; roads in, 79; housing styles in, 80; Anglican Church in, 83, 85, 106; economic depression in, 88–91, 104–5; governance of, 97–98; Loyalists exiled in, 98, 113; impact of Revolution on, 98–100, 103, 104–5, 110, 113; Great Awakening in, 101–13
Nyack, New York, 357

O

Occum, Samson, 26, 32, 33, 342
Odessa, New York, 182
Old Lights, 14
Olmstead, Frederick Law, 280
O'Neill, Mary, 257n. 49
Onondaga, New York, 177, 182
Onondaga County, New York, 314, 381
Onslow, Nova Scotia, 109
Orangeburg, New York, 356, 358
Orange County, New York, 269, 355, 356, 358, 367, 373, 374, 375, 376, 377
Orangetown, New York, 373–74, 375
Orford, New Hampshire, xvi, 56, 60, 64, 313, 319, 321; founders, 134; settlers, 219–20, 220n. 99
Orford Parish, Connecticut, 114, 114n. 89, 116, 122, 193, 194, 315, 317
Osborn, Ann, 104
Oswego, New York, 176, 179
Otis, James, 405
Outwater, Thomas, 359
Oweneco [Owanco], 75, 404, 405
Oyster Bay, New York, 237, 366, 367, 368

P

Palermo, Sicily, xxii, 263–64, 275, 279, 327, 330
Palmer, Ann (Denison), 402
Palmer, Gershom, 402
Palmer, Martha, 56n. 100
Palmyra, New York, 322
Pancoast, Charles S., 251n. 30, 326
Pancoast, Elizabeth, 250, 251n. 30, 326
Pancoast, Samuel, 251n. 30
Paris, France, 327, 330, 331, 332
Parker, Daniel, 82
Parker, Elisha, 82
Parker, John, 68
Parker, Robert, 82
Parrish, Sol, 82
Partridge, Alden, 228–29
Pasadena, California, 329
Pasamaquoddy, 108, 109
Patten, Charlotte, 346
Patten, Eleazar Wheelock, 346
Patten, George Jaffrey, 346
Patten, Hannah (Hurlbut), 346
Patten, Mary, 346
Patten, Mary (—), 345
Patten, Nathaniel Wheelock, 346
Patten, Ruth, 346
Patten, Ruth (Wheelock), 64, 69, 343, 345–46, 347
Patten, Sarah, 346
Patten, William, 53n. 93, 345
Patten, William B., 346
Paxton, Joseph, 280
Peale, Charles Willson, 160, 369
Pease, Nina (Phelps), 290n. 133, 332
Pease, Richard, 332
Peck, Elisha, 228
Peck, Sarah, 291
Peck, Sarah (Ayres), 251n. 30
Pennington, New Jersey, 31
Pennock, Thankful, 350
Perkins, William, 217n. 90
Peters, Hannah, 149, 149n. 84

Peters, Hannah Delvena, 139, 139n. 61, 149, 149n. 84, 162n. 120
Peters, John, 132, 133n. 38
Peters, Joseph, 140
Peters, Samuel: exile in London, 44, 113n. 88; ministry, 45–46, 46n. 77, 134, 220n. 99; Phelps loan from, 66, 68; family, 132, 134, 149; correspondence with Davenport Phelps, 137–42, 153, 155, 155n. 97, 155n. 98, 319; bids for church appointments, 140, 142n. 67, 147, 153n. 96, 155, 155n. 98; property of, 220
pew rental, 194n. 24, 219
Phelps, Aaron, 393
Phelps, Abigail, 305, 306, 307, 308, 390, 391, 393, 397
Phelps, Abigail (Burnham), 391
Phelps, Abigail (Merrick), 391, 393
Phelps, Abigail (Pinney), 20, 307–8
Phelps, Abigail (Sloan), 313
Phelps, Abigail (Stebbins), 390
Phelps, Alexander, xii-xiv, 307, 308, 309, 330; career choice, 19, 22, 26–27, 310–11; dispute with Wheelock, 19, 51, 53–54, 56–58; elective offices held, 19, 35, 35n. 47, 36, 38, 58; marriages, 19, 29, 30, 310, 344; religious affiliations, 19, 20, 26, 41–42, 310; role in founding of Dartmouth College, 19, 49–56, 312; childhood and education, 20, 22, 27, 310; land transactions, 29, 38–39, 40–41, 41n. 67, 47–48, 58–59, 60, 63–64, 66, 70; travel, 32, 37, 38, 40–41; financial difficulties, 40, 41–42, 63–64, 66–68, 134, 311–12; military appointment, 42–43; political views, 46–47; move to New Hampshire, 47–48, 48, 58–60, 312; estate, 50, 56, 60–63, 66–68, 134, 312; death, 64, 310; children, 120, 188, 188n. 4, 313–14
Phelps, Alexander, Jr., 59, 69, 69n. 131
Phelps, Amelia Chamberlain, 255, 330
Phelps, Ann, 305, 306
Phelps, Ann (Dover), xi, 301–2, 303
Phelps, Ann (Gaylord), 301
Phelps, Anna (Horsford), 29n. 28, 310
Phelps, Anne, xiii, 29, 29n. 28, 310, 313
Phelps, Anne (Phelps) (Jones), xiii, 310, 313
Phelps, Annie Brown (Coleman), 274, 291n. 127, 328, 331, 332
Phelps, Anson Greene, 228, 243, 249, 263
Phelps, Aurelia, 322
Phelps, Benajah, xiv-xvi, 310, 314–16; selection as Cornwallis pastor, 40, 81, 83–84, 314–15; arrest and release during Revolution, 71, 108–9, 315; in Nova Scotia, 71–72, 85–97, 314; political views, 71–72, 100; biblical origin of name, 72n. 4; marriage, 77, 86, 314, 409, 411; lineage, 81, 310; children, 87, 108, 114, 193, 194, 194n. 19, 207, 316–17, 323; Crown land grant to, 87–88, 89, 315; land transactions, 88, 104, 104n. 74, 108, 114–15, 116, 315; correspondence with Eleazar Wheelock, 89, 90; financial difficulties, 89, 91, 104, 114, 115, 116, 315–16; departure from Cornwallis, 95, 96, 103, 104, 106, 315; sermon on death of Jane Chipman, 95–97, 315; appeal to Connecticut for compensation, 106–7, 110n. 87, 111–13, 114–15; return to Connecticut, 109–10, 111, 114–16, 315; childhood and education, 115, 309, 314; retirement, death, and burial, 115–16, 233, 235, 314; elective offices held, 116; inheritance, 309
Phelps, Caroline Eliza. *See* Haring, Caroline Eliza (Phelps)
Phelps, Catharine (—) (Hickock), 391
Phelps, Catharine (Tiffany), xvii, 317–18, 321; children, 120, 136, 156, 321–22; marriage, 135, 317; in Upper Canada, 135, 153–56; left as single parent, 142–43; siblings' move to Upper Canada, 155–56; widowhood, 183

Phelps, Charles Haring, 257n. 49, 265, 274, 279, 280, 290, 290n. 124, 290n. 125, 291, 291n. 127, 328, 331–32

Phelps, Charles Haring, Jr., 290n. 124, 332

Phelps, Charles Haring [III], 265n. 68

Phelps, Cornelius, 303, 305, 306

Phelps, Daniel, 201, 202, 396

Phelps, Davenport, xvi-xviii, 313–14, 317–21; influence of Joseph Brant on, 34; religious affiliations, 34, 44, 120, 141–42, 153, 155, 161–65, 169, 173; naming of, 35, 120–21, 121n. 3; childhood and education, 55, 58, 59, 64, 66, 120–21, 188, 318; inheritance, 65, 67, 69; political views, 119–20, 138–41, 319; military service and appointments, 122, 122n. 9, 125, 126, 129, 136, 148, 318; correspondence with E. Wheelock, 126, 127, 128–29; recruitment of students for Dartmouth, 126, 127–29; elective offices held, 134, 135; land transactions, 135, 140–41, 148, 153, 154, 156–57, 174n. 149, 178, 183; legal career, 135, 136, 148, 162; marriage, 135, 317; in Upper Canada, 135, 137, 142–44, 147–49, 153, 154, 156–57, 319, 350; business ventures, 135–36, 148–49, 319, 320, 350; Masonic affiliation, 136–37, 152; in Geneva, New York, 137, 320; correspondence with Samuel Peters, 137–42, 153, 155, 155n. 97, 155 n. 98, 319; in Piermont, New Hampshire, 141; ministry to Indians, 157–65, 169–74; candidacy and ordination, 161–65, 169, 173; Episcopal mission to western New York, 165–82, 320; financial difficulties, 178; death and estate, 182–85, 321; slaves of, 184, 321; Hobart's tribute to, 184–85

Phelps, Dean Wheelock, 178, 322

Phelps, Denison, 87, 316

Phelps, Dorothy, 397

Phelps, Edward Lewis, 178, 322

Phelps, Eleanor, 395, 397

Phelps, Eleazar Wheelock, xviii-xxi, 236–37, 323–24; childhood and education, 35, 59, 69, 188, 188n. 4, 189, 206, 323; marriage, 115, 189, 193–95, 196, 316, 323; business career in Europe, 184; correspondence with wife, 186, 187; legal career, 187, 188, 198, 201, 202, 205–6, 221, 323–24, 396; residences in New York City, 187, 324; violent acts against, 187, 214–21; residence in Stafford, 187–88, 194, 323; turnpike project, 188, 197, 204, 209, 211, 212–13, 214–15, 221, 323–24; religious affiliations, 194n. 23; land transactions, 194n. 24, 206–8, 213, 221, 222; pew rental, 194n. 24, 219; children, 205, 234–35, 235n. 132, 324–26; personal property inventory, 205, 206, 217–19; public offices held, 205–6, 323, 324; estate executor for John Phelps, 207–8, 323; charges against, 208–9, 211, 323; in Europe, 221–23, 324; businesses in New York City, 223, 324; business in Havana, 225, 324; steward at West Point, 228–30, 234; death, 232–33, 324; lineage, 313

Phelps, Elisabeth, 309, 310

Phelps, Elisabeth (Greene), 397

Phelps, Eliza, 205, 222, 223n. 104, 233, 235n. 132, 324–25

Phelps, Eliza (Ayres): marriage, xxi-xxii, 250, 326; in Fairfield, 237, 239; portrait, 239, 287, 289; lineage, 250, 250n. 29, 251n. 30, 326; children, 250–51, 252, 254, 255, 256, 256n. 44, 264–65, 272–74, 275, 329–33, 387; widowhood, 257n. 49, 328; death and estate, 273n. 89, 290, 291–92, 326, 328

Phelps, Elizabeth, 391

Phelps, Elizabeth (—), 394, 395

Phelps, Elizabeth [Betsey], 87, 108, 114, 309, 316

Phelps, Elizabeth (—) (Copley), 303, 389–90

Phelps, Elizabeth (M—), 333
Phelps, Emelia, 35, 59, 70, 313, 325
Phelps, Emma Ayres, 255, 273, 274, 290, 329
Phelps, Ephraim, 309
Phelps, Esther, 396
Phelps, Eunice, 87, 108, 114, 235n. 133, 317
Phelps, Frances (—), 301
Phelps, Frank, 260, 264–65, 265n. 68, 274, 279, 284n. 115, 290, 291, 328, 331, 388
Phelps, Frank George, 290n. 124, 332
Phelps, George, 301, 330
Phelps, George Alexander, xxi-xxiii, 236, 325, 331, 388; childhood and education, 205, 233, 241, 270, 292, 325; business career, 222, 238–39, 240, 243, 249–50, 259–63, 326–27; residences in Fairfield, 234, 235, 237, 239, 256–58, 264–65, 272, 285–88, 327; residences in New York City, 234, 238–39, 241, 242, 250, 251, 252, 254, 255, 259, 264, 272, 274, 275, 277, 327; portrait, 239, 287, 289; marriage, 250, 326; children, 250–51, 252, 254, 255, 256, 256n 44, 264–65, 272–74, 275, 329–33, 387; land transactions, 255n. 42, 255n. 43, 256, 257, 271n. 81, 285–86; retirement, 261, 279, 285, 288; political activities, 261–63; Palermo office, 263, 327; will and estate, 273, 289–90, 291, 328; guardian of granddaughter, 284n. 115; death, 288–89, 326
Phelps, George Alexander, Jr.: childhood and education, 255, 328; business activities, 260, 275; in Europe, 263–64, 264n. 65, 284, 330; marriage and children, 272, 272n. 87, 274, 329–30; in Liverpool, 279, 280, 330; inheritance, 290, 328
Phelps, George Davenport, 143, 183, 321–22
Phelps, Grace, 391, 393
Phelps, Grace (Martin), 391
Phelps, Hannah, 305, 306, 308, 309, 310
Phelps, Hannah (Bissell), 306, 308
Phelps, Hannah (Newton), 303
Phelps, Harley, 330
Phelps, Harriet, 205, 223n. 104, 234, 257, 288, 325
Phelps, Harriet Augusta, 251, 255, 273, 273n. 90, 274, 290, 291, 291n. 127, 328, 329
Phelps, Helen, 265n. 64, 330
Phelps, Helen (Clark), 272, 272n. 87, 274, 284, 330
Phelps, Henry Curtis, 331
Phelps, Henry Davenport, 205, 222, 233, 237, 288, 325–26; picture of, 239
Phelps, Henry Demarest, 255–56, 330
Phelps, Henry Rodolphus, 178, 322
Phelps, Howard, 260, 261, 265, 273, 274, 279, 284, 290, 328, 332
Phelps, Howard, Jr., 333
Phelps, Isaac, 301
Phelps, Isabel (Wilson), 302, 303
Phelps, Jennie I. (Bierne), 274, 332
Phelps, Joel, 309, 310
Phelps, John, xix, 29, 29n. 28, 39, 59, 68, 323, 393; elective offices and political appointments, 29n. 28, 199, 201; marriages, 29n. 28, 394; commercial enterprises, 192, 198, 201–3, 394–95; land transactions, 198n. 38, 206; religious affiliations, 198n. 38, 394; political views, 199; death and estate of, 199–200, 207–8, 394–96; legal cases involving, 201–2; personal property, 203, 204
Phelps, John, Jr., 29n. 28, 396
Phelps, John Augustus, 178
Phelps, Jonathan [Jr.], political views, 100
Phelps, Joseph, 303, 305, 307
Phelps, Joseph, Jr., 307
Phelps, Joseph Augustus, 322
Phelps, Joshua, 66n. 121, 308, 309, 310

Phelps, Josiah, 395, 397
Phelps, Julia (Edus), 322
Phelps, Julia Maria, 205, 239, 250–51, 255, 272–73, 274–75, 290, 325, 328, 329
Phelps, Julie [Groschen], 290n. 124, 332
Phelps, Lucey, 35, 42, 313
Phelps, Lucy, 136, 143, 183, 321
Phelps, Lucy (Kent), 393
Phelps, Lydia, 391
Phelps, Lydia (Morey), 134–35, 135n. 44
Phelps, Mabel Marston, 332
Phelps, Marion Bradley, 331
Phelps, Martha, 305, 306
Phelps, Martha (Moses), 322
Phelps, Mary, 304, 306, 331, 390, 393, 397
Phelps, Mary (—), 301, 303
Phelps, Mary A. Bradley (Curtiss [Curtis]), 274, 331
Phelps, Mary Amelia, 205, 233, 235n. 132, 290n. 124, 325
Phelps, Mary (Curtice), 81, 308, 309, 310
Phelps, Mary (Edwards), 391
Phelps, Mary (Griswold), 304, 305
Phelps, Mary (Moray [Morey]), 310
Phelps, Mary (Richardson), 198n. 38, 394, 396
Phelps, Mary (—) (Salmon), 303
Phelps, Mary (Stephenson), 117, 317
Phelps, Mehitabel, 307, 308
Phelps, Mercy, 390
Phelps, Nathaniel, xii, xiv, 20, 27n. 26, 303, 306–8, 389–90, 391
Phelps, Nathaniel [Jr.], 81, 81n. 27, 307, 308–10, 390–91
Phelps, Nina, 290n. 124, 332
Phelps, Phebe, 87, 108, 114, 115, 205, 223n. 104, 233, 234, 235, 257, 290, 316, 323, 324, 325, 328. *See also* Phelps, Phebe (Denison); Phelps, Phebe (Phelps)
Phelps, Phebe (Denison): marriage, xv, 77, 186, 314, 409, 411; death, xvi, 233; lineage, 86, 116, 235, 314, 316; children, 87, 108, 114, 193, 194n. 19, 316–17, 323; land transactions, 104, 104n. 74, 108; alone in Nova Scotia, 108, 109–10
Phelps, Phebe (Phelps): childhood, xix, 84, 108, 114, 115, 194, 194n. 19; marriage, xviii, 115, 189, 193–95, 196, 316, 323; widowhood and death, xx, 233–35, 257, 328; in New York City, 187, 241n. 6; children, 205, 234–35, 235n. 132, 324–26; household skills, 217; in Europe, 222; claim for West Point debt, 229–30, 234; portrait, 235
Phelps, Rachel (Sawyer), 308–9
Phelps, Ralph Rodolphus, 184, 313–14, 317; birth and education, 59–60, 313; legal career, 69–70, 171, 194, 194n. 24, 216, 217n. 90, 235, 314; death and burial, 117, 235; move to New York State, 171, 314
Phelps, Richard, 302
Phelps, Roxey [Roxane] (Newcomb), 395, 397
Phelps, Ruth (Barnard), 394
Phelps, Ruth (Hathaway), 393
Phelps, Sally, 114, 117
Phelps, Samuel, 68, 134–35, 303, 305, 306, 309, 310, 391
Phelps, Samuel S., 393
Phelps, Samuel Ward, 396
Phelps, Sarah, 304, 305, 306, 309, 313, 322, 391
Phelps, Sarah Allen, 256n. 44, 330
Phelps, Sarah Ann (Selby), 322
Phelps, Sarah (Griswold), 303
Phelps, Sarah Maria (Rees), 321
Phelps, Sarah (Pinney), 302, 303
Phelps, Sarah [Sally], 59, 64, 65–66, 70, 235, 317
Phelps, Seth, 393
Phelps, Sherman, 87, 316
Phelps, Solomon, 307, 308
Phelps, Susan A. (DeRose), 325–26
Phelps, Susannah (Wells), 393

Phelps, Sylvester Oliver, 143, 321
Phelps, Temperance (Barbur [Barber]), 308
Phelps, Theodora, 156, 313, 322
Phelps, Theodora, 35, 59, 65, 66, 70, 309
Phelps, Theodora (Wheelock), xiii, 309, 310, 312, 313; lineage, 19, 30–32, 310; marriages, 19, 30–31, 69, 188, 310, 344; children, 34–35, 59–60, 120, 188, 188n. 4, 313; appeals for father's assistance, 42, 43, 67; settlement of husband's estate, 64–69, 121, 312; death, 69, 195, 310; inheritance, 343
Phelps, Theodotia, 29n. 28, 313
Phelps, Thomas, 390
Phelps, Thomas Coleman, 290n. 124, 332
Phelps, Timothy, 29n. 28, 36, 198n. 37, 201, 208, 208n. 70, 304–6, 307, 391–93, 394, 397
Phelps, Timothy [Jr.], 393
Phelps, William, xi, xxvii, 301–4, 305, 306, 390
Phelps, William Alexander, 143, 183, 321, 322
Phelps, William Chamberlain, 256n. 44, 330
Phelps, William Sr., 29n. 28
Phelps Brothers & Co., 278, 279, 327, 330, 331, 332
Phelps family plot, East Cemetery, Fairfield, Connecticut, 234
Phelps Furnace and Foundry, 198, 201, 203–4, 207, 323, 394
Phenix, Anne (Bogert), 370
Phenix, Jacob, 370
Philadelphia, Pennsylvania, 21, 132, 326, 374
Philmont, New Hampshire, 69
Pierce, Pelatiah, 68
Piermont, New Hampshire, 69n. 129, 133n. 38, 135, 136, 143, 153, 319, 320, 344
Pierson, Abigail, 31
Pinney, Abigail, 20, 307–8
Pinney, Oliver, 307
Pinney, Sarah, 302, 303
Pirshallon, John, 68
Pitkin, William, 39, 68
Pitkin, William, Jr., 39n. 59
Pitkins, Colln, 42
Plimpton, Priscilla, 336
Pomeroy, Abigail (Wheelock), 16, 20n. 2, 339
Pomeroy, Benjamin, 15, 16, 20, 20n. 2, 25n. 15, 29, 43, 44, 45n. 73, 53, 142, 339, 342
Pomfret, Connecticut, 332
Porter, Elisha, 82
Porter, Lydia, 59n. 108, 220n. 99
Porter, Thos., 68
Portor, Samuel, 82
Portor, Simeon, 82
Portsmouth, New Hampshire, 19, 38
Port William, Nova Scotia, 76, 78
Poughkeepsie, New York, 165, 168, 320, 367, 376, 377
Powell, Abigail, 321
Prentice, Sarah, 403
Presbyterian Church: ministry in Bermuda, 41; westward movement, 167–68
Preston, Connecticut, 337
Preston, Northamptonshire, England, 401
Princeton University, 31n. 34
privateering: impact of, 104–5; raid on Cornwallis, 105–8; in Caribbean, 231–32
Protestant Episcopal Church, 165–82, 185
Puerto Rico, 230
Pulteney estates, 143n. 69, 176n. 153
Pultneyville, New York, 182, 183, 317, 318, 321, 322
Putnam County, Georgia, 321
Putten. *See* Van Putten
Pynchon, Major William, 389

Q

Quebec, Canada: military campaign against, 118, 125–26, 128, 128n. 26, 318
Queens Loyal Rangers, 132
Queenston, Upper Canada, 139n. 61
Quick, Theunis Jacobsen, 354
Quick, Vroutje (Haring), 354

R

Ramapo lands, 377
Rast, Jehial, 82
Rawlyk, George, 92, 99
rebirth, 23, 24
Red Jacket, 172
Reed, Mary, 339
Rees, Abigail (Powell), 321
Rees, Sarah Maria, 321
Rees, William, 321
Reeve, Tapping, 206
Rehoboth, Massachusetts, 336
religion: church and state issues, 6–8; revivals, 13–15; access to church meetings, 23; westward movement, 167–68, 177; civilizing influence of, 168–69; in nineteenth-century Connecticut, 196–97
Revere, Paul, xvii, 136
Revolutionary War, 12, 270, 373; causes of, xiv; battle of Bennington, xvi, 131–33, 318; service in, xvi, 132, 133n38, 159, 339, 349, 408; Connecticut during, xvi, 191; response of Nova Scotia to, 98–100, 103, 104–5, 110, 113; plight of women during, 108; campaign against Quebec, 118, 125–26, 128, 128 n. 26, 318; land grants to veterans of, 179, 380, 381; New York City action, 258; Lexington alarm, 309; military engagements, 318, 326, 408
Rhode Island, 104
Richardson, Charles I., 382
Richardson, Mary, 198n. 38, 394, 396
Richmond, Indiana, 329
Ripley, Abigail (Wheelock), 343, 348
Ripley, Anna (Denison) (Minor) (Denison), 404
Ripley, Hannah (Sturtevant), 348
Ripley, Jere, 404
Ripley, Jonathan, 348
Ripley, Sylvanus, 124n. 17, 127, 128n. 26, 129, 130, 343, 348
roads. *See* turnpikes
Robinson, __, 260
Robinson, John, 88
Rockland County, New York, 269, 270, 271, 370, 371, 372, 380
Rockwell, Jonathan, 82
Rogers, Dorothy (Denison), 407
Rogers, Ebeneezer, 407
Rogers, James, 405
Rogers, John, 277n. 100
Rogers, Lucy (Denison), 407
Rogers, Samuel, 407
Rogers, Samuel, Jr., 405
Romney, George, 159
Roome, Maria, 370
Roosevelt, Cornelius, 363, 365
Roosevelt, Cornelius C., 364, 365
Roosevelt, Elbert, 364, 365
Roosevelt, Elizabeth, 364, 365
Roosevelt, Hilletje (Sjoerts), 365
Roosevelt, Jacobus, 365
Roosevelt, Johannes, 365
Roosevelt, John, 361, 365
Roosevelt, Margaret (Herring), 271, 363, 364, 365
Roosevelt, Mary, 365
Roosevelt, Theodore, 271
Rose, Rachel, 379
Rowland, James, 286n. 119
Rowland, Mary, 286n. 119
Roxbury, Massachusetts, 335, 345, 398, 399, 400, 401
Russell, Peter, 162–63
Rutgers College, 373
Ryder, Elizabeth, 364

## S


Salisbury, Connecticut, 339
Salmon, Mary (—), 303
Samson, __, 316
Samson, Elizabeth (Phelps), 87, 108, 114, 316
Saratoga, 133
Saugerties, New York, 332
Sawyer, Jonathan, 68
Sawyer, Rachel, 308–9
Saxton, Hannah (Denison) (Cheesbrough), 402
Saxton, Joseph, 402
Saybrook, Connecticut, 37n. 53, 403, 406
Schenectady, New York, 165
Schermerhorn, Simon, 243
Schieffelin, Hannah (Lawrence), 127n. 25
Schieffelin, Jacob, 127n. 25
Schoharie, New York, 171, 313
schooling, in colonial New England, 8, 8n. 16, 20, 32
Schraalenburgh, New Jersey, 379, 381
Schuyler, __, 123
Schuyler, Philip, 122, 123
Scotland, Connecticut, 332
Scott, John Morin, 374
Scoville, Joseph A., 249, 250
Seargeant, John, 68
Seccombe, John, 94, 94n. 57, 100, 100n. 65
Selby, Sarah Ann, 322
Selleck, Martha (Gould), 31
Selyns, Henricus, 352n. 481
Seneca Indians, 172
Shays's Rebellion, 141n. 65
Sheldon, New York, 174, 182
Sherman, David, 407
Sherman, Mercy (Wheeler), 407
Sherman, Prudence, 86, 314, 407, 410
Sherwin, Hannah (Phelps), 308
Sherwin, Jacob, 308
shipping: impact of Revolution on, 104–5; on waterways in New York State, 176, 244; transatlantic, 224–28, 243, 244–48, 259, 277–80. *See also* privateering
Shorpshire, England, 334
Simcoe, Elizabeth, 149, 150–51; watercolors of, 145, 150, 151, 151n. 87; on Joseph Brant, 157–58
Simcoe, John Graves, 142n. 67, 145–48, 149, 152, 160
Simsbury, Connecticut, 303, 304
Six Nations, 143, 144n. 72
Sjoerts, Hilletje, 365
slaves and servants, 42, 184, 257, 257n. 49, 321, 343
Sloan, Abigail, 313
smallpox, 128, 129, 130
Smiley, Eliza P[helps], 290n. 124, 326, 328
Smith, Brechtje (Haring), 356
Smith, Elizabeth, 380
Smith, Elizabeth (Denison), 410
Smith, Gerrit, 356
Smith, Israel, 68
Smith, Lambert, 356, 358
Smith, Margaritje (—), 356, 358
Smith, Nathan, 410
Smith, Steel, 68
Smith, William, Jr., 366
Society for the Propagation of the Gospel in Foreign Parts, 45n. 73, 83, 85
Sodus Point, New York, 322
Somers, Connecticut, 196, 219, 221, 397
Southampton, Lord Charles, 277n. 99
Southampton, Long Island, 370
Southold, Long Island, 25n. 15
Spann, Edward K., 245
SPG. *See* Society for the Propagation of the Gospel in Foreign Parts
Springfield, Massachusetts, 213–14, 392
Sproull, John, 383
St. Bartholomew, West Indies, 384
St. Peter's Church, Hebron, Connecticut, 44, 45
St. Peter's Church, Albany, New York, 170, 173, 174

St. Thomas, West Indies, 349
Stafford, Connecticut, xix, xx, xxi, 115, 187, 188, 194, 202, 206, 211, 223n. 104, 316, 323, 325, 326, 394, 395, 396; turnpike and roads through, 116, 212–13; population, 193; description of, 195–97; mineral springs, 197–98, 211–12; straw braid manufacture, 217
Stafford Springs, Connecticut, xix, 195
Stamford, Connecticut, 45n. 74, 139, 291, 331, 384; Upper Canada families from, 149
Stamp Act of 1765, xiii, 12, 26, 46–47, 89, 97
standing order, xii, 200–5
Standish, Ann (Allen), 337
Standish, Josiah, 337
Standish, Mercy, 337–38, 340
Standon, Hertfordshire, England, 399
Stanton, Borodell (Denison), 403
Stanton, Dorothy, 404, 407
Stanton, Joanna, 404, 406
Stanton, Joanna (Gardiner), 404
Stanton, Mary, 404
Stanton, Robert, 404
Stanton, Samuel, 403
Stanton, Sarah (Denison), 402, 404
Stanton, Thomas, Jr., 402, 404
Stark, John, 131, 132, 133
Stark, John A., 318
Starr, Samuel, 82, 105n. 78, 105–6, 106n. 79
Starr's Point, Cornwallis, Nova Scotia, 106
steam-powered transportation, 224, 256, 259, 264
Stebbins, Abigail, 390
Stephenson, Mary, 117, 317
Steward, Gordon, 99
Steward, Joseph, 33
Stiles, Aaron, 68, 135
Stiles, Ezra, 24n. 14, 57–58, 58n. 102, 341
Stiles, Nathan, 82
Stodder, Hannah, 335
Stodder, John, 335
Stonington, Connecticut, 401, 402, 404
Stony Brook, Connecticut, 405
Stprs, Aarpm, 68
Stratford, Connecticut, 25n. 15, 371, 407
straw hats and baskets, 217
Strong, John, 68
Strong, Samuel, 215, 216
Strong, Stephen, 82
Stuart, Gilbert, 159
Sturtevant, Hannah, 348
Stuyvesant, Peter, 352, 352n. 482
Suffield, Connecticut, 196, 198, 339, 391, 393
Suhm, Christian, 349
Suhm, Maria Malleville, 349
Suhm, Maria (Malleville), 349
Sullivan, John, 143, 143n. 71
Susquehannah Company, xiii, 29–30
Syracuse, New York, 171n. 141

## T

Talman, Brechtje (Haring), 354
Talman, Dirkje, 355
Talman, Dirkje (Teunis), 354
Talman, Douwe, 354
Talman, Grietje (Minneus), 355
Talman, Harmen, 355
Talman, Teunis, 354
Tappaen Indians, 353
Tappan, New York, 270, 352, 353, 354, 355, 356, 357, 359, 360, 366, 369, 370, 371, 372, 374, 376, 377, 378, 379, 380
Tappan Patent, 269, 353, 354
tariffs, opposition to, 261
Taylor, Josesph G., 277n. 100
Teaneck, New Jersey, 378
Terhune, Stephen, 378
Tery, John, 82
Teunis, Dirkje, 354
textile industry, 247–48
Thayendanegea, 157. *See also* Brant, Joseph

Thayer, Sylvanus, 228
Thetford, New York [Vermont], 47, 65, 311
Theuniszen, Harmen, 352
Thompson, Alice (Freeman), 401
Thompson, Bridget, 401, 402
Thompson, John, 401
Thompson, Mary, 410
Thorp, Oliver, 82
Thresher, Ebeneezer, 202
Ticonderoga, 39, 132
Tiffany, Catharine: *See also* Phelps, Catharine (Tiffany)
Tiffany, George, 155n. 99, 156
Tiffany, Gideon, 135, 135n. 47, 155, 156n. 100, 318, 351
Tiffany, Lucinda, 156n. 100
Tiffany, Lucy, 135n. 47, 351
Tiffany, Oliver, 155, 155n. 99, 156n. 100, 183, 321
Tiffany, Sarah Dean (Farrar), 135n. 47, 318, 351
Tiffany, Silvester, 155–56, 156n. 100
Tillotson, Daniel, 39n. 59, 56, 68, 134
Tinnent, Gilbert, 24
Tocqueville, Alexis de, 119, 252
Tolland, Connecticut, 196, 211
Tolland, Massachusetts, 213
Tories. *See* Loyalists [Tories]
Toronto, Canada. *See* York, Upper Canada
Townsend, Catharine L., 277n. 100
Townsend, John D. P., 277n. 100
Townshend Decrees, 97
Trask, Samuel, 206
Treat, Robert, 402
Treaty of Ghent, 223
Treaty of Paris (1763), 74
Trerice, John, Sr., 404
Trinity Church, Geneva, New York, 169, 170, 180–82, 320, 321
Trinity Church, New York City, 165, 169, 180, 320
Truman, Cornelia (Haring), 356
Truman, Peter, 356
Truman, Richard, 356
Trumbull, Benjamin, 13, 15, 16
Trumbull, Jonathan, 211
Truro, Nova Scotia, 84
Tryon, William, 258
Tully, Sarah (Fenny), 403
Tupper, Eliakim, Jr., 82
Turk, Ellen, 366
turnpikes, 209–14; building of, 188, 191, 192, 192n. 15; construction practices, 214–15
Tuscarora Indians, 172
Tuttle, George Montgomery, 284

U

Union, Connecticut, 26
Universalist Church, 197
Upper Canada: partial map of, 118, 166; settlement of, 144–48
*Upper Canada Gazette or American Oracle,* 152, 155, 156n. 100
Utica, New York, 143, 176, 371

V

Van der Beck, Henry, 379
Van der Beck, Martyntje [Margaret] (Haring), 378, 379
Van Hoorn, Neesje, 359
Van Houten, Claes, 356
Van Houten, Grietje Pieters (Haring), 356
Van Lent. *See* Lent
Van Putten, Cosyn Gerritsen, 352
Van Putten, Vroutje Gerritson, 352
Van Twiller, Worter, 361
Varick, Richard, 367
Verbryck, Samuel G., 378
Vermont, 118, 134n. 41, 166
Verveelen, Maria, 357

W

Wade, Sarah (Phelps), 304
Wade, William, 304
Wait, John, 243

Waite, Marcus Warren, 349
Wakefield, John, 335
Wakefield, Peregrina (Wheelock), 335
Wampanaug Indians, 402
Wansey, Henry, 201
Warner, Frederic Chester, 393
Warner, Lydia (Phelps), 391
Warner, Mark, 391
War of 1812, xxviii, 183, 222–23, 269, 382–83, 385
Warren, Experience (Wheelock), 335
Warren, Joseph, 335
Warren, Peter, 277n. 100
Warterous, John, 68
Warwick Presbyterian Church, 41
Washington, George, 123, 124, 126, 136, 271, 376
Waterbury, Connecticut, xxvi-xxvii, 45n74, 288, 333, 388
Waters, Israel, 213, 213n. 82
Wattles, Abigail (Denison), 407
Wattles, William, 407
Wayne, Anthony, 152n. 92
Webb, Joseph, 66, 68
Weber, Max, xxiii
Webster, Daniel, 349
Weld, Elizabeth, 400
Weld, Isaac: on Newark, Upper Canada, 151–52
Wells, Susannah, 393
Wentworth, John, 48, 48n. 81, 50, 54, 66, 68, 121, 133n. 38, 312
West, Stephen, 82
West, Wm., 82
Westchester, New York, 165
West Country, England, xi, xxvii
Westerly, Rhode Island, 403
Westfield, Massachusets, 301, 302
West Indies, xx, 11, 223, 230–32, 349, 384, 406
Westmoreland, Connecticut [Pennsylvania], 30
Westneck, Long Island, 368
Weston, Amaziah, 201
West Point, 228–30
West Ward, New York City, 370
Wetherald, Eliza Phelps (Winter), 239, 274, 329
Wetherald, James Taylor, 329
Wetherell, Mary, 403
Wetmore, ___, 282
Wharton, Edith, 276
Wheaton, Calub, 82
Wheeler, Mercy, 407
Wheelock, Abigail, 16, 20n. 2, 337, 339, 343, 348
Wheelock, Abigail (Kinsman), 351
Wheelock, Eleazar, xiii, xv, 114, 311, 312, 314, 318, 319, 335–36, 337, 338, 339, 340–44, 347, 350; and Dartmouth College, 19, 49–56, 121, 123–24, 131; itinerant preacher, 15–16; descriptions of, 16, 57–58; dispute with Alexander Phelps, 19, 51, 53–54, 56–58; religious affiliations and opinions, 20, 26, 168, 342; childhood and education, 20n. 2; relatives of, 24; land acquisitions, 29; children, 30, 336–37, 344–51; marriages, 30, 31, 335–36, 340, 350; *Narratives,* 32, 33; portrait, 33, 55; and Moor's Charity School, 33–34, 49, 123–24, 131, 158, 342, 343, 344, 346, 347; on Joseph Brant, 34; financial assistance to Alexander Phelps, 41–42; slaves and servants of, 42, 343; death and will, 69, 343–44; correspondence, 71, 89, 90, 126, 127, 128–29, 130; role in selecting Cornwallis pastor, 80, 81; on smallpox, 128–29
Wheelock, Eleazar [Jr.], xvii, 135, 136, 138, 138n. 58, 140, 344
Wheelock, Elizabeth, 336, 338
Wheelock, Elizabeth (Colburn), 336
Wheelock, Elizabeth (Fuller), 335–36
Wheelock, Ephraim, 336
Wheelock, Experience, 335
Wheelock, Experience (Bullard), 336

Wheelock, Gershon [Gershom], 335
Wheelock, Gideon, 135n. 47
Wheelock, Hannah (Stodder), 335
Wheelock, James, xvii, 129; childhood and education, 128, 129, 351; trip to Upper Canada, 128, 142, 319, 351; business ventures in Hartford, 135, 350; marriage, 135n. 47, 351; debts of, 136, 140; land transactions, 153, 154, 156–57
Wheelock, John, 56, 164, 188–89, 222, 339, 343, 344, 347, 349–50
Wheelock, Lucy (Tiffany), 135n. 47, 351
Wheelock, Maria Malleville, 350
Wheelock, Maria Malleville (Suhm), 349
Wheelock, Mary, 335, 336, 340, 347–48
Wheelock, Mary (Brinsmaid), 340, 341–42, 343, 347
Wheelock, Mary (Chenery), 336
Wheelock, Mary (—) (Ilis), 336
Wheelock, Mercy, 344
Wheelock, Mercy (Standish), 337–38, 340
Wheelock, Miriam (Bullen), 336
Wheelock, Peregrina, 335
Wheelock, Priscilla (Plimpton), 336
Wheelock, Radulphus [Ralph Rodolphus], 346–47
Wheelock, Ralph, 64, 334–35, 336, 337–38
Wheelock, Rebecca, 335, 337
Wheelock, Rebecca (Clarke), 334, 335
Wheelock, Record, 335
Wheelock, Ruth, 64, 69, 338, 339, 343, 345–46, 347
Wheelock, Ruth (Huntington), 337, 338
Wheelock, Sarah, 339
Wheelock, Sarah (Davenport) (Maltby), 30, 31, 310, 340, 341, 344
Wheelock, Sarah (Kendrick), 335
Wheelock, Silvester, 135n. 47
Wheelock, Thankful (Pennock), 350
Wheelock, Theodora. *See* Phelps, Theodora (Wheelock)
Wheelock, Tryphena (Young), 344, 350
White, Elizabeth, 251n. 30, 326
White, Elizabeth Wade, 221
White, George Luther, 284, 284n. 117, 288, 333, 388
White, Henry Wade, 286n. 119
White, Jane Amelia (Moses), 333, 388
White, John, 302
White, Julia Phelps (Haring): portrait, xxv, xxvii, 239, 283, 285, 287; family notebook of, xxviii-xxix, 250n. 29, 251n. 30, 326; trip to Europe, 264, 284; childhood, 271, 272, 274, 275, 281–85; correspondence, 272; marriage and children, 284, 284n. 117, 288, 328, 333, 388; inheritance, 284n. 115, 290, 291, 292, 328
White, Luther Chapin, 288, 333, 388
White, Mary, 251n. 30, 326
White, Stanford, 286n. 119
Whitefield, George, 20n. 2, 22–24, 342
Whitney, Eli, 248
Whitney, John, 104n. 74
Wickwire, Petter, 82
Willard, Abijah, 198, 198n. 38, 394
Willard, John, 196, 197, 383
Willard, Samuel, 196, 207, 209, 211–12, 220
Willard, Sydney, 198
Willes, Henry, 68
Williams, Isaac, 404
Williams, Sarah (Denison), 404
Williams, Solomon, 80, 91n. 48, 92, 93, 93n. 53
Williamson, Charles, 143n. 69, 176n. 153
Williamsport, Pennsylvania, 326
Willie, Agnes, 398
Wilmington, Vermont, 393
Wilson, Isabel, 302, 303
Wilton, South Carolina, 341
Windham, Connecticut, 12, 337, 338, 339, 340, 342
Windham County, Connecticut, 37

Windsor, Connecticut, xi, xxvii, 4, 5, 9, 29n. 28, 302, 303, 304, 305, 306, 317, 389, 390
Windsor, Nova Scotia, 408
Winter, Eliza Phelps, 239, 274, 329
Winter, Emma, 239, 329
Winter, Julia Maria (Phelps), 205, 239, 250–51, 255, 272–73, 274–75, 290, 325, 328, 329
Winter, Royal, 272, 329
Winthrop, John, xi, 19
Wolfville, Nova Scotia, 78
women: colonial, duties of, xxiii, 8; independence of, 194
Wonalonscet, New Hampshire, 332
Wood, John, 68
Wood, Jonathan, 82
Woodward, Bezaleel, 343, 347
Woodward, Mary (Wheelock), 343, 347–48
Woodworth, Amasa, 82
Woodworth, Benj., 82
Woodworth, Silas, 82
Woodworth, William, 82
Wooster, David, 127, 128
Worcester, Massachusetts, 394; network of roads to, 116, 196, 212–13
Worcester & Stafford Turnpike Corporation, xix, xx, 212, 215, 221
Wramplingham, Norfolk, England, 334, 335
Wright, Elizabeth (Phelps), 391
Wyllys, George, 113

## Y

Yale College, 20, 21, 22, 22n. 7, 24–25, 58, 81, 83, 83n. 29
Yankee boy, characteristics of, 249, 250
Yankee Planters. *See* New England Planters
York, Dorothy, 400
York, Upper Canada, 144, 148n. 79
Young, John, 67, 69, 344, 350
Young, Susannah (Gretchell), 344, 350
Young, Theodora (Wheelock) (Phelps). *See* Phelps, Theodora (Wheelock)
Young, Tryphena, 344, 350

## Z

Zabiskie, Christian, 359
Zabriskie, Henry, 359
Zabriskie, Lea Hedridge (Hoppe), 359
Zabriskie, Mary (Haring), 359

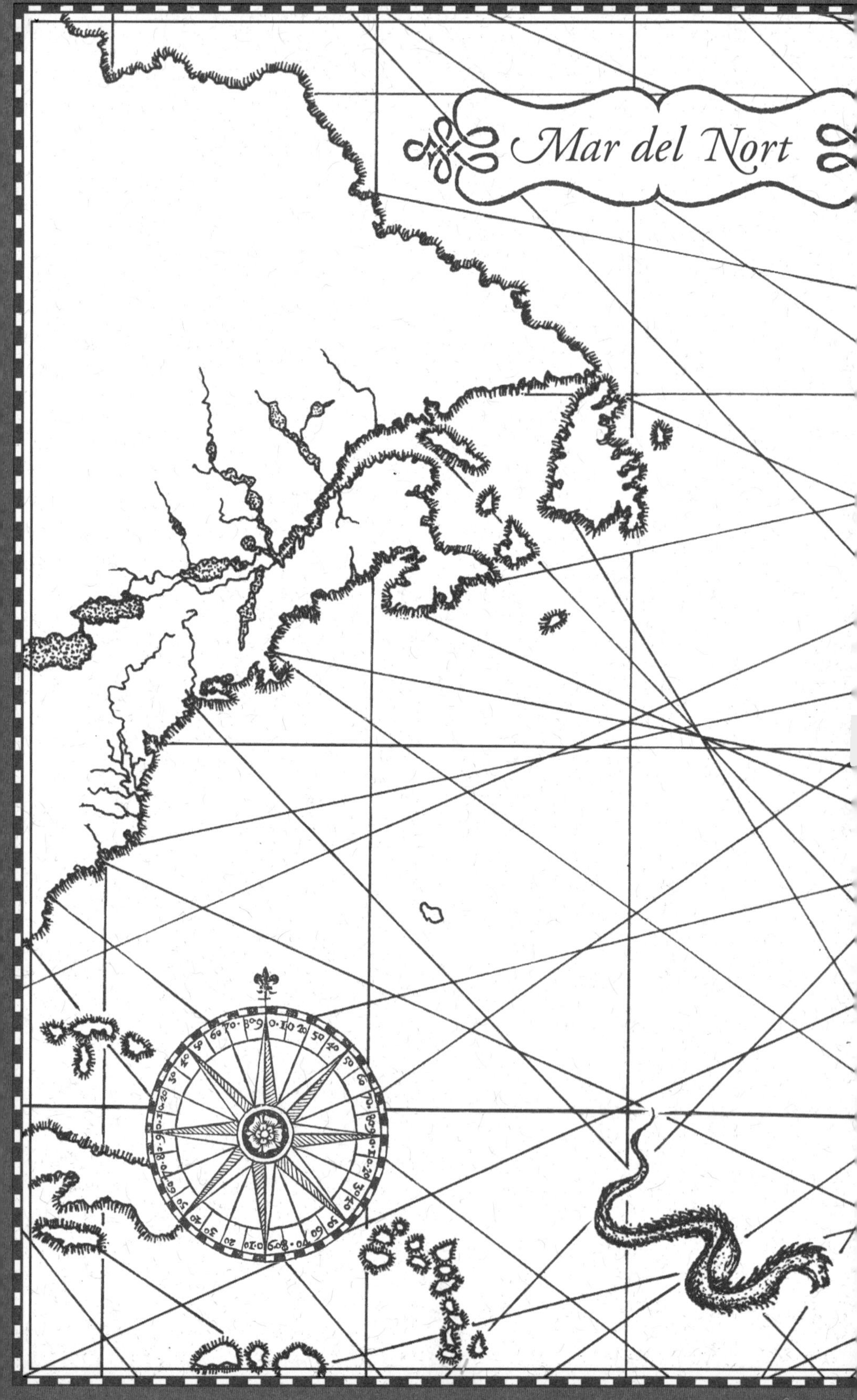
Mar del Nort